DICTIONARY

OF

CONTEMPORARIES

DICTIONNAIRE DES CONTEMPORAINS
LEXICON DER ZEITGENOSSEN
DIZIONARIO DI CONTEMPORANEI
DICCIONARIO DE CONTEMPORANEOS
СЛОВАРЬ СОВРЕМЕННИКОВ

COMPILED BY
A. J. LAUNAY

CENTAUR PRESS LTD.

First published in 1967 by the
Centaur Press Ltd. of Fontwell, Sussex
and 11-14 Stanhope Mews West, London, S.W.7

Printed in Great Britain
by T. J. Winterson Co.

DICTIONARY OF CONTEMPORARIES

PREFACE

THE aim of this dictionary is to show who were the contemporaries of any writer, artist, composer, philosopher or other influentially creative person of note, born at any time before 1900 A.D.

By alphabetical arrangement of names with dates, in sections of twenty-five years, a simple check can be made not only on a subject's contemporaries and his year of birth and death, but also on who preceded and followed him and so could have influenced, or been influenced by, his own work and ideas. This, indeed, is the book's major purpose.

In each section of twenty-five years, writers, artists and composers are given separate headings, and the sections are preceded throughout the book by a general list that includes major events, kings, presidents, heads of State, reigning popes, and notable persons.

Under the heading of Writers are included authors of novels, biographies and non-fiction, poets, historians, theologians and philosophers — in short, anyone who has written anything which can be said to have contributed significantly to the ethos of his own or a subsequent time. The same criterion has been applied to Artists (which heading includes painters, sculptors, architects and others who have created visually) and to Composers.

In the Index all writers, artists and composers are again listed with their dates to provide reference to the appropriate twenty-five-year section.

Up to 1501 Events and Prominent People were comparatively few. In order to simplify the periods prior to this, therefore, the twenty-five-year sections are preceded by Events and Prominent People listed in chronological order and in spans of 500 years up to the year 1001 A.D., and in spans of 100 years up to 1501, after which they are listed alphabetically every twenty five years.

While the attempt has been made to list the name of every creative person whose work has been recognised as contributory to the cultural climate of his or her era (the hard core of the internationally famous presenting no problems of selection), the vast number of lesser-known people has given rise to the question "Were

5

they influential enough to be included?" Clearly some limitation of numbers has had to be accepted, and it is likely that some readers will feel that notable persons have wrongly been omitted. The Editor can but hope that this dictionary will nevertheless serve its basic purpose in the eyes of that audience at whom it is primarily directed — students, biographers, historians, and indeed all serious readers who are concerned with assessing, through a realisation of the key figures in the creative field, the artistic and inspirational ethos of a given period.

Acknowledgements

I wish to express my grateful thanks to all those who assisted me in the compilation of this work, especially M. A. Henderson who checked through the whole dictionary for omissions, E. Launay who helped me search for and file the names, and C. Taylor-Whitehead and M. Melbourn who helped me read through the proofs.

A.J.L.

Publisher's Note

It has not been possible to refer to any one source in checking the orthography, accents and dates of certain subjects in this dictionary, surprising inconsistencies being found in even the most respectable sources. Existing authorities are also contradictory as to the first names of certain persons included.

While every reasonable effort has been made to avoid inconsistencies and errors, readers are advised to use the dictionary for its essential purpose in tracing contemporaries, and not as a final authority as to the spelling of names or the dates of births and deaths.

It has in fact been found that there are so many errors and contradictions in the accenting of names in the works of different authorities, that it is less misleading to omit accents altogether.

B.C. 3000	Early Minoan Age.
	Gold, Silver, Copper in use. Pictographical writing.
B.C. 2900	Great Pyramid Age begins.
B.C. 2850	Golden Age of China begins.
B.C. 2205	Hsai dynasty in China.
B.C. 2200	Linear writing with pen and ink. Copper in use.
B.C. 1766	Shang dynasty in China.
B.C. 1600	Bronze in use.
B.C. 1280	Iron in use.
B.C. 1220	Exodus of Israelites from Egypt.
B.C. 1190	Fall of Troy.
B.C. 1000	Jerusalem capital of Israel. King David.
B.C. 973	Solomon's Temple built in Jerusalem.
B.C. 846	Carthage founded.
B.C. 776	First Olympiad.
B.C. 753	Rome founded.
B.C. 675	Byzantium founded.
B.C. 660	Japanese history begins. First Mikado.
B.C. 597	Jerusalem destroyed.
B.C. 525	Persian conquest of Egypt.

PROMINENT PEOPLE

Pythagoras	582-500	Gautama (Buddah)	563-483

CHINESE DYNASTIES

The Five Sovereigns		Shang or Yin	1766-1122
(Legendary Epoch)	2697-2205	Chou	1122-255
Hsia	2205-1766		

WRITERS

Aeschylus	525-456	Heraclitus	540-475
Aesop	620-560	Hesiodus	c. 735
Alcaeus	c. 600	Hipponax	546-520
Alcmaeon	c. 520	Homer	c. 850
Alcman	c. 620	Laotse (Lao Tsu)	c. 500
Anacreon	c. 560	Parmenides of Elea	513-c. 430
Anaxagoras	500-428	Pindar	522-440
Anaximander	611-547	Sappho	c. 600
Anaximenes	c. 500	Simonides of Ceos	556-469
Archilochus	720-676	Stesichorus	c. 630-556
Bacchylides	c. 500	Thales	c. 580
Choerilus	c. 500	Theognis	fl. 544-541
Confucius	551-479	Tso Chiuming	c. 600
Cratinus	520-423	Tyrtaeus	fl. 685-668
Epicharmus	540-450	Xenophanes	576-480
Hecataeus of Miletus	550-476		

ARTISTS

Archermus	c. 500	Dipoenus	fl. 560
Bathycles	c. 600	Endoeus	c. 500
Chersiphron	c. 600		

B.C. 430	Great Plague in Egypt.
B.C. 390	Gauls sack Rome.
B.C. 331	Alexandria founded.
B.C. 264	First Punic war.
B.C. 221	Emperior Chi Huang Ti. Great Wall of China.
B.C. 218	Second Punic war.
B.C. 205	Rosetta Stone.
B.C. 202	Punic war ends.
B.C. 166	Tartar invasion of China.
B.C. 146	Carthage destroyed.
B.C. 60	First Triumvirate. Caesar, Pompey, Crassus.
B.C. 58	Caesar's victories in Gaul.
B.C. 55	Caesar's invasion of Britain.
B.C. 48	Defeat of Pompey in Egypt by Caesar.
B.C. 47	Cleopatra enthroned by Caesar.
B.C. 44	Caesar assassinated.
B.C. 30	Deaths of Anthony and Cleopatra.
B.C. 4	Birth of JESUS CHRIST.
B.C. 1	Christian era begins.

PROMINENT PEOPLE

Pericles	490-429	Julius Caesar	102-44
Alexander the Great	356-323	Herod the Great	73-4
Archimedes	287-212	Cleopatra	69-30
Euclid	died 282	Augustus	63-14
Hannibal	247-183	Jesus Christ	B.C. 4-33 A.D.

CHINESE DYNASTIES

Chou	1122-255	Han	B.C. 206-A.D. 220
Ch'in	255-206		

WRITERS

Aeschylus	525-456	Heraclitus	540-475
Choerilus	c. 500	Herodotus	484-425
Confucius	551-479	Pindar	522-440
Cratinus	520-423	Protagoras	481-411
Empedocles	490-430	Simonides of Ceos	556-469
Epicharmus	540-450	Sophocles	495-406
Euripides	484-407	Xenophanes	576-480
Gorgias	485-380		

ARTISTS

Antenor	fl. 500

WRITERS

Aeschylus	525-456	Herodotus	484-425
Cratinus	520-423	Magnes	fl. 460
Democritus	born 460	Pindar	522-440
Empedocles	490-430	Protagorus	481-411
Epicharmus	540-450	Simonides of Ceos	556-469
Euripedes	484-407	Socrates	470-399
Gorgias	485-380	Sophocles	495-406
Heraclitus	540-475	Thucydides	460-400

ARTISTS

Agatharcus	460-415	Polygnotus	470-440

WRITERS

Agathon	448-400	Herodotus	484-425
Antisthenes	444-365	Isocrates	436-338
Aristippus	435-356	Philoxenus	435-380
Aristophanes	448-385	Pindar	522-440
Cratinus	520-423	Plato	428-348
Democritus	born 460	Plato (Poet)	428-389
Empedocles	490-430	Protagoras	481-411
Epicharmus	540-450	Socrates	470-399
Euclid	450-374	Sophocles	495-406
Eupolis	446-411	Sophron	460-420
Euripedes	484-407	Thucycides	460-400
Gorgias	485-380	Xenophon	430-357

ARTISTS

Agatharcus	460-415	Polygnotus	470-440

WRITERS

Agathon	448-400	Iophon	fl. 405
Antisthenes	444-365	Isocrates	436-338
Aristippus	435-356	Philoxenus	435-380
Aristophanes	448-385	Plato	428-348
Cratinus	520-423	Plato (Poet)	428-389
Diogenes	412-323	Protagoras	481-411
Euclid	450-374	Socrates	470-399
Eupolis	446-411	Sophocles	495-406
Euripides	484-407	Sophron	460-420
Gorgias	485-380	Xenophon	430-357
Herodotus	484-425		

ARTISTS

Agatharcus	460-415	Hippodamus	fl. 420
Alcamenes	fl. 420		

WRITERS

Agathon	448-400	Isocrates	436-338
Antisthenes	444-365	Leucippus	fl. 400
Archelaus of Miletus	fl. 400	Phidias	c. 400
Aristippus	435-356	Philoxenus	435-380
Aristophanes	448-385	Plato	428-348
Aristotle	384-322	Plato (Poet)	428-389
Ctesias	fl. 400	Socrates	470-399
Diogenes	412-323	Theopompus	378-300
Ephorus	400-330	Xenocrates	396-314
Euclid	450-374	Xenophon	430-357
Gorgias	485-380	Zeno of Elea	fl. 400
Iophon	fl. 405		

ARTISTS

Ictinus	c. 400	Nicomachus	390-340

WRITERS

Antisthenes	444-365	Euclid	450-374
Aristippus	435-356	Isocrates	436-338
Aristotle	384-322	Plato	428-348
Callistheles	360-328	Theophrastus	372-286
Diogenes	412-323	Theopompus	378-300
Ephorus	400-330	Xenocrates	396-314
Eubulus	fl. 370	Xenophon	430-357

ARTISTS

Nicomachus	390-340

WRITERS

Aristotle	384-322	Plato	428-348
Callistheles	360-328	Pyrrho	360-270
Diogenes	412-323	Theopompus	378-300
Diphilus	342-291	Theophrastus	372-286
Ephorus	400-330	Timaeus	345-250
Epicurus	341-270	Xenocrates	396-314
Isocrates	436-338	Zeno of Citium	342-270
Menander	349-291		

ARTISTS

Leochares	fl. 350-338	Nicomachus	390-340

WRITERS

Aeneas, Tacticus	c. 300	Patrocles	312-261
Arcesilas	316-241	Pyrrho	360-270
Aristotle	384-322	Rhinthon	323-285
Cleanthes	301-232	Theopompus	378-300
Dicaerchus	c. 320	Theophrastus	372-286
Diogenes	412-323	Timaues	345-250
Diphilus	342-291	Timon	320-230
Epicurus	341-270	Xenocrates	396-314
Menander	349-291	Zeno of Citium	342-270

ARTISTS

Apelles	c. 325	Protogenes	fl. 332-300

WRITERS

Apollodorus of Carystus	300-260	Mencius	c. 300
Arcesilas	316-241	Patrocles	312-261
Chrysippus	280-207	Pyrrho	360-270
Cleanthes	301-232	Rhinton	323-285
Crantor	fl. 300	Sositheus	c. 284
Diphilus	342-291	Speusippus	c. 300
Epicurus	341-270	Theocritus	fl. 285
Eratosthenes of Alexandria	276-194	Theophrastus	372-286
Hecataeus of Abdera	c. 300	Timaeus	345-250
Livius Andronicus	284-204	Timon	320-230
Menander	349-291	Zeno of Citium	342-270

ARTISTS

Eutychides	c. 300	Protegenes	fl. 332-300

B

Apollodorus of Carystus	300-260	Naevius, Gnaeus	264-194
Arcesilas	316-241	Patrocles	312-261
Aratus of Soli	fl. 270	Plautus, Titus Maccius	250-184
Chrysippus	280-207	Pyrrho	360-270
Cleanthes	301-232	Rhianus	275-195
Epicurus	341-270	Timaeus	345-250
Eratosthenes of Alexandria	276-194	Timon	320-230
Fabius, Pictor Quintus	c. 254	Zeno of Citium	342-270
Livius Andronicus	284-204		

WRITERS

Antigonus of Carystus	241-197	Eratosthenes of Alexandria	276-194
Arcesilas	316-241	Livius Andronicus	284-204
Ariston	c. 250	Naevius, Gnaeus	264-194
Callimachus	c. 250	Plautus, Titus Maccius	250-184
Chrysippus	280-207	Rhianus	275-195
Cleanthes	301-232	Timaeus	345-250
Ennius, Quintus	239-170	Timon	320-230

ARTISTS

Aetion	fl. 250

Antigonus of Carystus	241-197	Livius Andronicus	284-204
Apollonius of Rhodes	fl222-181	Naevius, Gnaeus	264-194
Carneades	214-129	Pacuvius, Marcus	220-130
Chrysippus	280-207	Plautus, Titus Maccius	250-184
Ennius, Quintus	239-170	Polybius	201-120
Erastophones of Alexandria	276-194	Posidippus	fl. 225
Hostius	c. 225	Rhianus	275-195

Agatharchides	181-146	Naevius, Gnaeus	264-194
Antigonus of Carystus	241-197	Nicander	185-135
Apollonius of Rhodes	222-181	Pacuvius, Marcus	220-130
Carneades	214-129	Plautus, Titus Maccius	250-184
Critolaus	197-111	Polybius	200-120
Ennius, Quintus	239-170	Rhianus	275-195
Eratosthenes of Alexandria	276-194	Terence (Publius Terentius	
Lucilius, Gaius	180-103	Afer)	c. 190-159

Accius, Lucius	born 170	**Lucilius,** Gaius	180-103
Agatharchides	181-146	**Nicander**	185-135
Aristobulus	c. 160	**Pacuvius,** Marcus	220-130
Carneades	214-129	**Polybius**	200-120
Critolaus	197-111	**Terence** (Publius Terentius	
Ennius, Quintus	239-170	Afer)	c. 190-159

Agatharchides	181-146	Nicander	185-135
Aristeides	150-100	Pacuvius, Marcus	220-130
Carneades	214-129	Polybius	200-120
Critolaus	197-111	Posidonius	131-51
Lucilius, Gaius	180-103	Ssu-Ma Ch'ien	145-87

Archias, Aulus, Licinius	born 120	**Laberius,** Decimus	105-43
Aristeides	150-100	**Lucilius,** Gaius	180-103
Atticus, Titus Pomponius	109-32	**Polybius**	200-120
Bibaculus, Marcus Furius	born 103	**Posidonius**	131-51
Cicero, Marcus Tullius	106-43	**Ssu-Ma Ch'ien**	145-87
Critolaus	197-111	**Varro,** Marcus Terentius	116-27

Aenesidemus	c. 100	Hirtius, Aulus	90-43
Afranius, Lucius	fl. 100	Laberius, Decimus	105-43
Aristeides	150-100	Licinius, Macer Valvus Gaius	82-47
Atta, Titus, Quintus	died 77	Lucretius	98-55
Atticus, Titus Pomponius	109-32	Nepos, Cornelius	99-24
Cato, Marcus, Porcius	95-46	Pollio, Gaius Asinius	B.C. 76-5 A.D.
Cato, Publius Valerius	fl. 100	Posidonius	131-51
Catullus, Gaius Valerius	84-54	Sallust	86-34
Cicero, Marcus Tullius	106-43	Ssu-Ma Ch'ien	145-87
Dionysius of Halicarnasus	fl. 100	Varro, Marcus, Terentius	116-27
Dionysius, Thrax	fl. 100		

Andronicus	fl. 70-50	Livy	B.C. 59-17 A.D.
Athenodorus, Cananites		**Messalla,** Corvinus, Marcus	
	B.C. 74-7 A.D.	Valerius	B.C. 64-8 A.D.
Atticus, Titus Pomponius	109-32	**Nepos,** Cornelius	99-24
Cato, Marcus Porcius	95-46	**Pollio,** Gaius, Asinius	B.C. 76-5 A.D.
Catullus, Gaius Valerius	84-54	**Posidonius**	131-51
Cicero, Marcus Tullius	106-43	**Rufus,** Lucius, Varius	74-14
Diodorus, Siculus	fl. 60	**Sallust**	86-34
Fenestella	B.C. 52-19 A.D.	**Seneca,** Annaeus	B.C. 54-39 A.D.
Gallus, Cornelius	70-26	**Strabo**	B.C. 60-21 A.D.
Hirtius, Aulus	90-43	**Tibullus,** Albius	54-19
Horace	65-8	**Varro,** Marcus, Terentius	116-27
Laberius, Decimus	105-43	**Virgil**	70-19
Licinius, Macer Calvus Gaius	82-47		

WRITERS

Andronicus	fl. 70-50	Messalla, Corvinus Marcus	
Athenodorus, Cananites B.C. 74-7 A.D.		Valerius	B.C. 64-8 A.D.
Atticus, Titus Pomponis	109-32	Nepos, Cornelius	99-24
Cato, Marcus, Porcius	95-46	Ovid	B.C. 43-17 A.D.
Cicero, Marcus Tullius	106-43	Pollio, Gaius, Asinius	B.C. 76-5 A.D.
Cordus, Aulus Cremutius	fl. 43-18	Propertius, Sextus	48-15
Fenestella	B.C. 52-19 A.D.	Rufus, Lucius, Varius	74-14
Gallus, Cornelius	70-26	Sallust	86-34
Hirtius, Aulus	90-43	Seneca, Annaeus	B.C 54-39 A.D.
Horace	65-8	Strabo	B.C. 60-21 A.D.
Laberius, Decimus	105-43	Tibullus, Albius	54-19
Licinius, Macer, Calvus, Gaius	82-47	Varro, Marcus Terentius	116-27
Livy	B.C. 59-17 A.D.	Virgil	70-19

ARTISTS

Agesander   42-21

WRITERS

Asconius, Pedianus, Quintus
                                B.C. 9-A.D. 76
Athenodorus, Cananites B.C. 74-A.D. 7
Cordus, Aulus, Cremutius   fl. 43-18
Fenestella   B.C. 52-19 A.D.
Horace   65-8
Livy   B.C. 59-17 A.D.
Macer, Aemilius   died 16
Mesalla, Corvinus Marcus
   Valerius   B.C. 64-8 A.D.
Nepos, Cornelius   99-24
Ovid   B.C. 43-17 A.D.

Pollio, Gaius, Asinius   B.C. 76-5 A.D.
Propertius, Sextus   48-15
Rufus, Lucius, Varius   74-14
Seneca, Annaeus   B.C. 54-39 A.D.
Seneca, Lucius Annaeus
                           B.C. 4-65 A.D.
Strabo   B.C. 60-21 A.D.
Tibullus, Albius   54-19
Velleius, Paterculus Marcus
                          B.C. 19-31 A.D.
Virgil   70-19

ARTISTS

Agesander   42-21

33	The Crucifixion.
43	Claudius invades Britain.
51	St. Paul begins missionary travels.
64	Nero burns Rome. Persecution of Christians.
78	Agricola governor of Britain.
79	Pompeii and Herculaneum destroyed.
80	Colosseum in Rome built.
105	Paper invented by Tsai Lun.
121	Hadrian in Britain. Hadrian's wall.
212	Roman citizenship accorded to all free subjects.
238	Goths invade Eastern Europe.
253	Franks invade Gaul.
259	Destruction of the Temple of Diana at Esphesus.
285	Division of Empire, East and West.
292	Quadruple partition of the Empire.
350	Huns invade Europe.
364	Empire divided again. Emperors in East and West.
365	Picts and Scots in Britain.
397	Confessions of St. Augustine of Hippo.
406	Franks overrun Gaul.
410	Rome sacked by Alaric.
432	St. Patrick missionary in Ireland.
449	Britain invaded by Angles, Saxons and Jutes.
484	First schism. Eastern and Western churches.

PROMINENT PEOPLE

Jesus Christ	B.C. 4-33 A.D.	**Boadicea**	died 62 A.D.
Hadrian	76-139	**St. Augustine**	353-430
St. Patrick	385-461		

Han   B.C. 206-220 A.D.

ROMAN EMPERORS
Tiberius   14-37

WRITERS

Asconius Pedianus,		**Pliny** the Elder	23-79
Quintus	B.C. 9-76 A.D.	**Pollio,** Gaius	
Athenodorus,		Asinius	B.C. 76-5 A.D.
Cananties	B.C. 74-7 A.D.	Seneca, Annaeus	B.C. 54-39 A.D.
Fenestella	B.C. 52-19 A.D.	**Seneca,** Lucius	
Horace	B.C. 65-8 A.D.	Annaeus	B.C. 4-65 A.D.
Livy	B.C. 59-17 A.D.	Silius, Italicus	25-101
Messalla Corvinus,		**Strabo**	c. B.C. 60-21 A.D.
Marcus Valerius	B.C. 64-8 A.D.	**Velleius,** Paterculus	
Ovid	B.C. 43-17 A.D.	Marcus	B.C. 19-31 A.D.

Han   B.C. 206-220 A.D.

ROMAN EMPERORS

Caligula   37-41   Claudius   41-54

WRITERS

Asconius, Pedianus		Plutarch	46-120
Quintus	B.C. 9-76 A.D.	Quintilian, Marcus Fabius	
Curtius, Quintus	fl.41-54	Quintilianus	c. 35-100
Frontinus, Sextus Iulius	40-103	Seneca, Annaeus	B.C. 54-39 A.D.
Josephus, Flavius	37-95	Seneca, Lucius	
Lucan	39-65	Annaeus	B.C. 4-65 A.D.
Martial, Marcus Valerius		Silius, Italicus	25-101
Martialis	40-104	Statius, Publius Papinus	c. 45-96
Mela, Pomponius	fl. 40	Velleius, Paterculus	
Pan Chao, Ts'as Ta Ku	45-114	Marcus	B.C. 19-31 A.D.
Pliny the Elder	23-79		

Han   B.C. 206-220 A.D.

ROMAN EMPERORS

Claudius	41-54	Otho	68
Nero	54-68	Vitellius	68
Galba	68	Vespasian	68-79

POPES

St. Peter	64-c. 67	St. Linus	67-c. 79

WRITERS

Asconius, Pedianus	
Quintus B.C. 9-76 A.D.	
Bassus, Aufidius d.60	
Curtius, Quintus fl. 41-54	
Epictetus fl. 60	
Frontinus, Sestus Iulius 40-103	
Josephus, Flavius 37-95	
Juvenal 60-140	
Lucan 39-65	
Martial, Marcus Valerius	
Martialis 40-104	
Pan Chao, Ts'as Ta Ku 45-114	

Pliny the Elder   23-79
Pliny the Younger   61-113
Plutarch   46-120
Quintilian, Marcus Fabius
  Quintilianus   c. 35-100
Seneca, Lucius
  Annaeus   B.C. 4-65 A.D.
Silius, Italicus   25-101
Statius, Publius Papinius   c. 45-96
Suetonius, Tranquillus Gaius   75-160
Tacitus, Cornelius   55-120

Han   B.C. 206-220 A.D.

ROMAN EMPERORS

Vespasian	68-79	Nerva	96-98
Titus	79-81	Trajan	98-117
Domitian	81-96		

POPES

St. Linus	67-c. 79	St. Clement I	92-c. 101
St. Anacletus	79-c. 91	St. Evaristus	101-105

WRITERS

Apollonius of Tyana	fl. 76	Pan Chao, Ts'as Ta Ku	45-114
Arrianus, Flavius	90-c. 160	Pliny the Elder	23-79
Asconius Pedianus,		Pliny the younger	61-113
Quintus	B.C. 9-76 A.D.	Plutarch	46-120
Celsus	fl. 100	Quintilian, Marcus Fabius	
Frontinus, Sesxtus Iulius	40-103	Quintilianus	c. 35-100
Josephus, Flavius	37-95	Silius, Italicus	25-101
Juvenal	60-140	Statius, Publius Papinius	c. 45-96
Martial, Marcus Valerius		Suetonius, Tranquillus Gaius	75-160
Martialis	40-104	Tacitus, Cornelius	55-120

C

Han   B.C. 206-220 A.D.

ROMAN EMPERORS

Trajan   98-117   Hadrian   117-138

POPES

St. Clement I   92-101   St. Alexander   105-115
St. Evaristus   101-105 St. Sixtus I   115-125

WRITERS

Arrianus, Flavius	90-c. 160	Pan Chao, Ts'as Ta Ku	45-114
Basilides	fl. 125	Pliny the Younger	61-113
Frontinus, Sextus Iulius	40-103	Plutarch	46-120
Juvenal	60-140	Suetonius, Tranquilus Gaius	75-160
Lucian	125-190	Silius Italicus	25-101
Marcus Aurelius, Antoninus	121-180	Tacitus, Cornelius	55-120
Martial, Marcus Valerius			
Martialis	40-104		

ARTISTS

Apollorodus of Damascus   104-129

Han   B.C. 206-220 A.D.

ROMAN EMPERORS

Hadrian   117-138   Antoninus Pius   138-161

POPES

St. Telesphorus   125-136   St. Pius I.   140-155
St. Hyginus   136-140

WRITERS

Apuleius	fl. 150	Hegesippus	150-180
Arrianus, Flavius	90-c. 160	Juvenal	60-140
Cassius Dio, Cocceianus	150-235	Lucian	125-190
Clement of Alexandria	c. 150	Marcus Aurelius, Antoninus	121-180
Gellius Aulus	130-180		

ARTISTS

Appolodorus of Damascus   104-129

Han   B.C. 206-220 A.D.

ROMAN EMPERORS

Antoninus, Pius	138-161	Marcus Aurelius	161-180

POPES

St. Pius	140-155	St. Soter	166-175
St. Anicetus	155-166	St. Eleutherius	175-189

WRITERS

Africanus, Sextus Julius	170-240	Gellius, Aulus	130-180
Alciphron	fl. 180	Hegesippus	150-180
Ammonius	175-242	Lucian	125-190
Apuleius	fl. 150	Marcus Aurelius, Antoninus	121-180
Arrianus, Flavius	90-c. 160	Philostratus	170-245
Cassius Dio, Cocceianus	150-235	Tertullian	c. 160-230

Han   B.C. 206-220 A.D.

ROMAN EMPERORS

Marcus Aurelius	161-180	Pertinax	193
Commodus	180-193	Niger	193
Didius Julianus	193	Septimus Severus	193-211

POPES

St. Eleutherius	175-189	St. Zephyrinus	199-211
St. Victor I	189-199		

WRITERS

Africanus, Sextus Julius	170-240	Herodianus	180-c. 238
Ammonius	175-242	Lucian	125-190
Bhasa	fl. 200	Marcus Aurelius, Antoninus	121-180
Cassius Dio, Cocceianus	150-235	Origen	185-254
Gellius Aulus	130-180	Philostratus	170-245
Hegesippus	150-180	Tertullian	c. 160-230

Han   B.C. 206-220 A.D.   San Kuo (Epoch of
                                             the three kingdoms)   220-265

ROMAN EMPERORS

Septimus Severus	193-211	Macrinus	217-218
Caracalla	} 211-217	Elegalabus	218-222
Geta		Alexander Severus	222-235

POPES

St. Zephyrinus	199-217	St. Hyppolytus	
St. Calixtus I	217-222	(anti-pope)	217-235
		St. Urban I	222-230

WRITERS

Aelienus, Claudius	d. 222	Longinus, Dyonisius Cassius	213-273
Africanus, Sextus Julius	170-240	Origen	185-254
Ammonius	175-242	Philostratus	170-245
Cassius Dio, Cocceianus	150-235	Plotinus	205-270
Dexippus, Publius Herrenius	210-273	Tertullian	c. 160-230
Herodianus	180-238		

San Kuo (Epoch of
the three kingdoms)   220-265

ROMAN EMPERORS

Alexander, Severus	222-265	Gordian III.	238-244
Maximus I	235-238	Philip	244-249
Gordian I		Decius	249-251
Gordian II			
Balbinus	238		
Pupienus			

POPES

St. Urban I	222-230	St. Anteros	235-236
St. Pontianus	230-235	St. Fabian	236-250

WRITERS

Africanus, Sextus Juilus	170-240	Origen	185-254
Ammonius	175-242	Philostratus	170-245
Cassius Dio, Cocceianus	150-235	Plotinus	205-270
Dexippus, Publius Herennius	210-273	Porphyry	233-304
Herodianus	180-c. 238	Tertullian	c. 160-230
Longinus, Dyonisius Cassius	213-273		

San Kuo (Epoch of   Tsin   265-420
  the three kingdoms)   220-265

ROMAN EMPERORS

Decius	249-251	Gallienus	260-268
Gallus	251-253	Claudius II	268-270
Aemilian ⎫		Aurelian	270-275
Valerian ⎬	253-260	Tacitus	275-276
Gallienus ⎭			

POPES

Novatian (anti-pope)	251-	St. Sixtus II	257-258
St. Cornelius	251-253	St. Dionysius	259-268
St. Lucius I	253-254	St. Felix I	269-274
St. Stephen I	254-257	St. Eutychianus	275-283

WRITERS

Dexippus, Publius Herennius	210-273	Origen	185-254
Eusebius of Caesarea	264-340	Plotinus	205-270
Lactantius, Firmianus	260-340	Porphyry	233-304
Longinus, Dyonisius Cassius	213-273		

Tsin   265-420

ROMAN EMPERORS

Tacitus	275-276	Maximian	}	284-286
Florian	276	Diocletian		
Probus	276-282	Diocletian		286-305
Carus	282-284			
Carinus	}	284		
Numerian				

POPES

St. Eutychianus	275- c.283	St. Marcellinus	296-304
St. Gaius	283-c. 296		

WRITERS

Agathangelus, Agathange	c. 300	Lactantius, Firmianus	260-340
Athanasius (St.)	c. 296-373	Nemesianus, Marcus Aurelius	
Cato, Dionysius	c. 300	Olympus	fl. 283
Crysanthius	c. 300	Quintus, Smyrnaeus	c. 300
Eusebius of Caesarea	264-340	Porphyry	233-304

Tsin   265-420

ROMAN EMPERORS

Diocletian	286-305	Constantine The Great ⎤	
Constantius ⎱	305-306	Licinius	
Galerius ⎰		Maximin	
Severus	306	Galerius ⎬ 309-323	
Constantine The Great	306-307	Maxentius	
Licinius	307-308	Maximian ⎦	
Maximin	308-309	Constantine The Great	323-337

POPES

St. Marcellinus	296-304	St. Miltiades	311314
St. Marcellus I.	308-309	St. Sylvester I	314-335
St. Eusebius	309-310		

WRITERS

Athanasius (St.)	c. 296-373	Lactantius, Firmianus	260-340
Ausonius, Decimus Magnus	310-395	Porphyry	233-304
Eusebius of Caesarea	264-340		

Tsin   265-420

ROMAN EMPERORS

Constantine The Great   323-337

Constantine II
Constantius II }   337-353
Constans

POPES

St. Sylvester I	314-335	St. Julius I	337-352
St. Marcus	336		

WRITERS

Ammianus, Marcellines	330-390	Lactantius, Firmianus	260-340
Athanasius (St.)	c. 296-373	Plutarch of Athens	350-430
Ausonius, Decimus Magnus	310-395	Prudentius, Marcus Aurelius	
Eusebius of Caesarea	264-340	Clemens	348-410
Iamblicus	d. 338	Victorinus, Gaius Marius	fl. 350
Jerome (St.)	c. 340-420		

Tsin   265-420

ROMAN EMPERORS

Constantine II ⎫		Valens ⎫		
Constantius II ⎬	337-353	Valentinian I. ⎬		364-367
Constans ⎭		Valentinian I ⎱		
Constantius II	353-361	Gratian ⎰		367-375
Julian	361-363	Gratian ⎱		
Jovian	363-364	Valentinian II ⎰		375-379

POPES

St. Julius I	337-352	St. Damasus I	366-384
St. Liberius	352-366	Ursinus (anti-pope)	366-367
Felix II. (anti-pope)	355-365		

WRITERS

Aedesius	d. 355	Jerome (St.)	c. 340-420
Ammianus, Marcellines	330-390	Pelagius	c. 360-c. 420
Athanasius (St.)	c. 296-373	Plutarch of Athens	350-430
Augustine of Hippo (St.)	353-430	Prudentius, Marcus Aurelius	
Ausonius, Decimus Magnus	310-395	Clemens	348-410
Ephraem, Syrus	d. 373	Severus, Sulpicius	363-425
Eutropius	364-c. 378	Synesius	375-413
Hypatia	370-c. 415		

Tsin   265-420   Northern   386-581

ROMAN EMPERORS

Gratian   }   375-379   Theodosius The Great   379-395
Valentinian II   }   Honorius   393-423

POPES

St. Damasus I   366-384   St. Anastasius I   399-401
St. Siricius   384-399

WRITERS

Ammianus, Marcellines	330-390	Nemesius	fl. 390
Ammonius	c. 400	Pelagius	c. 360-c. 420
Augustine of Hippo (St.)	353-430	Plutarch of Athens	350-430
Ausonius, Decimus Magnus	310-395	Prudentius, Marcus Aurelius	
Claudianus, Claudius	fl. 395	Clemens	348-410
Dracontius, Blossius Aemilius	c. 400	Rutilius, Claudius	
Eutropius	364-378	Namatianus	c. 400
Fa Hsien	fl. 399-414	Severus, Sulpicius	363-425
Hypatia	370-415	Synesius	375-413
Jerome (St.)	c. 340-420	Theodoret	c. 393-458
Macrobius, Ambrosius			
Theodosius	395-423		

Tsin	265-420	Southern	420-589
Northern	386-581		

ROMAN EMPERORS
(Western)

Honorius	393-423	John (Usurper)	423-425
Constantine III (Usurper)	407-411	Valentinian III	425-455
Constantius III	421		

POPES

St. Anastasius I	399-401	St. Boniface I	418-422
St. Innocent I	401-417	Eulalius (anti-pope)	418-419
St. Zosimus	417-418	St. Celestine I	422-432

WRITERS

Augustine of Hippo (St.)	353-430	Pelagius	c. 360-c. 420
Fa Hsien	fl. 399-414	Plutarch of Athens	350-430
Hypatia	370-415	Proclus	412-485
Isaac of Antioch	408-450	Prudentius, Marcus Aurelius	
Jerome (St.)	c. 340-420	Clemens	348-410
Macrobius, Ambrosius		Severus, Sulpicius	363-425
Theodosius	395-423	Synesius	375-413
Orosius, Paulus	c. 415	Theodoret	c. 393-458

Northern   386-581   Southern   420-589

ROMAN EMPERORS

Valentinian III   425-455

POPES

St. Celestine I	422-432	St. Leo I	440-461
St. Sixtus III	432-440		

WRITERS

Achilles Tatius	fl. 450	Plutarch of Athens	350-430
Asclepigenia	430-485	Proclus,	412-485
Augustine of Hippo (St.)	353-430	Theodoret	c. 393-458
Isaac of Antioch	408-450		

| Northern | 386-581 | Southern | 420-589 |

ROMAN EMPERORS
(Western)

Valentinian III	425-455	Anthemius	467-472
Maximus (Usurper)	455	Olybrius (Usurper)	472-473
Avitus	455-456	Glycerius (Usurper)	473
Majorian	457-461	Julius Nepos	473-480
Severus (Usurper)	461-465	Romulus (Usurper)	475-476

POPES

| St. Leo I | 440-461 | St. Simplicius | 468-483 |
| St. Hilarius | 461-468 | | |

WRITERS

Asclepigenia	430-485	Jacob of Serugh	451-521
Ennodius, Magnus Felix	475-521	Kalidasa	fl. 450
Hesychius of Miletus	fl. 450	Proclus	412-485

Northern   356-581   Southern   420-589

ROMAN EMPERORS
Julius Nepos (Last emperor)   473-480

POPES

St. Simplicius	468-483	Anastasius II	496-498
St. Felix III	483-492	St. Symmachus	498-514
St. Gelasius I	492-496	Laurentius (anti-pope)	498-c. 505

FRANCE. HEADS OF STATE
Merovingian Dynasty   481-751

WRITERS

Amru 'Ul Quais	c. 500	Gildas	493-570
Antarah Ibn Shaddad	c. 500	Jacob of Serugh	451-521
Asclepigenia	430-485	Lydus, Joannes Laurentius	490-565
Boethius, Ancius Manlius		Nabigha Dhubyani	c. 500
Severinus	480-524	Philolaus	fl. 480
Cristodorus	491-518	Proclus	412-485
Corippus, Flavius Cresconius	c. 500	Procopius	499-656
Ennodius, Magnus Felix	475-521		

D

529   Code of Justinian.
542   Great plague in the East.
568   Lombard Kingdom founded.
622   The First year of the Mohammedan era.
787   Danish attacks on English coasts.
857   Papacy disputes.   Roman and Greek Empires.
888   France separated from Empire.
980   Viking attacks on English coasts.
991   Venice an independent kingdom.

PROMINENT PEOPLE

Mohammed   570-632   **St. Augustine**   d. 604
                                                (1st Archbishop of Canterbury)

| Northern | 386-581 | Southern | 420-589 |

POPES

| St. Symmachus | 498-514 | St. Hormisdas | 514-523 |
| Laurentius (anti-pope) | 498-c. 505 | St. John I | 523-526 |

FRANCE. HEADS OF STATE

| Merovingian Dynasty | 481-751 |

WRITERS

Boethius, Ancius Manlius		Gildas	493-570
Severinus	480-524	Jacob of Serugh	451-521
Christodorus	491-518	Lydus, Joannes Laurentius	490-565
Ennodius, Magnus Felix	475-521	Procopius	499-565

CHINESE DYNASTIES

Northern	386-581	Southern	420-589

POPES

St. John I	523-526	John II	533-535
St. Felix IV	526-530	St. Agapetus I	535-536
Dioscorus (anti-pope)	530	St. Silverius	536-537
Boniface II	530-532	Vigilius	537-555

FRANCE. HEADS OF STATE

Merovingian Dynasty	481-751

WRITERS

Agathias	536-582	Gildas	493-570
Alqama Al-Fahl	c. 550	Gregory, St. of Tours	538-594
Anaximenes of Miletus	c. 550	Jordanes	fl. 530
Columban	543-615	Lydus, Joannes Laurentius	490-565
Evagrius	536-600	Procopius	499-565

Northern	386-581	Southern	420-589

POPES

Vigilius	537-555	John III	561-574
Pelagius I	555-561	Benedict I	574-579

FRANCE. HEADS OF STATE

Merovingian Dynasty	481-751

WRITERS

Agathias	536-582	Gregory St. of Tours	538-594
Columban	543-615	Isidore of Seville	560-636
Evagrius	536-600	Lydus, Joannes Laurentius	490-565
Gildas	493-570	Procopius	499-565

CHINESE DYNASTIES   576-600

| Northern | 386-581 | Sui | 581-618 |
| Southern | 420-589 | | |

POPES

| Benedict I | 574-579 | St. Gregory I | 590-604 |
| Palagius II | 579-590 | | |

FRANCE. HEADS OF STATE

| Merovingian Dynasty | 481-751 |

WRITERS

Agathias	536-582	Evagrius	536-600
Aneurin	fl. 600	George Pisida	c. 600
Bhartrihari	fl. 600	Gregory St. of Tours	538-594
Columban	543-615	Isidore of Seville	560-636

Sui	581-618	T'Ang	618-907

POPES

St. Gregory I	590-604	St. Deusdedit	615-618
St. Sabinian	604-606	Boniface V	619-625
Boniface III	607-608	Honorius I	625-638
St. Boniface IV	608-615		

FRANCE. HEADS OF STATE

Merovingian Dynasty	481-751

WRITERS

Adamnan St.	625-704	Isidore of Seville	560-636
Columban	543-615	Simocatta, Theophylact	610-640
Hsuan Tsung	c. 605		

T'Ang   618-907

POPES

Honorius I	625-638	Theodore I	642-649
Severinus	638-640	St. Martin I	649-655
John IV	640-642		

FRANCE. HEADS OF STATE

Merovingian Dynasty   481-751

WRITERS

Adamnan St.	625-704	Isidore of Seville	560-636
Aldhelm St.	c. 640-709	Simocatta, Theophylact	610-640
Farazdaq	641-728		

T'Ang   618-907

POPES

St. Martin I, d. in exile	649-655	St. Vitalian	657-672
St. Eugenius I	654-657	Adeodatus II	672-676

FRANCE. HEADS OF STATE

Merovingian Dynasty   481-751

WRITERS

Adamnan St.	625-704	Farazdaq	641-728
Aldhelm St.	c. 640-709	Hassan Ibn, Thabit	d. 674
Bede, The Venerable	673-735		

T'Ang   618-907

POPES

Adeodatus II	672-676	John V	685-686
Donus	676-678	Conon	686-687
St. Agatho	678-681	Theodore and Paschal	
St. Leo II	681-683	(anti-popes)	687
St. Benedict II	683-685	St. Sergius I	687-701

FRANCE. HEADS OF STATE

Merovingian Dynasty   418-751

WRITERS

Adamnan St.	625-704	Caedmon	d. 680
Akahito, Yamobe	fl. 700	Farazdaq	641-728
Aldhelm St.	c.640-709	John of Damascus	c. 676-c. 754
Bede, The Venerable	673-735	Li-Po	700-762

ARTISTS

Wang-Wei   699-759

T'Ang   618-907

POPES

St. Sergius I	687-701	Sisinnius	708
John VI	701-705	Constantine	708-715
John VII	705-707	St. Gregory II	715-731

FRANCE. HEADS OF STATE

Merovingian Dynasty   418-751

WRITERS

Adamnan St.	625-704	John of Damascus	c. 676-c. 754
Aldhelm St.	c. 640-709	Li Po	700-762
Bede, The Venerable	673-735	Paulus Diaconus	720-800
Farazdaq	641-728		

ARTISTS

Wang Wei   699-759

T'Ang   618-907

POPES

St. Gregory II	715-731	Stephen II	752-757
St. Gregory III	731-741	St. Paul I	757-767
St. Zacharias	741-752		

FRANCE. HEADS OF STATE

Merovingian Dynasty   481-751

WRITERS

Abu-L-Atahiya	748-828	Farazdaq	641-728
Alcuin	735-804	Jarir Ibn Atiyya, Ul-Khaffi	d. 728
Bede, The Venerable	673-735	John of Damascus	c. 676-c. 754
Bhavabuti	fl. 730	Li Po	700-762
Cynewulf	737-780	Paulus Diaconus	720-800

ARTISTS

Wang Wei   699-759

T'Ang   618-907

POPES

St. Stephen	752-757	Philip (anti-pope)	768
St. Paul I	757-767	Stephen III	768-772
Constantine (anti-pope)	767-768	Adrian I	772-795

FRANCE. HEADS OF STATE

Merovingian Dynasty	481-751	Carolingian Dynasty	751-987

WRITERS

Abu-L-Atahiya	748-828	Ibn Ishaq	d. 768
Abu Nuwas	756-810	John of Damascus	c. 676-c. 754
Alcuin	735-804	Li Po	700-762
Cynewulf	737-780	Paulus Diaconus	720-800
Einhard	770-840	Po Chu I	772-846

ARTISTS

Wang Wei	699-759

CHINESE DYNASTIES

T'Ang   618-907

POPES
Adrian I   772-795   St. Leo III   795-816

FRANCE. HEADS OF STATE
Carolingian Dynasty   751-987

WRITERS

Abu-L-Atahiya	748-828	Einhard	770-840
Abu Nuwas	756-810	Nicephorus, Patriarcha	789-829
Alcuin	735-804	Paulus, Diaconus	720-800
Cynewulf	737-780	Po Chu I	772-846

T'Ang   618-907

POPES

St. Leo III	795-816	St. Paschal I	817-824
Stephen IV	816-817	Eugenius II	824-827

FRANCE. HEADS OF STATE

Carolingian Dynasty   751-987

HOLY ROMAN EMPERORS

Charles I (Charlemagne)   800-814   Louis I   814-840

ENGLISH SOVEREIGNS

Egbert   802-839

WRITERS

Abu-L-Atahiya	748-828	Einhard	770-840
Abu Nuwas	756-810	Erigena, Johannes Scotus	815-877
Abutamman, Habbib Ibn		Hisham Ibn Al-Kalbi	d. 819
Aus	807-c. 850	Nicephorus, Patriarcha	789-829
Alcuin	735-804	Po Chu I	772-846
Buaturi, Al Walid Ibn			
Ubaid-Allah	820-897		

T'Ang   618-907

POPES

Eugenius II	824-827	John (anti-pope)	844
Valentinus	827	Sergius II	844-847
Gregory IV	827-844	St. Leo IV	847-855

FRANCE. HEADS OF STATE

Carolingian Dynasty   751-987

HOLY ROMAN EMPERORS

Louis I   814-840   Lothar   840-855

ENGLAND. SOVEREIGNS

Egbert   802-839   Ethelwulf   839-858

SWEDEN. KINGS

Olaf and Edmund   850-882

WRITERS

Abu-L-Atahiya	748-828	Ibn, Duraid	837-934
Abutamman Habib Ibn		Ibn, Qutaiba	828-889
Aus	807-c. 850	Israeli, Isaac Ben Solomon	845-940
Alfred the Great	849-899	Nicephorus, Patriarcha	789-829
Buaturi, Al Walid Ibn		Po Chu I	772-846
Ubaid Allah	820-897	Tabari, Abu Jofar Mohammed	
Einhard	770-840	Ben Jarirol	839-923
Erigena, Johannes Scotus	815-877		

T'Ang   618-907

POPES

St. Leo IV	847-855	St. Nicholas I	858-867
Anastasius (anti-pope)	855	Adrian II	867-872
Benedict III	855-858	John VIII	872-882

FRANCE. HEADS OF STATE

Carolingian Dynasty   751-987

HOLY ROMAN EMPERORS

Lothar	840-855	Charles II	875-881
Louis II	855-875		

ENGLAND. SOVEREIGNS

Ethelwulf	839-858	Ethelred I	865-870
Ethelbald	858-860	Alfred the Great	870-899
Ethelbert	860-865		

SWEDEN. KINGS

Olaf and Edmund   850-882

WRITERS

Alfred the Great	849-899	Ibn, Duraid	837-934
Arethas	860-940	Ibn, Qutaiba	828-889
Buaturi, Ali-Walid Ibn		Israeli, Isaac Ben Solomon	845-940
Ubaid-Allah	820-897	Kindi, Abu Yusuf Ya Qubibn	
Erigena, Johannes Scotus	815-877	Ibn Ishaq Ul-Kindi	c. 873
Farabi	870-950	Tabari, Abu Jofar Mohammed	
Ibn'Abd Rabbihi	860-940	Ben Jarirol	839-923

E

T'Ang   618-907

POPES

John VIII	872-882	Boniface VI	c. 896
Marinus I	882-884	Stephen VI	896-897
St. Adrian III	884-885	Romanus	897
Stephen V	885-891	Theodore II	897
Formosus	891-896	John IX	898-900

FRANCE. HEADS OF STATE

Carolingian Dynasty   751-987

HOLY ROMAN EMPERORS

Charles II	875-881	Lambert	894-896
Charles III	882-887	Arnulf	896-899
Guido	887-894	Louis the child	899-901

ENGLAND. SOVEREIGNS

Alfred the Great   870-899   Edward the Elder   899-925

SWEDEN. KINGS

Olaf and Edmund   850-882   Eric Edmundsson   882-905

WRITERS

Abu'L Faraj Al-Isfahani	897-967	Ibn'Abd Rabbihi	860-940
Alfred the Great	849-899	Ibn, Duraid	837-934
Arethas	860-940	Ibn, Qutaiba	828-889
Buaturi, Al-Walid Ibn		Israeli, Isaac Ben Solomon	845-940
Ubaid-Allah	820-897	Tabari, Abu Jofar Mohammed	
Erigena, Johannes Scotus	815-877	Ben Jarirol	839-923
Farabi	870-950	Ya Qubi	d. 891

T'Ang	618-907	Wu Tai (Epoch of the five Dynasties)	907-960

POPES

John IX	898-900	Sergius III	904-911
Benedict IV	901-903	Anastasius III	911-913
Leo V	903	Lando	913-914
Christoph (anti-pope)	903-904	John X	914-928

FRANCE. HEADS OF STATE

Carolingian Dynasty	751-987

HOLY ROMAN EMPERORS

Louis the Child	899-901	Berengar	915-918
Louis III	901-911	Henry I	918-936
Conrad I	911-915		

ENGLAND. SOVEREIGNS

Edward the Elder	899-925	Athelstan	925-939

SWEDEN. KINGS

Eric Edmundsson	882-905	Bjorn Ericsson and Ring	905-950

WRITERS

Abu'L Faraj Al-Isfahani	897-967	Israeli, Isaac Ben Solomon	845-940
Arethas	860-940	Liudprand	922-972
Farabi	870-950	Tabari, Abu Jofar Mohammed	
Ibn'Abd Rabbihi	860-940	Ben Jarirol	839-923
Ibn Duraid	837-934		

Wu Tai (Epoch of
    the five Dynasties)   907-960

POPES

John X	914-928	Leo VII	936-939
Leo VI	928	Stephen VIII	939-942
Stephen VII	928-931	Marinus II	942-946
John XI	931-935	Agapetus II	946-955

FRANCE. HEADS OF STATE

Carolingian Dynasty   751-987

HOLY ROMAN EMPERORS

Henry I   918-936 Otto I   936-973

ENGLAND. SOVEREIGNS

Athelstan	925-939	Edred	946-955
Edmund I	939-946		

SWEDEN. KINGS

Bjorn Ericsson and Ring   905-950 Eric the Victorious   950-993

WRITERS

Abbon of Fleury	945-1004	Hrosvitha	935-1002
Abu'L Faraj Al-Isfahani	897-967	Ibn-Abd Rabbihi	860-940
Arathas	860-940	Ibn Duraid	837-934
Farabi	870-950	Israeli, Isaac Ben Solomon	845-940
Firdausi	c. 950-1020	Liudprand	922-972

Wu Tai (Epoch of the five Dynasties)	907-960	Sung	960-1279

POPES

Agapetus II	946-955	John XIII	965-972
John XII	955-964	Benedict VI	973-974
Leo VIII	963-965	Boniface VII (anti-pope)	974
Benedict V	966	Benedict VII	974-983

FRANCE. HEADS OF STATE

Carolingian Dynasty	751-987

HOLY ROMAN EMPERORS

Otto I	936-973	Otto II	973-983

ENGLAND. SOVEREIGNS

Edred	946-955	Edgar	959-975
Edwy	955-959	Edward the Younger	975-978

SWEDEN. KINGS

Eric the Victorious	950-993

WRITERS

Abbon of Fleury	945-1004	Hamadhani	967-1007
Abu'L Faraj Al-Isfahani	897-967	Hrosvitha	935-1002
Abu-L-UL-Maarri	973-1057	Ibn Faradi	962-1012
Aelfric	955-c. 1020	Liudprand	922-972
Aimoin	960-1010	Masudi, Abul-Hasan	d. 956
Firdausi	c. 950-1020		

Sung 960-1279

POPES

Benedict VII	974-983	Gregory V	996-999
John XIV	983-984	John XVI (anti-pope)	997-998
Boniface VII (anti-pope)	984-985	Sylvester II	999-1003
John XV	985-996		

FRANCE. HEADS OF STATE

Carolingian Dynasty	751-987	Robert	996-1031
Hugh Capet	987-996		

HOLY ROMAN EMPERORS

Otto II	973-983	Otto III	983-1002

ENGLAND. SOVEREIGNS

Edward the Younger	975-978	Ethelred II	979-1016

SWEDEN. KINGS

Eric the Victorious	950-993	Olaf Scatt-King	999-1022
Period of Confusion	933-999		

WRITERS

Abbon of Fleury	945-1004	Firdausi	c. 950-1020
Abu-L-Ala UL-Maarri	973-1057	Hamadhani	967-1007
Aelfric	955-c. 1020	Hrosvitha	935-1002
Aimoin	960-1010	Ibn Faradi	962-1012
Avicenna Ibn Sina	980-1037	Murasaki Shikibu	978-1031

COMPOSERS

Guido Aretinus of Arezzo	990-1050

1001   Norse discovery of Nova Scotia.
1009   Danes attack London.
1028   Canute conquers Norway.
1054   Separation of Latin and Greek churches.
1066   Battle of Hastings.
1086   Domesday book.
1099   Capture of Jerusalem.   Knights of St. John instituted.
1100   William II killed in New Forest.

PROMINENT PEOPLE

El Cid	1035-1099	**Lady Godiva**	1040-1080
Godfrey of Bouillon	1061-1100		

Sung   960-1279

POPES

Sylvester II	999-1003	Gregory (anti-pope)	1012
John XVII	1003-1004	Benedict VIII	1012-1024
John XVIII	1004-1009	John XIX	1024-1032
Sergius IV	1009-1012		

FRANCE. HEADS OF STATE

Robert   996-1031

HOLY ROMAN EMPERORS

Otto III	983-1002	Conrad II	1024-1037
Henry II	1002-1024		

ENGLAND. SOVEREIGNS

Ethelred II	979-1016	Canute	1016-1035
Edmund II	1016		

SWEDEN. KINGS

Olaf Scatt-King	999-1022	Anund Jacob	1022-1050

WRITERS

Abbon of Fleury	945-1004	Hamadhani	967-1007
Abu-L-Ala Ul-Maarri	973-1057	Hrosvitha	935-1002
Adhemar De Chabannes	988-c. 1034	Ibn Faradi	962-1012
Aelfric	955-c. 1020	Ibn Gabirol	1021-1058
Aimoin	960-1010	Murasaki Shikibu	978-1031
Avicebron	fl. 1020-1070	Psellus, Michael	
Avicenna Ibn Sina	980-1037	Constantine	1018-1079
Firdausi	c. 950-1020		

COMPOSERS

Guido Aretinus of Arezzo	990-1050

Sung   960-1279

POPES

John XIX	1024-1032	Clement II	1046-1047
Benedict IX	1032-1044	Benedict IX (restored)	1047-1048
Sylvester III	1045	Damasus II	1048
Gregory VI	1045-1046	St. Leo IX	1049-1054

FRANCE. HEADS OF STATE

Robert   996-1031   Henry I   1031-1060

HOLY ROMAN EMPERORS

Conrad II   1024-1037   Henry III   1037-1056

ENGLAND. SOVEREIGNS

Canute	1016-1035	Harthacanute	1040-1042
Harold	1035-1040	Edward the Confessor	1042-1066

SWEDEN. KINGS

Anund Jacob   1022-1050   Edmund the Old   1050-1060

WRITERS

Abu-L-Ala Ul-Maarri	973-1057	Bahya, Ibn Pauda	c. 1040
Adalberon	d. 1030	Ibn Gabirol	1021-1058
Adhemar De Chabannes	c. 988-1034	Murasaki Shikibu	978-1031
Anselm St.	1033-1109	Omar Khayam	1050-1123
Avicebron	fl. 1020-1070	Psellus, Michael	
Avicenna Ibn Sina	980-1037	Constantine	1018-1079

COMPOSERS

Guido Aretinus of Arezzo   990-1050

Sung   960-1279

POPES

St. Leo IX	1049-1054	Nicholas II	1059-1061
Victor II	1055-1057	Honorius II (anti-pope)	1061-1072
Stephen IX	1057-1058	Alexander II	1061-1073
Benedict X (anti-pope)	1058-1059	St. Gregory VII	1073-1085

FRANCE. HEADS OF STATE

Henry I	1031-1060	Philip I	1060-1108

HOLY ROMAN EMPERORS

Henry III	1037-1056	Henry IV	1056-1106

ENGLAND. SOVEREIGNS

Edward the Confessor	1042-1066	William I	1066-1087
Harold II	1066		

SWEDEN. KINGS

Edmund the Old	1050-1060	Period of Confusion	1066-1080
Stenkil	1060-1066		

WRITERS

Abu-L-Ala Ul-Maarri	973-1057	Hariri, Abu Mohammed	1054-1122
Adam of Bremen	fl. 1075	Ibn Gabirol	1021-1058
Anselm St.	1033-1109	Omar Khayam	1050-1123
Avicebron	fl. 1020-1070	Orderic Vitalis	1075-1142
Bryennius, Nicephorus	1062-1137	Psellus, Michael	
Eadmer	1060-1124	Constantine	1018-1079
Ghazali	1058-1111		

Sung   960-1279

POPES

St. Gregory VII	1073-1085	Clement III (anti-pope)	1084-1100
Victor III	1086-1087	Theodoric (anti-pope)	1100
Urban II	1088-1099	Paschal II	1099-1118

FRANCE. HEADS OF STATE
Philip I   1060-1108

HOLY ROMAN EMPERORS
Henry IV   1056-1106

ENGLAND. SOVEREIGNS

William I	1066-1087	Henry I	1100-1135
William II	1087-1100		

SWEDEN. KINGS

Period of Confusion	1066-1080	Inge the Good	1090-1118
Halstan	1080-1093		

WRITERS

Abelard, Peter	1079-1142	Halevi, Judah Ben	
Abenezra	1093-1167	Samuel	c. 1085-1140
Albert of Aix	c. 1100	Hariri, Abu Mohammed	1054-112
Anna, Comnena	1083-1148	Heinrich Von Veldecke	c. 1100
Anselm St.	1033-1109	Omar Khayam	1050-1123
Bernard of Clairvaux, St.	1090-1153	Orderic Vitalis	1075-1142
Bryennius, Nicephorus	1062-1137	Psellus, Michael	
Chretien De Troyes	c. 1100	Constantine	1018-1079
Eadmer	1060-1124	Tzetzes, Johannes	1120-1183
Ghazali	1058-1111	William of Malmesbury	c. 1095-1143

1147   Second Crusade.
1170   Thomas a Becket assassinated.
1180   Carthusian monastries established in England.
1187   Third Crusade.

PROMINENT PEOPLE

Thomas A Becket   1118-1170   Jenghiz Khan   1162-1227
Saladin   1137-1193

Sung   960-1279

POPES

Paschal II	1099-1118	Gregory VIII (anti-pope)	1118-1121
Albert (anti-pope)	1102	Calixtus II	1119-1124
Sylvester IV (anti-pope)	1105-1111	Honorius II	1124-1130
Gelasius II	1118-1119	Celestine II (anti-pope)	1124

FRANCE. HEADS OF STATE

Philip I	1060-1108	Louis VI	1108-1137

HOLY ROMAN EMPERORS

Henry IV	1056-1106	Lothar II	1125-1138
Henry V	1106-1125		

ENGLAND. SOVEREIGNS

Henry I	1100-1135

SWEDEN. KINGS

Inge the Good	1090-1118	Inge II Halstansson	1118-1130

WRITERS

Abelard, Peter	1079-1142	Geoffrey of Monmouth	c. 1100-1154
Abenezra	1093-1167	Ghazali	1058-1111
Abraham, Ibn Doud	1110-1180	Halevi, Judah Ben	
Ailred, Ethelred	1109-1166	Samuel	c. 1085-1140
Anna, Comnena	1083-1148	Hariri, Abu Mohammed	1054-1122
Anselm, St.	1033-1109	Hilarius	c. 1125
Benoit de St. Maure	fl. c. 1150	Omar Khayam	1050-1123
Bernard of Clairvaux, St.	1090-1153	Orderic Vitalis	1075-1142
Bryennius, Nicephorus	1062-1137	Tzestzes, Johannes	1120-1183
Eadmer	1060-1124	Wace, Robert	c. 1115-c. 1183
Farid Ud-Din Attar	1119-1229	William of Malmesbury	c. 1095-1143

Kao Tsung
  (Sung Dynasty)   1127-1162

POPES

Honorius II	1124-1130	Celestine II	1143-1144
Innocent II	1130-1143	Lucius II	1144-1145
Anacletus II (anti-pope)	1130-1138	Eugenius III	1145-1153
Victor IV (anti-pope)	1138		

FRANCE. HEADS OF STATE

Louis VI	1108-1137	Louis VII	1137-1180

HOLY ROMAN EMPERORS

Lothar II	1125-1138	Conrad III	1138-1152

ENGLAND. SOVEREIGNS

Henry I	1100-1135	Stephen	1135-1154

SWEDEN. KINGS

Inge II Halstansson	1118-1130	Sverker	1132-1155

PORTUGAL. KINGS

Alfonso I	1139-1185

WRITERS

Aagesen, Svend	fl. 1130	Geoffrey of Monmouth	c. 1100-1154
Abelard, Peter	1079-1142	Giraldus, Cambrensis	1146-1220
Abenezra	1093-1167	Halevi, Judah Ben	
Abraham, Ibn Doud	1110-1180	Samuel	1085-1140
Acominatus, Michael	1140-1220	Ibn Athir Majd Ud-Din	1149-1210
Ailred, Ethelred	1109-1166	Maimonides	1135-1204
Anna, Comnena	1083-1148	Map, Walter	1137-1209
Avempace, Ibn Bajjah	c. 1138	Orderic Vitalis	1075-1142
Averhoes, Ibn Ruoshd	1126-1198	Saxo Grammaticus	1150-1206
Bernard of Clairvaux, St.	1090-1153	Thomas	fl. 1150
Bryennius, Nicephorus	1062-1137	Tzestzes, Johannes	1120-1183
Chang Chun Kiu	1148-1227	Wace, Robert	c. 1115-c. 1183
Cinnamus, John	c. 1143-1180	William of Malmesbury	c. 1095-1143
Daniel, Arnaut	fl. 1150	William of Newburgh	1135-1200
Fakhr Ud Din Razi	1149-1209	William of Tyre	1137-1190
Farid Ud-Din Attar	1119-1229		

Kao Tsung		Hsaio Tsung	
(Sung Dynasty)	1127-1162	(Sung Dynasty)	1162-1189

POPES

Eugenius III	1145-1153	Victor IV (anti-pope)	1159-1164
Anastasius IV	1153-1154	Paschal III (anti-pope)	1164-1168
Adrian IV	1154-1159	Calixtus III (anti-pope)	1168-1178
Alexander III	1159-1181		

FRANCE. HEADS OF STATE

Louis VII	1137-1180

HOLY ROMAN EMPERORS

Conrad III	1138-1152	Frederick I	1152-1190

ENGLAND. SOVEREIGNS

Stephen	1135-1154	Henry II	1154-1189

SWEDEN. KINGS

Sverker	1132-1155	Charles VII	1160-1167
Eric IX (Saint)	1150-1160	Knut Ericsson	1167-1196

PORTUGAL. KINGS

Alfonso I	1139-1185

WRITERS

Abd-Ul-Latif	1162-1231	Hartmann, Von Aue	1170-1215
Abenezra	1093-1167	Ibn Arabi	1165-1240
Abraham, Ibn Doud	1110-1180	Ibn Athir	1160-1234
Acominatus, Michael	1140-1220	Ibn Athir, Diya Ud-Din	1163-1239
Ailred, Ethelred	1109-1166	Ibn Athir, Majd, Ud-Din	1149-1210
Averhoes, Ibn Ruoshd	1126-1198	Maimonides	1135-1204
Bar-Salibi, Jacob	d. 1171	Map, Walter	1137-1209
Bernard of Clairvaux, St.	1090-1153	Marie De France	c. 1175-1190
Brakelond, Jocelyn De	1173-1202	Saxo Grammaticus	1150-1206
Chang Chun Kiu	1148-1227	Tzestzes, Johannes	1120-1183
Cinnamus, John	c. 1143-1180	Villehardouin, Geoffroy De	1160-1213
Fakhr Ud-Din Razi	1149-1209	Wace, Robert	c. 1115-c. 1183
Farid Ud-Din Attar	1119-1229	Walther, Von Der	
Geoffrey of Monmouth	c. 1100-1154	Vogelweide	1170-1230
Giraldus, Cambrensis	1146-1220	William of Newburgh	1135-1200
Grosseteste, Robert	c. 1175-1253	William of Tyre	1137-1190

Hsaio Tsung (Sung Dynasty)	1162-1189	Kuang Tsung (Sung Dynasty	1189-1194
Ning Tsung (Sung Dynasty)	1194-1224		

POPES

Calixtus III (anti-pope)	1168-1178	Gregory VIII	1187
Innocent III (anti-pope)	1179-1180	Clement III	1187-1191
Lucius III	1181-1185	Celestine III	1191-1198
Urban III	1185-1187	Innocent III	1198-1216

FRANCE. HEADS OF STATE

Louis VII	1137-1180	Philip II	1180-1223

HOLY ROMAN EMPERORS

Frederick I.	1152-1190	**Philip** } (Rivals)	1197-120
Henry VI	1190-1197	**Otto IV**	

ENGLAND. SOVEREIGNS

Henry II	1154-1189	John	1199-1216
Richard I	1189-1199		

SWEDEN. KINGS

Knut Ericsson	1167-1196	Sverker Carlsson	1196-1205

PORTUGAL. KINGS

Alfonso I	1139-1185	Sancho I	1185-1211

Abd-Ul-Latif	1162-1231
Abraham, Ibn Doud	1110-1180
Acominatus, Michael	1140-1220
Adam, Scotus	c. 1180
Ambrose	c. 1190
Andre Le Chapelain	1180-1223
Anwari	d. 1196
Averhoes, Ibn Ruoshd	1126-1198
Beha Ud-Din Zuhair	1186-1258
Berceo, Gonsalo De	1180-1246
Brakelond, Jocelyn de	1173-1202
Chand Bardai	c. 1200
Chang Chun Kiu	1148-1227
Cinnamus, John	c. 1143-1180
Fakhr, Ud-Din Razi	1149-1209
Farid Ud-Din Attar	1119-1229
Garland, John	1195-1272
Giraldus, Cambrensis	1146-1220
Gottfried, Von Strassburg	fl. 1200
Grosseteste, Robert	c. 1175-1253
Hartmann, Von Aue	1170-1215
Ibn Arabi	1165-1240
Ibn Athir	1160-1234
Ibn Athir, Diya Ud-Din	1163-1239
Ibn Athir, Majd Ud-Din	1149-1210
Ibn Farid	1181-1235
Ibn Tufail	d. 1185
Maimonides	1135-1204
Map, Walter	1137-1209
Marie De France	c. 1175-1190
Montreuil, Gerbert De	c. 1200
Paris, Matthew	1200-1259
Sa'Di	1184-1291
Saxo Grammaticus	1150-1206
Snorri Sturluson	1179-1241
Tzestzes, Johannes	1120-1183
Villehardouin, Geoffroy De	1160-1213
Wace, Robert	c. 1115-c. 1183
Walther, Von De Vogelweide	1170-1200
William of Newburgh	1135-1200
William of Tyre	1137-1190
Wolfar Von Eschenbach	fl. 1200

ARTISTS

Hsai Kuei	1180-1230

F

1202	Fourth Crusade. France and England at War.
1203	Crusaders conquer Constantinople.
1206	Mogul Empire founded.
1209	Franciscan order established.
1215	Magna Carta signed by King John.
1216	First Parliament in England.
1217	Fifth Crusade.
1228	Sixth Crusade.
1229	Jerusalem ceded to Christians.
1248	Seventh Crusade.
1253	Jews driven out of France.
1265	Battle of Evesham.
1282	Sicilian Vespers massacre.
1290	Jews driven out of England.
1297	Battle of Stirling.
1298	Battle of Falkirk.

PROMINENT PEOPLE

Jenghiz Khan	1162-1227	Bruce, Robert	1274-1329
Marco Polo	1256-1323		

Ning Tsung		T'Ai Tsu (Jenghiz Kahn—	
(Sung Dynasty)	1194-1224	Mongol Dynasty)	1206-1229
Li Tsung			
(Sung Dynasty)	1224-1264		

POPES

Innocent III	1198-1216	Honorius III	1216-1227

FRANCE. HEADS OF STATE

Philip II	1180-1223	Louis VIII	1223-1226

HOLY ROMAN EMPERORS

Philip	} (Rivals)	1197-1208	Otto IV	1208-1212
Otto IV			Frederick II	1212-1250

ENGLAND. SOVEREIGNS

John	1199-1216	Henry III	1216-1272

SWEDEN. KINGS

Sverker Carlsson	1196-1205	Period of Confusion	1205-1250

PORTUGAL. KINGS

Sancho I	1185-1211	Sancho II	1223-1248
Alphonso II	1211-1223		

WRITERS

Abd-Ul-Latif	1162-1231	Ibn Athir	1160-1234
Acominatus, Michael	1140-1220	Ibn Athir, Diya Ud-Din	1163-1239
Albertus Magnus	1206-1280	Ibn Athir, Majd Ud-Din	1149-1210
Andre Le Chapelain	1180-1223	Ibn Farid	1181-1235
Aquinus, Thomas	1225-1275	Jalal Ad-Din Rumi	1207-1273
Bacon, Roger	1214-1294	Joinvile, Jean	1224-1319
Beha Ud-Din Zuhair	1186-1258	Latini, Brunetto	1210-1294
Berceo, Gonzalo De	1180-1246	Maimonides	1135-1204
Brakelond, Jocelyn De	1173-1202	Map, Walter	1137-1209
Busri	1211-1294	Paris, Matthew	c. 1200-1259
Chang Chun Kiu	1148-1227	Rumi	1207-1273
Elmacin, George	1223-1274	Sa'Di	1184-1291
Fakhr Ud-Din Razi	1149-1209	Saxo Grammaticus	1150-1206
Farid Ud-Din Attar	1119-1229	Snorri, Sturluson	1179-1241
Garland, John	1195-1272	Thomas the Rhymer	
Gervase of Tilbury	c. 1211	(of Ercelduone)	c. 1220-c. 1297
Giraldus Cambrensis	1146-1220	Villehardouin,	
Gottfried, Von Strassburg	c. 1210	Geoffrey De	1160-1213
Grosseteste, Robert	c. 1175-1253	Walther, Von Der	
Hartmann, Von Aue	1170-1215	Vogelsweide	1170-1230
Ibn Arabi	1165-1240		

ARTISTS

Hsia Kuei	1180-1230	Pisano, Niccola	1225-1278

Li Tsung (Sung Dynasty)	1224-1264	T'Ai Tsung (Ogotai Khan—	
T'Ai Tsu (Jenghiz Khan—		Mongol Dynasty)	1229-1246
Mongol Dynasty)	1206-1229	Ting Tsung (Kuyak Khan—	
		Mongol Dynasty)	1246-1251

POPES

Honorius III	1216-1227	Celestine IV	1241
Gregory IX	1227-1241	Innocent IV	1243-1254

FRANCE. HEADS OF STATE

Louis VIII	1223-1226	Louis IX	1226-1270

HOLY ROMAN EMPERORS

Frederick II	1212-1250	Conrad IV	1250-1254

ENGLAND. SOVEREIGNS

Henry III	1216-1272

SWEDEN. KINGS

Period of Confusion	1205-1250	Valdemar	1250-1275

PORTUGAL. KINGS

Sancho II	1223-1248	Alphonso III	1248-1279

WRITERS

Abano, Pietro D'	1250-1316	Ibn Athir, Diya Ud-Din	1163-1239
Abdul Latif	1162-1231	Ibn Farid	1181-1235
Abul Faraj	1226-1286	Jacopone, Da Todi	1230-1306
Albertus Magnus	1206-1280	Jalal Ad-Din Rumi	1207-1273
Aquinas, Thomas	1225-1275	Joinville, Jean	1224-1319
Bacon, Roger	1214-1294	Latini, Brunetto	1210-1294
Beha Ud-Din Zuhair	1186-1258	Lully, Raymond	c. 1232-1315
Berceo, Gonsalo De	1180-1246	Maerlant, Jacob Van	1235-1300
Busri	1211-1294	Meung, Jean De	1250-1305
Cavalcanti, Guido	1230-1300	Paris, Matthew	c. 1200-1259
Chang Chun Kiu	1148-1227	Rumi	1207-1273
Elmacin, George	1223-1274	Sa'Di	1184-1291
Farid Ud-Din Attar	1119-1229	Siger De Brabant	1235-1281
Garland, John	1195-1272	Snorri, Sturluson	1179-1241
Grosseteste, Robert	c. 1175-1253	Thomas the Rhymer	
Guillaume De Lorris	c. 1230	(of Ercelduone)	c. 1220-c. 1297
Guittone D'Arezzo	1230-1294	Walther, Von Der	
Ibn Arabi	1165-1240	Vogelweide	1170-1230
Ibn Athir	1160-1234		

Arnoflo Di Cambio	1232-1301	Pisano, Giovanni	1249-1320
Cimabué, Giovanni	1240-1302	Pisano, Niccola	1225-1278
Hsia Kuei	1180-1230		

COMPOSERS

Hallé, Adam de la	1235-1287

Li Tsung (Sung Dynasty)   1224-1264   Hsien Tsung (Mangu Khan—
Tu Tsung (Sung Dynasty)   1264-1274   Mongol Dynasty)   1251-1260
Kung Ti (Sung Dynasty)   1274-1276   Shih Tsu (Kublai Khan—
Ting Tsung (Kuyak Khan—   Mongol Dynasty)   1260-1294
   Mongol Dynasty)   1246-1251

POPES

Innocent IV   1243-1254   Clement IV   1265-1268
Alexander IV   1254-1261   St. Gregory X   1271-1276
Urban IV   1261-1264

FRANCE. HEADS OF STATE

Louis IX   1226-1270   Philip III   1270-1285

HOLY ROMAN EMPERORS

Conrad IV   1250-1254   Rudolf I   1273-1291
Interregnum

ENGLAND. SOVEREIGNS

Henry III   1216-1272   Edward I   1272-1307

SWEDEN. KINGS

Valdemar   1250-1275   Magnus I Ladulas 1275-1290

PORTUGAL. KINGS

Alphonso III   1248-1279

WRITERS

Abano, Pietro D'	1250-1316	Guittone D'Arezzo	1230-1294
Abul Faraj	1226-1286	Immanuel Ben Solomon	1265-1330
Abul Feda, Ismail Ibn Ali	1273-1331	Jacopone, Da Todi	1230-1306
Albertus, Magnus	1206-1280	Jalal Ad-Din Rumi	1207-1273
Aquinas, Thomas	1225-1275	Joinville, Jean	1224-1319
Angioleri, Cello	1260-1312	Latini, Brunetto	1210-1294
Bacon, Roger	1214-1294	Lully, Raymond	c. 1232-1315
Bedaresi, Yedaiah	1270-1340	Maerlant, Jacob Van	1235-1300
Beha Ud-Din Zuhair	1186-1258	Mannyng, Robert	1264-1340
Busri	1211-1294	Meung, Jean De	1250-1305
Cavalcanti, Guido	1230-1300	Paris, Matthew	c. 1200-1259
Cecco D'Ascoli	1257-1327	Philes, Manuel	1275-1345
Celano, Thomas de	c. 1255	Robert of Gloucester	fl. 1260-1300
Cino Da Pistoia	1270-1336	Rumi	1207-1273
Dante, Aligheiri	1265-1321	Sa'Di	1184-1291
Duns Scotus, Johannes	c. 1265-1308	Siger De Brabant	1235-1281
Eckhart, Johannes	1260-1327	Thomas the Rhymer	
Elmacin, George	1223-1274	(of Erceldoune)	c. 1220-c. 1297
Garland, John	1195-1272	Villani, Giovanni	1275-1348
Grosseteste, Robert	c. 1175-1253		

Arnoflo Di Cambio	1232-1301	Giotto	1267-1337
Cavallini, Pietro	1259-1344	Pisano, Andrea	1270-1348
Cimabué, Giovanni	1240-1302	Pisano, Giovanni	1249-1314
Duccio Di Buoninsegna	1255-1319	Pisano, Niccola	1225-1278
Gaddi, Gaddeo	1260-1332		

COMPOSERS

Hallé, Adam de la	1235-1287

Kung Ti (Sung Dynasty)	1274-1276	Shih Tsu (Kublai Khan—	
Tuan Tsung		Mongol Dynasty)	1260-1294
(Sung Dynasty)	1278-1279	Ch'Eng Tsung	
Ti-Ping		(Mongol Dynasty)	1294-1307
(Sung Dynasty	1278-1279		

POPES

St. Gregory X	1271-1276	Martin IV	1281-1285
Adrian V	1276	Honorius IV	1285-1287
St. Innocent V	1276	Nicholas IV	1288-1292
John XXI	1276-1277	St. Celestine V	1294
Nicholas III	1277-1280	Boniface VIII	1294-1303

FRANCE. HEADS OF STATE

Philip III	1270-1285	Philip IV	1285-1314

HOLY ROMAN EMPERORS

Rudolf I	1273-1291	Albert I	1298-1308
Adolf of Nassau	1292-1298		

ENGLAND. SOVEREIGNS

Edward I	1272-1307

SWEDEN. KINGS

Magnus I Ladulas	1275-1290	Birger	1290-1318

PORTUGAL. KINGS

Alphonso III	1248-1279	Diniz	1279-1325

WRITERS

Abano, Pietro D'	1250-1316	Guittone D'arezzo	1230-1294
Abul Faraj	1226-1286	Hampole, Richard	
Abul Feda, Ismail-Ibn-Ali	1273-1331	Rolle De	1290-1349
Albertus, Magnus	1206-1280	Immanuel Ben Solomon	1265-1330
Angiolieri, Cecco	1260-1312	Jacopone Da Todi	1230-1306
Aungervyle, Richard	1287-1345	Joinville, Jean	1224-1319
Bacon, Roger	1214-1294	Latini, Brunetto	1210-1294
Bedaresi, Yedaiah	1270-1340	Lully, Raymond	c. 1232-1315
Buridan, Jean	1295-1366	Machaut, Guillaume De	1300-1377
Busri	1211-1294	Maerlant, Jacob Van	1235-1300
Cavalcanti, Guido	1250-1300	Mannyng, Robert	1264-1340
Cecco D'Ascoli	1257-1327	Meung, Jean De	1250-1305
Cino Da Pistoia	1270-1336	Philes, Manuel	1275-1345
Clanvowe, Sir Thomas	c. 1300	Robert of Gloucester	fl. 1260-1300
Conrad of Wurzburg	d. 1287	Ruis, Juan	1283-1350
Dafydd Ab Gwylym	c. 1300	Sa'Di	1184-1291
Dante, Alighieri	1265-1321	Siger De Brabant	1235-1281
Duns Scotus, Johannes	1265-1308	Thomas the Rhymer	
Eckhart, Johannes	1260-1327	(of Erceldoune)	c. 1220-c. 1297
Gersonides, Levi	1288-1344	Villani, Giovanni	1275-1348
Gregoras, Nicephorus	1295-1360		

Agnolo	c. 1300	Giotto	1267-1337
Agostino	c. 1300	Lorenzetti, Ambrogio	1300-1348
Arnolfo Di Cambio	1232-1301	Lorenzetti, Pietro	1280-1348
Cavallini, Pietro	1259-1344	Martini, Simone	1284-1344
Cimabue	1240-1302	Pisano, Andrea	1270-1348
Daddi, Bernardo	1290-1350	Pisano, Giovanni	1249-1314
Duccio Di Buoninsegna	1255-1319	Pisano, Niccola	1225-1278
Gaddi, Gaddeo	1260-1332	Strode, Ralph	c. 1300
Gaddi, Taddeo	1300-1366		

COMPOSERS

Hallé, Adam de la	1235-1278

1302   Battle at Courtrai.
1314   Battle of Bannockburn.
1346   Battle of Crecy.
1347   English capture Calais.
1348   Black Death plague.
1350   Order of the Garter instituted.
1351   Statute of labourers passed in England.
1354   Rienzi killed.
1356   Battle of Poitiers.
1381   Poll Tax established in England.
       Wat Tyler and peasant uprising.
1388   Battle of Otterburn.
1397   Duke of Gloucestershire murdered.
1400   Owen Glendower leads Welsh revolt.

PROMINENT PEOPLE

Marco Polo	1256-1323	**Rienzi, Cola di**	1313-1354
Bruce, Robert	1274-1329		

[MONGOL (Yuan) DYNASTY]

Ch'Eng Tsung	1294-1307	Ying Tsung	1320-1323
Wu Tsung	1307-1311	T'Ai Ting Ti	1323-1328
Jen Tsung	1311-1320		

POPES

Boniface VIII	1294-1303	Clement V	
St. Benedict XI	1303-1304	(Avignon 1309)	1305-1314
		John XXII (Avignon)	1316-1334

FRANCE. HEADS OF STATE

Philip IV	1285-1314	Philip V	1316-1322
Louis X	1314-1316	Charles IV	1322-1328
John I	1316		

HOLY ROMAN EMPERORS

Albert I	1298-1308	Louis IV of Bavaria	1314-1347
Henry VII of Luxemburg	1308-1313		

ENGLAND. SOVEREIGNS

Edward I	1272-1307	Edward II	1307-1327

SWEDEN. KINGS

Birger	1290-1318	Magnus II	1319-1365

PORTUGAL. KINGS

Diniz	1279-1325	Alphonso IV	1325-1357

SCOTLAND. KINGS

Robert I (The Bruce)	1306-1329

WRITERS

Abano, Pietro D'	1250-1316	Guittone D'Areezo	1230-1394
Abulfeda, Ismail-Ibn-Ali	1273-1331	Hampole, Richard	
Angliolieri, Cecco	1260-1312	Rolle De	1290-1349
Aungervyle, Richard	1287-1345	Immanuel Ben Solomon	1265-1330
Barbour, John	1316-1395	Jacopone, Da Todi	1230-1306
Bedaresi, Yedaiah	1270-1340	Joinville, Jean	1224-1319
Boccaccio, Giovanni	1313-1375	Lully, Raymond	c. 1232-1315
Boner, Ulrich	1324-1349	Machaut, Guillaume De	1300-1377
Buridan, Jean	1295-1366	Mannyng, Robert	1264-1340
Cecco D'Ascoli	1257-1327	Pegolotti, Francesco	
Cino Da Pistoia	1270-1336	Balducci	1315-1340
Dante, Alighieri	1265-1321	Petracht	1304-1374
Duns Scotus, Johannes	c. 1265-1308	Philes, Manuel	1275-1345
Eckhart, Johannes	1260-1327	Ruis, Juan	1283-1350
Gersonides, Levi	1288-1344	Villani, Giovanni	1275-1348
Gregoras, Nicephorus	1295-1360	Wycliffe, John	c. 1320-1384
Guiart, Guillaume	d. 1316		

Arnolfo Di Cambio	1232-1301	**Giotto**	1267-1337
Cavallini, Pietro	1259-1344	**Lorenzetti,** Ambrogio	1300-1348
Cimabue, Giovanni	1240-1302	**Lorenzetti,** Pietro	1250-1348
Daddi, Bernardo	1290-1350	**Martini,** Simone	1284-1344
Duccio Di Buoninsegna	1255-1319	**Orcagna**	1308-1368
Gaddi, Gaddeo	1260-1332	**Pisano,** Andrea	1270-1348
Gaddi, Taddeo	1300-1366	**Pisano,** Giovanni	1249-1314

T'Ai Ting Ti	1323-1328	Wen Tsung	1329-1332
Yu Chu	1328	Ning Tsung	1332-1333
Ming Tsung	1328-1329	Shun Ti	1333-1368

POPES

John XXII (Avignon)	1316-1334	Benedict XII (Avignon)	1334-1342
Nicholas V		Clement VI (Avignon)	1342-1352
(anti-pope in Italy)	1328-1330		

FRANCE. HEADS OF STATE

| Charles IV | 1322-1328 | John | 1350-1364 |
| Philip VI | 1328-1350 | | |

HOLY ROMAN EMPERORS

| Louis IV of Bavaria | 1314-1347 | Charles IV of Luxumberg | 1347-1378 |

ENGLAND. SOVEREIGNS

| Edward II | 1307-1327 | Edward III | 1327-1377 |

SWEDEN. KINGS

| Magnus II | 1319-1365 |

PORTUGAL. KINGS

| Alphonso IV | 1325-1357 |

SCOTLAND. KINGS

| Robert I (The Bruce) | 1306-1329 | David II | 1329-1371 |

WRITERS

Abulfeda, Ismail Ibn Ali	1273-1331	Johannes Von Saaz	1350-1415
Aungervyle, Richard	1287-1345	Langland, William	1332-1400
Barbour, John	1316-1395	Lopez De Ayala,	
Bedaresi, Yedaiah	1270-1340	Don Pedro	1332-1407
Boccaccio, Giovanni	1313-1375	Machaut, Guillaume De	1300-1377
Boner, Ulrich	fl. 1324-1349	Mannyng, Robert	1264-1340
Buridan, Jean	1295-1366	Mezieres, Phillipe De	1327-1405
Cecco D'Ascoli	1257-1327	Michel of Northgate,	
Chaucer, Geoffrey	1340-1400	Dan	c. 1340
Cino Da Pistoia	1270-1336	Minot, Laurence	1333-1352
Crescas, Hasdai		Niem, Dietrich of	1345-1418
Ben Abraham	1340-1410	Pegolotti, Francesco	
Deschamps, Eustache	1346-1406	Balducci	1315-1340
Eckhart, Johannes	1260-1327	Petracht	1304-1374
Froissart, Jean	1338-1410	Philes, Manuel	1275-1345
Gersonides, Levi	1288-1344	Ruis, Juan de	1283-1350
Gregoras, Nicephorus	1295-1360	Sachetti, Franco	1330-1400
Hampole, Richard		Villani, Giovanni	1275-1348
Rolle De	1290-1349	Wycliffe, John	c. 1320-1384
Ibn Khaldun	1332-1406	Wyntoun, Andrew of	c. 1350-1420
Immanuel Ben Solomon	1265-1330		

Altichiero Da Zevio	1320-1385	Lorenzetti, Ambrogio	1300-1348
Cavallini, Pietro	1259-1344	Lorenzetti, Pietro	1280-1348
Daddi, Bernardo	1290-1350	Martini, Simone	1284-1344
Gaddi, Aquolo	1333-1396	Orcagna	1308-1368
Gaddi, Gaddeo	1260-1332	Pisano, Andrea	1270-1348
Gaddi, Taddeo	1300-1366	Sluter, Claus	1350-1405
Giotto	1267-1337	Spinelo, Aretino	1330-1410

Shun Ti [Mongol (Yuan) Dynasty]	1333-1368	T'Ai Tsu (Ming Dynasty)	1368-1398

POPES

Clement VI (Avignon)	1342-1352	Urban V (Avignon)	1362-1370
Innocent VI (Avignon)	1352-1362	Gregory XI	1370-1378

FRANCE. HEADS OF STATE

John	1350-1364	Charles V	1364-1380

HOLY ROMAN EMPERORS

Charles IV of Luxemberg   1347-1378

ENGLAND. SOVEREIGNS

Edward III   1327-1377

SWEDEN. KINGS

Magnus	1319-1365	Albert of Mecklenburg	1365-1388

PORTUGAL. KINGS

Alphonso IV	1375-1357	Ferdinand	1367-1383
Pedro I	1357-1367		

SCOTLAND. KINGS

David II	1329-1371	Robert II	1371-1390

WRITERS

Barbour, John	1316-1395	Langland, William	1332-1400
Bartoli, Taddeo	1362-1422	Lopez De Ayala,	
Boccaccio, Giovanni	1313-1375	Don Pedro	1332-1407
Bruni, Leonardo	1369-1444	Lydgate, John	1373-1450
Buridan, Jean	1295-1366	Machaut, Guillaume De	1300-1377
Chaucer, Geoffrey	1340-1400	Mezieres, Phillippe De	1327-1405
Crescas, Hasdai, Ben		Minot, Laurence	1333-1352
Abraham	1340-1410	Niem, Dietrich of	1345-1418
Deschamps, Eustache	1346-1406	Petracht	1304-1374
Froissart, Jean	1338-1410	Pisan, Christine De	1364-1430
Gregoras, Nicephorus	1295-1360	Sachetti, Franco	1330-1400
Hoccleve, Thomas	1368-1450	Wycliffe, John	c. 1320-1384
Ibn, Khaldun	1332-1406	Wyntoun, Andrew of	1350-1420
Johannes Von Saaz	1350-1415		

ARTISTS

Altichiero Da Zevio	1320-1385	Gaddi, Taddeo	1300-1366
Campin, Robert	1375-1444	Lorenzo, Monaco	1370-1425
Della Quercia, Jacopo	1374-1438	Orcagna	1308-1368
Eyck Van, Hubert	1366-1426	Sluter, Claus	1350-1405
Fabriano, Gentile Da	1370-1427	Spinelo, Arenito	1330-1410
Gaddi, Aquolo	1333-1396		

EMPERORS OF CHINA 1376-1400

T'Ai Tsu	1368-1398	Hui Ti	1398-1402

POPES

Gregory XI	1370-1378	Boniface IX	1389-1404
Urban VI	1378-1389	Benedict XIII (anti-pope)	1394-1423
Clement VII (anti-pope)	1378-1394		

FRANCE. HEADS OF STATE

Charles V	1364-1380	Charles VI	1380-1422

HOLY ROMAN EMPERORS

Charles IV of Luxemberg	1347-1378	Rupert of the Palatinate	1400-1410
Wenzel of Luxemberg	1378-1400		

ENGLAND. SOVEREIGNS

Edward III	1327-1377	Henry IV	1399-1413
Richard II	1377-1399		

SWEDEN. KINGS

Albert of Mecklenburf	1365-1388	Eric of Pomerania (XIII)	1397-1439
Margaret	1389-1397		

PORTUGAL. KINGS

Ferdinand	1367-1383	John I	1385-1433
Civil War	1383-1385		

KINGS OF SCOTLAND

Robert II	1371-1390	Robert III	1390-1406

WRITERS

Alphonsus, A Sancta Maria	1396-1456	Ibn, Khaldun	1332-1406
Barbour, John	1316-1395	Johannes, Von Saaz	1350-1415
Bartoli, Taddeo	1362-1422	Langland, William	1332-1400
Basselin, Olivier	1400-1450	La Sale, Antoine De	c. 1398-1470
Berners, Juliana	c. 1388	Lopez De Ayala Don Pedro	1332-1407
Bruni, Leonardo	1369-1444	Lydgate, John	1373-1450
Capgrave, John	1393-1464	Machaut, Guillaume De	1300-1377
Chartier, Alain	1392-1430	Madhava, Acharya	1380-
Chaucer, Geoffrey	1340-1400	March, Auzias	1379-1459
Codinus, George	c. 1400	Mezieres, Phillippe De	1327-1405
Crescas, Hasdai Ben Abraham	1340-1410	Niem, Dietrich of	1345-1418
Deschamps, Eustache	1346-1406	d'Orleans, Charles	1391-1465
Flavius, Blondus	1388-1463	Petracht	1304-1374
Froissart, Jean	1338-1410	Pisan, Christine de	1364-1431
George of Trebizond	1395-1484	Poggio (Bracciolini)	1380-1459
Hafiz	fl. 1388	Sachetti, Franco	1330-1400
Hans Der Guheler	c. 1400	Schiltberger, Johann	1381-1440
Hardyng, John	1378-1465	Thomas A Kempis	1380-1471
Hilton, Walter	d. 1396	Villena, Enrique De	1384-1433
Hoccleve, Thomas	1368-1450	Wycliffe, John	c. 1320-1384
		Wyntoun, Andrew of	1350-1420

ARTISTS

Angelico, Fra	1387-1455	Gaddi, Aquolo	1333-1396
Altichiero, Da Zievo	1320-1385	Ghiberti, Lorenzo	1378-1455
Bonfigli, Benedetto	c. 1400	Limburg, Pol De	c. 1400
Bouts, Dierick	1400-1475	Limburg, Hennequin de	c. 1400
Brunelleschi, Filippo	1377-1446	Limburg, Hermann de	c. 1400
Campin, Robert	1375-1444	Lochner, Stephan	1400-1451
Carpi, Ugo Da	c. 1400	Lorenzo, Monaco	1370-1425
Castagno, Andrea del	1409-1480	Masolino Da Panicale	1383-1447
Christus, Peter	1400-1473	Michelozzo Di Martolommeo	1396-1472
Della Quercia, Jacopo	1374-1438	Pisano, Vittore	1397-1455
Della Robbia, Luca	1399-1482	Sasseta, Stefano Di Giovanni	1392-1450
Diamante, Fra	c. 1400	Spinelo, Arenito	1330-1410
Donatello	1386-1466	Squarcione, Francesco	1394-1474
Eyck, Van Hubert	1366-1426	Uccello, Paolo	1397-1475
Eyck, Van Jan	1385-1441	Weyden, Rogier, Van Der	1400-1464
Fabriano, Gentile Da	1370-1427		
Filarete, Antonio	1400-1470		
Francke, Meister	c. 1400		

COMPOSERS

Wilkinson, Robert	c. 1400

G

1403   Battle of Shrewsbury.
1414   Council of Constance.
1415   Battle of Agincourt.
1428   English seige of Orleans.
1431   Joan of Arc burnt at stake.
1437   James I of Scotland murdered.
1438   First printing at Haarlem.
1440   Eton College founded.
1455   The start of the Wars of the Roses.   Battle of St. Albans.
1460   Battle of Northampton.
       Battle of Wakefield.
1461   Second Battle of St. Albans.
       Battle of Towton Field.
1464   Battle of Hexham.
1471   Battle of Barnet.
       Battle of Tewkesbury.
1476   Caxton begins printing.
1478   Spanish inquisition begins.
1483   Edward V. murdered.
1485   Battle of Bosworth Field.
1497   Newfoundland discovered by the Cabots.
       Cape of Good Hope rounded by Vasco de Gama.
1498   Columbus discovers America.

PROMINENT PEOPLE

Joan of Arc	1412-1431	Copernicus, Nicolaus	1473-1543
Caxton, William	1422-1491	Warbeck, Perkin	1474-1499
Columbus, Christopher	1446-1506	Cabot, Sebastian	1474-1557
Savonarola, Fra Giralamo	1452-1498	Borgia, Cesare	1476-1507
Vascoe De Gama	1460-1524	More, Sir Thomas	1478-1535
Pizarro, Francesco	1471-1541	Borgia, Lucrece	1480-1519
Wolsey, Thomas, Cardinal	1471-1530		

T'Ai Tsu	1368-1398	Jen Tsung	1424-1425
Hui Tui	1398-1402	Hsuan Tsung	1425-1435
Ch'Eng Tsu	1402-1424		

POPES

Boniface IX	1389-1404	Alexander V (anti-pope)	1409-1410
Benedict XIII (anti-pope)	1394-1423	Martin V	1417-1431
Innocent VII	1404-1406	Clement VIII (anti-pope)	1423-1429
Gregory XII	1406-1415	Benedict XIV (anti-pope)	1425-1430
John XXIII (anti-pope)	1410-1415		

FRANCE. HEADS OF STATE

Charles VI	1380-1422	Charles VII	1422-1461

HOLY ROMAN EMPERORS

Rupert of the Palatinate	1400-1410	Sigismund of Luxumberg	1410-1437

ENGLAND. SOVEREIGNS

Henry IV	1399-1413	Henry VI	1422-1461
Henry V	1413-1422		

SWEDEN. KINGS

Eric of Pomerania	1397-1439

PORTUGAL. KINGS

John I	1385-1433

KINGS OF SCOTLAND

Robert III	1309-1406	James I	1406-1437

ELECTORS OF BRANDENBURG

Frederick I	1415-1440

WRITERS

Alberti, Leon Battista	1404-1472	Hardyng, John	1378-1465
Alphonsus, A Sancta	1396-1456	Hoccleve, Thomas	1368-1450
Bartoli, Taddeo	1362-1422	Ibn, Khaldun	1332-1406
Basselin, Olivier	1400-1450	Jami	1414-1492
Bruni, Leonardo	1369-1444	Johannes Von Saaz	1350-1415
Capgrave, John	1393-1464	La Salle, Antoine De c. 1398-1470	
Chartier, Alain	1392-1430	Lopez De Ayala, Don Pedro 1332-1407	
Chastellain, Georges	1415-1475	Lydgate, John	1373-1450
Conti, Niccolo De	1419-1444	March, Auziàs	1397-1459
Deschamps, Eustache	1346-1406	Mena, Juan De	1411-1456
Dlugosz, Jan	1415-1480	Mezieres, Phillipe De	1327-1405
Flavius, Blondus	1388-1463	Niem, Dietrich of	1345-1418
Froissart, Jean	1338-1410	d'Orleans, Charles	1391-1465
George of Trebizond	1395-1484	Pecock, Reginald	1395-1460
Gower, John	d. 1408	Pisan, Christine De	1364-1430

Poggio, (Bracciolini)	1380-1459	Villena, Enrique De	1384-1433
Schiltberger, Johann	1381-1440	Worcester, William	1415-1482
Thomas A Kempis	1379-1471	Wyntoun, Andrew of	1350-1420

ARTISTS

Angelico, Fra	1387-1455	Lochner, Stefan	1400-1451
Bouts, Dierick	1400-1475	Lorenzo, Monaco	1370-1425
Brunelleschi, Filippo	1377-1446	Marmion, Simon	1425-1489
Campin, Robert	1375-1444	Masaccio	1401-1428
Castagno, Andrea Del	1409-1480	Michelozzi, Michelozzo	
Della Quercia, Jacopo	1367-1438	Di Bartolommeo	1396-1472
Della Robbia, Luca	1399-1482	Piero Della Francesca	1420-1492
Donatello	1386-1466	Pisano, Vittore	1397-1455
Eyck, Hubert Van	1366-1426	Rossellino, Bernado	1409-1464
Eyck, Jan Van	1385-1441	Sasseta, Stefano	
Fabriano, Gentile Da	1370-1427	Di Giovanni	1392-1450
Filarete, Antonio	1400-1470	Sluter, Claus	1350-1405
Fra Filippo Lippi	1406-1469	Spinelo, Aretino	1330-1410
Fouquet, Jean	1415-1485	Squarcione, Francesco	1394-1474
Ghiberti, Lorenzo	1378-1455	Uccello, Paolo	1397-1475
Gozzoli, Benozzo	1420-1497	Weyden, Rogier, Van Der	1400-1464

| Hsuan Tsung | 1425-1435 | Tai Tsung | 1449-1457 |
| Ying Tsung | 1435-1449 | | |

POPES

Martin V	1417-1431	Eugenius IV	1431-1447
Clement VIII (anti-pope)	1423-1429	Nicholas V	1447-1455
Benedict XIV (anti-pope)	1425-1430	Felix V (anti-pope)	1439-1449

FRANCE. HEADS OF STATE

| Charles VII | 1422-1461 |

HOLY ROMAN EMPERORS

| Sigismund of Luxumberg | 1410-1437 | Frederick III | 1440-1493 |
| Albert II | 1438-1440 | | |

ENGLAND. SOVEREIGNS

| Henry VI | 1422-1461 |

SWEDEN. KINGS

| Eric of Pomerania | 1397-1439 | Charles VIII | 1448-1457 |
| Christopher of Bavaria | 1439-1448 | | |

PORTUGAL. KINGS

| John I | 1385-1433 | Alphonso V | 1438-1481 |
| Edward | 1433-1438 | | |

SCOTLAND. KINGS

| James I | 1401-1437 | James II | 1437-1460 |

ELECTORS OF BRANDENBURG

| Frederick I | 1415-1440 | Frederick II | 1440-1470 |

WRITERS

Abarbanel, Isaac Ben Jehudah	1437-1508	Ficino, Marsilio	1433-1499
Alberti, Leon Battista	1404-1472	Flavius, Blondus	1388-1463
Alphonsus, A Sancta Maria	1396-1456	George of Trebizond	1395-1484
Alunno, Niccolo	1430-1502	Hardyng, John	1378-1465
Auvergne, Martial de	1430-1508	Hay, Gilbert	1450
Basselin, Olivier	1400-1450	Hoccleve, Thomas	1368-1450
Boiardo, Matteo Maria	1434-1494	Holland, Richard	1450
Bradshaw, Henry	1450-1513	Jami	1414-1492
Bruni, Leonardo	1369-1444	Krantz, Albert	1450-1517
Capgrave, John	1393-1464	La Salle, Antoine De	1398-1470
Chartier, Alain	1392-1430	Lydgate, John	1373-1450
Chastellain, Georges	1415-1475	Manrique, Gomez	1415-1490
Comines, Phillippe De	c. 1445-1509	Manrique, Jorge	1440-1479
Conti, Nicolo De	1419-1444	March, Auziàs	1397-1459
Dlugosz, Jan	1415-1480	Mena, Juan De	1411-1456
Ducas	1450	Molinet, Jean	1433-1507
		d'Orleans, Charles	1391-1465

WRITERS

Pecock, Reginald	1395-1460	Schiltberger, Johann	1381-1440
Pisan, Christine De	1364-1430	Thomas A Kempis	1379-1471
Poggio, (Bracciolini)	1380-1459	Villena, Enrique De	1384-1433
Pontanus, Jovianus	1426-1503	Villon, Francois	1431-1463
Pulci, Luigi	1432-1484	Worcester, William	1415-1482
Ros, Sir Richard	1429-		

ARTISTS

Angelico, Fra	1387-1455	Gozzoli, Benozzo	1420-1497
Antonello Da Messina	1430-1479	Liberale, Antonio	1445-1526
Baldovinetti, Alessio	1427-1499	Lochner, Stefan	1400-1451
Bellini, Gentile	1429-1507	Mantegna, Andrea	1431-1506
Bellini, Giovanni	1430-1516	Marmion, Simon	1425-1489
Botticelli, Sandro	1444-1510	Masaccio	1401-1428
Bouts, Dierick	1400-1475	Melozzo, Da Forli	1438-1494
Bramante, Douato	1444-1514	Memlinc, Hans	1430-1494
Brunelleschi, Filippo	1377-1446	Michelozzi, Michelozzo	
Campin, Robert	1375-1444	Di Bartolommeo	1396-1472
Castagno, Andrea Del	1409-1480	Mino Da Fiesola	1430-1484
Christus, Peter	1400-1473	Montagna, Bartolomeo	1450-1523
Civitali, Matteo	1435-1501	Morone, Domenico	1442-1517
Cossa, Francesco Del	1435-1477	Perugino, Pietro	1450-1524
Costa, Lorenzo	1460-1535	Piero Della Francesca	1420-1492
Crivelli, Carlo	1433-1493	Pisano, Vittore	1397-1455
Della Quercia, Jacopo	1367-1438	Rossellino, Antonio	1427-1479
Della Robbia, Andrea	1435-1525	Rossellino, Bernado	1409-1464
Della Robbia, Luca	c. 1400-1482	Sasseta, Stefano	
Desiderio Da Settignano	1428-1464	Di Giovanni	1392-1450
Domenico, Veneziano	1438-1461	Schongauer, Martin	1445-1491
Donatello	1386-1466	Signorelli, Luca	1450-1523
Eyck, Hubert Van	1366-1426	Sluter, Claus	1350-1405
Eyck, Jan Van	1385-1441	Spinelo, Aretino	1330-1410
Fabriano, Gentile Da	1370-1427	Squarcione, Francesco	1394-1474
Filarete, Antonio	1400-1470	Stoss, Veit	1438-1533
Fouquet, Jean	1415-1485	Tura, Cosimo	1430-1498
Florenzo Di, Lorenzo	1445-1525	Uccello, Paolo	1397-1475
Foppa, Vincenzo	1427-1515	Van Der Goes, Hugo	1440-1482
Fra Filippo Lippi	1406-1469	Verrocchio, Andrea Del	1435-1488
Francia	1450-1517	Vivarini, Antonio	1440-1476
Ghiberti, Lorenzo	1378-1455	Vivarini, Bartolommeo	fl. 1450-1499
Ghirlandajo, Domenico	1449-1494	Weyden, Rogier Van Der	1400-1464
Giocondo, Fra Giovanni	1433-1515	Wohlgemuth, Michael	1434-1519

COMPOSERS

Des Pres, Josquin	1450-1521	Obrecht, Jakob	1430-1500
Isaac, Heinrich	1450	Okheghem, Joannes	1430-1495

Ying Tsung (Restored)   1457-1464   Hsien Tsung   1464-1487

POPES

Nicholas V	1447-1455	Paul II	1464-1471
Calextus III	1455-1458	Sixtus IV	1471-1484
Pius II	1458-1464		

FRANCE. HEADS OF STATE

Charles VII   1422-1461   Louis XI   1461-1483

HOLY ROMAN EMPERORS

Frederick III   1440-1493

ENGLAND. SOVEREIGNS

Henry VI (deposed)	1422-1461	Henry VI (again)	1470-1471
Edward IV	1461-1470	Edward IV	1471-1483

SWEDEN. KINGS

Charles VIII	1448-1457	Regency under Sten Sture	
Christian I	1457-1464	the elder	1470-1497
Charles VIII (again)	1464-1465		
	1467-1470		

PORTUGAL. KINGS

Alphonso V   1438-1481

SCOTLAND. KINGS

James II   1437-1460   James III   1460-1488

ELECTORS OF BRANDENBURG

Frederick II   1440-1470   Albert Achilles   1470-1486

RUSSIA. TSARS

Ivan III, The Great   1462-1505

WRITERS

Abarbanel, Isaac Ben		Boyce, Hector	1465-1536
Jehudah	1437-1508	Bradshaw, Henry	1450-1513
Accolti, Bernardo	1465-1536	Brant, Sebastian	1457-1521
Achillini, Alessandro	1463-1512	Capgrave, John	1393-1464
Alberti, Leone Battista	1404-1472	Castellesi, Adriano	1460-1521
Alunno, Niccolo	1430-1502	Celtes, Konrad	1459-1508
Ariosto, Lodovico	1474-1533	Chastellain, Georges	1415-1475
Auvergne, Martial D'	1430-1508	Comines, Phillipe De	c. 1445-1509
Azurara, Gomez Eannes D'	d. 1474	Copernicus, Nicolas	1473-1543
Bembo, Pietro	1470-1547	Delmedigo, Elijah	1460-1497
Boiardo, Matteo Maria	1434-1494	Dlugosz, Jan	1415-1480

Douglas, Gavin	1474-1522	Murner, Thomas	1475-1537
Dunbar, William	1460-1520	Nifo, Agostino	1473-1538
Dunstable, John	d. 1453	d,Orleans, Charles	1391-1465
Encina, Juan Del	1468-1529	Pecock, Reginald	1395-1466
Erasmus, Desiderius	1466-1536	Peter, Martyr Anglerius	1459-1525
Ficino, Marsilio	1433-1499	Pico Della Mirandola,	
Flavius, Blondus	1388-1463	Giovanni	1463-1494
George of Trebizond	1395-1484	Poggio (Bracciolini)	1380-1459
Gringoire, Pierre	1475-1539	Politian, Angelo Ambrogini	1454-1494
Harry, The Minstrel	1470-1490	Pontanus, Jovianus	1426-1503
Henryson, Robert	fl. 1470-1500	Pulci, Bernardo	1438-1488
Jami	1414-1492	Pulci, Luigi	1432-1484
Kennedy, Walter	1460-1508	Rastell, John	1475-1536
Krantz, Henry	1450-1517	Resende, Garcia De	1470-1536
Hay, Gilbert	1450	Reuchlin, Johann	1455-1522
Holland, Richard	1450	Ros, Sir Richard	1429-
La Salle, Antoine de	1398-1470	Ruccelai, Giovanni	1475-1525
Le Maire De Belges, Jean	1473-1525	Sannazaro, Jacopo	1458-1530
Machiavelli, Niccolo	1469-1527	Sanuto, Marino	1466-1533
Major, John	1470-1550	Savonarola, Girolamo	1452-1498
Malory, Sir Thomas	-1471	Skelton, John	1460-1529
Manrique, Gomez	1415-1490	Thomas A Kempis	1379-1471
Manrique, Jorge	1440-1479	Villon, Francois	1431-1463
March, Auziàs	1397-1459	Vincente, Gil	1465-1536
Molinet, Jean	1433-1507	Virgil, Polydore	1470-1555
Medwall, Henry	1462-1505	Worcester, William	1415-1482
Mena, Juan De	1411-1456		

ARTISTS

Albertinelli, Mariotto	1474-1515	Cranach, Lucas	1472-1553
Angelico, Fra	1387-1455	Credi, Lorenzo Di	1457-1537
Antonello Da Messina	1430-1479	Crivelli, Carlo	1433-1493
Baccio D'Agnolo	1460-1543	Della Robbia, Andrea	1435-1525
Baldovinetti, Alessio	1427-1499	Della Robbia, Giovanni	1469-1529
Bartolommeo, Di Paghlo		Della Robbia, Luca	c. 1400-1482
Fra	1475-1517	Desiderio Da Settignano	1428-1464
Bellini, Gentile	1429-1507	Domenico, Veneziano	1438-1461
Bellini, Giovanni	1430-1516	Donatello	1386-1466
Bianchiferrari, Francesco		Durer, Albrecht	1471-1528
de	1460-1510	Filarete, Antonio	1400-1470
Boltraffio, Giovanni		Fiorenzo Di Lorenzo	1445-1525
Antonio	1467-1516	Foppa, Vincenzo	1427-1515
Borgdgnone, Ambrogio	1473-1524	Fouquet, Jean	1415-1485
Bosch, Hieronymus	1460-1516	Fra Fillipo Lippi	1406-1469
Botticelli, Sandro	1444-1510	Francia	1450-1517
Bouts, Dierick	1400-1475	Froment, Nicolas	1450-1490
Bramante, Donato	1444-1514	Geertgen, Van Haarlem	1465-1493
Briosco, Andrea	1470-1532	Ghiberti, Lorenzo	1378-1455
Burgkmair, Hans	1473-1531	Ghirlandajo, Domenico	1449-1494
Carpaccio, Vittorio	1465-1522	Giocondo, Fra Giovanni	1433-1515
Castagno, Andrea Del	1409-1480	Gozzoli, Benozzo	1420-1497
Catena, Vincenzo		Holbein, Hans	
Di Biagio	1470-1531	the elder	1460-1524
Christus, Peter	1400-1473	Krafft, Adam	1455-1509
Cima, Giambattista	1459-1517	Leonardo Da Vinci	1452-1519
Civitali, Matteo	1435-1501	Liberale Antonio	1445-1526
Cossa, Francesco Del	1435-1477	Lippi, Fillipino	1458-1504
Costa, Lorenzo	1460-1535	Lochner, Stephan	1400-1451

Luini, Barnardino	1475-1532	Pisano, Vitorre	1397-1455
Mabuse, Jan	1472-1534	Riemenschneider, Tilman	1460-1531
Mantegna, Andrea	1431-1506	Roberti, Ercole Di	1455-1496
Marmion, Simon	1425-1489	Rossellino, Antonio	1427-1479
Matsys, Quentin	1466-1530	Rossellino, Bernardo	1409-1464
Melozzo Da Forli	1438-1494	Sansovino, Andrea	1460-1529
Memlinc, Hans	1430-1494	Schongauer, Martin	1445-1491
Michelangelo	1475-1564	Signorelli, Luca	1450-1523
Michelozzi, Michelozzo		Solario, Andrea Da	1460-1520
Di Bartolomeo	1396-1472	Squarcione, Francesco	1394-1474
Mino Da Fiesola	1430-1484	Stoss, Veit	1438-1533
Montagna, Bartolomeo	1450-1523	Suardi, Bartolommeo	1455-1536
Morone, Domenico	1442-1517	Torrigiano, Pietro	1472-1522
Morone, Francesco	1471-1529	Tura, Cosimo	1430-1498
Moulins, Master of	1460-1529	Van Der Goes, Hugo	1440-1482
Pacher, Michael	1465-1498	Verrocchio, Andrea Del	1435-1488
Patinir, Joachim De	1475-1524	Vivarini, Antonio	1440-1476
Perugino, Pietro	1450-1524	Vivarini, Bartolommeo	1450-1499
Piero Della Francesca	1420-1492	Vivarini, Luigi	1457-1503
Piero Di Cosimo	1462-1521	Weyden, Rogier Van Der	1400-1464
Pinturicchio	1454-1513	Wohlgemuth, Michael	1434-1519

COMPOSERS

Binchois, Gilles	d. 1460	Obrecht, Jakob	1430-1500
Cornyshe, William	1465-1523	Okhegem, Joannes	1430-1495
Despres, Josquin	1450-1521		

EMPERORS OF CHINA (MING DYNASTY)   1476-1500

| Hsien Tsung | 1464-1487 | Hsiao Tsung | 1487-1505 |

POPES

| Sixtus IV | 1471-1484 | Alexander VI | 1492-1503 |
| Innocent VIII | 1484-1492 | | |

FRANCE. HEADS OF STATE

| Louis XI | 1461-1483 | Louis XII | 1498-1515 |
| Charles VIII | 1483-1498 | | |

HOLY ROMAN EMPERORS

| Frederick III | 1440-1493 | Maximilian I | 1493-1519 |

ENGLAND. SOVEREIGNS

| Edward IV | 1471-1483 | Richard III | 1483-1485 |
| Edward V | 1483 | Henry VII | 1485-1509 |

SWEDEN. KINGS

| Regency under Sten Sture | | John II | 1497-1501 |
| the Elder | 1470-1497 | | |

PORTUGAL. KINGS

| Alphonso V | 1438-1481 | Manoel I | 1495-1521 |
| John II | 1481-1495 | | |

SCOTLAND. KINGS

| James III | 1460-1488 | James IV | 1488-1513 |

ELECTORS OF BRANDENBURG

| Albert Achilles | 1486-1499 | John Cicero | 1499-1535 |

RUSSIA. TSARS

| Ivan III the Great | 1462-1505 |

Abarbanel, Isaac Ben Jehudah	1437-1508
Accolti, Bernardo	1465-1536
Accorso, Mariangelo	1490-1544
Achillini, Alessandro	1463-1512
Aconsio, Jacopo	1500-1566
Agrippa Von Nettesheim, Henry Cornelius	1486-1535
Agricola (Magister Islebius) Johann	1492-1566
Alamanni, Luigi	1495-1556
Alberus, Erasmus	1500-1553
Alunno, Niccolo	1430-1502
Arason, Jon	1484-1551
Aretino, Pietro	1492-1556
Ariosto, Lodovico	1474-1533
Auvergne, Martial D'	1430-1508
Aventius	1477-1534
Avila, Juan De	1500-1569
Avila Y Zuniga, Luis	1490-1560
Baldung, Grun Hans	1476-1545
Bale, John	1495-1563
Bandello, Matteo	1480-1562
Bandinelli, Baccio	1493-1560
Barclay, Alexander	1476-1552
Barros, Joao De	1496-1570
Bembo, Pietro	1470-1547
Berni, Francesco	1497-1536
Biel, Gabriel	-1495
Boiardo, Matteo, Maria	1434-1494
Boone, Andrew	1490-1549
Boscan-Almogauer, Juan	1490-1542
Boscanalmogaver, Juan	1490-1542
Boyce, Hector	1465-1536
Bradshaw, Henry	1450-1513
Brant, Sebastian	1457-1521
Castellesi, Adriano	1460-1521
Castiglioni, Baldassare	1478-1529
Castillejo, Cristobal De	1490-1550
Cavendish, George	1500-1562
Celtes, Konrad	1459-1508
Colonna, Vittoria	1490-1547
Comines, Philippe De	1445-c. 1509
Copernicus, Nicolas	1473-1543
Coverdale, Miles (trans bible)	1488-1569
Cranmer, Thomas	1489-1556
Delmedigo, Elijah	1460-1497
Des Periers, Bonaventure	1500-1544
Diaz Del Castillo, Bernal	1492-1581
Dlugosz, Jan	1415-1480
Douglas, Gavin	1474-1522
Dunbar, William	1460-1520
Elyot, Sir Thomas	1490-1546
Encina, Juan Del	1468-1529
Erasmus, Desiderius	1466-1536
Ficino, Marsilo	1433-1499
Firenzuola, Agnolo	1493-1545
Fleuranges, Robert De La Marck	1491-1537

Folengo, Theofilo	1491-1544
George of Trebizond	1395-1484
Giraldi, Giglio Gregorio	1479-1552
Gringoire, Pierre	1475-1539
Guevara, Antonio De	1490-1545
Guicciardini, Francesco	1483-1540
Guidiccioni, Giovanni	1480-1541
Hall, Edward	1499-1547
Harry The Minstrel	1470-1492
Hay, Gilbert	1450-
Henryson, Robert	fl. 1470-1500
Hessus, Helius, Eobanus	1488-1540
Heywood, John	1497-1580
Holland, Richard	1450-
Hughes, Thomas	1500-
Jami	1414-1492
Jovius, Paulus	1483-1552
Kennedy, Walter	1460-1508
Krantz, Albert	1450-1517
Latimer, Hugh	c. 1485-1555
Le Maine De Belges, Jean	1473-1525
Loyala, Ignatius de	1491-1556
Luther, Martin	1483-1546
Lyndsay, Sir David	1490-1555
Machiavelli, Niccolo	1469-1527
Magnus	1490-1558
Maitland, Sir Richard	1496-1586
Major, John	1470-1550
Manrique, Gomez	1415-1490
Manrique, Jorge	1440-1479
Marguerite of Navarre	1492-1549
Marot, Clement	1496-1544
Medwall, Henry	1462-1505
Melanchthon, Philip	1497-1560
Molinet, Jean	1433-1507
More, Sir Thomas	1478-1535
Murner, Thomas	1475-1537
Nardi, Jacopo	1476-
Nifo, Agostino	1473-1538
Oviedo Y Valdes, Gonzales Fernandez De	1478-1557
Paracelsus	1493-1541
Pedersen, Christiern	1480-1554
Peter, Martyr Anglerius	1459-1525
Picco Della Mirandola, Giovanni	1463-1494
Politian, Angelo Ambrogini	1454-1494
Pulci, Bernardo	1438-1488
Pulci, Luigi	1432-1484
Rabelais, Francois	1495-1553
Rastell, John	1475-1536
Resende, Garcia De	1470-1536
Reuchlin, Johann	1455-1522
Ribeiro, Bernardim	1482-1552
Ros, Sir Richard	1429-
Ruccelai, Giovanni	1475-1525
Sachs, Hans	1494-1576
Sa De Miranda, Francisco De	1485-1558

Sannazaro, Jacopo	1458-1530	Torres Naharro	
Sanuto, Marino	1466-1533	Bartolome De	1480-1530
Savonarola, Girolamo	1452-1495	Valdes, Juan De	1500-1541
Sceve, Maurice	1500-1564	Vida, Marco, Girolamo	1489-1566
Sepulveda, Juan Gines De	1490-1574	Vincente, Gil	1465-1536
Skelton, John	1460-1529	Virgil, Polydore	1470-1555
Stewart, William	1480-1550	Vives, Juan Luis	1492-1540
Stumpf, Johann	1500-1576	Worcester, William	1415-1482
Tasso, Bernardo	1493-1569	Zwingli, Huldreich	1484-1531

ARTISTS

Albertinelli, Mariotto	1474-1515	Cousin, Jean	1500-1590
Altdorfer, Albrecht	1480-1538	Coxcie, Michael	1499-1592
Antonello Da Messina	1430-1479	Cranach, Lucas	1472-1553
Baccio D'Agnolo	1460-1543	Credi, Lorenzo Di	1457-1537
Bagnacavallo,		Crivelli, Carlo	1433-1493
Bartolommeo	1484-1545	Della Colle, Raffaellino	1490-
Baldovinetti, Alessio	1427-1499	Delle Robbia, Andrea	1435-1525
Bandinelli, Baccio	1493-1560	Della Robbia, Giovanni	1469-1529
Bartolommeo Di Paghlo,		Della Robbia, Girolamo	1488-1566
Fra	1475-1517	Della Robbia, Luca	c. 1400-1482
Bartolommeo, Veneto	1480-1555	Dosso Dossi, Giovanni	1479-1542
Beccafumi, Domenico		Durer, Albrecht	1471-1528
Di Pace	1486-1551	Ferrari, Gaudenzio	1480-1546
Bellini, Gentile	1429-1507	Fiorenzo Di Lorenzo	1445-1525
Bellini, Giovanni	1430-1516	Foppa, Vincenzo	1427-1515
Bianchiferrari,		Fouquet, Jean	1415-1485
Francesco De	1460-1510	Francia	1450-1517
Boltraffio, Giovanni		Franciabigio	1482-1525
Francesco de	1467-1516	Froment, Nicolas	1450-1490
Bordone, Paris	1500-1571	Garofalo	1481-1559
Borgdgnone, Ambrogio	1473-1524	Geertgen, Van Haarlem	1465-1493
Bosch, Hieronymus	1460-1516	Genga, Girolamo	1476-1551
Botticelli, Sandro	1444-1510	Ghirlandajo, Domenico	1449-1494
Bramante, Donato	1444-1514	Ghirlandajo, Ridolfo	1483-1561
Briosca, Andrea	1470-1532	Giocondo, Fra Giovanni	1433-1515
Burgkmair, Hans	1473-1531	Giorgione	1478-1511
Campagnola, Domenico	1484-1563	Guilio, Romano	1499-1546
Caravagio, Polidoro Da	1500-1543	Gozzoli, Benozzo	1420-1497
Carpaccio, Vittorio	1465-1522	Grunewald, Mathias	1480-1528
Caroto, Giovanni		Heemskerk, Marten	
Francesco	1480-1555	Jacobisz	1498-1574
Castagno, Andrea Del	1409-1480	Holbein, Hans The elder	1460-1524
Castello, Giovanni Battista	1500-1569	Holbein, Hans	1497-1543
Catena, Vincenzo Di		Joos Van Cleve	1480-1540
Biagio	1470-1531	Krafft, Adam	1455-1509
Cavazzola, Paolo Morando	1486-1522	Leonardo Da Vinci	1452-1519
Cellini, Benvenuto	1500-1571	Liberale, Antonio	1445-1526
Cima, Giambattista	1459-1517	Lippi, Fillipine	1458-1504
Civerchio, Vincinzo	1500-	Lotto, Lorenzo	1480-1556
Civitali, Matteo	1435-1501	Lucas, Van Leyden	1494-1533
Cleve, Van Joos		Luini, Barnardino	1475-1532
Van Der Beke	1480-1540	Mabuse, Jan	1472-1534
Clouet, Jean	1485-1541	Mantegna, Andrea	1431-1506
Cornelisz, Lucas	1495-1552	Manuel, Nikolaus	1484-1550
Corregio	1494-1534	Marmion, Simon	1425-1489
Cossa, Francesco Del	1435-1477	Matsys, Quentin	1466-1530
Costa, Lorenzo	1460-1535	Melozzo Da Forli	1438-1494

Memlinc, Hans	1430-1494	Roberti, Ercole De	1455-1496
Michelangelo	1475-1564	Rossellino, Antonio	1427-1479
Mino Da Fiesola	1430-1484	Rossi, Giovanni	
Montagna, Bartolomeo	1450-1523	Battista De	1494-1541
Moretto Il	1494-1554	Sanmichele, Michele	1484-1559
Morone, Domenico	1442-1517	Sansovino, Andrea	
Morone, Francesco	1471-1529	Contucci Del Monte	1460-1529
Moulins, Master of	1460-1529	Sansovino, Jacopo	1486-1570
Orley, Bernard Van	1490-1540	Sarto, Andrea del	1486-1531
Pacchia, Girolamo Del	1477-1535	Schongauer, Martin	1445-1491
Pacher, Michael	1465-1498	Signorelli, Luca	1450-1523
Palma, Jacopo	1480-1528	Sodoma, Il	1477-1549
Patinir, Joachim De	1475-1524	Solaria, Andrea Da	1460-1520
Perino Del Vaga	1500-1547	Stoss, Veit	1438-1533
Peruzzi, Baldassare	1481-1536	Suardi, Bartolommeo	1455-1536
Perugino, Pietro	1450-1524	Titian	1477-1576
Piero Della Francesca	1420-1492	Torrigiano, Pietro	1472-1522
Piero Di Cosimo	1462-1521	Tura, Cosimo	1430-1498
Pinturicchio	1454-1513	Van Der Goes, Hugo	1440-1482
Piombo, Sebastian Del	1485-1547	Verrocchio, Andrea Del	1435-1488
Pontormo, Jacopo Da	1494-1552	Vivarini, Antonio	1440-1476
Pordenone, Il	1483-1539	Vivarini, Bartolommeo	1450-1499
Raphael, Sanzio	1483-1520	Vivarini, Luigi	1457-1503
Riemenschneider, Tilman	1460-1531	Wohlgemuth, Michael	1434-1519

COMPOSERS

Animuccia, Giovanni	1490-1571	Jimenez De Quesada	
Cornyshe, William	1465-1523	Gonzalo	1500-1579
Despres, Josquin	1450-1521	Obrecht, Jakob	1430-1500
Festa, Constanzo	1495-1545	Okhegem, Johannes	1430-1495
		Taverner, John	1495-1545

1500   Portuguese discover Brazil.
1506   Building of St. Peters, Rome.
1513   Battle of Flodden.
1519   Cortes conquers Mexico.
1521   Luther. Diet of Worms.

PROMINENT PEOPLE

Borgia, Cesare	1476-1507	Luther, Martin	1483-1546
Borgia, Lucrece	1480-1519	More, Sir Thomas	1478-1535
Cabot, Sebastian	1474-1557	Nostradamus	1503-1566
Calvin, John	1509-1564	Pizarro, Francesco	1471-1541
Colombus, Christopher	1446-1506	Vasco De Gama	1460-1524
Copernicus, Nicolaus	1473-1543	Wolsey, Thomas, Cardinal	1471-1530
Cortes, Hernando	1485-1547		

EMPERORS OF CHINA

Hsiao Tsung	1487-1505	Shih Tsung	1521-1566
Wu Tsung	1505-1521		

POPES

Alexander VI	1492-1503	Leo X	1513-1521
Pius III	1503	Adrian VI	1522-1523
Julius II	1503-1513	Clement VII	1523-1534

FRANCE. HEADS OF STATE

Louis XII	1498-1515	Francis I	1515-1547

HOLY ROMAN EMPERORS

Maximilian I	1493-1519	Charles V	1519-1558

ENGLAND. SOVEREIGNS

Henry VII	1485-1509	Henry VIII	1509-1547

SWEDEN. KINGS

John II	1497-1501	Regency under Sten Sture The Younger	1512-1520
Regency under Sten Sture The Elder	1501-1503	Christian II	1520-1523
Regency under Svante Sture	1504-1512	Gustavius	1523-1560

PORTUGAL. KINGS

Manoel I	1495-1521	John III	1521-1557

SCOTLAND. KINGS

James IV	1488-1513	James V	1513-1542

ELECTORS OF BRANDENBURG

Joachim, I	1499-1535

Isabella	d. 1504	Charles V	1516-1556
Ferdinand	d. 1516		

RUSSIA. TSARS

Ivan III, The Great	1462-1505	Vassili III	1505-1533

WRITERS

Abarbanel, Isaac Ben		Cavendish, George	1500-1562
Jehudah	1437-1508	Cecchi, Giammaria	1518-1587
Accolti, Bernardo	1465-1536	Celtes, Konrad	1459-1508
Accorso, Mariangelo	1490-1544	Cetina, Gutierre De	1518-1572
Achillini, Alessandro	1463-1512	Chaloner, Sir Thomas	1521-1565
Aconzio, Jacopo	1500-1566	Churchyard, Thomas	1520-1604
Adams, Clement	1519-1587	Cieza De Leon, Pedro De	1519-1560
Adriani, Giovanni Baptista	1513-1579	Colonna, Vittoria	1490-1547
Agrippa Von Nettesheim,		Comines, Phillipe De	c. 1445-1509
Henry Cornelius	1486-1535	Cooper, Thomas	1517-1594
Agricola (Magister Islebius)		Copernicus, Nicolas	1473-1543
Johann	1492-1566	Costanzo, Angelo Di	1507-1591
Alamanni, Luigi	1495-1556	Coverdale, Miles	
Alberus, Erasmus	1500-1553	(trans. bible)	1488-1569
Alunno, Niccolo	1430-1502	Cranmer, Thomas	1489-1556
Amyot, Jacques	1513-1593	Daurat, Jean	1508-1588
Arason, Jon	1484-1551	Della Casa, Giovanni	1503-1556
Aretino, Pietro	1492-1556	Des Periers, Bonaventure	1500-1544
Ariosto, Lodovico	1474-1533	Diaz Del Castillo, Bernal	1492-1581
Ascham, Roger	1515-1568	Dolce, Lodovico	1508-1568
Auvergne, Martial d'	1430-1508	Douglas, Gavin	1474-1522
Aventius	1477-1534	Du Bellay, Joachim	1522-1560
Avila, Juan de	1500-1569	Dunbar, William	1460-1520
Avila Y Zuniga, Luis	1490-1560	Edwards, Richard	1523-1566
Baldung, Grun Hans	1476-1545	Elyot, Sir Thomas	1490-1546
Bale, John	1495-1563	Encina, Juan Del	1468-1529
Bandello, Matteo	1480-1562	Erasmus, Desiderius	1466-1536
Bandinelli, Baccio	1493-1560	Fabricius, Georg	1516-1571
Barclay, Alexander	1476-1552	Fabyan, Robert	d. 1513
Barros, Joao De	1496-1570	Falcao, Christovam	1512-1553
Bellay, Joachim Du	1522-1560	Firenzuola, Agnolo	1493-1545
Bembo, Pietro	1470-1547	Fleuranges, Robert de la	
Berni, Francesco	1497-1536	Marck	1491-1537
Blois, Louis De	1506-1566	Folengo, Theofil	1491-1544
Boone, Andrew	1490-1549	Foxe, John	1516-1587
Boscan-Almogaver, Juan	1490-1542	Gesner, Konrad Von	1516-1565
Boyce, Hector	1465-1536	Giraldi, Giovanni Battista	1504-1573
Bradshaw, Henry	1450-1513	Giraldi, Giglio Gregorio	1479-1552
Brant, Sebastian	1457-1521	Grazzini, Antonio	
Buchanan, George	1506-1582	Francesco	1503-1583
Busbecq, Ogier		Grimald, Nicholas	1519-1562
Ghislain De	1522-1592	Gringoire, Pierre	1475-1539
Calvin, John	1509-1564	Guevara, Antonio De	1490-1545
Camoens, Louis De	1524-1580	Guicciardini, Francesco	1483-1540
Caro, Annibale	1507-1566	Guidiccioni, Giovanni	1480-1541
Casa, Giovanni Della	1503-1556	Hall, Edward	1499-1547
Castellesi, Adriano	1460-1521	Hawes, Stephen	1502-1521
Castiglioni, Baldassare	1478-1529	Hessus, Helius Eobanus	1488-1540
Castillejo, Cristobal De	1490-1550	Heywood, John	1497-1580
		Hughes, Thomas	1500-

Jewell, John	1522-1571	Reuchlin, Johann	1455-1522
Jovius, Paulus	1483-1552	Ribeiro, Bernardim	1482-1552
Kennedy, Walter	1460-1508	Ronsard, Pierre De	1524-1585
Knox, John	1513-1572	Ruccelai, Giovanni	1475-1525
Krantz, Albert	1450-1517	Rueda, Lope De	1510-1565
Languet, Hubert	1518-1581	Ruzzante	1502-1542
Latimer, Hugh	c. 1485-1555	Sachs, Hans	1494-1576
Leland, John	1506-1552	Sa De Miranda,	
Le Maire De Belges, Jean	1473-1525	Francisco De	1485-1558
Lemnius	1505-1550	Sannazaro, Jacopo	1458-1530
Lopez De Gomara,		Sanuto, Marino	1466-1533
Francisco	1511-1557	Sceve, Maurice	1500-1564
Loyala, Ignatius de	1491-1556	Sepulveda, Juan Gines De	1490-1574
Luther, Martin	1483-1546	Skelton, John	1460-1529
Lyndsay, Sir David	1490-1555	Sleidanus, Johannes	1506-1556
Machiavelli, Niccolo	1469-1527	Stewart, William	1480-1550
Magnus	1490-1558	Stow, John	1525-1605
Maitland, Sir Richard	1496-1586	Surrey, Henry Howard,	
Major, John	1470-1550	Earl of	c. 1517-1547
Marguerite of Navarre	1492-1549	Tasso, Bernardo	1493-1569
Marot, Clement	1496-1544	Taverner, Richard	1505-1575
Medwall, Henry	1462-1505	Telesio, Bernardio	1509-1588
Melanchthon, Philip	1497-1560	Theresa (St.)	1515-1582
Mendoza, Diego Hurtado		Torres Naharro, Bartolome	
De	1503-1575	De	1480-1530
Molinet, Jean	1433-1507	Tschudi, Giles	1505-1572
Montemor, Jorge	1520-1561	Tusser, Thomas	1524-1580
More, Sir Thomas	1478-1535	Tyard, Pontus De	1521-1605
Murner, Thomas	1475-1537	Udal, Nicholas	1504-1556
Nardi, Jacopo	1476-	Valdes, Juan De	1500-1541
Nifo, Agostino	1473-1538	Varthema, Ludovico Di	1502-1510
Ovideo Y Valdes,		Vaux of Harrowdene,	
Gonzales Fernandez De	1478-1557	Thomas Vaux	1510-1556
Paracelsus	1493-1541	Vega, Garcilaso De La	1503-1536
Pedersen, Christiern	1480-1554	Vida, Marco Girolamo	1489-1566
Peter Martyr Anglerius	1459-1525	Vincente, Gil	1465-1536
Pontanus, Jovianus	1426-1503	Virgil, Polydore	1470-1555
Porta, Guglielmo Della	1516-1577	Vives, Juan Luis	1492-1540
Rabelais, Francois	1495-1553	Winzet, Ninian	1518-1592
Rastell, John	1475-1536	Wyatt, Sir Thomas	1503-1542
Resende, Garcia De	1470-1536	Zwingli, Huldreich	1484-1531

ARTISTS

Aartsen, Pieter	1507-1573	Bartolommeo, Veneto	1480-1555
Abatti, Niccolo	1512-1571	Bassano, Giacomo Da	
Albertinelli, Mariotto	1474-1515	Ponte	1510-1592
Aldegraf, Heinrich	1502-1558	Beccafumi, Domenico Di	
Alessi, Galeazzo	1512-1572	Pace	1486-1551
Altdorfer, Albrecht	1480-1538	Bellini, Gentile	1429-1507
Amalteo, Pomponio	1505-1584	Bellini, Giovanni	1430-1516
Ammanati, Bartolomeo	1511-1592	Bianchiferrari, Francesco	
Baccio D'Agnolo	1460-1543	De	1460-1510
Bagnacavallo,		Bologna, Giovanni Da	1524-1608
Bartolommeo	1484-1545	Boltraffio, Giovanni	
Bandinelli, Baccio	1493-1560	Antonio	1467-1516
Barocchio, Giacomo	1507-1573	Bordone, Paris	1500-1571
Bartolommeo Di Paghlo,		Borgdgnone, Ambrogio	1473-1524
Fra	1475-1517	Bosch, Hieronymous	1460-1516

Botticelli, Sandro	1444-1510
Bramante, Douato	1444-1514
Briosco, Andrea	1470-1532
Bronzino, Il	1503-1572
Brueghel, Pieter	1525-1569
Burgkmair, Hans	1473-1531
Campagnola, Domenico	1484-c. 1563
Campi, Giulio	1502-1572
Caravaggio, Polidoro Da	1500-1543
Carpaccio, Vittorio	1465-1522
Caroto, Giovanni Francesco	1480-1555
Castello, Giovanni Battista	1500-1569
Catena, Vincenzo Di Biagio	1470-1531
Cattaneo, Danese Di Michele	1509-1573
Cavazzola, Paolo, Morando	1486-1522
Cellini, Benvenuto	1500-1571
Cima, Giambattista	1459-1517
Civerchio, Vincinzo	1500-
Civitali, Matteo	1435-1501
Cleve, Van Cornelis	1520-1567
Cleve, Van Joos Van Der Beke	1480-1540
Clouet, Jean	1485-1541
Cockx, Hieronymus	1510-1570
Coello, Alonso Sanchez	1515-1590
Cornelisz, Lucas	1495-1552
Corregio	1492-1534
Costa, Lorenzo	1460-1535
Cousin, Jean	1500-1590
Coxcie, Michael	1499-1592
Cranach, Lucas	1472-1553
Credi, Lorenzo Di	1457-1537
David, Gerard	-1523
Della Colle, Raffaellino	1490-
Delle Robbia, Andrea	1435-1525
Della Robbia, Giovanni	1469-1529
Della Robbia, Girolamo	1488-1566
De L'Orme, Philibert	1510-1570
Dosso Dossi, Giovanni	1479-1542
Durer, Albrecht	1471-1528
Farinato, Paolo	1524-1606
Ferrari, Gaudenzio	1480-1546
Fiorenzo Di Lorenzo	1445-1525
Fontana, Prospero	1512-1597
Foppa, Vincenzo	1427-1515
Francia	1450-1517
Franciabigio	1482-1525
Garofalo	1481-1559
Genga, Giralamo	1476-1551
Ghirlandajo, Ridolfo	1483-1501
Giocondo, Fra Giovanni	1433-1515
Giorgione	1478-1511
Giulio, Romano	1499-1546
Goujon, Jean	1520-1566
Grunewald, Mathias	1500-1530
H	

Heemskerk, Marten Jacobsz	1498-1574
Holbein, Hans, The elder	1460-1524
Holbein, Hans	1497-1543
Joos Van Cleve	1480-1540
Krafft, Adam	1455-1509
Kempener, Peter De	1505-1580
Leonardo Da Vinci	1452-1519
Leoni, Leone	1509-1590
Leopardi, Alessandro	1512
Lescot, Pierre	1510-1578
Liberale, Antonio	1445-1526
Limousin, Leonard	1505-1577
Lippi, Filippino	1457-1504
Lotto, Lorenzo	1480-1556
Lucas Van Leyden	1494-1533
Luini, Barnardino	1475-1532
Mabuse, Jan	1472-1534
Mantegna, Andrea	1431-1506
Manuel, Hans Rudolf	1525-1571
Manuel, Nikolaus	1484-1550
Matsys, Quentin	1466-1530
Michelangelo	1475-1564
Montagna, Bartolomeo	1450-1523
Morales, Luis D	1509-1586
Moretto, Il	1494-1554
Moro, Antonio	1512-1575
Morone, Domenico	1442-1517
Morone, Francesco	1471-1529
Moroni, Giambattista	1525-1578
Moulins, Master of	1460-1529
Orley, Bernard Van	1490-1540
Pacchia, Girolamo Del	1477-1535
Palissy, Bernard (Potter)	1510-1589
Palladio, Andrea	1518-1580
Palma, Jacopo	1480-1528
Parmigiano	1504-1540
Patinir, Joachim De	1475-1524
Perino Del Vaga	1500-1547
Peruzzi, Baldassare	1481-1536
Perugino, Pietro	1450-1524
Piero Di Cosimo	1462-1521
Pinturicchio	1454-1513
Piombo, Sebastian Del	1485-1547
Pontormo, Jacopo Da	1494-1552
Pordenone, Il	1483-1539
Primaticcio, Francesco	1504-1570
Procaccini, Ercole	1520-1591
Raphael, Sanzio	1483-1520
Riemenschneider, Tilman	1460-1531
Rossi, Giovanni Battista De	1494-1541
Sanmichele, Michele	1484-1559
Sansovino, Andrea Contucci	1460-1529
Sansovino, Jacopo	1486-1570
Sarto, Andrea del	1486-1531
Signorelli, Luca	1450-1523
Sodoma, Il	1477-1549

Solario, Andrea Da	1460-1520	Vasari, Giorgio	1511-1574
Stoss, Veit	1483-1533	Vignola, Giacomo	
Suardi, Bartolommeo	1455-1536	Barozzi Da	1507-1573
Titian	1477-1576	Vivarini, Luigi	fl. 1417-1503
Tintoretto, Jacopo Robusti	1518-1594	Volterra, Daniele Da	1509-1566
Torrigiano, Pietro	1472-1522	Wohlgemuth, Michael	1434-1519

COMPOSERS

Animuccia, Giovanni	1490-1571	Gabrieli, Andrea	1510-1586
Arcadelt, Jakob	1514-1575	Goudimel, Claude	1510-1572
Cabezon, Antonio De	1510-1566	Jimenez De Queseda,	
Cornyshe, William	1465-1523	Gonzalo	1500-1579
Des Pres, Josquin	1450-1521	Tallis, Thomas	1515-1585
Festa, Constanzo	1495-1545	Taverner, John	1495-1545

1526   Tyndale's New Testament published.
1528   Conquest of Peru.
1529   Fall of Wolsey.
1534   Papal power abolished in England.   Act of Supremacy.
1535   More executed.   First English Bible published.
         Loyola founds Jesuits.
1536   Catherine of Aragon dies.   Anne Boleyn executed.
         Henry VIII marries Jane Seymore.
1537   Death of Jane Seymore.
         Mount Etna in eruption.
1538   Henry VIII Excommunicated.
         Parish registers established in England.
1539   Revolt of Ghent.
1540   Henry VIII marries Anne of Cleves.
         Henry VIII marries Catherine Howard.
1544   Henry VIII invades France.
1545   Needles first produced in England.
1549   Act of Uniformity.

PROMINENT PEOPLE

Cabot, Sebastian	1474-1557	More, Sir Thomas	1478-1535
Calvin, John	1509-1564	Nostradamus	1503-1566
Copernicus, Nicolaus	1473-1543	Pizarro, Francesco	1471-1541
Cortes, Hernando	1485-1547	Tyndale, William	1492-1536
Loyola, St. Ignatius	1491-1556	Wolsey, Thomas, Cardinal	1471-1530
Luther, Martin	1483-1546		

EMPERORS OF CHINA (MING DYNASTY)

Shih Tsung	1521-1566

POPES

Clement VII	1523-1534	Julius III	1550-1555
Paul III	1534-1549		

FRANCE. HEADS OF STATE

Francis I	1515-1547	Henry II	1547-1559

HOLY ROMAN EMPERORS

Charles V	1519-1558

ENGLAND. SOVEREIGNS

Henry VIII	1509-1547	Edward VI	1547-1553

SWEDEN. KINGS

Gustavius I	1523-1560

PORTUGAL. KINGS

John III	1521-1557

James V　　　　　1513-1542　Mary　　　　　　　1542-1567

ELECTORS OF BRANDENBURG

Joachim I　　　　1499-1535　Joachim II　　　　　1535-1571

RUSSIA. TSARS

Vasili II　　　　1505-1533　Ivan IV, The Terrible　1533-1584

SPAIN. SOVEREIGNS

Charles V　　　　1516-1556

WRITERS

Accolti, Bernardo	1465-1536	Berni, Francesco	1497-1536
Accorso, Mariangelo	1490-1544	Blois, Louis De	1506-1566
Aconzio, Jacopo	1500-1566	Bodin, Jean	1530-1596
Acosta, Jose De	1539-1600	Boone, Andrew	1490-1549
Adams, Clement	1519-1587	Boscan-Almogaver, Juan	1490-1542
Adriani, Giovanni		Boyce, Hector	1465-1536
Baptista	1513-1579	Brantome, Pierre De	
Aemilius, Paulus	-1529	Bourdeilles	1530-1614
Agrippa Von Nettesheim,		Breton, Nicholas	1545-1626
Henry Cornelius	1486-1535	Bruno, Giordano	1548-1600
Agricola (Magister Islebius)		Bryskett, Lodowyck	1545-1612
Johann	1492-1566	Buchanan, George	1506-1582
Alamanni, Luigi	1495-1556	Busbecq, Ogier Ghislain	
Alberus, Erasmus	1500-1553	De	1522-1592
Alcazar, B. Del	1530-1606	Calvin, John	1509-1564
Aleman, Mateo	1547-1609	Camoens, Louis De	1524-1580
Allori, Alessandro	1535-1607	Caro, Annibale	1507-1566
Alvarez Do Oriente,		Casa, Giovanni Della	1503-1556
Fernao	1540-1595	Castiglioni, Baldassare	1478-1529
Ammirato, Scipione	1531-1601	Castillejo, Cristobal De	1490-1550
Amyot, Jacques	1513-1593	Cavendish, George	1500-1562
Arason, Jon	1484-1551	Cecchi, Giammaria	1518-1587
Aretino, Pietro	1492-1556	Cervantes, Saavedra,	
Ariosto, Lodovico	1474-1533	Miguel De	1547-1616
Ascham, Roger	1515-1568	Cetina, Gutierre De	1518-1572
Aventus	1477-1534	Chaloner, Sir Thomas	1521-1565
Avila, Juan de	1500-1569	Charron, Pierre	1541-1603
Avila Y Zuniga, Luis	1490-1560	Chrestien, Florent	1541-1596
Baif, Jean Antoine De	1532-1589	Churchyard, Thomas	1520-1604
Baldung, Grun Hans	1476-1545	Cieza De Leon, Pedro De	1510-1560
Bale, John	1495-1563	Colonna, Vittoria	1490-1547
Balfour, Robert	1550-1625	Cooper, Thomas	1517-1594
Bandello, Matteo	1480-1562	Copernicus, Nicolas	1473-1543
Bandinelli, Baccio	1493-1560	Corte-Real, Jeronymo	1533-1588
Barohona De Soto, Luis	1548-1595	Costanzo, Angelo Di	1507-1591
Barclay, Alexander	1476-1552	Coverdale, Miles	1488-1569
Baronius, Caeser	1538-1607	(trans bible)	
Barros, Joao De	1496-1570	Craig, Sir Thomas	1530-1608
Bellay, Joachim Du	1522-1560	Cranmer, Thomas	1489-1556
Belleau, Remy	1528-1577	Cueva, Juan De La	1550-1610
Bellenden, John	1533-1587	Daurat, Jean	1508-1588
Bembo, Pietro	1470-1547	Dee, John	1527-1608

Della Casa, Giovanni	1503-1556	Knox, John	1513-1572
Deloney, Thomas	1550-1600	Kochanowski, Jan	1530-1589
Des Periers, Bonaventure	1500-1544	Languet, Hubert	1518-1581
Desportes, Phillipe	1546-1606	Larivey, Pierre	1550-1612
Diaz Del Castillo, Bernal	1492-1581	La Taille, Jean De	1540-1608
Dolce, Lodovico	1508-1568	Latimer, Hugh	c. 1485-1555
Dorleans, Louis	1544-1629	Leland, John	1506-1552
Du Bartas, Guillaume		Leon, Luis Ponce De	1527-1591
De Salluste	1544-1590	Lindesay, Robert	1530-1590
Du Bellay, Joachim	1522-1560	Lopez De Gomara	
Edwards, Richard	1523-1566	Francisco	1511-1557
Elyot, Sir Thomas	1490-1546	Loyala, Ignatius de	1491-1556
Encina, Juan Del	1468-1529	Luther, Martin	1483-1546
Erasmus, Desiderius	1466-1536	Lyndsay, Sir David	1490-1555
Ercilla Y Zuniga,		Machiavelli, Niccolo	1469-1527
Alonso De	1533-1594	Magnus	1490-1558
Espinel, Vincente Martinez	1550-1624	Maitland, Sir Richard	1496-1586
Fabricius, Georg	1516-1571	Major, John	1470-1550
Falcao, Christovam	1512-1553	Manzolli, Pier Angelo	1543
Fenton, Sir Geoffrey	1539-1608	Marguerite of Navarre	1492-1549
Ferreira, Antonio	1528-1569	Mariana, Juan De	1536-1624
Figueroa, Francisco De	1536-1617	Marot, Clement	1496-1544
Firenzuola, Agnolo	1493-1545	Mazzonni, Giacomo	1548-1598
Fischart, Johann	1545-1591	Medwall, Henry	1490-
Fletcher, Giles	1548-1611	Melanchthon, Philip	1497-1560
Fleuranges, Robert		Mendoza, Diego Hurtado	
De La Marck	1491-1537	De	1503-1575
Folengo, Theofilo	1491-1544	Molina, Luis	1535-1600
Foxe, John	1516-1587	Montaigne, Michel De	1533-1592
Francheville, Pierre	1548-1616	Montemor, Jorge	1520-1561
Frischlin, Philipp		Montgomerie, Alexander	1550-1610
Nikodemus	1547-1590	More, Sir Thomas	1478-1535
Garnier, Robert	1534-1590	Murner, Thomas	1475-1537
Gascoigne, George	1535-1577	Nardi, Jacopo	1476-
Gesner, Konrad Von	1516-1565	Nifo, Agostino	1473-1538
Gil Polo, Gaspar	1530-1591	Norton, Thomas	1532-1584
Giraldi, Giovanni Battista	1504-1573	Oviedo Y Valdes, Gonzales	
Giraldi, Giglio Gregorio	1479-1552	Fernandez De	1478-1557
Googe, Barnabe	1540-1594	Paracelsus	1493-1541
Grazzini, Antonio		Pasquier, Etienne	1529-1615
Francesco	1503-1583	Passerat, Jean	1534-1602
Grevin, Jacques	1539-1570	Patrizzi, Francesco	1529-1597
Grimald, Nicholas	1519-1562	Paynter, William	1540-1594
Gringoire, Pierre	1475-1539	Pedersen, Christiern	1480-1554
Guarini, Giovanni Battista	1538-1612	Perez De Hita, Gines	1544-1619
Guevara, Antonio De	1490-1545	Pibrac, Guy De Faur	1529-1584
Guicciardini, Francesco	1483-1540	Rabelais, Francois	1495-1553
Guidiccioni, Giovanni	1480-1541	Rastell, John	1475-1536
Hall, Edward	1499-1547	Resende, Garcia De	1470-1536
Harvey, Gabriel	1545-1630	Ribeiro, Bernadim	1482-1552
Herrera, Antoine De	1549-1625	Rich, Barnabe	1540-1617
Herrera, Fernando De	1534-1597	Ronsard, Pierre De	1524-1585
Hessus, Helius Eobanus	1488-1540	Rueda, Lope De	1510-1565
Heywood, John	1497-1580	Ruzzante	1502-1542
Hughes, Thomas	1500-	Sachs, Hans	1494-1576
Hurtardo, Luis	1530-1598	Sackville, Thomas	1530-1608
Jewell, John	1522-1571	Sa De Miranda,	
Jodelle, Etienne	1532-1573	Francisco De	1485-1558
Jovius, Paulus	1483-1552	Sanders, Nicholas	1530-1581
Knolles, Richard	1545-1610	Sannazaro, Jacopo	1458-1530

Sanuto, Marino	1466-1533	Turberville George	1540-1610
Sceve, Maurice	1500-1564	Tusser, Thomas	1524-1580
Scot, Reginald	1538-1599	Tyard, Pontus De	1521-1605
Scott, Alexander	1550-	Tyndale, William	-1536
Sepuvelda, Juan Gines de	1490-1574	Udal, Nicholas	1504-1556
Skelton, John	1460-1529	Valdes, Juan De	1500-1541
Sleidanus, Johannes	1506-1556	Vauquelin De La Fresnaye,	
Stewart, William	1480-1550	Jean	1536-1608
Stow, John	1525-1605	Vaux of Harrowdene,	
Stumpf, Johann	1500-1576	Thomas, Vaux	1510-1556
Surrey, Henry Howard,		Vega, Garcilaso De La	1503-1536
Earl of	c. 1517-1547	Vega, Garcilaso, De La	
Tasso, Bernardo	1493-1569	El Inca	1535-1611
Tasso, Torqueto	1544-1595	Victoria, Thomas Luis De	
Taverner, Richard	1505-1575	Vida, Marco Girolamo	1489-1566
Telesio, Bernardio	1509-1588	Vincente, Gil	1465-1536
Theresa (St.)	1515-1582	Virgil, Polydore	1470-1555
Torres Naharro,		Vives, Juan Luis	1492-1540
Bartolome, de	1480-1530	Winzet, Ninian	1518-1592
Tschudi, Giles	1505-1572	Zwingli Huldreich	1484-1531
Tulsi, Das	1532-1623	Wyatt, Sir Thomas	1503-1542

ARTISTS

Aartsen, Pieter	1507-1573	Cattaneo, Danese	
Abati, Niccolo	1512-1571	Di Michele	1509-1573
Aldegraf, Heinrich	1502-1558	Cellini, Benvenuto	1500-1571
Alessi, Galeazzo	1512-1572	Cespedes, Pablo de	1536-1608
Altdorfer, Albrecht	1480-1538	Civerchio, Vincinzo	1500-
Amalteo, Pomponio	1505-1584	Clouet, Jean	1485-1541
Amman, Jost	1539-1591	Cockx, Hieronymus	1510-1570
Ammanati, Bartolomeo	1511-1592	Coello, Alonso Sanchez	1515-1590
Baccio D'Agnolo	1460-1543	Colins, Alexandre	1526-1612
Bagnacavallo, Bartolommeo	1484-1545	Coninxloo, Gillis Van	1544-1605
Bandinelli, Bartolommeo	1493-1560	Cornelisz, Jakob	fl. 1530
Barocci, Federigo	1528-1612	Cornelisz, Lucas	1495-1552
Barrocchio, Giacomo	1507-1573	Correggio	1494-1534
Bartolommeo, Veneto	1480-1555	Costa, Lorenzo	1460-1535
Bassano, Giacomo DaPonte	1510-1592	Cousin, Jean	1500-1590
Beccafumi, Domenico		Coxcie, Michael	1499-1592
Di Pace	1486-1551	Cleve, Van Cornelis	1520-1567
Bologna, Giovanni Da	1524-1608	Cleve, Van Joos	
Bordone, Paris	1500-1571	Van Der Beke	1480-1540
Brill, Mattys	1550-1584	Cranach, Lucas	1472-1553
Briosco, Andrea	1470-1532	Credi, Lorenzo Di	1457-1537
Bronzino, Il	1503-1572	Della Colle, Raffaellino	1490-
Brueghel, Pieter	1525-1569	Della Robbia, Giovanni	1469-1529
Burgkmair, Hans	1473-1531	Della Robbia, Girolamo	1488-1566
Calvart, Denis	1540-1619	De L'Orme, Philibert	1510-1570
Cambiasi, Luca	1527-1585	Dosso Dossi, Giovanni	1479-1542
Campagna, Gerolamo	1549-1626	Durer, Albrecht	1471-1528
Campagnola, Domenico	1484-c. 1563	Farinato, Paolo	1524-1606
Campi, Giulio	1502-1572	Ferrari, Gaudenzio	1480-1546
Campi, Vincenzo	1536-1591	Fontana, Prospero	1512-1597
Caracci, Annibale	1540-1609	Fontana, Domenico	1543-1607
Caroto, Giovanni Francesco	1480-1555	Garofalo	1481-1559
Castello, Giovanni Battista	1500-1569	Genga, Girolamo	1476-1551
Catena, Vincenzo		Giulio, Romano	1499-1546
Di Biagio	1470-1531	Goujon, Jean	1520-1566

Grunewald, Mathias	1500-1530	Perino Del Vaga	1500-1547
Heemskerk, Marten Jacobz	1498-1574	Peruzzi, Baldassare	1481-1536
Hilliard, Nicholas	1537-1619	Pilon, Germain	1537-1590
Hoefnagel, Joris	1542-1600	Piombo, Sebastian Del	1485-1547
Holbein, Hans	1497-1543	Pontormo, Jacopo Da	1494-1552
Kempener, Peter De	1505-1580	Pordenone, Il	1483-1539
Leoni, Leone	1509-1590	Porta, Giacomo Della	1541-1604
Leopardi, Alessandro	1512-	Primaticcio, Francesco	1504-1570
Lescot, Pierre	1510-1578	Procaccini, Camilio	1546-1629
Liberale, Antonio	1445-1526	Procaccini, Ercole	1520-1591
Limousin, Leonard	1505-1577	Ribalta, Francisco De	1550-1628
Lucas Van Leyden	1494-1533	Riemenschneider, Tilman	1460-1531
Luini, Barnardino	1475-1532	Rossi, Giovanni Battista De	1494-1541
Mabuse, Jan	1472-1534	Sanmichele, Michele	1484-1559
Mander, Carel Van	1548-1606	Sansovino, Andrea Contucci	1460-1529
Manuel, Hans Rudolf	1525-1571	Sansovino, Jacopo	1486-1570
Manuel, Nikolaus	1484-1530	Sarto, Andrea del	1486-1531
Matsys, Quentin	1466-1530	Sebastiano, Del Piombo	1485-1547
Michelangelo	1475-1564	Sodoma, Il	1477-1549
Morales, Luis De	1509-1586	Steenwijk, Hendrik Van c.	1550-1603
Moretto, Il	1494-1554	Stoss, Veit	1483-1533
Moro. Antonio	1512-1575	Suardi, Bartolommeo	1455-1536
Morone, Francesco	1471-1529	Theotocopouli, Domenico	
Moroni, Giambattista	1525-1578	(El Greco)	1542-1614
Moulins, Master of	1460-1529	Titian	1477-1576
Muziano, Girolamo	1528-1592	Tintoretto, Jacopo Robusti	1517-1594
Navarrette, Juan		Vasari, Giorgio	1511-1574
Fernandez De	1526-1579	Veronese, Paolo	1528-1588
Orley, Bernard Van	1490-1540	Vignola, Giacomo	
Pacchia, Girolamo Del	1477-1535	Barozzi Da	1507-1573
Palladio, Andrea	1518-1580	Volterra, Daniele Da	1509-1566
Palma, Jacopo	1480-1528	Wyatt, Sir Thomas	1503-1542
Palissy, Bernard	1510-1589	Zuccaro, Frederico	1539-1609
(Potter)		Zuccaro, Tadeo	1529-1566
Parmigiano	1504-1540		

COMPOSERS

Animuccia, Giovanni	1490-1571	Guerrero, Francisco	1528-1599
Arcadelt, Jakob	1514-1575	Handl, Jacob	1550-1591
Artusi, Giovanni Maria	1540-1613	Jimenez De Quesada,	
Byrd, William	1543-1623	Gonzalo	1500-1579
Cabezon, Antonio De	1510-1566	Lasso, Orlando	1530-1594
Cavalieri, Emilio De	1550-1599	Palestrina, Giovanni	
Festa, Constanzo	1495-1545	Pierluigi Da	1526-1594
Gabrieli, Andrea	1510-1586	Tallis, Thomas	1515-1585
Goudimel, Claude	1510-1572	Taverner, John	1495-1545

1554 Lady Jane Grey Executed.
1555 Diet of Augsburg.
1557 Battle of St. Quentin.
1560 Reformation established in Scotland.
1568 Revolt of Moors in Spain.
1569 Battle of Jarnac.
1572 St. Bartholomew massacre.
1573 Siege of La Rochelle.

PROMINENT PEOPLE

Cabot, Sebastian	1474-1557	Loyola, St. Ignatius	1491-1556
Calvin, John	1509-1564	Nostradamus	1503-1566
Knox, John	1505-1572	Catherine De Medici	1519-1589

EMPERORS OF CHINA (Ming Dynasty)

Mu Tsung	1566-1572	Shen Tsung	1572-1620

POPES

Julius III	1550-1555	Pius IV	1559-1565
Marcellus II	1555-	St. Pius V	1566-1572
Paul IV	1555-1559	Gregory XIII	1572-1585

FRANCE. HEADS OF STATE

Henry II	1547-1559	Charles IX	1560-1574
Francis II	1559-1560	Henry III	1574-1589

HOLY ROMAN EMPERORS

Charles V	1519-1558	Maximilian II	1564-1576
Ferdinand I	1558-1564		

ENGLAND. SOVEREIGNS

Edward VI	1547-1553	Elizabeth I	1558-1603
Mary I	1553-1558		

SWEDEN. KINGS

Gustavius I	1523-1560	John III	1568-1592
Eric XIV	1560-1568		

PORTUGAL. KINGS

John III	1521-1557	Sebastian	1557-1578

SCOTLAND. KINGS

Mary (Abdicated)	1542-1567	James VI	1567-1603

ELECTORS OF BRANDENBURG

Joachim II	1535-1571	John George	1571-1598

Ivan IV, The Terrible　　1533-1584

SPAIN. SOVEREIGNS

Charles V　　　　　　1516-1556　Philip II　　　　　　1556-1598

WRITERS

Aconzio, Jacopo	1500-1566	Bodin, Jean	1530-1596
Acosta, Jose De	1539-1600	Bracciolini, Francesco	1566-1645
Adams, Clement	1519-1587	Brantome, Pierre De	
Adriani, Giovanni		Bourdeilles	1530-1614
Baptista	1513-1579	Breton, Nicholas	1545-1626
Agricola (Magister		Broke, Arthur	-1563
Islebius) Johann	1492-1566	Brosse, Salomon De	1565-1626
Alabaster, William	1567-1640	Bruno, Giordano	1548-1600
Alamanni, Luigi	1495-1556	Bryskett, Lodowyck	1545-1612
Alberus, Erasmus	1500-1553	Buchanan, George	1506-1582
Alcazar, D. Del	1530-1606	Busbecq, Ogier	
Aleman, Mateo	1547-1609	Ghislain De	1522-1592
Allori, Alessandro	1535-1607	Calderwood, David	1575-1650
Alvarez Do Oriente,		Calvin, John	1509-1564
Fernao	1540-1595	Camden, William	1551-1623
Ammirato, Scipione	1531-1601	Camoens, Louis De	1524-1580
Amyot, Jacques	1513-1593	Campanella, Tommaso	1568-1639
Andrews, Lancelot	1555-1626	Campion, Thomas	1567-1620
Arason, Jon	1484-1551	Carew, Richard	1555-1620
Aretino, Pietro	1492-1556	Caro, Annibale	1507-1566
Argensola, Lupercio		Casa, Giovanni Della	1503-1556
Leonardo De	1559-1613	Castro Y Bellvis,	
Arminius, Jacobus	1560-1609	Guillen De	1569-1631
Arquijo, Juan De	1564-1623	Cavendish, George	1500-1562
Ascham, Roger	1515-1568	Cecchi, Giammaria	1518-1587
Aubigne, Theodore		Cervantes Saavedra,	
Agrippa De	1552-1630	Maguel De	1547-1616
Avila Juan De	1500-1569	Cetina, Gutierre De	1518-1572
Avila, Y Zuniga, Louis	1490-1560	Chaloner, Sir Thomas	1521-1565
Ayton, Sir Robert	1570-1638	Chapman, George	1559-1634
Bacon, Francis	1561-1626	Charron, Pierre	1541-1603
Baif, Jean Antoine De	1532-1589	Chettle, Henry	1560-1607
Baker, Sir Richard	1568-1645	Chiabrera, Gabriello	1552-1638
Balassa, Balint	1551-1594	Chrestien, Florent	1541-1596
Balbuena, Bernardo De	1568-1627	Churchyard, Thomas	1520-1604
Baldi, Bernardino	1553-1617	Cieza De Leon, Pedro De	1519-1560
Bale, John	1495-1563	Constable, Henry	1562-1613
Balfour, Robert	1550-1625	Cooper, Thomas	1517-1594
Bandello, Matteo	1480-1562	Corte-Real, Jeronymo	1533-1588
Bandinelli, Baccio	1493-1560	Costanzo, Angelo Di	1507-1591
Barahona De Soto, Luis	1548-1595	Coverdale, Miles	1488-1569
Barclay, Alexander	1476-1552	(trans bible)	
Baronius, Caesar	1538-1607	Craig, Sir Thomas	1530-1608
Barnfield, Richard	1574-1627	Cranmer, Thomas	1489-1556
Barros, Joao De	1496-1570	Cueva, Juan De La	1550-1610
Bellay, Joachim Du	1522-1560	Daniel, Samuel	1562-1619
Belleau, Remy	1528-1577	Daurat, Jean	1508-1588
Bellenden, John	1533-1587	Davies, John	1565-1618
Bellenden, William	1555-1633	Davies, Sir John	1569-1626
Blois, Louis De	1506-1566	Day, John	1574-1640
Boccalini, Trajano	1556-1613	Dee, John	1527-1608

Dekker, Thomas	c. 1570-1641	Hakluyt, Richard	1552-1616
Della Casa, Giovanni	1503-1556	Hales, John	-1571
Deloney, Thomas	1550-1600	Hall, Joseph	1574-1656
Dempster, Thomas	1570-1625	Hardy, Alexandre	1569-1631
Desportes, Philippe	1546-1606	Harington, Sir John	1561-1612
Diaz Del Castillo, Bernal	1492-1581	Harvey, Gabriel	c. 1545-1630
Dolce, Lodovico	1508-1568	Hayward, Sir John	1560-1627
Donne, John	1573-1631	Herrera, Antoine De	1549-1625
Dorleans, Louis	1544-1629	Herrera, Fernando De	1534-1597
Drayton, Michael	1563-1631	Heywood, John	1497-1580
Du Bartas, Guillaume		Heywood, Thomas	1574-1641
De Sallust؛	1544-1590	Hollinshed, Raphael	d. c. 1580
Du Bellay, Joachim	1522-1560	Hooker, Richard	1553-1600
Du Vair, Guillaume	1556-1621	Hughes, Thomas	1500-
Edwards, Richard	1523-1566	Hume, Alexander	1557-1609
Ercilla Y Zuniga,		Hurtado, Luis	1530-1598
Alonso De	1533-1594	Jewell, John	1522-1571
Espinel, Vincente		Jodelle, Etienne	1532-1573
Martinez	1550-1624	Johnson, Richard	1573-1659
Fabricius, Georg	1516-1571	Jonson, Ben	1573-1637
Falcao, Christovam	1512-1553	Jovius, Paulus	1483-1552
Fenton, Sir Geoffrey	1539-1608	Kirke, Edward	1553-1613
Ferishta, Mohammed		Knolles, Richard	1545-1610
Kasim	1570-1611	Knox, John	1513-1572
Ferreira, Antonio	1528-1569	Kochanowski, Jan	1530-1584
Figueroa, Francisco De	1536-1617	Kyd, Thomas	1558-1594
Fischart, Johann	1545-1591	Labé, Louis Charlin Perrin	-1566
Fletcher, Giles	1548-1611	Languet, Hubert	1518-1581
Florio, John	c. 1553-1625	Larivey, Pierre	1550-1612
Fludd, Robert	1575-1637	La Taille, Jean De	1540-1608
Fowler, William	1560-1614	Latimer, Hugh	c. 1485-1555
Foxe, John	1516-1587	Laud, William (Archbishop	
Francheville, Pierre	1548-1616	of Canterbury)	1573-1645
Francis of Sales	1567-1622	Leland, John	1506-1552
Fraunce, Abraham	1558-1663	Leon, Luis Ponce De	1527-1591
Frischlin, Philipp		Lindesay, Robert	1530-1590
Nikodemus	1547-1590	Lodge, Thomas	1558-1625
Galilei, Galileo	1564-1642	Lopez De Gomara	
Garnier, Robert	1534-1590	Francisco	1511-1557
Gascoigne, George	1535-1577	Loyala, Ignatius de	1491-1556
Gesner, Konrad Von	1516-1565	Lyly, John	1553-1606
Gil Polo, Gaspar	1530-1591	Lyndsay, Sir David	1490-1555
Giraldi, Giovanni Battista	1504-1573	Magnus	1490-1558
Giraldi, Giglio Gregorio	1479-1552	Maitland, Sir Richard	1496-1586
Godwin, Francis	1562-1633	Malherbe, Francois De	1555-1628
Gongora Y Argote,		Manzolli, Pier Angelo	1543-
Luis De	1561-1627	Mariana, Juan De	1536-1624
Googe, Barnabe	1540-1594	Marini, Giovani Battista	1569-1625
Gosson, Stephen	1554-1624	Markham, Gervase	1568-1637
Grazzini, Antonio		Marlowe, Christopher	1564-1593
Francesco	1503-1583	Marston, John	1575-1634
Greene, Robert	1558-1592	Mazzoni, Giacomo	1548-1598
Greville, Sir Fulke	1554-1628	Melanchthon, Philip	1497-1560
Grevin, Jacques	1539-1570	Mendoza, Diego Hurtado	
Grimald, Nicholas	1519-1562	De	1503-1575
Guarini, Giovanni		Meres, Francis	1565-1647
Battista	1538-1612	Middleton, Thomas	1570-1627
Guevara, Louis Velez de	1570-1644	Molina, Luis	1535-1600
Guidiccioni, Giovanni	1480-1541	Montaigne, Michel De	1533-1592

Montchretien, Antoine De	1575-1621
Montemor, Jorge	1520-1561
Montgomerie, Alexander	1550-1610
Moryson, Fynes	1566-1630
Munday, Anthony	1553-1633
Nashe, Thomas	1567-1601
Norton, Thomas	1532-1584
Oviedo Y Valdes,	
Gonzales Fernandez De	1478-1557
Pasquier, Etienne	1529-1615
Passerat, Jean	1534-1602
Patrizzi, Francesco	1529-1597
Paynter, William	1540-1594
Pedersen, Christiern	1480-1554
Peele, George	1558-1597
Perez De Hita, Gines	1544-1619
Pibrac, Guy De Faur	1529-1584
Rabelais, Francois	1495-1553
Regnier, Mathurin	1573-1613
Ribeiro, Bernadim	1482-1552
Rich, Barnabe	1540-1617
Rinuccini, Attavio	1562-1621
Rolland, John	1560-
Ronsard, Pierre De	1524-1585
Rueda, Lope De	1510-1565
Sachs, Hans	1494-1576
Sackville, Thomas	1530-1608
Sa De Miranda,	
Francisco De	1485-1558
Sanders, Nicholas	1530-1581
Sceve, Maurice	1500-1564
Scot, Reginald	1538-1599
Scott, Alexander	1550-
Sepuvelda, Juan Gines De	1490-1574
Shakespeare, William	1564-1616
Sidney, Sir Philip	1554-1586
Sleidanus, Johannes	1506-1556
Sousa, Luiz De	1555-1632
Southwell, Robert	1561-1595
Speed, John	1552-1629
Spenser, Edmund	1552-1599
Stevenson, William	-1575
Stirling, William	
Alexander	1567-1640
Stow, John	1525-1605
Straparola, Giovan	
Francesco	-1557
Stumpf, Johann	1500-1576
Sylvester, Joshua	1563-1618
Tasso, Bernardo	1493-1569
Taverner, Richard	1505-1575
Telesio, Bernardio	1509-1588
Theresa (St.)	1515-1582
Thou, Jacques Auguste De	1553-1617
Tirso De Molina	1571-1648
Totnes, George Carew	1555-1629
Tourneur, Cyril	1575-1626
Tschudi, Giles	1505-1572
Tulsi, Das	1532-1623
Turberville, George	1540-1610
Tusser, Thomas	1524-1580
Tyard, Pontus De	1521-1605
Udal, Nicholas	1504-1556
Urfe, Honore D'	1568-1625
Vauquelin De La	
Fresnaye, Jean	1536-1608
Vaux of Harrowdene,	
Thomas Vaux	1510-1556
Vega Carpio, Lope	
Felix De	1562-1635
Vega, Garcilaso	
De La El Inca	1535-1616
Victoria, Tomas Luis De	1535-1611
Vida, Marco Girolamo	1489-1566
Virgil, Polydore	1470-1555
Watson, Thomas	1557-1592
Whetstone, George	1551-1587
Winzet, Ninian	1518-1592
Wotton, Sir Henry	1568-1639

ARTISTS

Aartsen, Pieter	1507-1573
Abati, Niccolo	1512-1571
Aldegraf, Heinrich	1502-1558
Alessi, Galeazzo	1512-1572
Amalteao, Pomponio	1505-1584
Amman, Jost	1539-1591
Ammanati, Bartolomeo	1511-1592
Anna, Baldasarre	1560-1639
Balen, Henry Van	1560-1632
Bandinelli, Bartolommeo	1493-1560
Barocci, Federigo	1528-1612
Barocchio, Giacomo	1507-1573
Bartolommeo, Veneto	1480-1555
Bassano, Giacomo Da	
Ponte	1510-1592
Beccafumi, Domenico Di	
Pace	1486-1551
Bloemart, Abraham	1564-1651
Bologna, Giovanni Da	1524-1608
Bordone, Paris	1500-1571
Brill, Mattys	1550-1584
Brill, Paul	1554-1626
Brozino, Il	1503-1572
Brueghel, Pieter	1525-1569
Caluart, Denis	1540-1619
Cambiasi, Luca	1527-1585
Campagna, Gerolamo	1549-1626
Campagnola, Domenico	c. 1484-1563
Campi, Giulio	1502-1572
Campi, Vincenzo	1536-1591
Caracci, Agostino	1557-1602

Caracci, Annibale	1540-1609	Jones, Inigo	1573-1651
Caracci, Ludovico	1555-1619	Kempener, Peter De	1505-1580
Caravaggio, Michel Angelo	1573-1610	Keyser, Hendrik De	1565-1621
Carducci, Bartolommeo	1568-1610	Leoni, Leone	1509-1590
Caroto, Giovanni		Leopardi, Alessandro	1512-
Francesco	1480-1555	Lescot, Pierre	1510-1578
Castello, Bernado	1557-1629	Limousin, Leonard	1505-1577
Castello, Giovanni		Mander, Carel Van	1548-1606
Battista	1500-1569	Manuel, Hans Rudolf	1525-1571
Cattaneo, Danese Di		Michelangelo	1475-1564
Michele	1509-1573	Mierevelt, Michiel	
Cellini, Benvenuto	1500-1571	Jansz Van	1567-1641
Cesari, Giuseppe	1568-1640	Moretto, Il	1494-1554
Cespedes, Pablo De	1536-1608	Morales, Luis De	1509-1586
Civerchio, Vincinzo	1500-	Moro, Antonio	1512-1575
Cigoli, Lodovico Cardi Da	1559-1613	Moroni, Giambattista	1525-1578
Cleve, Van Cornelis	1520-1567	Muziano, Girolamo	1528-1592
Clouet, Francois	-1572	Navarrete, Juan	
Cockx, Hieronymus	1510-1570	Fernandez De	1526-1579
Coello, Alonso Sanchez	1515-1590	Pacheco, Francisco	1571-1654
Colins, Alexandre	1526-1612	Palladio, Andrea	1518-1580
Coninxloo, Gillis Van	1544-1605	Palissy, Bernard	1510-1589
Corenzio, Belisario	1558-1643	(Potter)	
Cornelisz, Cornelisz	1562-1638	Pilon, Germain	1537-1590
Cornelisz, Lucas	1495-1552	Pontormo, Jacopo Da	1495-1552
Cousin, Jean	1500-1590	Porta, Giacomo Della	1541-1604
Coxcie, Michael	1499-1592	Procaccini, Camilio	1546-1629
Cranach, Lucas	1472-1553	Procaccini, Ercole	1520-1591
Crespi, Giovanni Battista	1557-1633	Primaticcio, Francesco	1504-1570
Della Robbia, Girolamo	1488-1566	Reni, Guido	1575-1642
De L'Orme, Philibert	1510-1570	Ribalta, Francesco de	1550-1628
Farinato, Paolo	1524-1606	Sanmichele, Michele	1484-1559
Fontana, Domenico	1543-1607	Sansovino, Jacopo	1486-1570
Fontana, Lavinia	1552-1614	Steenwijk, Hendrik Van	c. 1550-1603
Fontana, Prospero	1512-1597	Theotocopouli, Domenico	
Garofalo	1481-1559	(El Greco)	1542-1614
Genga, Girolamo	1476-1551	Titian	1477-1576
Gentileschi, Orazio De	1562-1647	Tintoretto, Jacopo Robusti	1518-1594
Gheeraerts, Marcus	1561-1635	Van Veen, Otto	1556-1634
Goujon, Jean	1520-1566	Vasari, Giorgio	1511-1574
Heemskerk, Marten		Veronese, Paolo	1528-1588
Jacobsz	1498-1574	Vignola, Giacomo	
Hilliard, Nicholas	1537-1619	Barozzi Da	1507-1573
Hoefnagel, Joris	1542-1600	Volterra, Daniele Da	1509-1566
Janssens, Van Nuyssen		Zuccaro, Frederigo	1539-1609
Abraham	1575-1632	Zuccaro, Taddep	1529-1566

COMPOSERS

Aichinger, Gregor	1565-1628	Carlton, Richard	1560-1638
Animuccia, Giovanni	1490-1571	Cavalieri, Emilio De	1550-1599
Arcadelt, Jacob	1514-1575	Cooper, John	1570-1627
Artusi, Giovanni Maria	1540-1613	Dowland, John	1563-1626
Basile, Giambattista	1575-1632	Eccard, Johann	1553-1611
Bateson, Thomas	1570-1630	Farmer, John	1565-1605
Bull, John	1562-1628	Farnaby, Giles	c. 1560-1600
Byrd, William	1543-1623	Gabrieli, Andrea	1510-1586
Cabezon, Antonio De	1510-1566	Gesualdo, Don Carlos	1560-1613
Caccini, Guilio	1558-1615	Goudimel, Claude	1510-1572

Guerrero, Francisco	1528-1599	Palestrina, Giovanni	
Handl, Jacob	1550-1591	Pierluigi Da	1526-1594
Hassler, Hans Leo	1564-1612	Peri, Jacopo	1561-1633
Jimenez De Quesada,		Praetorius, Michael	1571-1621
Gonzalo	1500-1579	Sweelinck, Jan Pieter	1562-1621
Lasso, Orlando	1530-1594	Tallis, Thomas	1515-1585
Marenzio, Luca	1560-1599	Tomkins, Thomas	1572-1656
Monteverdi, Claudio	1567-1643	Wilbye, John	1574-1638
Morley, Thomas	1558-1603		

1577 Drake's first voyage round the world.
1586 Battle of Zutphen.
1588 Defeat of the Spanish Armada.
1590 Battle of Ivry.
1595 Tyrone rebellion.
1600 English East India Company formed.

PROMINENT PEOPLE

Catherine De Medici	1519-1589	Richelieu, Jean Du Plessis	
Drake, Sir Francis	1540-1596	Cardinal Duc De	1585-1642

EMPERORS OF CHINA

Shen Tsung	1572-1620

POPES

Gregory XIII	1572-1585	Gregory XIV	1590-1591
Sixtus V	1585-1590	Innocent IX	1591
Urban VII	1590	Clement VIII	1592-1605

FRANCE. HEADS OF STATE

Henry III	1574-1589	Henry IV	1589-1610

HOLY ROMAN EMPERORS

Maximilian II	1564-1576	Rudolf II	1576-1612

ENGLAND, SOVEREIGNS

Elizabeth I	1558-1603

PORTUGAL. KINGS

Sebastian	1557-1578	Under Spanish Suzerainty	1581-1640
Henry	1578-1580		

SCOTLAND. KINGS

James VI	1567-1603

ELECTORS OF BRANDENBURG

John George	1571-1598	Joachim III Frederick	1598-1608

RUSSIA. TSARS

Ivan IV, The Terrible	1533-1584	Boris	1598-1605
Theodore I	1584-1598		

SPAIN. SOVEREIGNS

Philip II	1556-1598	Philip III	1598-1621

John III	1568-1592	Charles IX	1600-1611
Sigismund	1592-1599		

WRITERS

Acosta, Jose De	1539-1600	Brathwait, Richard	1588-1673
Adams, Clement	1519-1587	Breton, Nicholas	1545-1626
Adriani, Giovani Baptista	1513-1579	Brosse, Salomon De	1565-1626
Aitzema, Lieuwe Van	1600-1669	Browne, William	1591-1643
Alabaster, William	1567-1640	Bruno, Giordano	1548-1600
Alarcon Y Mendoza,		Bryskett, Lodowyck	1545-1612
Jean Ruiz de	1580-1639	Buchanan, George	1506-1582
Alcazar, B. Del	1530-1606	Burton, Robert	1577-1640
Aleman, Mateo	1547-1609	Busbecq, Ogier Ghislain	
Allori, Allesandro	1535-1607	De	1522-1592
Alvarez Do Oriente,		Calderon, De La Barca	
Fernao	1540-1595	Pedro	1600-1681
Ammirato, Scipione	1531-1601	Calderwood, David	1575-1650
Amyot, Jacques	1513-1593	Camden, William	1551-1623
Andrewes, Lancelot	1555-1626	Camoens, Louis De	1524-1580
Argensola, Lupercio		Campanella, Tommaso	1568-1639
Leonardo De	1559-1613	Campion, Thomas	1567-1620
Arminius, Jacobus	1560-1609	Carew, Richard	1555-1620
Arrebo, Anders		Carew, Thomas	1595-1638
Christiensen	1587-1637	Caro, Annibale	1507-1566
Arquijo, Juan De	1564-1623	Castillo, Solorzano,	
Aubigne, Theodore		Alonso De	1584-1647
Agrippa De	1552-1630	Castro Y Bellvis,	
Avercamp, Hendrik	1585-1634	Guillen De	1569-1631
Avila, Gil Gonzalez De	1577-1658	Cats, Jakob	1577-1660
Ayton, Sir Robert	1570-1638	Cecchi, Giammaria	1518-1587
Bacon, Francis	1561-1626	Cervantes Saavedra,	
Baif, Jean Antoine De	1532-1589	Miguel De	1547-1616
Baillie, Robert	1599-1662	Cespedes Y Meneses,	
Baker, Sir Richard	1568-1645	Gonzalo De	1585-1638
Balassa, Balint	1551-1594	Chapman, George	1559-1634
Balbuena, Bernardo De	1568-1627	Chapelaine, Jean	1595-1674
Baldi, Bernardino	1553-1617	Charron, Pierre	1541-1603
Balfour, Robert	1550-1625	Chettle, Henry	1560-1607
Balzac, Jean Louis		Chiabrera, Gabriello	1552-1638
Guez De	1594-1654	Chrestien, Florent	1541-1596
Barahona De Soto, Luis	1548-1595	Churchyard, Thomas	1520-1604
Baronus, Caesar	1538-1607	Cluwer, Philip	1580-1623
Barnfield, Richard	1574-1627	Comenius, Johann Amos	1592-1670
Bassompiere, Francois De	1579-1646	Constable, Henry	1562-1613
Baudier, Michel	1589-1645	Constanzo, Angelo D.	1507-1591
Beaumont, Francis	1584-1616	Cooper, Thomas	1517-1594
Beaumont, Sir John	1583-1627	Corbet, Richard	1582-1635
Belleau, Remy	1528-1577	Corte-Real, Jeronymo	1533-1588
Bellenden, John	1533-1587	Coryate, Thomas	1577-1617
Bellenden, William	1555-1633	Cotton, John	1584-1652
Boccalini, Trajano	1556-1613	Craig, Sir Thomas	1530-1608
Bodin, Jean	1530-1596	Cueva, Juan De La	1550-1610
Boisrobert, Francois Le		Daniel, Samuel	1562-1619
Metel De	1592-1662	Daurat, Jean	1508-1588
Bracciolini, Francesco	1566-1645	Davies, John	1565-1618
Bradford, William	1590-1657	Davies, Sir John	1569-1626
Brantome, Pierre De		Davila, Enrico Caterino	1576-1613
Bourdeille	c. 1540-1640		

Day, John	1574-1640	Grotius, Hugo	1583-1645
Dee, John	1527-1608	Guarini, Giovanni	
Dekker, Thomas	1570-1641	Battista	1538-1612
Delmedigo, Joseph		Guevara, Luis De Velez	1570-1644
Soloman	1591-1655	Gundulic, Ivan	1588-1638
Deloney, Thomas	1550-1600	Hajji, Khalifa c.	1599-1658
Dempster, Thomas	1570-1625	Hake, Edward	1579
Descartes, Rene	1596-1650	Hakluyt, Richard	1552-1616
Desmarets, Jean	1595-1676	Hall, Joseph	1574-1656
Desportes, Philippe	1546-1606	Hardy, Alexandre	1569-1631
Diaz Del Castillo, Bernal	1492-1581	Harington, Sir John	1561-1612
Donne, John	1573-1631	Harlib, Samuel	1599-1670
Dorleans, Louis	1544-1629	Harvey, Gabriel c.	1545-1630
Drayton, Michael	1563-1631	Harvey, William	1578-1657
Drummond, William	1585-1649	Haughton, William	1598
Du Bartas, Guillaume		Hayward, Sir John	1560-1627
De Salluste	1544-1590	Heemskerk, Johan Van	1597-1656
Duchesne, Andre	1584-1640	Herbert, George	1593-1633
Du Vair, Guillaume	1556-1621	Herbert of Cherbury	1583-1648
Ercilla Y Zuniga,		Herrera, Antoine De	1549-1625
Alonso De	1533-1594	Herrera, Fernando De	1534-1597
Espinel, Vincente Martinez	1550-1624	Herrick, Robert	1591-1674
Fairfax, Edward	1580-1635	Heylyn, Peter	1600-1662
Faria Y Sousa, Manuel De	1590-1649	Heywood, Thomas	1574-1641
Fenton, Sir Geoffrey	1539-1608	Hobbes, Thomas	1588-1679
Ferishta, Mohammed		Holinshed, Raphael	d. c. 1580
Kasim	1570-1611	Holles, Denzil Holles	1599-1680
Field, Nathan	1587-1619	Hooft, Pieter Cornelissen	1581-1647
Figueroa, Francisco De	1536-1617	Hooker, Richard	1553-1600
Filmer, Sir Robert	1590-1653	Howell, James	1594-1666
Fischart, Johann	1545-1591	Hume, Alexander	1557-1609
Flecknoe, Richard	1600-1678	Hunnis, William	-1597
Fletcher, Giles	1548-1611	Hortado, Luis	1530-1598
Fletcher, Giles	1584-1623	Huygens, Sir Constantijn	1596-1687
Fletcher, John	1579-1625	Jansen, Cornelius	1585-1638
Fletcher, Phineas	1582-1650	Jauregui, Juan De	1583-1641
Florio, John c.	1553-1625	Johnson, Richard	1573-1659
Fludd, Robert	1575-1637	Jonson, Ben	1573-1637
Ford, John	1586-1640	Knolles, Richard	1545-1610
Fowler, William	1560-1614	Kochanowski, Jan	1530-1584
Foxe, John	1516-1587	Kyrke, Edward	1553-1613
Francheville, Pierre	1548-1616	Kydd, Thomas	1558-1594
Francis of Sales	1567-1622	La Mothe Le Vayer,	
Fraunce, Abraham	1558-1663	Francois De	1588-1672
Frischlin, Philipp		Languet, Hubert	1518-1581
Nikodemus	1547-1590	Larivey, Pierre	1550-1612
Galilei, Galileo	1564-1642	La Taille, Jean De	1540-1608
Garnier, Robert	1534-1590	Laud, William (Archbishop	
Gascoigne, George	1535-1577	of Canterbury)	1573-1645
Gassendi, Pierre	1592-1655	Leon, Luis Ponce De	1527-1591
Gil Polo, Gaspar	1530-1591	Lindesay, Robert	1530-1590
Godwin, Francis	1562-1633	Lobo, Francisco	
Gongora Y Argote,		Rodriguez	1580-1622
Luis De	1561-1627	Lodge, Thomas	1558-1625
Googe, Barnabe	1540-1594	Lyly, John	1553-1606
Gasson, Stephen	1554-1624	Maitland, Sir Richard	1496-1586
Grazzini, Antonio		Makkari, Ahmed El	1585-1631
Francesco	1503-1583	Malherbe, Francois De	1555-1628
Greene, Robert	1558-1592	Manzolli, Pier Angelo	1543-
Greville, Sir Fulke	1554-1628	Marca, Pierre De	1594-1662

Mariana, Juan De	1536-1624	Scot, Reginald	1538-1599
Marini, Giovanni Battista	1569-1625	Scott, Alexander	1550-
Markham, Gervase	1568-1637	Selden, John	1584-1654
Marlowe, Christopher	1564-1593	Shakespeare, William	1564-1616
Marston, John	1575-1634	Shirley, James	1596-1666
Massinger, Philip	1583-1640	Sidney, Sir Philip	1554-1586
May, Thomas	1595-1650	Smith, John	1580-1631
Mazzoni, Giacomo	1548-1598	Sorel, Charles	1597-1674
Meres, Francis	1565-1647	Sousa, Luiz De	1555-1632
Middleton, Thomas	1570-1627	Southwell, Robert	1561-1595
Mira De Amescua,		Spenser, Edmund	1552-1599
Antonio	1578-1644	Speed, John	1552-1629
Molina, Luis	1535-1600	St. Jernhjelm, Georg	1598-1672
Montainge, Michel De	1533-1592	Stirling, William	
Montchretien, Antoine De	1575-1621	Alexander	1567-1640
Montgomerie, Alexander	1550-1610	Stow, John	1525-1605
Moryson, Fynes	1566-1630	Stumpf, Johann	1500-1576
Munday, Anthony	1553-1633	Sylvester, Joshua	1563-1618
Mure, Sir William	1594-1657	Tasso, Torqueto	1544-1595
Mytens, Daniel	1590-1642	Taylor, John	1580-1653
Najara, Israel Ben Moses	1587-	Telesio, Bernardio	1509-1588
Nashe, Thomas	1567-1601	Theresa (St.)	1515-1582
Norton, Thomas	1532-1584	Thou, Jacques Auguste De	1553-1617
Ogilby, John	1600-1676	Tirso De Molina	1571-1648
Opitz, Von Boberfeld,		Totnes, George Carew	1555-1629
Martin	1597-1639	Tourneur, Cyril	1575-1626
Overbury, Sir Thomas	1581-1613	Tulsi, Das	1532-1623
Parker, Martin	1600-1656	Turberville, George	1540-1610
Pasquier, Etienne	1529-1615	Tusser, Thomas	1524-1580
Passerat, Jean	1534-1602	Tyard, Pontus De	1521-1605
Patrizzi, Francesco	1529-1597	Urfe, Honore D'	1568-1625
Paynter, William	1540-1594	Vaugelas, Claude Faure	1596-1650
Peacham, Henry	1576-1643	Vaughan, William	1577-1641
Peele, George	1558-1597	Vauquelin De La	
Perez De Hita, Gines	1544-1619	Fresnaye, Jean	1536-1608
Pibrac, Guy De Faur	1529-1584	Vega Carpio, Lope	
Purchas, Samuel	1577-1626	Felix De	1562-1635
Puttenham, George	-1590	Vega, Garcilaso De La	
Quarles, Francis	1592-1644	(El Inca)	1535-1616
Quevedo Y Villegas,		Velez De Guevara, Luis	1579-1644
Francisco Gomez De	1580-1645	Viau, Theophile de	1590-1626
Racan, Honore De Bueil	1589-1670	Victoria, Tomas Luis de	1535-1611
Regnier, Mathurin	1573-1613	Villamediana Count De	1580-1622
Rich, Barnabe	1540-1617	Voiture, Vincent	1598-1648
Rinuccini, Ottavio	1562-1621	Vondel, Joost Van Den	1587-1679
Rolland, John	1560-	Walton, Izaak	1593-1683
Ronsard, Pierre De	1524-1585	Watson, Thomas	1557-1692
Rowley, William	1585-1642	Whetstone, George	1551-1587
Sachs, Hans	1494-1576	Wilson, Robert	-1600
Sackville, Thomas	1530-1608	Winslow, Edward	1595-1655
Saint-Amant, Marc		Winthrop, John	1588-1649
Antoine De Gerard	1594-1661	Winzet, Ninian	1518-1592
Sanders, Nicholas	1530-1581	Wither, George	1588-1667
Sandys, George	1578-1644	Wotton, Sir Henry	1568-1639

ARTISTS

Albani, Francesco	1578-1660	Amalteo, Pomponio	1505-1584
Allori, Christofand	1577-1621	Amman, Jost	1539-1591

I

Ammanati, Bartolomeo	1511-1592	Gentileschi, Orazio De	1562-1647
Anna, Baldasarre	1560-1639	Gheeraerts, Marcus	1561-1635
Badalocchio, Sisto	1581-1647	Goyen, Jan Josephszoon	
Balen, Henry Van	1560-1632	Van	1596-1656
Barbieri, Giovanni		Guercino	1590-1666
Francesco	1591-1666	Hals, Frans	1580-1666
Barocci, Federigo	1528-1612	Heem, Jan Davidz Van	1600-1683
Bassano, Giacomo		Hernandes, Gregorio	1576-1636
Da Ponte	1510-1592	Hilliard, Nicholas	1537-1619
Bernini, Giovanni Lorenzo	1598-1680	Hoefnagel, Joris	1542-1600
Bloemart, Abraham	1564-1651	Honthorst, Gerard, Van	1590-1656
Bologna, Giovanni Da	1524-1608	Iwasa, Matahei	1578-1650
Borromini, Francesco	1599-1667	Jameson, John	1588-1644
Brill, Mattys	1550-1584	Janssen, Cornelis	1593-1664
Brill, Paul	1554-1626	Janssens, Van Nuyssen	
Caluart, Denis	1540-1619	Abraham	1575-1632
Callot, Jacques	c. 1594-1635	Jones, Inigo	1573-1651
Cambiasi, Luca	1527-1585	Jonson, Cornelis	
Camp, Huysen Dirk		Van Ceulen	1593-1662
Rafelsz	1586-1627	Jordaens, Jacob	1593-1678
Campi, Vincenzo	1536-1591	Kempener, Peter De	1505-1580
Caravaggio, Michel		Keyser, Hendrik De	1565-1621
Angelo	1573-1610	Laar, Pieter Van	1590-1658
Carducci, Bartolommeo	1568-1610	Lanfranco, Giovanni	1581-1647
Carracci, Agostino	1557-1602	Leoni, Leone	1509-1590
Carracci, Annibale	1540-1609	Lescot, Pierre	1510-1578
Carracci, Lodovico	1555-1619	Limousin, Leonard	1505-1577
Castello, Bernado	1557-1629	Mander, Carel Van	1548-1606
Cavedone, Jacopo	1577-1660	Mansart, Francois	1598-1666
Cesari, Giuseppe	1568-1640	Mierevelt, Michiel Jansz	
Cespedes, Pablo De	1536-1608	Van	1567-1641
Cigoli, Lodovico		Montanes, Juan Martinez	1580-1649
Cardi Da	1559-1613	Morales, Luis De	1509-1586
Claude-Lorraine	1600-1682	Moroni, Giambatista	1525-1578
Codde, Pieter	1599-1678	Muziano, Girolamo	1528-1592
Coello, Alonso Sanchez	1515-1590	Navarrete, Juan	
Colins, Alexandre	1526-1612	Fernandez De	1526-1579
Coninxloo, Gillis Van	1544-1605	Pacheco, Francisco	1571-1654
Corenzio, Belisario	1558-1643	Palladio, Andrea	1518-1580
Cornelisz, Cornelis	1562-1638	Palissy, Bernard	1510-1589
Cousin, Jean	1500-1590	(potter)	
Cortona, Pietro		Pilon, Germain	1537-1590
Berrettini Da	1596-1669	Porta, Giacomo Della	1541-1604
Coxcie, Michael	1499-1592	Poussin, Nicolas	1594-1665
Crayer, Gaspard De	1584-1669	Procaccini, Camillo	1546-1629
Crespi, Daniele	1590-1630	Procaccini, Ercole	1520-1591
Crespi, Giovanni Battista	1557-1633	Procaccini, Ercole the	
De Keyser, Thomas	1596-1667	younger	1596-1676
Diaz, Diego Valentin	1585-1660	Quesnoy, Francois Du	1594-1646
Diepenbeek, Abraham Van	1596-1675	Reni, Guido	1575-1642
Domenichino, Zampieri	1581-1641	Ribalta, Francisco De	1550-1628
Duck, Jacob	1600-1660	Ribera, Josepe De	1588-1656
Elsheimer, Adam	1579-1620	Rubens, Peter Paul	1577-1640
Elstracke, Renold	c. 1590-1630	Sacchi, Andrea	1600-1661
Falcone, Aniello	1600-1656	Sarrazin, Jacques	1588-1660
Farinato, Paolo	1524-1606	Snyders, Frans	1579-1657
Fontana, Domenico	1543-1607	Steenwijk, Hendrik Van c.	1550-1603
Fontana, Lavinia	1552-1614	Stone, Nicholas	1587-1647
Fontana, Prospero	1512-1597	Teniers, David the elder	1582-1649
Gentileschi, Artemisia	1597-1651	Terbrugghen, Hendrik	1588-1629

Theotocopouli, Domenico		Velasquez, Diego	
(El Greco)	1542-1614	Rodriguez	1599-1660
Titian	1477-1576	Veronese, Paolo	1528-1588
Tintoretto, Jacopo Rubusti	1518-1594	Vos, Cornelis De	1585-1651
Van De Velde, Jan	1593-1641	Vouet, Simon	1590-1649
Van Dyck, Anthony Sir	1599-1641	Zuccaro, Frederigo	1539-1609
Van Veen, Otto	1556-1634	Zurbaran, Francisco De	1598-1669

COMPOSERS

Aichinger, Gregor	1565-1628	Guerrero, Francisco	1528-1599
Allegri, Gregorio	1582-1652	Handl, Jacob	1550-1591
Artusi, Giovanni Maria	1540-1613	Hassler, Hans Leo	1564-1612
Basile, Giambattista	1575-1632	Jenkins, John	1592-1678
Bateson, Thomas	1570-1630	Jimenes De Quesada,	
Bull, John	1562-1628	Gonzalo	1500-1579
Byrd, William	1543-1623	Lasso, Orlando	1530-1594
Caccini, Guilio	1558-1615	Lawes, Henry	1596-1662
Carlton, Richard	1560-1638	Marenzio, Luca	1560-1599
Cavalieri, Emilio De	1550-1599	Monteverdi, Claudio	1567-1643
Cooper, John	1570-1627	Morley, Thomas	1558-1603
Cruger, Johann	1598-1662	Palestrina, Giovanni	
Dowland, John	1563-1626	Pierluigi Da	1526-1594
East, Michael	1580-1648	Peri, Jacopo	1561-1633
Eccard, Johann	1553-1611	Praetorius, Michael	1571-1621
Farmer, John	1565-1605	Ravencroft, Thomas	1590-1633
Farrant, Richard	d. 1580	Schutz, Heinrich	1585-1672
Ford, Thomas	1580-1648	Sweelinck, Jan Pieter	1562-1621
Frescobaldi, Girolmo	1583-1644	Tallis, Thomas	1515-1585
Gabrieli, Andrea	1510-1586	Tomkins, Thomas	1572-1656
Gabrieli, Giovani	1557-1612	Wilbye, John	1574-1638
Gesualdo, Don Carlos	1560-1613	Wilson, John	1595-1674
Gibbons, Orlando	1583-1625		

1603   England and Scotland united.
1605   Gunpowder plot.
1607   Dutch destroy Spanish fleet at Gibraltar.
1618   Thirty years war begins. Sir Walter Raleigh executed.
1620   Treaty of Ulm. Pilgrim Fathers land in New England.
1624   Barbadoes colonised by English.
1625   Parliament dissolved by Charles I.

PROMINENT PEOPLE

Cromwell, Oliver	1599-1658	Richelieu, Armand Jean	
Raleigh, Sir Walter	1552-1618	Du Plessis Cardinal	
		Duc De	1585-1642

EMPERORS OF CHINA
(Ming Dynasty)

Shen Tsung	1572-1620	Hsi Bung	1620-1627
Kuang Tsung	1620		

POPES

Clement VIII	1592-1605	Gregory XV	1621-1623
Leo XI	1605	Urban VIII	1623-1644
Paul V	1605-1621		

FRANCE. HEADS OF STATE

Henry IV	1589-1610	Louis XIII	1610-1643

HOLY ROMAN EMPERORS

Rudolf II	1576-1612	Ferdinand II	1619-1637
Matthias	1612-1619		

ENGLAND. SOVEREIGNS

Elizabeth I	1558-1603	Charles I	1625-1649
James I	1603-1625		

SWEDEN. KINGS

Charles IX	1600-1611	Gustavius II	1611-1632

PORTUGAL. KINGS

Under Spanish Suzerainty	1581-1640

SCOTLAND. KINGS

James VI	1567-1603

ELECTORS OF BRANDENBURG

Joachim III Frederick	1598-1608	George William	1619-1640
John Sigismund	1608-1619		

Boris	1598-1605	Michael	1613-1645
Theodore II	1605	Alexis	1645-1676
Interregnum	1605-1613		

SPAIN. SOVEREIGNS

Philip III	1598-1621	Philip IV	1621-1665

WRITERS

Aitzema, Lieuwe Van	1600-1669	Boccalini, Trajano	1556-1613
Alabaster, William	1567-1640	Boisrobert, Francois Le	
Alarcon Y Mendoza,		Metel De	1592-1662
Jean Ruiz De	1580-1639	Bracciolini, Francesco	1566-1645
Alcazar, B. Del	1530-1606	Bradford, William	1590-1657
Aleman, Mateo	1547-1609	Bradstreet, Ann	1612-1672
Allori, Allesandro	1535-1607	Brantome, Pierre De	
Ammirato, Scipione	1531-1601	Bourdeille	c. 1540-1640
Angelus, Silecius	1624-1677	Brathwaite, Richard	1588-1673
Andrewes, Lancelot	1555-1626	Breton, Nicholas	1545-1626
Argensola, Lupercio		Brome, Alexander	1620-1666
Leonardo De	1559-1613	Brosse, Salomon De	1565-1626
Arminius, Jacobus	1560-1609	Browne, Sir Thomas	1605-1682
Arnault, Antoine	1612-1694	Browne, William	1591-1643
Arrebo, Anders		Bryskett, Lodowyck	1545-1612
Christiensen	1587-1637	Bulstrode, Sir Richard	1610-1711
Arquijo, Juan De	1564-1623	Burton, Robert	1577-1640
Ashmole, Elias	1617-1692	Bussy, Roger de Rabutin	1618-1693
Aubignac, Francois		Butler, Samuel	1612-1680
Hedelin Abbe De	1604-1676	Calderon, De La Barca	
Aubigne, Theodore		Pedro	1600-1681
Agrippa De	1562-1630	Calderwood, David	1575-1650
Avercamp, Hendrik	1585-1634	Calprenede, Gautier Des	
Avila, Gil Gonzales De	1577-1658	Costes De La	1610-1663
Ayrer, Jakob	-1605	Camden, William	1551-1623
Ayton, Sir Robert	1570-1638	Campanella, Tommaso	1568-1639
Bacon, Francis	1561-1626	Campion, Thomas	1567-1620
Baillie, Robert	1599-1662	Carew, Richard	1555-1620
Baker, Sir Richard	1568-1645	Carew, Thomas	1595-1638
Balbuena, Bernardo De	1568-1627	Cartwright, William	1611-1643
Baldinucci, Filippo	1624-1696	Castillo Solorzano,	
Balfour, Robert	1550-1625	Alonso De	1584-1647
Baldi, Bernardino	1553-1617	Castro Y Bellvis,	
Balzac, Jean Louis		Guillen De	1569-1631
Guez De	1594-1654	Cats, Jakob	1577-1660
Barclay, Robert	1648-1690	Cervantes Saavedra,	
Baronius, Caesar	1538-1607	Miguel De	1547-1616
Barnfield, Richard	1574-1627	Cespedes Y Menses,	
Bartoli, Danielle	1608-1685	Gonzalo De	1585-1638
Bassompiere, Francois De	1579-1646	Chamberlayne, William	1619-1679
Baudier, Michel	1589-1645	Chapman, George	1559-1634
Beaumont, Francis	1584-1616	Chapelaine, Jean	1595-1674
Beaumont, Sir John	1583-1627	Charron, Pierre	1541-1603
Beaumont, Joseph	1616-1699	Chettle, Henry	1560-1607
Bellenden, William	1555-1633	Chiabreka, Gabriello	1552-1638
Benlowes, Edward	1603-1676	Churchyard, Thomas	1520-1640
Benserade, Isaac De	1613-1691	Clarendon, Edward Hyde	
Bergerac, Cyrano,		(1st Earl)	1609-1674
Savinien De	1619-1655	Clauberg, Johann	1622-1665

Cleveland, John	1613-1658	Fleming, Paul	1609-1640
Cluwer, Philip	1580-1623	Fletcher, Giles	1548-1611
Coello, Antonio	1611-1652	Fletcher, Giles	1584-1623
Cokain, Sir Aston	1608-1684	Fletcher, John	1579-1625
Comenius, Johann Amos	1592-1670	Fletcher, Phineas	1582-1650
Constable, Henry	1562-1613	Florio, John	c. 1553-1625
Corbet, Richard	1582-1635	Fludd, Robert	1575-1637
Corneille, Pierre	1606-1684	Ford, John	1586-1640
Corneille, Thomas	1625-1709	Fowler, William	1560-1614
Coryate, Thomas	1577-1617	Fox, George	1624-1691
Cotton, John	1584-1652	Francheville, Piere	1548-1616
Cowley, Abraham	1618-1667	Francis of Sales	1567-1622
Craig, Sir Thomas	1530-1608	Fraunce, Abraham	1558-1663
Crashaw, Richard	1613-1649	Froberger, Johann Jakob	1616-1667
Cudworth, Ralph	1617-1688	Fuller, Thomas	1608-1661
Cueva, Juan De La	1550-1610	Furetiere, Antoine	1619-1688
Culpeper, Nicholas	1616-1654	Galilei, Galileo	1564-1642
Dach, Simon	1605-1659	Garcilaso De La Vega,	
Daniel, Samuel	1562-1619	El Inca	1540-1616
Davenant, Sir William	1606-1668	Gassendi, Pierre	1592-1655
Davenport, Robert	1623-1639	Gauden, John	1605-1662
Davies, John	1565-1618	Gerhardt, Paul	1607-1676
Davies, Sir John	1569-1626	Geulincx, Arnold	1624-1669
Davila, Enrico Caterino	1576-1631	Godwin, Francis	1562-1633
Day, John	1574-1640	Gongora Y Argote,	
Dee, John	1527-1608	Luis De	1561-1627
Dekker, Thomas	1570-1641	Gosson, Stephen	1554-1624
Delmedigo, Joseph		Gracian Y Morales,	
Soloman	1591-1655	Baltasar	1601-1658
Dempster, Thomas	1570-1625	Greville, Sir Fulke	1554-1628
Denham, Sir John	1615-1669	Grimmelshausen, Hans	
Descartes, Rene	1596-1650	Jakob Christof Fel Von	1625-1676
Desmarets, Jean	1595-1676	Grotius, Hugo	1583-1645
Desportes, Phillippe	1546-1606	Gryphius, Andreas	1616-1664
Digby, Sir Kenelm	1603-1665	Guarini, Giovanni Battista	1538-1612
Donne, John	1573-1631	Guericke, Otto Von	1602-1686
Dorleans, Louis	1544-1629	Guevara, Luis Velez De	1570-1644
Drayton, Michael	1563-1631	Gundulic, Ivan	1588-1638
Drummond, William	1585-1649	Gyongyosi, Istvan	1620-1704
Duchesne, Andre	1584-1640	Habingdon, William	1605-1654
Dugdale, Sir William	1605-1686	Hajji, Khalifa	c. 1599-1658
Du Ryer, Pierre	1606-1658	Hake, Edward	1579-
Du Vair, Guillaume	1556-1621	Hakluyt, Richard	1552-1616
Enriquez, Gomes Antonio	1602-1662	Hall, Joseph	1574-1656
Espinel, Vincente Martinez	1550-1624	Hardy, Alexandre	1569-1631
Evelyn, John	1620-1706	Harington, Sir John	1561-1612
Fairfax, Edward	1580-1635	Harlib, Samuel	1599-1670
Falkland, Lucius Cary		Harrington, James	1611-1677
Viscount	1610-1643	Harsdorffer, Georg Philipp	1607-1658
Fanshawe, Sir Richard	1608-1666	Harvey, Gabriel	c. 1545-1630
Faria Y Sousa, Manuel De	1590-1649	Harvey, William	1578-1657
Felltham, Owen	1602-1668	Haughton, William	1598-
Fenton, Sir Geoffrey	1539-1608	Hayward, Sir John	1560-1627
Ferishta, Mohammed		Heemskerk, Johan Van	1597-1656
Kasim	1570-1611	Herbert, George	1593-1633
Field, Nathan	1587-1619	Herbert of Cherbury	1583-1648
Figueroa, Francisco De	1536-1617	Herbert, Sir Thomas	1608-1682
Filmer, Sir Robert	1590-1653	Herrera, Antoine De	1549-1625
Flecknoe, Richard	1600-1678	Herrick, Robert	1591-1674

Heylyn, Peter	1600-1662
Heywood, Thomas	1574-1641
Hobbes, Thomas	1588-1679
Holles, Denzil Holles	1599-1680
Hooft, Pieter Cornelissen	1581-1647
Howell, James	1594-1666
Hume, Alexander	1557-1609
Huygens, Sir Constantijn	1596-1687
Jansen, Cornelius	1585-1638
Janssen, Geraert	fl. 1616
Jauregui, Juan De	1583-1641
Johnson, Richard	1573-1659
Jonson, Ben	1573-1637
Jordan, Thomas	1612-1685
Killigrew, Thomas	1612-1683
Killigrew, Sir William	1606-1695
Kirke, Edward	1553-1613
Knolles, Richard	1545-1610
La Calprenede, Gauthier De Costes	1610-1663
La Fontaine, Jean De	1621-1695
La Mothe Le Vayer, Francois De	1588-1672
Larivey, Pierre	1550-1612
La Rochefoucauld, Francois De	1613-1680
La Taille, Jean De	1540-1608
La Tour, Georges de	1593-1652
Laud, William (Archbishop of Canterbury)	1573-1645
L'Estrange, Sir Roger	1616-1704
Lobo, Francisco Rodrigues	1580-1622
Lodge, Thomas	1558-1625
Lovelace, Richard	1618-1658
Lyly, John	1553-1606
Maimbourg, Louis	1610-1686
Mairet, Jean De	1604-1686
Makkari, Ahmed El	1585-1631
Malherbe, Francois De	1555-1628
Manuel De Mello, Don Francisco	1608-1666
Marca, Pierre De	1594-1662
Mariana, Juan De	1536-1624
Marini, Giovanni Battista	1569-1625
Markham, Gervase	1568-1637
Marston, John	1575-1634
Marvell, Andrew	1621-1678
Massinger, Philip	1583-1640
Matos, Fragoso, Juan De	1608-1689
May, Thomas	1595-1650
Melo, Francisco Manuel De	1608-1666
Meres, Francis	1565-1647
Middleton, Thomas	1570-1627
Milton, John	1608-1674
Mira De Amescua, Antonio	1578-1644
Moliere, (Jean Baptiste Poquelin)	1622-1673
Montchretien, Antoine De	1575-1621

Montgomerie, Alexander	1550-1610
More, Henry	1613-1687
Moreto Y Cavana, Agustin	1618-1669
Moryson, Fynes	1566-1630
Moscherrosch, Johann Michael	1601-1669
Motteville, Francoise Bertraut De	1621-1689
Munday, Anthony	1553-1633
Mure, Sir William	1594-1657
Mytens, Daniel	1590-1642
Najara, Israel Ben Moses	1587-
Nashe, Thomas	1567-1601
Ogilby, John	1600-1676
O'Higgin, Tadhg, Dall	-1616
Opitz Von Boberfield, Martin	1597-1639
Overbury, Sir Thomas	1581-1613
Pallavicino, Ferrante	1618-1644
Pallavicino, Pietro Sforza	1607-1667
Parker, Martin	1600-1656
Pascal, Blaise	1623-1662
Pasquier, Etienne	1529-1615
Passerat, Jean	1534-1602
Peacham, Henry	1576-1643
Perez, De Hita, Gines	1544-1619
Purchas, Samuel	1577-1626
Quarles, Francis	1592-1644
Quevedo Y Villegas, Francisco Gomez De	1580-1645
Racan, Honore De Bueil	1589-1670
Randolph, Thomas	1605-1635
Regnier, Mathurin	1573-1613
Retz, Cardinal de	1614-1679
Rich, Barnabe	1540-1617
Rich, Richard	1610-
Rinuccini, Ottavio	1562-1621
Rolland, John	1560-
Rotrou, Jean De	1609-1650
Rowley, William	1585-1642
Rushworth, John	1612-1690
Sackville, Thomas	1530-1608
Saint-Amant, Marc Antoine De Gerard	1594-1661
Saint Evremond, Charles Marquetel De Saint Denis- Segnieur De	1610-1703
Sandys, George	1578-1644
Sarasin, Jean Francois	1614-1654
Scarron, Paul	1610-1660
Scudery, Georges De	1601-1667
Scudery, Madeleine De	1607-1701
Selden, John	1584-1654
Shakespeare, William	1564-1616
Shirley, James	1596-1666
Smith, John	1580-1631
Solis Y Ribadeneyra, Antonio De	1610-1686
Sorel, Charles	1597-1674
Sousa, Louiz De	1555-1632

Speed, John	1552-1629	Vaughan, Henry	1622-1695
St. Jernhjelm, George	1598-1672	Vaughan, William	1577-1641
Stanley, Thomas	1625-1678	Vauquelin, De La Fresnaye	
Stow, John	1525-1605	Jean	1536-1608
Strode, William	1602-1645	Vega Carpio, Lope	
Sturling, William Alexander	1567-1640	Felix De	1562-1635
Suckling, Sir John	1609-1642	Vega, Garcilaso De La	
Sylvester, Joshua	1563-1618	(El Inca)	1535-1616
Tallemant, Gedeon Sieur		Velez De Guevara, Luis	1579-1644
Des Reaux	1619-1692	Viau, Theophile de	1590-1626
Taylor, Jeremy	1613-1667	Victoria, Tomas Luis De	1553-1611
Taylor, John	1580-1653	Vieira, Antonio	1608-1697
Thomas, Nabbes	1605-	Villamediana Count De	1580-1622
Thou, Jacques, Auguste De	1553-1617	Voiture, Vincent	1598-1648
Tirso De Molina	1571-1648	Vondel, Joost Van Den	1587-1679
Totnes, George Carew	1555-1629	Waller, Edmund	1606-1687
Tourneur, Cyril	1575-1626	Walton, Izaak	1593-1683
Tulsi Das	1532-1623	Webster, John	1602-1624
Turberville, George	1540-1610	Whichcote, Benjamin	1609-1683
Tyard, Pontus De	1521-1605	Williams, Roger	c.1600-1683
Urfe, Honore D'	1568-1625	Winslow, Edward	1595-1655
Urquhart, Sir Thomas	1611-1660	Winthrop, John	1588-1649
Vane, Sir Henry	1613-1662	Wither, George	1588-1667
Vaugelas, Claude Faure	1596-1650	Wotton, Sir Henry	1568-1639

ARTISTS

Algardi, Alessandro	1602-1654	Castello, Bernado	1557-1629
Allori, Christofand	1577-1621	Castello, Valerio	1625-1659
Albani, Francesco	1578-1660	Cavedone, Jacopo	1577-1660
Anguier, Francois	1604-1669	Cesari	1568-1640
Anguier, Michel	1612-1686	Cespedes, Pablo de	1536-1608
Anna, Baldasarre	1560-1639	Champaign, Phillipe De	1602-1674
Badalocchio, Sisto	1581-1647	Cigoli, Lodovico, Cardi Da	1559-1613
Balen, Henry Van	1560-1632	Claude Lorrain	1600-1682
Barbieri, Giovanni		Codde, Pieter	1599-1678
Francesco	1591-1666	Colin, Alexandre	1526-1612
Barocci, Federigo	1528-1612	Coninxloo Gillis Van	1544-1605
Berchem, Nicolaes	1620-1683	Cooper, Samuel	1609-1672
Bernini, Giovanni Lorenzo	1598-1680	Coques, Gonzales	1614-1684
Bloemart, Abraham	1564-1651	Corenzio, Belisario	1558-1643
Bolagna, Giovanni Da	1524-1608	Cornelisz, Cornelis	1562-1638
Borromini, Francesco	1599-1667	Cortona, Pietro Berrettini	
Both, Jan	1618-1652	Da	1596-1669
Brill, Paul	1554-1626	Courtois, Jacques	1621-1676
Brouwer, Adrian	1606-1638	Crayer, Gaspard De	1584-1669
Callot, Jacques	c. 1594-1635	Crespi, Daniele	1590-1630
Caluart, Denis	1540-1619	Crespi, Giovanni Batista	1557-1633
Camphuysen, Dirk Rafelsz	1586-1627	De Keyser, Thomas	1596-1667
Cano, Alonzo	1601-1667	Dobson, William	1610-1646
Cantarini, Simone	1612-1648	Dolci, Carlo	1616-1686
Cappelle, Jan Van Der	1624-1679	Domenichino, Zampieri	1581-1641
Caracci, Agostino	1557-1602	Douw, Gerrit	1613-1675
Caracci, Annibale	1540-1609	Duck, Jacob	1600-1660
Caracci, Ludovico	1555-1619	Eekhout, Gerbrand	
Caravaggio, Michel Angelo	1573-1610	Van Den	1621-1674
Carducci, Bartolommeo	1568-1610	Elsheimer, Adam	1579-1620
Carreno De Miranda,		Elstracke, Renold	c. 1590-1630
Juan	1614-1685	Everdingen, Allart Van	1621-1675

Fabritius, Carel	1624-1654	Mignard, Pierre	1610-1695
Faithorne, William	1616-1691	Montanes, Juan Martinez	1580-1649
Falcone, Aniello	1600-1656	Murillo, Bartolome	
Farinato, Paolo	1524-1606	Esteban	1617-1682
Felibien, Andre	1619-1695	Oliver, Isaac Peter	d. 1617
Flemal, Bertholet	1614-1675	Ostade, Adriaan Van	1610-1685
Flinck, Govert	1615-1660	Pacheco, Francisco	1564-1654
Fontana, Domenico	1543-1607	Paolini, Pietro	1603-1682
Fontana, Lavinia	1552-1614	Pareja, Juan De	1606-1670
Franceschini, Baldassare	1611-1689	Petitot, Jean	1608-1691
Fresnoy, Charles		Porta, Giacomo Della	1541-1604
Alphonse Du	1611-1665	Post, Pieter	1608-1669
Fyt, Jan	1609-1661	Potter, Paul	1625-1654
Gentileschi, Artemisia	1597-1651	Poussin, Gaspar	1613-1675
Gentileschi, Orazio De	1562-1647	Poussin, Nicolas	1594-1665
Gheeraerts, Marcus	1561-1635	Procaccini, Camillo	1546-1629
Goyen, Jan Josephzoon Van	1596-1656	Procaccini, Ercole the	
Grimaldi, Giovanni		younger	1596-1676
Francesco	1606-1680	Puget, Pierre	1622-1694
Guercino	1590-1666	Quesnoy, Francois du	1594-1646
Hals, Franz	1580-1666	Rembrandt, Harmensz	
Heem, Jan Davidz Van	1600-1683	Van Rijn	1606-1669
Helst, Bartholomaens		Reni, Guido	1575-1642
Van Der	1613-1670	Ribalta, Francisco de	1550-1628
Hernandes, Gregorio	1576-1636	Ribera, Jusepe de	1588-1656
Herrera, Francisco		Rosa, Salvator	1615-1673
"El Mozo"	1622-1685	Rubens, Peter Paul	1577-1640
Hilliard, Nicholas	1537-1619	Sacchi, Andrea	1600-1661
Hollar, Wenceslaus	1607-1677	Sandrart, Joachim Van	1606-1688
Honthorst, Gerard Van	1590-1656	Sarrazin, Jacques	1588-1660
I Wasa, Matahei	1578-1650	Sassoferato	1605-1685
Jamesone, John	1588-1644	Snyders, Frans	1579-1657
Janssen, Cornelis	1593-1664	Steenwijk, Hendrik Van	c. 1550-1603
Janssens, Van Nuyssen		Stone, Nicholas	1587-1647
Abraham	1675-1632	Teniers, David the Elder	1582-1649
Jones, Inigo	1573-1651	Teniers, David the	
Jonson, Cornelis Van		Younger	1610-1690
Ceulen	1593-1662	Ter Borch, Gerard	1617-1681
Jordaens, Jacob	1593-1678	Terbrugghen, Hendrik	1588-1629
Keyser, Hendrik De	1565-1621	Theotocopouli, Domenico	
Koninck, Philips	1619-1688	(El Greco)	1542-1614
Laar, Pieter Van	1590-1658	Van De Velde, Jan	1593-1641
Lahire, Laurent De	1606-1656	Van De Velde, William	1611-1693
Lanfranco, Giovanni	1581-1647	Van Dyck, Sir Anthony	1599-1641
Le Brun, Charles	1619-1690	Van Veen, Otto	1556-1634
Lely, Sir Peter	1618-1680	Velasquez, Diego	
Le Sueur, Eustache	1616-1655	Rodriguez	1599-1660
Lievensz, Jan	1607-1674	Vos Cornelis De	1585-1651
Lorenzo, Lippi	1606-1664	Vovet, Simon	1590-1649
Mander, Carel Van	1548-1606	Weenix, Jan Baptist	1621-1660
Mansart, Francois	1598-1666	Wouwerman, Philip	1619-1668
Maratta, Carlo	1625-1713	Zuccaro, Frederigo	1539-1609
Mierevelt, Micheil		Zurbaran, Francisco De	1598-1669
Jansz Van	1567-1641		

COMPOSERS

Aichinger, Gregor	1565-1628	Allegri, Gregorio	1582-1652
Albert, Heinrich	1604-1651	Artusi, Giovanni Maria	1540-1613

Basile, Giambattista	1575-1632	Gibbons, Orlando	1583-1625
Bateson, Thomas	1570-1630	Hassler, Hans Leo	1564-1612
Bull, John	1562-1628	Holborn, Anthony	died c. 1602
Byrd, William	1543-1623	Jenkins, John	1592-1678
Caccini, Guilio	1558-1615	Lawes, Henry	1596-1662
Carissimi, Giacomo	1604-1674	Legrenzi, Giovanni	1625-1690
Carlton, Richard	1560-1638	Monteverdi, Claudio	1567-1643
Cavalli, Francesco	1602-1676	Morley, Thomas	1558-1603
Cesti, Marc'Antonio	1618-1669	Peri, Jacopo	1561-1633
Cooper, John	1570-1627	Praetorius, Michael	1571-1621
Cruger, Johann	1598-1662	Ravencroft, Thomas	1590-1633
Dowland, John	1563-1626	Schmelzer, Johann	
East, Michael	1586-1648	Heinrick	1623-1680
Eccard, Johann	1553-1611	Schutz, Heinrich	1585-1672
Farmer, John	1565-1605	Sweelinck, Jan Pieter	1562-1621
Ford, Thomas	1580-1648	Tomkins, Thomas	1572-1656
Frescobaldi, Girolamo	1583-1644	Weelkes, Thomas	d. 1623
Gabrieli, Giovanni	1557-1612	Wilbye, John	1574-1638
Gesualdo, Don Carlos	1560-1613	Wilson, John	1595-1674

1631   Battle of Leipsic.
1632   Battle of Lutzen.
1641   Coffee first drunk in England.
1642   New Zealand and Tasmania discovered.   Battle of Worcester.
       Battle of Edge Hill.
1643   Battle of Newbury.
1644   Battle of Marston Moor   2nd Battle of Newbury.
1645   Battle of Naseby.
1648   Battle of Preston.   Rump Parliament elected.
1649   Charles I executed.

PROMINENT PEOPLE

Cromwell, Oliver	1599-1658	Newton, Sir Isaac	1642-1727
Jeffrey, George (Judge)	1648-1689	Richelieu, Armand Jean Du	
Kidd, Captain William	1645-1701	Plessis, Cardinal Duc De	1585-1642

EMPERORS OF CHINA

Hsi Tsung		Shih Tsu [Manchu	
(Ming Dynasty)	1620-1627	(Ching) Dynasty]	1644-1661
Ssu Tsung			
(Ming Dynasty)	1627-1644		

POPES

Urban VIII	1623-1644	Innocent X	1644-1655

FRANCE. HEADS OF STATE

Louis XIII	1610-1643	Louis, XIV	1643-1715

HOLY ROMAN EMPERORS

Ferdinand II	1619-1637	Ferdinand III	1637-1657

ENGLAND. SOVEREIGNS

Charles I	1625-1649	Commonwealth &	
		Protectorate	1649-1660

SWEDEN. KINGS

Gustavius II	1611-1632	Christina	1632-1654

PORTUGAL. KINGS

Under Spanish Suzerainty	1581-1640	John IV	1640-1656

ELECTORS OF BRANDENBURG

George, William	1619-1640	Frederick William	1640-1688

RUSSIA. TSARS

Michael	1613-1645	Alexis	1645-1676

SPAIN. SOVEREIGNS

Philip IV	1621-1665

Acosta, Uriel	d. 1647	Brathwaite, Richard	1588-1673
Aitzema, Lieuwe Van	1600-1669	Breton, Nicholas	1545-1626
Alabaster, William	1567-1640	Broekhuizew, Jan Van	1649-1707
Alarcon Y Mendoza,		Brome, Alexander	1620-1666
Jean Ruiz de	1580-1639	Brosse, Salemon de	1565-1626
Alcoforado, Marianna	1640-1723	Browne, Sir Thomas	1605-1682
Alleine, Joseph	1634-1668	Browne, William	1591-1643
Amelot de la Houssaey,		Bulstrode, Sir Richard	1610-1711
Abraham Nicolas	1634-1706	Bunyan, John	1628-1688
Angelus, Silecius	1624-1677	Burnet, Gilbert	1643-1715
Arnault, Antoine	1612-1694	Burnet, Thomas	1635-1715
Arrebo, Anders		Burton, Robert	1577-1640
Christiensen	1587-1637	Butler, Samuel	1612-1680
Ashmole, Elias	1617-1692	Bussy, Roger de Rabutin	1618-1693
Aubignac, Francois		Calderon, De La Barca	
Hedelin Abbe de	1604-1676	Pedro	1600-1681
Aubigne, Theodore		Calderwood, David	1575-1650
Agrippa De	1562-1630	Calprenede, Gautier Des	
Aubrey, John	1626-1697	Costes De La	1610-1663
Aulnoy, Marie Catherine		Campanella, Tommaso	1568-1639
le Jumel de Barneuille		Castillo Solorzano,	
de la Motte	1650-1705	Alonso De	1584-1647
Auton, Sir Robert	1570-1638	Castro Y Bellvis,	
Avercamp, Hendrik	1585-1634	Guillen De	1569-1631
Avila Gil Gonzales De	1577-1658	Carew, Thomas	1595-1638
Bacon, Francis	1561-1626	Cartwright, William	1611-1643
Baillie, Robert	1599-1662	Cats, Jakob	1577-1660
Baker, Sir Richard	1568-1645	Cespedes Y Meneses,	
Balbuena, Bernardo De	1568-1627	Gonsalo De	1585-1638
Baldinucci, Filippo	1624-1696	Chamberlayne, William	1619-1679
Balzac, Jean Louis		Chapelaine, Jean	1595-1674
Guez De	1594-1654	Chapman, George	1559-1634
Barclay, Robert	1648-1690	Chaulieu, Guillaume	
Barnfield, Richard	1574-1627	Amfrye De	1639-1720
Bartoli, Danielle	1608-1685	Chiabreka, Gabriello	1552-1638
Bartoli, Pietro Santo	1635-1700	Choisy, Francois	
Bassompiere, Francois De	1579-1646	Timoleon Abbe De	1644-1724
Baudier, Michel	1589-1645	Clarendon, Edward Hyde	
Bayle, Pierre	1647-1706	1st Earl of	1609-1674
Beaumont, Sir John	1583-1627	Clauberg, Johann	1622-1665
Beaumont, Joseph	1616-1699	Cleveland, John	1613-1658
Behn, Aphra	1640-1689	Cocker, Edward	1631-1675
Bellenden, William	1555-1633	Coello, Antonio	1611-1652
Benlowes, Edward	1603-1676	Cokain, Sir Aston	1608-1684
Benserade, Isaac De	1613-1691	Comenius, Johann Amos	1592-1670
Bergerac, Cyrano de	1619-1655	Corbet, Richard	1582-1635
Blackmore, Sir Richard	1650-1729	Corneille, Pierre	1606-1684
Blount, Sir Thomas Pope	1649-1687	Corneille, Thomas	1625-1709
Boileau-Despreaux,		Cotton, Charles	1630-1687
Nicolas	1636-1711	Cowley, Abraham	1618-1667
Boirobert, Francois		Crashaw, Richard	1613-1649
Le Metel De	1592-1662	Crowne, John	1640-1703
Bossuet, Jacques Benigne	1627-1704	Cudworth, Ralph	1617-1688
Boursault, Edme	1638-1701	Culpeper, Nicholas	1616-1654
Boyle, Robert	1627-1691	Cumberland, Richard	1631-1718
Bracciolini, Francesco	1566-1645	Dach, Simon	1605-1659
Bradford, William	1590-1657	Dalgarno, George	1626-1687
Bradstreet, Ann	1612-1672	Daniel, Gabriel	1649-1728
Brantome, Pierre De		Dass, Petter	1647-1708
Bourdeille	1540-c. 1640	Davenant, Sir William	1606-1668

Davenport, Robert	1623-1639
Davies, Sir John	1569-1626
Davila, Enrico Caterino	1576-1631
Day, John	1574-1640
Dekker, Thomas	c. 1570-1641
Delmedigo, Joseph Soloman	1591-1655
Denham, Sir John	1615-1669
Descartes, Rene	1596-1650
Deshoulieres, Antoinette	1638-1694
Desmarets, Jean	1595-1676
Digby, Sir Kennelm	1603-1665
Dodwell, Henry	1641-1711
Donne, John	1573-1631
Dorleans, Louis	1544-1629
Drayton, Michael	1563-1631
Drummond, William	1585-1649
Dryden, John	1631-1700
Duchesne, Andre	1584-1640
Dugdale, Sir William	1605-1686
Du Ryer, Pierre	1606-1658
Ellwood, Thomas	1639-1714
Enriquez, Gomez Antonio	1602-1662
Etherege, Sir George	1635-1691
Evelyn, John	1620-1706
Fairfax, Edward	1580-1635
Falkland, Lucius Cary Viscount	1610-1643
Fanshawe, Sir Richard	1608-1666
Faria Y Sousa, Manuel De	1590-1649
Felltham, Owen	1602-1668
Filicaia, Vincenzo da	1642-1707
Filmer, Sir Robert	1590-1653
Flecknoe, Richard	1600-1678
Fleming, Paul	1609-1640
Fletcher, Phineas	1582-1650
Fleury, Claude	1640-1723
Fludd, Robert	1575-1637
Ford, John	1586-1640
Fox, George	1624-1691
Fraunce, Abraham	1558-1663
Froberger, Johann Jakob	1616-1667
Fuller, Thomas	1608-1661
Furetiere, Antoine	1619-1688
Galilei, Galileo	1564-1642
Gassendi, Pierre	1592-1655
Gauden, John	1605-1662
Gerhardt, Paul	1607-1676
Geulincx, Arnold	1624-1669
Glanville, Joseph	1636-1680
Glapthorne, Henry	1635-1642
Godwin, Francis	1562-1633
Gongora Y Argote, Luis De	1561-1627
Gracian Y Morales, Baltasar	1601-1658
Greville, Sir Fulke	1554-1628
Grimmelshausen, Hans Jacob Christof Felvon	1625-1676
Grotius, Hugo	1583-1645
Gryphius, Andreas	1616-1664
Guericke, Otto Von	1602-1686
Guevara, Luis Velez De	1570-1644
Guidi, Carlo Alessandro	1650-1712
Gundulic, Ivan	1588-1638
Guyon, Jeanne Marie Bouvier de la Mothe	1648-1717
Gyongyosi, Istvan	1620-1704
Habingdon, William	1605-1654
Hajji Khalifa	1599-c. 1658
Hake, Edward	1579-
Hall, Joseph	1574-1656
Hamilton, Anthony	1645-1720
Hardy, Alexander	1569-1631
Harlib, Samuel	1599-1670
Harrington, James	1611-1677
Harsdorffer, Georg Philipp	1607-1658
Harvey, Gabriel	1545-c. 1630
Harvey, William	1578-1657
Haughton, William	1598-
Hayward, Sir John	1560-1627
Heemskerk, Johan Van	1597-1656
Herbert, George	1593-1633
Herbert of Cherbury	1583-1648
Herbert, Sir Thomas	1608-1682
Herrick, Robert	1591-1674
Heylyn, Peter	1600-1662
Heywood, Thomas	1580-1641
Hobbes, Thomas	1588-1679
Holles, Denzil Holles	1599-1680
Hooft, Pieter Cornelissen	1581-1647
Howard, Sir Robert	1626-1698
Howell, James	1594-1666
Hoz Y Mota, Juan Claudio De La	1630-1714
Huygens, Sir Constantijn	1596-1687
Jansen, Cornelius	1585-1638
Jauregui, Juan De	1583-1641
Johnson, Richard	1573-1659
Jonson, Ben	1573-1637
Jordan, Thomas	1612-1685
Killigrew, Thomas	1612-1683
Killigrew, Sir William	1606-1695
Kingo, Thomas Hansen	1634-1703
Kirk, Robert	1641-1692
La Bruyere, Jean De	1645-1696
La Calprenede, Gauthier De Costes	1610-1663
La Fayette, Marie Madeleine	1634-1693
La Fontaine, Jean De	1621-1695
Lairesse, Gerard De	1641-1711
La Mothe Le Vayer, Francois De	1588-1672
La Rochefoucauld, Francois De	1613-1680
Latour, Georges de	1593-1652
Laud, William (Archbishop of Canterbury)	1573-1645
Leibniz, Gottfried Wilhelm	1646-1716

L'Estrange, Sir Roger	1616-1704	Quinault, Phillipe	1635-1688
Locke, John	1632-1704	Racan, Honore De Bueill	1589-1670
Lovelace, Richard	1618-1658	Racine, Jean	1639-1699
Maimbourg, Louis	1610-1686	Randolph, Thomas	1605-1635
Mairet, Jean De	1604-1686	Retz, Cardinal de	1614-1679
Makkari, Ahmed el	1585-1631	Rochester, John Wilmot	1647-1680
Malebranche, Nicolas	1638-1715	Roscommon, Wentworth	
Maleherbe, Francois De	1555-1628	Dillon	1630-1685
Manuel De Mello,		Rotrou, Jean De	1609-1650
Don Francisco	1608-1666	Rowley, William	1585-1642
Marca, Pierre De	1594-1662	Rushworth, John	1612-1690
Markham, Gervase	1568-1637	Rymer, Thomas	1641-1713
Marston, John	1575-1634	Saint Amant, Marc	
Marvell, Andrew	1621-1678	Antoine De Gerard	1594-1661
Massinger, Philip	1583-1640	Saint Evremond, Charles	
Mather, Increase	1639-1723	Marquetel de Saint	
Matos, Fragoso, Juan De	1608-1689	Denis Seigneur de	1610-1703
May, Thomas	1595-1650	Saint Real, Cesar Vichard	
Melo, Francisco		Abbé de	1631-1692
Manuel de	1608-1666	Sandys, George	1578-1644
Meres, Francis	1565-1647	Sarasin, Jean Francois	1614-1654
Middleton, Thomas	1570-1627	Scarron, Paul	1610-1660
Mira De Amescua,		Scudery, Georges De	1601-1667
Antonio	1578-1644	Scudery, Madeleine De	1607-1701
Milton, John	1608-1674	Sedley, Sir Charles	1639-1701
Moliere, (Jean Baptiste		Selden, John	1584-1654
Poquelin)	1622-1673	Settle, Elkanam	1648-1724
More, Henry	1614-1687	Sevigne, Marie De	
Moreto Y Cavana, Agustin	1618-1669	Rabutin-Chantal	1626-1696
Moryson, Fynes	1566-1630	Shadwell, Thomas	1642-1692
Moscherosch, Johann		Sherlock, William	1641-1707
Michael	1601-1669	Shirley, James	1596-1666
Motteville, Francoise		Smith, John	1580-1631
Bertaut De	1621-1689	Solis Y Ribadeneyra,	
Munday, Anthony	1553-1633	Antonio de	1610-1686
Mure, Sir William	1594-1657	Sorel, Charles	1597-1674
Mytens, Daniel	1590-1642	Sousa, Luiz De	1555-1632
Najara, Israel Ben Moses	1587-	Speed, John	1552-1629
Newton, Sir Isaac	1642-1727	Spinoza, Benedictus De	1632-1677
Ogilby, John	1600-1676	St. Jernhjelm, Georg	1598-1672
Opitz Von Boberfeld,		Stanley, Thomas	1625-1678
Martin	1597-1639	Stillingfleet, Edward	1635-1699
Pallavicino, Ferrante	1618-1644	Stirling, William	
Pallavicino, Pietro, Sforza	1607-1667	Alexander	1567-1640
Parker, Martin	1600-1656	Strode, William	1602-1645
Pascal, Blaise	1623-1662	Strype, John	1643-1737
Peacham, Henry	1576-1643	Suckling, Sir John	1609-1642
Penn, William	1644-1718	Tallemant, Gedeon	
Pepys, Samuel	1633-1703	Sieur Des Reaux	1619-1692
Perrault, Charles	1628-1703	Taylor, Jeremy	1613-1667
Philips, Katharine	1631-1664	Taylor, John	1580-1653
Phillips, Edward	1630-1696	Temple, Sir William	1628-1699
Phillips, John	1631-1706	Thomas, Nabbes	1605-
Pozzo, Andrea	1642-1709	Tillemont, Sebastian Le	
Puffendorf, Samuel		Nain De	1637-1698
Freiherr Von	1632-1694	Tirso De Molina	1571-1648
Quarles, Francis	1592-1644	Totnes, George Carew	1555-1629
Quesnel, Pasquier	1634-1719	Traherne, Thomas	1637-1674
Quevedo Y Villegas,		Tourneur, Cyril	1575-1626
Francisco Gomez De	1580-1645		

Urquhart, Sir Thomas	1611-1660	Waller, Edmund	1606-1687
Vane, Sir Henry	1613-1662	Walton, Izaak	1593-1683
Vaugelas, Claude Faure	1596-1650	Whichcote, Benjamin	1609-1683
Vaughan, Henry	1622-1695	Wigglesworth, Michael	1631-1705
Vaughan, William	1577-1641	Williams, Roger	c. 1600-1683
Vega Carpio, Lope		Winslow, Edward	1595-1655
Felix De	1562-1635	Winthrop, John	1588-1649
Velez De Guevara, Luis	1579-1644	Wither, George	1588-1667
Viau, Theophile De	1590-1626	Wood, Anthony	1632-1695
Vieira, Antonio	1608-1697	Wotton, Sir Henry	1568-1639
Voiture, Vincent	1598-1648	Wyncherley, William	1640-1716
Vodel, Joost Van Den	1587-1679	Young, Edward	1638-1765

ARTISTS

Algardi, Alessandro	1602-1654	Corenzio, Belisario	1558-1643
Albani, Francesco	1578-1660	Cortona, Pietro	
Anguier, Francois	1604-1669	Berrettini Da	1596-1669
Anguier, Michel	1612-1686	Cotton, John	1584-1652
Anna, Baldasarre	1560-1639	Courtois, Guillaume	1628-1679
Backhuysen, Ludolf	1631-1708	Courtois, Jacques	1621-1676
Badalocchio, Sisto	1581-1647	Coypel, Noel	1628-1707
Balen, Henry Van	1560-1632	Coysevox, Charles Antoine	1640-1720
Barbieri, Giovanni		Crayer, Gaspard De	1584-1669
Francesco	1591-1666	Crespi, Daniele	1590-1630
Beck, David	1621-1656	Crespi, Giovanni Battista	1557-1633
Berchem, Nicolaes	1620-1683	De Keyser, Thomas	1596-1667
Bernini, Giovanni		Dobson, William	1610-1646
Lorenzo	1598-1680	Dolci, Carlo	1616-1686
Bloemart, Abraham	1564-1651	Domenichino, Zampieri	1581-1641
Borromini, Francesco	1599-1667	Douw, Gerrit	1613-1675
Both, Jan	1618-1652	Duck, Jacob	1600-1660
Boulle, Andre Charles	1642-1732	Eeckhout, Gerbrand	
(cabinet maker)		Van Den	1621-1674
Bourse, Esaias	1630-1673	Elstracke, Renold	c. 1590-1630
Brill, Paul	1554-1626	Everdingen, Allart Van	1621-1675
Brouwer, Adrian	1606-1638	Fabritius, Carel	1624-1654
Callot, Jacques	c. 1594-1635	Faed, John	died 1626
Camphuysen, Dirk Rofelsz	1586-1627	Faithorne, William	1616-1691
Cano, Alonzo	1601-1667	Falcone, Aniello	1600-1656
Cantarini, Simone	1612-1648	Felibien, Andre	1619-1695
Cappelle, Jan Van Der	1624-1679	Ferri, Ciro	1634-1689
Carreno De Miranda,		Flatman, Thomas	1637-1688
Juan	1614-1685	Flemal, Bertholet	1614-1675
Castello, Bernado	1557-1629	Flinck, Govert	1615-1660
Castello, Valerio	1625-1659	Fontana, Carlo	1638-1714
Cavedone, Jacopo	1577-1660	Franceschini, Baldassare	1611-1689
Cesari, Giuseppe	1568-1640	Franceschini, Marco	
Champaign, Phillipe De	1602-1674	Antonio	1648-1729
Churriguera, Don José	1650-1725	Fresnoy, Charles Alphonse	1611-1665
Cibber, Caius Gabriel	1630-1700	Fruytiers, Philip	1627-1666
Cignani, Carlo	1628-1719	Fyt, Jan	1609-1661
Claude, Lorrain	1600-1682	Gentileschi, Artemisia	1597-1651
Cleve, Van Jan	1646-1716	Gentileschi, Orazioi De	1562-1647
Codde, Pieter	1599-1678	Gheeraerts, Marcus	1561-1635
Coello, Claudio	1630-1693	Gibbons, Grinling	1648-1721
Cooper, Samuel	1609-1672	Giordano, Luca	1632-1705
Coques, Gonzales	1614-1684	Girardon, Francois	1628-1715
Cornelisz, Cornelis	1562-1638		

Goyen, Jan Josephzoon Van	1596-1656	Montanes, Juan Martinez	1580-1649
Grimaldi, Giovanni Francesco	1606-1680	Murillo, Bartolome Esteban	1617-1682
Guernico	1590-1666	Netscher, Gaspar	1639-1684
Hals, Franz	1580-1666	Ostade, Adriaan Van	1610-1685
Heem, Jan Davidz Van	1600-1683	Pacheco, Francisco	1564-1654
Helst, Bartholomaeus, Van Der	1613-1670	Paolini, Pietro	1603-1682
		Pareja, Juan De	1606-1670
Hernandes, Gregorio	1576-1636	Petitot, Geacomo Della	1541-1604
Herrera, Francisco "El Mozo"	1622-1685	Post, Pieter	1608-1669
		Potter, Paul	1625-1654
Heyden, Jan Van Der	1637-1712	Poussin, Gaspar	1613-1675
Hilliard, Lawrence	-1640	Prieur, Pierre	1626-1676
Hobbema, Meyndert	1638-1709	Procaccini, Camillo	1546-1629
Hollar, Wenceslaus	1607-1677	Procaccini, Ercole the younger	1596-1676
Hondecoeter, Melchior D'	1636-1695	Poussin, Nicolas	1594-1665
Honthorst, Gerard, Van	1590-1656	Puget, Pierre	1622-1694
Hooch, Pieter De	1629-1683	Quesnoy, Francois du	1594-1646
Hoogstraten, Samuel Dirksz Van	1627-1678	Rembrandt, Harmensz Van Rijn	1606-1669
Huchtenburg, John Van	1647-1733	Reni, Guiedo	1575-1642
Huysmans, Cornelius	1648-1727	Ribalta, Francisco de	1550-1628
Huysmans, Jacob	1633-1696	Ribera, Jusepe de	1588-1656
I Wasa Matahei	1578-1650	Rosa, Salvatore	1615-1673
Jamesone, John	1588-1644	Rubens, Peter Paul	1577-1640
Janssen, Cornelis	1593-1664	Ruysdael, Jacob Van	1628-1682
Janssens, Van Nuyssen Abraham	1575-1632	Sacchi, Andrea	1600-1661
		Sandrart, Joachim Van	1606-1688
Jones, Inigo	1573-1651	Sarrazin, Jacques	1588-1660
Jonson, Cornelius Van Ceulen	1593-1662	Sassoferato	1605-1685
		Snyders, Frans	1579-1657
Jordaens, Jacob	1593-1678	Steen, Jan Havicksz	1626-1679
Jouvenet, Jean	1644-1717	Stone, Nicholas	1587-1647
Kneller, Sir Godfrey	1648-1723	Stradivari, Antonio (Violin maker)	1644-1737
Koninck, Philips	1619-1688	Teniers, David the elder	1582-1649
Laar, Pieter Van	1590-1658	Teniers, David the younger	1610-1690
Lafosse, Charles De	1640-1716		
Lahire, Laurent De	1606-1656	Ter Borch, Gerard	1617-1681
Lanfranco, Giovanni	1581-1647	Ter Brugghen, Hendrik	1588-1629
Le Brun, Charles	1619-1690	Van De Velde, Adrian	1636-1672
Lely, Sir Peter	1618-1680	Van De Velde, Jan	1593-1641
Le Sueur, Eustache	1616-1655	Van De Velde, the younger	1633-1707
Lievensz, Jan	1607-1674	Van Dyck, Sir Anthony	1599-1641
Lorenzo, Lippi	1606-1664	Van Veen, Otto	1556-1634
Maes, Nicholas	1632-1693	Velasquez, Diego Rodriguez	1599-1660
Mansard, Joels Hardouin	1646-1708		
Mansart, Francois	1598-1666	Vermeer, Jan Van Der Meer	1632-1675
Maratta, Carlo	1625-1713	Verrio, Antonio	1639-1707
Metsu, Gabriel	1630-1667	Vos, Cornelis de	1585-1651
Meulen, Adam Frans Van Der	1632-1690	Vouet, Simon	1590-1649
		Weenix, Jan Baptist	1621-1660
Mierevelt, Michiel Jansz Van	1567-1641	Wouwerman, Philip	1619-1668
Mieris, Frans Van	1635-1681	Wren, Sir Christopher	1632-1723
Mignard, Pierre	1610-1695	Zurbaran, Francisco De	1598-1669
Mignon, Abraham	1640-1697		
Mile, Jean Francois	1642-1679		

Aichinger, Gregor	1565-1628
Albert, Heinrich	1604-1651
Alegri, Gregorio	1582-1652
Basile, Giambattista	1575-1632
Bateson, Thomas	1570-1630
Biber, Heinrich Johann	
Franz Von	1644-1704
Blow, John	1648-1708
Bononcini, Giovanni	
Maria	1642-1678
Bull, John	1562-1628
Cambert, Robert	1628-1677
Carissimi, Giacomo	1604-1674
Carlton, Richard	1560-1638
Cavalli, Francesco	1602-1676
Cesti, Marc'Antoni	1618-1669
Cooper, John	1570-1627
Couperin, Charles	1638-1679
Cruger, Johann	1598-1662
East, Michael	1580-1648

Eccles, John	1650-1735
Ferrabosco, Alfonso	d. 1628
Ford, Thomas	1580-1648
Frescobaldi, Girolamo	1583-1644
Jenkins, John	1592-1678
Lawes, Henry	1596-1662
Legrenzi, Giovanni	1625-1690
Locke, Matthew	1630-1677
Lully, Jean-Baptiste	1639-1687
Monteverdi, Claudio	1567-1643
Peri, Jacopo	1561-1633
Pilkington, Francis	1638-
Ravencroft, Thomas	1590-1633
Schmeltzer, Johann	
Heinrich	1623-1680
Schütz, Heinrich	1585-1672
Stradella, Allessandro	1645-1682
Tomkins, Thomas	1572-1656
Wilbye, John	1574-1638
Wilson, John	1595-1674

K

1652   England at War with the Dutch.
1654   England and Holland at Peace.
1658   Richard Cromwell made protector.
1660   Charles II proclaimed.
1664   England and Holland at War.
1665   Great Plague in London.   London Gazette first published.
1666   France declares war on England.   Great Fire of London.
1668   Triple Alliance. England, Holland and Sweden.
1670   Hudson Bay Co. formed.
1672   England and France form treaty. Join forces against Dutch.
1674   England and Holland at Peace.

PROMINENT PEOPLE

Cromwell, Oliver	1599-1658	Marlborough, John	
Cromwell, Richard	1626-1712	Churchill 1st Duke	1650-1722
Kidd, Captain William	1645-1701	Newton, Sir Isaac	1642-1727

EMPERORS OF CHINA
[Manchu (Ch-ing) Dynasty]

Shih Tsu	1644-1661	Kang Tsi	1662-1722

POPES

Innocent X	1644-1655	Clement IX	1667-1669
Alexander VII	1655-1667	Clement X	1670-1676

FRANCE. HEADS OF STATE

Louis XIV	1643-1715

HOLY ROMAN EMPERORS

Ferdinand III	1637-1657	Leopold I	1658-1705

ENGLAND. SOVEREIGNS

Commonwealth &		Charles II	1660-1685
Protectorate	1649-1660		

SWEDEN. KINGS

Christina	1632-1654	Charles XI	1660-1697
Charles X	1654-1660		

PORTUGAL. KINGS

John IV	1640-1656	Alphonso VI	1656-1683

ELECTORS OF BRANDENBURG

Frederick William	1640-1688

RUSSIA. TSARS

Alexis	1645-1676

WRITERS

Addison, Joseph	1672-1719	Burnet, Gilbert	1643-1715
Aguesseau, Henri		Burnet, Thomas	1635-1715
François d'	1668-1751	Butler, Samuel	1612-1680
Ainsworth, Robert	1660-1743	Bussy, Roger de Rabutin	1618-1693
Aitzema, Lieuwe Van	1600-1669	Byrd, William	1674-1744
Alcoforado, Marianna	1640-1723	Calderon De La Barca,	
Alleine, Joseph	1634-1668	Pedro	1600-1681
Amelot de la Houssaey,		Calprenede, Gautier Des	
Abraham Nicolas	1634-1706	Costes De La	1610-1633
Angelus, Silecius	1624-1677	Campistron, Jean	
Arbuthnot, John	1667-1735	Galbert De	1656-1723
Arnault, Antoine	1612-1694	Cats, Jakob	1577-1660
Asgill, John	1659-1738	Centlivre, Susanna	1667-1723
Ashmole, Elias	1617-1692	Chamberlayne, William	1619-1679
Astell, Mary	1668-1731	Chapelaine, Jean	1595-1674
Atterbury, Francis	1663-1732	Chaulieu, Guillaume	
Aubignac, Francois		Amerye De	1639-1720
Hedelin Abbe De	1604-1676	Coisy, Francois Timoleon	
Aubrey, John	1626-1697	Abbe de	1644-1724
Aulnoy, Marie Cathrine	1650-1705	Cibber, Colley	1671-1757
Baillie, Lady Grizel	1665-1746	Clarendon, Edward Hyde	
Baillie, Robert	1599-1662	(1st Earl of)	1609-1674
Baldinucci, Filippo	1624-1696	Clarke, Samuel	1675-1729
Balzac, Jean-Louis		Clauberg, Johann	1622-1665
Guez De	1594-1654	Cleland, William	1661-1689
Barclay, Robert	1648-1690	Cleveland, John	1613-1658
Bartoli, Danielle	1608-1685	Cocker, Edward	1631-1675
Bartoli, Pietro Santo	1635-1700	Coello, Antonio	1611-1652
Bayle, Pierre	1647-1706	Cokain, Sir Aston	1608-1684
Beaumont, Joseph	1616-1699	Comenius, Johann Amos	1592-1670
Behn, Aphra	1640-1689	Congreve, William	1670-1729
Benlowes, Edward	1603-1676	Corneille, Pierre	1606-1684
Benserade, Isaac De	1613-1691	Cornielle, Thomas	1625-1709
Bentley, Richard	1662-1742	Cotton, John	1584-1652
Bergerac, Cyrano de	1619-1655	Cotton, Charles	1630-1687
Blackmore, Sir Richard	1650-1729	Cowley, Abraham	1618-1667
Blount, Sir Thomas Pope	1649-1697	Crebillon, Prosper Jolyot	
Boileau-Despreaux		De	1674-1762
Nicolas	1636-1711	Crescimbeni, Giovanni	
Boisrobert, Francois Le		Mario	1663-1728
Metel De	1592-1662	Crousaz, Jean Pierre	1663-1748
Bossuet, Jacques Benigne	1627-1704	Crowne, John	1640-1703
Boulainvilliers, Henri	1658-1722	Cudworth, Ralph	1617-1688
Boursault, Edme	1638-1701	Culpeper, Nicholas	1616-1654
Boyle, Robert	1627-1691	Cumberland, Richard	1631-1718
Bradford, William	1590-1657	Cutts of Gowran,	
Bradstreet, Ann	1612-1672	John Cutts	1661-1707
Brady, Nicholas	1659-1726	Dach, Simon	1605-1659
Brathwait, Richard	1588-1673	Dahlstjerna, Gunno	1661-1709
Broekhuizen, Jan Van	1649-1707	Dalgarno, George	1626-1687
Brome, Alexander	1620-1666	Dampier, William	1652-1715
Brome, Richard	-1652	Dancourt, Florent Carton	1661-1725
Browne, Sir Thomas	1605-1682	Daniel, Gabriel	1649-1728
Bulstrode, Sir Richard	1610-1711	Dass, Petter	1647-1708
Bunyan, John	1628-1688	Davenant, Sir William	1606-1668

Defoe, Daniel	1659-1731
Delmedigo, Joseph	
Soloman	1591-1655
Denman, Sir John	1615-1669
Dennis, John	1657-1734
Deshoulieres, Antoinette	1638-1694
Desmartes, Jean	1595-1676
Digby, Sir Kenelm	1603-1665
Dodwell, Henry	1641-1711
Dryden, John	1631-1700
Dugdale, Sir William	1605-1686
Dupin, Louis Ellies	1657-1719
D'Urfey, Thomas	1654-1723
Du Ryer, Pierre	1606-1658
Ellwood, Thomas	1639-1714
Enriquez, Gomez Antonio	1602-1662
Etherege, Sir George	1635-1691
Evelyn, John	1620-1706
Fanshawe, Sir Richard	1608-1666
Felltham, Owen	1602-1668
Fénelon, François de	
Salignac de la Mothe	1651-1715
Filicaia, Vincenzo da	1642-1702
Filmer, Sir Robert	1590-1653
Flacknoe, Richard	1600-1678
Fleury, Claude	1640-1723
Folard, Jean Charles	1669-1752
Fontenelle, Bernard Le	
Bovier De	1657-1757
Fortiguerra, Nicolo	1674-1735
Fox, George	1624-1691
Fraunce, Abraham	1558-1663
Froberger, Johann Jakob	1616-1667
Gassendi, Pierre	1592-1655
Gauden, John	1605-1662
Gerhardt, Paul	1607-1676
Geulincx, Arnold	1624-1669
Glanville, Joseph	1636-1680
Gracian Y Morales,	
Baltasar	1601-1658
Grimmelshausen, Hans	
Jakob Christof Flevon	1625-1676
Gryphius, Andreas	1616-1664
Guericke, Otto Von	1602-1686
Guidi, Carlo Alessandro	1650-1712
Guyon, Jeanne Marie	
Bouvier De La Mothe	1640-1717
Gyongyosi, Istvan	1620-1704
Habingdon, William	1605-1654
Hajji Khalifa	1599-c. 1658
Hake, Edward	1579-
Halifax, Charles Montague	1661-1715
Hall, Joseph	1574-1656
Hamilton, Anthony	1645-1720
Harlib, Samuel	1599-1670
Harvey, William	1578-1657
Harrington, James	1611-1677
Harris, John	1666-1719
Harsdorffer, Georg Philipp	1607-1658
Heemskerk, Johan Van	1597-1656
Helyot, Pierre	1660-1716
Herbert, Sir Thomas	1608-1682
Herrick, Robert	1591-1674
Heylyn, Peter	1600-1662
Hobbes, Thomas	1588-1679
Holles, Denzil Holles	1599-1680
Howard, Sir Robert	1626-1698
Howell, James	1594-1666
Hoz Y Mota, Juan	
Claudio De La	1630-1714
Huygens, Sir Constantijn	1596-1687
Johnson, Richard	1573-1659
Jordan, Thomas	1612-1685
Killigrew, Thomas	1612-1683
King, William	1663-1712
Kingo, Thomas Hansen	1634-1703
Kirk, Robert	1641-1692
La Bruyere, Jean De	1645-1696
La Calprenede, Gauthier	
De Costes	1610-1663
La Fayette, Marie-	
Madeleine	1634-1693
La Fontaine, Jean De	1621-1695
Lairesse, Gerard De	1641-1711
La Mothe Le Vayer,	
Francois De	1588-1672
La Motte, Antoine	
Houder De	1672-1731
La Rochefoucauld,	
Francois De	1613-1680
La Tour, Georges De	1593-1652
Lee, Nathaniel	1653-1692
Leibniz, Gottfried	
Wilhelm	1646-1716
Le Sage, Alain Rene	1668-1747
L'Estrange, Sir Roger	1616-1704
Locke, John	1632-1704
Lockhart, George	1673-1731
Lovelace, Richard	1618-1658
Maffei, Francesco	
Scipione	1675-1755
Magnusson, Arni	1663-1730
Maimbourg, Louis	1610-1686
Mairet, Jean De	1604-1686
Malebranche, Nicholas	1638-1715
Mandeville, Bernard De	1670-1733
Manley, Mary	
De La Riviere	1663-1724
Manuel De Mello, Don	
Francisco	1608-1666
Marais, Marin	1656-1728
Marca, Pierre De	1594-1662
Marsigli, Luigi	
Ferdinando	1658-1730
Marvell, Andrew	1621-1678
Mather, Cotton	1663-1728
Mather, Increase	1639-1723
Matos, Fragoso, Juan De	1608-1689
Melo, Francisco	
Manuel de	1608-1666

Milton, John	1608-1674	Saint Evremond, Charles	
Moliere, (Jean Baptiste,		Marquetel de Saint	
Poquelin)	1622-1673	Denis Seignieur de	1610-1703
More, Henry	1614-1687	Saint, Pierre, Charles	
Moreto Y Cavana,		Irenee Castel	1658-1743
Agustin	1618-1669	Saint Real, Cesar, Vichard	
Moscherosch, Johann		Abbé De	1631-1692
Michael	1601-1669	Saint-Simon, Louis De	
Motteux, Pierre Antoine	1663-1718	Rouvroy	1675-1755
Motteville, Francois		Scarron, Paul	1610-1660
Bertaut De	1621-1689	Scudery, Georges De	1601-1667
Muratori, Ludovico		Scudery, Madeleine De	1607-1701
Antonio	1672-1750	Sedley, Sir Charles	1639-1701
Mure, William (Sir)	1594-1657	Selden, John	1584-1654
Najara, Israel Ben Moses	1587-	Settle, Elkanah	1648-1724
Newton, Sir Isaac	1642-1727	Sevigne, Marie De	
Norris, John	1657-1711	Rabutin Chantal	1626-1696
North, Roger	1653-1734	Sewall, Samuel	1652-1730
O'Carolan, Turlogh	1670-1738	Shadwell, Thomas	1642-1692
Ogilby, John	1600-1676	Shaftesbury, Anthony	
Oldham, John	1653-1683	Ashley Cooper 3rd Earl	1671-1713
Oldmixon, John	1673-1742	Sherlock, William	1641-1707
Otway, Thomas	1652-1685	Shirley, James	1596-1666
Pallavicino, Pietro Sforza	1607-1667	Solis Y Ribadeneyra	
Parker, Martin	1600-1656	Antonio De	1610-1686
Pascal, Blaise	1623-1662	Somerville, William	1675-1742
Paterson, William	1658-1719	Sorel, Charles	1597-1674
Penn, William	1644-1718	Southerne, Thomas	1660-1746
Pepusch, Johann		Speke, Hugh	1656-1724
Christoph	1667-1752	Spinoza, Benedictus De	1632-1677
Perrault, Charles	1628-1703	St. Jernhjelm, Georg	1598-1672
Philips, Ambrose	1675-1749	Stanley, Thomas	1625-1678
Philips, Katharine	1631-1664	Steel, Sir Richard	1672-1729
Phillips, Edward	1630-1696	Stillingfleet, Edward	1635-1699
Phillips, John	1631-1706	Strype, John	1643-1737
Pitcairn, Archibald	1652-1713	Tallemant, Gedeon Sieur	
Pomfret, John	1667-1702	Des Reaux	1619-1692
Pozzo, Andrea	1642-1709	Tate, Nahum	1652-1715
Prior	1664-1721	Taylor, Jeremy	1613-1667
Puffendorf, Samuel		Taylor, John	1580-1653
Freiherr Von	1632-1694	Temple, Sir William	1628-1699
Quesnel, Pasquier	1634-1719	Thomas, Nabbes	1605-
Quinault, Phillipe	1635-1688	Thomasius, Christian	1655-1728
Racan, Honore De Beuil	1589-1670	Tillemont, Sebastian	
Racine, Jean	1639-1699	Le Nain De	1637-1698
Rapin, Paul De	1661-1725	Tindal, Matthew	1656-1733
Regnard, Jean Francois	1655-1709	Traherne, Thomas	1637-1674
Retz, Cardinal de	1614-1679	Urquhart, Sir Thomas	1611-1660
Rochester, John Wilmot	1647-1680	Vanbrugh, Sir John	1664-1726
Rollin, Charles	1661-1741	Vane, Sir Henry	1613-1662
Roscommon, Wentworth		Vaughan, Henry	1622-1695
Dillon	1630-1685	Vico, Giovanni Battista	1668-1744
Rousseau, Jean Baptiste	1671-1741	Vieira, Antonio	1608-1697
Rowe, Nicholas	1674-1718	Vondel, Joost Van Den	1587-1679
Rushworth, John	1612-1690	Waller, Edmund	1606-1687
Rymer, Thomas	1641-1713	Walton, Izaak	1593-1683
Saint Amant, Marc		Watts, Isaac	1674-1748
Antoine Gerard	1594-1661	Wharton, Henry	1664-1695
		Whichcote, Benjamin	1609-1683
		Wigglesworth, Michael	1631-1705

Williams, Roger	c. 1600-1683	Woolaston, William	1654-1724
Winchelsea, Anne Finch	1661-1720	Wood, Anthony	1632-1695
Winslow, Edward	1595-1655	Wyncherley, William	1640-1716
Wither, George	1588-1667	Young, Edward	1638-1765

ARTISTS

Albani, Francesco	1578-1660	Dolci, Carlo	1616-1686
Algardi, Alessandro	1602-1654	Douw, Gerrit	1613-1675
Allou, Gilles	1670-1751	Duck, Jacob	1600-1660
Anguier, Francois	1604-1669	Dusart, Cornelis	1660-1704
Anguier, Michel	1612-1686	Eekhout, Gerbrand Van	
Archer, Thomas	1668-1743	Den	1621-1674
Backhuysen, Ludolf	1631-1708	Everingen, Allart Van	1621-1675
Barbieri, Giovanni		Fabritius, Carel	1624-1654
Francesco	1591-1666	Faithorne, William	1616-1691
Beck, David	1621-1556	Falcone, Aniello	1600-1656
Berchem, Nicholaes	1620-1683	Felibien, Andre	1619-1695
Bernini, Giovanni Lorenzo	1598-1680	Ferri, Ciro	1634-1689
Bloeman, Jan Frans Van	1662-1740	Fischer, Johann Berhard	1656-1723
Bloemart, Abraham	1564-1651	Flatman, Thomas	1637-1688
Borromini, Francesco	1599-1667	Flemal, Bertholet	1614-1675
Both, Jan	1618-1652	Flinck, Govert	1615-1660
Bouchardon, Edme	1698-1762	Fontana, Carlo	1638-1714
Boulle, Andre Charles	1642-1732	Franceschini, Baldassare	1611-1689
(cabinet maker)		Franceschini, Marco	
Bourse, Esaias	1630-1673	Antonio	1648-1729
Cano, Alonzo	1601-1667	Fresnoy, Charles	
Cappelle, Jan Van Der	1624-1679	Alphonse Du	1611-1665
Carreno De Miranda, Juan	1614-1685	Fruytiers, Philip	1627-1666
Carriera, Rosalba	1675-1757	Fyt, Jan	1609-1661
Cassana, Niccolo	1659-1714	Gentileschi, Artemisia	1597-1651
Castello, Valerio	1625-1659	Gibbons, Grinling	1648-1721
Cavedone, Jacopo	1577-1660	Gillot, Claude	1673-1722
Champaign, Phillipe De	1602-1674	Giordano, Luca	1632-1705
Churriguera, Don Jose	1650-1725	Girardon, Francois	1628-1715
Cibber, Caius Gabriel	1630-1700	Goven, Jan Josephzoon	
Cignani, Carlo	1628-1719	Van	1596-1656
Claude, Lorrain	1600-1682	Grimaldi, Giovanni	
Cleve, Van Jan	1646-1716	Francesco	1606-1680
Closterman, John	1656-1713	Guercino	1590-1666
Codde, Pieter	1599-1678	Hals, Frans	1580-1666
Coello, Claudio	1630-1693	Hawksmoor, Nicholas	1661-1736
Cooper, Alexander	-1660	Heem, Jan Davidz Van	1600-1683
Cooper, Samuel	1609-1672	Herrera, Francisco	
Coques, Gonzales	1614-1684	"El Mozo"	1622-1685
Cornelisz, Cornelis	1562-1638	Helst, Batholomaens	
Cortona, Pietro		Van Der	1613-1670
Berrettini Da	1596-1669	Hevden, Jan Van Der	1637-1712
Courtois, Guillaume	1628-1679	Hobbema, Mevndert	1638-1709
Courtois, Jacques	1621-1676	Hollar, Wenceslaus	1607-1677
Coustou, Nicolas	1658-1733	Hondecoeter, Melchior De	1636-1695
Coypel, Antoine	1661-1722	Honthorst, Gerard Van	1590-1656
Coypel, Noel	1628-1707	Hooch, Pieter De	1629-1683
Coysevoy, Charles Antoine	1640-1720	Hoogstraten, Samuel	
Craver, Gaspard De	1584-1769	Dirksz Van	1627-1678
Crespi, Giusenpi, Maria	1665-1747	Houbraken, Arnold	1660-1719
Dahl, Michael	1656-1743	Huchtenburg, John Van	1647-1733
De Keyser, Thomas	1596-1667	Huysmans, Jacob	1633-1696

Huysmans, Jan Baptist	1654-1716	Pareja, Juan De	1606-1670
Huysmans, Cornelius	1648-1727	Petitot, Jean	1608-1691
Janssen, Cornelis	1593-1664	Post, Pieter	1608-1669
Janssens, Victor Honorius	1658-1736	Potter, Paul	1625-1654
Jones, Inigo	1573-1651	Poussin, Gaspar	1613-1675
Jonson, Cornelis		Prieur, Pierre	1626-1676
Van Ceulen	1593-1662	Procaccini, Ercole the	
Jordaens, Jacob	1593-1678	younger	1596-1676
Jouvenet, Jean	1644-1717	Poussin, Nicholas	1594-1665
Kneller, Sir William	1648-1723	Puget, Pierre	1622-1694
Koninck, Philips	1619-1688	Rembrandt, Harmensz	
Laar, Pieter Van	1590-1658	Van Rijn	1606-1669
Lafosse, Charles De	1640-1716	Ribera, Jusepe De	1588-1656
Laguerre, Louis	1663-1721	Rigaud, Hyacinthe	1659-1743
Lahire, Laurent De	1606-1656	Rosa, Salvator	1615-1673
Largilliere, Nicolas	1656-1746	Ruysdael, Jacob Van	1628-1682
Le Brun, Charles	1619-1690	Sacchi, Andrea	1600-1661
Legros, Pierre	1656-1719	Sandrart, Joachim Van	1606-1688
Lely, Sir Peter	1618-1680	Sarrazin, Jacques	1588-1660
Le Sueur, Eustache	1616-1655	Sassoferato	1605-1685
Lievensz, Jan	1607-1674	Smybert, John	1584-1651
Lorenzo, Lippi	1606-1664	Snyders, Frans	1579-1657
Maes, Nicholas	1632-1693	Steen, Jan Havicksz	1626-1679
Magnasco, Alessandro	1667-1749	Stradivari, Antonio	1644-1737
Mansard, Jules Hardouin	1646-1708	(violin maker)	
Mansart, Francois	1598-1666	Ter Borch, Gerard	1617-1681
Maratta, Carlo	1625-1713	Teniers, David the	
Marot, Daniel	1661-1712	younger	1610-1690
Metsu, Gabriel	1630-1667	Vanbrugh, Sir John	1664-1726
Meulen, Adam Frans		Van De Velde, Adrian	1636-1672
Van Der	1632-1690	Van Der Velde,	
Mieris, Frans Van	1635-1681	William the younger	1633-1707
Mignard, Pierre	1610-1695	Velasquez, Diego	
Mignon, Abraham	1640-1697	Rodriguez	1599-1660
Mile, Jean Francois	1642-1679	Vermeer, Jan Van Der	
Murillo, Bartolome		Meer	1632-1675
Esteban	1617-1682	Verrio, Antonio	1639-1707
Nash, Richard	1674-1762	Vos, Cornelis De	1585-1651
Netscher, Gaspar	1639-1684	Walker, Robert	-1658
Ostade, Adriaan Van	1610-1685	Weenix, Jan Baptist	1621-1660
Pacheco, Francisco	1564-1654	Wouwerman, Philip	1619-1668
Palomino De Castro,		Wren, Sir Christopher	1632-1723
Antonio	1653-1726	Zurbaran, Francisco De	1598-1669
Paolini, Pietro	1603-1682		

COMPOSERS

Albert, Heinrich	1604-1651	Campra, Anore	1660-1744
Albinoni, Tommaso	1674-1745	Carissimi, Giacomo	1604-1674
Allegri, Gregorio	1582-1652	Cavalli, Francesco	1602-1676
Ariosti, Attilio	1660-	Cesti, Marc'Antonio	1618-1669
Blow, John	1648-1708	Clari, Giovanni Carlo	
Bononcini, Giovanni		Maria	1669-1745
Battista	1670-1755	Clarke, Jeremiah	1659-1707
Bononcini, Giovanni		Corelli, Arcangelo	1653-1713
Maria	1642-1678	Couperin, Charles	1638-1679
Bononcini, Marc Antonio	1675-1726	Couperin, Francois	1668-1733
Caldara, Antonio	1670-1736	Cruger, Johann	1598-1662
Cambert, Robert	1628-1677	Eccles, John	1650-1735

Garth, Sir Samuel	1661-1719	Pachelbel, Johan	1653-1706
Innes, Thomas	1663-1744	Purcell, Henry	1659-1695
Jenkins, John	1592-1678	Scarlatti, Alessandro	1659-1725
Keiser, Reinhold	1673-1739	Schmelzer, Johann	
Lawes, Henry	1596-1662	Heinrich	1623-1680
Legrenzi, Giovanni	1625-1690	Steffani, Agostino	1653-1728
Locke, Matthew	1630-1677	Stradella, Alessandro	1645-1682
Lotti, Antonio	1667-1740	Tomkins, Thomas	1572-1656
Lully, Jean-Baptiste	1639-1687	Wilson, John	1595-1674

1678 English and Dutch Alliance.
1679 Habeas Corpus Act.
1685 Battle of Sedgemoor.
      Bloody Assizes.
1688 Smyrna destroyed by earthquake.
1689 Battle of Killiecrankie.
      Bill of Rights passed.
1690 Battle of the Boyne.
      Siege of Limerick.
1692 Massacre of Glencoe.
      Battle of La Hogue.
      Battle of Steinkirk.
1694 Bank of England incorporated.

PROMINENT PEOPLE

Cromwell, Richard	1626-1712	**Marlborough,** John	
Fahrenheit, Gabriel Daniel	1686-1736	Churchill, 1st Duke	1650-1722
Kidd, Captain William	1645-1701	Newton, Sir Isaac	1642-1727
		Penn, William	1644-1718

EMPERORS OF CHINA
[Manchu (Ching) Dynasty]

Kang Tsi   1662-1722

POPES

Clement X	1670-1676	**Alexander VIII**	1689-1691
Innocent XI	1676-1689	**Innocent XII**	1691-1700

FRANCE. HEADS OF STATE

Louis XIV   1643-1715

HOLY ROMAN EMPERORS

Leopold I   1658-1705

ENGLAND. SOVEREIGNS

Charles II	1660-1685	**William III & Mary**	1689-1694
James II	1685-1688	**William III**	1694-1702

SWEDEN. KINGS

Charles XI   1660-1697   **Charles XII**   1697-1718

PORTUGAL. KINGS

Alphonso VI   1656-1683   **Pedro II**   1683-1706

ELECTORS OF BRANDENBURG

Frederick William   1640-1688   **Frederick III**   1688-1713

RUSSIA. TSARS

Alexis	1645-1676	**Ivan II**	1682-1689
Theodore III	1676-1682	**Peter the Great 1**	1682-1725

Charles II　　　　　　　　1665-1700

WRITERS

Abauzit, Firmin	1679-1767	Bulstrode, Sir Richard	1610-1711
Addison, Joseph	1672-1719	Bunyan, John	1628-1688
Aguesseau, Henry		Burnet, Gilbert	1643-1715
François d'	1668-1751	Burnet, Thomas	1635-1715
Ainsworth, Robert	1660-1743	Butler, Samuel	1612-1680
Alcoforado, Marianna	1640-1723	Bussy, Roger de Rabutin	1618-1693
Amelot de la Houssaey,		Byrd, William	1674-1744
Abraham Nicolas	1634-1706	Byrom, John	1692-1763
Ames, Joseph	1689-1759	Calderon De La Barca,	
Amhurst, Nicholas	1697-1742	Pedro	1600-1681
Amory, Thomas	1691-1788	Campistron, Jean	
Arbuthnot, John	1667-1735	Galbert De	1656-1723
Arnault, Antoine	1612-1694	Canizares, Jose De	1676-1750
Asgill, John	1659-1738	Carey, Henry	1690-1743
Ashmole, Elias	1617-1692	Carte, Thomas	1686-1754
Astell, Mary	1688-1731	Centlivre, Susanna	1667-1723
Atterbury, Francis	1663-1732	Challoner, Richard	1691-1781
Aubignac, Francois		Chamberlayne, William	1619-1679
Hedelin Abbe De	1604-1676	Chaulieu, Guillaume	
Aubrey, John	1626-1697	Amfrye De	1639-1720
Aulnoy, Marie Cathrine		Chesterfield, Philip	
Le Jumel	1650-1705	Dormer Stanhope	
Bachaumont, Louis		(4th Earl of)	1694-1773
Petit De	1690-1771	Choisy, Francois	
Baillie, Lady Grizel	1665-1746	Timoleon, Abbe De	1644-1724
Baldinucci, Filippo	1624-1696	Cibber, Colley	1671-1757
Barclay, Robert	1608-1685	Clarke, Samuel	1675-1729
Bartoli, Danielle	1608-1685	Cleland, William	1661-1689
Bartoli, Pietro Santo	1635-1700	Cokain, Sir Aston	1608-1684
Bayle, Pierre	1647-1706	Colden, Cadwallader	1688-1776
Beaumont, Joseph	1616-1699	Collier, Arthur	1680-1732
Behn, Aphra	1640-1689	Congreve, William	1670-1729
Benserade, Isaac De	1613-1691	Corneille, Pierre	1606-1684
Bentley, Richard	1662-1742	Cornielle, Thomas	1635-1709
Berkeley, George	1685-1753	Cotton, Charles	1630-1687
Bilfinger, George		Crebillon, Prosper	
Bernhard	1693-1750	Jolyot De	1674-1762
Blackmore, Sir Richard	1650-1729	Crescimbeni, Giovanni	
Blair, Robert	1699-1746	Mario	1663-1728
Blount, Sir Thomas Pope	1649-1697	Crousaz, Jean Pierre	1663-1748
Bodmer, Johann Jakob	1698-1783	Crowne, John	1640-1703
Boileau-Despreaux,		Cudworth, Ralph	1617-1688
Nicolas	1636-1711	Cumberland, Richard	1631-1718
Bolingbroke, Henry St. John	1678-1751	Cutts of Gowran, John	
Bossuet, Jacques Benigne	1627-1704	Cutts	1661-1707
Boston, Thomas	1677-1732	Dahlstjerna, Gunno	1661-1709
Boulainvilliers, Henri	1658-1722	Dalgarno, George	1626-1687
Boursault, Edme	1638-1701	Dampier, William	1652-1715
Boyle, Robert	1627-1691	Dancourt, Florent Carton	1661-1725
Brady, Nicholas	1659-1726	Daniel, Gabriel	1649-1728
Brockes, Barthold Heinrich	1680-1747	Dass, Petter	1647-1708
Broekhuizen, Jan Van	1649-1707	Defoe, Daniel	1659-1731
Brorson, Hans Adolf	1694-1764	Dennis, John	1657-1734
Browne, Sir Thomas	1605-1682	Deshoulieres, Antoinette	1638-1694
Brucker, Johann Jakob	1696-1770	Desmartes, Jean	1595-1676

Destouches, Phillipe	1680-1754	Huygens, Sir Constantijn	1596-1687
Dodwell, Henry	1641-1711	Jordan, Thomas	1612-1685
Dryden, John	1631-1700	Kames, Henry Home	1696-1782
Dupin, Louis Ellies	1657-1719	Killigrew, Thomas	1612-1683
D'Urfey, Thomas	1653-1723	King, William	1663-1712
Dyer, John	1699-1757	Kingo, Thomas Hansen	1634-1703
Ellwood, Thomas	1639-1714	Kirk, Robert	1641-1692
Etherege, Sir George	1635-1691	La Bruyere, Jean De	1645-1696
Eusden, Laurence	1688-1730	La Chaussee, Pierre Claude	
Evelyn, John	1620-1706	Nivelle De	1692-1754
Farquhar, George	1677-1707	La Fayette, Marie	
Fénelon, François de Salignac		Madeleine	1634-1693
de la Mothe	1651-1715	La Fontaine, Jean De	1621-1695
Fenton, Elijah	1683-1730	Lagrange-Chancel, Francois	
Filicaia, Vincenzo Da	1642-1707	Joseph	1677-1758
Flecknoe, Richard	1600-1678	Lairesse, Gerard De	1641-1711
Fleury, Claude	1640-1723	Lamotte, Antoine Houdar	
Folard, Jean Charles	1669-1752	De	1672-1731
Fontenelle, Bernard		La Rochefoucauld,	
Le Bovier De	1657-1757	Francois De	1613-1680
Fortiguerra, Nicolo	1674-1735	Law, William	1686-1761
Fox, George	1624-1691	Lee, Nathaniel	1653-1692
Frugoni, Carlo Innocenzo		Leibniz, Gottfried	
Maria	1692-1768	Wilhelm	1646-1716
Gay, John	1685-1732	Le Sage, Alain Rene	1668-1747
Gerhardt, Paul	1607-1676	L'Estrange, Sir Roger	1616-1704
Giannone, Pietro	1676-1748	Lillo, George	1693-1739
Glanville, Joseph	1636-1680	Locke, John	1632-1704
Gottsched, Johann		Lockhart, George	1673-1731
Churtaph	1700-1766	Macklin, Charles	1697-1797
Green, Matthew	1696-1737	Maffei, Francesco	
Grimmelshausen, Hans Jakob		Scipione	1675-1755
Christof Felvon	1625-1676	Magnusson, Arni	1663-1730
Guericke, Otto Von	1602-1686	Maimbourg, Louis	1610-1686
Guidi, Carlo Alessandro	1650-1712	Mairet, Jean De	1604-1686
Gunther, Johann Christian	1695-1723	Malebranchie, Nicholas	1638-1715
Guyon, Jeanne Marie	1648-1717	Mandeville, Bernard De	1670-1733
Gyongvosi, Istvan	1620-1704	Manley, Mary De La	
Hake, Edward	1579-	Riviere	1663-1724
Halifax, Charles Montague	1661-1715	Marais, Marin	1656-1728
Hamilton, Anthony	1645-1720	Marivaux, Pierre,	
Harrington, James	1611-1677	Carlet De Chamlain De	1688-1763
Harris, John	1666-1719	Marsigli, Luigi Fernando	1658-1730
Haywood, Eliza	1693-1756	Marvell, Andrew	1621-1678
Hearne, Thomas	1678-1735	Mather, Cotton	1663-1728
Heylot, Pierre	1660-1716	Mather, Increase	1639-1723
Henault, Charles Dean		Matos, Fragoso, Juan De	1608-1689
Francois	1685-1770	Metastasio	1698-1782
Herbert, Sir Thomas	1608-1682	Montagu, Lady Mary	
Hervey of Ickworth, John		Wortley	1689-1762
Hervey	1696-1743	Montesquieu, Charles Louis	
Hill, Aaron	1685-1750	De Secondat	1689-1755
Hobbes, Thomas	1588-1679	More, Henry	1614-1687
Holberg, Ludvig Holberg	1684-1754	Motteux, Pierre Antoine	1663-1718
Holles, Denzil Holles	1599-1680	Motteville, Francoise	
Howard, Sir Robert	1626-1698	Bertaut De	1621-1689
Hoz Y Mota, Juan Claudio		Muratori, Ludovico	
De La	1630-1714	Antonio	1672-1750
Hughes, John	1677-1720	Neal, Daniel	1678-1743
Hutcheson, Francis	1694-1746	Newton, Sir Isaac	1642-1727

Norris, John	1657-1711
North, Roger	1653-1734
O'Carolan, Turlough	1670-1738
Ogilby, John	1600-1776
Oldham, John	1653-1683
Oldmixon, John	1673-1742
Orrery, Charles Boyle	1676-1731
Ottway, Thomas	1652-1685
Patlock, Robert	1697-1767
Parnell, Thomas	1679-1718
Paterson, William	1658-1719
Pellisson, Paul	1624-1693
Penn, William	1644-1718
Pepusch, Johann Christolph	1667-1752
Pepys, Samuel	1633-1703
Perrault, Charles	1628-1703
Philips, Ambrose	1675-1749
Philips, John	1676-1708
Phillips, Edward	1630-1696
Phillips, John	1631-1706
Piron, Alexis	1689-1773
Pitcairn, Archibald	1652-1713
Pomfret, John	1667-1702
Pontoppidan, Erik	1698-1764
Pope, Alexander	1688-1744
Pozzo, Andrea	1642-1709
Prevost, Antoine Francois	1697-1763
Prior, Matthew	1664-1721
Puffendorf, Samuel Frieherr Von	1632-1694
Quesnel, Pasquier	1634-1719
Quinault, Phillipe	1635-1688
Racine, Jean	1639-1699
Racine, Louis	1692-1763
Ramsay, Allan	1686-1758
Ramsay, Andrew Michael	1686-1743
Rapin, Paul de	1661-1725
Regnard, Jean Francois	1655-1709
Reimarus, Hermann Samuel	1694-1768
Retz, Cardinel de	1614-1679
Richardson, Samuel	1689-1761
Rochester, John Wilmot	1647-1680
Rollin, Charles	1661-1741
Roscommon, Wentworth Dillon	1630-1685
Rousseau, Jean Baptiste	1671-1741
Rowe, Nicholas	1674-1718
Rushworth, John	1612-1690
Rymer, Thomas	1641-1713
Saint Evremond, Charles Marquetel de Saint Denis Seigneur de	1610-1703
Saint-Pierre, Charles Irenee Castel	1658-1743
Saint Real, Cesar Vichard Abbé de	1631-1692
Saint-Simon, Louis de Rouvroy	1675-1755
Savage, Richard	1697-1743
Sedley, Sir Charles	1639-1701

Settle, Elkanah	1648-1724
Sevigne, Marie de Rabutin-Chantal	1626-1696
Sewall, Samuel	1652-1730
Shadwell, Thomas	1642-1692
Shaftesbury, Anthony Ashley Cooper, 3rd Earl	1671-1713
Sherlock, William	1641-1707
Solis Y Ribadeneyra, Antonio De	1610-1686
Somervile, William	1675-1742
Southern, Thomas	1660-1746
Speke, Hugh	1656-1724
Spence, Joseph	1699-1768
Spinoza, Benedictus De	1632-1677
Staal, Marguerite Jeanne Cordier De Launay	1684-1750
Steele, Sir Richard	1672-1729
Stillingfleet, Edward	1635-1699
Strype, John	1643-1737
Swedenborg, Emanuel	1688-1772
Swift, Jonathan	1676-1745
Tallemant, Gedeon Sieur Des Reaux	1619-1692
Tate, Nahum	1652-1715
Temple, Sir William	1628-1699
Tencin, Claudine Alexandrine Guerin De	1681-1749
Theobald, Lewis	1688-1744
Thomasius, Christian	1655-1728
Thomson, James	1700-1748
Tickell, Thomas	1686-1740
Tillemont, Sebastian le Nain De	1637-1698
Tindal, Matthew	1656-1733
Torres Y Villaroel, Diego De	1696-1759
Vanbrugh, Sir John	1664-1726
Vaughan, Henry	1622-1695
Vilo, Giovanni Battista	1668-1744
Vieira, Antonio	1608-1697
Voltaire, Francois Marie Arouet De	1694-1788
Vondel, Joost Van Den	1587-1679
Waller, Edmund	1606-1687
Walton, Izaak	1593-1683
Watts, Isaac	1674-1748
Wharton, Henry	1664-1695
Whichcote, Benjamin	1609-1683
Wigglesworth, Michael	1631-1705
Williams, Roger	c. 1600-1683
Winchelsea, Anne Finch	1661-1720
Wodrow, Robert	1619-1734
Wollaston, William	1659-1724
Wolff, Christian	1679-1754
Wood, Anthony	1632-1695
Wyncherley, William	1640-1716
Young, Edward	1638-1765
Zinzendorf, Nicolaus Ludwig Grafron	1700-1760

Allou, Gilles	1670-1751	Franceschini, Marco	
Anguier, Michael	1612-1686	Antonio	1648-1729
Archer, Thomas	1668-1743	Gabriel, Jacques Ange	1698-1782
Backhuysen, Ludolf	1631-1708	Gibbons, Grinling	1648-1721
Berchem, Nicolaes	1620-1683	Gibbs, James	1682-1754
Bernini, Giovanni Lorenzo	1598-1680	Gillot, Claude	1673-1722
Bloeman, Jan Frans Van	1662-1740	Giordano, Luca	1632-1705
Bouchardon, Edme	1698-1762	Girardon, Francois	1628-1715
Boulle, Andre Charles	1642-1732	Grimaldi, Giovanni	
(Cabinet maker)		Francesco	1606-1680
Bredael, Jan Frans Van	1683-1750	Hawksmoor, Nicholas	1661-1736
Briseux, Charles Etienne	1680-1754	Heem, Jan Davidz Van	1600-1683
Burlington, Richard Boyle		Herrera, Francisco	
3rd Earl of	1695-1753	"El Moso"	1622-1685
Caffieri, Jacques	1678-1755	Heyden, Jan Van Der	1637-1712
Canaletto	1697-1768	Highmore, Joseph	1692-1780
Cappelle, Jan Van Der	1624-1679	Hobbema, Meyndert	1638-1709
Carreno De Miranda, Juan	1614-1685	Hogarth, William	1697-1764
Carriera, Rosalba	1675-1757	Hollar, Wenceslaus	1607-1677
Cassana, Niccolo	1659-1714	Hondecoetter, Melchoir D'	1636-1695
Chardin, Jean Baptiste		Hooch, Pieter, De	1629-1683
Simeon	1699-1779	Hoogstraten, Samuel	
Churriguera, Don Jose	1650-1725	Dirksz Van	1627-1678
Cibber, Caius Gabriel	1630-1700	Houbraken, Arnold	1660-1719
Cignani, Carlo	1628-1719	Huchtenburg, John Van	1647-1733
Claude, Lorrain	1600-1682	Huysmans, Cornelius	1648-1727
Cleve, Van Jan	1646-1716	Huysmans, Jacob	1633-1696
Closterman, John	1656-1713	Huysmans, Jan Baptist	1654-1716
Codde, Pieter	1599-1678	Huysum, Jan Van	1682-1749
Coello, Claudio	1630-1693	Janssens, Victor Honorius	1658-1736
Coques, Gonzales	1614-1684	Jordaens, Jacob	1593-1678
Cortona, Pietro Benettini da	1596-1669	Jouvenet, Jean	1644-1717
Courtois, Guillaume	1628-1679	Kent, William	1685-1748
Courtois, Jacques	1621-1676	Kneller, Sir Godfrey	1648-1723
Coustou, Guillaume	1678-1746	Koninck, Philips	1619-1688
Coustou, Nicholas	1658-1733	Lafosse, Charles De	1640-1716
Coypel, Antoine	1661-1722	Laguerre, Louis	1663-1721
Coypel, Charles Antoine	1694-1752	Lancret, Nicholas	1690-1743
Coypel, Noel	1628-1707	Largilliere, Nicolas	1656-1746
Coypel, Noel Nicholas	1692-1734	Le Brun, Charles	1619-1690
Coysevoy, Charles Antoine	1640-1720	Le Gros, Pierre	1656-1719
Crespi, Giuseppe Maria	1665-1747	Lely, Sir Peter	1618-1680
Cressent, Charles	1685-1768	Lemoine, Francois	1688-1737
Cuvilles, Francois De	1698-1767	Limborch, Hendrick Van	1680-1758
Dahl, Michael	1656-1743	Maes, Nicholas	1632-1693
Diaz, Diego Valentin	1685-1660	Magnasco, Alessandro	1667-1749
Diepenbeek, Abraham Van	1596-1675	Mansard, Jules Hardouin	1646-1708
Dolci, Carlo	1616-1686	Maratta, Carlo	1625-1713
Donner, Raphael George	1693-1741	Marot, Daniel	1661-1712
Dusart, Cornelis	1660-1704	Meissonier, Juste Aurele	1693-1750
Faithorne, William	1616-1691	Mena, Pedro De	1693-
Falens, Karel Van	1683-1733	Meulen, Adam Frans Van	
Felibien, Andre	1619-1695	Der	1632-1690
Ferri, Ciro	1634-1689	Mieris, Frans Van	1635-1681
Fischer, Johann Bernard		Mignard, Pierre	1610-1695
Von Erlach	1656-1723	Mignon, Abraham	1640-1697
Flatman, Thomas	1637-1688	Mile, Jean Francois	1642-1679
Flitcroft, Henry	1679-1769	Murillo, Bartolome Esteban	1617-1682
Fontana, Carlo	1638-1714	Nash, Richard	1674-1762
Frenceschini, Baldassare	1611-1689	Nattier, Jean Marc	1685-1766

Netscher, Gaspar	1639-1684	Scheemakers, Pieter	1691-1770
Neumann, Balthasar	1687-1753	Steen, Jan Havicksz	1626-1679
Ostade, Adriaan Van	1610-1685	Stradivari, Antonio	1644-1737
Palomino De Castro,		(Violin maker)	
Antonio	1653-1726	Subleyras, Pierre	1699-1749
Paolini, Pietro	1603-1682	Teniers,	
Pater, Jean Baptiste Joseph	1695-1736	David the younger	1610-1690
Pergolesi, Michael Angelo	1700-1736	Ter Borch, Gerard	1617-1681
Petitot, Jean	1608-1691	Thornhill, Sir James	1676-1734
Prieur, Pierre	1626-1676	Tiepolo, Giovanni Battista	1692-1769
Procaccini,		Vanbrugh, Sir John	1664-1726
Ercole the younger	1596-1676	Van Der Velde,	
Puget, Pierre	1622-1694	Willem the Younger	1633-1707
Rigaud, Hyacinthe	1659-1743	Van Goyen, Jan Josephzem	1696-1756
Roubillac, Louis Francois	1695-1762	Van Loo, Jean Baptiste	1684-1745
Ruysdael, Jacob Van	1628-1682	Verrio, Antonio	1639-1707
Rysbrack, Michael	1693-1770	Watteau, Antoine	1684-1721
Sandrart, Joachim Van	1606-1688	Wren, Sir Christopher	1632-1723
Sassoferato	1605-1685		

COMPOSERS

Albinoni, Tommaso	1674-1745	Jenkins, John	1592-1678
Astorga, Emanuele	1680-1755	Keiser, Reinhold	1673-1739
Bach, Johan Sebastian	1685-1750	Lawes, Henry	1596-1662
Barsanti, Francesco	1690-1775	Leclair, Jean Marie	1697-1764
Blow, John	1648-1708	Legrenzi, Giovanni	1625-1690
Bononcini, Giovanni		Leo, Leonardo	1694-1744
Baptista	1670-1755	Locke, Matthew	1630-1677
Bononcini, Giovanni Maria	1642-1678	Logroscino, Nicola	1700-1763
Bononcini, Marc Antonio	1675-1726	Lotti, Antonio	1667-1740
Caldara, Antonio	1670-1736	Lully, Jean-Baptiste	1639-1687
Cambert, Robert	1628-1677	Marcello, Benedetto	1686-1739
Campra, Anore	1660-1744	Mattheson, Johann	1681-1764
Cavalli, Francesco	1602-1676	Pachebel, Johann	1653-1706
Clari, Giovanni Carlo		Porpora, Niccola Antonio	1686-1767
Maria	1669-1745	Purcell, Henry	1659-1695
Clarke, Jeremiah	1659-1707	Quantz, Johann Joachim	1697-1773
Corelli, Arcangelo	1653-1713	Rameau, Jean Philippe	1683-1764
Croft, William	1678-1727	Roman, Johan Helmich	1694-1758
Couperin, Charles	1638-1679	Scarlatti, Alessandro	1659-1725
Couperin, Francois	1668-1733	Scarlatti, Guiseppe	
Daquin, Louis Claude	1694-1772	Domenico	1685-1757
Durante, Francesco	1684-1755	Schmeltzer, Johann	
Fasch, Johann Friedrich	1688-1758	Heinrich	1623-1680
Finger, Godfrey	1685-1717	Schütz, Heinrich	1585-1672
Garth, Sir Samuel	1661-1719	Steffani, Agostino	1653-1728
Greene, Maurice	1695-1755	Stradella, Alessandro	1645-1682
Handel, George Frederick	1685-1759	Tartini, Giuseppe	1692-1770
Hasse, Johann Adolph	1699-1783	Telemann, Georg Philip	1681-1767
Heinicken, Johann David	1683-1729	Vivaldi, Antonio	1678-1741
Innes, Thomas	1663-1744		

1701　War of the Spanish succession.
1702　England declares war on France and Spain.
1703　Battle of Pultusk.
1704　Battle of Blenheim.
1705　Battle of Cassano.
1706　Battle of Ramillies.
1707　First Parliament of Great Britain.
1708　Battle of Oudenarde.
1709　Battle of Malplaquet.
1710　Battle of Saragossa.
1713　Peace of Utrecht.
1715　Riot Act passed.
　　　Battle of Sheriffmuir.
　　　Battle of Preston.
1717　Triple Alliance. England, France and Holland.
1718　Quadruple Alliance. Great Britain, France, Holland and the Emperor.
　　　England declares war against Spain.
1719　France declares war against Spain.
1720　Spain joins Quadruple Alliance.
　　　South Sea Bubble bursts.

PROMINENT PEOPLE

Clive, Lord Robert	1725-1774	Marlborough, John	
Cromwell, Richard	1626-1712	Churchill, 1st Duke	1650-1722
Fahrenheit, Gabriel Daniel	1686-1736	Newton, Sir Isaak	1642-1727
Kidd, Captain William	1645-1701	Penn, William	1644-1718
		Turpin, Dick	1705-1739

EMPERORS OF CHINA (MANCHU (Ch'ing) DYNASTY)

Kang Tsi	1662-1722	Yung Cheng	1723-1735

POPES

Clement XI	1701-1721	Benedict XIII	1724-1730
Innocent XIII	1721-1724		

FRANCE. HEADS OF STATE

Louis XIV	1643-1715	Louis XV	1715-1774

HOLY ROMAN EMPERORS

Leopold I	1658-1705	Charles VI	1711-1740
Joseph I	1705-1711		

ENGLAND. SOVEREIGNS

William III	1694-1702	George I	1714-1727
Anne	1702-1714		

SWEDEN. KINGS

Charles XII	1697-1718	Frederick I	1720-1751
Ulrica Eleanora	1718-1720		

PORTUGAL. KINGS

Pedro II	1683-1706	John V	1706-1750

Frederick I (Frederick III   Frederick William I   1713-1740
Elector of Brandenburg) 1701-1713

RUSSIA. TSARS

Peter the Great I   1682-1725   Catherine I   1725-1727

SPAIN. SOVEREIGNS

Philip V   1700-1724   Philip V   1724-1746
Luis   1724

WRITERS

Abauzit, Firmin	1679-1767	Blomefield, Francis	1705-1752
Abel, Karl Friedrich	1725-1787	Boccage, Marie Anne	
Adam, Jean	1710-1765	Fiquet du	1710-1802
Addison, Joseph	1672-1719	Bodmer, Johann Jakob	1698-1783
Aepinus, Franz Ulrich		Boileau-Despreaux, Nicolas	1636-1711
Theodor	1724-1802	Bolingbroke, Henry	
Aguesseau, Henri		St. John	1678-1751
François d'	1668-1751	Bossuet, Jacques Benigne	1627-1704
Ainsworth, Robert	1660-1743	Boston Thomas	1677-1732
Akenside, Mark	1721-1770	Boulainvilliers, Henri	
Alcoforado, Marianna	1640-1723	Compte de	1658-1722
Alembert, Jean Le Rond D'	1717-1783	Boursault, Edme	1638-1701
Algarotti, Francesco,		Brady, Nicholas	1659-1726
Count	1712-1764	Brockes, Barthold	
Amelot de la Houssaey,		Heinrich	1680-1747
Abraham Nicholas	1634-1706	Broekhuizen, Jan Van	1649-1707
Ames, Joseph	1689-1759	Brooke, Henry	1703-1783
Amhurst, Nicholas	1697-1742	Brorson, Hans Adolf	1694-1764
Amory, Thomas	1691-1788	Brosses, Charles de	1709-1777
Anquetil, Louis Pierre	1723-1808	Brown, John	1715-1766
Anstey, Christopher	1724-1805	Browne, Isaac Hawkins	1705-1760
Arbuthnot, John	1667-1735	Brucker, Johann Jakob	1696-1770
Argens, Jean Baptiste		Bryant, Jacob	1715-1804
de Boyer, Marquis de	1704-1771	Bulstrode, Sir Richard	1610-1711
Armstrong, John	1709-1779	Buonafede, Appiano	1716-1793
Asgill, John	1659-1738	Burnet, Gilbert	1643-1715
Astell, Mary	1668-1731	Burnet, Thomas	1635-1715
Atterbury, Francis	1663-1732	Byrd, William	1674-1744
Aubrey, John	1626-1697	Byrom, John	1692-1763
Aulnoy, Marie Cathrine	1650-1705	Cambridge, Richard	
Bachaumont, Louis		Owen	1717-1802
Petit de	1690-1771	Campistron, Jean	
Baillie, Grizel, Lady	1665-1746	Galbert De	1656-1723
Barthelemy, Jean Jakob	1716-1795	Canizares, Jose De	1676-1750
Baumgarten, Alexander		Carey, Henry	1690-1743
Gottlieb	1714-1762	Carte, Thomas	1686-1754
Bayle, Pierre	1647-1706	Carter, Elizabeth	1717-1806
Bentley, Richard	1662-1742	Casanova De Seingalt,	
Berkeley, George	1685-1753	Giovanni Jacopo	1725-1798
Bilfinger, George		Casti, Giovanni Battista	1724-1803
Bernhard	1693-1750	Cazotte, Jacques	1719-1792
Birch, Thomas	1705-1766	Centlivre, Susanna	1667-1723
Blacklock, Thomas	1721-1791	Challoner, Richard	1691-1781
Blackmore, Sir Richard	1650-1729	Chaulieu, Guillaume	
Blair, Robert	1699-1746	Amfrye De	1639-1720

Chesterfield, Philip Dormer		Folard, Jean Charles	1669-1752
Stanhope (4th Earl of)	1694-1713	Fontenelle, Bernard Le	
Choisy, Francois		Bovier De	1657-1757
Timoleon Abbe De	1644-1724	Foote, Samuel	1720-1777
Cibber, Colley	1671-1757	Fortiguera, Nicolo	1674-1735
Cibber, Theophilus	1703-1758	Franklin, Benjamin	1706-1790
Clarke, Samuel	1675-1729	Frugoni, Carlo Innocenzo	
Clement, Francois	1714-1793	Maria	1692-1768
Cockburn, Alicia	1713-1794	Gay, John	1685-1732
Colden, Cadwallader	1688-1776	Gellert, Christian	
Colle, Charles	1709-1783	Furchtegott	1715-1769
Collier, Arthur	1680-1732	Genovesi, Antonio	1712-1769
Collier, John	1708-1786	Giannone, Pietro	1676-1748
Collins, William	1721-1759	Gleim, Johann Wilhelm	
Condillac, Etienne		Ludwig	1719-1803
Bonnot De	1715-1780	Glover, Richard	1712-1785
Congreve, William	1670-1729	Goldoni, Carlo	1707-1793
Cooke, Thomas	1703-1756	Gottsched, Johann	
Cornielle, Thomas	1625-1709	Christoph	1700-1766
Correa Garcao, Pedro		Gotz, Johann Nikolaus	1721-1781
Antonio Joaquim	1724-1772	Gozzi, Carlo	1720-1806
Crebillon, Prosper		Graves, Richard	1715-1804
Jolyot De	1674-1762	Gray, Thomas	1716-1771
Crescimbeni, Giovanni		Green, Matthew	1696-1737
Mario	1663-1728	Gresset, Jean Baptiste	
Crousaz, Jean Pierre	1663-1748	Louis	1709-1777
Crowne, John	1640-1703	Grimm, Friedrich	
Cruden, Alexander	1701-1770	Melchior	1723-1807
Crusius, Christian August	1715-1775	Guidi, Carlo Alessandro	1650-1712
Cumberland, Richard	1631-1718	Gunther, Johann	
Cutts of Gowran,		Christian	1695-1723
John Cutts	1661-1707	Guyon, Jeanne Marie	
Dahlstjerna, Gunno	1661-1709	Bouvier De La Mothe	1648-1717
Dalin, Olof Von	1708-1763	Gyongyosi, Istvan	1620-1704
Dampier, William	1652-1715	Hagedorn, Friedrich Von	1708-1754
Dancourt, Florent Carton	1661-1725	Halifax, Charles Montague	1661-1715
Daniel, Gabriel	1649-1728	Hamilton, Anthony	1645-1720
Dass, Petter	1647-1708	Hamilton, William	1704-1754
Defoe, Daniel	1659-1731	Hanbury, Williams,	
Dennis, John	1657-1734	Sir Charles	1708-1759
Destouches, Phillipe	1680-1754	Harris, John	1666-1719
Diderot, Denis	1713-1784	Hartley, David	1705-1757
Dodsley, Robert	1703-1764	Hawkesworth, John	1715-1773
Dodwell, Henry	1641-1711	Hawkins, Sir John	1719-1789
Dupin, Louis Ellies	1657-1719	Haywood, Eliza	1693-1756
D'Urfey, Thomas	1653-1723	Hearne, Thomas	1678-1735
Dyer, John	1699-1757	Helvetius, Claude Adrien	1715-1771
Edwards, Jonathan	1703-1758	Helyot, Pierre	1660-1716
Ekhof, Konrad	1720-1778	Hemsterhuis, Francois	1721-1790
Ellwood, Thomas	1639-1714	Henault, Charles Jean	
Eusden, Laurence	1688-1730	Francois	1685-1770
Evelyn, John	1620-1706	Hervey of Ickworth,	
Farquhar, George	1677-1707	John Hervey	1696-1743
Farvart, Charles Simon	1710-1792	Hill, Aaron	1685-1750
Fénelon, François de		Hill, John	1716-1775
Salignac de la Mothe	1651-1715	Holbach, Paul Heinrich	
Fenton, Elijah	1683-1730	Dietrich	1723-1789
Ferguson, Adam	1723-1816	Holberg, Ludvig Holberg	1684-1754
Fielding, Henry	1707-1754	Home, John	1722-1808
Filicaia, Vincenzo da	1642-1707	Hontheim, Johann	
Fleury, Claude	1640-1723	Nikolaus Von	1701-1790

L

Hoz Y Mota, Juan	
Claudio De La	1630-1714
Hughes, John	1677-1720
Hume, David	1711-1776
Hurd, Richard	1720-1808
Hutcheson, Francis	1694-1746
Isla, Jose Francisco De	1703-1781
Jenyns, Soame	1704-1787
Johnson, Samuel	1709-1784
Kames, Henry Home	1696-1782
Kant, Immanuel	1724-1804
King, William	1663-1712
Kingo, Thomas Hansen	1634-1703
Kleist, Ewald Christian	
Von	1715-1759
Klopstock, Friedrich	
Gottlieb	1724-1803
La Chaussee, Pierre	
Claude Nivelle De	1692-1754
La Grange-Chancel,	
Francois Joseph	1677-1758
Lairesse, Gerard De	1641-1711
Lamettrie, Julien	
Offray De	1709-1751
La Motte, Antoine	
Houdar De	1672-1731
Law, William	1686-1761
Leibnitz, Gottfried	
Wilhelm	1646-1716
Lennox, Charlotte	1720-1804
Le Sage, Alain Rene	1668-1747
L'Estrange, Sir Roger	1616-1704
Lillo, George	1693-1739
Linnaeus, Carl	1707-1778
Locke, John	1632-1704
Lockhart, George	1673-1731
Lomonosov, Mikhail	
Vasilievich	1711-1765
Luzan Claramunt, De	
Suelves Y Guerea	
Ignaccio	1702-1754
Luzzatto, Moses Hayim	1707-1747
Lyttelton, George,	
1st Baron	1709-1773
Macklin, Charles	1697-1797
Mably, Gabriel Bonnot De	1709-1785
Maffei, Francesco	
Scipione	1675-1755
Magnusson, Arni	1663-1730
Malebranche, Nicolas	1638-1715
Mallet, David	1705-1765
Mandeville, Bernard De	1670-1733
Manley, Mary De La	
Riviere	1663-1724
Marais, Marin	1656-1728
Marivaux, Pierre Carlet	
De Chamblain De	1688-1763
Marmontel, Jean Francois	1723-1799
Marsigli, Luigi Ferdinando	1658-1730
Mason, William	1725-1797
Mather, Cotton	1663-1728
Mather, Increase	1639-1723
Metastasio	1698-1782
Michell, John	1724-1793
Mirabeau, Victor Riqueti	1715-1789
Montagu, Elizabeth	1720-1800
Montagu, Lady Mary	
Wortley	1689-1762
Montesquieu, Charles Louis	
De Secondat	1689-1755
Moore, Edward	1712-1757
Motteux, Pierre Antoine	1663-1718
Muratori, Ludovico	
Antonio	1672-1750
Neal, Daniel	1678-1743
Newton, Sir Isaac	1642-1727
Norris, John	1657-1711
North, Roger	1653-1734
O'Carolan, Turlogh	1670-1738
Oldmixon, John	1673-1742
Orrery, Charles Boyle	1676-1731
Paltock, Robert	1697-1767
Parnell, Thomas	1679-1718
Paterson, William	1658-1719
Payne, Henry Neville	died c. 1710
Penn, William	1644-1718
Pepusch, Johann	
Christoph	1667-1752
Pepys, Samuel	1633-1703
Perrault, Charles	1628-1703
Philips, Ambrose	1675-1749
Philips, John	1676-1708
Phillips, John	1631-1706
Piranesi, Giambattista	1720-1778
Piron, Alexis	1689-1773
Pitcairn, Archibald	1652-1713
Pomfret, John	1667-1702
Pontoppidan, Erik	1698-1764
Pope, Alexander	1688-1744
Pozzo, Andrea	1642-1709
Prevost, Antoine Francois	1697-1763
Price, Richard	1723-1791
Prior, Matthew	1664-1721
Quesnel, Pasquier	1634-1718
Racine, Louis	1692-1763
Ramsay, Allan	1686-1758
Ramsay, Andrew Michael	1686-1743
Rapin, Paul De	1661-1725
Raynal, Guillaume	
Thomas Francois	1713-1796
Regnard, Jean Francois	1655-1709
Reid, Thomas	1710-1796
Reimarus, Hermann	
Samuel	1694-1768
Richardson, Samuel	1689-1761
Robertson, William	1721-1793
Rollin, Charles	1661-1741
Rousseau, Jean Baptiste	1671-1741
Rousseau, Jean Jacques	1712-1778
Rowe, Nicholas	1674-1718
Rymer, Thomas	1641-1713

Saint Evremond, Charles Marquetul de Saint Denis Seigneur de	1610-1703
Saint-Lambert, Jean Francois De	1716-1803
Saint-Pierre, Charles Irenee Castel	1658-1743
Saint-Simon, Louis De Rouvroy	1675-1755
Savage, Richard	1697-1743
Sedaine, Michel Jean	1719-1797
Sedley, Sir Charles	1639-1701
Semler, Johann Salomo	1725-1791
Settle, Elkanan	1648-1724
Sewall, Samuel	1672-1730
Shaftesbury, Anthony Ashley Cooper, 3rd Earl of	1671-1713
Shenstone, William	1714-1763
Sheridan, Thomas	1719-1788
Sherlock, William	1641-1707
Silva, Antonio Jose Da	1705-1739
Smart, Christopher	1722-1771
Smith, Adam	1723-1790
Smollet, Tobias George	1721-1771
Somerville, William	1675-1742
Southerne, Thomas	1660-1746
Speke, Hugh	1656-1724
Spence, Joseph	1699-1768
Staal, Marguerite Jeanne Cordier De Launay	1684-1750
Steele, Sir Richard	1672-1729
Sterne, Laurence	1713-1768
Stillingfleet, Benjamin	1702-1771
Strype, John	1643-1737
Swedenborg, Emanuel	1688-1772
Swift, Jonathan	1676-1745
Tate, Nahum	1652-1715
Tencin, Claudine Alexandrine Guerin De	1681-1749
Theobald, Lewis	1688-1744
Tickell, Thomas	1686-1740
Tindal, Matthew	1656-1733
Thomasius, Christian	1655-1728
Thomson, James	1700-1748
Torres Y Villaroel, Diego De	1696-1759
Uz, Johann Peter	1720-1796
Vanbrugh, Sir John	1664-1726
Vilo, Giovanni Battista	1668-1744
Voltaire, Francois Marie Arouet De	1694-1778
Walpole, Horace	1717-1797
Warton, Joseph	1722-1800
Watts, Isaak	1674-1748
Wesley, John	1703-1791
White, Gilbert	1720-1793
Whitehead, Paul	1710-1774
Whitehead, William	1715-1785
Wigglesworth, Michael	1631-1705
Winchelsea, Anne Finch	1661-1720
Wodrow, Robert	1679-1734
Wolff, Christian	1679-1754
Wollaston, William	1659-1724
Wyncherley, William	1640-1716
Young, Edward	1638-1765
Zinzendorf, Nicolaus Ludwig, Graf von	1700-1760

ARTISTS

Allou, Gilles	1670-1751
Archer, Thomas	1668-1743
Backhuysen, Ludolf	1631-1708
Batoni, Pompeo Grolamo	1708-1787
Blondel, Jacques Francois	1705-1774
Bouchardon, Edme	1698-1762
Boucher, Francois	1703-1770
Boulle, Andre Charles (cabinet maker)	1642-1732
Boydell, John	1719-1804
Bredael, Jan Frans Van	1683-1750
Briseux, Charles Etienne	1680-1754
Brown, Lancelot ("Capability") (landscape gardener)	1715-1783
Burlington, Richard Boyle, 3rd Earl of	1695-1753
Caffieri, Jacques	1678-1755
Camus De Mezieres, Nicolas Le	1721-1789
Canaletto	1697-1768
Canaletto, Bernardo Beleto	1720-1780
Carriera, Rosalba	1675-1757
Cassana, Niccolo	1659-1714
Chardin, Jean Baptiste Simeon	1699-1779
Chippendale, Thomas (cabinet maker)	1718-1779
Churriguera, Don Josi	1650-1725
Cignani, Carlo	1628-1719
Closterman, John	1656-1713
Coustou, Guillaume I	1678-1746
Coustou, Guillaume II	1716-1777
Coustou, Nicolas	1658-1733
Coypel, Antoine	1661-1722
Coypel, Charles Antoine	1694-1752
Coypel, Noel	1628-1707
Coypel, Noel Nicholas	1692-1734
Coysevoy, Charles Antoine	1640-1720
Crespi, Giuseppi Maria	1665-1747
Cressent, Charles	1685-1768
Cuvilles, Francois De	1698-1767
Dahl, Michael	1656-1743
Dietrich, Christian Wilhelm Ernst	1712-1774
Donner, Raphael Georg	1693-1741

Dusart, Cornelis	1660-1704	Longhi, Petro	1702-1785
Falconet, Ettienne		Magnasco, Alessandro	1667-1749
Maurice	1716-1791	Mansard, Jules, Hardouin	1645-1708
Falens, Karel Van	1683-1733	Maratta, Carlo	1625-1713
Fischer, Johann Bernard	1656-1723	Marot, Daniel	1661-
Flitcroft, Henry	1679-1769	Meissonier, Juste Aurele	1693-1750
Fontana, Carlo	1638-1714	Mena, Pedro De	1693-
Franceschini, Marco		Nash, Richard	1674-1762
Antonio	1648-1729	Nattier, Jean Marc	1685-1766
Gabriel, Jacques Ange	1698-1782	Neumann, Balthasar	1687-1753
Gibbons, Grinling	1648-1721	Palomino De Castro,	
Gibbs, James	1682-1754	Antonio	1653-1726
Gillot, Claude	1673-1722	Pater, Jean Baptiste	
Giordano, Luca	1632-1705	Joseph	1695-1736
Girardon, Francois	1628-1715	Pergolesi, Michael Angelo	1700-
Greuze, Jean Baptiste	1725-1805	Pigalle, Jean Baptiste	1714-1785
Guardi, Francesco	1712-1793	Ramsay, Allan	1713-1784
Hawksmoor, Nicholas	1661-1736	Reynolds, Sir Joshua	1723-1792
Heyden, Jan Van Der	1637-1712	Rigaud, Hyacinthe	1659-1743
Highmore, Joseph	1692-1780	Roubillac, Louis Francois	1695-1762
Hobbema, Meyndert	1638-1709	Rysbrack, Michael	1693-1770
Hogarth, William	1697-1764	Sandby, Paul	1725-1809
Houbraken, Arnold	1660-1719	Scheemakers, Pieter	1691-1770
Huchtenburg, John Van	1647-1733	Stradivari, Antonio	1644-1737
Huysmans, Cornelius	1648-1727	(violin maker)	
Huysmans, Jan Baptist	1654-1716	Soufflot, Jacques Germain	1709-1780
Huysum, Jan Van	1682-1749	Stuart, James	1713-1788
Janssens, Victor Honorius	1658-1736	Subleyras, Pierre	1699-1749
Jouvenet, Jean	1644-1717	Thornhill, Sir James	1676-1734
Kent, William	1685-1748	Tiepolo, Giovanni Battista	1692-1769
Kneller, Sir Godfrey	1648-1723	Vanbrugh, Sir John	1664-1726
Lafosse, Charles De	1640-1716	Van Der Velde, Willem	
Laguerre, Louis	1663-1721	the younger	1633-1707
La Grenee, Jean Louis		Van Goyen, Jan Josephzoon	1696-1756
Francois	1724-1805	Van Loo, Charles Andre	1705-1765
Lancret, Nicolas	1690-1743	Van Loo, Jean Baptiste	1684-1745
Largilliere, Nicolas	1656-1746	Vernet, Claude Joseph	1714-1789
La Tour, Maurice		Verrio, Antonio	1639-1707
Quentin De	1704-1788	Watteau, Antoine	1684-1721
Legros, Pierre	1656-1719	Wilson, Richard	1714-1782
Lemoine, Francois	1688-1737	Wood, John	1705-1754
Lemoyne, Jean Baptiste	1704-1778	Wren, Sir Christopher	1632-1723
Limborch, Hendrick Van	1680-1758	Zuccarelli, Francesco	1702-1788
Liotard, Jean Etienne	1702-1789		

COMPOSERS

Alberti, Domenico	1710-1740	Bononcini, Giovanni	
Albinoni, Tommaso	1674-1745	Battista	1670-1755
Arne, Thomas Augustine	1710-1778	Bononcini, Marc Antonio	1675-1726
Astorga, Emanuele		Boyce, William	1710-1779
Gioacchino	1680-1755	Caldara, Antonio	1670-1736
Bach Johann Sebastian	1685-1750	Campra, Anore	1660-1744
Bach, Karl Philipp		Clari, Giovanni Carlo	
Emanuel	1714-1788	Maria	1669-1745
Bach, Wilhelm Friedmann	1710-1784	Clarke, Jeremiah	1659-1707
Barsanti, Francesco	1690-1775	Corelli, Arcangelo	1653-1713
Benda, Georg	1722-1795	Croft, William	1678-1727
Blow, John	1648-1708	Couperin, Francois	1668-1733
		Daquin, Louis Claude	1694-1772

Durante, Francesco	1684-1755	Mattheson, Johann	1681-1764
Eberlin, Johann Ernst	1702-1762	Nardini, Pietro	1722-1793
Fasch, Johann Friedrich	1688-1758	Nares, James	1715-1783
Finger, Godfrey	1685-1717	Pachebel, Johan	1653-1706
Galuppi, Baldassare	1706-1785	Pergolesi, Giovanni	
Garth, Sir Samuel	1661-1719	Battista	1710-1736
Gluck, Christoph Willibald	1714-1787	Porpora, Niccola Antonio	1686-1767
Graun, Karl Heinrich	1701-1759	Quantz, Johann Joachim	1697-1773
Greene, Maurice	1695-1755	Rameau, Jean	1683-1764
Handel, George Frederick	1685-1759	Roman, Johan Helmich	1694-1758
Hasse, Johann Adolph	1699-1783	Scarlatti, Alessandro	1659-1725
Heinichen, Johann David	1683-1729	Scarlatti, Guiseppe	
Innes, Thomas	1663-1744	Domenico	1685-1757
Jommelli, Niccolo	1714-1774	Schobert, Johann	1720-1767
Keiser, Reinhold	1673-1739	Stamitz, Johann	1717-1757
Leclair, Jean Marie	1697-1764	Stanley, John	1713-1786
Leo, Leonardo	1694-1744	Steffan, Agostino	1653-1728
Logroscino, Nicola	1700-1763	Tartini, Giuseppe	1692-1770
Lotti, Antonio	1667-1740	Telemann, George Philipp	1681-1767
Marcello, Benedetto	1686-1739	Vivaldi, Antonio	1678-1741

1729   Peace between Britain, France and Spain.
1734   Siege of Dantzig.
1738   Lorraine ceded to France.
1739   England goes to war with Spain.
1742   France declares war against Maria Theresa of Austria, England and Holland.
1745   Battle of Fontenoy.
          Battle of Prestonpans.
1746   Battle of Falkirk.
          Battle of Culloden.
1748   Peace concluded at Aix la Chapelle.

PROMINENT PEOPLE

Clive, Lord Robert	1725-1774	Newton, Sir Isaac	1642-1727
Cook, Captain James	1728-1770	Turpin, Dick	1705-1739
Fahrenheit, Gabrielle		Wilkes, John	1727-1797
Daniel	1686-1736	Wolfe, General James	1727-1759
Hastings, Warren	1732-1818		

EMPERORS OF CHINA (MANCHU (Ch'ing) DYNASTY)

Yung Cheng	1723-1735	Kao Tsung	1735-1795

POPES

Benedict XIII	1724-1730	Benedict XIV	1740-1758
Clement XII	1730-1740		

FRANCE. HEADS OF STATE

Louis XV	1715-1774

HOLY ROMAN EMPERORS

Charles VI	1711-1740	Francis I of Lorraine	1745-1765
Charles VII of Bavaria	1742-1745		

ENGLAND. SOVEREIGNS

George I	1714-1727	George II	1727-1760

SWEDEN. KINGS

Frederick I	1720-1751

PORTUGAL. KINGS

John V	1706-1750	Joseph	1750-1777

PRUSSIA. KINGS

Frederick William I	1713-1740	Frederick II	1740-1786

RUSSIA. TSARS

Catherine I	1725-1727	Ivan VI	1740-1741
Peter II	1727-1730	Elizabeth	1741-1762
Anne	1730-1740		

WRITERS

Abauzit, Firmin	1679-1767	Bickerstaffe, Isaac	1735-1812
Abel, Karl Friedrich	1725-1787	Bilfinger, George Bernhard	1693-1750
Adam, Alexander	1741-1809	Birch, Thomas	1705-1766
Adam, Jean	1710-1765	Blacklock, Thomas	1721-1791
Adams, John	1735-1826	Blackmore, Sir Richard	1650-1729
Adanson, Michel	1727-1806	Blair, Robert	1699-1746
Aepinus, Franz Ulrich		Blamire, Susanna	1747-1794
Theodor	1724-1802	Blomefield, Francis	1705-1752
Aguesseau, Henri		Boccage, Marie Anne	
Francois d'	1668-1751	Fiquet De	1710-1802
Aikin, John	1747-1822	Bodmer, Johann Jakob	1698-1783
Ainsworth, Robert	1660-1743	Boie, Heinrich Christian	1744-1806
Akenside, Mark	1721-1770	Bolingbroke, Henry	
Alembert, Jean Le		St. John	1678-1751
Rond D'	1717-1783	Bolyai, Wolfgang	1775-1856
Alfireri, Vittorio, Count	1749-1803	Bonstetten, Charles	
Algarotti, Francesco,		Victor De	1745-1832
Count	1712-1764	Boston, Thomas	1677-1732
Ames, Joseph	1689-1759	Boswell, James	1740-1795
Amhurst, Nicholas	1697-1742	Brady, Nicholas	1659-1726
Amory, Thomas	1691-1788	Brockes, Barthold Heinrich	1680-1747
Anderson, John	1726-1796	Brooke, Henry	1703-1783
Anderson, Robert	1750-1830	Brorson, Hans Adolf	1694-1764
Andrews, James Pettit	1737-1797	Brosses, Charles de	1709-1777
Anquetil, Louis Pierre	1723-1808	Brown, John	1715-1766
Anspach, Elizabeth,		Browne, Isaac Hawkins	1705-1760
Margravine of	1750-1828	Bruce, Micheal	1746-1767
Anstey, Christopher	1724-1805	Brucker, Johann Jakob	1696-1770
Arbuthnot, John	1667-1735	Bryant, Jacob	1715-1804
Archenholz, Johann		Buonafede, Appiano	1716-1793
Wilhelm Von	1743-1812	Burger, Gottfried August	1747-1794
Argens, Jean Baptiste		Burke, Edmund	1729-1797
De Boyer, Marquis D'	1704-1771	Byrd, William	1674-1744
Armstrong, John	1709-1779	Byrom, John	1692-1763
Asgill, John	1659-1738	Cadalso, Vasquez Jose	1741-1782
Astell, Mary	1668-1731	Cambridge, Richard	
Atterbury, Francis	1663-1732	Owen	1717-1802
Bachaumont, Louis		Canizares, Jose De	1676-1750
Petit De	1690-1771	Carey, Henry	1690-1743
Baillie, Lady Grizel	1665-1746	Carte, Thomas	1686-1754
Barbauld, Anna Letitia	1743-1825	Carter, Elizabeth	1717-1806
Barnard, Lady Anne	1750-1825	Casanova De Seingalt,	
Barthelemy, Jean-Jacques	1716-1795	Giovanni Jacopo	1725-1798
Baumgarten, Alexander		Casti, Giovanni Battista	1724-1803
Gottlieb	1714-1762	Cazotte, Jacques	1719-1792
Beattie, James	1735-1803	Cerutti, Giuseppe	1728-1792
Beaumarchais, Pierre		Cesarotti, Melchiore	1730-1808
Augustin Caron De	1732-1799	Challoner, Richard	1697-1781
Beccaria, Cesare		Chamfort, Sebastien Roch	
Marchese De	1738-1794	Nicolas	1741-1794
Bekker, Elizabeth	1738-1804	Chapone, Hester	1727-1801
Bellman, Karl Mikael	1740-1795	Charriere, Isabelle De	1740-1805
Belloy, Dormont De	1727-1775	Churchill, Charles	1731-1764
Bentham, Jeremy	1748-1832	Cibber, Colley	1671-1757
Bentley	1662-1742	Cibber, Theophilus	1703-1758
Berkeley, George	1685-1753	Clarke, Samuel	1675-1729

Claudius, Matthias	1740-1815
Clement, Francois	1714-1793
Cockburn, Alicia	1713-1794
Colden, Cadwallader	1688-1776
Coleman, George	1732-1794
Collé, Charles	1709-1783
Collier, Arthur	1680-1732
Collier, John	1708-1786
Collins, William	1721-1759
Colman, George the Elder	1732-1794
Combe, William	1741-1823
Condorcet, Marie Jean Antoine, Marquis De	1743-1794
Condillac, Etienne Bonnot De	1715-1780
Congreve, William	1670-1729
Cooke, Thomas	1703-1756
Correa, Garcao, Pedro Antonio Joaquim	1724-1772
Cowley, Hannah	1743-1809
Cowper, William	1731-1800
Coxe, William	1747-1828
Crauford, Quintin	1743-1819
Crebillon, Prosper Jolyot De	1674-1762
Crescimbeni, Giovanni Mario	1663-1728
Crousaz, Jean Pierre	1663-1748
Cruden, Alexander	1701-1770
Crusius, Christian August	1715-1775
Cruz E Silva, Antonio Diniz Da	1731-1799
Cruz, Raymon De La	1731-1794
Cumberland, Richard	1732-1811
Dalin, Olof Von	1708-1763
Daniel, Gabriel	1649-1728
Da Ponté, Lorenzo	1749-1838
Darwin, Erasmus	1731-1802
Dashkova, Catherina Romanovna	1744-1810
Day, Thomas	1748-1789
Defoe, Daniel	1659-1731
Delille, Jacques	1738-1813
Delolme, Jean Louis	1740-1806
Denina, Carlo Giovanni Maria	1731-1813
Dennis, John	1657-1734
Denis, Michael	1729-1800
Derzhavin, Gavrila Romanovich	1743-1816
Desforges, Pierre Jean Baptiste Choudard	1746-1806
Destouches, Phillipe	1680-1754
Diderot, Denis	1713-1784
Diniz Da Cruz E Silva, Antonio	1731-1799
Dodsley, Robert	1703-1764
Dorat, Claude Joseph	1743-1780
Ducis, Jean Francois	1733-1816
Dupuis, Charles Francois	1742-1809
Durao, Jose De Santa Rita	1737-1784
Dutens, Louis	1730-1812
Dyer, John	1699-1757
Eberhard, Johann Augustus	1739-1809
Edgeworth, Richard Lovell	1744-1817
Edwards, Bryan	1743-1800
Edwards, Jonathan	1703-1758
Ekhof, Konrad	1720-1778
Elliot, Jean	1727-1805
Engel, Johann Jakob	1741-1802
Epinay, Louise Florence Petronille Tardieu d'esclavelles D'	1726-1783
Erskine, Henry	1746-1817
Eschenburg, Johann Joachim	1743-1820
Eusden, Laurence	1688-1730
Ewald, Johannes	1743-1781
Fabroni, Angelo	1732-1803
Falconer, William	1732-1769
Farvart, Charles Simon	1710-1792
Fawkes, Francis	1720-1777
Fenton, Elijah	1683-1730
Ferguson, Adam	1723-1816
Fergusson, Robert	1750-1774
Fielding, Henry	1707-1754
Folard, Jean Charles	1669-1752
Fontenelle, Bernard Le Bovier De	1657-1757
Fortiguera, Niccolo	1674-1735
Foote, Samuel	1720-1777
Francois De Neufchateau, Nicolas Louis	1750-1828
Franklin, Benjamin	1706-1790
Frugoni, Carlo Innocenzo Maria	1692-1768
Garat, Dominique Joseph	1749-1833
Garcia De La Huerta, Vincente Antonio	1734-1787
Gay, John	1685-1732
Gellert, Christian Furchtegott	1715-1769
Genlis, Stephanie Felicite Ducrest De St. Aubin	1746-1830
Genovesi, Antonio	1712-1769
Gerard, Alexander	1728-1795
Gerstenberg, Heinrich Wilhelm Von	1737-1823
Giannone, Pietro	1676-1748
Gibbon, Edward	1737-1794
Gillies, John	1747-1836
Ginguenne, Pierre Louis	1748-1815
Gleim, Johann Wilhelm Ludwig	1719-1803
Glover, Richard	1712-1785
Goethe, Johann Wolfgang Von	1749-1832
Goldoni, Carlo	1707-1793
Goldsmith, Oliver	1728-1774
Gottsched, Johann Christoph	1700-1766

Gotter, Friedrich Wilhelm	1746-1797
Gotz, Johann Nikolaus	1721-1781
Gozzi, Carlo	1720-1806
Graves, Richard	1715-1804
Gray, Thomas	1716-1771
Green, Matthew	1696-1737
Gresset, Jean Baptiste Louis	1709-1777
Grimm, Friedrich Melchior	1723-1807
Hagedorn, Friedrich Von	1708-1754
Hamann, Johann Georg	1730-1788
Hamilton, William	1704-1754
Hanbury, Williams, Sir Charles	1708-1759
Hartley, David	1705-1757
Hasted, Edward	1732-1812
Hawkesworth, John	1715-1773
Hawkins, Sir John	1719-1789
Hayley, William	1745-1820
Haywood, Eliza	1693-1756
Hearne, Thomas	1678-1735
Heinse, Johann, Jakob Wilhelm	1749-1803
Helvetius, Claude Adrien	1715-1771
Hemstehuis, Francois	1721-1790
Henault, Charles Jean Francois	1685-1770
Herder, Johann Gottfried Von	1744-1803
Hervey of Ickworth, John Hervey	1696-1743
Hill, Aaron	1685-1750
Hill, John	1716-1775
Hippel, Theodor Gottlieb Von	1741-1796
Holbach, Paul Heinrich Dietrich	1723-1789
Holberg, Ludvig Holberg	1684-1754
Holcroft, Thomas	1745-1809
Holland, Henry	1746-1806
Holty, Ludwig Heinrich Cristoph	1748-1776
Home, John	1722-1808
Hontheim, Johann Nikolaus Von	1701-1790
Hook, James	1746-1827
Hopkinson, Francis	1737-1791
Huerta, Vincente Garcia de la	1730-1787
Hume, David	1711-1776
Hurd, Richard	1720-1808
Hutcheson, Francis	1694-1746
Iriarte, Tomas De	1750-1791
Isla, Jose Francisco De	1703-1781
Jacobi, Friedrich Heinrich	1743-1819
Jacobi, Johann Georg	1740-1814
Jefferson, Thomas	1743-1826
Jenyns, Soame	1704-1787
Jephson, Robert	1736-1803
Johnson, Samuel	1709-1784

Jovellanos, Gaspar Melchor De	1744-1811
Kames, Henry Home	1696-1782
Kant, Immanuel	1724-1804
Kelly, Hugh	1739-1777
King, Thomas	1730-1805
Kleist, Ewald Christian Von	1715-1759
Klopstock, Friedrich Gottlieb	1724-1803
Knebel, Karl Ludwig Von	1744-1834
La Chaussee, Pierre Claude Nivelle De	1692-1754
Laclos, Pierre Amboise Francois	1741-1803
Lagrange-Chancel, Francois Joseph	1677-1758
Lamarck, Jean Chevalier de	1744-1829
Lamettrie, Julien Offray De	1709-1751
La Motte, Antoine Houdar De	1672-1731
Langhorne, John	1735-1779
Lavater, Johann Kaspar	1741-1801
Law, William	1686-1761
Lee, Sophia	1750-1824
Lemierre, Antoine Marin	1733-1793
Lennox, Charlotte	1720-1804
Le Sage, Alain Rene	1668-1747
Lespinasse, Julie De	1732-1776
Lessing, Gotthold Ephraim	1729-1781
Lichtenberg, Georg Christoph	1742-1799
Ligne, Charles Joseph	1735-1814
Lillo, George	1693-1739
Linnaeus, Carl	1707-1778
Lockhart, George	1673-1731
Logan, John	1748-1788
Lomonosov, Mikhail Vasilievich	1711-1765
Luzan Claramunt, De Suelves Y Gurrea Ignacio	1702-1754
Luzzatto, Moses Hayim	1707-1747
Lyttelton, George, 1st Baron	1709-1773
Mably, Gabriel Bennet De	1709-1785
Mackenzie, Henry	1745-1831
Macklin, Charles	1697-1797
Macpherson, James	1736-1796
Madan, Martin	1726-1790
Maffei, Francesco Scipione	1675-1755
Magnusson, Arni	1663-1730
Mallet, David	1705-1765
Mandeville, Bernard De	1670-1733
Marais, Marin	1656-1728
Marivaux, Pierre Carlet De Chamblain De	1688-1763
Marmontel, Jean Francois	1723-1799
Marsigli, Luigi Ferdinando	1658-1730

Masdeu, Juan Francisco De	1744-1817	Raynal, Guillaume Thomas Francois	1713-1796
Mason, William	1725-1797	Reeve, Clara	1729-1807
Mather, Cotton	1663-1728	Reid, Thomas	1710-1796
Mendelsshon, Moses	1729-1786	Reimarus, Hermann Samuel	1694-1768
Mercier, Sebastien	1740-1814		
Merck, Johann Heinrich	1741-1791	Restif, Nicolas Edme	1734-1806
Metastasio	1698-1782	Richardson, Samuel	1689-1761
Michell, John	1724-1793	Robertson, William	1721-1793
Mickle, William Julius	1735-1788	Rollin, Charles	1661-1741
Mirabeau, Victor Riqueti	1715-1789	Rousseau, Jean Baptiste	1671-1741
Mitford, William	1744-1827	Rousseau, Jean Jacques	1712-1778
Montagu, Elizabeth	1720-1800	Rulhiere, Claude Carloman De	1735-1791
Montagu, Lady Mary Wortley	1689-1762		
Montesquieu, Charles Louis De Secondat	1689-1755	Sade, Donatien Alphonse Francois, Marquis De	1740-1814
		Saint-Lambert, Jean Francois De	1716-1803
Moore, Edward	1712-1757		
Moore, John	1729-1802	Saint-Martin, Louis Claude De	1743-1803
More, Hannah	1745-1833		
Morellet, Andre	1727-1819	Saint-Pierre, Bernardin De	1737-1814
Muller, Friedrich	1749-1825	Saint-Pierre, Charles Irenee Castel	1658-1743
Muratori, Ludovico Antonio	1672-1750		
Murphy, Arthur	1727-1805	Saint-Simon, Louis De Rouvroy	1675-1755
Musaus, Johann Karl August	1735-1787	Salomon, Johann Peter	1745-1815
		Savage, Richard	1697-1743
Nascimento, Francisco Manoel De	1734-1819	Schlozer, August Ludwig Von	1735-1809
Neal, Daniel	1678-1743	Schubart, Christian Friedrich Daniel	1739-1791
Newton, Sir Isaac	1642-1727		
Nichols, John	1745-1826	Sedaine, Michel Jean	1719-1797
Nicolai, Christoph Friedrich	1733-1811	Semler, Johann Salomo	1725-1791
		Senac De Meilhan, Gabriel	1736-1803
North, Roger	1653-1734	Sewall, Samuel	1652-1730
O'Carolan, Turlogh	1670-1738	Seward, Anna	1747-1809
Oldmixon, John	1673-1742	Shenstone, William	1714-1763
Orme, Robert	1728-1801	Sheridan, Thomas	1719-1788
Orrery, Charles Boyle	1676-1731	Silva, Antonio Jose Da	1705-1739
Paine, Thomas	1737-1809	Smart, Christopher	1722-1771
Paley, William	1743-1805	Smith, Adam	1723-1790
Paltock, Robert	1697-1767	Smith, Charlotte	1749-1806
Parini, Giuseppe	1729-1799	Smith, John Stafford	1750-1836
Pepusch, Johann Christoph	1667-1752	Smollett, Tobias George	1721-1771
Percy, Thomas	1729-1811	Somervile, William	1675-1742
Philips, Ambrose	1675-1749	Southerne, Thomas	1660-1746
Piozzi, Hester Lynch	1741-1821	Spence, Joseph	1699-1768
Piranesi, Giambattista	1720-1778	Staal, Marguerite Jeanne Cordier De Launay	1684-1750
Piron, Alexis	1689-1773		
Pontoppidan, Erik	1698-1764	Steele, Sir Richard	1672-1729
Pope, Alexander	1688-1744	Sterne, Laurence	1713-1768
Prevost, Antoine Francois	1697-1763	Stilling, Heinrich	1740-1817
Price, Richard	1723-1791	Stillingfleet, Benjamin	1702-1771
Priestly, Joseph	1733-1804	Stolberg, Friedrich Leopold	1750-1819
Prior, Matthew	1664-1721		
Proud, Robert	1728-1813	Struensee, Johan Frederick	1737-1772
Pye, Henry James	1745-1813	Strutt, Joseph	1742-1802
Racine, Louis	1692-1763	Strype, John	1643-1737
Ramsay, Allan	1686-1758	Swedenborg, Emanuel	1688-1772
Ramsay, Andrew Michael	1686-1743	Swift, Jonathan	1676-1745
Raspe, Rudolf Erich	1737-1794		

Tencin, Claudine	
Alexandrine Guerin De	1681-1749
Theobald, Lewis	1688-1744
Thomasius, Christian	1655-1728
Thomson, James	1700-1748
Tickell, Thomas	1686-1740
Tindal, Matthew	1656-1733
Torres Y Villaroel,	
Diego De	1696-1759
Trumbull, John	1750-1831
Uz, Johann Peter	1720-1796
Vanbrugh, Sir John	1664-1726
Vico, Giovanni Battista	1668-1744
Voltaire, Francois Marie	
Arouet De	1694-1778
Walker, John	1732-1807
Walpole, Horace	1717-1797
Warton, Joseph	1722-1800
Warton, Thomas	1728-1790

Washington, George	1732-1799
Watts, Isaac	1674-1748
Wesley, John	1703-1791
West, Benjamin	1738-1820
White, Gilbert	1720-1793
Wieland, Christoph	
Martin	1733-1813
Whitehead, Paul	1710-1774
Whitehead, William	1715-1785
Wodrow, Robert	1679-1734
Wolcot, John	
(Peter Pindar)	1738-1819
Wolff, Christian	1679-1754
Young, Arthur	1741-1820
Young, Edward	1638-1765
Zimmermann, Johan Georg,	
Ritter Van	1728-1795
Zinzendorf, Nicolaus	
Ludwig, Graf von	1700-1760

ARTISTS

Abilgaard, Nicolaj	
Abraham	1744-1809
Adam, James	1730-1794
Adam, Robert	1728-1792
Allan, David	1744-1796
Allou, Gilles	1670-1751
Alvarez, Don Manuel	1727-1797
Archer, Thomas	1668-1743
Bacon, John	1740-1799
Banks, Thomas	1735-1805
Barker, Robert	1739-1806
Barry, James	1741-1806
Bartolozzi, Francesco	1727-1815
Batoni, Pompeo Girolamo	1708-1787
Blondel, Jacques Francois	1705-1774
Bonomi, Giuseppe	1739-1808
Bouchardon, Edme	1698-1762
Boucher, Francois	1703-1770
Boulle, Andre Charles	
(cabinet maker)	1642-1732
Boydell, John	1719-1804
Bredael, Jan Frans Van	1683-1750
Briseux, Charles Etienne	1680-1754
Brown, Lancelot	
("Capability")	
(landscape gardener)	1715-1783
Burlington, Richard Boyle,	
3rd Earl of	1695-1753
Burney, Charles	1726-1814
Caffieri, Jacques	1678-1755
Camus, De Mezieres	
Nicolas Le	1721-1789
Canaletto	1697-1768
Canaletto, Bernardo Belleto	1720-1780
Carriera, Rosalba	1675-1757
Casanova De Seingalt,	
Francesco	1727-1805

Casanova De Seingalt,	
Giovanni Batista	1728-1795
Chambers, Sir William	1726-1796
Chardin, Jean Simeon	1699-1779
Chippendale, Thomas	
(cabinet maker)	1718-1779
Chodowiecki, Daniel	
Nicolas	1726-1801
Cipriani, Giovanni Batista	1727-1785
Cleveland, John	1747-1786
Cleveland, Robert	1747-1809
Copley, John Singleton	1737-1815
Coustou, Guillaume I	1678-1746
Coustou, Guillaume II	1716-1777
Coustou, Nicolas	1658-1733
Cosway, Richard	1742-1821
Coypel, Charles Antoine	1694-1752
Coypel, Noel Nicholas	1692-1734
Crespi, Giuseppi Maria	1665-1747
Cressent, Charles	1685-1768
Cuvilles, Francois De	1698-1767
Dahl, Michael	1656-1743
Damer, Anne Seymour	1749-1828
Dance, George	1741-1825
Daniell, Thomas	1749-1840
David, Jacques Louis	1748-1825
De Loutherbourg, Philip	
James	1740-1812
Denon, Dominique Vivant	1747-1825
Dietrich, Christian	
Wilhelm Ernts	1712-1774
Donner, Raphael Georg	1693-1741
Downman, John	1750-1824
Doyen, Gabriel Francois	1726-1806
Earlom, Richard	1743-1822
Falconet, Ettienne Maurice	1716-1791
Falens, Karel Van	1683-1733
Farington, Joseph	1747-1821

Fiorillo, Johann Dominicus	1748-1821
Flitcroft, Henry	1679-1769
Fragonard, Jean Honore	1732-1806
Franceschini, Marco	
Antonio	1648-1729
Fuseli, Henry	1741-1835
Gabriel, Jacques Ange	1698-1782
Gainsborough, Thomas	1727-1788
Gessner, Salomon	1730-1788
Gibbs, James	1682-1754
Goya Y Lucientes,	
Francisco	1746-1828
Greuze, Jean Baptiste	1725-1805
Guardi, Francesco	1712-1793
Hawksmoor, Nicholas	1661-1736
Highmore, Joseph	1692-1780
Hogarth, William	1697-1764
Houdon, Jean Antoine	1740-1828
Huchtenburg, John Van	1647-1733
Humphrey, Ozias	1742-1810
Huysmans, Cornelius	1648-1727
Huysum, Jan Van	1682-1749
Janssens, Victor Honorius	1658-1736
Kauffmann, Angelica	1741-1807
Kent, William	1685-1748
La Grenee, Jean Louis	
Francois	1724-1805
Lancret, Nicolas	1690-1743
Largilliere, Nicolas	1656-1746
La Tour, Maurice	
Quentin De	1704-1788
Lemoine, Francois	1688-1737
Lemoyne, Jean Baptiste	1704-1778
Limborch, Hendrick Van	1680-1758
Liotard, Jean Etienne	1702-1789
Longhi, Pietro	1702-1785
Magnasco, Alessandro	1667-1749
Meissonier, Juste Aurele	1693-1750
Mena, Pedro de	1693-
Mengs, Antony Raphael	1728-1779
Michel, Claude	1738-1814
Nash, Richard	1674-1762
Nattier, Jean Marc	1685-1766
Neumann, Balthazar	1687-1753
Nollekens, Joseph	1737-1823

Northcote, James	1746-1831
Pajou, Augustin	1730-1809
Palomino Decastro,	
Antonio	1653-1726
Pater, Jean Baptiste	
Joseph	1695-1736
Peale, Charles Willson	1741-1827
Pergolesi, Michael Angelo	1700-1736
Pigalle, Jean Baptiste	1714-1785
Pine, Robert Edge	1730-1788
Ramsay, Allan	1713-1784
Reynolds, Sir Joshua	1723-1792
Rigaud, Hyacinthe	1659-1743
Robert, Hubert	1733-1808
Romney, George	1734-1802
Rousseau, De La Rottiere	
Jean Simeon	1747-
Roubillac, Louis Francois	1695-1762
Rysbrack, Michael	1693-1770
Sandby, Paul	1725-1809
Scheemakers, Pieter	1691-1770
Smart, John	1740-1811
Soufflot, Jacques Germain	1709-1780
Stradivari, Antonio	
(violin maker)	1644-1737
Stuart, James	1713-1788
Subleyras, Pierre	1699-1749
Thornhill, Sir James	1676-1734
Tiepolo, Giovanni Battista	1692-1769
Towne, Francis	1739-1816
Vanbrugh, Sir John	1664-1726
Van Goyen, Jan	
Josephzoon	1696-1756
Van Loo, Charles Andrew	1705-1765
Van Loo, Jean Baptiste	1684-1745
Vernet, Claude Joseph	1714-1789
Wedgewood, Josiah	
(potter)	1730-1795
Wilson, Richard	1714-1782
Wood, John	1705-1754
Wright, Joseph	1734-1797
Wyatt, James	1746-1813
Zuccarelli, Francesco	1702-1788
Zoffany, Johann	1733-1810
Zucchi, Antonio Pietro	1726-1795

COMPOSERS

Albrechtberger, Johann	
Gregory	1736-1809
Alberti, Domenico	1710-1740
Albinoni, Tommaso	1674-1745
Arne, Thomas Augustine	1710-1778
Arnold, Samuel	1740-1802
Astorga, Emanuele	
Giocchino	1680-1755
Avison, Charles	1710-1770
Bach, Johann Christian	1735-1782
Bach, Johann Sebastian	1685-1750
Bach, Wilhelm Friedmann	1710-1784

Bach, Karl Philip	
Emanuel	1714-1788
Barsanti, Francesco	1690-1775
Batishill, Jonathan	1738-1801
Benda, Georg	1722-1795
Boccherini, Luigi	1743-1805
Bononcini, Giovanni	
Battista	1670-1755
Boyce, William	1710-1779
Caldara, Antonio	1670-1736
Cambini, Giovanni	
Giuseppe	1746-1825

Campra, Anore	1660-1744	Leo, Leonardo	1694-1744
Cannabich, Christian	1731-1798	Linley, Thomas	1732-1795
Cimarosa, Domenico	1749-1801	Logroscino, Nicola	1700-1763
Clari, Giovanni Carlo		Lotti, Antonio	1667-1740
Maria	1669-1745	Lucchesi, Andrea	1741-1800
Corri, Domenico	1746-1825	Marcello, Benedetto	1686-1739
Couperin, Francois	1668-1733	Mattheson, Johann	1681-1764
Croft, William	1678-1727	Monsigny, Pierre	
Daquin, Louis Claude	1694-1772	Alexandre	1729-1817
Dibdin, Charles	1745-1814	Nardini, Pietro	1722-1793
Dittersdorf, Karl		Nares, James	1715-1783
Ditters Von	1739-1799	Paisiello, Giovanni	1741-1816
Durante, Francesco	1684-1755	Pergolesi, Giovanni	
Eberlin, Johann Ernst	1702-1762	Battista	1710-1736
Fasch, Friedrich	1688-1758	Philidor, Francois Andre	
Galuppi, Baldassare	1706-1785	Danican	1726-1795
Gazzaniga, Giuseppe	1743-1818	Piccinni, Niccola	1728-1800
Giordani, Giuseppe	1744-1798	Porpora, Niccola Antonio	1686-1767
Gluck, Christoph		Quantz, Johann Joachim	1697-1773
Willibald	1714-1787	Rameau, Jean Phillipe	1683-1764
Gossec, Francois Joseph	1734-1829	Roman, Johan Helmich	1694-1758
Gow, Niel	1727-1807	Sacchini, Antonio Maria	
Graun, Karl Heinrich	1701-1759	Gaspare	1734-1786
Greene, Maurice	1695-1755	Salieri, Antonio	1750-1825
Gretry, Andre Ernest		Sarti, Giuseppe	1729-1802
Modeste	1741-1813	Scarlatti, Guiseppe	
Handel, George Frederick	1685-1759	Domenico	1685-1757
Hasse, Johann Adolph	1699-1783	Schobert, Johann	1720-1767
Haydn, Franz Joseph	1732-1809	Shield, William	1748-1829
Haydn, Michael	1737-1806	Stamitz, Carl Philipp	1745-1801
Heinichen, Johann David	1683-1729	Stamitz, Johann	1717-1757
Hiller, Johann Adam	1728-1804	Stanley, John	1713-1786
Innes, Thomas	1663-1744	Tartini, Giuseppe	1692-1770
Jommelli, Niccolo	1714-1774	Telemann, Georg Philipp	1681-1767
Jackson, Wilhelm	1730-1803	Vivaldi, Antonio	1678-1741
Keiser, Reinhold	1673-1739	Vogler, George Joseph	1749-1814
Leclair, Jean Marie	1697-1764		

1752   Great Britain adopts new style calendar.
1755   Lisbon earthquake.
       Etna erupts.
1756   Great Britain declares war against France.
       Seven Years' War begins.
       Black Hole of Calcutta atrocity.
1759   Battle of Minden.
       Battle of Quebec.
1762   Great Britain declares war against Spain.
1763   Treaty of Peace between Great Britain, France, Spain and Portugal.
1770   Discovery of New South Wales.
1772   Treaty for partition of Poland between Austria, Prussia and Russia.
1773   Boston tea party.
1775   Battle of Lexington.
       Battle of Bunker's Hill.

PROMINENT PEOPLE

Clive, Robert, Lord	1725-1774	Marat, Jean Paul	1743-1793
Cook, Captain James	1728-1770	Marie Antoinette	1755-1793
Danton, Georges Jacques	1759-1794	Mirabeau, Gabriel,	
Hastings, Warren	1732-1818	Comte de	1749-1791
Hood, Samuel, Admiral,		Nelson, Horatio ,Viscount	1758-1805
1st Viscount	1724-1816	Wellington, Duke of	1769-1852
Jenner, Edward	1749-1823	Wilkes, John	1727-1797
Josephine, Empress	1763-1814	Wolfe, General James	1727-1759

EMPERORS OF CHINA (MANCHU (Ch'ing) DYNASTY)
Kao Tsung   1735-1795

POPES

Benedict XIV	1740-1758	Clement XIV	1769-1774
Clement XIII	1758-1769	Pius VI	1775-1799

FRANCE. HEADS OF STATE
Louis XV   1715-1774   Louis XVI   1774-1793

HOLY ROMAN EMPERORS
Francis I of Lorraine   1745-1765   Joseph II   1765-1790

ENGLAND. SOVEREIGNS
George II   1727-1760   George III   1760-1820

SWEDEN. KINGS
Frederick I   1720-1751   Gustavius III   1771-1792
Adolphus Frederick   1751-1771

PORTUGAL. KINGS
Joseph   1750-1777

PRUSSIA. KINGS
Frederick II   1740-1786

Elizabeth	1741-1762	Catherine the Great II	1762-1796
Peter III	1762-		

SPAIN. SOVEREIGNS

Ferdinand VI	1746-1759	Charles III	1759-1788

WRITERS

Abauzit, Firmin	1679-1767	Barrington, George	
Abel, Karl Friedrich	1725-1787	(Waldren)	1755-1804
Abernethy, John	1764-1831	Barthelemy, Jean-Jacques	1716-1795
Adam, Alexander	1741-1809	Baumgarten, Alexander	
Adam, Jean	1710-1765	Gottlieb	1714-1762
Adams, Hannah	1755-1831	Beattie, James	1735-1803
Adams, John	1735-1826	Beauchamp, Alphonse De	1767-1832
Adams, John Quincy	1767-1848	Beaumarchais, Pierre	
Adanson, Michel	1725-1806	Augustin Caron De	1732-1799
Aepinus, Franz Ulrich		Beaumont, Sir George	
Theodor	1724-1802	Howland	1753-1827
Adolphus, John	1768-1845	Beccaria, Cesare,	
Aikin, John	1747-1822	Marchese De	1738-1794
Akenside, Mark	1721-1770	Beck, Christian Daniel	1757-1832
Alembert, Jean Le		Beck, Jakob Sigismund	1761-1840
Rond D'	1717-1783	Beckford, William	1760-1844
Alfireri, Vittorio, Count	1749-1803	Beechey, Sir William	1753-1839
Algarotti, Francesco,		Beffroy De Reigny, Louis	
Count	1712-1764	Abel	1757-1811
Ames, Joseph	1689-1759	Bekker, Elizabeth	1738-1804
Amory, Thomas	1691-1788	Bellman, Karl Mikael	1740-1795
Ancillon, Johann Peter		Belloy, Dormont De	1727-1775
Friedrich	1766-1836	Bentham, Jeremy	1748-1832
Anderson, John	1726-1796	Berkeley, George	1685-1753
Anderson, Robert	1750-1830	Berry, Mary	1763-1852
Andrews, James Pettit	1737-1797	Bickerstaffe, Isaac	1735-1812
Andrieux, Francois		Bignon, Louis Pierre	
Guillaume Jean		Edouard	1771-1841
Stanislas	1759-1833	Bilderijk, Willem	1756-1831
Anquetil, Louis Pierre	1723-1808	Birch, Thomas	1705-1766
Anstey, Christopher	1724-1805	Blacklock, Thomas	1721-1791
Archenholz, Johann		Blake, William	1757-1827
Wilhelm Von	1743-1812	Blamire, Susanna	1747-1794
Argens, Jean Baptiste de		Blomefield, Francis	1705-1752
Boyer, Marquis d'	1704-1771	Bloomfield, Robert	1766-1823
Armstrong, John	1709-1779	Bocage, Manvel Maria	
Arnault, Antoine Vincent	1766-1834	Barbosa De	1765-1805
Arndt, Ernst Moritz	1769-1860	Boccage, Marie Anne	
Anspach, Elizabeth		Fiquet De	1710-1802
Maravine of	1750-1828	Bodmer, Johann Jakob	1698-1783
Austen, Jane	1775-1817	Boie, Heinrich Christian	1744-1806
Azais, Pierre Hyacinthe	1766-1845	Bolingbroke, Henry	
Bachaumont, Louis Petit		St. John	1678-1751
De	1690-1771	Bolyai, Wolfgang	1775-1856
Bacsanyi, Janos	1763-1845	Bonald, Louis Gabriel	
Baggesen, Jens Immanuel	1764-1826	Ambrose	1754-1840
Baillie, Joanna	1762-1851	Bonneville, Nicholas De	1760-1828
Barbauld, Anna Letitia	1743-1825	Bonstetten, Charles	
Barker, Thomas of Bath	1769-1847	Victor De	1745-1832
Barlow, Joel	1754-1812	Boswell, James	1740-1795
Barnard, Lady Anne	1750-1825		

Botta, Carlo Guiseppe Guglielmo	1766-1837
Bouilly, Jean-Nicolas	1763-1842
Bouterwek, Friedrich	1765-1828
Bowdler, Thomas (editor)	1754-1825
Bowles, William Lisle	1762-1850
Bree, Mathias Ignatius Van	1773-1839
Brillat-Savarin, Anthelme	1755-1826
Brissot de Warville, Jacques Pierre	1754-1793
Brooke, Henry	1703-1783
Brorson, Hans Adolf	1694-1764
Brosses, Charles de	1709-1777
Brown, Charles Brockden	1771-1810
Brown, John	1715-1766
Browne, Isaac Hawkins	1705-1760
Bruce, Micheal	1746-1767
Brucker, Johann Jakob	1696-1770
Bryant, Jacob	1715-1804
Brydges, Sir Samuel Egerton	1762-1837
Buonafede, Appiano	1716-1793
Burger, Gottfried August	1747-1794
Burke, Edmund	1729-1797
Burney, Charles	1726-1814
Burney, Fanny (Madame D'Arblay)	1752-1840
Burns, Robert	1759-1796
Bury, Lady Charlotte Susan Maria	1775-1861
Byrom, John	1692-1763
Cadalso, Vasquez Jose	1741-1782
Cambridge, Richard Owen	1717-1802
Campan, Jeanne Louise Henriette	1752-1822
Campbell, Thomas	1777-1844
Carte, Thomas	1686-1754
Carter, Elizabeth	1717-1806
Casanova De Seingalt, Giovanni Jacopo	1725-1798
Casti, Giovanni Battista	1724-1803
Cazotte, Jacques	1719-1792
Cerutti, Giuseppe	1738-1792
Cesarotti, Melchiore	1730-1808
Challoner, Richard	1691-1781
Chalmers, Alexander	1759-1834
Chamfort, Sebastien Roch Nicolas	1741-1794
Chapone, Hester	1727-1801
Charriere, Isabelle De	1740-1805
Chateaubriand, Francois Rene	1768-1848
Chatterton, Thomas	1752-1770
Chenedolle, Charles Julien Lioult De	1769-1833
Chenier, Marie Andre De	1762-1794
Chenier, Marie-Joseph Blaise De	1764-1811
Chesterfield, Philip Dormer Stanhope (4th Earl of)	1694-1773
Churchill, Charles	1731-1764
Cibber, Colley	1671-1757
Cibber, Theophilus	1703-1758
Clarke, Edward Daniel	1769-1822
Claudius, Matthias	1740-1815
Clement, Francois	1714-1793
Cobbett, William	1763-1835
Cockburn, Alicia	1713-1794
Colden, Cadwallader	1688-1776
Coleman, George	1732-1794
Coleridge, Samuel Taylor	1772-1834
Collé, Charles	1709-1783
Collier, John	1708-1786
Collin, Heinrich Joseph Von	1771-1811
Collin D'Harleville, Jean Francois	1755-1806
Collins, William	1721-1759
Colma, George the Elder	1732-1794
Colman, George	1762-1836
Combe, William	1741-1823
Condorcet, Marie Jean Antoine Nicolas Caritat Marquis De	1743-1794
Condillac, Etienne Bonnot De	1715-1780
Constant De Rebecque, Henri Benjamin	1767-1830
Cooke, Thomas	1704-1756
Correa Garcao, Pedro Antonio Joaquim	1724-1772
Cottin, Marie	1770-1807
Courier, Paul Louis	1773-1825
Cowley, Hannah	1743-1809
Cowper, William	1731-1800
Coxe, William	1747-1828
Crabbe, George	1754-1832
Craufurd, Quintin	1743-1819
Crebillon, Prosper Jolyot De	1674-1762
Creevey, Thomas	1768-1838
Creuzer, George Friedrich	1771-1858
Crocker, Hannah Mather	1752-1829
Croft, Sir Herbert	1751-1816
Cruden, Alexander	1701-1770
Crusius, Christian August	1715-1775
Cruz E Silva, Antonio Diniz Da	1731-1799
Cruz, Raymon De La	1731-1794
Csokonai, Mihaly Vitez	1773-1805
Cumberland, Richard	1732-1811
Cuvier, Georges (Leopold)	1769-1832
Dalin, Olof Von	1708-1763
Da Ponte, Lorenzo	1749-1838
Daru, Piere Antoine Comte	1767-1829
Darwin, Erasmus	1731-1802
Dashkova, Catherina Romanovna	1744-1810

Daunov, Pierre Claude		Fabre D'Eglantine,	
Francois	1761-1840	Philippe Francois	
Day, Thomas	1748-1789	Nazaire	1755-1794
Delarue, Gervais	1751-1835	Fabroni, Angelo	1732-1803
Delille, Jacques	1738-1813	Falconer, William	1732-1769
Delolme, Jean Louis	1740-1806	Falk, Johann Daniel	1768-1826
Denina, Carlo Giovanni		Farvart, Charles Simon	1710-1792
Maria	1731-1813	Fawkes, Francis	1720-1777
Denis, Michael	1729-1800	Feith, Rhijnvis	1753-1824
Derzhavin, Gavrila		Fejer, Gyorgy	1766-1852
Romanovich	1743-1816	Ferguson, Adam	1723-1816
Desagiers, Marc Antoine		Fergusson, Robert	1750-1774
Madeleine	1772-1827	Feuerbach, Paul Johann	
Desforges, Pierre Jean		Anselm	1775-1833
Baptiste Choudard	1746-1806	Fichte, Johann Gottlieb	1762-1814
Destouches, Phillipe	1680-1754	Florian, Jean Pierre	
Dibdin, Thomas John	1771-1841	Claris De	1755-1794
Diderot, Denis	1713-1784	Fontanes, Louis	1757-1821
Diniz Da Cruz E Silva	1731-1799	Fontenelle, Bernard Le	
D'Israeli, Isaac	1766-1848	Bovier De	1657-1757
Dmitriev, Ivan Ivanovich	1760-1837	Foote, Samuel	1720-1777
Dodsley, Robert	1703-1764	Forner, Juan Pablo	1756-1797
Dorat, Claude Joseph	1734-1780	Forster, Johann George	
Drake, Nathan	1766-1836	Adam	1754-1794
Drinkwater, Betthune		Foster, John	1770-1843
John	1762-1844	Fourier, Francois Marie	
Droz, Francois-Xavier	1773-1850	Charles	1772-1837
Ducis, Jean Francois	1733-1816	Frampton, Mary	1773-1846
Dumont, Pierre Etienne		Francois De Neufchateau,	
Louis	1759-1829	Nicolas Louis	1750-1828
Dunlap, William	1766-1839	Franklin, Benjamin	1706-1790
Dupuis, Charles Francois	1742-1809	Franzen, Frans Michael	1772-1847
Durao, Jose De Santa Rita	1737-1784	Freneau, Philip Morin	1752-1832
Dutens, Louis	1730-1812	Frere, John Hookham	1769-1846
Duval, Alexandre Vincent		Fries, Jakob Friedrich	1773-1843
Pineux	1767-1842	Frugoni, Carlo Innicenzo	
Dwight, Timothy	1752-1817	Maria	1692-1768
Dyer, John	1699-1757	Gagern, Hans Christoph	
Eberhard, Christian August		Ernst	1766-1852
Gottlob	1769-1845	Galluppi, Pasquale	1770-1846
Eberhard, Johann		Garat, Dominique Joseph	1749-1833
Augustus	1739-1809	Garcia De La Huerta,	
Edgeworth, Maria	1767-1849	Vincente Antonio	1734-1787
Edgeworth, Richard Lovell	1744-1817	Gellert, Christian	
Edwards, Bryan	1743-1800	Furchtegott	1715-1769
Edwards, Jonathan	1703-1758	Genlis, Stephanie Felicité	
Egan, Pierce	1772-1849	Ducrest De St. Aubin	1746-1830
Ekhof, Konrad	1720-1778	Genovesi, Antonio	1712-1769
Elliot, Jean	1727-1805	Gerard, Alexander	1728-1795
Ellis, George	1753-1815	Gerstenberg, Heinrich	
Engel, Johann Jakob	1741-1802	Wilhelm Von	1737-1823
Epinay, Louise Florence		Gibbon, Edward	1737-1794
Petronille Tardieu		Gifford, William	1756-1826
d'esclavelles D'	1726-1783	Gilbert, Nicolas Joseph	
Erskine, Henry	1746-1817	Laurent	1751-1780
Eschenburg, Johann		Gillies, John	1747-1836
Joachim	1743-1820	Ginguene, Pierre Louis	1748-1815
Eschenmayer, Adam Karl		Gioja, Melchiorre	1767-1829
August Von	1768-1852	Giordani, Pietro	1774-1848
Escoquiz, Juan	1762-1820	Gleim, Johann Wilhelm	
Ewald, Johannes	1743-1781	Ludwig	1719-1803

M

Glover, Richard	1712-1785	Home, John	1722-1808
Godwin, Mary		Hontheim, Johann	
Wollstonecraft	1759-1797	Nikolaus Von	1701-1790
Godwin, William	1756-1836	Hook, James	1746-1827
Goethe, Johann Wolfgang		Hopkinson, Francis	1737-1791
Von	1749-1832	Huerta, Vincente	
Goldoni, Carlo	1707-1793	Garcia de la	1730-1787
Goldsmith, Oliver	1728-1774	Humboldt, Friedrich	
Good, John Mason	1764-1827	(Baron Von)	1769-1859
Gotter, Friedrich Wilhelm	1746-1797	Humboldt, Karl Wilhelm	
Gottsched, Johann		Von	1767-1835
Christoph	1700-1766	Hume, David	1711-1776
Gotz, Johann Nikolaus	1721-1781	Hurd, Richard	1720-1808
Gozzi, Carlo	1720-1806	Iffland, August Wilhelm	1759-1814
Grant, Anne	1755-1838	Inchbald, Elizabeth	1753-1821
Graves, Richard	1715-1804	Iriarte, Tomas De	1750-1791
Gray, Thomas	1716-1771	Isla, Jose Francisco De	1703-1781
Gresset, Jean Baptiste		Jacobi, Friedrich Heinrich	1743-1819
Louis	1709-1777	Jacobi, Johann Georg	1740-1814
Grimm, Friedrich		Jakob, Ludwig Heinrich	
Melchior	1723-1807	Von	1759-1827
Gyllembourg-Ehrensvard,		Jefferson, Thomas	1743-1826
Thomasine Christine	1773-1856	Jenyns, Soame	1704-1787
Hamilton, Elizabeth	1758-1816	Jephson, Robert	1736-1803
Hagedorn, Friedrich Von	1708-1754	Johnson, Samuel	1709-1784
Hamann, Johann Georg	1730-1788	Joubert, Joseph	1754-1824
Hamilton, William	1704-1754	Jouy, Victor Joseph	
Hanbury, Williams,		Etienne De	1764-1846
Sir Charles	1708-1759	Jovellanos, Gaspar	
Hartley, David	1705-1757	Melchor De	1744-1811
Hasted, Edward	1732-1812	Kames, Henry Home	1696-1782
Hawkesworth, John	1715-1773	Kant, Immanuel	1724-1804
Hawkins, Sir John	1719-1789	Karamzin, Nicolai	
Hayley, William	1745-1820	Mikhailovich	1765-1826
Haywood, Eliza	1693-1756	Karman, Jozsef	1769-1795
Heeren, Arnold Hermann		Kazinczy, Ferencz	1759-1831
Ludwig	1760-1842	Kellgren, Johan Henrik	1751-1795
Hegel, Georg Wilhelm		Kelly, Hugh	1739-1777
Friedrich	1770-1831	King, Thomas	1730-1805
Heinse, Johann Jakob		Kisfaludy, Sandor	1772-1844
Wilhelm	1749-1803	Kleist, Ewald Christian	
Helmers, Jan Frederick	1767-1813	Von	1715-1759
Helvetius, Claude Adrien	1715-1771	Klinger, Friedrich	
Hemsterhuis, Francois	1721-1790	Maximilian Von	1752-1831
Henault, Charles Jean		Klopstock, Friedrich	
Francois	1685-1770	Gottlieb	1724-1803
Herder, Johann Gotfried		Knebel, Karl Ludwig Von	1744-1834
Von	1744-1803	Knigge, Adolf Franz	
Hill, John	1716-1775	Friedrich	1752-1796
Hippel, Theodor Gottlieb		Kotzebue, August Friedrich	
Von	1741-1796	Ferdinand Von	1761-1819
Hogg, James	1770-1835	Krug, Wilhelm Traugott	1770-1842
Holbach, Paul Heinrich		Krylov, Ivan Andreevich	1768-1844
Dietrich	1723-1789	Lacepede, Bernard De	
Holberg, Ludvig Holberg	1684-1754	Laville, Compte De	1756-1825
Holcroft, Thomas	1745-1809	La Chaussee, Pierre Claude	
Holderlin, Johann		Nivelle De	1692-1754
Christian Friedrich	1770-1843	Laclos, Piere Amboise	
Holland, Henry	1746-1806	Francois	1741-1803
Holty, Ludwig Heinrich		Lacretelle, Jean Charles	
Cristoph	1748-1776	Dominique de	1766-1855

Lagrange-Chancel, Francois	
Joseph	1677-1758
La Harpe, Frederic Cesare	1754-1838
Laing, Malcolm	1762-1818
Lamarck, Jean Chevalier	
de	1744-1829
Lamb, Charles	1775-1834
Lamettrie, Julien Offray	
De	1709-1751
Landor, Walter Savage	1775-1864
Langhorne, John	1735-1779
Laromiguiere, Pierre	1756-1837
Las Cases, Emmanuel	
Diendonné, Compte de	1766-1842
Lavater, Johann Kaspar	1741-1801
Law, William	1686-1761
Laya, Jean Louis	1761-1833
Lee, Harriet	1757-1851
Lee, Sophia	1750-1824
Lemercier, Nepomucene	1771-1840
Lemierre, Antoine Marin	1733-1793
Lennox, Charlotte	1720-1804
Lenz, Jakob Michael	
Reinhold	1751-1792
Les Pinasse, Lulie De	1732-1776
Lessing, Gotthold Ephraim	1729-1781
Lewis, Matthew Gregory	1775-1818
Leyden, John	1775-1811
Lichtenberg, Georg	
Christoph	1742-1799
Ligne, Charles Joseph	1735-1814
Lingard, John	1771-1851
Linnaeus, Carl	1707-1778
Lista y Aragon, Alberto	1775-1848
Lodge, Edmund	1756-1839
Lofft, Capel	1751-1824
Logan, John	1748-1788
Lomonosov, Mikhail	
Vasilievich	1711-1765
Louvet De Couvrai, Jean	
Baptiste	1760-1797
Luttrel, Henry	1765-1851
Luzan, Claramunt de	
Suelves Y Gurrea	
Ignacio	1702-1754
Lyttelton, George,	
1st Baron	1709-1773
Mably, Gabriel Bennet De	1709-1785
Macedo, Jose Agostinho	
De	1761-1831
Mackenzie, Henry	1745-1831
Mackintosh, Sir James	1765-1832
Macklin, Charles	1697-1797
Macpherson, James	1736-1796
M'crie, Thomas	1772-1835
Madan, Martin	1726-1790
Maffei, Francesco	
Scipione	1675-1755
Maimon, Salomon	1754-1800
Maine De Biran, Francois	
Pierre Gonthier	1766-1824
Maistre, Joseph De	1754-1821
Maistre, Xavier De	1763-1852
Mallet, David	1705-1765
Malthus, Thomas Robert	1766-1834
Manuel, Louis Pierre	1751-1793
Marivaux, Pierre Carlet	
De Chamblain De	1688-1763
Marmontel, Jean Francois	1723-1799
Martin, Francois Xavier	1762-1846
Masdeu, Jean Francisco	
De	1744-1817
Mason, William	1725-1797
Matthisson, Friedrich Von	1761-1831
Melendez Valdes, Juan	1754-1817
Mendelssohn, Moses	1729-1786
Mercier, Sebastien	1740-1814
Merck, Johann Heinrich	1741-1791
Metastasio	1698-1782
Michaud, Joseph Francois	1767-1839
Michell, John	1724-1793
Mickle, William Julius	1735-1788
Mill, James	1773-1836
Mirabeau, Victor Riqueti	1715-1789
Mitford, William	1744-1827
Montagu, Elizabeth	1720-1800
Montagu, Lady Mary	
Wortley	1689-1762
Montefiore, Joshua	1762-1843
Montesquieu, Charles	
Louis De Secondat	1689-1755
Montgomery, James	1771-1854
Monti, Vincenzo	1754-1828
Moore, Edward	1712-1757
Moore, John	1729-1802
Moratin, Leandro	
Fernandez De	1760-1820
More, Hannah	1745-1833
Morellet, Andre	1727-1819
Moritz, Karl Philipp	1757-1793
Morton, Thomas	1764-1838
Muller, Friedrich	1749-1825
Muller, Johannes Von	1752-1809
Murphy, Arthur	1727-1805
Musaus, Johann Karl	
August	1735-1787
Nascimento, Francisco	
Manoel De	1734-1819
Nicholas, John	1745-1826
Nicholson, William	1753-1815
Nicolai, Christoph	
Friedrich	1733-1811
Opie, Amelia	1769-1853
Orme, Robert	1728-1801
Paine, Thomas	1737-1809
Paley, William	1743-1805
Paltock, Robert	1697-1767
Parini, Giuseppe	1729-1799
Pepusch, Johann	
Christoph	1667-1752
Percy, Thomas	1729-1811
Pindemonte, Ippolito	1753-1828

Piozzi, Hester Lynch	1741-1821	Schlozer, August Ludwig	
Piranezi, Giambattista	1720-1778	Von	1735-1809
Piron, Alexis	1689-1773	Schubart, Christian	
Pontoppidan, Erik	1698-1764	Friedrich Daniel	1739-1791
Prevost, Antoine Francois	1697-1763	Scott, Sir Walter	1771-1832
Price, Richard	1723-1791	Sedaine, Michel Jean	1719-1797
Priestley, Joseph	1733-1804	Seguier, William	1771-1843
Proud, Robert	1728-1813	Semler, Johann Salomo	1725-1791
Pye, Henry James	1745-1813	Senac De Meilhan, Gabriel	1736-1803
Pyne, William Henry	1769-1843	Senancour, Etienne Pivert	
Quincy, Josiah	1772-1864	De	1770-1846
Quintana, Manuel José	1772-1857	Seward, Anna	1747-1809
Racine, Louis	1692-1763	Shenstone, William	1714-1763
Radcliffe, Ann	1764-1823	Sheridan, Richard	
Ramsay, Allan	1686-1758	Brinsley Butler	1751-1816
Raspe, Rudolf Erich	1737-1794	Sheridan, Thomas	1719-1788
Raynal, Guillaume		Sherwood, Mary Martha	1775-1851
Thomas Francois	1713-1796	Shiels, Robert	-1753
Raynouard, Francois		Sismondi, Jean Charles	
Juste Marie	1761-1836	Leonard Simonde	1773-1842
Reeve, Clara	1729-1807	Smart, Christopher	1722-1771
Reid, Thomas	1710-1796	Smith, Adam	1723-1790
Reimarus, Hermann		Smith, Charlotte	1749-1806
Samuel	1694-1768	Smith, James	1775-1839
Restif, Nicolas Edme	1734-1806	Smith, John Stafford	1750-1836
Richardson, Samuel	1689-1761	Smith, Sidney	1771-1845
Richmond, Legh	1772-1827	Smollett, Tobias George	1721-1771
Richter, Johann Paul		Southey, Robert	1774-1843
Friedrich	1763-1825	Souza-Botelho, Adelaide	
Rivarol, Antoine De	1753-1801	Filleul	1761-1836
Robertson, William	1721-1793	Spence, Joseph	1699-1768
Rogers, Samuel	1763-1855	Stael, Madame De	1766-1817
Roscoe, William	1753-1831	Steffens, Henrik	1773-1845
Rouget De Lisle, Claude		Sterne, Laurence	1713-1768
Joseph	1760-1836	Stewart, Dugald	1753-1828
Rousseau, Jean Jacques	1712-1778	Stilling, Heinrich	1740-1817
Royer-Collard, Pierre		Stillingfleet, Benjamin	1702-1771
Paul	1763-1845	Stolberg, Friedrich	
Rulhiere, Claude		Leopold	1750-1819
Carloman De	1735-1791	Struensee, Johan	1737-1772
Russell, Thomas	1762-1788	Strutt, Joseph	1742-1802
Sade, Donatien Alphonse		Swedenborg, Emanuel	1688-1772
Francois, Marquis De	1740-1814	Tannahill, Robert	1774-1810
Saint-Lambert, Jean		Taylor, William	1765-1836
Francois De	1716-1803	Tieck, Johann Ludwig	1773-1853
Saint-Mattin, Louis		Torres Y Villaroel,	
Claude De	1743-1803	Diego De	1696-1759
Saint-Pierre, Bernardin De	1737-1814	Trumbull, John	1750-1831
Saint-Simon, Louis De		Turner, Sharon	1768-1847
Rouvroy	1675-1755	Uz, Johann Peter	1720-1796
Salomon, Johann Peter	1745-1815	Volney, Constantin	
Savage, Richard	1743-	Francois Chasseboeuf	
Schelling, Friedrich		Compte de	1757-1820
Wilhelm Joseph Von	1775-1854	Voltaire, Francois Marie	
Schiller, Johann Cristoph		Arouet De	1694-1778
Friedrich Von	1759-1805	Voss, Johann Heinrich	1751-1826
Schlegel, August		Wackenroder, Wilhelm	
Wilhelm Von	1767-1845	Heinrich	1773-1798
Schlegel, Friedrich Von	1772-1829	Walker, John	1732-1807
Schleiermacher, Friedrich		Walpole, Horace	1717-1797
Daniel Ernst	1768-1834	Warton, Joseph	1722-1800

Warton, Thomas	1728-1790	Wolcott, John	
Washington, George	1732-1799	(Peter Pinder)	1738-1819
Webster, Noah	1758-1843	Wollaston, William Hyde	1766-1828
Werner, Zacharias	1768-1823	Wordsworth, Dorothy	1771-1855
Wesley, John	1703-1791	Wordsworth, William	1770-1850
West, Benjamin	1738-1820	Wraxall, Sir Nathaniel	
White, Gilbert	1720-1793	William	1751-1831
Whitehead, Paul	1710-1774	Young, Arthur	1741-1820
Whitehead, William	1715-1785	Young, Edward	1683-1765
Wieland, Christoph		Zimmerman, Johan Georg	
Martin	1733-1813	Ritter Van	1728-1795
Wilberforce, William	1759-1833	Zinzendorf, Nicolaus	
Wilson, Alexander	1766-1813	Ludwig Graf Von	1700-1760
Wirt, William	1772-1834	Zschokke, Johann	
		Heinrich Daniel	1771-1848

ARTISTS

Abilgaard, Nicolaj		Canaletto, Bernardo	
Abraham	1744-1809	Balleto	1720-1780
Adam, James	1730-1794	Canova, Antonio	1757-1822
Adam, Robert	1728-1792	Carriera, Rosalba	1675-1757
Allan, David	1744-1796	Carstens, Armus Jacob	1754-1798
Allou, Gilles	1670-1751	Casanova De Seingalt,	
Alvarez, Don Emanuel	1727-1797	Francois	1727-1805
Alvarez, Don Jose	1768-1827	Casanova De Seingalt,	
Appiani, Andrea	1754-1817	Giovanni Battista	1728-1795
Bacon, John	1740-1799	Catlin, George	1796-1872
Baltard, Louis Pierre	1764-1846	Chambers, Sir William	1726-1796
Banks, Thomas	1735-1805	Chardin, Jean Baptiste	
Barker, Robert	1739-1806	Simeon	1699-1779
Baroni, Pompeo		Chippendale, Thomas	
Girolamo	1708-1787	(cabinet maker)	1718-1779
Barry, James	1741-1806	Chodowiecki, Daniel	
Bartolini, Lorenzo	1777-1850	Nicolas	1726-1801
Bartolozzi, Francesco	1727-1815	Cipriani, Giovanni Batista	1727-1785
Bewick, Thomas	1753-1828	Cleveland, John	1747-1786
Bird, Edward	1772-1819	Cleveland, Robert	1747-1809
Blondel, Jacques Francois	1705-1774	Copley, John Singleton	1737-1815
Bone, Henry	1755-1834	Corbould, Richard	1757-1831
Bonomi, Giuseppe	1739-1808	Cosway, Richard	1742-1821
Bosio, Francois Joseph		Coypel, Charles Antoine	1694-1752
Baron	1769-1845	Cozens, John Robert	1752-1797
Bouchardon, Edme	1698-1762	Cressent, Charles	1685-1768
Boucher, Francois	1703-1770	Crome, John	1768-1821
Boydell, John	1719-1809	Cuvilles, Francois De	1698-1767
Briseux, Charles Etienne	1680-1754	Damer, Anne Seymour	1749-1828
Brown, Lancelot		Dance, George	1741-1825
(" Capability ")		Daniell, Samuel	1775-1811
landscape gardener	1715-1783	Daniell, Thomas	1749-1840
Bulfinch, Charles	1763-1844	Daniell, William	1769-1837
Burlington, Richard		Dannecker, Johann	
Boyle, 3rd Earl of	1695-1753	Heinrich Von	1758-1841
Caffieri, Jacques	1678-1755	David, Jacques Louis	1748-1825
Cagnola, Luigi	1762-1833	De Loutherbourg, Philip	
Camuccini, Vincenzo	1773-1844	James	1740-1812
Camus De Mesieres,		Denon, Dominique Vivant	1747-1825
Nicolas De	1721-1789	Desmoulins, Camille	1760-1794
Canaletto	1697-1768	Dietrich, Christian	
		Wilhelm Ernst	1712-1774

Downman, John	1750-1824	Liotard, Jean Etienne	1702-1789
Doyen, Gabriel Francois	1726-1806	Longhi, Pietro	1702-1785
Drouais, Jean Germain	1763-1788	Manwaring, Robert	
Dumont, Francois	1751-1831	(cabinet maker)	1760-
Earlom, Richard	1743-1822	Mena, Pedro De	1693-
Engleheart, George	1752-1829	Mengs, Antony Raphael	1728-1779
Exshaw, Charles	-1771	Michel, Claude	1738-1814
Falconet, Ettienne		Morland, George	1763-1804
Maurice	1716-1791	Motte, William de la	1775-1863
Farington, Joseph	1747-1821	Nash, John	1752-1835
Fiorillo, Johann		Nash, Richard	1674-1762
Dominicus	1748-1821	Nasmyth, Alexander	1758-1840
Flaxman, John	1755-1826	Nattier, Jean Marc	1685-1766
Flitcroft, Henry	1679-1769	Neumann, Balthazar	1687-1753
Fontaine, Pierre Francois		Nollekens, Joseph	1737-1823
Leonard	1762-1853	Northcote, James	1746-1831
Fragonard, Jean Honore	1732-1806	Opie, John	1761-1807
Friedrich, Caspar David	1774-1840	Pajou, Augustin	1730-1809
Fuseli, Henry	1741-1825	Peale, Charles Willson	1741-1837
Gabriel, Jacques Ange	1698-1782	Percier, Charles	1764-1838
Gainsborough, Thomas	1727-1788	Pergolesi, Michael Angelo	1700-
Gerard, Francois	1770-1837	Pigalle, Jean Baptiste	1714-1785
Gessner, Salomon	1730-1788	Pine, Robert Edge	1730-1788
Gibbs, James	1682-1754	Plimer, Andrew	1763-1837
Gillray, James	1757-1815	Porter, Robert Ker	1775-1842
Girodet De Roussy, Anne		Prud'hon, Pierre	1758-1823
Louis	1767-1824	Raeburn, Sir Henry	1756-1823
Girtin, Thomas	1775-1802	Ramsay, Allan	1713-1784
Goya Y Lucientes,		Reynolds, Sir Joshua	1723-1792
Francisco	1746-1828	Robert, Hubert	1733-1808
Granet, Francois Marius	1775-1849	Romney, George	1734-1802
Greuze, Jean Baptiste	1725-1805	Rousseau, De La Rottiere	
Gros, Antoine Jean	1771-1835	Jean Simeon	1747-
Guardi, Francesco	1712-1793	Roubillac, Louis Francois	1695-1762
Guerin, Pierre Narcisse	1774-1833	Rowlandson, Thomas	1756-1827
Hansen, Christian		Rysbrack, Michael	1693-1770
Frederik	1756-1845	Sandby, Paul	1725-1809
Heaphy, Thomas	1775-1835	Schadow, Johann Gottfried	1764-1850
Hepplewhite, George		Scheemakers, Pieter	1691-1770
(cabinet maker)	-1786	Shee, Sir Martin Archer	1769-1850
Highmore, Joseph	1692-1780	Sheraton, Thomas (cabinet	
Hogarth, William	1697-1764	maker)	1751-1806
Hokusai, Katsushika	1760-1849	Smart, John	1740-1811
Hoppner, John	1758-1810	Smith, John Raphael	1752-1812
Houdon, Jean Antoine	1740-1828	Soane, Sir John	1753-1837
Humphrey, Ozias	1742-1810	Soufflot, Jacques Germain	1709-1780
Ince, William (cabinet		Sowerby, James	1757-1822
maker)	1762-	Stothard, Thomas	1755-1834
Isabey, Jean Baptiste	1767-1855	Stuart, Gilbert	1755-1828
Kauffmann, Angelica	1741-1807	Stuart, James	1713-1788
La Grenee, Jean Louis		Thorvaldsen, Bertol	1770-1844
Francois	1742-1805	Tiepolo, Giovanni Battista	1692-1769
La Tour, Maurice		Towne, Francis	1739-1816
Quentin De	1704-1788	Trumbull, John	1756-1843
Lawrence, Sir Thomas	1769-1830	Turner, Joseph Mallord	
Le Brun, Marie Elizabeth		William	1775-1851
Louise	1755-1842	Utamaro	1754-1806
Lejeune, Louis Francois	1775-1848	Vangoyen, Jan Josephzoon	1696-1756
Lemoyne, Jean Baptiste	1704-1778	Vanloo, Charles Andrew	1705-1765
L'Enfant, Pierre Charles	1754-1835	Vernet, Antoine Charles	
Limborch, Hendrick Van	1680-1758	Horace	1758-1835

Vernet, Claude Joseph	1714-1789
Vigee-Lebrun, Marie Anne Elizabeth	1755-1842
Wedgewood, Josiah (potter)	1730-1795
Westmacott, Sir Richard	1775-1856
Wilson, Richard	1714-1782
Wood, John	1705-1754
Wright, Joseph	1734-1797
Wyatt, James	1746-1813
Zoffany, Johann	1733-1810
Zuccarelli, Francesco	1702-1786
Zucchi, Antonio Pietro	1726-1795

COMPOSERS

Albrechtberger, Johann Gregory	1736-1809
Arne, Thomas Augustine	1710-1778
Arnold, Samuel	1740-1802
Asioli, Bonifacio	1769-1832
Astorga, Emannuele Gioacchino	1680-1755
Attwood, Thomas	1765-1838
Avison, Charles	1710-1770
Bach, Johann Christian	1735-1782
Bach, Karl Philipp Emanuel	1714-1788
Bach, Wilhelm Friedemann	1710-1784
Baini, Guiseppe	1775-1844
Barsanti, Francesco	1690-1775
Batishill, Jonathan	1738-1801
Beethoven, Ludwig Van	1770-1827
Benda, Georg	1722-1795
Boccherini, Luigi	1743-1805
Boieldieu, Francois Adrien	1775-1834
Bononcini, Giovanni Baptista	1670-1755
Boyce, William	1710-1779
Callcott, John Wall	1766-1821
Cambini, Giovanni Giuseppe	1746-1825
Campenhout, Francois Von	1779-1849
Cannabich, Christian	1731-1798
Cherubini, Maria Luigi	1760-1842
Cimarosa, Domenico	1749-1801
Clementi, Muzio	1752-1832
Corri, Domenico	1746-1825
Crotch, William	1775-1847
Daquin, Louis Claude	1694-1772
Dibdin, Charles	1745-1814
Dittersdorf, Karl Ditters Von	1739-1799
Durante, Francesco	1684-1755
Dussek, Jan Ladislav	1761-1812
Eberlin, Johann Ernst	1702-1762
Eberwein, Traugott Maximilian	1775-1831
Fasch, Johann Friedrich	1688-1758
Galuppi, Baldassare	1706-1785
Garcia, Manoel	1775-1832
Gazzaniga, Giuseppe	1743-1818
Giordanni, Giuseppe	1744-1798
Gluck, Christoph Willibald	1714-1787
Gossec, Francois Joseph	1734-1829
Gow, Niel	1727-1807
Graun, Karl Heinrich	1701-1759
Greene, Maurice	1695-1755
Gretry, Andre Ernest Modeste	1741-1813
Handel, George Frederick	1685-1759
Hasse, Johann Adolph	1699-1783
Haydn, Franz Joseph	1732-1809
Haydn, Michael	1737-1806
Hiller, Johann Adam	1728-1804
Himmel, Frederick Henry	1765-1814
Jackson, Wilhelm	1730-1803
Jommelli, Niccolo	1714-1774
Kelly, Michael	1762-1826
Leclair, Jean Marie	1697-1764
Lesueur, Jean Francois	1760-1837
Linley, Thomas	1732-1795
Logroscino, Nicola	1700-1763
Lucchesi, Andrea	1741-1800
Mattheson, Johann	1681-1764
Mehul, Etienne Nicolas	1763-1817
Monsigny, Pierre Alexandre	1729-1817
Mozart, Wolfgang Amadeus	1756-1791
Nardini, Pietro	1722-1793
Nares, James	1715-1783
Paer, Ferdinando	1771-1839
Paisiello, Giovanni	1741-1816
Philidor, Francois Andre Danican	1726-1795
Piccini, Niccola	1728-1800
Pleyel, Ignaz Joseph	1757-1831
Porpora, Niccola Antonio	1686-1767
Quantz, Johann Joachim	1697-1773
Rameau, Jean Philippe	1683-1764
Roman, Johan Helmich	1694-1758
Sacchini, Antonio Maria	1734-1786
Salieri, Antonio	1750-1825
Sarti, Giuseppe	1729-1802
Scarlatti, Guiseppe Domenico	1685-1757
Schobert, Johann	1720-1767
Shield, William	1748-1829
Spontini, Gasparo Luigi	1774-1851
Stamitz, Carl Philipp	1745-1801
Stamitz, Johann	1717-1757

Stanley, John	1713-1786	Viotti, Giovanni Battista	1753-1824
Steibelt, Daniel	1764-1823	Vogler, Georg Joseph	1749-1814
Storace, Stephen	1763-1796	Wesley, Samuel	1766-1837
Tartini, Giuseppe	1692-1770	Zingarelli, Niccolo	1752-1837
Telemann, Georg Philipp	1681-1767		

1776	Declaration of American Independence.
	Battle of Trenton.
1777	Battle of Brandy Wine.
	Battle or Germantown.
1778	France declares war against Great Britain.
1779	Spain declares war against England.
1780	Gordon riots in London.
1783	Peace established between England and U.S.
	France and Spain agree on terms of peace.
1788	" Times " first published.
1789	Mutiny of the Bounty.
	French revolution begins. Bastille destroyed.
1791	New French constitution adopted by National Assembly.
1793	Reign of terror starts in France. Marat assassinated.
	Marie Antoinette executed.
1794	Danton executed. End of reign of terror.
1796	Battle of Lodi.
	Spain declares war on England.
	Battle of Arcola.
1797	Battle of Rivoli.
	Vaccination introduced.
1798	Battle of the Pyramids.
	Battle of the Nile.
	Rebellion in Ireland.
1799	Battle of Aboukir.
	Income Tax.
1800	Battle of Marengo.
	Battle of Hohenlinden.

PROMINENT PEOPLE

Beau Brummell, George Bryan	1778-1840	Josephine, Empress	1763-1814
Danton, Georges Jacques	1759-1794	Marat, Jean Paul	1743-1793
Emmett, Robert	1778-1803	Marie Antoinette	1755-1793
Faraday, Michael	1791-1867	Mirabeau, Gabriel, Comte de	1749-1791
Hastings, Warren	1732-1818	Nelson, Horatio, Viscount	1758-1805
Hood, Samuel, 1st Viscount, Admiral	1724-1816	Paganini, Nicolo	1782-1840
Jenner, Edward	1749-1823	Wellington, Duke of	1769-1852

EMPERORS OF CHINA (MANCHU (Ch'ing) DYNASTY)

Kao Tsung	1735-1795	Jen Tsung	1795-1820

POPES

Pius VI	1775-1799	Pius VII	1800-1823

FRANCE. HEADS OF STATE

Louis XVI	1774-1793	The Directors	1795-1799
Robespierre	1792-1794	The Consulate	1799-1804

HOLY ROMAN EMPERORS

Joseph II	1765-1790	Francis II	1792-1806
Leopold II	1790-1792		

George III   1760-1820

SWEDEN. KINGS

Gustavius III   1771-1792   Gustavius IV   1792-1809

PORTUGAL. KINGS

Joseph   1750-1777   Maria I   1777-1816
Pedro III   1777-1786

PRUSSIA. KINGS

Frederick II   1740-1786   Frederick William III   1797-1840
Frederick William II   1786-1797

RUSSIA. TSARS

Catherine the Great II   1762-1796   Paul   1796-1801

SPAIN. SOVEREIGNS

Charles III   1759-1788   Charles IV   1788-1808

U.S.A. PRESIDENTS

George Washington   1789-1797   John Adam   1797-1801

WRITERS

Abel, Karl Friedrich	1725-1787	Ancelot, Jacques Arsene	
Abernethy, John	1764-1831	Francois Polycarpe	1794-1854
Adam, Alexander	1741-1809	Ancillon, Johann Peter	
Adams, Hannah	1755-1831	Friedrich	1766-1836
Adams, John	1735-1826	Anderson, John	1726-1796
Adams, John Quincy	1767-1848	Anderson, Robert	1750-1830
Adanson, Michel	1727-1806	Andrews, James Pettit	1737-1797
Adolphus, John	1768-1845	Andrieux, Francois	
Adolphus, John Leycester	1795-1862	Guillaume Jean	
Aepinus, Franz Ulrich		Stanislas	1759-1833
Theodor	1724-1802	Anspach, Elizabeth,	
Afzelius, Aruid August	1785-1871	Margravine of	1750-1828
Aikin, John	1747-1822	Anquetil, Louis Pierre	1723-1808
Aikin, Lucy	1781-1864	Anstey, Christopher	1724-1805
Ainslie, Hew	1792-1878	Apperley, Charles James	
Aksakov, Sergei		(Nimrod)	1777-1843
Timofeyevich	1791-1859	Arago, Jacques Etienne	
Alaman, Lucas	1792-1853	Victor	1790-1855
Alcott, Amos Bronson	1799-1888	Archenholz, Johann	
Alembert, Jean Le		Wilhelm Von	1743-1812
Rond D'	1717-1783	Argens, Jean Baptiste De	
Alexis, Willibald	1798-1871	Boyer, Marquis D'	1704-1771
Alfireri, Vittorio, Count	1749-1803	Aribau, Bonaventura	
Alison, Sir Archibald	1792-1867	Carles	1795-1862
Almeida-Garrett, Joao		Armstrong, John	1709-1779
Battista da	1799-1854	Arnault, Antoine-Vincent	1766-1834
Almqvist, Karl Jonas		Arndt, Ernst Moritz	1769-1860
Ludwig	1793-1866	Arnim, Elizabeth	
Amory, Thomas	1691-1788	(Bettina) Von	1785-1859

Arnim, Ludwig Achim Von	1781-1831
Arnold, Thomas	1795-1842
Atkinson, Thomas Witlam	1799-1861
Austen, Jane	1775-1817
Austin, Sarah	1793-1867
Azais, Pierre Hyacinthe	1766-1845
Azeglio, Massimo Taparelli, Marquis D'	1798-1866
Bacsanyi, Janos	1763-1845
Baggesen, Jens Immanuel	1764-1826
Bahr, Johann Christian Felix	1798-1872
Bailey, Samuel	1791-1870
Ballanche, Pierre Simon	1776-1847
Baillie, Joanna	1762-1851
Balbo, Cesare, Count	1789-1853
Balzac, Honore De	1799-1850
Banim, John	1798-1842
Barante, Amable Guillaume Propser Brugiere	1782-1866
Barker, Thomas of Bath	1769-1847
Barlow, Joel	1754-1812
Barlow, Peter	1776-1862
Barnard, Lady Anne	1750-1825
Barnes, William	1800-1886
Barrington, George (Waldren)	1755-1804
Barthelemy, Auguste Marseille	1796-1867
Barthelemy, Jean-Jacques	1716-1795
Barton, Bernard	1784-1849
Basevi, George	1794-1845
Baudissin, Wolf Heinrich	1789-1878
Batyushkov, Konstantin Nikolaievitch	1787-1855
Baumgarten, Alexander Gottlieb	1714-1762
Bautain, Louis Eugene Marie	1796-1867
Bayly, Thomas Haynes	1797-1839
Beattie, James	1735-1803
Beauchamp, Alphonse De	1767-1832
Beaufort, Louis De	-1795
Beaumarchais, Pierre Augustin Caron De	1732-1799
Beaumont, Sir George Howland	1753-1827
Beccaria, Cesare, Marchese De	1738-1794
Beck, Christian Daniel	1757-1832
Beck, Jakob Sigismund	1761-1840
Beckford, William	1760-1844
Beechey, Sir William	1753-1839
Beffroy, De Reigny Louis Abel	1757-1811
Bekker, Elizabeth	1738-1804
Belli, Giuseppe Gioachino	1791-1863
Bellman, Karl Mikael	1740-1795
Beneke, Friedrich Edouard	1798-1856
Bentham, Jeremy	1748-1832

Beranger, Pierre Jean De	1780-1857
Berard, Joseph Frederic	1789-1828
Berchet, Giovanni	1783-1851
Berry, Mary	1763-1852
Berzsenyi, Daniel	1776-1836
Beskow, Bernhard Von	1796-1868
Bibaud, Michel	1782-1857
Bickerstaffe, Isaac	1735-1812
Bignon, Louis Pierre Edouard	1771-1841
Bilderdijk, Willem	1756-1831
Bissen, Herman Vilhelm	1798-1868
Bitzius, Albrecht	1797-1854
Blacklock, Thomas	1721-1791
Blake, William	1757-1827
Blamire, Susanna	1747-1794
Blessington, Marguerite	1789-1849
Blicher, Steen Steensen	1782-1848
Bloomfield, Robert	1766-1823
Blore, Edward	1787-1879
Bocage, Manuel Maria Barbosa De	1765-1805
Boccage, Marie Anne Fiquet de	1710-1802
Bodmer, Johann Jakob	1698-1783
Boerne, Karl Ludwig	1786-1837
Boie, Heinrich Christian	1744-1806
Bolyai, Wolfgang	1775-1856
Bonald, Louis Gabriel Ambroise	1754-1840
Bonneville, Nicholas de	1760-1828
Bonstetten, Charles Victor De	1745-1832
Borne, Ludwig	1786-1837
Bostrom, Christoffer Jacob	1797-1866
Boswell, James	1740-1795
Botta, Carlo Guiseppe Guglielmo	1766-1837
Bouilly, Jean-Nicolas	1763-1842
Bouterwek, Friedrich	1765-1828
Bowdich, Thomas Edward	1790-1824
Bowdler, Thomas (editor)	1754-1825
Bowles, William Lisle	1762-1850
Bree, Matthias Ignatius Van	1773-1839
Brentano, Clemens	1778-1842
Breton, de Los Herreros, Manuel	1796-1873
Brillat-Savarin, Anthelme	1755-1826
Brissot de Warville, Jacques Pierre	1754-1793
Brooke, Henry	1703-1783
Brosses, Charles de	1709-1777
Broughton, John Cam Hobhouse	1786-1869
Brown, Charles Brockden	1771-1810
Brown, Thomas	1778-1820
Browne, James	1793-1841
Brunton, Mary	1778-1818

Bryant, Jacob	1715-1804	Claudius, Matthias	1740-1815
Bryant, William Cullen	1794-1878	Clausewitz, Karl Von	1780-1831
Brydges, Sir Samuel		Clement, Francois	1714-1793
Egerton	1762-1837	Cobbett, William	1763-1835
Buchez, Philippe Benjamin		Cockburn, Alicia	1713-1794
Joseph	1796-1865	Colden, Cadwallader	1688-1776
Buckingham, James Silk	1786-1855	Coleman, George	1732-1794
Bulgarin, Thaddeus	1789-1859	Coleridge, Hartley	1796-1849
Buonafede, Appiano	1716-1793	Coleridge, Samuel-Taylor	1772-1834
Burger, Gottfried August	1747-1794	Colle, Charles	1709-1783
Burke, Edmund	1729-1797	Collier, John	1708-1786
Burney, Charles	1726-1814	Collier, John Payne	1789-1883
Burney, Fanny		Collin, Heinrich Joseph	
(Madame D'Arblay)	1752-1840	Von	1771-1811
Burns, Robert	1759-1796	Collin D'Harleville, Jean	
Bury, Lady Charlotte		Francois	1755-1806
Susan Maria	1775-1861	Collins, William	1788-1847
Byron, George Gordon		Colma, George the Elder	1732-1794
Byron	1788-1824	Colman, George	1762-1836
Caballero, Fernan	1796-1877	Combe, William	1741-1823
Cadalso, Vasquez Jose	1741-1782	Comte, Auguste	1798-1857
Cambridge, Richard Owen	1717-1802	Condorcet, Marie Jean	
Campan, Jeanne Louise		Antoine Nicolas Caritat,	
Henriette	1752-1822	Marquis De	1743-1794
Campbell, Thomas	1777-1844	Condillac, Etienne Bonnot	
Canina, Luigi	1795-1856	De	1715-1780
Carleton, William	1794-1869	Constant De Rebecque,	
Carlyle, Thomas	1795-1881	Henri Benjamin	1767-1830
Carter, Elizabeth	1717-1806	Cooper, James Fenimore	1789-1851
Casanova De Seingalt,		Costello, Louisa Stuart	1799-1870
Giovanni Jacopo	1725-1798	Cottin, Marie	1770-1807
Castelli, Ignaz Franz	1781-1862	Courier, Paul Louis	1773-1825
Casti, Giovanni Battista	1724-1803	Cousin, Victor	1792-1867
Cazotte, Jacques	1719-1792	Cowley, Hannah	1743-1809
Cerutti, Giuseppe	1738-1792	Cowper, William	1731-1800
Cesarotti, Melchiore	1730-1808	Coxe, William	1747-1828
Challoner, Richard	1691-1781	Cozens, Alexander	died 1782
Chalmers, Alexander	1759-1834	Crabbe, George	1754-1832
Chalybaus, Heinrich		Craufurd, Quintin	1743-1819
Moritz	1796-1862	Creevey, Thomas	1768-1838
Chamfort, Sebastien Roch		Creuzer, George Friedrich	1771-1858
Nicolas	1741-1794	Crocker, Hannah Mather	1752-1829
Chamier, Fredrick	1796-1870	Croft, Sir Herbert	1751-1816
Chamisso, Adelbert Von	1781-1838	Croker, John Wilson	1780-1857
Channing, William		Croker, Thomas Crofton	1798-1854
Ellery	1780-1842	Crusenstolpe, Magnus	
Chapone, Hester	1727-1801	Jakob	1795-1865
Charriere, Isabelle De	1740-1805	Cruz E Silva, Antonio	
Chasles, Philarete	1798-1873	Diniz Da	1731-1799
Chateaubriand, Francois		Cruz, Raymon De La	1731-1794
Rene	1768-1848	Csokonai, Mihaly Vitez	1773-1805
Chatterton, Thomas	1752-1770	Cumberland, Richard	1732-1811
Chenedolle, Charles		Cunningham, Allan	1784-1842
Julien Lioult De	1769-1833	Cunninghame-Graham,	
Chenier, Marie Andre de	1762-1794	Robert	-1797
Chenier, Marie Joseph		Cuvier, Georges	
Blaise De	1764-1811	(Leopold)	1769-1832
Christopoulos, Athanasios	1772-1847	Da Costa, Isaak	1798-1860
Clare, John	1793-1864	Dahlgren, Karl Frederik	1791-1844
Clarke, Charles Cowden	1787-1877	Dahlmann, Friedrich	
Clarke, Edward Daniel	1769-1822	Christoph	1785-1860

Da Ponte, Lorenzo	1749-1838
Darley, George	1795-1846
Daru, Pierre Antoine, Comte	1767-1829
Darwin, Erasmus	1731-1802
Dashkova, Catherina Romanovna	1744-1810
D'Aubigné, Jean Henri Merle	1794-1872
Daunov, Pierre Claude Francois	1761-1840
David, Pierre Jean	1789-1856
Day, Thomas	1748-1789
Delarue, Gervais	1751-1835
Delavigne, Jean Francois Casimir	1793-1843
Delille, Jacques	1738-1813
Delolme, Jean Louis	1740-1806
Delvig, Anton Antonovich, Baron Von	1798-1831
Denina, Carlo Giovanni Maria	1731-1813
Denis, Michael	1729-1800
De Quincey, Thomas	1785-1859
Derzhavin, Gavrila Romanovich	1743-1816
Desagiers, Marc Antoine Madeleine	1772-1827
Desforges, Pierre Jean Baptiste Choudard	1746-1806
Deschamps, Emile	1791-1871
Dibdin, Thomas John	1771-1841
Diderot, Dennis	1713-1784
Diniz Da Cruz E Silva, Antonio	1731-1799
D'Israeli, Isaac	1766-1848
Dmitriev, Ivan Ivanovich	1760-1837
Dollinger, Johann Joseph Ignaz Von	1799-1890
Dorat, Claude Joseph	1734-1780
Drake, Nathan	1766-1836
Drinkwater, Betthune John	1762-1844
Droste-Hulshoff, Annette Elizabeth	1797-1848
Droz, Francois-Xavier	1773-1850
Ducange, Victor Henri Joseph Brahain	1783-1833
Ducis, Jean Francois	1733-1816
Dumont, Pierre Etienne Louis	1759-1829
Dunlap, William	1766-1839
Dupuis, Charles Francois	1742-1809
Durao, Jose De Santa Rita	1737-1784
Dutens, Louis	1730-1812
Duval, Alexandre Vincent Pineux	1767-1842
Dwight, Timothy	1752-1817
Eberhard, Christian August Gottlob	1769-1845

Eberhard, Johann Augustus	1739-1809
Eckermann, Johann Peter	1792-1864
Edgeworth, Maria	1767-1849
Edgeworth, Richard Lovell	1744-1817
Edwards, Bryan	1743-1800
Egan, Pierce	1772-1849
Eichendorff, Joseph Freiherr Von	1788-1857
Ekhof, Konrad	1720-1778
Elliot, Jean	1727-1805
Elliott, Ebenezer	1781-1849
Ellis, George	1753-1815
Elphinstone, Mountstuart	1779-1859
Engel, Johann Carl Ludwig	1778-1840
Engel, Johann Jakob	1741-1802
Ennemoser, Joseph	1787-1855
Epinay, Louise Florence Petronille Tardieu D'Esclavelles D'	1726-1783
Erskine, Henry	1746-1817
Erskine, Thomas	1788-1870
Eschenburg, Johann Joachim	1743-1820
Eschenmayer, Adam Karl August Von	1768-1852
Escoquiz, Juan	1762-1820
Estebanez, Caldren Serafin	1799-1867
Etienne, Charles Guillaume	1777-1845
Everett, Alexander Hill	1790-1847
Ewald, Johannes	1743-1781
Fabre D'Eglantine, Philippe Francois Nazaire	1755-1794
Fabriani, Severino	1792-1849
Fabroni, Angelo	1732-1803
Fahlcrantz, Christian Erik	1790-1866
Fain, Agathon Jean Francois	1778-1837
Falk, Johann Daniel	1768-1826
Fallmerayer, Jakob Phillip	1790-1861
Farvart, Charles Simon	1710-1792
Fauriel, Claude Charles	1782-1844
Fawkes, Francis	1720-1777
Fay, Andreas	1786-1864
Feith, Rhijnvis	1753-1824
Fejer, Gyorgy	1766-1852
Ferguson, Adam	1723-1816
Fergusson, Robert	1750-1774
Ferrier, Susan Edmonstone	1782-1854
Feuerbach, Paul Johann Anselm	1775-1833
Fichte, Immanuel Hermann Von	1796-1879
Fichte, Johann Gottlieb	1762-1814

Fielding, Anthony Van Dyke Copley	1787-1855
Finlay, George	1799-1875
Fitzball, Edward	1792-1873
Florian, Jean Pierre Claris De	1755-1794
Foa, Eugene Rodriguez-Gradis	1798-1853
Follen, Adolf Ludwig	1794-1855
Follen, Karl	1795-1840
Fontanes, Louis	1757-1821
Foote, Samuel	1720-1777
Ford, Richard	1796-1858
Forner, Juan Pablo	1756-1797
Forster, Friedrich Christoph	1791-1868
Forster, Johann Georg Adam	1754-1794
Foscolo, Ugo	1778-1827
Foster, John	1770-1843
Fouque, Friedrich Heinrich Karl De La Motte	1777-1843
Fourier, Francois Marie Charles	1772-1837
Frampton, Mary	1773-1846
Francois De Neufchateau, Nicolas Louis	1750-1828
Franklin, Bejamin	1706-1790
Franzen, Frans Michael	1772-1847
Fraser, James Baillie	1783-1856
Freneau, Philip Morin	1752-1832
Frere, John Hookham	1769-1846
Fries, Jakob Friedrich	1773-1843
Froebel, Friedrich Wilhelm August	1782-1852
Frohlich, Abraham Emanuel	1796-1865
Frugoni, Carlo Innocenzo Maria	1692-1768
Fryxell, Anders	1795-1881
Gagern, Hans Christoph Ernst	1766-1852
Galluppi, Pasquale	1770-1846
Galt, John	1779-1839
Garat, Dominique Joseph	1749-1833
Garcia De La Huerta, Vincente Antonio	1734-1787
Garrett, Joao Baptista Da Silva Leitao De Almeida	1799-1854
Geiser, Eric Gustav	1783-1877
Genlis, Stephanie Felicite Ducrest De St. Aubin	1746-1830
Gerard, Alexander	1728-1795
Gerstenberg, Heinrich Wilhelm Von	1737-1823
Gesenius, Friedrich Heinrich Wilhelm	1786-1842
Gibbon, Edward	1737-1794
Gieseler, Johan Karl Ludwig	1792-1854
Gifford, William	1756-1826

Gilbert, Nicolas Joseph Laurent	1751-1780
Gillies, John	1747-1836
Ginguene, Pierre Louis	1748-1815
Gioja, Melchiorre	1767-1829
Giordani, Pietro	1774-1848
Giraud, Giovanni	1776-1834
Gleig, George Robert	1796-1888
Gleim, Johann Wilhelm Ludwig	1719-1803
Glen, William	1789-1826
Glinka, Fedor Nikolayevich	1788-1880
Glover, Richard	1712-1785
Godwin, Mary Wollstonecraft	1759-1797
Godwin, William	1756-1836
Goethe, Johann Wolfgang Von	1749-1832
Goldoni, Carlo	1707-1793
Good, John Mason	1764-1827
Goodrich, Samuel Griswold	1793-1860
Gore, Catherine Grace Frances	1799-1861
Gorres, Joseph Von	1776-1848
Gotter, Friedrich Wilhelm	1746-1797
Gotz, Johann Nikolaus	1721-1781
Gozzi, Carlo	1720-1806
Grant, Anne	1755-1838
Graves, Richard	1715-1804
Gresset, Jean Baptiste Louis	1709-1777
Greville, Charles Cavendish Fulke	1794-1865
Griboyedov, Alexander Sergeyevich	1795-1829
Grimm, Friedrich Melchior	1723-1807
Grimm, Jacob Ludwig Carl	1785-1863
Grimm, Wilhelm Carl	1786-1859
Grossi, Tommaso	1791-1853
Grote, George	1794-1871
Grundtvig, Nikolai Frederik Severin	1783-1872
Guizot, Francois Pierre Guillaume	1787-1874
Gyllembourg-Eh Rensvard, Thomasine Christine	1773-1856
Hale, Sarah Josepha	1788-1879
Haliburton, Thomas Chandler	1796-1865
Hall, Basil	1788-1844
Hallam, Henry	1777-1859
Halleck, Fitz-Green	1790-1867
Hamilton, Elizabeth	1758-1816
Hamilton, Thomas	1789-1842
Hamilton, Sir William	1788-1856
Hamann, Johann Georg	1730-1788
Hardwyck, Philip	1792-1870

Haring, George Wilhelm Heinrich	1798-1871
Hasted, Edward	1732-1812
Hawkins, Sir John	1719-1789
Hazlitt, William	1778-1830
Hayley, William	1745-1820
Heeren, Arnold Hermann Ludwig	1760-1842
Hegel, Georg Wilhelm Friedrich	1770-1831
Heiberg, Johan Ludvig	1791-1860
Heine, Heinrich	1797-1856
Heinse, Johann Jakob Wilhelm	1749-1803
Helmers, Jan Frederik	1767-1813
Hemans, Dorothea Felicia	1793-1835
Hemsterhuis, Francois	1721-1790
Herbart, Johann Friedrich	1776-1841
Herder, Johann Gottfried Von	1744-1803
Hertz, Henrik	1797-1870
Hinrichs, Hermann Friedrich Wilhelm	1794-1861
Hippel, Theodor Gottlieb Von	1741-1796
Hoffman, August Heinrich	1798-1874
Hoffman, Ernst Theodor Wilhelm	1776-1822
Hogg, James	1770-1835
Hogg, Thomas Jefferson	1792-1862
Holbach, Paul Heinrich Dietrich	1723-1789
Holcroft, Thomas	1745-1809
Holderlin, Johann Christian Friedrich	1770-1843
Holland, Henry	1746-1806
Holland, Sir Henry	1788-1873
Holtei, Karl Eduard Von	1798-1880
Holty, Ludwig Heinrich Christoph	1748-1776
Home, John	1722-1808
Hone, William	1780-1842
Hontheim, Johann Nikolaus Von	1701-1790
Hood, Thomas	1799-1845
Hook, James	1746-1827
Hook, Theodore Edward	1788-1841
Hopkinson, Francis	1737-1791
Hormayr, Joseph Frerherr Von	1782-1848
Howitt, Mary	1799-1888
Howitt, William	1792-1879
Huerta, Vincente Garcia de la	1730-1787
Humboldt, Friedrich (Baron Von)	1769-1839
Humboldt, Karl Wilhelm Von	1767-1835
Hume, David	1711-1776
Hunt, James Henry Leigh	1784-1859
Hunter, Joseph	1783-1861
Hurd, Richard	1720-1808
Hyslop, James	1798-1827
Iffland, August Wilhelm	1759-1814
Immermann, Karl Leberecht	1796-1840
Inchbald, Elizabeth	1753-1821
Ingemann, Bernhard Severin	1789-1862
Ingoldsby, Thomas	1788-1845
Innes, Cosmo	1798-1874
Iriarte, Tomas De	1750-1791
Irving, Washington	1783-1859
Isla, Jose Francisco De	1703-1781
Jacobi, Friedrich Heinrich	1743-1819
Jacobi, Johann, Georg	1740-1814
Jakob, Ludwig Heinrich Von	1759-1827
James, George Payne Rainsford	1799-1860
Jameson, Anna Brownell	1794-1860
Jasmin, Jacques	1798-1864
Jefferson, Thomas	1743-1826
Jenyns, Soame	1704-1787
Jephson, Robert	1736-1803
Jesse, Edward	1780-1868
Johnson, Samuel	1709-1784
Josika, Miklos	1794-1865
Joubert, Joseph	1754-1824
Jouffroy, Theodore Simon	1796-1842
Jouy, Victor Joseph Etienne De	1764-1846
Jovellanos, Gaspar Mechor De	1744-1811
Kames, Henry Home	1696-1782
Kant, Immanuel	1724-1804
Karadzic, Viek Stefanovic	1787-1864
Karamzin, Nicolai Mikhailovich	1765-1826
Karman, Jozsef	1769-1795
Kazinczy, Ferencz	1759-1831
Keats, John	1795-1821
Keble, John	1792-1866
Keightley, Thomas	1789-1872
Kellgren, Johan Henrik	1751-1795
Kelly, Hugh	1739-1777
Kenney, James	1780-1849
Kerner, Justinus Andreas Christian	1786-1862
Key, Francis Scott	1779-1843
King, Thomas	1730-1805
Kisfaludy, Karoly	1788-1830
Kisfaludy, Sandor	1772-1844
Kleist, Heinrich Wilhelm Von	1777-1811
Klinger, Friedrich Maximilian Von	1752-1831
Klopstock, Friedrich Gottlieb	1724-1803
Knebel, Karl Ludwig Von	1744-1834

Knigge, Adolf Franz Friedrich	1752-1796	
Knight, Charles	1791-1873	
Knowles, James Sheridan	1784-1862	
Kock, Charles Paul De	1793-1871	
Kolcsey, Ferencz	1790-1888	
Kopisch, August	1799-1853	
Korner, Karl Theodor	1791-1813	
Kotzebue, August Friedrich Ferdinand Von	1761-1819	
Krause, Karl Christian Friedrich	1781-1832	
Krug, Wilhelm Traugott	1770-1842	
Kuhlau, Friedrich	1786-1832	
Krylou, Ivan Andreevich	1768-1844	
Lacepede, Bernard De Laville, Compte De	1756-1825	
Laclos, Rene Amboise Francois	1741-1803	
Laharpe, Frederic Cesar	1754-1838	
Laing, Malcolm	1762-1818	
Lacretelle, Jean Charles Dominique de	1766-1855	
Lamarck, Jean Chevalier de	1744-1829	
Lamartine, Alphonse De	1790-1869	
Lamb, Charles	1775-1834	
Lamennais, Hugues Felicite Robert De	1782-1854	
Landor, Walter Savage	1775-1864	
Langhorne, John	1735-1779	
Lappenberg, Johann Martin	1794-1865	
Laromibuiere, Pierre	1756-1837	
Las Cases, Emmanuel Dieudonné, Compte de	1766-1842	
Lauder, Sir Thomas Dick	1784-1848	
Lavater, Johann Kaspar	1741-1801	
Laya, Jean Louis	1761-1833	
Lee, Harriet	1757-1851	
Lee, Sophia	1750-1824	
Le Mercier, Nepomuvene	1771-1840	
Lemierre, Antoine Marin	1733-1793	
Lennoz, Charlotte	1720-1804	
Lenz, Jakob Michael Reinhold	1751-1792	
Leo, Heinrich	1799-1878	
Leopardi, Giacomo	1798-1837	
Leroux, Pierre	1798-1871	
Lespinasse, Julie De	1732-1776	
Lessing, Gotthold Ephraim	1729-1781	
Lewis, Matthew Gregory	1775-1818	
Leyden, John	1775-1811	
Lichtenberg, Georg Christoph	1742-1799	
Ligne, Charles Joseph	1735-1814	
Lingard, John	1771-1851	
Linnieus, Carl	1707-1778	
Lista Y Aragon, Alberto	1775-1848	
Lyttleton, George, 1st Baron	1709-1773	
Lockhart, John Gibson	1794-1854	
Lodge, Edmund	1756-1839	
Lofft, Capel	1751-1824	
Logan, John	1748-1788	
Louvet De Couvrai, Jean Baptiste	1760-1797	
Lover, Samuel	1797-1868	
Luttrell, Henry	1765-1851	
Mably, Gabriel Bennet De	1709-1785	
Macedo, Jose Agostinho De	1761-1831	
Mackenzie, Henry	1745-1831	
Mackintosh, Sir James	1765-1832	
Maclaren, Charles	1782-1866	
Macpherson, James	1736-1796	
Madan, Martin	1726-1790	
M'Crie, Thomas	1772-1835	
Maggin, William	1793-1842	
Magny, Claude Drigon	1797-1879	
Maine De Biran, Francois-Pierre Gonthier	1766-1824	
Maistre, Joseph De	1754-1821	
Maistre, Xavier De	1763-1852	
Majlath, Janos	1786-1855	
Malthus, Thomas Robert	1766-1834	
Manuel, Louis Pierre	1751-1793	
Manzoni, Alessandro	1785-1873	
Markham, Mrs.	1780-1837	
Marmontel, Jean Francois	1723-1799	
Marryat, Frederick	1792-1848	
Martin, Francois Xavier	1762-1846	
Martin, Martin	fl.1790	
Martinez De La Rosa, Francisco De Paula	1787-1862	
Masdeu, Juan Francisco De	1744-1817	
Mason, William	1725-1797	
Matthisson, Friedrich Von	1761-1831	
Maturin, Charles Robert	1782-1824	
Maurer, Georg Ludwig Von	1790-1872	
Melendez Valdes, Juan	1754-1817	
Mendelsshon, Moses	1729-1786	
Menzel, Wolfgang	1798-1873	
Mercier, Sebastien	1740-1814	
Merck, Johann Heinrich	1741-1791	
Metastasio	1698-1782	
Michaud, Joseph Francois	1767-1839	
Michelet, Jules	1798-1874	
Michell, John	1724-1793	
Mickiewicz, Adam	1798-1855	
Mickle, William Julius	1735-1788	
Mignet, Francois Auguste Marie	1796-1884	
Mill, James	1773-1836	
Milman, Henry Hart	1791-1868	
Mirabeau, Victor Riqueti	1715-1789	
Mitford, John	1781-1859	
Mitford, Mary Russell	1787-1855	
Mitford, William	1744-1827	
Moir, David Macbeth	1798-1851	
Moller, Poul Martin	1794-1838	

Montagu, Elizabeth	1720-1800	Prescott, William Hickling	1796-1859
Montefiore, Joshua	1762-1843	Price, Richard	1723-1791
Montgomery, James	1771-1854	Priestley, Joseph	1733-1809
Monti, Vincenzo	1754-1828	Pringle, Thomas	1789-1834
Moore, John	1729-1802	Procter, Bryan Waller	1787-1874
Moore, Thomas	1779-1852	Proud, Robert	1728-1813
Moratin, Leandro		Pushkin, Alexander	1799-1837
Fernandez De	1760-1828	Pye, Henry James	1745-1813
More, Hannah	1745-1833	Pyne, William Henry	1769-1843
Morellet, Andre	1727-1819	Quincy, Josiah	1772-1864
Morgan, Lady Sydney	1783-1859	Quintana, Manuel Jose	1772-1857
Morier, James	1780-1849	Radcliffe, Ann	1764-1823
Moritz, Karl Philipp	1757-1793	Ranke, Leopold Von	1795-1886
Morton, Thomas	1764-1838	Raspe, Rudolf Erich	1737-1794
Motherwell, William	1797-1835	Rauch, Christian Daniel	1777-1875
Muller, Friedrich	1749-1825	Raumer, Friedrich Ludwig	
Muller, Johannes Von	1752-1809	George Van	1781-1873
Muller, Wilhelm	1794-1827	Raynal, Guillaume Thomas	
Murphy, Arthur	1727-1805	Francois	1713-1796
Musaus, Johann Karl		Raynouard, Francois Juste	
August	1735-1787	Marie	1761-1836
Nairne, Carolina Oliphant	1766-1845	Reeve, Clara	1729-1807
Nascimento, Francisco		Reid, Thomas	1710-1796
Manoel De	1734-1819	Remusat, Charles Francois	
Nasmyth, Patrick	1787-1831	Marie	1797-1875
Neal, John	1793-1876	Restif, Nicolas Edme	1734-1806
Neander, Johann	1789-1850	Richmond, Legh	1772-1827
Nichols, John	1745-1826	Richter, Johann Paul	
Nicholson, William	1753-1815	Freidrich	1763-1825
Nicolai, Christoph		Ritter, Heinrich	1791-1869
Friedrich	1733-1811	Rivarol, Antoine De	1753-1801
Niebuhr, Barthold Georg	1776-1831	Rivas, Angel De Saavedra	1791-1865
Nitzsch, Karl Immanuel	1787-1868	Robertson, William	1721-1793
Nodier, Charles	1780-1844	Rogers, Samuel	1763-1855
Normanby, Constantine		Roscoe, William	1753-1831
Henry Phipps	1797-1863	Rosmini-Serbati, Antonio	1797-1855
Ohlenschlager, Adam		Rossetti, Gabriele	1783-1854
Gottlob	1779-1850	Rouget De Lisle, Claude	
Olmedo, Jose Joaquin De	1780-1847	Joseph	1760-1836
Opie, Amelia	1769-1853	Rousseau, Jean Jacques	1712-1778
Orme, Robert	1728-1801	Royer-Collard, Pierre Paul	1763-1845
Paine, Thomas	1737-1809	Rückert, Freidrich	1788-1866
Palacky, Frantisek	1798-1876	Rulhiere, Claude	
Paley, William	1743-1805	Carloman De	1735-1791
Palfrey, John Gorham	1796-1881	Russell, Thomas	1762-1788
Palgrave, Sir Francis	1788-1861	Sade, Donatien Alphonse	
Parini, Giuseppe	1729-1799	Francois, Marquis De	1740-1814
Paulding, James Kirke	1778-1860	Safarik, Pavel Joseph	1795-1861
Payne, John Howard	1791-1852	Saintine, Joseph Xavier	1798-1865
Peacock, Thomas Love	1785-1866	Saint-Lambert, Jean	
Pellico, Silvio	1788-1854	Francois De	1716-1803
Percival, James Gates	1795-1856	Saint-Martin, Louis	
Percy, Thomas	1729-1811	Claude De	1743-1803
Pertz, Georg Heinrich	1795-1876	Saint-Pierre, Bernardin De	1737-1814
Picken, Andrew	1788-1833	Salomon, Johann Peter	1745-1815
Pindemonte, Ippolito	1753-1828	Schelling, Friedrich	
Piozzi, Hester Lynch	1741-1821	Wilhelm Joseph Von	1775-1854
Piranesi, Giambattista	1720-1778	Schiller, Johann Cristoph	
Planche, James Robinson	1796-1880	Friedrich Von	1759-1805
Porter, Anna Maria	1780-1832	Schimmelpenninck, Mary	
Porter, Jane	1776-1850	Ann	1778-1856

N

Schlegel, August Wilhelm Von	1767-1845
Schlegel, Friedrich Von	1772-1829
Schleiermacher, Friedrich Daniel Ernst	1768-1834
Schlozer, August Ludwig Von	1735-1809
Schopenhaur, Arthur	1788-1860
Schubart, Christian Friedrich Daniel	1739-1791
Scott, Sir Walter	1771-1832
Scribe, Eugene	1791-1861
Sedaine, Michel Jean	1719-1797
Seguir, William	1771-1843
Segur, Philippe Paul, Comte De	1780-1873
Semler, Johann, Salomo	1725-1791
Senac De Meilhan, Gabriel	1736-1803
Senancour, Etienne Pivert De	1770-1846
Seward, Anna	1747-1809
Sheil, Richard Lalor	1791-1851
Shelley, Mary Wollstonecraft	1797-1851
Shelley, Percy Bysshe	1792-1822
Sheridan, Richard Brinsley Butler	1751-1816
Sheridan, Thomas	1719-1788
Sherwood, Mary Martha	1775-1851
Sigourney, Lydia Huntley	1791-1865
Sismondi, Jean Charles Leonard Simonde	1773-1842
Smith, Adam	1723-1790
Smith, Charlotte	1749-1806
Smith, Horace	1779-1849
Smith, James	1775-1839
Smith, John Stafford	1750-1836
Smith, Sydney	1771-1845
Southey, Robert	1774-1843
Souza-Botelo, Adelaide Filleul	1761-1836
Sparks, Jared	1789-1866
Stael, Madame De	1766-1817
Steffens, Henrik	1773-1845
Stendhal, Marie Henry Beyle	1783-1842
Stewart, Dugald	1753-1828
Stilling, Heinrich	1740-1817
Stolberg, Friedrich Leopold	1750-1819
Struensee, Johan Frederick	1737-1772
Strutt, Joseph	1742-1802
Swetchine, Madame	1782-1857
Talfourd, Sir Thomas Noon	1795-1854
Tannahill, Robert	1774-1810
Taylor, Ann	1782-1866
Taylor, Isaak	1787-1865
Taylor, Jane	1783-1824
Taylor, William	1765-1836
Tegner, Essaias	1782-1846
Tennant, William	1784-1848

Thierry, Jacques Nicolas Augustin	1795-1856
Thiers, Louis Adolph	1797-1877
Thirlwall, Connop	1797-1875
Thompson, William c.	1785-1833
Ticknor, George	1791-1871
Tieck, Johann Ludwig	1773-1853
Topffer, Rodolphe	1799-1846
Toreno, Jose Maria Queipo De Llano	1786-1843
Trelawny, Edward John	1792-1881
Trollope, Frances	1780-1863
Trumbull, John	1750-1831
Turner, Sharon	1768-1847
Uhland, Johann Ludwig	1787-1862
Uz, Johann Peter	1720-1796
Varnhagen Von Ense, Karl August	1785-1858
Verplanck, Gulian Crommelin	1786-1870
Vigny, Alfred De	1797-1863
Villemain, Abel Francois	1790-1870
Volney, Constantin Francois Chasseboeuf, Compte De	1757-1820
Voltaire, Francois Marie Arouet De	1694-1778
Voss, Johann Heinrich	1751-1826
Waagen, Gustav Friedrich	1794-1868
Wackenroder, Wilhelm Heinrich	1773-1798
Walker, John	1732-1807
Walker, Thomas	1784-1836
Walpole, Horace	1717-1797
Warton, Joseph	1722-1800
Warton, Thomas	1728-1790
Washington, George	1732-1799
Webster, Noah	1758-1843
Wells, Charles Jeremiah	1798-1879
Werner, Zacharias	1768-1823
Wesley, John	1703-1791
West, Benjamin	1738-1820
Whately, Richard	1787-1863
Whewell, William	1794-1866
White, Gilbert	1720-1793
White, Henry Kirke	1785-1806
Whitehead, Paul	1710-1774
Whitehead, William	1715-1785
Wieland, Christoph Martin	1733-1813
Wilberforce, William	1759-1833
Wilson, Alexander	1766-1813
Wilson, John	1785-1854
Winther, Christian	1796-1876
Wirt, William	1772-1834
Wolcot, John (Peter Pindar)	1738-1819
Wolfe, Charles	1791-1823
Wollaston, William Hyde	1766-1828
Wordsworth, Dorothy	1771-1855
Wordsworth, William	1770-1850
Wraxall, Sir Nathaniel William	1751-1831

Wyss, Johann	1781-1830	Zimmermann, Johan Georg	
Young, Arthur	1741-1820	Ritter Von	1728-1795
Zhukovsky, Vasili		Zschokke, Johann Heinrick	
Andreyevich	1783-1852	Daniel	1771-1848

ARTISTS

Abildgaard, Nicolaj		Chambers, Sir William	1726-1796
Abraham	1744-1809	Chantrey, Sir Francis	
Adam, James	1730-1794	Legatt	1781-1841
Adam, Robert	1728-1792	Chardin, Jean Baptiste	
Allan, David	1744-1796	Simeon	1699-1779
Allan, Sir William	1782-1850	Charlet, Nicolas Toussaint	1792-1845
Allston, Washington	1779-1843	Chippendale, Thomas	
Alvarez, Don Jose	1768-1827	(cabinet maker)	1718-1779
Alvarez, Don Manuel	1727-1797	Chisholm, Alexander	1792-1847
Appiani, Andrea	1754-1817	Chodowiecki, Daniel	
Audubon, John James	1785-1851	Nicolas	1726-1801
Bacon, John	1740-1799	Cipriani, Giovanni Bastista	1727-1785
Baily, Edward Hodges	1788-1867	Cleveland, John	1747-1786
Baltard, Louis Pierre	1764-1846	Cleveland, Robert	1747-1809
Banks, Thomas	1735-1805	Cockerell, Charles Robert	1788-1863
Barker, Robert	1739-1806	Constable, John	1776-1837
Barry, Sir Charles	1795-1860	Cooper, Abraham	1787-1868
Barry, James	1741-1806	Corbould, Richard	1757-1831
Bartolini, Lorenzo	1777-1850	Cornelius, Peter Von	1783-1867
Bartolozzi, Francesco	1727-1815	Corot, Jean-Baptiste	
Barye, Antoine Louis	1796-1875	Camille	1796-1875
Batoni, Pompeo Girolamo	1708-1787	Cosway, Richard	1742-1821
Begas, Karl	1794-1854	Cotman, John Sell	1782-1842
Bewick, Thomas	1753-1828	Cox, David	1783-1859
Bird, Edward	1772-1819	Cozens, Alexander	d. 1782
Bone, Henry	1755-1834	Cozens, John Robert	1752-1797
Bonomi, Giuseppe	1739-1808	Crome, John	1768-1821
Bosio, Francois Joseph,		Cruikshank, George	1792-1878
Baron	1769-1845	Daguerre, Louis Jacques	
Bossi, Giuseppe	1777-1816	Mande	1789-1851
Boydell, John	1719-1804	Dahl, Johann Kristen	
Brown, Lancelot		Clausen	1788-1857
(" Capability ") (land-		Damer, Anne Seymour	1749-1828
scape gardener)	1715-1783	Danby, Francis	1793-1861
Bulfinch, Charles	1763-1844	Dance, George	1741-1825
Burn, William	1789-1870	Daniell, Samuel	1775-1811
Bystrom, Johan Niklas	1783-1848	Daniell, Thomas	1749-1840
Cagnola, Luigi	1762-1833	Daniell, William	1769-1837
Callcott, Sir Augustus Wall	1779-1844	Dannecker, Johann	
Calvert, Charles	1785-1852	Heinrich Von	1758-1841
Calvert, Edward	1799-1883	Dantan, Antoine Laurent	1798-1878
Camuccini, Vincenzo	1773-1844	Darly, Matthew	-1781
Camus De Mezieres,		David, Jacques Louis	1748-1825
Nicolas Le	1721-1789	Delacroix, Ferdinand	
Canaletto, Bernardo		Victor Eugene	1798-1863
Belleto	1720-1780	Delaroche, Hippolyte	1797-1856
Canova, Antonio	1757-1822	De Loutherbourg, Philip	
Carstens, Armus Jacob	1754-1798	James	1740-1812
Casanova De Seingalt,		Denon, Dominique Vivant,	
Francesco	1727-1805	Baron de	1747-1825
Casanova De Seingalt,		Des Moulins, Camillo	1760-1794
Giovanni Battista	1728-1795	Downman, John	1750-1824
Cattermole, George	1800-1868	Doyen, Gabriel Francois	1726-1806

Drouais, Jean Germain	1763-1788
Dumont, Francois	1751-1831
Durand, Asher Brown	1796-1886
Earlom, Richard	1743-1822
Eastlake, Sir Charles Lock	1793-1865
Eckersberg, Kristoffer	1783-1853
Engleheart, George	1752-1829
Etty, William	1787-1849
Falconet, Ettienne	
Maurice	1716-1791
Farington, Joseph	1747-1821
Fielding, Copley	1787-1855
Fiorillo, Johann Dominicus	1748-1821
Flaxman, John	1755-1826
Fogelberg, Benedict Erland	1786-1854
Fontaine, Pierre Francois	
Leonard	1762-1853
Fowler, Charles	1792-1867
Fragonard, Jean Honore	1732-1806
Friedrich, Caspar David	1774-1840
Fuseli, Henry	1741-1825
Gabriel, Jacques Ange	1698-1782
Gainsborough, Thomas	1727-1788
Gerard, Francois	1770-1837
Gericault, Theodore	1791-1824
Gessner, Salomon	1730-1788
Gibson, John	1790-1866
Gillray, James	1757-1815
Girodet De Roussy, Anne	
Louis	1767-1824
Gordon, Sir John Watson	1788-1864
Girtin, Thomas	1775-1802
Goya Y Lucientes,	
Francisco	1746-1828
Granet, Francois Marius	1775-1849
Greuze, Jean Baptiste	1725-1805
Gros, Antoine Jean	1771-1835
Guardi, Francesco	1712-1793
Guerin, Pierre Narcisse	1774-1833
Gwilt, Joseph	1784-1863
Hansen, Christian	
Frederick	1756-1845
Harding, Chester	1792-1866
Harlow, George Henry	1787-1819
Haydon, Benjamin Robert	1786-1846
Hayter, Sir George	1792-1871
Heaphy, Thomas	1775-1835
Hepplewhite, George	
(cabinet maker)	-1786
Highmore, Joseph	1692-1780
Hilton, William	1786-1839
Hiroshige, Audo	1797-1858
Hittorff, Jacques Ignace	1792-1867
Hokusai, Katsushika	1760-1849
Hoppner, John	1758-1810
Houdon, Jean Antoine	1740-1828
Humphry, Ozias	1742-1810
Hunt, William Henry	1790-1864
Ingres, Jean Auguste	
Dominique	1780-1867
Isabey, Jean Baptiste	1767-1855

Kauffmann, Angelica	1741-1807
Kirkup, Seymour Stocker	1788-1880
La Grenee, Jean Louis	
Francois	1724-1805
La Tour, Maurice	
Quentin De	1704-1788
Lawrence, Sir Thomas	1769-1830
Le Brun, Marie Elizabeth	
Louise	1755-1842
Lejeune, Louis Francois	1775-1848
Lemaire, Philippe Honoré	1798-1880
Lemoyne, Jean Baptiste	1704-1778
L'Enfant, Pierre Charles	1754-1825
Leslie, Charles Robert	1794-1859
Linnell, John	1792-1882
Liotard, Jean Etienne	1702-1789
Longhi, Pietro	1702-1785
Martin, John	1789-1854
Mengs, Antony Raphael	1728-1779
Michel, Claude	1738-1814
Moore, William	1790-1851
Morland, George	1763-1804
Morse, Samuel Finley	
Breese	1791-1872
Motte, William De La	1775-1863
Mulready, William	1786-1863
Nash, John	1752-1835
Nasmyth, Alexander	1758-1840
Nollekens, Joseph	1737-1823
Northcote, James	1746-1831
Opie, John	1761-1807
Overbeck, Johann	
Friedrich	1789-1869
Pajou, Augustin	1730-1809
Peale, Charles Willson	1741-1827
Peale, Rembrandt	1778-1860
Percier, Charles	1764-1838
Pigalle, Jean Baptiste	1714-1785
Pine, Robert Edge	1730-1788
Pinelli, Bartolomeo	1781-1834
Playfair, William Henry	1789-1857
Plimer, Andrew	1763-1837
Porta, Carlo	1776-1821
Porter, Robert Ker	1775-1842
Prout, Samuel	1783-1852
Prud'Hon, Pierre	1758-1823
Raeburn, Sir Henry	1756-1823
Ramsay, Allan	1713-1784
Reynolds, Sir Joshua	1723-1792
Rickman, Thomas	1776-1841
Robert, Hubert	1733-1808
Roberts, David	1796-1864
Romney, George	1734-1802
Rousseau De La Rottiere,	
Jean Simeon	1747-
Rowlandson, Thomas	1756-1827
Rude, Francois	1784-1855
Sandby, Paul	1725-1809
Schadow, Friedrick	
Wilhelm	1798-1862
Schadow, Johann Gottlieb	1764-1850

Schadow, Rudolf	1786-1822	Utamaro	1754-1806
Scheffer, Ary	1795-1858	Vanderlyn, John	1776-1852
Schnorr Von Karolsfeld,		Varley, John	1778-1842
Julius	1794-1872	Veit, Philipp	1793-1877
Severn, Joseph	1793-1879	Verboeckhoven, Eugen	
Shee, Sir Marin Archer	1769-1850	Joseph	1798-1881
Sheraton, Thomas		Vernet, Antoine Charles	
(cabinet maker)	1751-1806	Horace	1758-1835
Smart, John	1740-1811	Vernet, Claude Joseph	1714-1789
Smirke, Sir Robert	1781-1867	Vernet, Emile Jean	
Smith, John Raphael	1752-1812	Horace	1789-1863
Soane, Sir John	1753-1837	Vigee-Lebrun, Marie-Anne	
Soufflot, Jacques Germain	1709-1780	Elizabeth	1755-1842
Sowerby, James	1757-1822	Wainewright, Thomas	
Stanfield, William		Griffiths	1794-1852
Clarkson	1794-1867	Waldo, Samuel Lovett	1783-1861
Stark, James	1794-1859	Wedgewood, Josiah	
Stothard, Thomas	1755-1834	(potter)	1730-1795
Stuart, Gilbert	1755-1828	Westmacott, Sir Richard	1775-1856
Stuart, James	1713-1788	Wilkie, Sir David	1785-1841
Sully, Thomas	1783-1872	Wilson, Richard	1714-1782
Thorvaldsen, Bertel	1770-1844	Wint, Peter De	1784-1849
Tite, Sir William	1798-1873	Wright, Joseph	1734-1797
Trumbull, John	1756-1843	Wyatt, James	1746-1813
Towne, Francis	1739-1816	Zoffany, Johann	1733-1810
Turner, Joseph Mallord		Zuccarelli, Francesco	1702-1788
William	1775-1851	Zucchi, Antonio Pietro	1726-1795

COMPOSERS

Albrechtberger, Johann		Corri, Domenico	1746-1825
Gregory	1736-1809	Crotch, William	1775-1847
Arne, Thomas Augustine	1710-1778	Czerny, Karl	1791-1857
Arnold, Samuel	1740-1802	Diabelli, Anton Antonio	1781-1858
Asioli, Bonifacio	1769-1832	Dibdin, Charles	1745-1814
Attwood, Thomas	1765-1838	Dittersdorf, Karl Ditters	
Auber, Daniel Francois		Von	1739-1799
Eprit	1782-1871	Donizetti, Gaetano	1797-1848
Bach, Johann Christian	1735-1782	Dussek, Jan Ladislav	1761-1812
Bach, Karl Philipp		Eberwein, Traugott	
Emanuel	1714-1788	Maximilian	1775-1831
Bach, Wilhelm Friedmann	1710-1784	Fetis, Francois Joseph	1784-1871
Baini, Guiseppe	1775-1844	Field, John	1782-1837
Batishill, Jonathan	1738-1801	Galuppi, Baldassare	1706-1785
Beethoven, Ludwig Van	1770-1827	Gansbacher, Johann	
Benda, Georg	1722-1795	Baptist	1778-1844
Bishop, Sir Henry Rowley	1786-1855	Garcia, Manoel	1775-1832
Boccherini, Luigi	1743-1805	Gazzaniga, Giuseppe	1743-1818
Boieldieu, Francois Adrien	1775-1834	Geddes, Andrew	1783-1844
Boyce, William	1710-1779	Giordani, Guiseppe	1744-1798
Callcott, John Wall	1766-1821	Gluck, Christoph	
Cambini, Giovanni		Willibald	1714-1787
Giuseppe	1746-1825	Gossec, Francois Joseph	1734-1829
Cannabich, Christian	1731-1798	Gow, Niel	1727-1807
Cherubini, Maria Luigi	1760-1842	Gretry, Andre Ernest	1741-1813
Cimarosa, Domenico	1749-1801	Halevy, Jacques Francois	1799-1862
Campenhout, Francois		Hasse, Johann Adolph	1699-1783
Von	1779-1849	Hauptmann, Moritz	1792-1868
Clementi, Muzio	1752-1832	Haydn, Franz Joseph	1732-1809
Corbould, Henry	1787-1844	Haydn, Michael	1737-1806

Herold, Louis Joseph	1791-1833	**Philidor,** Francois Andre	
Hiller, Johann Adam	1728-1804	Danican	1726-1795
Himmel, Fredrick Henry	1765-1814	**Piccinni,** Niccola	1728-1800
Horn, Charles Edward	1786-1849	**Pleyel,** Ignaz Joseph	1757-1831
Hummel, Johann		**Retzsch,** Friedrich August	
Nepomuk	1778-1837	Moritz	1779-1857
Jackson, Wilhelm	1730-1803	**Rossini,** Gioachino	
Kelly, Michael	1762-1826	Antonio	1792-1868
Kreutzer, Konradin	1780-1849	**Salieri,** Antonio	1750-1825
Lesueur, Jean Francois	1760-1837	**Sarti,** Giuseppe	1729-1802
Linley, Thomas	1732-1795	**Sacchini,** Antonio Maria	
Loewe, Johann Karl		Gaspare	1734-1786
Gottfried	1796-1869	**Schinkel,** Karl Friedrich	1781-1841
Lucchesi, Andrea	1741-1800	**Schubert,** Franz Peter	1797-1828
Marschner, Heinrich		**Shield,** William	1748-1829
August	1795-1861	**Spohr,** Ludwig	1784-1859
Mehul, Etienne Nicolas	1763-1817	**Spontini,** Gasparo Luigi	
Meyebeer, Giacomo	1791-1864	Pacifico	1774-1851
Monsigny, Pierre		**Stamitz,** Carl Philipp	1745-1801
Alexandre	1729-1817	**Stanley,** John	1713-1786
Mozart, Wolfgang		**Steibelt,** Daniel	1764-1823
Amadeus	1756-1791	**Storace,** Stephen	1763-1796
Nardini, Pietro	1722-1793	**Viotti,** Giovanni Battista	1753-1824
Nares, James	1715-1783	**Vogler,** Georg Joseph	1749-1814
Nathan, Isaac	1791-1864	**Weber,** Carl Maria	1786-1826
Paer, Ferdinando	1771-1839	**Wesley,** Samuel	1766-1837
Paisiello, Giovanni	1741-1816	**Zingarelli,** Niccolo	1752-1837
Pearsall, Robert Lucas De	1795-1856		

1801	Battle of Alexandria.
	Treaty of Peace between Great Britain and France.
1803	Napoleon sells Louisiana to U.S.
	Britain declares war on France.
1804	Code Napoleon published.
	Napoleon and Josephine crowned.
	Spain declares war on Britain.
1805	Battle of Trafalgar.
	Battle of Austerlitz.
1806	Battle of Jena.
1807	Battle of Eylau.
	Battle of Friedland.
1808	Battle of Vimiera.
1809	Battle of Corunna.
	Napoleon excommunicated.
	France and Austria sign peace treaty.
1811	Battle of Fuentes d'Onore.
	Battle of Albuera.
	Luddite riots.
1812	United States declare war on Great Britain.
	Napoleon declares war on Russia.
	Battle of Salamanca.
	Battle of Borodino. Burning of Moscow.
1813	Execution of Luddites.
	Battle of Lutzen.
	Battle of Vittorio.
	Battle of the Pyrenees.
	Battle of Leipsic.
1814	Battle of Orthez.
	Napoleon deposed, banished to Elba.
	Peace between Great Britain and U.S.
1815	Battle of New Orleans.
	Napoleon escapes from Elba. Declares new constitution.
	Battle of Ligny.
	Battle of Quatre Bras.
	Battle of Waterloo.
	Napoleon sent to St. Helena.
1817	Riots at Manchester.
	Battle of Mehudpore.
1819	Florida ceded to U.S. by Spain.
	" Peterloo."
1822	Massacre by Turks at Scio.

PROMINENT PEOPLE

Brown, John	1800-1859	Lessep, Vicomte Ferdinande de	1805-1894
Brummell, 'Beau,' George Bryan	1778-1840	Livingstone, Dr. David	1813-1873
Emmett, Robert	1778-1803	Manning, Henry Edward, Cardinal	1808-1892
Faraday, Michael	1791-1863		
Hastings, Warren	1732-1818	Nelson, Horatio, Viscount	1758-1805
Hood, Samuel, 1st Viscount, Admiral	1724-1816	Paganini, Nicolo	1782-1840
		Smith, Joseph	1805-1844
Jenner, Edward	1749-1823	Wellington, Duke of	1769-1852
Josephine, Empress	1763-1814		

EMPERORS OF CHINA (MANCHU (Ch'ing) DYNASTY)

Jen Tsung	1795-1820	Hsuan Tsung	1820-1850

POPES

Pius VII   1800-1823   Leo XII   1823-1829

FRANCE. HEADS OF STATE

The Consulate	1799-1804	Louis XVIII	1814-1824
Napoleon I	1804-1814	Charles X	1824-1830

HOLY ROMAN EMPERORS

Francis II (abdicated)   1792-1806

ENGLAND. SOVEREIGNS

George III   1760-1820   George IV   1820-1830

SWEDEN. KINGS

Gustavius IV	1792-1809	Charles XIV (Bernadotte)	1818-1844
Charles XIII	1809-1818		

PORTUGAL. KINGS

Maria I   1777-1816   John VI   1816-1826

PRUSSIA. KINGS

Frederick William III   1797-1840

RUSSIA. TSARS

Paul	1796-1801	Nicholas I	1825-1855
Alexander I	1801-1825		

SPAIN. SOVEREIGNS

Ferdinand VII	1808	Ferdinand VII	1813-1833
Joseph Bonaparte	1808-1812		

U.S.A. PRESIDENTS

John Adams	1797-1801	James Monroe	1817-1825
Thomas Jefferson	1801-1809	John Quincy Adams	1825-1829
James Maddison	1809-1817		

AUSTRIA. EMPERORS

Franz I   1804-1835

NETHERLANDS. SOVEREIGNS

William I   1815-1840

WRITERS

Aarestrup, Emil	1800-1856	Abbot, Jacob	1803-1879
Aasen, Ivar	1813-1896	A'Beckett, Gilbert, Abbot	1811-1856

Abernethy, John	1764-1831
Ackermann, Louise	
Victorine Choquet	1813-1890
Adam, Alexander	1741-1809
Adams, Hannah	1755-1831
Adams, John	1735-1826
Adams, John Quincy	1767-1848
Adams, Sarah Flower	1805-1848
Adams, William Taylor	1822-1897
Adanson, Michel	1727-1806
Adolphus, John	1768-1845
Adolphus, John Leycester	1795-1862
Aepinus, Franz Ulrich	
Theodor	1724-1802
Afzelius, Aruid August	1785-1871
Agassiz, Jean Louis	
Rodolphe	1807-1873
Aikin, John	1747-1822
Aikin, Lucy	1781-1864
Aimard, Gustave	1818-1883
Ainslie, Hew	1792-1872
Ainsworth, William	
Harrison	1805-1882
Aird, Thomas	1802-1876
Agoult, Marie Catherine	
Sophie, Countess de	
Flavigny	
(Daniel Stern)	1805-1876
Aguilar, Grace	1816-1847
Aguilo Y Fuster, Marian	1825-1897
Akers, Benjamin Paul	1825-1861
Aksakov, Sergei	
Timofeyevich	1719-1859
Aksakov, Ivan Sergeyevich	1823-1886
Aksakov, Konstantin	1817-1860
Alaman, Lucas	1792-1853
Alcott, Amos Bronson	1799-1888
Alden, Joseph	1807-1885
Aleardi, Aleardo	1812-1878
Alecsandri, Vasile	1821-1890
Alexander, Cecil Francis	1818-1895
Alexis, Willibald	1798-1871
Alfireri, Vittorio, Count	1749-1803
Alison, Sir Archibald	1792-1867
Allibone, Samuel Austin	1816-1889
Allingham, William	1824-1889
Allmers, Hermann	1821-1902
Almeida-Garrett, Joao	
Baptista Da	1799-1854
Almqvist, Karl Jonas	
Ludwig	1793-1866
Ampere, Jean Jacques	1800-1864
Ancelot, Jacques Arsene	
Francois Polycarpe	1794-1854
Ancillon, Johann Peter	
Friedrich	1766-1836
Andersen, Hans Christian	1805-1875
Anderson, Robert	1750-1830
Andrieux, Francois	
Guillaume Jean Stanislas	1759-1833
Anquetil, Louis Pierre	1723-1808
Anspach, Elizabeth,	
Magravine of	1750-1828
Anstey, Christopher	1724-1805
Apperley, Charles James	
(Nimrod)	1777-1843
Arago, Jacques Etienne	
Victor	1790-1855
Arany, Janos	1817-1882
Archenholz, Johann	
Wilhelm Von	1743-1812
Aribau, Bonaventura	
Carles	1798-1862
Armitage, Edward	1817-1896
Arnason, Jon	1819-1888
Arnault, Antoine Vincent	1766-1834
Arndt, Ernst Moritz	1769-1860
Arneth, Alfred	1819-1897
Arnim, Elizabeth	
(Bettina) Von	1785-1859
Arnim, Ludwig Achim	
Von	1781-1831
Arnold, Matthew	1822-1888
Arnold, Thomas	1795-1842
Arthur, Timothy Shay	1809-1885
Asbjornsen, Peter Christian	1812-1885
Atkinson, Thomas Witlam	1799-1861
Auerbach, Berthold	1812-1882
Auersperg, Anton	
Alexander	1806-1876
Augier, Guillaume Victor	
Emile	1820-1889
Austen, Jane	1775-1817
Austin, Sarah	1793-1867
Autran, Joseph	1813-1877
Avellanida, Gertrudis	
Gomez D'	1814-1873
Aytoun, William	
Edmonstoun	1813-1865
Azais, Pierre Hyacinthe	1766-1845
Azeglio, Massimo	
Taparelli, Marquis D'	1798-1866
Bacon, Delia Salter	1811-1859
Bacon, Leonard	1802-1881
Bacsanyi, Janos	1763-1845
Baedeker, Karl	1801-1859
Baggesen, Jens Immanuel	1764-1826
Bahr, Johann Christian	
Felix	1798-1872
Bailey, Philip James	1816-1902
Bailey, Samuel	1791-1870
Baillie, Joanna	1762-1851
Bain, Alexander	1818-1903
Balaguer y Cirera, Victor	1824-1901
Balbo, Cesare, Count	1789-1853
Balfe, Michael Willen	1808-1870
Ballanche, Pierre Simon	1776-1847
Ballantine, James	1808-1877
Ballantyne, Robert	
Michael	1825-1894
Balmes, Jaime Luciano	1810-1848
Balzac, Honore De	1799-1850

Bancroft, George	1800-1891
Banim, John	1798-1842
Banville, Theodore Faullain De	1823-1891
Barante, Amable Guillaume Prosper Brugiere	1782-1866
Baratynski, Yevgeniy Abramovich	1800-1844
Barbauld, Anna Letitia	1743-1825
Barbey D'Aurevilly, Jules Amedee	1808-1889
Barbier, Henri Auguste	1805-1882
Barbier, Paul Jules	1825-1901
Barker, Thomas, of Bath	1769-1847
Barker, Thomas Jones Barker	1815-1882
Barlow, Joel	1754-1812
Barlow, Peter	1776-1862
Barnard, Lady Anne	1750-1825
Barnes, William	1800-1886
Barrington, George (Waldron)	1755-1804
Barthelemy, Auguste Marseille	1796-1867
Barthelemy, Saint Hilaire Jules	1805-1895
Barton, Bernard	1784-1849
Basevi, George	1794-1845
Batyushkov, Konstantin Nikolaievitch	1787-1855
Baudelaire, Charles Pierre	1821-1867
Baudissin, Wolf Heinrich	1789-1878
Bauer, Bruno	1809-1882
Bauernfeld, Eduard Von	1802-1890
Bautain, Louis Eugene Marie	1796-1867
Bayly, Thomas Haynes	1797-1839
Beattie, James	1735-1803
Beauchamp, Alphonse De	1767-1832
Beaumont, Sir George Howland	1753-1827
Beauvoir, Roger De	1809-1866
Beck, Christian Daniel	1757-1832
Beck, Jakob Sigismund	1761-1840
Beckford, William Thomas	1760-1844
Beddoes, Thomas Lovell	1803-1849
Beecher, Henry Ward	1813-1887
Beechey, Sir William	1753-1839
Beets, Nikolaas	1814-1903
Beffroy De Reigny, Louis Abel	1757-1811
Bekker, Elizabeth	1738-1804
Bell, Henry Glassford	1803-1874
Bell, Robert	1800-1867
Belli, Giuseppe Gioachino	1791-1863
Benedix, Julius Roderich	1811-1873
Beneke, Friedrich Edward	1798-1856
Bentham, Jeremy	1748-1832
Beranger, Pierre Jean De	1780-1857
Berard, Joseph Frederic	1789-1828
Berchet, Giovanni	1783-1851

Bernard, Charles De	1804-1850
Berry, Mary	1763-1852
Bertrand, Jacques Louis Napoleon	1807-1841
Berzsenyi, Daniel	1776-1836
Beskow, Bernhard Von	1796-1868
Bibaud, Michel	1782-1857
Bickerstaffe, Isaac	1735-1812
Biedermann, Friedrich Karl	1812-1901
Bignon, Louis Pierre Edouard	1771-1841
Bilderdijk, Willem	1756-1831
Billings, Robert William	1813-1874
Bissen, Herman Vilhelm	1798-1868
Bitzius, Albrecht	1797-1854
Blackie, John Stuart	1809-1895
Blackmore, Richard Doddridge	1825-1900
Blake, William	1757-1827
Blanc, Jean Joseph Charles Louis	1811-1882
Blanchard, Samuel Laman	1804-1845
Blessington, Marguerite	1789-1849
Blicher, Steen Steensen	1782-1848
Bloomfield, Robert	1766-1823
Blore, Edward	1787-1879
Bocage, Manuel Maria Barbosa De	1765-1805
Boccage, Marie Anne Fiquet De	1710-1802
Bodenstedt, Friedrich Martin Von	1819-1892
Boerne, Karl Ludwig	1786-1837
Boie, Heinrich Christian	1744-1806
Boisgobey, Fortune Abraham Du	1824-1891
Boker, George Henry	1823-1890
Bonald, Louis Gabriel Ambroise	1754-1840
Bonneville, Nicholas De	1760-1828
Bonstetten, Charles Victor De	1745-1832
Borel, Petrus	1809-1859
Borne, Ludwig	1786-1837
Bornier, Henri	1825-1901
Borrow, George Henry	1803-1881
Bosboom-Toussaint, Anna Louisa Geertruida	1812-1886
Bostrom, Christoffer Jacob	1797-1866
Botta, Carlo Guiseppe Guglielmo	1766-1837
Boucicault, Dion	1822-1890
Bouilhet, Louis Hyacinthe	1822-1869
Bouilly, Jean-Nicolas	1763-1842
Bouterwek, Friedrich	1765-1828
Bowdich, Thomas Edward	1790-1824
Bowdler, Thomas (editor)	1754-1825
Bowen, Francis	1811-1890
Bowles, William Lisle	1762-1850
Boyd, Andrew Kennedy Hutchinson	1825-1899

Boylai, Wolfgang	1775-1856	Campoamor Y Campoosorio,	
Bree, Matthias Ignatius		Raymon De	1819-1901
Van	1773-1839	Canina, Luigi	1795-1856
Bremer, Fredrika	1801-1865	Cannon, Charles James	1800-1860
Brentano, Clemens	1778-1842	Cantu, Cesare	1804-1895
Breton de Los Herreros,		Capefigue, Jean-Baptiste	
Manuel	1796-1873	Honore Raymond	1801-1872
Brierley, Benjamin	1825-1896	Capern, Edward	1819-1894
Brillat-Savarin, Anthelme	1755-1826	Carlen, Emilia Smith	
Brizeux, Julien Auguste		Flygare	1807-1892
Pelage	1803-1858	Carleton, William	1794-1869
Bronte, Anne	1820-1849	Carlyle, Thomas	1795-1881
Bronte, Charlotte	1816-1855	Carrer, Luigi	1801-1850
Bronte, Emily	1818-1848	Carriere, Moritz	1817-1895
Brooks, Charles William		Carter, Elizabeth	1717-1806
Shirley	1816-1874	Cary, Alice	1820-1871
Broughton, John Cam		Castelli, Ignaz Franz	1781-1862
Hobhouse	1786-1869	Castello, Branco Camillo	1825-1890
Brown, Charles Brockden	1771-1810	Casti, Giovanni Battista	1724-1803
Brown, Samuel Morison	1817-1856	Cattaneo, Carlo	1801-1869
Brown, Thomas	1778-1820	Cavalcaselle, Giovanni	
Browne, James	1793-1841	Battista	1820-1897
Browning, Elizabeth		Cesarotti, Melchiore	1730-1808
Barrett	1806-1861	Chalmers, Alexander	1759-1834
Browning, Robert	1812-1889	Chalybaus, Heinrich	
Brownson, Orestes		Moritz	1796-1862
Augustus	1803-1876	Chambers, Robert	1802-1871
Brunton, Mary	1778-1818	Chamier, Frederick	1796-1870
Bryant, Jacob	1715-1804	Chamisso, Adelbert Von	1781-1838
Bryant, William Cullen	1794-1878	Champfleury	1821-1889
Brydges, Sir Samuel		Channing, William Ellery	1780-1842
Egerton	1762-1837	Chapone, Hester	1727-1801
Buchez, Philippe Benjamin		Charriere, Isabelle De	1740-1805
Joseph	1796-1865	Chasles, Philarete	1798-1873
Buchner, Ludwig	1824-1899	Chateaubriand, Francois	
Buckhardt, Jakob	1818-1897	Rene	1768-1848
Buckingham, James Silk	1786-1855	Chenedolle, Charles Julien	
Buckle, Henry Thomas	1821-1862	Lioult De	1769-1833
Buckstone, John Baldwin	1802-1879	Chenier, Marie-Joseph	
Bulgarin, Thaddeus	1789-1859	Blaise De	1764-1811
Bulwer, Henry Lytton	1801-1872	Cheruel, Pierre Adolphe	1809-1891
Burney, Charles	1726-1814	Child, Francis James	1825-1896
Burney, Fanny		Child, Lydia Maria	1802-1874
(Madame D'Arblay)	1752-1840	Christopoulos, Athanasios	1772-1847
Burrows, Montagu	1819-1905	Cibrario, Luigi, Count	1802-1870
Burton, John Hill	1809-1881	Clare, John	1793-1864
Burton, Sir Richard		Clark, William George	1821-1878
Francis	1821-1890	Clarke, Charles Cowden	1787-1877
Burton, William Evans	1804-1860	Clarke, Edward Daniel	1769-1822
Bury, Lady Charlotte		Claudius, Matthias	1740-1815
Susan Maria	1775-1861	Clausewitz, Karl Von	1780-1831
Byron, George Gordon	1788-1824	Clive, Caroline	1801-1873
Caballero, Fernan	1796-1877	Clough, Arthur Hugh	1819-1861
Caird, John	1820-1898	Cobbe, Frances, Power	1822-1904
Cairns, John Elliot	1823-1875	Cobbett, William	1763-1835
Calvert, George Henry	1803-1889	Cockton, Henry	1807-1853
Calvo, Carlos	1824-1906	Cole, Sir Henry	1808-1882
Cambridge, Richard Owen	1717-1802	Coleridge, Hartley	1796-1849
Campan, Jeanne Louise		Coleridge, Samuel Taylor	1772-1834
Henriette	1752-1822	Coleridge, Sara	1802-1852
Campbell, Thomas	1777-1844	Colet, Louise	1810-1876

Collett, Jacobine Camilla	1813-1895	Darwin, Erasmus	1731-1802
Collier, John Payne	1789-1883	Dashkova, Catherina	
Collin, Heinrich Joseph		Romanovna	1744-1810
Von	1771-1811	D'Aubigné, Jean Henri	
Collin D'Harleville, Jean		Merle	1794-1872
Francois	1755-1806	Daumer, Georg Friedrich	1800-1875
Collins, William	1788-1847	Daunov, Pierre Claude	
Collins, William Wilkie	1824-1889	Francois	1761-1840
Colman, George	1762-1836	David, Pierre Jean	1789-1856
Combe, William	1741-1823	Davis, Thomas Osborne	1814-1845
Comte, Auguste	1798-1857	De Geer, Louis Gerhard,	
Conscience, Hendrik	1812-1883	Baron	1818-1896
Constant De Rebecque,		Dekker, Edward Douwes	1820-1887
Henri Benjamin	1767-1830	Delarue, Gervais	1751-1835
Cooper, James Fenimore	1789-1851	Delavigne, Jean Francois	
Coppee, Henry	1821-1895	Casimir	1793-1843
Costello, Louisa Stuart	1799-1870	Delille, Jacques	1738-1813
Cottin, Marie	1770-1807	Delolme, Jean Louis	1740-1806
Courier, Paul Louis	1773-1825	Delvig, Anton Antonovich,	
Cousin, Victor	1792-1867	Baron Von	1798-1831
Cowley, Hannah	1743-1809	Demogeot, Jacques Claude	1808-1894
Coxe, William	1747-1828	Denina, Carlo Giovanni	
Craven, Pauline	1808-1891	Maria	1731-1813
Crabbe, George	1754-1832	Dennery, Adolphe Philippe	1811-1899
Craufurd, Quintin	1743-1819	De Quincey, Thomas	1785-1859
Creasy, Sir Edward		Derzhavin, Gavrila	
Shepherd	1812-1878	Romanovich	1743-1816
Creevey, Thomas	1768-1838	Desagiers, Marc Antoine	
Cremazie, Octave	1822-1879	Madeleine	1772-1827
Creuzer, George Friedrich	1771-1858	Desforges, Pierre Jean	
Crocker, Hannah Mather	1752-1829	Baptiste Choudard	1746-1806
Croft, Sir Herbert	1751-1816	Deschamps, Emile	1791-1871
Crocker, John Wilson	1780-1857	De Vere, Aubrey Thomas	1814-1902
Croker, Thomas Crofton	1798-1854	Dexter, Henry Martyn	1821-1890
Crowe, Catherine	1800-1870	Dibdin, Thomas John	1771-1841
Crusenstolpe, Magnus		Dickens, Charles John	
Jakob	1795-1865	Huffam	1812-1870
Csengery, Antal	1822-1880	Digby, Kenelm Henry	1800-1880
Csokonai, Mihaly Vitez	1773-1805	Dingelstedt, Franz Von	1814-1881
Cullum, George Washington	1809-1892	Disraeli, Benjamin	1804-1881
Cumberland, Richard	1732-1811	D'Israeli, Isaac	1766-1848
Cunningham, Allan	1784-1842	Dixon, William Hepworth	1821-1879
Curtis, George William	1824-1892	Dmitriev, Ivan Ivanovich	1760-1837
Curtius, Ernst	1814-1896	Dobell, Sydney Thompson	1824-1874
Curtius, Georg	1820-1885	Dollinger, Johann Joseph	
Cuvier, Georges (Léopold)	1769-1832	Ignaz Von	1799-1890
Da Costa, Isaac	1798-1860	Domett, Alfred	1811-1887
Dahlgren, Karl Fredrik	1791-1844	Donoso, Cortez Juan	1809-1853
Dahlmann, Friedrich		Doran, John	1807-1878
Christoph	1785-1860	Dostoievsky, Fyodor	
Dalling and Bulwer,		Mikhaylovich	1821-1881
Baron	1801-1872	Douglas, Sir William Fettes	1822-1891
Dall'Ongaro, Francesco	1808-1873	Doyle, Sir Francis	
Dana, Richard Henry	1815-1882	Hastings Charles	1810-1888
Da Ponte, Lorenzo	1749-1838	Drake, Friedrich	1805-1882
Dareste De La Chavanne,		Drake, Nathan	1766-1836
Cleophas	1820-1882	Draper, William	1811-1882
Darley, George	1795-1846	Drinkwater, Bethune John	1762-1844
Daru, Pierre Antoine		Drobisch, Moritz Wilhelm	1802-1896
Comte	1767-1829	Droste-Hulshoff, Annette	
Darwin, Charles Robert	1809-1882	Elizabeth	1797-1848

Droysen, Johann Gustav	1808-1884
Droz, Francois Xavier	1773-1850
Du Camp, Maxime	1822-1894
Ducange, Victor Henri	
Joseph Brahain	1783-1833
Ducasse, Pierre Emmanuel	
Albert	1813-1893
Ducis, Jean Francois	1733-1816
Dumas, Alexandre	1802-1870
Dumas, Alexandre (fils)	1824-1895
Dumont, Augustin	
Alexandre	1801-1884
Dumont, Pierre Etienne	
Louis	1759-1829
Duncker, Maximilian	
Wolfgang	1811-1886
Dunlap, William	1766-1839
Dupuis, Charles Francois	1742-1809
Dupont, Pierre	1821-1870
Duruy, Jean Victor	1811-1894
Dutens, Louis	1730-1812
Dutt, Michael Madhu	
Sudan	1824-1873
Duval, Alexandre Vincent	
Pineux	1767-1842
Dwight, Timothy	1752-1817
Eberhard, Christian	
August Gottlob	1769-1845
Eberhard, Johann	
Augustus	1739-1809
Eckermann, Johann Peter	1792-1864
Eddy, Mary Baker Glover	1821-1910
Edgeworth, Maria	1767-1849
Edgeworth, Richard Lovell	1744-1817
Egan, Pierce	1772-1849
Eichendorff, Joseph	
Freiherr Von	1788-1857
Eliot, George	
(Marian Evans)	1819-1880
Elliot, Jean	1727-1805
Elliott, Ebenezer	1781-1849
Ellis, Alexander John	1814-1890
Ellis, George	1753-1815
Elphinstone, Mountstuart	1779-1859
Emerson, Ralph Waldo	1803-1882
Engel, Johann Carl	
Ludwig	1778-1840
Engel, Johann Jakob	1741-1802
Engels, Friedrich	1820-1895
English, Thomas Dunn	1819-1902
Ennemoser, Joseph	1787-1855
Eotvos, Jossef, Baron	1813-1871
Erckmann, Emile	1822-1899
Erdelyi, Janos	1814-1868
Erdmann, Johann Eduard	1805-1892
Erskine, Henry	1746-1817
Erskine, Thomas	1788-1870
Eschenburg, Johann	
Joachim	1743-1820
Eschenmayer, Adam Karl	
August Von	1768-1852
Escoiquiz, Juan	1762-1820
Espronceda, Jose De	1808-1842
Esquiros, Henri Francois	
Alphonse	1812-1876
Estebanez Caldren, Serafin	1799-1867
Etienne, Charles	
Guillaume	1777-1845
Everett, Alexander Hill	1790-1847
Fabriani, Severino	1792-1849
Fabroni, Angelo	1732-1803
Fahlcrantz, Christian Erik	1790-1866
Fain, Agathon Jean	
Francois	1778-1837
Falk, Johann Daniel	1768-1826
Falke, Johann Friedrich	
Gottlieb	1823-1876
Fallmerayer, Jakob Phillip	1790-1861
Falloux, Frederic Alfred	
Pierre	1811-1886
Farini, Luigi Carlo	1812-1866
Fauriel, Claude Charles	1782-1844
Fay, Andreas	1786-1864
Fechner, Gustav Theodor	1801-1887
Feith, Rhijnvis	1753-1824
Fejer, Gyorgy	1766-1852
Ferguson, Adam	1723-1816
Ferguson, Sir Samuel	1810-1886
Fergusson, James	1808-1886
Ferrari, Giuseppe	1812-1876
Ferrari, Paolo	1822-1889
Ferrier, Susan Edmonstone	1782-1854
Feuchtersleben, Ernst	1806-1849
Feuerbach, Ludwig	
Andreas	1804-1872
Feuerbach, Paul Johann	
Anselm	1775-1833
Feuillet, Octave	1821-1890
Feval, Paul Henri	
Corentin	1817-1887
Feydeau, Ernest Aime	1821-1873
Fichte, Immanuel	
Hermann Von	1796-1879
Fichte, Johann Gottlieb	1762-1814
Fielding, Anthony Vandyke	
Copley	1787-1855
Fields, James Thomas	1817-1881
Figuier, Louis	1819-1894
Finlay, George	1799-1875
Fisher, Ernst Kuno	
Berthold	1824-1907
Fitzball, Edward	1792-1873
Fitzgerald, Edward	1809-1883
Flaubert, Gustave	1821-1880
Foa, Eugenie Rodriguez	
Gradis	1798-1853
Follen, Adolf Ludwig	1794-1855
Follen, Karl	1795-1840
Fontan, Louis Marie	1801-1839
Fontane, Theodor	1819-1898
Fontanes, Louis	1757-1821
Ford, Richard	1796-1858

Forster, Friedrich	
Christoph	1791-1868
Forster, John	1812-1876
Fortlage, Karl	1806-1881
Foscolo, Ugo	1778-1827
Foster, John	1770-1843
Fouque, Friedrich Heinrich	
Karl De La Motte	1777-1843
Fourier, Francois Marie	
Charles	1772-1837
Frampton, Mary	1773-1846
Francois De Neufchateau,	
Nicolas Louis	1750-1828
Frankl, Ludwig August	1810-1894
Franzen, Frans Michael	1772-1847
Fraser, Alexander	
Campbell	1819-1914
Fraser, James Baillie	1783-1856
Freeman, Edward	
Augustus	1823-1892
Freiligrath, Ferdinand	1810-1876
Freneau, Philip Morin	1752-1832
Frere, John Hookham	1769-1846
Freytag, Gustav	1816-1895
Fries, Jakob Friedrich	1773-1843
Froebel, Friedrich Wilhelm	
August	1782-1852
Frohlich, Abraham	
Emanuel	1796-1865
Frohschammer, Jakob	1821-1893
Frothingham, Octavius	
Brooks	1822-1895
Froude, James Anthony	1818-1894
Fryxell, Anders	1795-1881
Fuller, Margaret	1810-1850
Fullerton, Lady Georgiana	
Charlotte	1812-1885
Gachard, Louis Prosper	1800-1885
Gagern, Hans Christoph	
Ernst	1766-1852
Galluppi, Pasquale	1770-1846
Galt, John	1779-1839
Garat, Dominique Joseph	1749-1833
Garay, Janos	1812-1853
Gareau, Francois Xavier	1806-1866
Garrett, Joao Baptista Da	
Silva Leita De Almeida	1799-1854
Gaskell, (Mrs.) Elizabeth	
Cleghorn	1810-1865
Gatty, Margaret	1809-1893
Gautier, Theophile	1811-1872
Geibel, Emanuel	1815-1884
Geiser, Eric Gustav	1783-1877
Genlis, Stephanie Felicité	
Ducrest de St. Aubin	1746-1830
Gerstacker, Friedrich	1816-1877
Gerssenberg, Heinrich	
Wilhelm Von	1737-1823
Gervinus, Georg Gottfried	1805-1871
Gesenius, Friedrich	
Heinrich Wilhelm	1786-1842

Gfrorer, August Friedrich	1803-1861
Giacometti, Paolo	1816-1882
Giesebrecht, Wilhelm Von	1814-1889
Gifford, William	1756-1826
Gilbert, William	1804-1889
Gillies, John	1747-1836
Gilchrist, Alexander	1828-1861
Gilchrist, Anne	1828-1885
Ginguene, Pierre Louis	1748-1815
Gioberti, Vincenzo	1801-1852
Gioja, Melchiorre	1767-1829
Giordani, Pietro	1774-1848
Girardin, Delphine De	1804-1855
Giraud, Giovanni	1776-1834
Gieseler, Johann Karl	
Ludwig	1792-1854
Giudici, Paolo Emiliano	1812-1872
Giusti, Guiseppi	1809-1850
Glassbrenner, Adolf	1810-1876
Gleig, George Robert	1796-1888
Gleim, Johann Wilhelm	
Ludwig	1719-1803
Glen, William	1789-1826
Glinka, Fedor Nikolayevich	1788-1880
Godwin, William	1756-1836
Goethe, Johann Wolfgang	
Von	1749-1832
Gogol, Nikolai Vasilievich	1809-1852
Goldschmidt, Aaron Meier	1819-1887
Goltz, Bogumil	1801-1870
Goncalves Dias, Antonio	1823-1864
Goncharov, Ivan	
Alexandrovich	1812-1891
Goncourt De, Edmond	
Louis Antoine Huot	1822-1896
Good, John Mason	1764-1827
Goodrich, Samuel	
Griswold	1793-1860
Gore, Catherine Grace	
Frances	1799-1861
Gorres, Joseph Von	1776-1848
Gottschall, Rudolf Von	1823-1908
Gould, John	1804-1881
Gozlan, Leon	1803-1866
Gozzi, Carlo	1720-1806
Grabbe, Christian Dietrich	1801-1836
Grant, Anne	1755-1838
Grant, James	1822-1887
Graves, Richard	1715-1804
Gratz, Heinrich	1817-1891
Greene, George Washington	1811-1883
Green, Mary Ann Evrett	1818-1895
Greg, William Rathbone	1809-1881
Gregorovius, Ferdinand	1821-1891
Greville, Charles	
Cavendish Fulke	1794-1865
Griboyedov, Alexander	
Sergeyevich	1795-1829
Griffin, Gerald	1803-1840
Grigorovich, Dmitri	
Vaslievich	1822-1900

Grimm, Friedrich Melchior	1723-1807
Grimm, Jacob Ludwig Carl	1785-1863
Grimm, Wilhelm Carl	1786-1859
Grossi, Tommaso	1791-1853
Grote, George	1794-1871
Grub, George	1812-1892
Grundtvig, Nikolai Frederik Severin	1783-1872
Guerin Du Cayla, Georges Maurice De	1810-1839
Guerrazzi, Francesco Domenico	1804-1873
Guest, Edwin	1800-1880
Guizot, Francois Pierre Guillaume	1787-1874
Gutzkow, Karl Ferdinand	1811-1878
Guys, Constantin	1805-1892
Gyllembourg-Eh Rensvard, Thomasine Christine	1773-1856
Hacklander, Friedrich Wilhelm Von	1816-1877
Hagenbach, Karl Rudolf	1801-1874
Hahn-Hahn, Ida	1805-1880
Hake, Thomas Gordon	1809-1895
Hale, Edward Everett	1822-1909
Hale, Sarah Josepha	1788-1879
Halevy, Jean	1804-1883
Haliburton, Thomas Chandler	1796-1865
Hall, Anna Maria	1800-1881
Hall, Basil	1788-1844
Hall, Samuel Carter	1800-1889
Hallam, Henry	1777-1859
Hallgrimson, Jonas	1807-1845
Hamilton, Elizabeth	1758-1816
Hamilton, Thomas	1789-1842
Hamilton, Sir William	1788-1856
Hamley, Sir Edward Bruce	1824-1893
Hammer, Julius	1810-1862
Hardwick, Philip	1792-1870
Haring, George Wilhelm Heinrich	1798-1871
Hartmann, Moritz	1821-1872
Hartzenbusch, Juan Eugenio	1806-1880
Hasselt, Andre Henri Constant Van	1806-1874
Hasted, Edward	1732-1812
Hauch, Johannes Carsten	1790-1872
Hauff, Wilhelm	1802-1827
Haureau, Barthelemy	1812-1896
Hausser, Ludwig	1818-1867
Hawker, Robert Stephen	1803-1875
Hawthorne, Nathaniel	1804-1864
Hayley, William	1745-1820
Haym, Rudolf	1821-1901
Hayward, Abraham	1801-1884
Hazard, Rowland Gibson	1801-1888
Hazlitt, William	1778-1830
Hebbel, Christian Friedrich	1813-1863
Heeren, Arnold Hermann Ludwig	1760-1842
Hegel, Georg Wilhelm Friedrich	1770-1831
Heiberg, Johan Ludvig	1791-1860
Heine, Heinrich	1797-1856
Heinse, Johann Jakob Wilhelm	1749-1803
Hellck, Fitz-Greene	1790-1867
Helmers, Jan Frederik	1767-1813
Helmholtz, Hermann Ludwig Ferdinand Von	1821-1894
Helps, Sir Arthur	1813-1875
Hemans, Felicia Dorothea	1793-1835
Herbart, Johann Friedrich	1776-1841
Herculano De Carvalno, E Araujo Alexandre	1810-1877
Herder, Johann Gottfried Von	1744-1803
Heredia Y Heredia, Jose Maria	1803-1839
Hertz, Henrik	1797-1870
Herwegh, Georg	1817-1875
Herzen, Alexander Ivanovich	1812-1870
Higginson, Thomas Wentworth	1823-1911
Himly, Louis-Auguste	1823-1906
Hinrichs, Hermann Friedrich Wilhelm	1794-1861
Hoffman, August Heinrich	1798-1874
Hoffman, Ernst Theodor Wilhelm	1776-1822
Hoffmann, Heinrich	1809-1894
Hogg, James	1770-1835
Hogg, Thomas Jefferson	1792-1862
Holbach, Paul Heinrich Dietrich	1723-1789
Holcroft, Thomas	1745-1809
Holderlin, Johann Christian Friedrich	1770-1843
Holland, Henry	1746-1806
Holland, Sir Henry	1788-1873
Holland, Josiah Gilbert	1819-1881
Holmes, Oliver Wendell	1809-1894
Holtei, Karl Eduard Von	1798-1880
Home, John	1722-1808
Hone, William	1780-1842
Hood, Thomas	1799-1845
Hook, James	1746-1827
Hook, Theodore Edward	1788-1841
Hormayr, Joseph Freiherr Von	1782-1848
Horne, Richard Henry	1803-1884
Hostrup, Jens Christion	1818-1894
Hotho, Heinrich Gustav	1802-1873
Houghton, Richard Monckton Milnes	1809-1885
Houssaye, Arsene	1815-1896
Howe, Julia Ward	1819-1910
Howitt, Mary	1799-1888

Howitt, William	1792-1879	Kazinczy, Ferencz	1759-1831
Hughes, Thomas	1822-1896	Keats, John	1795-1821
Hugo, Victor Marie	1802-1885	Keble, John	1792-1866
Humboldt, Freidrich,		Keightley, Thomas	1789-1872
Baron Von	1769-1859	Keller, Gottfried	1819-1890
Humboldt, Karl Wilhelm		Kemble, John Mitchell	1807-1857
von	1767-1835	Kenealy, Edward Vaughan	
Hunt, James Henry Leigh	1784-1859	Hyde	1819-1880
Hunter, Joseph	1783-1861	Kenney, James	1780-1849
Hurd, Richard	1720-1808	Kerner, Justinus Andreas	
Huxley, Thomas Henry	1825-1895	Christian	1786-1862
Hyslop, James	1798-1827	Kervyn De Lettenhove,	
Iffland, August Wilhelm	1759-1814	Constantine Bruno	1817-1891
Ihne, Wilhelm	1821-1902	Key, Francis Scott	1779-1843
Immermann, Karl Lebrecht	1796-1840	Kierkegaard, Soren Aaby	1813-1855
Inchbald, Elizabeth	1753-1821	King, Thomas	1730-1805
Ingelby, Clement Manfred	1823-1886	Kinglake, Alexander	
Ingelow, Jean	1820-1897	William	1809-1891
Ingemann, Bernhard		Kingsley, Charles	1819-1875
Severin	1789-1862	Kingston, William Henry	
Ingoldsby, Thomas	1788-1845	Giles	1814-1880
Ingraham, Joseph Holt	1809-1860	Kinkel, Johann Gottfried	1815-1882
Innes, Cosmo	1798-1874	Kisfaludy, Karoly	1788-1830
Irving, Washington	1783-1859	Kisfaludy, Sandor	1772-1844
Jacobi, Freidrich Heinrich	1743-1819	Kitto, John	1804-1854
Jacobi, Johann Georg	1740-1814	Klaczko, Julian	1825-1906
Jahn, Otto	1813-1869	Kleist, Bernd Heinrich	
Jakob, Ludwig Heinrich		Wilhelm Von	1777-1811
Von	1759-1827	Klinger, Friedrich	
James, George Payne		Maximilian Von	1752-1831
Rainsford	1799-1860	Klopstock, Friedrich	
Jameson, Anna Brownell	1794-1860	Gottlieb	1724-1803
Janin, Jules Gabriel	1804-1874	Knebel, Karl Ludwig Von	1744-1834
Jasmin, Jacques	1798-1864	Knight, Charles	1791-1873
Jefferson, Thomas	1743-1826	Knowles, James Sheridan	1784-1862
Jephson, Robert	1736-1803	Kock, Charles Paul De	1793-1871
Jerrold, Douglas William	1803-1857	Kolcsey, Ferencz	1790-1888
Jesse, Edward	1780-1868	Kopisch, August	1799-1853
Jewsbury, Geraldine Endsor	1812-1880	Korner, Karl Theodor	1791-1813
Joinville, Francois Fernand		Kotzebue, August Friedrich	
D'Orleans	1818-1900	Ferdinand Von	1761-1819
Jokai, Maurus	1825-1904	Krasinski, Zygmunt, Count	1812-1859
Jones, Ebenezer	1820-1860	Kraszweski, Joseph	
Jones, Ernest	1819-1869	Ignatius	1812-1887
Jordan, Wilhelm	1819-1904	Krause, Karl Christian	
Josika, Miklos	1794-1865	Friedrich	1781-1832
Joubert, Joseph	1754-1824	Krug, Wilhelm Traugott	1770-1842
Jouffroy, Theodore Simon	1796-1842	Krylov, Ivan Andreevich	1768-1844
Jouy, Victor Joseph		Kuhlau, Friedrich	1786-1832
Etienne De	1764-1846	Kurz, Hermann	1813-1873
Jovellanos, Gaspar		Labiche, Eugene Marin	1815-1888
Melchor De	1744-1811	Lacaita, Sir James	1813-1895
Judson, Edward Zane		Lacepede, Bernard De	
Carroll	1823-1886	Laville, Compte De	1756-1825
Kant, Immanuel	1724-1804	Laclos, Pierre Amboise	
Karadzil, Viek Stefanovich	1787-1864	Francois	1741-1803
Karamzin, Nicolai		Lacretelle, Jean Charles	
Mikhailovich	1765-1826	Dominique de	1766-1855
Karr, Alphonse	1808-1890	La Farina, Giuseppe	1815-1863
Kate, Jan Jacob		La Harpe, Frederic	
Lodewijk Ten	1819-1889	Cesare	1754-1838

Laing, Malcolm	1762-1818	Lippincott, Sara Jane	
Laing, Samuel	1810-1897	Clarke	1823-1904
Lamarck, Jean Chevalier		Lista Y Aragon, Alberto	1775-1848
de	1744-1829	Lister, Thomas Henry	1800-1842
Lamartine, Alphonse De	1790-1869	Littre, Maximilien Paul	
Lamb, Charles	1775-1834	Emile	1801-1881
Lamennais Felicite		Livingstone, David	1813-1873
Robert De	1782-1854	Ljunggren, Gustaf Kaken	
Landon, Letitia Elizabeth	1802-1838	Jordan	1823-1905
Landor, Walter Savage	1775-1864	Locker-Lampson, Frederick	1821-1895
Lane, Edward William	1801-1876	Lockhart, John Gibson	1794-1854
Langhorne, John	1735-1779	Lodge, Edmund	1756-1839
Lappenberg, Johann		Lofft, Capel	1751-1824
Martin	1794-1865	Longfellow, Henry	
Laprade, Pierre Marin		Wadsworth	1807-1882
Victor Richard De	1812-1883	Lönnrot, Elias	1802-1884
Laromiguire, Pierre	1756-1837	Lossing, Benson John	1813-1891
Larousse, Pierre Athanase	1817-1875	Lotze, Rudolf Hermann	1817-1881
Larra, Mariano Jose De	1809-1837	Lover, Samuel	1797-1868
Las Cases, Emmanuel		Lowell, James Russell	1819-1891
Dieudonné Compte De	1766-1842	Ludwig, Otto	1813-1865
Laube, Heinrich	1806-1884	Luttrell, Henry	1765-1851
Lauder, Sir Thomas Dick	1784-1848	Lytton, Edward George	
Laurent, Francois	1810-1887	Lytton Bulwer-Lytton	1803-1873
Lavater, Johann Kaspar	1741-1801	Macaulay, Thomas	
Laya, Jean Louis	1761-1833	Babington Macaulay	1800-1859
Layard, Sir Austen Henry	1817-1894	Macedo, Jose Agostinho	
Lazarus, Moritz	1824-1903	De	1761-1831
Lea, Henry Charles	1825-1909	MacCarthy, Denis Florence	1817-1882
Leconte De Lisle, Charles		McCord, Louise Sussana	
Marie Rene	1818-1894	Cheves	1810-1879
Lee, Harriet	1757-1851	Macdonald, George	1824-1905
Lee, Sophia	1750-1824	McGee, Thomas D'Arcy	1825-1868
Le Fanu, Joseph Sheridan	1814-1873	Macgregor, John	1825-1892
Legouve, Gabriel Jean		Mackay, Charles	1814-1889
Baptiste Ernest Wilfrid	1807-1903	Mackenzie, Henry	1745-1831
Leland, Charles Godfrey	1824-1903	Mackintosh, Sir James	1765-1832
Lemercier, Nopmucene	1771-1840	Maclaren, Charles	1782-1866
Le Moine, James		M'Cosh, James	1811-1894
MacPherson	1825-1912	M'Crie, Thomas	1772-1835
Lemon, Mark	1809-1870	Madach, Imre	1823-1864
Lenau, Nikolaus	1802-1850	Maginn, William	1793-1842
Lennep, Jacob Van	1802-1868	Magny, Claude Drigon	1797-1879
Lennox, Charlotte	1720-1804	Maine De Biran, Francois-	
Leo, Heinrich	1799-1878	Pierre Gonthier	1766-1824
Leopardi, Giacomo	1798-1837	Maine, Sir Henry James	
Lermontov, Mikhail		Sumner	1822-1888
Yurevich	1814-1841	Maistre, Joseph De	1754-1821
Leroux, Pierre	1798-1871	Maistre, Xavier De	1763-1852
Lever, Charles James	1806-1872	Maitland, Edward	1824-1897
Lewald, Fanny	1811-1889	Majlath, Janos	1786-1855
Lewes, George Henry	1817-1878	Major, Richard Henry	1818-1891
Lewis, Sir George Corwall	1806-1863	Malleson, George Bruce	1825-1898
Lewis, Matthew Gregory	1775-1818	Malthus, Thomas Robert	1766-1834
Leyden, John	1775-1811	Mangan, James Clarence	1803-1849
Lieber, Francis	1800-1872	Maning, Frederick Edward	1812-1883
Liebrecht, Felix	1812-1890	Mansel, Henry Longueville	1820-1871
Ligne, Charles Joseph	1735-1814	Manzoni, Alessandro	1785-1873
Lincoln, Abraham	1809-1865	Mapu, Abraham	1808-1867
Lindo, Mark Prager	1819-1879	Markham, Mrs.	1780-1837
Lingard, John	1771-1851	Marquardt, Joachim	1812-1882

o

Marryat, Frederick	1792-1848	More, Hannah	1745-1833
Marston, John Westland	1819-1890	Moreau, Hegesippe	1810-1838
Martin, Francois Xavier	1762-1846	Morellet, Andre	1727-1819
Martin, Henri	1810-1883	Morgan, Lady Sydney	1783-1859
Martin, Sir Theodore	1816-1909	Morier, James	1780-1849
Martineau, Harriet	1802-1876	Morike, Eduard Friedrich	1804-1875
Martineau, James	1805-1900	Morley, Henry	1822-1894
Martinez De La Rosa,		Morton, John Maddison	1811-1891
Francisco De Paula	1787-1862	Morton, Thomas	1764-1838
Marx, Karl Heinrich	1818-1883	Mosen, Julius	1803-1867
Masdeu, Juan Francisco		Motherwell, William	1797-1835
De	1744-1817	Motley, John Lothrop	1814-1877
Masson, David	1822-1907	Muller, Friedrich	1749-1825
Matthisson, Friedrich Von	1761-1831	Muller, Johannes Von	1752-1809
Maturin, Charles Robert	1782-1824	Muller, Wilhelm	1794-1827
Maurer, Georg Ludwig		Munch-Bellinghausen,	
Von	1790-1872	Eligius Franz Joseph	1806-1871
Mayhew, Henry	1812-1887	Murger, Henry	1822-1861
Melendez Valdez, Juan	1754-1817	Murphy, Arthur	1727-1805
Melville, Herman	1819-1891	Musset, Alfred De	1810-1857
Menard, Louis Nicolas	1822-1901	Nairne, Carolina Oliphant	1766-1845
Menzel, Wolfgang	1798-1873	Nascimento, Francisco	
Mercier, Sebastien	1740-1814	Manoel De	1734-1819
Merimee, Prosper	1803-1870	Nasmyth, Patrick	1787-1831
Merivale, Charles	1808-1893	Neal, John	1793-1876
Mesonero-Romanos,		Neander, Johann	1789-1850
Ramon De	1803-1882	Nekrasov, Nikolai	
Meurice, Paul	1818-1905	Alexeyevich	1821-1877
Meyer, Conrad Ferdinand	1825-1898	Nerval, Gerard de	1808-1855
Michaud, Joseph Francois	1767-1839	Nestroy, Johann	1801-1862
Michelet, Jules	1798-1874	Newman, Francis William	1805-1897
Mickiewicz, Adam	1798-1855	Newman, John Henry	
Mignet, Francois Auguste		(Cardinal)	1801-1890
Marie	1796-1884	Nicholas, John	1745-1826
Mill, James	1773-1836	Nicholson, William	1753-1815
Mill, John Stuart	1806-1873	Nicolai, Christoph	
Miller, Hugh	1802-1856	Friedrich	1733-1811
Milman, Henry Hart	1791-1868	Nicoll, Robert	1814-1837
Mitchell, Donald Grant	1822-1908	Niebuhr, Barthold Georg	1776-1831
Mitford, John	1781-1859	Nitzsch, Karl Immanuel	1787-1868
Mitford, Mary Russell	1787-1855	Nitzsch, Karl Wilhelm	1818-1880
Mitford, William	1744-1827	Noailles, Paul, Duke de	1802-1885
Moir, David Macbeth	1798-1851	Nodier, Charles	1780-1844
Molesworth, William		Normanby, Constantine	
Nassau	1816-1890	Henry Phipps	1797-1863
Moller, Paul Martin	1794-1838	Norton, Caroline Elizabeth	
Mommsen, Theodor	1817-1903	Sarah	1808-1877
Montalembert, Charles		Ohlenschlager, Adam	
Forbes Rene De	1810-1870	Gottlob	1779-1850
Montanelli, Giuseppe	1813-1862	Olmedo, Jose Joaquin De	1780-1847
Montefiore, Joshua	1762-1843	Opie, Amelia	1769-1853
Montgomery, James	1771-1854	Opzoomer, Cornelius	
Montgomery, Robert	1807-1855	William	1821-1892
Monti, Vincenzo	1754-1828	Orme, Robert	1728-1801
Monticelli, Adolphe		Ostrovsky, Alexander	
Joseph Thomas	1824-1886	Nikolaevich	1823-1886
Montufar, Lorenzo	1823-1898	Ozanam, Antoine Frederic	1813-1853
Moore, John	1729-1802	Paine, Thomas	1737-1809
Moore, Thomas	1779-1852	Palacky, Frantisek	1798-1876
Moratin, Leandro		Paley, William	1743-1805
Fernandez De	1760-1828	Palfrey, John Gorham	1796-1881

Palgrave, Sir Francis	1788-1861	Raugh, Christian Daniel	1777-1875
Palgrave, Francis Turner	1824-1897	Raumer, Friedrick Ludwig	
Paludan-Muller, Frederick	1809-1876	George Van	1781-1873
Parker, Theodore	1810-1860	Ravaison-Mollien, Jean	
Parkman, Francis	1823-1893	Gaspard Felix	1813-1900
Parton, James	1822-1891	Rawlinson, George	1812-1902
Patmore, Coventry Kersey		Raynouard, Francois Juste	
Dighton	1823-1896	Marie	1761-1836
Pattison, Mark	1813-1884	Reade, Charles	1814-1884
Paulding, James Kirke	1778-1860	Redgrave, Richard	1804-1888
Pauli, Reinhold	1823-1882	Reeve, Clara	1729-1807
Payne, John Howard	1791-1852	Reid, Thomas Mayne	1818-1883
Paz Soldan, Mariano		Remusat, Charles Francois	
Felipe	1821-1886	Marie	1797-1875
Peabody, Andrew Preston	1811-1893	Renan, Ernest	1823-1892
Peacock, Thomas Love	1785-1866	Renouvier, Charles	
Peesemsky, Alexey		Bernard	1815-1903
Feofilactovich	1820-1881	Restif, Nicolas Edme	1734-1806
Pellico, Silvio	1788-1854	Reuter, Fritz	1810-1874
Percival, James Gates	1795-1856	Richmond, Legh	1772-1827
Percy, Thomas	1729-1811	Richter, Johann Paul	
Pertz, Georg Heinrich	1795-1876	Friedrich	1763-1825
Petofi, Alexander	1823-1849	Ritter, Heinrich	1791-1869
Picken, Andrew	1788-1833	Rivarol, Antoine De	1753-1801
Pindemonte, Ippolito	1753-1828	Rivas, Angel De Saavedra	1791-1865
Piozzi, Hester Lynch	1741-1821	Rogers, Randolph	1825-1892
Planche, James Robinson	1796-1880	Rogers, Samuel	1763-1855
Poe, Edgar Allan	1809-1849	Roscoe, William	1753-1831
Poerico, Alessandro	1802-1848	Rosenkranz, Karl	1805-1879
Ponsard, Francois	1814-1867	Rosmini-Serbatil, Antonio	1797-1855
Poole, William Frederick	1821-1894	Rossetti, Gabriele	1783-1854
Porter, Anna Maria	1780-1832	Rouget de Lisle, Claude	
Porter, Jane	1776-1850	Joseph	1760-1836
Porter, Noah	1811-1892	Roumanile, Joseph	1818-1891
Potgieter, Everhardes		Royer-Collard, Pierre Paul	1763-1845
Johannes	1808-1875	Rückert, Friedrich	1788-1866
Potthast, August	1824-1898	Ruffini, Giovanni	
Praed, Winthrop		Domenico	1807-1881
Mackworth	1802-1839	Ruge, Arnold	1802-1880
Prantl, Karl Von	1820-1888	Runeberg, Johan Ludvig	1804-1877
Prati, Giovanni	1815-1884	Ruskin, John	1819-1900
Prescott, William Hickling	1796-1859	Sade, Donatien Alphonse	
Priestley, Joseph	1733-1804	Francois (Marquis De)	1740-1814
Pringle, Thomas	1789-1834	Safarik, Pavel Josef	1795-1861
Procter, Adelaide Anne	1825-1864	Sainte-Beuve, Charles	
Procter, Bryan Waller	1787-1874	Augustin	1804-1869
Proud, Robert	1728-1813	Saintine, Joseph Xavier	1798-1865
Proudhon, Pierre Joseph	1809-1865	Saint-Lambert, Jean	
Pusey, Edward Bouverie	1800-1882	Francois De	1716-1803
Pushkin, Alexander	1799-1837	Saint-Marc, Girardin	1801-1873
Pye, Henry James	1745-1813	Saint-Martin, Louis Claude	
Pyne, William Henry	1769-1843	De	1743-1803
Quicherat, Jules Etienne		Saint-Pierre, Bernardin De	1737-1814
Joseph	1814-1882	Salomon, Johann Peter	1745-1815
Quincy, Josiah	1772-1864	Sand, George (Dudevant)	1804-1876
Quinet, Edgar	1803-1875	Sandeau, Leonard Sylvain	
Quintana, Manuel Josè	1772-1857	Julien	1811-1883
Radcliffe, Ann	1764-1823	Sant, James	1820-1916
Ragabe, Alexandros-Rizos	1810-1892	Sarmiento, Domingo	
Rands, William Brighty	1823-1882	Faustino	1811-1888
Ranke, Leopold Von	1795-1886	Saxe, John Godfrey	1816-1887

Schelling, Friedrich Wilhelm Joseph Von	1775-1854
Schiller, Johann Cristoph Friedrich Von	1759-1805
Schimmelpenninck, Mary Ann	1778-1856
Schlegel, August Wilhelm Von	1767-1845
Schlegel, Friedrich Von	1772-1829
Schleiermacher, Friedrich Daniel Ernst	1768-1834
Schlozer, August Ludwig Von	1735-1809
Schopenhauer, Arthur	1788-1860
Scott, Sir Walter	1771-1832
Scribe, Eugene	1791-1861
Seguier, William	1771-1843
Segur, Philippe Paul, Comte de	1780-1873
Sellar, William Young	1825-1890
Senac de Meilhan, Gabriel	1736-1803
Senancour, Etienne Pivert De	1770-1846
Settembrini, Luigi	1813-1877
Seward, Anna	1747-1809
Sewell, Anna	1820-1878
Shairp, John Campbell	1819-1885
Shaw, Henry Wheeler	1818-1885
Sheil, Richard Lalor	1791-1851
Shelley, Mary Wollstonecraft	1797-1851
Shelley, Percy Bysshe	1792-1822
Sheridan, Richard Brinsley Butler	1751-1816
Sherwood, Mary Martha	1775-1851
Shevchenko, Taras	1814-1861
Sigourney, Lydia Huntley	1791-1865
Simms, William Gilmore	1806-1870
Simon, Jules Francois	1814-1896
Simrock, Karl Joseph	1802-1876
Sismondi, Jean Charles Leonard Simonde	1773-1842
Skene, William Forbes	1809-1892
Slowacki, Juljusz	1809-1849
Smiles, Samuel	1812-1904
Smith, Charlotte	1749-1806
Smith, Goldwin	1823-1910
Smith, Horace	1779-1849
Smith, James	1775-1839
Smith, John Stafford	1750-1836
Smith, Sidney	1771-1845
Smith, Walter Chalmers	1824-1908
Smith, Sir William	1813-1893
Soloviev, Sergei Mikhailovich	1820-1879
Southey, Robert	1774-1843
Souza-Botelmo, Adelaide Filleul	1761-1836
Sparks, Jared	1789-1866
Spencer, Herbert	1820-1903
Stael, Madame De	1766-1817
Stahl, Frierich Julius	1802-1861
Stanhope, Philip Henry Stanhope	1805-1875
Stanley, Arthur Penrhyn	1815-1881
Steffens, Henrik	1773-1845
Stendhal, (Marie Henry Beyle)	1783-1842
Sterling, John	1806-1844
Stern, Daniel (Agoult)	1805-1876
Stewart, Dugald	1753-1828
Stifter, Adalbert	1805-1868
Stilling, Heinrich	1740-1817
Stirling, James Hutchinson	1820-1909
Stirling-Maxwell, Sir William Bart	1818-1878
Stirner, Max	1806-1856
Stoddard, Richard Henry	1825-1903
Stolberg, Friedrich Leopold	1750-1819
Storm, Theodor Wolsden	1817-1888
Stowe, Harriet Elizabeth Beecher	1811-1896
Strachwitz, Moritz Karl Wilhelm Anton	1822-1847
Strauss, David Friedrich	1808-1874
Street, Alfred Billings	1811-1881
Strickland, Agnes	1806-1874
Strutt, Joseph	1742-1802
Stubbs, William	1825-1901
Sue, Eugene	1804-1857
Surtees, Robert Smith	1803-1864
Swanwick, Anna	1813-1899
Swetchine, Madame	1782-1857
Sybel, Heinrich Von	1817-1895
Talfourd, Sir Thomas Noon	1795-1854
Tannahill, Robert	1774-1810
Taylor, Ann	1782-1866
Taylor, Bayard	1825-1878
Taylor, Sir Henry	1800-1886
Taylor, Isaak	1787-1865
Taylor, Isaak	1829-1901
Taylor, Jane	1783-1824
Taylor, Tom	1817-1880
Taylor, William	1765-1836
Tegner, Esaias	1782-1846
Tennant, William	1784-1848
Tennyson, Alfred Tennyson	1809-1892
Thackeray, William Makepeace	1811-1863
Thierry, Jacques Nicolas Augustin	1795-1856
Thiers, Louis Adolph	1797-1877
Thirlwall, Connop	1797-1875
Thompson, William	c. 1785-1833
Thoreau, Henry David	1817-1862
Ticknor, George	1791-1871
Tieck, Johann Ludwig	1773-1853
Tischendorf, Lobegott	1815-1874
Tocqueville, Alexis Charles Henri Clérel	1805-1859

Tolstoy, Alexei		Walker, John	1732-1807
Konstantinovich	1817-1875	Walker, Thomas	1784-1836
Tommaseo, Niccolo	1802-1874	Wallace, Alfred Russel	1823-1913
Tompa, Mihaly	1817-1868	Wallon, Henri Alexandre	1812-1904
Topelius, Zachris	1818-1898	Warburton, Eliot	1810-1852
Topffer, Rodolphe	1799-1846	Warner, Susan Bogert	1819-1895
Toreno, Jose Maria		Warren, Samuel	1807-1877
Queipo De Llano	1786-1843	Waugh, Edwin	1817-1890
Trelawny, Edward John	1792-1881	Webster, Noah	1758-1843
Trench, Richard Chevenix	1807-1886	Welhaven, Johann Sebastian	
Trendelenburg, Friedrich		Cammermeyer	1807-1873
Adolf	1802-1872	Wells, Charles Jeremiah	1798-1879
Trollope, Anthony	1815-1882	Wennerberg, Gunnar	1817-1901
Trollope, Frances	1780-1863	Wergeland, Henrik Arnold	1808-1845
Trollope, Thomas		Werner, Zacharias	1768-1823
Adolphus	1810-1892	West, Benjamin	1738-1820
Trumbull, John	1750-1831	Whately, Richard	1787-1863
Tucker, Charlotte Marie	1821-1893	Whewell, William	1794-1866
Tupper, Martin Farquhar	1810-1889	White, Henry Kirke	1785-1806
Turgenev, Ivan		White, Richard Grant	1821-1885
Sereyevich	1818-1883	Whitehead, Charles	1804-1862
Turner, Charles Tennyson	1808-1879	Whitman, Walt	1819-1892
Turner, Sharon	1768-1847	Whittier, John Greenleaf	1807-1892
Tyndall, John	1820-1893	Wieland, Christoph	
Tyuchev, Fydor Ivanovich	1803-1873	Martin	1733-1813
Uhland, Johann Ludwig	1787-1862	Wilberforce, William	1759-1833
Vacherot, Etienne	1809-1897	Willis, Nathaniel Parker	1806-1867
Valera Y Alcala, Galiano		Wilson, Alexander	1766-1813
Juan	1824-1905	Wilson, John	1785-1854
Van Beers, Jan	1821-1888	Winther, Christian	1796-1876
Vaperau, Louis Gustave	1819-1906	Wirt, William	1772-1834
Varnhagen, Francisco		Wolcot, John (Peter	
Adolpho De	1816-1878	Pinder)	1738-1819
Varnhagen, Von Ense		Wolfe, Charles	1791-1823
Karl August	1785-1858	Wollaston, William Hyde	1766-1828
Verplanck, Gulian		Wood, Mrs. Henry	1814-1887
Crommelin	1786-1870	Wordsworth, Dorothy	1771-1855
Vidyasagar, Iswar		Wordsworth, William	1770-1850
Chandra	1820-1891	Wraxall, Sir Nathaniel	
Vigny, Alfred De	1797-1863	William	1751-1831
Villemain, Abel Francois	1790-1870	Wright, Thomas	1810-1887
Vinje, Aasmund Olavson	1816-1870	Wyatt, Sir Matthew Digby	1820-1877
Vischer, Friedrich		Wyss, Johann	1781-1830
Theodor	1807-1887	Yonge, Charlotte Mary	1823-1901
Volney, Constantin		Young, Arthur	1741-1820
Francois Chasseboeuf,		Zeller, Eduard	1814-1908
Compte de	1757-1820	Zhukovsky, Vasili	
Voss, Johann Heinrich	1751-1826	Andreyevich	1783-1852
Waagen, Gustav Friedrich	1794-1868	Zorrilla, Jose	1817-1893
Wackenroder, Wilhelm		Zschokke, Johann	
Heinrich	1773-1798	Heinrick Daniel	1771-1848

ARTISTS

Achenbach, Andreas	1815-1910	Ansdell, Richard	1815-1885
Ainmuller, Maximilian		Appiani, Andrea	1754-1817
Emmanuel	1807-1870	Armitage, Edward	1817-1896
Allan, Sir William	1782-1850	Audubon, John James	1785-1851
Allston, Washington	1779-1843	Baily, Edward Hodges	1788-1867
Alvarez, Don Jose	1768-1827	Ball, Thomas	1819-1911

Baltard, Louis Pierre	1764-1846
Bandel, Ernst Von	1800-1876
Banks, Thomas	1735-1805
Barker, Robert	1739-1806
Barry, Sir Charles	1795-1860
Barry, James	1741-1806
Bartolini, Lorenzo	1777-1850
Bartolozzi, Francesco	1727-1815
Barye, Antoine Louis	1796-1875
Begas, Karl	1794-1854
Bell, John	1811-1895
Beverley, William Roxby	1814-1889
Bewick, Thomas	1753-1828
Birch, Samuel	1813-1885
Bird, Edward	1772-1819
Bone, Henry	1755-1834
Bonomi, Giuseppe	1739-1808
Bonheur, Rosa	1822-1899
Bonington, Richard Parkes	1801-1828
Bosio, Francois Joseph, Baron	1769-1845
Bossi, Giuseppe	1777-1816
Boudin, Louis Eugene	1824-1898
Bough, Samuel	1822-1878
Bouguereau, Adolphe William	1825-1905
Boydell, John	1719-1804
Brascassat, Jacques Raymond	1804-1867
Brierly, Sir Oswald Walters	1817-1894
Bright, Henry	1814-1873
Brodie, William	1815-1881
Brown, Ford Madox	1821-1893
Brown, George Loring	1814-1889
Brown, Henry Kirke	1814-1886
Browne, Hablot Knight	1815-1882
Bulfinch, Charles	1763-1844
Burn, William	1789-1870
Burton, Decimus	1800-1881
Butterfield, William	1814-1900
Bystrom, Johan Niklas	1783-1848
Cabanel, Alexandre	1823-1889
Cagnola, Luigi	1762-1833
Calame, Alexandre	1810-1864
Callcott, Sir Augustus Wall	1779-1844
Calvert, Charles	1785-1852
Calvert, Edward	1799-1883
Camphausen, Wilhelm	1818-1885
Camuccini, Vincenzo	1773-1844
Canova, Antonio	1757-1822
Capronnier, Jean Baptiste	1814-1891
Casanova de Seingalt, Francesco	1727-1805
Catlin, George	1796-1872
Cattermole, George	1800-1868
Chantrey, Sir Charles Legatt	1781-1841
Charlet, Nicolas Toussaint	1792-1845

Chasseriau, Theodore	1819-1856
Chisholm, Alexander	1792-1847
Chodowiecki, Daniel Nicolas	1726-1801
Clays, Paul Jean	1819-1900
Cockerell, Charles Robert	1788-1863
Cole, Thomas	1801-1848
Constable, John	1776-1837
Cooper, Abraham	1787-1868
Cooper, Thomas Sidney	1803-1902
Cope, Charles West	1811-1890
Copley, John Singleton	1737-1815
Corbould, Edward Henry	1815-1905
Corbould, Henry	1787-1844
Corbould, Richard	1757-1831
Cornelius, Peter Von	1783-1867
Corot, Jean-Baptiste Camille	1796-1875
Cosway, Richard	1742-1821
Cotman, John Sell	1782-1842
Courbet, Gustav	1819-1877
Couture, Thomas	1815-1879
Crane, Thomas	1808-1859
Cox, David	1783-1859
Cox, David, the younger	1809-1885
Crome, John	1768-1821
Crawford, Thomas	1814-1857
Creswick, Thomas	1811-1869
Cruikshank, George	1792-1878
Daguerre, Louis Jacques Mande	1789-1851
Dahl, Johann, Kristen Clausen	1788-1857
Damer, Anne Seymour	1749-1828
Danby, Francis	1793-1861
Dance, George	1741-1825
Daniell, Samuel	1775-1811
Daniell, Thomas	1749-1840
Daniell, William	1769-1837
Dannecker, Johann Heinrich Von	1758-1841
Dantan, Antoine Laurent	1798-1878
Dantan, Jean Pierre	1800-1869
Darley, Felix Octavius Carr	1822-1888
Daubigny, Charles Francois	1817-1878
Daumier, Honore	1808-1879
David, Jacques Louis	1748-1825
Dawson, Henry	1811-1878
Decamps, Alexandra Gabriel	1803-1860
Delacroix, Ferdinand Victor Eugene	1798-1863
Delaroche, Hippolyte	1797-1856
De Loutherbourg, Philip James	1740-1812
Denon, Dominique Vivant	1747-1825
Diaz, Narcisse Virgile	1809-1876
Dobson, William Charles Thomas	1817-1898

Doyle, Richard	1824-1883
Duncan, Thomas	1807-1845
Dupre, Giovanni	1817-1882
Dupre, Jules	1811-1889
Dyce, William	1806-1864
Downman, John	1750-1824
Doyen, Gabriel Francois	1726-1806
Dumont, Francois	1751-1831
Durand, Asher Brown	1796-1886
Earlom, Richard	1743-1822
Eastlake, Sir Charles Lock	1793-1865
Eberz, Josef	1801-1882
Eckersberg, Kristoffer	1783-1853
Egg, Augustus Leopold	1816-1863
Engleheart, George	1752-1829
Elliott, Charles Loring	1812-1868
Etex, Antoine	1808-1888
Etty, William	1787-1849
Farington, Joseph	1747-1821
Fielding, Copley	1787-1855
Fiorillo, Johann Dominicus	1748-1821
Flandrin, Jean Hippolyte	1809-1864
Flaxman, John	1755-1826
Fogelberg, Benedict Erland	1786-1854
Foley, John Henry	1818-1874
Fontaine, Pierre Francois Leonard	1762-1853
Forster, Ernst	1800-1885
Foster, Myles Birkett	1825-1899
Fowler, Charles	1792-1867
Fragonard, Jean Honore	1732-1806
Francais, Francois Louis	1814-1897
Fremiet, Emmanuel	1824-1910
Friedrich, Caspar David	1774-1840
Fripp, Alfred Downing	1822-1895
Fripp, George Arthur	1814-1896
Fuseli, Henry	1741-1825
Frith, William Powell	1819-1909
Fromentin, Eugene	1820-1876
Frost, William Edward	1810-1877
Fuhrich, Joseph Von	1800-1876
Fuller, George	1822-1884
Gallait, Louis	1810-1887
Garnier, Jean Louis Charles	1825-1898
Gavarni, Paul	1801-1866
Geddes, Andrew	1783-1844
Gericault, Theodore	1791-1824
Gerome, Jean Leon	1824-1904
Gerrard, Francois	1770-1837
Gibson, John	1790-1866
Gilbert, Sir John	1817-1897
Gillray, James	1757-1815
Girodet De Roussy, Anne Louis	1767-1824
Girtin, Thomas	1775-1802
Gleyre, Charles	1806-1874
Goldschmidt, Hermann	1802-1866
Goodall, Frederick	1822-1904
Gordon, Sir John Watson	1788-1864

Goya Y Lucientes, Francisco	1746-1828
Granet, Francois Marius	1775-1849
Grant, Sir Francis	1803-1878
Greenough, Horatio	1805-1852
Greuze, Jean Baptiste	1725-1805
Gros, Antoine Jean	1771-1835
Gudin, Theodore	1802-1880
Guerin, Pierre Narcisse	1774-1833
Guillaume, Jean Baptiste Claude	1822-1905
Gwilt, Joseph	1784-1863
Haag, Carl	1820-1915
Hamon, Jean Louis	1821-1874
Hansen, Christian Frederik	1756-1845
Hansom, Joseph Aloysius	1803-1882
Harding, Chester	1792-1866
Harlow, George Henry	1787-1819
Harpignies, Henri	1819-1916
Harvey, Sir George	1806-1876
Haydon, Benjamin Robert	1786-1846
Hayter, Sir George	1792-1871
Heaphy, Thomas	1775-1835
Herbert, John Rogers	1810-1900
Hilderbrandt, Eduard	1818-1869
Hilton, William	1786-1839
Hiroshege, Ando	1797-1858
Hittorff, Jacques Ignace	1792-1867
Hokusai, Katsushika	1760-1849
Hook, James Clarke	1819-1907
Hoppner, John	1758-1810
Horsley, John Calcott	1817-1903
Houdon, Jean Antoine	1740-1828
Hubner, Julius	1806-1882
Huet, Paul	1804-1869
Humphry, Ozias	1742-1810
Hunt, William Henry	1790-1864
Hunt, William Morris	1824-1879
Huntingdon, Daniel	1816-1906
Hurlstone, Frederick Yeates	1800-1869
Ingres, Jean Auguste Dominique	1780-1867
Inman, Henry	1801-1846
Innes, George	1825-1894
Isabey, Jean Baptiste	1767-1855
Israel, Josef	1824-1911
Jacques, Charles	1813-1894
Jalabert, Charles Francois	1819-1901
Johnson, Eastman	1824-1906
Jonkind, Johann Barthold	1819-1891
Jordan, Rudolf	1810-1887
Kauffmann, Angelica	1741-1807
Kaulbach, Wilhelm Von	1805-1874
Keene, Charles Samuel	1823-1891
Kensett, John Frederick	1818-1872
Kirkup, Seymour Stocker	1788-1880
La Grenée, Jean Louis Francois	1724-1805
Landseer, Sir Edwin Henry	1802-1873

Lauder, Robert Scott	1803-1869
Lawrence, Sir Thomas	1769-1830
Lear, Edward	1812-1888
Le Brun, Marie Elizabeth Louise	1755-1842
Leech, John	1817-1864
Lehman, Rudolf	1819-1905
Lejeune, Louis Francois	1775-1848
Lemaire, Philippe Honoré	1798-1880
L'Enfant, Pierre Charles	1754-1825
Leslie, Charles Robert	1794-1859
Leutze, Emanuel	1816-1868
Leys, Hendrik	1815-1869
Lindsay, Sir Coutts	1824-1913
Linnell, John	1792-1882
Macculoch, Horatio	1805-1867
Maclise, Daniel	1806-1870
MacNee, Sir Daniel	1806-1882
Madrazo Y Kunt, Don Federico, De	1815-1894
Manes, Josef	1820-1871
Marochetti, Carlo	1805-1867
Marshall, William Calder	1813-1894
Martin, John	1789-1854
Meissonier, Jean Louis Ernst	1815-1891
Menzel, Adolph Friedrich Erdmann Von	1815-1905
Michel, Claude	1738-1814
Millet, Jean Francois	1814-1875
Moore, William	1790-1851
Morel La Deuil, Leonard	1820-1888
Morland, George	1763-1804
Morse, Samuel Finley Breese	1791-1872
Motte, William De La	1775-1863
Mount, William Sidney	1807-1868
Muller, William James	1812-1845
Mulready, William	1786-1863
Nash, John	1752-1835
Nasmyth, Alexander	1758-1840
Nicol, Erskine	1825-1904
Nollekens, Joseph	1737-1823
Northcote, James	1746-1831
Ondine, Eugene Andre	1810-1887
Opie, John	1761-1807
Overbeck, Johann Friedrich	1789-1869
Page, William	1811-1885
Pajou, Augustin	1730-1809
Palmer, Samuel	1805-1881
Paton, Sir Joseph Noel	1821-1901
Paxton, Sir Joseph	1801-1865
Peace, Charles Willson	1741-1827
Peale, Rembrandt	1778-1860
Pearson, John Loughborough	1817-1897
Percier, Charles	1764-1838
Pinelli, Bartolomeo	1781-1834
Playfair, William Henry	1789-1857
Plimer, Andrew	1763-1837

Poole, Paul Falconer	1807-1879
Porta, Carlo	1776-1821
Portaels, Jean Francois	1818-1895
Porter, Robert Ker	1775-1842
Powers, Hiram	1805-1873
Prout, Samuel	1783-1852
Prud'hon, Pierre	1758-1823
Pugin, Augustus Welby Northmore	1812-1852
Puvis, De Chavannes Pierre Cecile	1824-1898
Raeburn, Sir Henry	1756-1823
Renwick, James	1818-1895
Rethel, Alfred	1816-1859
Retzsch, Friedrich August Moritz	1779-1857
Richmond, George	1809-1896
Rickman, Thomas	1776-1841
Rietschel, Ernst	1804-1861
Robert, Hubert	1733-1808
Roberts, David	1796-1864
Romney, George	1734-1802
Rousseau, Pierre Etienne Theodore	1812-1867
Rowlandson, Thomas	1756-1827
Rude, Francois	1784-1855
Sandby, Paul	1725-1809
Schadow, Friedrich Wilhelm	1798-1862
Schadow, Johann Gottfried	1764-1850
Schadow, Rudolf	1786-1822
Scheffer, Ary	1795-1858
Schinkel, Karl Friedrich	1781-1841
Schnorr Von Karolsfeld, Julius	1794-1872
Schwanthaler, Ludwig Michael	1802-1848
Schwind, Moritz Von	1804-1871
Scott, David	1806-1849
Scott, Sir George Gilbert	1811-1878
Semper, Gottfried	1803-1873
Severn, Joseph	1793-1879
Shee, Sir Martin Archer	1769-1850
Sheraton, Thomas (cabinet maker)	1751-1806
Simson, William	1800-1847
Smart, John	1740-1811
Smillie, James David	1833-1909
Smirke, Sir Robert	1781-1867
Smith, John Raphael	1752-1812
Soane, Sir John	1753-1837
Sowerby, James	1757-1822
Stanfield, William Clarkson	1794-1867
Stark, James	1794-1859
Steell, Sir John	1804-1891
Steinle, Eduard	1810-1886
Story, William Wetmore	1819-1895
Stothard, Thomas	1755-1834
Street, George Edmund	1824-1881
Stuart, Gilbert	1755-1828

Sully, Thomas	1783-1872	Vigee Lebrun, Marie Anne	
Tenniel, Sir John	1820-1914	Elizabeth	1755-1842
Thorvaldsen, Bertel	1770-1844	Violet Le Duc, Eugen	
Tite, Sir William	1798-1873	Emmanuel	1814-1879
Towne, Francis	1739-1816	Vorosmarty, Mihaly	1800-1855
Travies De Villiers,		Wainewright, Thomas	
Charles Joseph	1804-1859	Griffiths	1794-1852
Troyon, Constant	1810-1865	Waldo, Samuel Lovett	1783-1861
Trumbull, John	1756-1843	Ward, George Frederic	1817-1904
Turner, Joseph Mallord		Weir, Robert Walter	1803-1889
William	1775-1851	Westmacott, Sir Richard	1775-1856
Uta Maro	1754-1806	Wiertz, Anton Joseph	1806-1865
Vanderlyn, John	1776-1852	Wilkie, Sir David	1785-1841
Varley, John	1778-1842	Willems, Florent Joseph	
Veit, Philipp	1793-1877	Marie	1823-1905
Verboeckhoven, Eugene		Wint, Peter De	1784-1849
Joseph	1798-1881	Winter Halter, Franz	
Vernet, Antoine Charles		Xavier	1806-1873
Horace	1758-1835	Wyatt, Johann	1746-1813
Vernet, Emile Jean		Ziem, Felix Francois	
Horace	1789-1863	George	1821-1911
		Zoffany, Johann	1733-1810

COMPOSERS

Abt, Franz	1819-1885	Cimarosa, Domenico	1749-1801
Adam, Adolphe Charles	1803-1856	Chopin, Frederic Francois	1810-1849
Albrechtberger, Johann		Clementi, Muzio	1752-1832
Gregory	1736-1809	Cornelius, Carl August	
Arditi, Luigi	1822-1903	Peter	1824-1874
Arnold, Samuel	1740-1802	Corri, Domenico	1746-1825
Arriaga, Juan	1806-1826	Costa, Sir Michael	1810-1884
Asioli, Bonifacio	1769-1832	Crotch, William	1775-1847
Attwood, Thomas	1765-1838	Czerny, Karl	1791-1857
Auber, Daniel Francois		Dargomijsky, Alexander	
Eprit	1782-1871	Sergeivich	1813-1869
Baini, Guiseppe	1775-1844	David, Felicien	1810-1876
Batishill, Jonathan	1738-1801	Diabelli, Anton Antonio	1781-1858
Barnett, John	1802-1890	Dibdin, Charles	1745-1814
Beethoven, Ludwig Van	1770-1827	Donizetti, Gaetano	1797-1848
Bellini, Vincenzo	1801-1835	Doppler, Albert Franz	1821-1883
Benedict, Sir Julius	1804-1885	Dreyschock, Alexander	1818-1869
Bennett, Sir William		Dussek, Jan Ladislav	1761-1812
Sterndale	1816-1875	Dykes, John Bacchus	1823-1876
Beriot, Charles Auguste		Eberwein, Traugott	
De	1802-1870	Maximilian	1775-1831
Berlioz, Hector	1803-1869	Elvey, Sir George Job	1816-1893
Bishop, Sir Henry Rowley	1786-1855	Ernst, Heinrich Wilhelm	1814-1865
Boccherini, Luigi	1743-1805	Fetis, Francois Joseph	1784-1871
Boieldieu, Francois Adrien	1775-1834	Field, John	1782-1837
Bottesini, Giovanni	1822-1889	Flotow, Friedrich Freiherr	1812-1883
Brabazon, Hercules		Franck, Cesar	1822-1890
Brabazon	1821-1906	Franz, Robert	1815-1892
Bruckner, Anton	1824-1896	Gade, Niels Vilhelm	1817-1890
Callcott, John Wall	1766-1821	Gansbacher, Johann	
Cambini, Giovanni		Baptist	1778-1844
Giuseppe	1746-1825	Garcia, Manoel	1775-1832
Campenhout, Francois		Gazzaniga, Giuseppe	1743-1818
Von	1779-1849	Glinka, Michael Ivanovich	1803-1857
Cherubini, Marcia Luigi	1760-1842	Goss, Sir John	1800-1880

Gossec, Francois Joseph	1734-1829
Gounod, Charles Francois	1818-1893
Gow, Niel	1727-1807
Gretry, Andre Ernest Modeste	1741-1813
Gung'l, Josef	1810-1889
Halevy, Jacques Francois	1799-1862
Hatton, John Liptrot	1809-1886
Hauptmann, Moritz	1792-1868
Haydn, Franz Joseph	1732-1809
Haydn, Michael	1737-1806
Heller, Stephen	1815-1888
Henselt, Adolf Von	1814-1889
Herold, Louis Joseph	1791-1833
Herve, Florimond Rounger	1825-1892
Herz, Henri	1806-1888
Hiller, Ferdinand	1811-1885
Hiller, Johann Adam	1728-1804
Himmel, Frederick Henry	1765-1814
Horn, Charles Edward	1786-1849
Hullah, John Pyke	1812-1884
Hummel, Johann Nepomuk	1778-1837
Jackson, William	1730-1803
Kelly, Michael	1762-1826
Kjeruf, Halfdan	1815-1868
Kreutzer, Konradin	1780-1849
Lacombe, Louis Trouillon	1818-1884
Lado, Edouard	1823-1892
Lemmens, Nicolas Jacques	1823-1881
Lesueur, Jean Francois	1760-1837
Liszt, Franz	1811-1886
Loewe, Johann Karl Gottfried	1796-1869
Lortzing, Albert	1801-1851
MacFarren, Sir George Alexander	1813-1887
Marschner, Heinrich August	1795-1861
Mehul, Etienne Nicolas	1763-1817
Mendelssohn, Bartholdi Jakob Ludwig Felix	1809-1847
Meyebeer, Giacomo	1791-1864
Monk, William Henry	1823-1889
Monsigny, Pierre Alexandre	1729-1817
Nathan, Isaac	1791-1864
Nicolai, Otto	1810-1849
Offenbach, Jacques	1819-1880
Ouseley, Sir Frederick Arthur Gore	1825-1889
Paer, Ferdinando	1771-1839
Paisiello, Giovanni	1741-1816
Pearsall, Robert Lucas De	1795-1856
Pierson, Henry Hugo	1815-1873
Pleyel, Ignaz-Joseph	1757-1831
Raff, Joseph Joachim	1822-1882
Reineck, Carl Heinrich	1824-1910
Rockstro, William Smith	1823-1895
Rossini, Gioachino Antonio	1792-1868
Salieri, Antonio	1750-1825
Sarti, Giuseppe	1729-1802
Schubert, Franz	1808-1878
Schubert, Franz Peter	1797-1828
Schumann, Clara Josephine	1819-1896
Schumann, Robert Alexander	1810-1856
Shield, William	1748-1829
Smetana, Bedrich	1824-1884
Spontini, Gasparo Luigi	1774-1851
Spohr, Ludwig	1784-1859
Spottiswoode, Alicia Anne, Lady John	1811-1900
Stamitz, Carl Philipp	1745-1801
Steibelt, Daniel	1764-1823
Strauss, Johann	1804-1849
Strauss, Johann the younger	1825-1899
Suppe, Franz Von	1820-1895
Thomas, Ambroise	1811-1896
Verdi, Giuseppe Fortunino	1813-1901
Viotti, Giovanni Battista	1753-1824
Vogler, George Joseph	1749-1814
Wagner, Wilhelm Richard	1813-1883
Wallace, William Vincent	1812-1865
Weber, Carl Maria Friedrich	1786-1826
Wesley, Samuel Sebastian	1810-1876
Wesley, Samuel	1766-1837
Zingarelli, Niccolo	1752-1837

1827   Kingdom of Greece founded.
       Battle of Navarino.
1830   Warsaw uprising.
1831   First epidemic of Asiatic cholera in England.
1833   Slavery abolished in British colonies.
       First Government grant aid to English schools.
1834   Faraday discovers electrical self-induction.
1837   Morse alphabet adopted.
1838   National Gallery opened.
1839   Gold discovered in Australia.
1840   Penny postage instituted.
1842   Khyber Pass incident.
1843   Battle of Meeanee.
       Battle of Maharajpore.
1845   Battle of Moodkee.
       Battle of Ferozeshah.
1846   Battle of Aliwal.
       Repeal of the Corn Laws.
1847   British Museum opened.
1848   Gold discovered in California.
1849   Hugary invaded by Russia.
1850   Submarine telegraph between England-France.

PROMINENT PEOPLE

Brown, John	1800-1859	Lessepes, Vicomte	
Bismarck, Prince Otto		Ferdinand de	1805-1894
Eduard Leopold Von	1815-1898	Lister, Lord	1827-1912
Booth, General William	1829-1912	Livingstone, Dr. David	1813-1873
Braille, Louis	1809-1852	Manning, Henry Edward,	
Brummell, 'Beau', George		Cardinal	1808-1892
Bryan	1778-1840	Paganini, Nicolo	1782-1840
Edison, Thomas Alva	1847-1931	Pasteur, Louis	1822-1895
Faraday, Michael	1791-1867	Rontgen, Prof. Welhelm	
Garibaldi, Giuseppe	1807-1882	Konrad	1845-1923
Kitchener of Khartoum	1850-1916	Smith, Joseph	1805-1844
		Wellington, Duke of	1769-1852

EMPERORS OF CHINA (MANCHU (Ch'ing) DYNASTY)

Hsuan Tsung   1820-1850

POPES

Leo XII	1823-1829	Pius IX	1830-1878
Pius VIII	1829-1830		

FRANCE. HEADS OF STATE

Charles X	1824-1830	Louis Napoleon Bonaparte	1848-1852
Louis Philippe	1830-1848		

ENGLAND. SOVEREIGNS

George IV	1820-1830	Victoria	1837-1901
William IV	1830-1837		

SWEDEN. KINGS

Charles XIV (Bernadotte)	1818-1844	Oscar I	1844-1859

John VI	1816-1826	Miguel	1828-1834
Pedro IV	1826-	Maria II (again)	1834-1853
Maria II	1826-1828		

RUSSIA. TSARS

| Nicholas I | 1825-1855 |

SPAIN. SOVEREIGNS

| Ferdinand VII | 1813-1833 | Isabella II | 1833-1868 |

U.S.A. PRESIDENTS

John Quincy Adams	1825-1829	J. Knox Polk	1845-1849
Andrew Jackson	1829-1837	Zachary Taylor	1849-1850
Martin Van Buren	1837-1841	Millard Fillimore	
W. H. Harrison	1841-	(Vice P.)	1850-1853
John Tyler (Vice P.)	1841-1845		

PRUSSIA. KINGS

| Frederick William III | 1797-1840 | Frederick William IV | 1840-1861 |

AUSTRIA. EMPERORS

| Franz I | 1804-1835 | Franz Josef | 1848-1916 |
| Ferdinand I | 1835-1848 | | |

NETHERLANDS. SOVEREIGNS

| William I | 1815-1840 | William III | 1849-1890 |
| William II | 1840-1849 | | |

BELGIUM. KINGS

| Leopold I | 1831-1865 |

WRITERS

Aarestrup, Emil	1800-1856	Adams, Hannah	1755-1831
Aasen, Ivar	1813-1896	Adams, Henry Brooks	1838-1918
Abbott, Edwin Abbott	1838-1926	Adams, John Quincy	1767-1848
Abbott, Evelyn	1843-1901	Adams, Sarah Flower	1805-1848
Abbott, Jacob	1803-1879	Adams, William Taylor	1822-1897
Abbott, Lyman	1835-1922	Adolphus, John	1768-1845
A'Beckett, Gilbert Abbott	1811-1856	Adolphus, John Leycester	1795-1862
Abernethy, John	1764-1831	Afanasiev, Alexander	
Aberigh Mackay, George		Nikolaievitch	1826-1871
Robert	1848-1881	Afzelius, Aruid August	1785-1871
About, Edmond Francois		Agassiz, Jean Louis	
Valentin	1828-1885	Rodolphe	1807-1873
Ackermann, Louise		Agoult, Marie Catherine	
Victorine Choquet	1813-1890	Sophie de Flavigny,	
Acton, John Emrich		Countess de (Daniel	
Edward Dolbey	1834-1902	Stern)	1805-1876
Adam, Juliette	1836-1936	Aguilar, Grace	1816-1847
Adams, Charles Follen	1842-1918	Aguilo I Fuster, Marian	1825-1897

Aicard, Jean Francois	
Victor	1848-1921
Aide, Hamilton	1830-1906
Aimard, Gustave	1818-1883
Ainger, Alfred	1837-1904
Ainslie, Hew	1792-1878
Ainsworth, William	
Harrison	1805-1882
Aird, Thomas	1802-1876
Akers, Benjamin Paul	1825-1861
Aksakov, Ivan Sergeyevich	1823-1886
Aksakov, Konstantin	1817-1860
Aksakov, Sergei,	
Timofeyevich	1791-1859
Alaman, Lucas	1792-1853
Alarcon, Pedro Antonio	1833-1891
Alcott, Amos Bronson	1799-1888
Alcott, Louisa May	1832-1888
Alden, Isabella	1841-1930
Alden, Joseph	1807-1885
Aldrich, Thomas Bailey	1836-1907
Aleardi, Aleardo	1812-1878
Alecsandri, Vasile	1821-1890
Alexander, Cecil Francis	1818-1895
Alexander, William	1826-1894
Alexis, Willibald	1798-1871
Alger, Horatio	1834-1899
Alin, Oscar Josef	1846-1900
Alison, Sir Archibald	1792-1867
Allen, Charles Grant	
Blairfindie	1848-1899
Allen, James Lane	1849-1925
Allibone, Samuel Austin	1816-1889
Allingham, William	1824-1889
Alma-Tadema, Sir	
Lawrence	1836-1912
Allmers, Hermann	1821-1902
Almeida-Garrett, Joao	
Baptista Da	1799-1854
Almqvist, Karl Jonas	
Ludwig	1793-1866
Amicis, Edmondo De	1846-1908
Amiel, Henri Frederic	1821-1881
Ampere, Jean Jacques	1800-1864
Ancelot, Jacques Arsene	
Francois Polycarpe	1794-1854
Ancillon, Johann Peter	
Friedrich	1766-1836
Ancona, Alessandro	1835-1914
Andersen, Hans	
Christian	1805-1875
Anderson, Robert	1750-1830
Andrieux, Francois	
Guillaume Jean	
Stanislas	1759-1833
Angelier, Auguste Jean	1848-1911
Anspach, Elizabeth	
Margravine	1750-1828
Antokolski Mark	
Matreevich	1843-1902
Anzengruber, Ludwig	1839-1889
Apperley, Charles James	
(Nimrod)	1777-1843
Arago, Jacques Etienne	
Victor	1790-1855
Arany, Janos	1817-1882
Arbois de Jubainville,	
Marie Henri d'	1827-1910
Arcault, Antoine-Vincent	1766-1834
Aribau, Bonaventura	
Carlos	1798-1862
Armitage, Edward	1817-1896
Arnason, Jon	1819-1888
Arndt, Ernst Moritz	1769-1860
Arneth, Alfred	1819-1897
Arnim, Elizabeth	
(Bettina) Von	1785-1859
Arnim, Ludwig Achim	
Von	1781-1831
Arnold, Sir Edwin	1832-1904
Arnold, Matthew	1822-1888
Arnold, Thomas	1795-1842
Arthur, Timothy Shay	1809-1885
Asbjornsen, Peter	
Christian	1812-1885
Ashe, Thomas	1836-1889
Asnyk, Adam	1838-1897
Atkinson, Thomas	
Witlam	1799-1861
Aubanel, Theodore	1829-1886
Augier, Guillaume Victor	
Emile	1820-1889
Aulard, Francois Victor	
Alphonse	1849-1928
Austin, Alfred	1835-1913
Austin, Sarah	1793-1867
Autran, Joseph	1813-1877
Avellanida, Gertrudis	
Gomez d'	1814-1873
Avenarius, Richard	
Heinrich Ludwig	1843-1896
Averbach, Berthold	1812-1882
Aversperg, Anton	
Alexander	1806-1876
Axelrod, Pavel	
Borriasovich	1850-1928
Ayala Y Herrera, Adelardo	
Lopez d'	1828-1879
Aytoun, William	
Edmonstoun	1813-1865
Azais, Pierre Hyacinthe	1766-1845
Azeglio, Massimo	
Taparelli, Marquis d'	1798-1866
Bacon, Delia Salter	1811-1859
Bacon, Leonard	1802-1881
Bacsanyi, Janos	1763-1845
Baedeker, Karl	1801-1859
Bagehot, Walter	1826-1877
Baggesen, Jens Immanuel	1764-1826

Bahr, Johann Christian		Beck, Jakob Sigismund	1761-1840
Felix	1798-1872	Beckford, William	1760-1840
Bailey, Samuel	1791-1870	Becque, Henry Francois	1837-1899
Bailey, Philip James	1816-1902	Becquer, Gustavo Adolfo	1836-1870
Baillie, Joanna	1762-1851	Beddoes, Thomas Lovell	1803-1849
Bain, Alexander	1818-1903	Beecher, Henry Ward	1813-1887
Baird, Henry Martin	1832-1906	Bede, Cuthbert	1827-1889
Balaguer, Victor	1824-1901	Beechey, Sir William	1753-1839
Balbo, Cesare, Count	1789-1853	Beeton, Mrs. Isabella	
Balfe, Michael William	1808-1870	Mary Mayson	1836-1865
Ballanche, Pierre Simon	1776-1847	Beets, Nikolaas	1814-1903
Ballantine, James	1808-1877	Beljame, Alexandre	1842-1906
Ballantyne, Robert		Bell, Henry Glassford	1803-1874
Michael	1825-1894	Bell, Robert	1800-1867
Balmes, Jaime Luciano	1810-1848	Bellamy, Edward	1850-1898
Balzac, Honore De	1799-1850	Belli, Giuseppe	
Bancroft, George	1800-1891	Gioachino	1791-1863
Bancroft, Hubert Howe	1832-1918	Benedix, Julius Roderich	1811-1873
Banim, John	1798-1842	Beneke, Friedrich Eduard	1798-1856
Banville, Theodore		Bentham, Jeremy	1748-1832
Faullain De	1823-1891	Bernhardi, Friedrich	
Barante, Amable Guillaume		Von	1849-1930
Prosper Brugiere	1782-1866	Beranger, Pierre Jean De	1780-1857
Baratynski, Yvegeniy		Berard, Joseph Frederic	1789-1828
Abramovich	1800-1844	Berchet, Giovanni	1783-1851
Barbey D' Aurevilly, Jules		Bernard, Charles De	1804-1850
Amedee	1808-1889	Berry, Mary	1763-1852
Barbier, Henri Auguste	1805-1882	Bertrand, Jacques Louis	
Barbier, Paul Jules	1825-1901	Napoleon	1807-1841
Baring-Gould, Sabine	1834-1924	Berzsenyi, Daniel	1776-1836
Barker, Thomas of Bath	1769-1847	Besant, Annie	1847-1933
Barker, Thomas James		Besant, Walter Sir	1836-1901
Barker	1815-1852	Beskow, Bernhard Von	1796-1868
Barlow, Peter	1776-1862	Bibaud, Michel	1782-1857
Barnes, William	1800-1886	Biedermann, Friedrich	
Barr, Amelia Edith	1831-1919	Karl	1812-1901
Barriere, Theodore	1823-1877	Bierce, Ambrose	1842-1916
Barrili, Antonio Giulio	1836-1908	Bignon, Louis Pierre	
Barthelemy, Auguste		Edouard	1771-1841
Marseille	1796-1867	Bilderdijk, Willem	1756-1831
Barthelemy, Saint		Billings, Robert William	1813-1874
Hilaire Jules	1805-1895	Birrell, Augustine	1850-1933
Barton, Bernard	1784-1849	Bishop, Isabella	1831-1904
Bascom, John	1827-1911	Bissen, Herman Vilhelm	1798-1868
Basevi, George	1794-1845	Bitzius, Albrecht	1797-1854
Bates, Arlo	1850-1918	Bjornson, Bjornstjerne	1832-1910
Batyushkov, Konstantin		Black, William	1841-1898
Nikolaievitch	1787-1855	Blackie, John Stuart	1809-1895
Baudelaire, Charles Pierre	1821-1867	Blackmore, Richard	
Baudissin, Wolf Heinrich	1789-1878	Doddridge	1825-1900
Bauer, Bruno	1809-1882	Blake, William	1757-1827
Bauernfeld, Eduard Von	1802-1890	Blanc, Jean Joseph	
Baumbach, Rudolf	1840-1905	Charles Louis	1811-1882
Bautain, Louis Eugene		Blanchard, Samuel Laman	1804-1845
Marie	1796-1867	Blavatsky, Helena Petrova	1831-1891
Bayly, Thomas Haynes	1797-1839	Blessington, Marguerite	1789-1849
Beauchamp, Alphonse De	1767-1832	Blicher, Steen Steensen	1782-1848
Beaumont, Sir George		Blind, Mathilde	1841-1896
Howland	1753-1827	Bliss, Philip Paul	1838-1876
Beauvoir, Roger De	1809-1866	Blood, Benjamin Paul	1832-1919
Beck, Christian Daniel	1757-1832	Blore, Edward	1787-1879

Blouet, Paul	1848-1903	Brooks, Phillips	1835-1893
Bloy, Leon	1846-1917	Broughton, John Cam	
Blunt, Wilfrid Scawen	1840-1922	Hobhouse	1786-1869
Bodenstedt, Friedrich		Broughton, Rhoda	1840-1920
Martin Von	1819-1892	Brown, Peter Hume	1850-1918
Boerne, Karl Ludwig	1786-1837	Brown, Samuel Morison	1817-1856
Boisgobey, Fortune		Brown, Thomas Edward	1830-1897
Abraham Du	1824-1891	Browne, James	1793-1841
Boker, George Henry	1823-1890	Browning, Elizabeth	
Boldrewood, Rolf	1826-1915	Barrett	1806-1861
Bolyai, Wolfgang	1775-1856	Browning, Oscar	1837-1923
Bonald, Louis Gabriel		Browning, Robert	1812-1889
Ambroise	1754-1840	Brownson, Orestes	
Bonghi, Ruggero	1828-1895	Augustus	1803-1876
Bonneville, Nicholas De	1760-1828	Brugsch, Heinrich Karl	1827-1894
Bonstetten, Charles		Brunner, Henry	1840-1915
Victor De	1745-1832	Bryant, William Cullen	1794-1878
Borel, Petrus	1809-1859	Brydges, Sir Samuel	
Borne, Ludwig	1786-1837	Egerton	1762-1837
Bornier, Henri	1825-1901	Buchanan, Robert	
Borrow, George Henry	1803-1881	Williams	1841-1901
Bosanquet, Bernard	1848-1923	Buchez, Philippe Benjamin	
Bosboom-Toussaint, Anna		Joseph	1796-1865
Louisa Geertruida	1812-1886	Buchner, Ludwig	1824-1899
Bostrom, Christoffer Jacob	1797-1866	Buckingham, James Silk	1786-1855
Botta, Carlo Guiseppe		Buckle, Henry Thomas	1821-1862
Guglielmo	1766-1837	Buckstone, John Baldwin	1802-1879
Boucicault, Dion	1822-1890	Bulgarin, Thaddeus	1789-1859
Bouilhet, Louis Hyacinthe	1822-1869	Bulwer, Henry Lytton	1801-1872
Bouilly, Jean Nicolas	1763-1842	Burckhardt, Jakob	1818-1897
Bouterwek, Friedrich	1765-1828	Burgess, John Bagnold	1830-1897
Bowen, Francis	1811-1890	Burnand, Frederick	
Boweles, William Lisle	1762-1850	Gustavus	1842-1885
Boyd, Andrew Kennedy		Burnett, Frances Eliza	
Hutchinson	1825-1899	Hodgson	1849-1924
Boyesen, Hjalmar	1848-1895	Burney, Fanny	
Braddon, Mary Elizabeth	1837-1915	(Madame D'Arblay)	1752-1840
Bradley, Edward	1827-1889	Burroughs, John	1837-1921
Bradley, Francis Herbert	1846-1924	Burrows, Montagu	1819-1905
Braga, Theophilo	1843-1924	Burton, John Hill	1809-1881
Brandes, Georg Maurice		Burton, Sir Richard	
Cohen	1842-1927	Francis	1821-1890
Bree, Matthias Ignatius		Burton, William Evans	1804-1860
Van	1773-1839	Bury, Lady Charlotte	
Bremer, Fredrika	1801-1865	Susan Maria	1775-1861
Brentano, Clemens	1778-1842	Butler, Samuel	1835-1902
Brentano, Franz	1838-1917	Byron, Henry James	1834-1884
Breton de Los Herreros,		Caballero, Fernan	1796-1877
Manuel	1796-1873	Cable, George	
Bridges, Robert Seymour	1844-1930	Washington	1844-1925
Brierley, Benjamin	1825-1896	Caird, Edward	1835-1908
Brillat-Savarin, Anthelme	1755-1826	Caird, John	1820-1898
Brizeux, Julien Auguste		Calderwood, Henry	1830-1897
Pelage	1803-1858	Calverley, Charles Stuart	1831-1884
Brokmeyer, Henry Conrad	1828-1906	Calvert, George Harris	1803-1889
Bronte, Anne	1820-1849	Calvo, Carlos	1824-1906
Bronte, Charlotte	1816-1855	Cairns, John Elliot	1823-1875
Bronte, Emily	1818-1848	Campbell, Thomas	1777-1844
Brooke, Stopford Augustus	1832-1916	Campoamor Y Campoosorio,	
Brooks, Charles William		Raymon De	1819-1901
Shirley	1816-1874	Canina, Luigi	1795-1856

Cannon, Charles James	1800-1860
Canth, Minna	1844-1897
Cantu, Cesare	1804-1895
Capefigue, Jean Baptiste Honore Raymond	1801-1872
Capern, Edward	1819-1894
Capuana, Luigi	1839-1915
Carducci, Giosue	1835-1907
Carey, Phoebe	1824-1871
Carlen, Emilia Smith Flygare	1807-1892
Carleton, Will	1845-1912
Carleton, William	1794-1869
Carlyle, Thomas	1795-1881
Carmen, Sylva	1843-1916
Carnegie, Andrew	1835-1910
Caro, Emile Marie	1826-1887
Carpenter, Edward	1844-1929
Carr, Joseph William Comyns	1849-1916
Carrer, Luigi	1801-1850
Carriere, Moritz	1817-1895
Cary, Alice	1820-1871
Castelli, Ignaz Franz	1781-1862
Castello, Branco Camillo	1825-1890
Cattaneo, Carlo	1801-1869
Cavalcaselle, Giovanni Battista	1820-1897
Cazalis, Henri	1840-1909
Chalmers, Alexander	1759-1834
Chalybaus, Heinrich Moritz	1796-1862
Chambers, Robert	1802-1871
Chamier, Fredrick	1796-1870
Chamisso, Adelbert Von	1781-1838
Champfleury	1821-1889
Channing, William Ellery	1780-1842
Chantavoine, Henri	1850-1918
Charles, Elizabeth	1828-1896
Chasles, Philarete	1798-1873
Chateaubriand, Francois Rene	1768-1848
Chatrian, Alexandre (Erckman-Chatrian)	1826-1890
Chatter Ji, Bankim Chandra	1838-1894
Chenedolle, Charles Julien Lioult De	1769-1833
Cherbuliez, Charles Victor	1829-1899
Chernyshevsky, Nikolay Gavrilovich	1828-1889
Cheruel, Pierre Adolphe	1809-1891
Chesney, Charles Cornwallis	1826-1876
Child, Francis James	1825-1896
Child, Lydia Maria	1802-1874
Christopoulos, Athanasios	1772-1847
Cibrario, Luigi, Count	1802-1870
Cladel, Leon	1835-1892
Clare, John	1793-1864
Clark, William George	1821-1878

Claretie, Jules Arsene Arnaud	1840-1913
Clarke, Charles Cowden	1787-1877
Clarke, Marcus Andrew Hislop	1846-1881
Clausewitz, Karl Von	1780-1831
Clifford, William Kingdon	1845-1879
Clive, Caroline	1801-1873
Clough, Arthur Hugh	1819-1861
Cobbe, Frances Power	1822-1904
Cobbett, William	1763-1835
Cockton, Henry	1807-1853
Cole, Sir Henry	1808-1882
Coleridge, Hartley	1796-1849
Coleridge, Samuel Taylor	1772-1834
Coleridge, Sara	1802-1852
Colet, Louise	1810-1876
Collett, Jacobine Camilla	1813-1895
Collier, John Payne	1789-1883
Collins, Charles Allston	1828-1873
Collins, Mortimer	1827-1876
Collins, William	1788-1847
Collins, William Wilkie	1824-1889
Colman, George	1762-1836
Colomb, Philip Howard	1831-1899
Comte, Auguste	1798-1857
Conscience, Hendrik	1812-1883
Constant, Benjamin Jean Joseph	1845-1902
Constant De Rebeque, Henri Benjamin	1767-1830
Conway, Hugh	1847-1885
Conway, Moncure Daniel	1832-1907
Cook, Edward Dutton	1829-1883
Cooke, John Esten	1830-1886
Cooke, Rose Terry	1827-1892
Coolidge, Susan	1835-1905
Cooper, James Fenimore	1789-1851
Coppee, Francois	1842-1908
Coppee, Henry	1821-1895
Cossa, Pietro	1830-1881
Costa, Joaquim	1846-1911
Costello, Louisa Stuart	1799-1870
Coster, Charles Theodore Henri De	1827-1879
Courthope, William John	1842-1917
Cousin, Victor	1792-1867
Cox, Sir George William	1827-1902
Coxe, William	1747-1828
Craddock, Charles Egbert	1850-1922
Craik, Dinah Maria	1826-1887
Crabbe, George	1754-1832
Craven, Pauline	1808-1891
Creasy, Sir Edward Shepherd	1812-1878
Creevey, Thomas	1768-1838
Creighton, Mandell	1843-1901
Cremazie, Octave	1822-1879
Cremer, Jakobus Jan	1827-1880
Creuzer, George Friedrich	1771-1858

Crocker, Hannah Mather	1752-1829
Croker, John Wilson	1780-1857
Croker, Thomas Crofton	1798-1854
Crowne, Catherine	1800-1870
Crozier, John Beattie	1849-1921
Crusenstolpe, Magnus Jakob	1795-1865
Csengery, Antal	1822-1880
Csiky, Gergoly	1842-1891
Cullum, George Washington	1809-1892
Cummins, Maria Suzanna	1827-1866
Cunningham, Allan	1784-1842
Curtis, George William	1824-1892
Curtius, Ernst	1814-1896
Curtius, Georg	1820-1885
Cuvier, Georges (Leopold)	1769-1832
Da Costa, Isaak	1798-1860
Dahlgreen, Karl Fredrik	1791-1844
Dahlmann, Friedrich Christoph	1785-1860
Dahn, Julius Sophus Felix	1834-1912
Dalling & Bulwer, Baron	1801-1872
Dall 'Ongaro, Francesco	1808-1873
D'Alviella, Count Goblet	1846-1925
Daly, Augustin	1838-1899
Dana, Richard Henry	1815-1882
Da Ponte, Lorenzo	1749-1838
Dareste De La Chavanne, Cleophas	1820-1882
Darley, George	1795-1846
Darmesteter, James	1849-1894
Daru, Pierre Antoine, Comte	1767-1829
Darwin, Charles Robert	1809-1882
D'Aubigné, Jean Henri	1794-1872
Daudet, Alphonse	1840-1897
Daudet, Ernest	1837-1921
Daumer, Georg Friedrich	1800-1875
Daunou, Pierre Claude Francois	1761-1840
David, Pierre Jean	1789-1856
Davidson, Thomas	1840-1900
Davis, Thomas Osborne	1814-1845
Decelles, Alfred Duclos	1843-1925
De Cort, Frans	1834-1878
De Geer, Louis Gerhard, Baron	1818-1896
Dekker, Edward Douwes	1820-1887
Delarue, Gervais	1751-1835
Delavigne, Jean Francois Casimir	1793-1843
Delbruck, Hans	1848-1929
Delisle, Leopold Victor	1826-1910
Delvig, Anton Antonovich, Baron Von	1798-1831
Demogeot, Jacques Claude	1808-1894

P

De Morgan, William Trend	1839-1917
Denifle, Heinrich Seuse	1844-1905
Dennery, Adolphe Philippe	1811-1899
Dent, John Charles	1841-1887
De Quincey, Thomas	1785-1859
Deroulede, Paul	1846-1914
Desagiers, Marc Antoine Madeleine	1772-1827
Deschamps, Emile	1791-1871
De Tabley, John Byrne Leicester Warren	1835-1895
Deussen, Paul	1845-1919
De Vere, Aubrey Thomas	1814-1902
Dexter, Henry Martyn	1821-1890
Dibdin, Thomas John	1771-1841
Dicey, Edward	1832-1911
Dickens, Charles John Huffam	1812-1870
Dickinson, Emily	1830-1886
Dierx, Leon	1838-1912
Digby, Kenelm Henry	1800-1880
Dilthey, Wilhelm	1833-1911
Dingelstedt, Franz Von	1814-1881
Dionne, Narcisse Eutrope	1848-1917
Disreali, Benjamin	1804-1881
D'Israeli, Isaac	1766-1848
Dixon, Richard Watson	1833-1900
Dixon, William Hepworth	1821-1879
Dmitriev, Ivan Ivanovich	1760-1837
Dobell, Sydney Thompson	1824-1874
Dobson, Henry Austin	1840-1921
Dodge, Mary	1838-1905
Dodge, Theodore Ayrault	1842-1909
Dollinger, Johann Joseph Ignaz Von	1799-1890
Domett, Alfred	1811-1887
Donoso, Cortes Juan	1809-1853
Doran, John	1807-1878
Dostoievsky, Fyodor Mikhaylovich	1821-1881
Doughty, Charles Montagu	1843-1926
Douglas, Sir William Fettes	1822-1891
Dove, Alfred	1844-1916
Dowden, Edward	1843-1913
Doyle, Sir Francis Hastings Charles	1810-1888
Drachmann, Holger Henrik Herboldt	1846-1908
Dragomirov, Micheal Ivanovich	1830-1905
Drake, Friedrich	1805-1882
Drake, Nathan	1766-1836
Draper, William	1811-1882
Drinkwater, Bethune John	1762-1844
Drobisch, Moritz Wilhelm	1802-1896

Droste-Hulshoff, Annette	
Elizabeth	1797-1848
Droysen, Johann Gustav	1808-1884
Droz, Francois-Xavier	1773-1850
Duboc, Julius	1829-1903
Du Camp, Maxime	1822-1894
Ducange, Victor Henri	
Joseph Brahain	1783-1833
Ducasse, Pierre Emmanuel	
Albert	1813-1893
Duff, Sir Mountstuart	
Elphinstone Grant	1829-1906
Duff-Gordon, Lucy	1829-1869
Duhring, Eugen Karl	1833-1921
Dumas, Alexandre	1802-1870
Dumas, Alexandre (fils)	1824-1895
Du Maurier, George Louis	
Palmella Busson	1834-1896
Dummler, Ernst Ludwig	1830-1902
Dumont, Augustin	
Alexandre	1801-1884
Dumont, Pierre Etienne	
Louis	1759-1829
Duncker, Maximilian	
Wolfgang	1811-1886
Dunlap, William	1766-1839
Dupont, Pierre	1821-1870
Duruy, Jean Victor	1811-1894
Dutt, Michael Madhu	
Sudan	1824-1873
Duval, Alexandre Vincent	
Pineux	1767-1842
Eberhard, Christian	
August Gottlob	1769-1845
Ebers, Georg Moritz	1837-1898
Ebner-Eschenbach, Marie	1830-1916
Eca De Queiroz, Jose	
Maria	1843-1900
Echegaram Y Ezaguire,	
José	1833-1916
Eckermann, Johann Peter	1792-1864
Eddy, Mary Baker Glover	1821-1910
Edgeworth, Maria	1767-1849
Edgren-Leffler, Anne	
Charlotte	1849-1892
Edwards, Amelia	1831-1892
Egan, Pierce	1772-1849
Eggleston, Edward	1837-1902
Eichendorff, Joseph	
Freiherr Von	1788-1857
Eliot, George	
(Marian Evans)	1819-1880
Elliott, Ebenezer	1781-1849
Ellis, Alexander John	1814-1890
Elphinstone, Mountstuart	1779-1859
Emerson, Ralph Waldo	1803-1882
Eminescu, Mihail	1849-1889
Engel, Johann Carl	
Ludwig	1778-1840
Engels, Friedrich	1820-1895
English, Thomas Dunn	1819-1902

Ennemoser, Joseph	1787-1855
Eotvos, Jozsef, Baron	1813-1871
Erckmann, Emile	1822-1899
Erdelyi, Janos	1814-1868
Erdmann, Johann Eduard	1805-1892
Erskine, Thomas	1788-1870
Eschenmayer, Adam Karl	
August Von	1768-1852
Espronceda, Jose De	1808-1842
Esquiros, Henri Francois	
Alphonse	1812-1876
Estebanez, Caldren Serafin	1799-1867
Etienne, Charles	
Guillaume	1777-1845
Eucken, Rudolf Christoph	1846-1926
Everett, Alexander Hill	1790-1847
Ewing, Juliana, Horatia	
Orr	1841-1885
Fabre, Ferdinand	1830-1898
Fabriani, Severino	1792-1849
Fagniez, Gustav Charles	1842-1927
Faguet, Emile	1847-1916
Fahlcrantz, Christian Erik	1790-1866
Fain, Agathon Jean	
Francois	1778-1837
Falk, Johann Daniel	1768-1826
Falke, Johann, Friedrich	
Gottlieb	1823-1876
Fallmerayer, Jakob Phillip	1790-1861
Falloux, Frederic	
Alfred Pierre	1811-1886
Farina, Salvatore	1846-1918
Farini, Luigi Carlo	1812-1866
Farjeon, Benjamin Leopold	1838-1903
Farrar, Frederic William	1831-1903
Fauriel, Claude Charles	1782-1844
Fay, Andreas	1786-1864
Fazy, Henri	1842-1920
Fechner, Gustav Theodor	1801-1887
Fejer, Gyorgy	1766-1852
Fenn, George Manville	1831-1909
Ferguson, Sir Samuel	1810-1886
Fergusson, James	1808-1886
Ferrari, Giuseppe	1812-1876
Ferrari, Paolo	1822-1889
Ferri, Luigi	1826-1895
Ferrier, Paul	1843-1920
Ferrier, Susan	
Edmonstone	1782-1854
Feuchtersleben, Ernst	1806-1849
Feuerbach, Ludwig	
Andreas	1804-1872
Feurbacj, Paul Johann	
Anselm	1775-1833
Feuillet, Octave	1821-1890
Feval, Paul Henri	
Corentin	1817-1887
Feydeau, Ernest Aime	1821-1873
Fichte, Immanuel	
Hermann Von	1796-1879
Field, Eugene	1850-1895

Fielding, Anthony	
Vandyke Copley	1787-1855
Fields, James Thomas	1817-1881
Figuier, Louis	1819-1894
Filon, Augustin	1841-1916
Finlay, George	1799-1875
Fiske, John	1842-1901
Fisher, Ernst Kuno	
Berthold	1824-1907
Fitzball, Edward	1792-1873
Fitzgerald, Edward	1809-1883
Fitzgerald, Perry	
Hetherington	1834-1925
Flach, Geoffroi Jacques	1846-1919
Flammarion, Nicolas	
Camille	1842-1925
Flaubert, Gustave	1821-1880
Foa, Eugenie	
Rodriguez-Gradis	1798-1853
Fogazzaro, Antonio	1842-1911
Follen, Adolf Ludwig	1794-1855
Follen, Karl	1795-1840
Fontan, Louis Marie	1801-1839
Fontane, Theodor	1819-1898
Ford, Richard	1796-1858
Forsell, Hans Ludwig	1843-1901
Forster, Friedrich	
Christoph	1791-1868
Forster, John	1812-1876
Fortlage, Karl	1806-1881
Foscolo, Ugo	1778-1827
Foster, John	1770-1843
Fouillee, Alfred Jules	
Emile	1838-1912
Fouque, Friedrich Heinrich	
Karl De La Mote	1777-1843
Fourier, Francois Marie	
Charles	1772-1837
Fowler, Thomas	1832-1904
Frampton, Mary	1773-1846
France, Anatole	1844-1924
Francois De Neufchateau,	
Nicolas Louis	1750-1828
Frankl, Ludwig August	1810-1894
Franzen, Frans Michael	1772-1847
Franzos, Karl Emil	1848-1904
Fraser, Alexander	
Campbell	1819-1914
Fraser, James Baillie	1783-1856
Frechette, Louis Honore	1839-1908
Freeman, Edward	
Augustus	1823-1892
Freiligraph, Ferdinand	1810-1876
Freneau, Philip Morin	1752-1832
Frere, John Hookham	1769-1846
Freytag, Gustav	1816-1895
Fries, Jakob Friedrich	1773-1843
Froebel, Friedrich	
Wilhelm August	1782-1852
Frohlich, Abraham	
Emanuel	1796-1865

Frohschammer, Jakob	1821-1893
Frothingham, Octavius	
Brooks	1822-1895
Froude, James Anthony	1818-1894
Fryxell, Anders	1795-1881
Fucini, Renato	1843-1921
Fuller, Margaret	1810-1850
Fullerton, Lady Georgiana	
Charlotte	1812-1885
Fustel De Coulanges,	
Numa Dennis	1830-1889
Fyffe, Charles Alan	1845-1892
Gaboriau, Emile	1835-1873
Gachard, Louis Prosper	1800-1885
Gagern, Hans Christoph	
Ernst	1766-1852
Gairdner, James	1828-1912
Galluppi, Pasquale	1770-1846
Galt, John	1779-1839
Garat, Dominique Joseph	1749-1833
Garay, Janos	1812-1853
Gardiner, Samuel Rawson	1829-1902
Gareau, Francois Xavier	1806-1866
Garnett, Richard	1835-1906
Garrett, Joao Baptista Da	
Silva Leitao De	
Almeida	1799-1854
Gaskell, (Mrs.) Elizabeth	
Cleghorn	1810-1865
Gatty, Margaret	1809-1873
Gautier, Leon	1832-1897
Gautier, Theophile	1811-1872
Geibel, Emanuel	1815-1884
Geijer, Eric Gustav	1783-1877
George, Henry	1839-1897
Genlis, Stephanie Felicité	
Ducrest De Staubin	1746-1830
Gesenius, Friedrich	
Heinrich Wilhelm	1786-1842
Gerstacker, Friedrich	1816-1877
Gervinus, Georg Gottfried	1805-1871
Gezelle, Guido	1830-1899
Gfrorer, August Friedrich	1803-1861
Ghika, Helena	1829-1888
Giacometti, Paolo	1816-1882
Giacosa, Guiseppe	1847-1906
Gibson, William Hamilton	1850-1896
Giesebrecht, Wilhelm	
Von	1814-1889
Gifford, William	1756-1826
Gilbert, Sir John Thomas	1829-1898
Gilbert, William	1806-1889
Gilbert, Sir William	
Schwenk	1836-1911
Gilchrist, Alexander	1828-1861
Gilchrist, Anna	1828-1885
Gilder, Richard Watson	1844-1909
Gillies, John	1747-1836
Gindley, Anton	1829-1892
Giner De Los Rios,	
Francisco	1840-1915

Gioberti, Vincenzo	1801-1852	Greville, Henry	1842-1902
Gioja, Melchiorre	1769-1829	Griboyedov, Alexander	
Giordani, Pietro	1774-1848	Sergeyevich	1705-1829
Girardin, Delphine De	1804-1855	Griffin, Gerald	1803-1840
Giraud, Giovanni	1776-1834	Grigorovich, Dmitri	
Gieseler, Johann Karl		Vaslievich	1822-1900
Ludwig	1792-1854	Grimm, Jacob Ludwig	
Giudici, Paolo Emiliano	1812-1872	Carl	1785-1863
Giusti, Giuseppi	1809-1850	Grimm, Wilhelm Carl	1786-1859
Glassbrenner, Adolf	1810-1876	Grossi, Tommaso	1791-1853
Glatigny, Joseph Albert		Grossmith, George	1847-1912
Alexandre	1839-1873	Grote, George	1794-1871
Gleig, George Robert	1796-1888	Grub, George	1812-1892
Glen, William	1789-1826	Grundtvig, Nikolai	
Glinka, Fedor		Fredrik Severin	1783-1872
Nikolayevich	1788-1880	Grundy, Sydney	1848-1914
Godwin, William	1756-1836	Gubernatis, Angelo De	1840-1913
Goethe, Johann Wolfgang		Guerin Du Cayla, Georges	
Von	1749-1832	Maurice De	1810-1839
Gogol, Nikolai		Guerrazzi, Francesco	
Vasilievich	1809-1852	Domenico	1804-1873
Goldschmidt, Aaron		Guerrini, Olinda	1845-1916
Meier	1819-1887	Guest, Edwin	1800-1880
Goltz, Bogumil	1801-1870	Guizot, Francois Pierre	
Gomperz, Theodor	1832-1912	Guillaume	1787-1874
Goncalves Dias, Antonio	1823-1864	Gutschmid, Alfred	1835-1887
Goncharov, Ivan		Gutzkow, Karl Ferdinand	1811-1878
Alexandrovich	1812-1891	Guys, Constantin	1805-1892
Goncourt De, Edmond		Gyllembourg Eh Rensvard,	
Louis Antoine Huot	1822-1896	Thomasine Christine	1773-1856
Goncourt De, Jules		Gyp	1849-1932
Alfred Huot	1830-1870	Habberton, John	1842-1921
Good, John Mason	1764-1827	Hacklander, Friedrich	
Goodrich, Samuel		Wilhelm Von	1816-1877
Griswold	1793-1860	Hagenbach, Karl Rudolf	1801-1874
Gordon, Adam Lindsay	1833-1870	Hahn, Ida	1805-1880
Gordon, Leon	1831-1892	Hake, Thomas Gordon	1809-1895
Gore, Catherine Grace		Hale, Edward Everett	1822-1909
Frances	1799-1861	Hale, Sarah Josepha	1788-1879
Gorres, Joseph Von	1776-1848	Halevy, Jean	1804-1883
Gosse, Sir Edmund	1849-1928	Halevy, Ludovic	1834-1908
Gottschall, Rudolf Van	1823-1908	Haliburton, Thomas	
Gould, John	1804-1881	Chandler	1796-1865
Gozlan, Leon	1803-1860	Hall, Anna Maria	1800-1881
Grabbe, Christian		Hall, Basil	1788-1844
Dietrich	1801-1836	Hall, Samuel Carter	1800-1889
Graf, Arturo	1848-1913	Hall, William Edward	1835-1894
Grant, Anne	1755-1838	Hallam, Henry	1777-1859
Grant, James	1822-1887	Halleck, Fitz-Greene	1790-1867
Gratz, Heinrich	1817-1891	Hallgrimson, Jonas	1807-1845
Graves, Alfred Percival	1846-1931	Halliday, Andrew	1830-1877
Gray, David	1838-1861	Hamerton, Philip Gilbert	1834-1894
Green, John Richard	1837-1883	Hamilton, Thomas	1789-1842
Green, Mary Ann Evrett	1818-1895	Hamilton, Sir William	1788-1856
Green, Thomas Hill	1836-1882	Hamley, Sir Edward	
Greene, George		Bruce	1824-1893
Washington	1811-1883	Hammer, Julius	1810-1962
Greg, William Rathbone	1809-1881	Hannay, James	1827-1873
Gregorovius, Ferdinand	1821-1891	Hardwick, Philip	1792-1870
Greville, Charles		Hardy, Thomas	1840-1928
Cavendish Fulke	1794-1865		

Ingoldsby, Thomas	1788-1845	Kerner, Justinus Andreas		
Ingraham, Joseph Holt	1809-1860	Christian	1786-1862	
Ingraham, Prentice	1843-1904	Kervyn De Lettenhove,		
Innes, Cosmo	1798-1874	Constantine Bruno	1817-1891	
Irving, Washington	1783-1859	Key, Ellen	1849-1926	
Isaacs, Jorge	1837-1895	Key, Francis-Scott	1779-1833	
Jackson, Helen Maria	1831-1885	Kielland, Alexander	1849-1906	
Jacobsen, Jens Peter	1847-1885	Kierkegaard, Soren Aaby	1813-1855	
Jahn, Otto	1813-1869	Kinglake, Alexander		
Jakob, Ludwig Heinrich		William	1809-1891	
Von	1759-1827	Kingsley, Charles	1819-1875	
James, George Payne		Kingsley, Henry	1830-1876	
Rainsford	1799-1860	Kingston, William Henry		
James, Henry	1843-1916	Giles	1814-1880	
James, William	1842-1910	Kinkel, Johann Gottfried	1815-1882	
Jameson, Anna Brownell	1794-1860	Kisfaludy, Karoly	1788-1830	
Janin, Jules Gabriel	1804-1874	Kisfaludy, Sandor	1772-1844	
Janssen, Johannes	1829-1891	Kitto, John	1804-1854	
Jasmin, Jacques	1798-1864	Kivi, Steuval	1834-1872	
Jebb, Sir Richard		Klaczko, Julian	1825-1906	
Claverhouse	1841-1905	Klinger, Friedrich		
Jefferies, Richard	1848-1887	Maximilian Von	1752-1831	
Jefferson, Thomas	1743-1826	Knebel, Karl Ludwig Von	1744-1834	
Jensen, Adolf	1837-1879	Knight, Charles	1791-1873	
Jensen, Wilhelm	1837-1911	Knowles, James Sheridan	1784-1862	
Jerrold, Douglas William	1803-1857	Kock, Charles Paul De	1793-1871	
Jesse, Edward	1780-1868	Kolcsey, Ferencz	1790-1888	
Jewett, Sarah Orne	1849-1909	Kopisch, August	1799-1853	
Jewsbury, Geraldine		Krasinski, Zygmunt,		
Endsor	1812-1880	Count	1812-1859	
Joinville, Francois		Kraszewski, Joseph		
Ferdinand d'Orleans	1818-1900	Ignatius	1812-1887	
Jokai, Maurus	1825-1904	Krause, Karl Christian		
Jones, Ebenezer	1820-1860	Friedrich	1781-1832	
Jones, Ernest	1819-1869	Kropotkin, Peter		
Jones, Henry	1831-1899	Alexeivich	1842-1921	
Jordan, Wilhelm	1819-1904	Krug, Wilhelm Traugott	1770-1842	
Josika, Miklos	1794-1865	Krylov, Ivan Andreevich	1768-1844	
Jouffroy, Theodore		Kuhlau, Friedrich	1786-1832	
Simon	1796-1842	Kurz, Hermann	1813-1873	
Jouy, Victor Joseph		Labiche, Eugene Marin	1815-1888	
Etienne De	1764-1846	Lacaita, Sir James	1813-1895	
Judson, Edward Zane		Lacretelle, Jean Charles		
Carroll	1823-1886	Dominique de	1766-1855	
Junqueiro, Abilio Guena	1850-1923	Ladd, George Tumbull	1842-1921	
Karadzic, Viek Stefanovic	1787-1864	La Farina, Giuseppe	1815-1863	
Karamzin, Nicolai		La Harpe, Frederic Cesare	1754-1838	
Mikhailovich	1765-1826	Laing, Samuel	1810-1897	
Karr, Alphonse	1808-1890	Lamarck, Jean		
Kate, Jan Jacob		Chevalier de	1744-1829	
Lodewyk Ten	1819-1889	Lamartine, Alphonse De	1790-1869	
Kazinczy, Ferencz	1759-1831	Lamb, Charles	1775-1834	
Keble, John	1792-1866	Lamennais, Hugues		
Keightley, Thomas	1789-1872	Felicite Robert De	1782-1854	
Keller, Gottfried	1819-1890	Landon, Letitia Elizabeth	1802-1838	
Kemble, John Mitchell	1807-1857	Landor, Walter Savage	1775-1864	
Kendall, Henry Clarence	1841-1882	Lane, Edward William	1801-1876	
Kenealy, Edward Vaughan		Lanfrey, Pierre	1828-1877	
Hyde	1819-1880	Lang, Andrew	1844-1912	
Kenney, James	1780-1849	Lange, Friedrich Albert	1828-1875	
		Langhorne, John	1735-1779	

Lanier, Sidney	1842-1881
Lappenberg, Johann Martin	1794-1865
Laprade, Pierre Marin Victor Richard De	1812-1883
Laromiguiere, Pierre	1756-1837
Larousse, Pierre Athanase	1817-1875
Larra, Mariano Jose De	1809-1837
Las Cases, Emmanuel Dieudonné, Compte de	1766-1842
Laube, Heinrich	1806-1884
Lauder, Sir Thomas Dick	1784-1848
Laurent, Francois	1810-1887
Lavisse, Ernest	1842-1922
Lawless, Emily	1845-1913
Lawrence, George Alfred	1827-1876
Laya, Jean Louis	1716-1833
Layard, Sir Austen Henry	1817-1894
Lazarus, Emma	1849-1887
Lazarus, Moritz	1824-1903
Lea, Henry Charles	1825-1909
Lecky, William Edward Hartpole	1838-1903
Leconte De Lisle, Charles Marie Rene	1818-1894
Lee, Harriet	1757-1851
Le Fanu, Joseph Sheridan	1814-1873
Legouve, Gabriel Jean Baptiste Ernest Wilfrid	1807-1903
Leleand, Charles Godfrey	1824-1903
Le Mercier, Nepomucene	1771-1840
Le Moine, James MacPherson	1825-1912
Lemon, Mark	1809-1870
Lemonnier, Antoine Louis Camille	1844-1913
Lenau, Nikolaus	1802-1850
Lennep, Jakob Van	1802-1868
Leo, Heinrich	1799-1878
Leopardi, Giacomo	1798-1837
Lermontov, Mikhail Yurevich	1814-1841
Leroux, Pierre	1798-1871
Leskov, Nikolai Semenovich	1831-1895
Lever, Charles James	1806-1872
Lewald, Fanny	1811-1889
Lewes, George Henry	1817-1878
Lewis, Sir George Cornwall	1806-1863
Lie, Jonas Lauritz Edemil	1833-1908
Lieber, Francis	1800-1872
Liebrecht, Felix	1812-1890
Liliencron, Detlev Von	1844-1909
Lincoln, Abraham	1809-1865
Lindau, Rudolf	1829-1910
Lindo, Mark Prager	1819-1879
Lingard, John	1771-1851
Lippincott, Sara Jane Clarke	1823-1904
Lista Y Aragon, Alberto	1775-1848
Lister, Thomas Henry	1800-1842
Littre, Maximilien Paul Emile	1801-1881
Livingstone, David	1813-1873
Ljunggren, Gustaf Haken Jordan	1823-1905
Locker-Lampson, Frederick	1821-1895
Lockhart, John Gibson	1794-1854
Lockhart, William Ewart	1846-1900
Lodge, Edmund	1756-1839
Lodge, Henry Cabot	1850-1924
Longfellow, Henry Wadsworth	1807-1882
Lönnrot, Elias	1802-1884
Lossing, Benson John	1813-1891
Loti, Pierre	1850-1923
Lotze, Rudolf Hermann	1817-1881
Lover, Samuel	1797-1868
Lowell, James Russell	1819-1891
Lubke, Wilhelm	1826-1893
Luchaire, Achille	1846-1908
Ludwig, Otto	1813-1865
Lund, Troels Frederik	1840-1921
Luttrell, Henry	1765-1851
Lytton, Edward George Lytton, Bulwer-Lytton	1803-1873
Lytton, Edward Robert Bulwer-Lytton	1831-1891
Macaulay, Thomas Babington Macaulay	1800-1859
MacCarthy, Denis Florence	1817-1882
M'Carthy, Justin	1830-1912
McCord, Louise Susanna Cheves	1810-1879
Macdonald, George	1824-1905
Macedo, Jose Agostinho De	1761-1831
Mach, Ernst	1838-1916
McGee, Thomas D'Arcy	1825-1868
McGonagall, William	1830-
MacGregor, John	1825-1892
Mackay, Charles	1814-1889
Mackaye, Steele	1842-1894
Mackenzie, Henry	1745-1831
Mackintosh, Sir James	1765-1832
Maclaren, Charles	1782-1866
MacNeill, John Gordon Swift	1849-1926
M'Cosh, James	1811-1894
M'Crie, Thomas	1772-1835
Madach, Imre	1823-1864
Maginn, William	1793-1842
Magny, Claude Drigon	1797-1879
Mahan, Alfred Thayer	1840-1914
Maine, Sir Henry James Sumner	1822-1888
Maiste, Xavier De	1763-1852
Maitland, Edward	1824-1897

Maitland, Frederic	
William	1850-1906
Majlath, Janos	1786-1855
Major, Richard Henry	1818-1891
Mallarme, Stephane	1842-1898
Malleson, George Bruce	1825-1898
Mallock, William Hurrell	1849-1923
Malthus, Thomas Robert	1766-1834
Mameli, Goffredo	1827-1849
Mangan, James Clarence	1803-1849
Maning, Frederick	
Edward	1812-1883
Mansel, Henry	
Longueville	1820-1871
Manzoni, Alessandro	1785-1873
Mapu, Abraham	1808-1867
Maris, Matthys	1839-1917
Maris, Willem	1843-1910
Markham, Mrs.	1780-1837
Marquardt, Joachim	1812-1882
Marryat, Florence	1838-1899
Marryat, Frederick	1792-1848
Marston, John Westland	1819-1890
Marston, Philip Bourke	1850-1887
Martin, Francois Xavier	1762-1846
Martin, Henri	1810-1883
Martin, Sir Theodore	1816-1909
Martineau, Harriet	1802-1876
Martineau, James	1805-1900
Martinez De La Rosa,	
Francisco De Paula	1787-1862
Martini, Ferdinando	1841-1928
Marx, Karl Heinrich	1818-1883
Massey, Gerald	1828-1907
Masson, David	1822-1907
Masson, Frederic	1847-1923
Matthisson, Friedrich	
Von	1761-1831
Maupassant, Henri Rene	
Albert Guy De	1850-1893
Maurer, Georg Ludwig	
Von	1790-1872
Mayhew, Henry	1812-1887
Mehring, Franz	1846-1919
Meilhac, Henri	1831-1897
Melville, Herman	1819-1891
Menard, Louis Nicolas	1822-1901
Mendes, Catulle	1841-1909
Menzel, Wolfgang	1798-1873
Meredith, George	1828-1909
Merimee, Propser	1803-1870
Merivale, Charles	1808-1893
Mesonero Romanos,	
Ramon De	1803-1882
Meurice, Paul	1818-1905
Meyer, Conrad Ferdinand	1825-1898
Meynell, Alice	1849-1922
Michaud, Joseph Francois	1767-1839
Michelet, Jules	1789-1874
Mickiewicz, Adam	1798-1855

Mignet, Francois Auguste	
Marie	1796-1884
Mill, James	1773-1836
Mill, John Stuart	1806-1873
Miller, Hugh	1802-1856
Miller, Joaquin	1841-1913
Milman, Henry Hart	1791-1868
Mirbeau, Octave Henri	
Marie	1850-1917
Mistral, Frederic	1830-1914
Mitchell, Donald Grant	1822-1908
Mitford, John	1781-1859
Mitford, Mary Russell	1787-1855
Mitford, William	1744-1827
Moir, David Macbeth	1798-1851
Molesworth, Mary Louisa	1839-1921
Molesworth, William	
Nassau	1816-1890
Moller, Poul Martin	1794-1838
Mommsen, Theodor	1817-1903
Monkhouse, William	
Cosmo	1840-1901
Monnier, Marc	1829-1885
Monod, Gabriel	1844-1912
Montalembert, Charles	
Forbes Rene De	1810-1870
Montanelli, Giuseppe	1813-1862
Montefiore, Joshua	1762-1843
Montgomery, James	1771-1854
Montgomery, Robert	1807-1855
Monti, Vincenzo	1754-1828
Monticelli, Adolphe	
Joseph Thomas	1824-1886
Montufar, Lorenzo	1823-1898
Moore, Thomas	1779-1852
Moratin, Leandro	
Fernandez De	1760-1828
More, Hannah	1745-1833
Moreau, Hegesippe	1810-1838
Morgan, Lady Sydney	1783-1859
Morier, James	1780-1849
Morike, Eduard Friedrich	1804-1875
Morley, Henry	1822-1894
Morley, John Morley	1838-1923
Morris, Sir Lewis	1833-1907
Morris, William	1834-1896
Morton, John Maddison	1811-1891
Morton, Thomas	1764-1838
Mosen, Julius	1803-1867
Motherwell, William	1797-1835
Motley, John Lothrop	1814-1877
Moulton, Louise Chandler	1835-1908
Muir, John	1838-1914
Munch-Bellinghausen,	
Eligius Franz Joseph	1806-1871
Murger, Henry	1822-1861
Musset, Alfred De	1810-1857
Myers, Frederic William	
Henry	1843-1901
Nairne, Carolina Oliphant	1766-1845
Nasmyth, Patrick	1787-1831

Neal, John	1793-1876	Pater, Walter Horatio	1839-1894
Neander, Johann	1789-1850	Patmore, Coventry Kersey	
Nekrasov, Nikolai		Dighton	1823-1896
Alexeyevich	1821-1877	Pattison, Mark	1813-1884
Neruda, Jan	1834-1891	Paul, Charles Kegan	1828-1902
Nerval, Gerard De	1808-1855	Pauli, Reinhold	1823-1882
Nestroy, Johann	1801-1862	Paulding, James Kirke	1778-1860
Nettleship, Richard Lewis	1846-1892	Paulsen, Friedrich	1846-1908
Newman, Francis William	1805-1897	Payn, James	1830-1898
Newman, John Henry		Payne, John Howard	1791-1852
(Cardinal)	1801-1890	Paz Soldan, Mariano	
Nichol, John	1833-1894	Felipe	1821-1886
Nichols, John	1745-1826	Peabody, Andrew Preston	1811-1893
Nicoll, Robert	1814-1837	Peacock, Thomas Love	1785-1866
Niebuhr, Barthold Georg	1776-1831	Peesemsky, Alexey	
Nietzsche, Friedrich		Feofilactovich	1820-1881
Wilhelm	1844-1900	Peirce, Charles Sanders	1839-1914
Nitzsch, Karl Immanuel	1787-1868	Pelham, Henry Francis	1846-1907
Nitzsch, Karl Wilhelm	1818-1880	Pellico, Silvio	1788-1854
Noailles, Paul, Duke of	1802-1885	Percival, James Gates	1759-1856
Nodier, Charles	1780-1844	Pereda, Jose Maria De	1833-1906
Noel, Roden Berkeley		Perez Galdos, Benito	1845-1920
Wriothesley	1834-1894	Pertz, Georg Heinrich	1795-1876
Nordau, Max Simon	1848-1923	Petofi, Alexander	1823-1849
Normanby, Constantine		Pfleiderer, Edmund	1842-1902
Henry Phipps	1797-1863	Picken, Andrew	1788-1833
Norris, William Edward	1847-1925	Pindemonte, Ippolito	1753-1828
Norton, Caroline Elizabeth		Planche, James Robinson	1796-1880
Sarah	1808-1877	Poe, Edgar Allan	1809-1849
Norton, Charles Eliot	1827-1908	Poerio, Alessandro	1802-1848
Nunez De Arce, Gaspar	1834-1903	Ponsard, Francois	1814-1867
O'Grady, Standish James	1846-1928	Poole, William Frederick	1821-1894
Ohlenschlager, Adam		Porter, Anna Maria	1780-1832
Gottlob	1779-1850	Porter, Jane	1776-1850
Ohnet, Georges	1848-1918	Porter, Noah	1811-1892
Oliphant, Laurence	1829-1888	Porto-Riche, Georges De	1849-1930
Oliphant, Margaret		Potgieter, Everhardes	
Oliphant	1828-1897	Johannes	1808-1875
Oliveira, Martins Joaquim		Potthast, August	1824-1898
Pedro De	1845-1894	Powell, Frederick York	1850-1903
Olmedo, Jose Joaquin De	1780-1847	Praed, Winthrop	
Opie, Amelia	1769-1853	Mackworth	1802-1839
Opzoomer, Cornelius		Prantl, Karl Von	1820-1888
William	1821-1892	Prati, Giovanni	1815-1884
Orzeszkowa, Eliza	1842-1910	Prel, Karl	1839-1899
O'Shaughnessy, Arthur		Prescott, Harriet	
William Edgar	1844-1880	Elizabeth	1835-1921
Ostrovsky, Alexander		Prescott, William Hickling	1796-1859
Nikolaevich	1823-1886	Pringle, Thomas	1789-1834
Ouida	1839-1908	Procter, Adelaide Anne	1825-1864
Ozanan, Antoine Frederic	1813-1853	Procter, Bryan Waller	1787-1874
Palacky, Frantisek	1798-1876	Proudhon, Pierre Joseph	1809-1865
Palfrey, John Gorham	1796-1881	Prus, Boleslaw	1847-1912
Palgrave, Sir Francis	1788-1861	Prutz, Hans	1843-1929
Palgrave, Francis Turner	1824-1897	Purnell, Thomas	1834-1889
Paludan-Muller, Frederik	1809-1876	Pusey, Edward Bouverie	1800-1882
Paoli, Cesare	1840-1902	Pushkin, Alexander	1799-1837
Paris, Gaston	1839-1903	Pyne, William Henry	1769-1843
Parker, Theodore	1810-1860	Quental, Anthero De	1842-1891
Parkman, Francis	1823-1893	Quicherat, Jules Etienne	
Parton, James	1822-1891	Joseph	1814-1882

Quincy, Josiah	1772-1864	Ruffini, Giovanni	
Quinet, Edgar	1803-1875	Domenico	1807-1881
Quintana, Marnel José	1772-1857	Ruge, Arnold	1802-1880
Raabe, Wilhelm	1831-1910	Runeberg, Johan Ludvig	1804-1877
Ragabe, Alexandros		Ruskin, John	1819-1900
Rizos	1810-1892	Rutherford, Mark	1829-1913
Rambaud, Alfred Nicolas	1842-1905	Rydberg, Abraham Viktor	1828-1895
Ranc, Arthur	1831-1908	Safarik, Pavel Josef	1795-1861
Randall, James Ryder	1839-1908	Sainte-Beuve, Charles	
Rands, William Brighty	1823-1882	Augustin	1804-1869
Ranke, Lepold Von	1795-1886	Saint-Marc, Girardin	1801-1873
Rauch, Christian Daniel	1777-1875	Saintsbury, George	
Raumer, Friedrich Ludwig		Edward Bateman	1845-1933
George Van	1781-1873	Sala, George Augustin	
Ravaisson-Mollien, Jean		Henry	1828-1895
Gaspard Felix	1813-1900	Saltykov, Micheal	
Rawlinson, George	1812-1902	Evgrafovich	1826-1889
Raynouard, Francois Juste		Sand, George (Dudevant)	1804-1876
Marie	1761-1836	Sandeau, Leonard	
Reade, Charles	1814-1884	Sylvain Julien	1811-1883
Realf, Richard	1834-1878	Sanday, William	1843-1920
Reclus, Jean Jacques		Sant, James	1820-1916
Elisée	1830-1905	Santine, Joseph Xavier	1798-1865
Redgrave, Richard	1804-1888	Sardou, Victorien	1831-1908
Reid, Thomas Mayne	1818-1883	Sarmiento, Domingo	
Remusat, Charles Francois		Faustino	1811-1888
Marie	1797-1875	Saxe, John Godfrey	1816-1887
Renan, Ernest	1823-1892	Scheffel, Joseph Viktor	
Renouvier, Charles		Von	1826-1886
Bernard	1815-1903	Schelling, Friedrich	
Reuter, Fritz	1810-1874	Wilhelm Joseph Von	1775-1854
Rice, James	1843-1882	Scherer, Wilhelm	1841-1886
Richepin, Jean	1849-1926	Schimmelpenninck, Mary	
Richmond, Legh	1772-1827	Ann	1778-1856
Riley, James Whitcomb	1849-1916	Schlegel, August Wilhelm	
Ritchie, Anne Isabella,		Von	1767-1845
Lady	1837-1919	Schlegel, Friedrich Von	1772-1829
Ritter, Heinrich	1791-1869	Schleiermacher, Friedrich	
Rivas, Angel De Saavedra	1791-1865	Daniel Ernst	1768-1834
Robertson, Thomas		Schopenhaur, Arthur	1788-1860
William	1829-1871	Schweitzer, Jean Baptista	
Roe, Edward Payson	1838-1888	Von	1833-1875
Rogers, Randolphe	1825-1892	Scott, Sir Walter	1771-1832
Rogers, Samuel	1763-1855	Scribe, Eugene	1791-1861
Roscoe, William	1753-1831	Seebohm, Frederick	1833-1912
Rosegger, Peter	1843-1918	Seeley, Sir John Robert	1834-1895
Rosenkranz, Karl	1805-1879	Seguier, William	1771-1843
Rosmini-Serbati, Antonio	1797-1855	Segur, Philippe Paul,	
Ross, Janet Anne	1842-1927	Comte de	1780-1873
Rossetti, Christina		Sellar, William Young	1825-1890
Georgina	1830-1894	Senancour, Etienne Pivert	
Rossetti, Dante Gabriele	1828-1882	De	1770-1846
Rossetti, Gabriele	1783-1854	Seth, Andrew	1850-1931
Rossetti, William Michael	1829-1919	Settembrini, Luigi	1813-1877
Rouget De Lisle, Claude		Sewell, Anna	1820-1878
Joseph	1760-1836	Shairp, John Campbell	1819-1885
Roumanville, Joseph	1818-1891	Shaw, Henry Wheeler	1818-1885
Royer-Collard, Pierre		Sheil, Richard Lalor	1791-1851
Paul	1763-1845	Shelley, Mary	
Rubinstein, Anton	1824-1894	Wollstonecraft	1795-1851
Rückert, Friedrich	1788-1866	Sherwood, Mary Martha	1775-1851

Shevshenko, Taras	1814-1861
Shorthouse, Joseph Henry	1834-1903
Sidwick, Henry	1838-1900
Sienkiewicz, Henryk	1846-1916
Sigourney, Lydia Huntley	1791-1865
Sill, Edward Rowland	1841-1887
Simms, William Gilmore	1806-1870
Simon, Jules Francois	1814-1896
Simrock, Karl Joseph	1802-1876
Sims, George Robert	1847-1922
Sismondi, Jean Charles	
Leonard Simonde	1773-1842
Skeat, Walter William	1835-1912
Skene, William Forbes	1809-1892
Slowacki, Juljusz	1809-1849
Smiles, Samuel	1812-1904
Smith, Alexander	1830-1867
Smith, John Stafford	1750-1836
Smith, Francis Hopkinson	1838-1915
Smith, Goldwin	1823-1910
Smith, Horace	1779-1849
Smith, James	1775-1839
Smith, Sidney	1771-1845
Smith, Walter Chalmers	1824-1908
Smith, Sir William	1813-1893
Snoilsky, Carl Johan	
Gustaf	1841-1903
Soloviev, Sergei	
Mikhailovich	1820-1879
Sorel, Albert	1842-1906
Sorel, Georges	1847-1922
Southey, Robert	1774-1843
Souza-Botelho, Adelaide	
Filleul	1761-1836
Sparks, Jared	1789-1866
Spencer, Henry	1820-1903
Spielhagen, Friedrich Von	1829-1911
Spitteler, Carl	1845-1924
Stahl, Friedrich Julius	1802-1861
Stanhope, Philip Henry	
Stanhope	1805-1875
Stanley, Arthur Penrhyn	1815-1881
Stanley, Sir Henry Morton	1841-1904
Stedman, Edmund	
Clarence	1833-1908
Steffens, Henrik	1773-1845
Stendhal, (Marie Henry	
Beyle)	1783-1842
Stephen, Sir Leslie	1832-1904
Sterling, John	1806-1844
Stevenson, Robert Louis	
Balfour	1850-1894
Stewart, Dugald	1753-1828
Stifter, Adalbert	1805-1868
Stirling, James	
Hutchinson	1820-1909
Stirling-Maxwell, Sir	
William, Bart.	1818-1878
Stirner, Max	1806-1856
Stockton, Francis Richard	1834-1902
Stoddard, John Lawson	1850-1931

Stoddard, Richard Henry	1825-1903
Stoddard, William Osborn	1835-1925
Storm, Theodor Wolsden	1817-1888
Stowe, Harriet Elizabeth	
Beecher	1811-1896
Strachwitz, Moritz Karl	
Wilhelm Anton	1822-1847
Strauss, David Friedrich	1808-1874
Street, Alfred Billings	1811-1881
Strickland, Agnes	1806-1874
Strindberg, John August	1849-1912
Stubbs, William	1825-1901
Sue, Eugene	1804-1857
Sully-Prudhomme, Rene	
Francois Armand	
Prudhomme	1839-1907
Surtees, Robert Smith	1803-1864
Suttner, Bertha	1843-1914
Swanwick, Anna	1813-1899
Swetchine, Madame	1782-1857
Sybel, Heinrich Von	1817-1895
Swinburne, Algernon	
Charles	1837-1909
Symonds, John Addington	1840-1893
Tabley, John Byrne	
Leicester Warren	1835-1895
Taine, Hippolyte Adolphe	1828-1893
Tamayo Y Baus, Manuel	1829-1898
Talfourd, Sir Thomas	
Noon	1795-1854
Taylor, Ann	1782-1866
Taylor, Bayard	1825-1878
Taylor, Sir Henry	1800-1886
Taylor, Isaak	1787-1865
Taylor, Isaak	1829-1901
Taylor, Tom	1817-1880
Taylor, William	1765-1836
Tedder, Henry Richard	1850-1924
Tegner, Esaias	1782-1846
Tennant, William	1784-1848
Tennyson, Alfred Lord	1809-1892
Thakaray, William	
Makepeace	1811-1863
Thaxter, Celia Laighton	1835-1894
Theuriet, Claude Adhemar	
Andre	1833-1907
Thierry, Jacques Nicolas	
Augustin	1795-1856
Thiers, Louis Adolph	1797-1877
Thirlwall, Connop	1797-1875
Thomas, Brandon	1849-1914
Thompson, William c.	1785-1833
Thomson, James	1834-1882
Thoreau, Henry David	1817-1862
Ticknor, George	1791-1871
Tieck, Johann Ludwig	1773-1853
Tischendorf, Lobegatt	1815-1874
Tocqueville, Alexis	
Charles Henri Clarel	1805-1859
Tolstoy, Alexei	
Konstantinovich	1817-1875

Tolstoy, Leo Nikolayevich	1828-1910
Tommaseao, Niccolo	1802-1874
Tompa, Mihaly	1817-1868
Topelius, Zachris	1818-1898
Topffer, Rodolphe	1799-1846
Toreno, Jose Maria	
Queipo De Llano	1786-1843
Traill, Henry Duff	1842-1900
Treitschke, Heinrich Von	1834-1896
Trelawny, Edward John	1792-1881
Trench, Richard Chenevix	1807-1886
Trendelenburg, Friedrich	
Adolf	1802-1872
Trevelyan, Sir George Otto	1838-1928
Trollope, Anthony	1815-1882
Trollope, Frances	1780-1863
Trollope, Thomas Adolphus	1810-1892
Trumbull, John	1750-1831
Tucker, Charlotte Marie	1821-1893
Tupper, Martin Farquehar	1810-1889
Turgenev, Ivan Sergeyevich	1818-1883
Turner, Charles Tennyson	1808-1879
Turner, Sharon	1768-1847
Twain, Mark	1835-1910
Tyler, Moses Coit	1835-1900
Tyndall, John	1820-1893
Tyuchev, Fydor Ivanovich	1803-1873
Uberweg, Friedrich	1826-1871
Uhland, Johann Ludwig	1787-1861
Uspenski, Gleb Ivanovich	1840-1902
Valera Y Alcala, Galiano	
Juan	1824-1905
Valles, Jules	1832-1885
Vacherot, Etienne	1809-1897
Van Beers, Jan	1821-1888
Vapereau, Louis Gustave	1819-1906
Varnhagen, Francisco	
Adolpho De	1816-1878
Varnhagen, Von Ense	
Karl August	1785-1858
Vazoff, Ivan	1850-1921
Veitch, John	1829-1894
Verdaguer, Mosen Jacinto	1845-1902
Verga, Giovanni	1840-1922
Verlaine, Paul	1844-1896
Verne, Jules	1828-1905
Verplanck, Gulian	
Crommelin	1786-1870
Viaud, Louis Marie Julien	1850-1923
Vidyasagar, Isaar Chandra	1820-1891
Vigfusson, Gudbrandr	1828-1889
Vigny, Alfred De	1797-1863
Villari, Pasquale	1827-1917
Villemain, Abel Francois	1790-1870
Villiers, De L'isle Adam	
Auguste, Compte De	1838-1889
Vinje, Aasmund Olavson	1816-1870
Vischer, Friedrich Theodor	1807-1887
Vogue, Eugene Melchior	1848-1910
Voss, Johann Heinrich	1751-1826
Waagen, Gustav Friedrich	1794-1868

Walker, Thomas	1784-1836
Wallace, Alfred Russel	1823-1913
Wallace, Lewis	1827-1905
Wallace, William	1844-1897
Wallon, Henri Alexandre	1812-1904
Warburton, Eliot	1810-1852
Ward, Artemus	1834-1867
Warner, Charles Dudley	1829-1900
Warner, Susan Bogert	1819-1895
Warren, Samuel	1807-1877
Watts-Dunton, Walter	
Theodore	1832-1914
Waugh, Edwin	1817-1890
Webster, Noah	1758-1843
Welhaven, Johann	
Sebastian Cammermeyer	1807-1873
Wells, Charles Jeremiah	1798-1879
Wennerberg, Gunnar	1817-1901
Wergeland, Henrik Arnold	1808-1845
Whately, Richard	1787-1863
Whewell, William	1794-1866
White, Richard Grant	1821-1885
White, William Hale	1831-1913
Whitehead, Charles	1804-1862
Whitman, Walt	1819-1892
Whittier, John Greenleaf	1807-1892
Widmann, Joseph Victor	1842-1911
Wieniawiski, Henri	1835-1880
Wilberforce, William	1759-1833
Wilde, Lady Jane Francesca	
"Speranza"	1826-1896
Wildenbruch, Ernst Van	1845-1909
Willis, Nathaniel Parker	1806-1867
Wills, William Gorman	1828-1891
Wilson, John	1785-1854
Wilcox, Ella	1850-1919
Winsor, Justin	1831-1897
Winther, Christian	1796-1876
Wirt, William	1772-1834
Wollaston, William Hyde	1766-1828
Wood, Mrs. Henry	1814-1887
Wordsworth, Dorothy	1771-1855
Wordsworth, William	1770-1850
Wraxall, Sir Nathaniel	
William	1751-1831
Wright, Thomas	1810-1887
Wright, William Aldis	1836-1914
Wundt, Wilhelm Max	1832-1920
Wyatt, Sir Matthew Digby	1820-1877
Wyss, Johann	1781-1830
Yates, Edmund	1831-1894
Yonge, Charlotte Mary	1823-1901
Yriarte, Charles	1832-1898
Zeller, Eduard	1814-1908
Zhukovsky, Vasili	
Andreyevich	1783-1852
Zola, Emile Edouard	
Charles Antoine	1840-1902
Zorrilla, Jose	1817-1893
Zschokke, Johann Heinrich	
Daniel	1771-1848

Achenbach, Andreas	1815-1910
Ainmuller, Maximilian Emmanuel	1807-1870
Allan, Sir William	1782-1850
Allston, Washington	1779-1843
Alvarez, Don Jose	1768-1827
Anderson, Sir Robert Rowland	1834-1921
Ansdell, Richard	1815-1885
Armitage, Edward	1817-1896
Armstead, Henry Hugh	1828-1905
Audubon, John James	1785-1851
Baily, Edward Hodges	1788-1867
Ball, Thomas	1819-1911
Baltard, Louis Pierre	1764-1846
Bandel, Ernst Von	1800-1876
Barry, Sir Charles	1795-1860
Bartolini, Lorenzo	1777-1850
Bartholdi, Auguste	1834-1904
Bartholome, Paul Albert	1848-1928
Barye, Antoine Louis	1796-1875
Bastien-Lepage, Jules	1848-1884
Bates, Harry	1850-1899
Baudry, Paul Jacques Aime	1828-1886
Begas, Karl	1794-1854
Begas, Rheinhold	1831-1911
Bell, John	1811-1895
Bellows, Albert F.	1829-1883
Bentley, John Francis	1839-1902
Besnard, Paul Albert	1849-1934
Beverley, William Roxby	1814-1889
Bewick, Thomas	1753-1828
Bierstadt, Albert	1830-1902
Birch, Samuel	1813-1885
Blakelock, Ralph Albert	1847-1919
Blashfield, Edwin Howland	1848-1936
Blomfield, Sir Arthur William	1829-1899
Boehm, Sir Joseph Edgar	1834-1890
Boeklin, Arnold	1827-1901
Bone, Henry	1755-1834
Bonheur, Rosa	1822-1899
Bonington, Richard Parkes	1801-1828
Bonnat, Leon Joseph Florentin	1833-1922
Bosio, Francois Joseph Baron	1769-1845
Boudin, Louis Eugene	1824-1898
Bough, Samuel	1822-1878
Boughton, George Henry	1833-1905
Bouguereau, Adolphe William	1825-1905
Bracquemond, Felix	1833-1914
Bradford, William	1827-1906
Braekeleer, Henri Jean Augustin De	1840-1888
Brascassat, Jacques Raymon	1804-1867
Breton, Jules Adolphe Aime Louis	1827-1906

Bridggman, Frederic Arthur	1847-1928
Brierly, Sir Oswald Walters	1817-1894
Bright, Henry	1814-1873
Brock, Sir Thomas	1847-1922
Brodie, William	1815-1881
Brown, George Loring	1814-1889
Brown, Ford Maddox	1821-1893
Brown, Henry Kirke	1814-1886
Brown, John George	1831-1913
Brown, Hablot Knight	1815-1882
Bruce-Joy, Albert	1842-1924
Brunner, Arnold William	1842-1919
Bulfinch, Charles	1763-1844
Burn, William	1789-1870
Burne-Jones, Sir Edward Burne	1833-1898
Burnham, Daniel Hudson	1846-1912
Burton, Decimus	1800-1881
Butterfield, William	1814-1900
Bystrom, Johan Niklas	1783-1848
Cabanel, Andreas	1815-1910
Cagnola, Luigi	1762-1833
Calame, Alexander	1810-1864
Caldecott, Randolph	1846-1886
Calderon, Philip Hermogenes	1833-1898
Callcott, Sir Augustus Wall	1779-1844
Calvert, Charles	1785-1852
Calvert, Edward	1799-1883
Camphausen, Wilhelm	1818-1885
Camuccini, Vincenzo	1773-1844
Capronnier, Jean-Baptiste	1814-1891
Carolus-Duran,	1837-1917
Carpeaux, Jean Baptiste	1827-1875
Carriere, Eugene	1849-1906
Cassatt, Mary	1845-1926
Catlin, George	1796-1872
Cattermole, George	1800-1868
Cazin, Jean Charles	1841-1901
Cezanne, Paul	1839-1906
Chalmers, George Paul	1836-1878
Chantrey, Sir Francis Legatt	1781-1841
Chapu, Henri	1833-1891
Charlet, Nicolas Toussaint	1792-1845
Chase, William Merrit	1849-1916
Chasseriau, Theodore	1819-1856
Chisholm, Alexander	1792-1847
Church, Frederick Edwin	1826-1900
Claus, Emile	1849-1924
Clays, Pal Jean	1819-1900
Cockerell, Charles Robert	1788-1863
Cole, Thomas	1801-1848
Cole, Vicat	1833-1893
Collier, Hon. John	1850-1934
Colman, Samuel	1832-1920
Constable, John	1776-1837
Cooper, Abraham	1787-1868
Cooper, Thomas Sidney	1803-1902

Cope, Charles West	1811-1890
Corbould, Edward Henry	1815-1905
Corbould, Henry	1787-1844
Corbould, Richard	1757-1831
Corman, John Sell	1782-1842
Cormon, Fernand	1845-1924
Cornelius, Peter Von	1783-1867
Corot, Jean-Baptiste Camille	1796-1875
Costa, Giovanni	1826-1903
Courbet, Gustav	1819-1877
Couture, Thomas	1815-1879
Cox, David the Elder	1783-1859
Cox, David the Younger	1809-1885
Crane, Thomas	1808-1859
Crane, Walter	1845-1915
Crauck, Gustav	1827-1905
Crawford, Thomas	1814-1857
Creswick, Thomas	1811-1869
Cruickshank, George	1792-1878
Daguerre, Louis Jacques Mande	1789-1851
Dahl, Johann Kristen Clausen	1788-1857
Dalou, Jules	1838-1902
Damer, Ann Seymour	1749-1828
Danby, Francis	1793-1861
Daniell, Thomas	1749-1840
Daniell, William	1769-1837
Dannecker, Johann Heinrich Von	1758-1841
Dantan, Antoine Laurent	1798-1878
Dantan, Edward Joseph	1848-1897
Dantan, Jean Pierre	1800-1869
Darley, Felix Octavius Carr	1822-1888
Daubigny, Charles Francois	1817-1878
Daumet, Pierre Jerome Honore	1826-1911
Daumier, Honore	1808-1879
Dawson, Henry	1811-1878
Decamps, Alexandra Gabriel	1803-1860
Defregger, Franz Von	1835-1921
Degas, Hilaire Germain Edgar	1834-1917
Delacroix, Ferdinand Victor Eugene	1798-1863
Delaroche, Hyppolyte	1797-1856
Delaunay, Elie	1828-1891
Detaille, Edouard	1848-1912
Diaz, Narcisse Virgile	1809-1876
Dielman, Frederick	1847-1935
Dillens, Julien	1849-1904
Dobson, William Charles Thomas	1817-1898
Dore, Paul Gustave	1832-1883
Doyle, Richard	1824-1883
Dubois, Paul	1829-1905
Dumont, Francois	1751-1831
Duncan, Thomas	1807-1845
Dupre, Giovanni	1817-1882
Dupre, Jules	1811-1889
Durand, Asher Brown	1796-1886
Duveneck, Frank	1848-1919
Dyce, William	1806-1864
Eakins, Thomas	1844-1916
East, Alfred	1849-1913
Eastlake, Sir Charles Lock	1793-1865
Eaton, Wyatt	1849-1896
Eberlein, Gustav	1847-1926
Ebrz, Josef	1801-1882
Eckenberg, Kristoffer	1783-1853
Egg, Augustus Leopold	1816-1863
Elliott, Charles Loring	1812-1868
Engleheart, George	1752-1829
Etex, Antoine	1809-1888
Etty, William	1787-1849
Faed, Thomas	1826-1900
Falguiere, Jean Alexandre Joseph	1831-1900
Fantin-Latour, Ignace Henri	1836-1904
Farquharson, David	1840-1907
Farquharson, Joseph	1846-1935
Feuerbach, Anselm	1829-1880
Fielding, Copley	1787-1855
Fildes, Sir Luke	1844-1927
Flandrin, Jean Hyppolyte	1809-1864
Flaxman, John	1755-1826
Fofelberg, Benedict Erland	1786-1854
Foley, John Henry	1818-1874
Fontaine, Pierre Francois Leonard	1762-1853
Forster, Ernst	1800-1885
Fortuny, Mariano Jose	1838-1874
Foster, Myles Byrkett	1825-1899
Fowler, Charles	1792-1867
Francais, Francois Louis	1814-1897
Fremiet, Emmanuel	1824-1910
French, Daniel Chester	1850-1931
Friedrich, Caspar David	1774-1840
Fripp, Alfred Downing	1822-1895
Fripp, George Arthur	1814-1896
Frith, William Powell	1819-1909
Fromentin, Eugene	1820-1876
Frost, William Edward	1810-1877
Fuhrich, Joseph Von	1800-1876
Fuller, George	1822-1884
Gallait, Louis	1810-1887
Garnier, Jean Louis Charles	1825-1898
Gauguin, Paul	1848-1903
Gavarni, Paul	1801-1866
Gebhardt, Eduard Von	1830-1925
Geddes, Andrew	1783-1844
Gerard, Francois	1770-1837
Gerome, Jean Leon	1824-1904
Gibson, John	1790-1866
Gifford, Robert Swain	1840-1905

Gilbert, Sir John	1817-1897
Gleyre, Charles	1806-1874
Goldschmidt, Hermann	1802-1866
Goodall, Frederick	1822-1904
Gordon, Sir John Watson	1788-1864
Goya Y Lucientes, Francisco	1746-1828
Granet, Francois Marius	1775-1849
Grant, Sir Francis	1803-1878
Greenaway, Kate	1846-1901
Gregory, Edward John	1850-1909
Gros, Antoine Jean	1771-1835
Gudin, Theodore	1802-1880
Guerin, Pierre Narcisse	1774-1833
Guillamin, Armand	1841-1927
Guillaume, Jean Baptiste Claude Eugene	1822-1905
Gwilt, Joseph	1784-1863
Haag Carl	1820-1915
Haas, Johannes Hubertus Leonhardus De	1832-1908
Habermann Hugo, Freiherr Von	1849-1929
Haider, Karl	1846-1912
Hamon, Jean Louis	1821-1874
Hansen, Christian Frederick	1756-1845
Hanson, Joseph Acosy, Aloysius	1803-1882
Harding, Chester	1792-1866
Harpignies, Henri	1819-1916
Hartley, Jonathan Scott	1845-1912
Harvey, Sir George	1806-1876
Haydon, Benjamin Robert	1786-1846
Hayter, Sir George	1792-1871
Hearphy, Thomas	1775-1835
Henner, Jean Jacques	1829-1905
Herbert, John Rogers	1810-1900
Herkomer, Sir Hubert Von	1849-1914
Hilderbrand, Adolf	1847-1921
Hildersbrand, Eduard	1818-1869
Hilton, William	1786-1839
Hiroshege,	1797-1858
Hittorff, Jacques Ignace	1792-1867
Hockert, Johan Frederick	1826-1866
Hokusai, Katsushika	1760-1849
Holiday, Henry	1839-1927
Holl, Frank	1845-1888
Homer, Winslow	1836-1910
Hook, James Clarke	1819-1907
Horsley, John Callcott	1817-1903
Hosmer, Harriet Goodhue	1830-1908
Houdon, Jean Antoine	1740-1828
Hovenden, Thomas	1840-1895
Hubner, Julius	1806-1882
Huet, Paul	1804-1869
Hughes, Arthur	1832-1915
Hunt, Alfred William	1830-1896
Hunt, Richard Morris	1828-1895
Hunt, William Henry	1790-1864

Hunt, William Holman	1827-1910
Huntingdon, Daniel	1816-1906
Hurlstone, Frederick Yeates	1800-1869
Ingres, Jean Auguste Dominique	1780-1867
Inman, Henry	1801-1846
Inness, George	1825-1894
Isabey, Jean Baptiste	1767-1855
Israels, Josef	1824-1911
Jackson, Sir Thomas Graham	1835-1924
Jalabert, Charles Francois	1819-1901
Johnson, Eastman	1824-1906
Jonkind, Johann Barthold	1819-1891
Jordan, Rudolf	1810-1887
Kaulbach, Wilhelm Von	1805-1874
Keene, Charles Samuel	1823-1891
Keller, Albert Von	1844-1920
Kensett, John Frederick	1818-1872
Kirkup, Seymore Stocker	1788-1880
Knaus, Ludwig	1829-1910
Knight, Daniel Ridgway	1845-1924
Knowles, Sir James	1831-1908
Kyosai, Sho Fu	1831-1889
La Farge, John	1835-1910
Landseer, Sir Edwin Henry	1802-1873
Lathrop, Francis	1849-1909
Lauder, Robert Scott	1803-1869
Laurens, Jean Paul	1838-1921
Lawrence, Sir Thomas	1769-1830
Lear, Edward	1812-1888
Le Brun, Marie, Elizabeth Louise	1755-1842
Leech, John	1817-1864
Legros, Alphonse	1837-1911
Lehman, Rudolf	1819-1905
Leibl, Wilhelm	1844-1900
Leighton, Frederick Leighton	1830-1896
Lejeune, Louis Francois	1775-1848
Lemaire, Philippe Honore	1798-1880
Lenbach, Franz Von	1836-1904
Leslie, Charles Robert	1794-1859
Leutze, Emanuel	1816-1868
Liebermann, Max	1847-1935
Lindsay, Sir Coutts	1824-1913
Linnell, John	1792-1882
Linton, Sir James Dromgole	1840-1916
Leys, Hendrik	1815-1869
Lucas, John Seymour	1849-1923
Macbeth, Robert Walker	1848-1910
Macculoch, Horatio	1805-1867
McEntee, Jervis	1828-1891
McKim, Charles Follen	1847-1909
Maclise, Daniel	1806-1870
Macnee, Sir Daniel	1806-1882
Mactaggart, William	1835-1910
Macwhirter, John	1839-1911
Madrazo, Y Kunt Don Fernando De	1815-1894

Makart, Hans	1840-1884
Manes, Josef	1820-1871
Manet, Edouard	1832-1883
Manson, George	1850-1876
Marees, Hans Von	1837-1899
Maris, Jacob	1837-1899
Marochetti, Carlo	1805-1867
Martin, Homer Dodge	1836-1897
Martin, John	1789-1854
Matejko, Jan Alois	1838-1893
Mauve, Anton	1838-1888
Marshall, William Calder	1813-1894
Mead, Larkin Goldsmith	1835-1910
Mead, William Rutherford	1846-1928
Meissonier, Jean Louis Ernest	1815-1891
Menzel, Adolph Fredrich Erdmann Von	1815-1905
Mercie, Marius Jean Antonin	1845-1916
Mesdag, Hendrik Willem	1831-1915
Meunier, Constantin	1831-1905
Millais, Sir John Everett	1829-1896
Millet, Francis Davis	1846-1912
Millet, Jean Francois	1814-1875
Monet, Claude	1840-1926
Moore, William	1790-1851
Moore, Henry	1831-1895
Moran, Edward	1829-1901
Moreau, Gustave	1826-1898
Morel-Ladeuil, Leonard	1820-1888
Morisot, Berthe Marie Pauline	1841-1895
Morriss, William	1834-1896
Morse, Samuel Finley Breese	1791-1872
Mosler, Henry	1841-1920
Motte, William de la	1775-1863
Mount, William Sydney	1807-1868
Muller, William James	1812-1845
Mulready, William	1786-1863
Munkacsy, Michael	1846-1900
Murray, Sir David	1849-1933
Nash, John	1752-1835
Nasmyth, Alexander	1758-1840
Nesfield, William Eden	1835-1888
Neuville, Alphonse Marie De	1836-1885
Nicol, Erskine	1825-1904
Northcote, James	1746-1831
Orchardson, Sir William	1832-1910
Oudine, Eugene Andre	1810-1887
Overbeck, Johann Frederich	1789-1869
Page, William	1811-1885
Palmer, Samuel	1805-1881
Parsons, Alfred	1847-1920
Paton, Sir Joseph Noel	1821-1901
Paxton, Sir, Joseph	1801-1865
Peale, Charles Willson	1741-1827
Peale, Rembrandt	1778-1860
Pearson, John Loughborough	1817-1897
Percier, Charles	1764-1838
Pettie, John	1839-1893
Piloty, Karl Von	1826-1886
Pinelli, Bartolomeo	1781-1834
Pinwell, George John	1842-1875
Pissaro, Camille	1831-1903
Playfair, William Henry	1789-1857
Plimer, Andrew	1763-1837
Portaels, Jean Francois	1818-1895
Post, George Browne	1837-1913
Powers, Hiram	1805-1873
Poynter, Sir Edward John	1836-1919
Pradilla, Francisco	1848-1921
Prinsep, Valentine Cameron	1838-1904
Prout, Samuel	1783-1852
Pugin, Augustus Welby Northmore	1812-1852
Puvis De Chavannes, Pierre Cecil	1824-1898
Redon, Odilon	1840-1916
Regnault, Henri	1843-1871
Reid, Sir George	1841-1913
Renoir, Pierre Auguste	1841-1919
Renwick, James	1818-1895
Repin, Ilya Yefimovich	1844-1930
Rethel, Alfred	1816-1859
Retsch, Frederich August Moritz	1779-1857
Richardson, Henry Hobson	1838-1886
Richmond, George	1809-1896
Richmond, Sir William Blake	1842-1921
Rickman, Thomas	1776-1841
Rietshel, Ernst	1804-1861
Riviere, Briton	1840-1920
Roberts, David	1796-1864
Rodin, Auguste	1840-1917
Rogers, John	1829-1904
Rops, Felicien	1833-1898
Rossetti, Dante Gabriel	1828-1882
Rousseau, Henri	1844-1910
Rousseau, Pierre Etienne Theodore	1812-1867
Rowlandson, Thomas	1756-1827
Rude, Francois	1784-1855
Ryder, Albert Pinkham	1847-1917
Schadow, Friedrich Wilhelm	1798-1862
Schadow, Johann Gottfried	1764-1850
Scheffer, Ary	1795-1858
Schilling, Johannes	1828-1910
Schinkel, Karl Friedrick	1781-1841
Schnorr, Von Karolsfeld Julius	1794-1873
Schreyer, Adolf	1828-1899

COMPOSERS

Q

Baini, Guiseppe	1775-1844	Faure, Gabriel	1845-1924
Balakirev, Milly		Fetis, Francois Joseph	1784-1871
Alexeivich	1836-1910	Fibich, Zdenko	1850-1900
Bargiel, Woldemar	1828-1897	Field, John	1782-1837
Barnby, Sir Joseph	1838-1896	Foster, Stephen Collins	1826-1864
Barnett, John	1802-1890	Flotow, Friedrich	
Barnett, John Francis	1837-1916	Freiherr Von	1812-1883
Beethoven, Ludwig Van	1770-1827	Franck, Cesar	1822-1890
Bellini, Vincenzo	1801-1835	Franz, Robert	1815-1892
Bendl, Karel	1838-1897	Gade, Niels Vilhelm	1817-1890
Benedict, Sir Julius	1804-1885	Gansbacher, Johann Baptist	1778-1844
Bennett, Sir William		Garcia, Manoel	1775-1832
Sterndale	1816-1875	Gazzaniga, Giuseppe	1743-1818
Benoit, Peter Leonard		Glinka, Michael Ivanovich	1803-1857
Leopold	1834-1901	Godard, Benjamin	1849-1895
Beriot, Charles Auguste De	1802-1870	Goldmark, Karl	1832-1915
Berlioz, Hector	1803-1869	Goss, Sir John	1800-1880
Bishop, Sir Henry Rowley	1786-1855	Gossec, Francois Joseph	1734-1829
Bizet, Georges	1838-1875	Gounod, Charles Francois	1818-1893
Boieldieu, Francois Adrien	1775-1834	Grieg, Edvard Hagerup	1843-1907
Boito, Arriego	1842-1918	Gung'l, Josef	1810-1889
Borodin, Alexander		Halevy, Jacques Francois	1799-1862
Porfyrievich	1834-1887	Hatton, John Liptrot	1809-1886
Bottesini, Giovanni	1822-1889	Hauptmann, Moritz	1792-1868
Brabazon, Hercules		Heller, Stephen	1815-1888
Brabazon	1821-1906	Henselt, Adolf Von	1814-1889
Brahms, Johannes	1833-1897	Herold, Louis Joseph	1791-1833
Bruch, Max	1838-1920	Herve, Florimond Rounger	1825-1892
Bruckner, Anton	1824-1896	Herz, Henri	1806-1888
Buck, Dudley	1839-1909	Hiller, Ferdinand	1811-1885
Campenhout, Francois Von	1779-1849	Horn, Charles Edward	1786-1849
Chabrier, Alexis Emmanuel	1841-1894	Hullah, John Pyke	1812-1884
Cherubini, Maria Luigi	1760-1842	Hummel, Johann Nepomuk	1778-1837
Chopin, Frederic Francois	1810-1849	Joachim, Joseph	1831-1907
Clay, Frederic	1838-1889	Joncières, Victorin	1839-1903
Clementi, Muzio	1752-1832	Kelly, Michael	1762-1826
Cornelius, Carl August		Kjerulf, Halfdan	1815-1868
Peter	1824-1874	Kreutzer, Konradin	1780-1849
Costa, Sir Michael	1810-1884	Lacombe, Louis Trouillon	1818-1884
Crotch, William	1817-1872	Lalo, Edouard	1823-1892
Cui, Cesar Antonovitch	1835-1918	Lassen, Eduard	1830-1904
Czerny, Karl	1791-1857	Lecocq, Alexandre Charles	1832-1918
Dargomijsky, Alexander		Lemmens, Nicolas Jacques	1823-1881
Sergeivich	1813-1869	Lesuer, Jean Francois	1760-1837
Damrosch, Leopold	1832-1885	Lindau, Paul	1839-1919
David, Felicien	1810-1876	Liszt, Franz	1811-1886
Delibes, Clement Philibert		Loewe, Johann Karl	
Leo	1836-1891	Gottfried	1796-1869
Diabelli, Anton Antonio	1781-1858	Lortzing, Albert	1801-1851
Donizetti, Gaetano	1797-1848	Macfarren, Sir George	
Doppler, Albert Franz	1821-1883	Alexander	1813-1887
Dreyschock, Alexander	1818-1869	Mackenzie, Sir Alexander	
Dubois, Francois Clement	1837-1924	Campbell	1847-1935
Dupark, Henri	1848-1933	Marschner, Heinrich	
Dvorak, Anton	1841-1904	August	1795-1861
Dykes, John Bacchus	1823-1876	Massenet, Jules Emile	1842-1912
Eberwein, Traugott		Mendelssohn, Bartholdi	
Maximilian	1775-1831	Felix	1809-1847
Eitner, Robert	1832-1905	Meyebeer, Giacomo	1791-1864
Elvey, Sir George Job	1816-1893	Monk, William Henry	1823-1889
Ernst, Heinrich Wilhelm	1814-1865	Mottl, Felix	1856-1911

Moussorgsky, Modest		Schumann, Robert	
Petrovich	1835-1881	Alexander	1810-1856
Napravnik, Edward	1839-1915	Sgambati, Giovanni	1843-1914
Nathan, Isaac	1791-1864	Shield, William	1748-1829
Nicolai, Otto	1810-1849	Smetana, Bedrich	1824-1884
Offenbach, Jacques	1819-1880	Soderman, August Johan	1832-1876
Ouseley, Sir Frederick	1825-1889	Spontini, Gasparo Luigi	
Paer, Ferdinando	1771-1839	Pacifico	1774-1851
Paisiello, Giovanni	1741-1816	Spohr, Ludwig	1784-1859
Parry, Sir Charles Hubert	1848-1918	Spottiswoode, Alicia Ann,	
Pearsall, Robert Lucas De	1795-1856	Lady Ann	1811-1900
Pedrell, Felipe	1841-1922	Strauss, Johann	1804-1849
Pierson, Henry Hugo	1815-1873	Strauss, Johann, the	
Planquette, Robert	1850-1903	younger	1825-1899
Pleyel, Ignaz Joseph	1757-1831	Sullivan, Sir Arthur	
Ponchielli, Amilcare	1834-1886	Seymour	1842-1900
Raff, Joseph Joachim	1822-1882	Suppe, Franz Von	1820-1895
Randegger, Alberto	1832-1911	Svendsen, Johan Severin	1840-1911
Reineck, Carl Heinrich	1824-1910	Thomas, Ambroise	1811-1896
Rheinberger, Joseph		Thomas, Arthur Goring	1850-1892
Gabriel	1839-1901	Tosti, Sir Francesco Paolo	1846-1916
Rimsky-Korsakov, Nicolas		Tschaikovsky, Peter Ilich	1840-1893
Andreevich	1844-1908	Verdi, Giuseppe Fortunino	
Rockstro, William Smith	1823-1895	Francesco	1813-1901
Rossini, Gioachino Antonio	1792-1868	Wagner, Wilhelm Richard	1813-1883
Rubinstein, Anton	1829-1924	Waldteuffel, Emil	1837-1915
Saint-Saens, Charles		Wallace, William Vincent	1812-1865
Camille	1835-1921	Weber, Carl Maria	1786-1826
Scharwenka, Xavier	1850-1924	Wesley, Samuel Sebastian	1810-1876
Schubert, Franz	1808-1878	Wesley, Samuel	1766-1837
Schubert, Franz Peter	1797-1828	Widor, Charles Marie	1845-1937
Schumann, Clara Josephine	1819-1896	Zingarelli, Niccolo	1752-1837

1854	France declares war on Russia.
	Great Britain declares war on Russia.
	Crystal Palace opened.
	Battle of the Alma.
	Seige of Sebastopol.
	Battle of Balaclava.
	Battle of Inkerman.
1856	Peace treaty signed in Paris.
1857	Indian mutiny.
	Relief of Lucknow.
1858	Atlantic cable.
1859	Battle of Montebello.
	Battle of Magenta.
	Battle of Solferino.
1860	Battle of Volturno.
1862	Battle of Williamsburg.
	Cotton famine in Lancashire.
	2nd Battle of Bull Run.
1863	Slavery abolished in U.S.
	Battle of Chatanooga.
1865	Lincoln assassinated.
	Antiseptic surgery introduced.
1866	Austria declares war on Prussia. Italy.
	Battle of Custozza.
	Battle of Sadowa.
	Battle of Lissa.
1867	Schleswig-Holstein annexed to Prussia.
	Dominion of Canada established.
1869	Suez Canal opened.
1870	France declares war on Prussia.
	Battle of Woerth
	Battle of Gravelotte.
	Battle of Sedan.
	Rome and Papal States annexed to Italy.
	Germany proclaimed a united empire.
1871	Communards destroy Tuileries, set fire to Louvre etc.
	Great fire of Chicago.
1872	The Ballot is introduced in England.
1873	Typewriter invented.

PROMINENT PEOPLE

Bismark, Prince Otto, Eduard Leopold Von	1815-1898	Lessepes, Vicomte Ferdinande de	1805-1894
Booth, General William	1829-1912	Lister, Lord	1827-1912
Braille, Louis	1809-1852	Livingstone, Dr. David	1813-1873
Brown, John	1800-1859	Lloyd George, David	1863-1945
Caruso, Enrico	1873-1921	Manning, Henry Edward Cardinal	1808-1892
Curie, Pierre	1859-1906		
Curie, Marie	1867-1934	Nobel, Alfred	1833-1896
Diaghilev, Sergei Pavlovich	1872-1929	Pankhurst, Emmeline	1858-1928
		Pasteur, Louis	1822-1895
Edison, Thomas Alva	1847-1931	Rasputin, Grigori Yefimovich	1871-1916
Faraday, Michael	1791-1867		
Gandhi, Mahandas Karamchand	1869-1948	Rhodes, Cecil	1853-1902
		Rontgen, Prof. Wilhelm Konrad	1845-1923
Garibaldi, Giuseppe	1807-1882		
Kitchener of Khartoum	1850-1916		

EMPEROS OF CHINA
(MANCHU (Ch'ing) DYNASTY)

| Wen Tsung | 1850-1861 | Mu Tsung | 1861-1875 |

POPES

| Piux IX | 1846-1878 |

FRANCE. HEADS OF STATE

Louis Napoleon		President Adolphe Thiers	1871-1873
Bonaparte	1848-1852	President Marshal	
Napoleon III	1852-1870	Macmahon	1873-1879

ENGLAND. SOVEREIGNS

| Victoria | 1837-1901 |

SWEDEN. KINGS

| Oscar I | 1844-1859 | Oscar II | 1872-1907 |
| Charles XV | 1859-1872 | | |

PORTUGAL. KINGS

| Maria II (Again) | 1834-1853 | Luiz I | 1861-1889 |
| Pedro V | 1853-1861 | | |

RUSSIA. TSARS

| Nicholas I | 1825-1855 | Alexander II | 1855-1881 |

SPAIN. SOVEREIGNS

| Isabella II | 1833-1868 | Alfonso XII | 1874-1885 |
| Interregnum | 1868-1874 | | |

U.S.A. PRESIDENTS

Millard Fillimore		Abraham Lincoln	1861-1865
(Vice P)	1850-1853	Andrew Johnson	
Franklin Pierce	1853-1857	(Vice P)	1865-1869
James Buchanan	1857-1861	Ulysses Grant	1869-1877

KINGS OF PRUSSIA

| Frederick William IV | 1840-1861 | William I | 1861-1888 |
| | | became Emperor of Germany 1861 | |

EMPERORS OF AUSTRIA

| Franz Josef | 1848-1916 |

NETHERLANDS. SOVEREIGNS

| William III | 1849-1890 |

Leopold I	1831-1865	Leopold II	1865-1909

KING OF ITALY

Victor Emmanuel II   1861-1878

WRITERS

Aakjaer, Jeppe	1866-1930	Aksakov, Konstantin	1817-1860
Aanrud, Hans	1863-1953	Aksakov, Sergei	
Aansen, Ivar	1813-1896	Timofeyevich	1791-1859
Aarestrup, Emil	1800-1856	Alaman, Lucas	1792-1853
Abbott, Edwin, Abbott	1838-1926	Alarcon, Pedro, Antonio	1833-1891
Abbott, Evelyn	1843-1901	Alas, Leopoldo	1852-1901
Abbott, Jacob	1803-1879	Albert, Eugen Francis	
Abbott, Lyman	1835-1922	Charles d'	1864-1932
Abbott, Wilbur, Cortez	1869-1947	Alcott, Amos Bronson	1799-1888
A Beckett, Gilbert, Abbott	1811-1856	Alcott, Louisa May	1832-1888
Aberigh-Mackay, George		Alcover, Joan	1854-1926
Robert	1848-1881	Alden, Isabella	1841-1930
About, Edmond Francois		Alden, Joseph	1807-1885
Valentin	1828-1885	Aldrich, Thomas Bailey	1836-1907
Ackermann, Louise		Aleardi, Aleardo	1812-1878
Victorine Choquet	1813-1890	Alecsandri, Vasile	1821-1890
Acton, John Emerich		Alexander, Cecil Francis	1818-1895
Edward Dolbey	1834-1902	Alexander, Samuel	1859-1938
Adam, Juliette	1836-1936	Alexander, William	1826-1894
Adam, Paul	1862-1920	Alexis, Willibald	1798-1871
Adams, Andy	1859-1935	Alger, Horatio	1834-1899
Adams, Charles Follen	1842-1918	Alin, Oscar, Josef	1846-1900
Adams, Henry Brooks	1838-1918	Alington, Cyril, Argentine	1872-
Adams, Oscar Fay	1855-1919	Alison, Sir Archibald	1792-1867
Adams, Samuel Hopkins	1871-1958	Allen, Charles Grant	
Adams, William Taylor	1822-1897	Blairfindie	1848-1899
Adamson, Robert	1852-1902	Allen, James Lane	1849-1925
Addams, Jane	1860-1935	Allibone, Samuel, Austin	1816-1889
Ade, George	1866-1944	Allingham, William	1824-1889
Adickes, Erich	1866-1928	Allmers, Hermann	1821-1902
Adolphus, John Leycester	1795-1862	Alma Tadema,	
Adler, Alfred	1870-1937	Sir Laurence	1836-1912
Afzelius, Aruid, August	1785-1871	Almeida-Garrett	
Agassiz, Jean Louis		Joao Baptista da	1799-1854
Rodolphe	1807-1873	Almqvist, Karl Jonas	
Agoult, Marie Catherine		Ludwig	1793-1866
Sophie de Flavigny	1805-1876	Alvarez Quintero,	
Aguilo I Fuster Marian	1825-1897	Joaquin	1873-1944
Aho, Juhani	1861-1921	Alvarez Quintero, Serafin	1871-1938
Aicard, Jean Francois		Amicis, Edmondo de	1846-1908
Victor	1848-1921	Amiel, Henri Frederic	1821-1881
Aide, Hamilton	1830-1906	Ampere, Jean, Jacques	1800-1864
Aimard, Gustave	1818-1883	Ancelot, Jacques Arsene	
Ainger, Alfred	1837-1904	Francois Polycarpe	1794-1854
Ainslie, Hew	1792-1878	Ancona, Alessandro	1835-1914
Ainsworth, William		Andersen, Hans Christian	1805-1875
Harrison	1805-1882	Andrews, Charles	
Aird, Thomas	1802-1876	McLean	1863-1943
Akers, Benjamin Paul	1825-1861	Andreyev, Leonid	
Aksakov, Ivan		Nicolaievich	1871-1919
Sergeyvich	1823-1886	Angell, Sir Norman	1874

Angellier, Auguste Jean	1848-1911	Bacon, Delia Salter	1811-1859
Angus, Marion	1866-1946	Bacon, Leonard	1802-1881
Anker-Larsen, Johannes	1874-1957	Baedeker, Karl	1801-1859
Annunzio, Gabrielle, D'	1863-1938	Bagehot, Walter	1826-1877
Anstey, Francis	1856-1935	Bahr, Hermann	1863-1934
Antokolski, Mark		Bahr, Johann, Christian	
Matveevich	1834-1902	Felix	1798-1872
Anzengruber, Ludwig	1839-1889	Bailey, Philip James	1816-1902
Arago, Jacques Etienne		Bailey, Samuel	1791-1870
Victor	1790-1855	Baillie, Joanna	1762-1851
Arany, Janos	1817-1882	Bain, Alexander	1818-1903
Arbois De Jubainville,		Baird, Henry Martin	1832-1906
Marie Henri d'	1827-1910	Baker, Sir Herbert	1862-1946
Archer, William	1856-1924	Baker, Ray Stannard	1870-1946
Aribau, Bonaventura		Balaguer, Victor	1824-1901
Carles	1798-1862	Balbo, Cesare Count	1789-1853
Arnason, Jon	1819-1888	Baldensperger, Fernand	1871-1958
Arndt, Ernst Moritz	1769-1860	Ballantine, James	1808-1877
Arneth, Alfred	1819-1897	Ballantyne, Robert	
Arnim, Elizabeth (Betinna)		Michael	1825-1894
Von	1785-1859	Balmont, Constantine	1867-1943
Arnold, Sir Edwin	1832-1904	Bancroft, George	1800-1891
Arnold, Matthew	1822-1888	Bancroft, Hubert Howe	1832-1918
Arthur, Timothy Shay	1809-1885	Bang, Hermann Joachim	1858-1912
Asbjornsen, Peter		Banville, Theodore	
Christian	1812-1885	Faullain, De	1823-1891
Ashbee, Charles Robert	1863-1942	Barante, Amable	
Ashe, Thomas	1836-1889	Guillaume Prosper	
Asnyk, Adam	1838-1897	Brugiere	1782-1866
Atherton, Gertrude		Barbey D'aurevilly, Jules	
Franklin	1857-1948	Amedee	1808-1889
Atkinson, Thomas		Barbier, Henri Auguste	1805-1882
Witlam	1799-1861	Barbier, Paul Jules	1825-1901
Aubanel, Theodore	1829-1886	Barbusse, Henri	1873-1935
Auerbach, Berthold	1812-1882	Baring, Maurice	1874-1946
Auersperg, Anton		Baring-Gould, Sabine	1834-1924
Alexander	1806-1876	Barlow, Jane	1860-1917
Augier, Guillaume, Victor		Barlow, Peter	1776-1862
Emile	1820-1889	Barnes, William	1800-1886
Aulard, Francois Victor		Baroja, Pio	1872-1956
Alphonse	1849-1928	Barr, Amelia Edith	1831-1919
Austin, Alfred	1835-1913	Barres, Maurice	1862-1923
Austin, Mary Hunter	1869-1934	Barrie, Sir James	
Austin, Sarah	1793-1867	Matthew	1860-1937
Autran, Joseph	1813-1877	Barriere, Theodore	1823-1877
Avellanida, Gertrudis		Barrili, Antonio Guilio	1836-1908
Gomez D'	1814-1873	Barthelemy, Auguste,	
Avenarius, Richard		Marseille	1796-1867
Heinrich Ludwig	1843-1896	Barthelemy, Saint-Hilaire	
Axelrod, Pavel		Jules	1805-1895
Borriasovich	1850-1928	Bascom, John	1827-1911
Ayala Y Herrera		Bashkirtsev, Marie	1860-1884
Adelardo Lopez d'	1828-1879	Bataille, Felix Henri	1872-1922
Aytoun, William		Bates, Arlo	1850-1918
Edmonstoun	1813-1865	Bates, Katharine Lee	1859-1929
Azeglio, Massimo		Bateson, Mary	1865-1906
Taparelli Marquis d'	1798-1866	Batyushkov, Konstantin	
Azorin, Jose Martinez Ruis	1874-	Nikolaievitch	1787-1855
Babbitt, Irving	1865-1933	Baudelaire, Charles	
Bacheller, Irving Addison	1859-1950	Pierre	1821-1867

Baudissin, Wolf Heinrich	1789-1878	
Bauer, Bruno	1809-1882	
Bauernfeld, Eduard, Von	1802-1890	
Baumbach, Rudolf	1840-1905	
Bautian, Louis Eugene Marie	1796-1867	
Bax, Ernest Belfort	1854-1926	
Bazin, Rene	1853-1932	
Beard, Charles Austin	1874-1948	
Beauvoir, Roger De	1809-1866	
Becker, Carl L.	1873-1945	
Becque, Henry Francois	1837-1899	
Becquer, Gustavo Adolfo	1836-1870	
Bede, Cuthbert	1827-1889	
Bédier, Joseph	1864-1938	
Beecher, Henry Ward	1813-1887	
Beerbohm, Sir Max	1872-1956	
Beeton (Mrs.) Isabella Mary Mayson	1836-1865	
Beets, Nikolaas	1814-1903	
Belasco, David	1854-1931	
Beljame, Alexandre	1842-1906	
Bell, Henry Glassford	1803-1874	
Bell, John Jay	1871-1934	
Bell, Robert, Sir	1800-1867	
Bellamy, Edward	1850-1898	
Belli, Giuseppe Gioachino	1791-1863	
Belloc, Joseph, Hilaire Pierre	1870-1953	
Belloc-Lowndes, Marie Adelaide	1868-1947	
Benavente Y Martinez, Jacinto	1866-1954	
Benedix, Julius Roderick	1811-1873	
Beneke, Frederich Eduard	1798-1856	
Bennett, Enoch Arnold	1867-1931	
Benoa, Julien	1867-	
Benson, Arthur Christopher	1862-1925	
Benson, Edward Frederic	1867-1940	
Benson, Robert Hugh	1871-1914	
Bentley, Edmond Clerihew	1875-1956	
Beranger, Pierre Jean De	1780-1857	
Berchet, Giovanni	1783-1851	
Berdyaev, Nikolas	1874-1948	
Berenson, Bernard	1865-1959	
Beresford, John Davys	1873-1947	
Bergman, Bo Hjalmar	1869-	
Bergson, Henri	1859-1941	
Bernard, Tristan	1866-1947	
Bernhardi, Friedrich Von	1849-1930	
Berry, Mary	1763-1852	
Bertrand, Louis	1866-1941	
Besant, Annie	1847-1933	
Besant, Walter Sir	1836-1901	
Beskow, Bernhard Von	1796-1868	
Bialik, Hayim Nachman	1873-1934	

Bibaud, Michel	1782-1857	
Biedermann, Friedrich Karl	1812-1901	
Bierce, Ambrose	1842-1916	
Billings, Robert William	1813-1874	
Binding, Rudolf Georg	1867-1938	
Binyon, Laurence	1869-1943	
Birrell, Augustine	1850-1933	
Bishop, Isabella	1831-1904	
Bitzius, Albrecht	1797-1854	
Bjornson, Bjornstjerne	1832-1910	
Black, William	1841-1898	
Blackie, John Stuart	1809-1895	
Blackmore, Richard Doddridge	1825-1900	
Blackwood, Algernon Henry	1869-1951	
Blanc, Jean Joseph Charles Louis	1811-1882	
Blavatsky, Helena Petrova	1831-1891	
Blind, Mathilde	1847-1896	
Bliss, Philip Paul	1838-1876	
Blok, Petrus Johannes	1855-1932	
Blondel, Maurice	1861-1939	
Blood, Benjamin Paul	1832-1919	
Blouet, Paul	1848-1903	
Bloy, Leon	1846-1917	
Blunt, Wilfrid Scawen	1840-1922	
Boas, Franz	1858-1942	
Bodenstedt, Friedrich Martin Von	1819-1892	
Boisgobey, Fortune Abraham Du	1824-1891	
Bojer, Johan	1872-1959	
Boker, George Henry	1823-1890	
Boldrewood, Rolf	1826-1915	
Bolyai, Wolfgang	1775-1856	
Bonghi, Ruggero	1828-1895	
Boothby, Guy Newell	1867-1905	
Bordeaux, Henri	1870-	
Borel, Petrus	1809-1859	
Borrow, George, Henry	1803-1881	
Bosanquet, Bernard	1848-1923	
Bosboom Toussaint, Anna Louisa Geertruida	1812-1886	
Bostrom, Christoffer Jacob	1797-1866	
Bottomley, Gordon	1874-1948	
Bouchor, Maurice	1855-1929	
Boucicault, Dion	1822-1890	
Bouilhet, Louis Hyacinthe	1822-1869	
Bourget, Paul Charles Joseph	1852-1935	
Bowen, Francis	1811-1890	
Boyd, Andrew Kennedy Hutchinson	1825-1899	
Boyesen, Hjalmar	1848-1895	
Boylesve, Rene	1867-1926	
Braddon, Mary Elizabeth	1837-1915	

Bradford, Gameliel	1863-1932
Bradley, Andrew Cecil	1851-1935
Bradley, Edward	1827-1889
Bradley, Francis Herbert	1846-1924
Braga, Theophilo	1843-1924
Brailsford, Henry Noel	1873-1958
Bramah, Ernest	1867-1942
Brandes, Gorge Maurice Cohen	1842-1927
Braun, Lily	1865-1916
Brazil, Angela	1868-1947
Breasted, James Henry	1865-1935
Bremer, Frederika	1801-1865
Bremond, Henri	1865-1933
Brentano, Franz	1838-1917
Breton de Los Herreros, Manuel	1796-1873
Bridges, Robert Seymour	1844-1930
Brierly, Benjamin	1825-1896
Brieux, Eugene	1858-1932
Brizeux, Julien Auguste Pelage	1803-1858
Brokmeyer, Henry Conrad	1828-1906
Bronte, Charlotte	1816-1855
Brooke, Stopford Augustus	1832-1916
Brooks, Charles William Shirley	1816-1874
Brooks, Phillips	1835-1893
Broughton, John Cam Hobhouse	1786-1869
Broughton, Rhoda	1840-1920
Brown, Alice	1857-1948
Brown, George Douglas	1869-1902
Brown, Oliver Maddox	1855-1874
Brown, Peter Hume	1850-1918
Brown, Samuel Morison	1817-1856
Brown, Thomas, Edward	1830-1897
Browning, Elizabeth Barrett	1806-1861
Browning, Oscar	1837-1923
Browning, Robert	1812-1889
Brownson, Orestes Augustus	1803-1876
Brugsch, Hienrick Karl	1827-1894
Brunner, Henry	1840-1915
Bryant, William Cullen	1794-1878
Bryce, Lloyd Stephens	1851-1917
Bryussov, Valery Yakovlevich	1873-1924
Buchan, John	1875-1940
Buchanan, Robert Williams	1841-1901
Buchez, Philippe Benjamin Joseph	1796-1865
Buchner, Ludwig	1824-1899
Buckingham, James Silk	1786-1855
Buckle, George Earle	1854-1935
Buckle, Henry Thomas	1821-1862

Buckstone, John Baldwin	1802-1879
Bulgarin, Thaddeus	1789-1859
Bunin, Ivan Alexeyevich	1870-1953
Bulwer, Henry Lytton	1803-1873
Burckhardt, Jakob	1818-1897
Burnand, Frederick Gustavus	1842-1885
Burnett, Frances Eliza Hodgson	1849-1924
Burroughs, Edgar Rice	1875-1950
Burroughs, John	1837-1921
Burrows, Montague	1819-1905
Burton, John Hill	1809-1881
Burton, Sir Richard Evans	1804-1860
Burton, Sir Richard Francis	1821-1890
Bury, Lady Charlotte Susan Maria	1775-1861
Bury, John Bagnell	1861-1927
Butler, Nicholas Murray	1862-1947
Butler, Samuel	1835-1902
Buysse, Cyriez	1859-1932
Byron, Henry James	1834-1884
Caballero, Fernan	1796-1877
Cable, George Washington	1844-1925
Caine, Sir Thomas Henry Hall	1853-1931
Caird, Edward	1835-1908
Caird, John	1820-1898
Cairns, John Elliot	1823-1875
Calderon, George	1868-1915
Calderwood, Henry	1830-1897
Calvert, George Henry	1803-1889
Calvet, Jean	1874-
Calvo, Carlos	1824-1906
Campoamor Y Campoosorio Raymon De	1819-1901
Canina, Luigi	1795-1856
Cannon, Charles James	1800-1860
Canth, Minna	1844-1897
Cantu, Cesare	1804-1895
Capfigue, Jean Baptiste Honore Raymond	1801-1872
Capern, Edward	1819-1894
Capuana, Luigi	1839-1915
Capus, Alfred	1858-1922
Caraglia, Joan	1852-1912
Carducci, Giosue	1835-1907
Carey, Phoebe	1824-1871
Carlen, Emilia Smith Flygare	1807-1892
Carleton, Will	1845-1912
Carleton, William	1794-1869
Carlyle, Thomas	1795-1881
Carman, Bliss	1861-1929
Carmen, Sylva	1843-1916
Carnegie, Andrew	1835-1918
Caro, Emile Marie	1826-1887
Carpenter, Edward	1844-1929

Carr, Joseph William	1849-1916
Carriere, Moritz	1817-1895
Carton, R. C.	1853-1928
Cary, Alice	1820-1871
Cassirer, Ernst	1874-1945
Castelli, Ignaz Franz	1781-1862
Castello, Branco Camillo	1825-1890
Castro, Eugenio de	1869-1944
Cattaneo, Carlo	1801-1869
Cavalcaselle, Giovanni Battista	1820-1897
Cazalis, Henri	1840-1909
Chalybaus, Heinrich Moritz	1796-1862
Chambers, Robert	1802-1871
Chamier, Frederick	1796-1870
Champfleury	1821-1889
Chantavoine, Henri	1850-1918
Chapman, John Jay	1862-1933
Charles, Elizabeth	1828-1896
Chasles, Philarete	1798-1873
Chatrian, Alexandre (Erckman, Chatrian)	1826-1890
Chatterji, Bankim Chandra	1838-1894
Chausson, Ernest	1855-1899
Chekhov, Anton Pavlovich	1860-1904
Cherbuliez, Charles Victor	1829-1899
Chernyshevsky, Nikolay Gavrilovich	1828-1889
Cheruel, Pierre Adolphe	1809-1891
Chesney, Charles Cornwallis	1826-1876
Chesterton, Gilbert Keith	1874-1936
Chiesa, Fransesco	1871-
Child, Francis James	1825-1896
Child, Lydia Maria	1802-1874
Chopin, Kate	1851-1904
Churchill, Winston	1871-1947
Churchill, Sir Winston Leonard Spencer	1874-1965
Cibrrio, Luigi Count	1802-1870
Cladel, Leon	1835-1892
Clare, John	1793-1864
Claretie, Jules Arsene Arnaud	1840-1913
Clarke, Charles Cowden	1787-1877
Clarke, Marcus Andrew Hislop	1846-1881
Clark, William George	1821-1878
Claudel, Paul	1868-1955
Claussen, Sophus Niels Christen	1865-1931
Clemencau, George	1841-1929
Clifford, William Kingdon	1845-1879
Clive, Caroline	1801-1873
Clough, Arthur Hugh	1819-1861
Clowes, Sir William Laird	1856-1905

Cobbe, Frances Power	1822-1904
Cockton, Henry	1807-1853
Cole, Sir Henry	1808-1882
Colerisge, Sara	1802-1852
Colet, Louise	1810-1876
Colette, Sidonie Gabrielle	1873-1954
Collett, Jacobine Camilla	1813-1895
Collier, John Payne	1789-1883
Collins, Charles Allston	1828-1873
Collins, Mortimer	1827-1876
Collins, William Wilkie	1824-1889
Colomb, Philip Howard	1831-1899
Comte, Auguste	1798-1857
Conrad, Joseph	1857-1924
Conscience Hendrik	1812-1883
Conway, Hugh	1847-1885
Conway, Moncure Daniel	1832-1907
Cook, Edward Dutton	1829-1883
Cook, Sir Edward Tyas	1857-1919
Cooke, John Esten	1830-1886
Cooke, Rose Terry	1837-1892
Coolidge, Susan	1835-1905
Coolus, Romaine	1868-1952
Cooper, James Fenimore	1789-1851
Coppee, Francois	1842-1908
Coppee, Henry	1821-1895
Corelli, Marie	1855-1924
Cossa, Pietro	1830-1881
Costa, Joaquim	1846-1911
Costello, Louisa Stuart	1799-1877
Coster, Charles Theodore Henri, De	1827-1879
Couperus, Louis	1863-1923
Courteline, Georges	1860-1929
Courthope, William John	1842-1917
Cousin, Victor	1792-1867
Cox, Sir George William	1827-1902
Craddock, Charles Egbert	1850-1922
Craig, Edward Gordon	1872-
Craigie, Pearl Mary Teresa	1867-1906
Craik, Dinah Maria	1826-1887
Crane, Stephen	1871-1900
Craven, Pauline	1808-1891
Crawford, Francis Marion	1854-1909
Creasy, Sir Edward Shepherd	1812-1878
Creighton, Mandell	1843-1901
Cremazie, Octave	1822-1879
Cremer, Jakobus Jan	1827-1880
Creuzer, George Friedrich	1771-1858
Croce, Benedetto	1866-1952
Crockett, Samuel Rutherford	1860-1914
Croker, John Wilson	1780-1857
Croker, Thomas Crofton	1798-1854
Crowe, Catherine	1800-1870
Crozier, John Beattie	1849-1921
Crusenstolpe, Magnus Jakob	1795-1865

Csengery, Antal	1822-1880
Csiky, Gregor	1842-1891
Cullum, George Washington	1809-1892
Cummins, Maria Suzanna	1827-1866
Cumont, Franz Valery Marie	1868-1947
Cunninghame, Graham Robert Bontine	1852-1936
Curel, Francois Vicomte, De	1854-1928
Curtis, George William	1824-1892
Curtius Ernst	1814-1896
Curtius, Georg	1820-1885
Cust, Sir Lionel Henry	1859-1929
Da Costa, Isaak	1798-1860
Dahlmann, Friedrich Christoph	1785-1860
Dahn, Julius Sophus Felix	1834-1912
Dall'ongaro, Francesco	1808-1873
D'Alviella, Count Goblet	1846-1925
Daly, Augustin	1838-1899
Dana, Richard Henry	1815-1882
D'Annunzio, Gabriele	1863-1938
Da Ponte, Lorenzo	1749-1838
Dareste De La Chavanne, Cleophas	1820-1882
Darmesteter, James	1849-1894
Darwin, Charles Robert	1809-1882
D'Aubigné, Sean Henri Merle	1794-1872
Daudet, Alphonse	1840-1897
Daudet, Ernest	1837-1921
Daudet, Leon	1867-1942
Daumer, Georg Friedrich	1800-1875
Davidson, John	1857-1909
Davidson, Thomas	1840-1900
Davies, Hubert Henry	1869-1917
Davies, William Henry	1871-1940
Davis, Henry William Carless	1874-1928
Davis, Richard Harding	1864-1916
Debosis, Adolfo	1863-1924
Decelles, Alfred Duclos	1843-1925
De Court, Frans	1834-1878
De Geer, Louis Gerhard Baron	1818-1896
Dehmel, Richard	1863-1920
Dekker, Edward Douwes	1820-1887
De La Mare, Walter John	1873-1956
Deland, Margaretta Wade	1857-1945
Delbruck, Hans	1848-1929
Deledda, Grazia	1875-1936
Delisle, Leopold Victor	1826-1910
Demogeot, Jacques Claude	1808-1894
De Morgan, William Frend	1839-1917
Denifle, Heinrich Seuse	1844-1905

Dennery, Adolphe Phillippe	1811-1899
Dent, John Charles	1841-1887
De Quincey, Thomas	1785-1859
Deroulede, Paul	1846-1914
Deschamps, Emile	1791-1871
De Tabley, John Byrne Leicester Warren	1835-1895
Deussen, Paul	1845-1919
Devere, Aubrey Thomas	1814-1902
Dewey, John	1859-1952
Dexter, Henry Martyn	1821-1890
Dicey, Edward	1832-1911
Dickens, Charles John Huffam	1812-1870
Dickinson, Emily	1830-1886
Dickinson, Goldsworthy Lowes	1862-1932
Dierx, Leon	1838-1912
Digby, Kenelm Henry	1800-1880
Dilthey, Wilhelm	1833-1911
Dingelstedt, Franz Von	1814-1881
Dionne, Narcisse Eutrope	1848-1917
Disreali, Benjamin	1804-1881
Dixon, Richard Watson	1833-1900
Dixon, William Hepworth	1821-1879
Dobell, Sydney Thompson	1824-1874
Dobson, Henry Austin	1840-1921
Dodge, Mary	1838-1905
Dodge, Theodore Ayault	1842-1909
Dodgson, Charles Lutwidge (Lewis Carroll)	1832-1898
Dollinger, Johann Joseph Ignaz Von	1799-1890
Domett, Alfred	1811-1887
Donnay, Charles Maurice	1859-1945
Donoso, Cortez Juan	1809-1853
Doran, John	1807-1878
Dostoievsky, Fyodor Mikhaylovich	1821-1881
Doughty, Sir Arthur George	1860-1936
Doughty, Charles Montegu	1843-1926
Douglas, Lord Alfred Bruce	1870-1945
Douglas, Norman	1868-1952
Douglas, Sir William Fettes	1822-1891
Dove, Alfred	1844-1916
Dowden, Edward	1843-1913
Dowson, Ernest	1867-1900
Doyle, Sir Arthur Conan	1859-1930
Doyle, Sir Francis Hastings Charles	1810-1888
Drachmann, Holger Henrick Herboldt	1846-1908
Dragomirov, Michael Ivanovich	1830-1905

Draper, William	1811-1882
Dreiser, Theodore	1871-1945
Drews, Arthur	1865-1935
Driesch, Hans Adolf	
Eduard	1867-1941
Drobisch, Moritz Wilhelm	1802-1896
Droysen, Johann Gustav	1808-1884
Drummond, Henry	1851-1897
Duboc, Julius	1829-1903
Dubois, William Edward	
Burghardt	1868-
Du Camp, Maxime	1822-1894
Ducasse, Pierre Emmanuel	
Albert	1813-1893
Duclauz, Agnes Mary	
Frances	1857-1944
Duff, Sir Mountstuart	
Elphinstone Grant	1829-1906
Duff-Gordon, Lucie	1829-1869
Duhring, Eugen Karl	1833-1921
Dumas, Alexandre	1802-1870
Dumas, Alexandre (fils)	1824-1895
Du Maurier, George Louis	
Palmella Busson	1834-1896
Dummler, Ernst Ludwig	1830-1902
Dunbar, Paul Laurence	1872-1906
Duncker, Maximilian	
Wolgang	1811-1886
Dunne, John William	1875-1949
Dupont, Pierre	1821-1870
Durkheim, Emile	1858-1917
Duruy, Jean Victor	1811-1894
Dutt, Michael Madhu	
Sudan	1824-1873
Ebers, Georg Moritz	1837-1898
Ebert, Karl Egon	1801-1882
Ebner-Eschenbach, Marie	1830-1916
Eca De Queiroz, Jose Maria	1843-1900
Echegaram Y Eizaguire,	
José	1833-1916
Eckermann, Johann Peter	1792-1854
Eddy, Mary Baker Glover	1821-1910
Edgren-Lffeler, Anne	
Charlotte	1849-1892
Edwards, Amelia	1831-1892
Eeden, Frederick	
Willem Van	1860-1932
Egan, Maurice Francois	1852-1924
Egge, Peter Andreas	1869-
Eggleston, Edward	1837-1902
Ehrenfels, Christian	
Freiherr Von	1859-1932
Eichendorff, Joseph	
Freiherr Von	1788-1857
Eisler, Rudolf	1873-1926
Eisner, Kurt	1867-1919
Eliot, Sir Charles Norton	
Edgcumbe	1864-1931
Eliot, George	
(Marian Evans)	1819-1880

Ellis, Alexander John	1814-1890
Ellis, Henry Havelock	1859-1939
Elphinstone, Mountstuart	1779-1859
Elton, Oliver	1861-1945
Emerson, Ralph Waldo	1803-1882
Eminescu, Mihail	1849-1889
Engels Friedrich	1820-1895
English, Thomas Dunn	1819-1902
Ennemoser, Joseph	1787-1855
Eotvos, Joseph Baron	1813-1871
Erckmann, Emile	
(Erckman-Chatrian)	1822-1899
Erdelyi, Janos	1814-1868
Erdmann, Benno	1851-1921
Erdmann, Johann Eduard	1805-1892
Ernle, Rowland Edmund	
Prothero	1851-1937
Ernst, Paul	1866-1933
Erskine, Thomas	1788-1870
Eschenmayer, Adam Karl	
August Von	1768-1852
Esher, Reginald Baliol	
Brett	1852-1930
Esquiros, Henri Francois	
Alphonse	1812-1876
Estaunie, Edouard	1862-1942
Estebanez, Caldren Serafin	1799-1867
Eucken, Rudolf Christoph	1846-1926
Evans, George Essex	1863-1909
Ewing, Juliana Horatia	
Orr	1841-1885
Fabre, Ferdinand	1830-1898
Fagan, James Bernard	1873-1933
Fagniez, Gustav Charles	1842-1927
Faguet, Emile	1847-1916
Fahlcrantz, Christian	
Erik	1790-1866
Falke, Gustave	1853-1916
Falke, Johann Friedrich	
Gottlieb	1823-1876
Fallmerayer, Jakob Phillip	1790-1861
Falloux, Frederic Alfred	
Pierre	1811-1886
Farina, Salvatore	1846-1918
Farini, Luigi Carlo	1812-1866
Farjeon, Benjamin	
Leopold	1838-1903
Farrar, Frederick	
William	1831-1903
Fay, Andreas	1786-1864
Fazy, Henri	1842-1920
Fechner, Gustav Theodor	1801-1887
Federer, Heinrich	1866-1928
Fejer, Gyorgy	1766-1852
Fenn, George Maniville	1831-1909
Ferguson, Sir Samuel	1810-1886
Fergusson, James	1808-1886
Ferrari, Giuseppe	1812-1876
Ferrari, Paolo	1822-1889
Ferrero, Guglielmo	1871-1942

Ferri, Luigi	1826-1895	Frazer, Sir James George	1854-1941
Ferrier, Paul	1843-1920	Frechette, Louis Honore	1839-1908
Ferrier, Susan		Frederic, Harold	1856-1896
Edmonstone	1782-1854	Freeman, Edward	
Feuerbach, Ludwig		Augustus	1823-1892
Andreas	1804-1872	Freeman, Mary Eleanor	
Feuillet, Octave	1821-1890	Wilkins	1852-1930
Feval, Paul Henri		Freiligrath, Ferdinand	1810-1876
Corentin	1817-1887	Frenssen, Gustav	1863-1945
Feydeau, Ernest-Aime	1821-1873	Freud, Sigmund	1856-1939
Fichte, Immanuel		Frey, Adolf	1855-1920
Hermann, Von	1796-1879	Freytag, Gustav	1816-1895
Field, Eugene	1850-1895	Fried, Alfred Hermann	1864-1921
Fields, James Thomas	1817-1881	Friedjung, Heinrich	1851-1920
Figuier, Louis	1819-1894	Froding, Gustav	1860-1911
Filon, Augustin	1841-1916	Froebel, Friedrich	
Finlay, George	1799-1875	Wilhelm August	1782-1852
Firth, Sir Charles		Frohlich, Abraham	
Harding	1857-1936	Emanuel	1796-1965
Fisher, Ernst Kuno		Frohschammer, Jakob	1821-1893
Berthold	1824-1907	Frost, Robert	1875-
Fisher, Herbert Albert		Frothingham, Octavious	
Laurens	1865-1940	Brooks	1822-1895
Fiske, John	1842-1901	Froude, James Anthony	1818-1894
Fitch, William Clyde	1865-1909	Fryxell, Anders	1795-1881
Fitzball, Edward	1792-1873	Fucini, Renato	1843-1921
Fitzgerald, Edward	1809-1883	Fullerton, Lady Georgiana	
Fitzgerald, Percy		Charlotte	1812-1885
Hetherington	1834-1925	Fustel, De Coulanges	
Flach, Geoffroi Jacques	1846-1919	Numa Denis	1830-1889
Flammarion, Nicolas		Fyffe, Charles Alan	1845-1892
Camille	1842-1925	Gaboriau, Emile	1835-1873
Flaubert, Gustave	1821-1880	Gachard, Louis Prosper	1800-1885
Flers, Robert, De La Motte		Gagern, Hans Christoph	
Ango	1872-1927	Ernst	1766-1852
Foa, Eugenie		Gairdner, James	1828-1912
Rodruguez-Gradis	1789-1853	Gale, Zona	1874-1938
Fogazzaro, Antonio	1842-1911	Galsworthy, John	1867-1933
Follen, Adolf Ludwig	1794-1855	Ganesh Datta Shastri,	
Fontaine, Theodor	1819-1898	Shri Jagadguru	1861-1940
Ford, Paul Leicester	1865-1902	Ganivet, Angel	1865-1898
Ford, Richard	1796-1858	Garay, Janos	1812-1853
Forsell, Hans Ludvig	1843-1901	Garborg, Arne Evensen	1851-1924
Forster, Friedrich		Gardiner, Samuel Rawson	1829-1902
Christoph	1791-1868	Gareau, Francois Xavier	1806-1866
Forster, John	1812-1876	Garland, Hamlin	1860-1940
Fort, Paul	1872-1960	Garnett, Edward	1868-1937
Fortescue, Sir John		Garnett, Richard	1835-1906
William	1859-1933	Garrett, Joao Baptista	
Fortlage, Karl	1806-1881	Da Silva Leitao	
Fouillee, Alfred Jules		De Almeida	1799-1854
Emile	1838-1912	Garshin, Vsevolod	
Fowler, Frank George	1871-1918	Mikhailovich	1855-1888
Fowler, Henry Watson	1858-1933	Gaskell (Mrs.) Elizabeth	
France, Anatole	1844-1924	Cleghorn	1810-1865
Frankl, Ludwig August	1810-1894	Gatty, Margaret	1809-1873
Franzos, Karl Emil	1848-1904	Gautier, Leon	1832-1897
Fraser, Alexander		Gautier, Theophile	1811-1872
Campbell	1819-1914	Geddes, Patrick	1854-1932
Fraser, James Baillie	1783-1856	Geibel, Emanuel	1815-1884

Geijer, Eric Gustav	1783-1877	Gosse, Sir Edmund	1849-1928
Gentile, Giovanni	1875-1944	Gottschall, Rudolf Von	1823-1908
George, Henry	1839-1897	Gould, John	1804-1881
George, Stefan	1868-1933	Gould, Nathaniel	1857-1919
Gerstacker, Friedrich	1816-1877	Gourmont, Remy De	1858-1915
Gervinus, Georg Gottfried	1805-1871	Gozlan, Leon	1803-1866
Gezelle, Guido	1830-1899	Grahame, Kenneth	1859-1922
Gfrorer, August Friedrich	1803-1861	Grand, Sarah	1862-1943
Ghika, Helena	1829-1888	Grant, James	1822-1887
Giacometti, Paolo	1816-1882	Gratz, Heinrich	1817-1891
Giacosa, Guiseppe	1847-1906	Graves, Alfred Percival	1846-1931
Gibson, William		Gray, David	1838-1861
Hamilton	1850-1896	Green, John Richard	1837-1883
Gide, Andre Paul		Green, Mary Ann Everett	1818-1895
Guillaume	1869-1951	Green, Thomas Hill	1836-1882
Giesebrecht, Wilhelm Von	1814-1889	Greene, George	
Gieseler, Johann Karl		Washington	1811-1883
Ludwig	1792-1854	Greg, William Rathbone	1809-1881
Gilbert, Sir John Thomas	1829-1898	Gregorovius, Ferdinand	1821-1891
Gilbert, William	1804-1889	Gregory, Isabella Augusta	1852-1932
Gilbert, Sir William		Greville, Charles Cavendish	
Schwenk	1836-1911	Fulke	1794-1865
Gilder, Richard Watson	1844-1909	Greville, Henry	1842-1902
Gilgik, Iwan	1858-1924	Grey, Zane	1872-1939
Gillette, William Hooker	1853-1937	Grigorovich, Dmitri	
Gindely, Anton	1829-1892	Vaslievich	1822-1900
Giner De Los Rios,		Grillparzer, Franz	1791-1872
Francisco	1840-1915	Grimm, Jacob Ludwig	
Gioberti, Vincenzo	1801-1852	Carl	1785-1863
Girardin, Delphine De	1804-1855	Grimm, Wilhelm Carl	1786-1859
Gissing, George Robert	1857-1903	Groome, Francis Hindes	1851-1902
Giudici, Paolo, Emiliano	1812-1872	Grossi, Tommaso	1791-1853
Gjellerup, Karl	1857-1919	Grossmith, George	1847-1912
Glasgow, Ellen	1874-1945	Grote, George	1794-1871
Glassbrenner, Adolf	1810-1876	Grub, George	1812-1892
Glatigny, Joseph Albert		Grundy, Sydney	1848-1914
Alexandre	1839-1873	Gruntvig, Nikolai Frederick	
Gleig, George Robert	1796-1888	Severin	1783-1872
Glinka, Fedor		Gubernatis, Angelo De	1840-1913
Nikolayevich	1788-1880	Guerin, Charles	1873-1907
Glyn, Elinor	1864-1943	Guerrazzi, Francesco	
Gogol, Nikolai Vasilievich	1809-1852	Domenico	1804-1873
Goldschmidt, Aaron Meier	1819-1887	Guerrini, Olinda	1845-1916
Goltz, Bogumil	1801-1870	Guest, Edwin	1800-1880
Gomperez, Theodor	1832-1912	Guimera, Angel	1849-1924
Goncalves, Dias Antonio	1823-1864	Guizot, Francois Pierre	
Goncharov, Ivan		Guillaume	1787-1874
Alexandrovich	1812-1891	Guthrie, Thomas Anstey	1856-1934
Goncourt De, Edmond	1822-1896	Gutschmid, Alfred	1835-1887
Goncourt De, Jules	1830-1870	Gutzkow, Karl Ferdinand	1811-1878
Gooch, George Peabody	1873-	Guyau, Jean Marie	1854-1888
Goodrich, Samuel		Gyllembourg Eh Rensvard,	
Griswold	1793-1860	Thomasine Christine	1773-1856
Gordon, Adam Lindsay	1833-1870	Gyp	1849-1932
Gordon, Leon	1831-1892	Habberton, John	1842-1921
Gore, Catherine Grace		Hacklander, Friedrich	
Frances	1799-1861	Wilhelm Von	1816-1877
Gorky, Maxim	1868-1936	Hagenbach, Karl Rudolf	1801-1874
Gorst, Harold	1868-1950	Haggard, Sir Henry	
Gorter, Herman	1864-1933	Rider	1856-1925

Hahn-Hahn, Ida	1805-1880	Hawker, Robert Stephen	1803-1875
Hake, Thomas Gordon	1809-1895	Hawthorne, Nathaniel	1804-1864
Haldane Elizabeth		Hay, John	1838-1905
Sanderson	1862-1937	Haym, Rudolf	1821-1901
Haldane, Richard Burdon		Hayward, Abraham	1801-1884
Haldane	1856-1928	Hazard, Rowland Gibson	1801-1888
Hale, Edward Everett	1822-1909	Hebbel, Christian	
Hale, Sarah Josepha	1788-1879	Friedrich	1813-1863
Halevy, Daniel	1872-1962	Heer, Jakob Christoph	1859-1925
Halevy, Elie	1870-1937	Heiberg, Gunnar Edvard	
Halevy, Leon	1802-1883	Rode	1857-1929
Halevy, Ludovic	1834-1908	Heiberg, Johan Ludvig	1791-1860
Haliburton, Thomas		Heidenstam, Verner Von	1859-1940
Chandler	1796-1865	Heijermans, Hermann	1864-1924
Hall, Anna Maria	1800-1881	Heine, Heinrich	1797-1856
Hall, Samuel Carter	1800-1889	Helmholtz, Hermann	
Hall, William Edward	1835-1894	Ludwig Ferdinand Von	1821-1894
Hallam, Henry	1777-1859	Helps, Sir Arthur	1813-1875
Halleck, Fitz-Greene	1790-1867	Henderson, William	
Halliday, Andrew	1830-1877	James	1855-1937
Hamerton, Philip Gilbert	1834-1894	Henley, William Ernest	1849-1903
Hamilton, Sir William	1788-1856	Henry, O.	1862-1910
Hamley, Sir Edward		Henty, George Alfred	1832-1902
Bruce	1824-1893	Herculano De Carvalho	
Hammer, Julius	1810-1862	E. Araujo Alexandre	1810-1877
Hammond, John Lawrence		Herczeg, Ferenc	1863-
Lebreton	1872-1949	Heredia, Jose Maria De	1842-1905
Hamsun, Knut	1859-1952	Hermant, Abel	1862-1950
Handel-Mazzetti, Enrica	1871-1955	Hernandez, Jose	1854-1886
Hannay, James	1827-1873	Herne, Jame A.	1840-1901
Hannay, James Owen	1865-1950	Herrick, Robert	1868-1938
Hanotaux, Albert Auguste		Hervieu, Paul	1857-1915
Gabriel	1853-1944	Hewlett, Maurice Henry	1861-1923
Hansson, Ola	1860-1925	Heyse, Paul Johann	
Hardwick, Philip	1792-1870	Ludwig Von	1830-1914
Hardy, Thomas	1840-1928	Hichens, Robert Smythe	1864-1950
Hare, Augustus John		Higginson, Thomas	
Cuthbert	1834-1903	Wentworth	1823-1911
Haring, Georg Wilhelm		Hill, George Birbeck	
Heinrich	1798-1871	Norman	1835-1903
Harland, Henry	1861-1905	Hillebrand, Karl	1829-1884
Harraden, Beatrice	1864-1936	Himly, Louis-Auguste	1823-1906
Harris, Frank	1856-1931	Hinrichs, Hermann	
Harris, Joel Chandler	1848-1908	Friedrich Wilhelm	1794-1861
Harrison, Frederic	1831-1923	Hippius, Zinaida	1869-1945
Hart, Albert Bushnell	1854-1942	Hobhouse, Leonard	
Harte, Francis Bret	1836-1902	Trelawney	1864-1929
Hartmann, Karl, Robert		Hocking, Silas Kitto	1850-1935
Eduard Von	1842-1906	Hodgkin, Thomas	1831-1913
Hartmann, Moritz	1821-1872	Hodgson, John Evan	1831-1895
Hartzenbusch, Juan		Hodgson, Ralph	1871-
Eugenio	1806-1880	Hodgson, Shadworth	
Hasselt, Andre Henri		Holloway	1832-1912
Constant Van	1806-1874	Hoffding, Harald	1843-1931
Hauch, Johannes Carsten	1790-1872	Hoffman, August	
Hauptmann, Gerhart	1862-1946	Heinrich	1798-1874
Haureau, Barthelemy	1812-1896	Hoffman, Heinrich	1809-1894
Hausser, Ludwig	1818-1867	Hofmannsthal, Hugo Von	1874-1929
Haverfield, Francis John	1860-1919	Holl, Karl	1866-1926
Havet, Julien	1853-1893	Holland, Sir Henry	1788-1873

Holland, Josiah Gilbert	1819-1881	Ivanov, Vyacheslav	
Holmes, Oliver Wendell	1809-1894	Ivanovich	1866-1949
Holtei, Karl Eduard Von	1798-1880	Jacks, Laurence Pearsall	1860-1955
Holst, Hermann, Eduard		Jackson, Frederick John	
Von	1841-1904	Foakes	1855-1941
Holz, Arno	1863-1929	Jackson, Helen Maria	1831-1885
Hope, Anthony	1863-1933	Jacob, Violet	1863-1946
Hopfen, Hans Von	1835-1904	Jacobs, William Wymark	1863-1943
Hopkins, Gerard Manley	1844-1889	Jacobsen, Jens Peter	1847-1885
Horne, Richard Henry	1803-1884	Jahn, Otto	1813-1869
Hornung, Ernest William	1866-1921	James, George Payne	
Hosmer, James Kendall	1834-1927	Rainsford	1799-1860
Hostrup, Jens Christian	1818-1892	James, Henry	1843-1916
Hotho, Heinrich Gustav	1802-1873	James, Montague Rhodes	1862-1936
Houghton, Richard		James, William	1842-1910
Monkton Milnes	1809-1885	Jameson, Anna Brownell	1794-1860
Housman, Alfred Edward	1859-1936	Jammes, Francis	1868-1938
Housman, Laurence	1865-1959	Jane, Frederick Thomas	1870-1916
Houssaye, Arsene	1815-1896	Janin, Jules Gabriel	1804-1874
Houssaye, Henry	1848-1911	Janssen, Johannes	1829-1891
Howe, Julia Ward	1819-1910	Jasmin, Jacques	1798-1864
Howells, William Dean	1837-1920	Jebavy, Vaclav	1868-1929
Howitt, Mary	1799-1888	Jebb, Sir Richard	
Howitt, William	1792-1879	Claverhouse	1841-1905
Hubbard, Elbert	1856-1915	Jefferies, Richard	1848-1887
Huch, Ricarda	1864-1947	Jensen, Johannes Vilhelm	1873-1950
Hudson, William Henry	1841-1922	Jensen, Wilhelm	1837-1911
Huggenberger, Alfred	1867-	Jerome, Jerome Klapka	1859-1927
Hughes, Clovis	1851-1907	Jerrold, Douglas William	1803-1857
Hughes, Thomas	1822-1896	Jesse, Edward	1780-1868
Hugo, Victor Marie	1802-1885	Jewett, Sarah Orne	1849-1909
Humboldt, Friedrich		Jewsbury, Geraldine	
Baron Von	1769-1850	Endsor	1812-1880
Hume, Fergus	1859-1932	Johnson, James Weldon	1871-1938
Hunt, James Henry Leigh	1784-1859	Johnson, Lionel Pigot	1867-1902
Hunter, Joseph	1783-1861	Joinville, Francois	
Hutton, Arthur Wollaston	1848-1912	Ferdinand d'Orlean	1818-1900
Hutton, Richard Holt	1826-1897	Jokai, Maurus	1825-1904
Huxley, Thomas Henry	1825-1895	Jones, Ebenezer	1820-1860
Huysmans, Joris Karl	1848-1907	Jones, Ernest	1819-1869
Hyde, Douglas	1860-1949	Jones, Henry	1831-1899
Hyne, Charles John Cutliffe		Jones, Henry Arthur	1851-1929
Wright	1865-1944	Jordan, Wilhelm	1819-1904
Ibanez, Vincent Blasco	1867-1928	Jorga, Nicolas	1871-1940
Ibsen, Henrik Johan	1828-1906	Jorgensen, Johannes	1866-1951
Ihne, Wilhelm	1821-1902	Josika Miklos	1794-1865
Ilg, Paul	1875-	Judson, Edward Zane	
Inge, William Ralph	1860-1954	Carroll	1823-1886
Ingelow, Jean	1820-1897	Jung, Carl Gustav	1875-1964
Ingemann, Bernhard		Junqueiro, Abilio Guena	1850-1923
Severin	1789-1862	Jusserand, Jean Adrien	
Ingleby, Clement		Antoine Jules	1855-1932
Manfried	1823-1886	Kahn, Gustave	1859-1936
Ingraham, Joseph Holt	1809-1860	Kang Yu-Wei	1857-1927
Ingraham, Prentice	1843-1904	Karadzk, Viek Stefanovic	1787-1864
Innes, Arthur Donald	1863-1938	Karlfeldt, Erik Axel	1864-1931
Innes, Cosmo	1798-1874	Karr, Alphonse	1808-1890
Iqbal, Sir Mohammed	1875-1938	Kate, Jacob Lodewykten	1819-1889
Irving, Washington	1783-1859	Keble, John	1792-1866
Isaacs, Jorge	1837-1895	Keightley, Thomas	1789-1872

Keller, Gottfried	1819-1890
Kemble, John Mitchell	1807-1857
Kendall, Henry Clarence	1841-1882
Kenealy, Edward Vaughan Hyde	1819-1880
Kerner, Justinus Andreas Christian	1786-1862
Kervyn De Lettenhove, Joseph	1817-1891
Key, Ellen	1849-1926
Kielland, Alexander	1849-1906
Kierkegaard, Soren Aaby	1813-1855
Kinck, Hans Ernst	1865-1926
Kinglake, Alexander William	1809-1891
Kingsley, Charles	1819-1875
Kingsley, Henry	1830-1876
Kingston, William Henry Giles	1814-1880
Kinkel, Johann Gottfried	1815-1882
Kipling, Rudyard	1865-1936
Kitto, John	1804-1854
Kivi, Steuval	1834-1872
Klaczko, Julian	1825-1906
Knight, Charles	1791-1873
Knoblock, Edward	1874-1945
Knowles, James Sheridan	1784-1862
Kock, Charles Paul De	1793-1871
Kolcsey, Ferencz	1790-1888
Korolenko, Vladimir Galaktionovich	1853-1921
Kpisch, August	1799-1853
Krasinski, Zygmunt Count	1812-1859
Kraszewski, Joseph Ignatius	1812-1887
Kraus, Karl	1874-1936
Krehbiel, Henry Edward	1854-1923
Kretzer, Marx	1854-1941
Kropotkin, Peter Alexeivich	1842-1921
Ku Hung-Ming	1856-1928
Kulpe, Oswald	1868-1915
Kuprin, Alexander Ivanovich	1870-1938
Kurz, Hermann	1813-1873
Labiche, Euegene Marin	1815-1888
Lacaita, Sir James	1813-1895
Lacretelle, Jean Charles Dominique de	1766-1855
Ladd, George Trumbull	1842-1921
La Farina, Giuseppe	1815-1863
Laforgue, Jules	1860-1887
Lagerlof, Selma	1858-1940
Laing, Samuel	1810-1897
Lamartine, Alphonse, De	1790-1869
Lamennais, Hugues Felicite Robert De	1782-1854
Landor, Walter Savage	1775-1864
Lane, Edward William	1801-1876
Lane-Poole, Reginald	1857-1939

R

Lane-Poole, Stanley	1854-1931
Lanfrey, Pierre	1828-1877
Lang, Andrew	1844-1912
Lange, Friedrich Albert	1828-1875
Lanier, Sidney	1842-1881
Lanson, Gustave	1857-1935
Lapidoth-Swarth, Helene	1859-1941
Lappenberg, Johann Martin	1794-1865
Laprade, Pierre Marin Victor Richard De	1812-1883
Larousse, Pierre Athanase	1817-1875
Laube, Heinrich	1806-1884
Lauff, Josef	1855-1933
Laurent, Francois	1810-1887
Lavedan, Henri Leon Emile	1859-1940
Lavisse, Ernest	1842-1922
Lawless, Emily	1845-1913
Lawrence, George Alfred	1827-1876
Lawson, Henry Hertzberg	1867-1922
Layard, Sir Austen Henry	1817-1894
Lazarus, Emma	1849-1887
Lazarus, Moritz	1824-1903
Lea, Henry Charles	1825-1909
Leacock, Stephen Butler	1869-1944
Lecky, William, Edward Hartpole	1838-1903
Leconte De Lisle, Charles Marie Rene	1818-1894
Lee, Sir Sidney	1859-1926
Lee, Vernon	1856-1935
Le Fanu, Joseph Sheridan	1814-1873
Le Gallienne, Richard	1866-1947
Legouve, Gabriel Jean Baptiste Ernest Wilfred	1807-1903
Leland, Charles Godfrey	1824-1903
Lemaitre, Jules	1853-1914
Le Moine, James MacPherson	1825-1912
Lemon, Mark	1809-1870
Lemonnier, Antoine Louis Camille	1844-1913
Lenin, Vladimir Ilyich (Ulyonov)	1870-1924
Lennep, Jacob Van	1802-1862
Leo, Heinrich	1799-1878
Le Queux, William Tufnell	1864-1927
Leroux, Pierre	1798-1871
Leskov, Nikolai Semenovich	1831-1895
Lever, Charles James	1806-1872
Levertin, Oscar Ivan	1862-1906
Levy-Bruhl, Lucien	1857-1939
Lewald, Fanny	1811-1889
Lewes, George Henry	1817-1878
Lie, Jonas Lauritz Edemil	1833-1908
Lieber, Francis	1800-1872

Liebrecht, Felix	1812-1890	Machar, Jan Svatopluk	1864-1942
Liliencron, Detlev Von	1844-1909	Mackay, Charles	1814-1889
Lincoln, Abraham	1809-1865	Mackaye, Percy	1875-
Lindau, Paul	1839-1919	Mackaye, Steele	1842-1894
Lindau, Rudolf	1829-1910	MacLaren, Charles	1782-1866
Lindo, Mark Prager	1819-1879	Macmaster, John Bach	1852-1932
Lingard, John	1771-1851	MacNeill, John Gordon	
Lippincott, Sara Jane		Swift	1849-1926
Clarke	1823-1904	M'Cosh, James	1811-1894
Lipps, Theodore	1851-1914	M'cTaggart, John	
Littlefiel, Walter	1867-1948	M'cTaggart Ellis	1866-1925
Littre, Maximilien Paul		Madach, Imre	1823-1864
Emile	1801-1881	Maeterlinck, Maurice	1862-1949
Livingstone, David	1813-1873	Magny, Claude Drigon	1797-1879
Ljunggren, Gustaf Haken		Mahan, Alfred Thayer	1840-1914
Jordan	1823-1905	Maine, Sir Henry James	
Locke, William John	1863-1930	Sumner	1822-1888
Locker-Lampson, Frederick	1821-1895	Maironis	1862-1932
Lockhart, John Gibson	1794-1854	Maistre, Xavier De	1763-1852
Lodge, Henry Cabot	1850-1924	Maitland, Edward	1824-1897
Longfellow, Henry		Maitland, Frederic	
Wadsworth	1807-1882	William	1850-1906
Lönnrot, Elias	1802-1884	Majlath, Janos	1786-1855
Lossing, Benson John	1813-1891	Major, Richard Henry	1818-1891
Losski, Nikolai		Malet, Lucas	1852-1931
Onufreivich	1870-	Mallarme, Stephane	1842-1898
Loti, Pierre	1850-1923	Malleson, George Bruce	1825-1898
Lotze, Rudolf Hermann	1817-1881	Mallock, William Hurrell	1849-1923
Louys, Pierre	1870-1925	Maning, Frederick	
Lover, Samuel	1797-1868	Edward	1812-1883
Lowell, Amy	1874-1925	Mann, Heinrich	1871-1950
Lowell, James Russell	1819-1891	Mann, Thomas	1875-1955
Lubke, Wilhelm	1826-1893	Mansel, Henry	
Lucas, Edward Verrall	1868-1938	Longueville	1820-1871
Luchaire, Achille	1846-1908	Manzoni, Alessandro	1785-1873
Ludwig, Emil	1861-1948	Mapu, Abraham	1808-1867
Ludwig, Otto	1813-1865	Marguerite, Paul	1860-1918
Lummis, Charles Fletcher	1859-1928	Marguerite, Victor	1866-1942
Lunacharsky, Anatoly		Markham, Edwin	1852-1940
Vasilievich	1875-1933	Marquardt, Joachim	1812-1882
Lund, Troels Frederick	1840-1921	Marradi, Giovanni	1852-1922
Luttrell, Henry	1765-1851	Marryat, Florence	1838-1899
Lyall, Edna	1857-1903	Marston, John Westland	1819-1890
Lytton, Edward George		Marston, Philip Bourke	1850-1887
Lytton Bulwer-Lytton	1803-1873	Martin, Henri	1810-1883
Lytton, Edward Robert		Martin, Sir Theodore	1816-1909
Bulwer-Lytton	1831-1891	Martin, Violet Florence	1862-1915
Maartens, Maarten	1858-1915	Martineau, Harriet	1802-1876
Macaulay, Thomas		Martineau, James	1805-1900
Babington Macaulay	1800-1859	Martinez De La Rosa	
MacCarthy, Denis		Francisco De Paula	1787-1862
Florence	1817-1882	Martini, Ferdinando	1841-1928
M'Carthy, Justin	1830-1912	Marx, Karl Heinrich	1818-1883
McCord, Louise Susanna		Mason, Alfred Edward	
Cheves	1810-1879	Woodley	1865-1948
MacDonald, George	1824-1905	Mason, Walt	1862-1939
McGee, Thomas D'Arcy	1825-1868	Massey, Gerald	1828-1907
MacGregor, John	1825-1892	Masson, David	1822-1907
Mach, Ernst	1838-1916	Masson, Frederic	1847-1923
Machado, Antonio	1875-1939	Masters, Edgar Lee	1869-1950

Matthews, Brander	1852-1929	Monod, Gabriel	1844-1912
Maugham, William		Monroe, Harriet	1860-1936
Somerset	1874-1965	Montague, Charles	
Maupassant, Henri Rene		Edward	1867-1928
Albert Guy de	1850-1893	Montalembert, Charles	
Maurer, Georg Ludwig		Forbes Rene De	1810-1870
Von	1790-1872	Montanelli, Giuseppe	1813-1862
Maurras, Charles	1868-1952	Montgomery, James	1771-1854
Mayhew, Henry	1812-1887	Montgomery, Robert	1807-1855
Medina, Jose Toribio	1852-1930	Montufar, Lorenzo	1823-1898
Mee, Arthur	1875-1943	Moody, William Vaughan	1869-1910
Mehring, Franz	1846-1919	Moore, George	1852-1933
Meilhac, Henri	1831-1897	Moore, George Edward	1873-1958
Meinong, Alexius Von	1853-1930	Moore, Thomas	1779-1852
Melville, Herman	1819-1891	More, Paul Elmer	1864-1937
Menard, Louis Nicolas	1822-1901	Moreas, Jean	1856-1910
Mendes, Catulle	1841-1909	Morgan, Lady Sydney	1783-1859
Menendez y Pelayo,		Morike, Eduard Friedrich	1804-1875
Marcelino	1856-1912	Morley, Henry	1822-1894
Menzel, Wolfgang	1798-1873	Morley, John Morley	1838-1923
Meredith, George	1828-1909	Morris, Sir Lewis	1833-1907
Merezhkovsky, Dmitri		Morris, William	1834-1896
Sergeievich	1865-1941	Morrison, Arthur	1863-1945
Merimee, Prosper	1803-1870	Morton, John Maddison	1811-1891
Merivale, Charles	1808-1893	Mosen, Julius	1803-1867
Merrick, Leonard	1864-1939	Motley, John Lothrop	1814-1877
Merrill, Stuart	1863-1915	Moulton, Louise Chandler	1835-1908
Merriman, Henry Seton	1862-1903	Muir, John	1838-1914
Mesonero Romanos,		Muirhead, John Henry	1855-1940
Ramon De	1803-1882	Munch-Bellinghausen,	
Meurice, Paul	1818-1905	Eligius Franz Joseph	1806-1871
Mew, Charlotte	1870-1928	Munro, Hector Hugh	
Meyer, Conrad Ferdinand	1825-1898	(Saki)	1870-1916
Meyer, Eduard	1855-1930	Munsterberg, Hugo	1863-1916
Meynell, Alice	1849-1922	Munthe, Axel	1857-1949
Meyrink, Gustav	1868-1932	Murger, Henry	1822-1861
Michelet, Jules	1798-1874	Murray, Gilbert	1866-1957
Mickiewicz, Adam	1798-1855	Musset, Alfred De	1810-1857
Mignet, Francois Auguste		Myers, Frederic William	
Marie	1796-1884	Henry	1843-1901
Mill, John Stuart	1806-1873	Naden, Constance Caroline	
Miller, Hugh	1802-1856	Woodhill	1858-1889
Miller, Joaquin	1841-1913	Neal, John	1793-1876
Milman, Henry Hart	1791-1868	Nekrasov, Nikolai	
Milyukov, Paul		Alexeyeivich	1821-1877
Nikolayevich	1859-1942	Neruda, Jan	1834-1891
Mirbeau, Octave Henri		Nerval, Gerard de	1808-1855
Marie	1850-1917	Nesbit, Edith	1858-1924
Mistral, Frederic	1830-1914	Nestroy, Johann	1801-1862
Mitchell, Donald Grant	1822-1908	Nettleship, Richard Lewis	1846-1892
Mitford, John	1781-1859	Newbolt, Sir Henry John	1862-1938
Mitford, Mary Russell	1787-1855	Newman, Francis William	1805-1897
Moir, David Macbeth	1798-1851	Newman, John Henry	
Molesworth, Mary Louisa	1839-1921	(Cardinal)	1801-1890
Molesworth, William		Nexo, Martin Andersen	1869-1954
Nassau	1816-1890	Nichol, John	1833-1894
Mommsen, Theodor	1817-1903	Nicholson, Meredith	1866-1947
Monkhouse, William		Nietzshe, Friedrich	
Cosmo	1840-1901	Wilhelm	1844-1900
Monnier, Marc	1829-1885	Nitzsch, Karl Immanuel	1787-1868

Nitzsch, Karl Wilhelm	1818-1880
Noailles, Paul Duke of	1802-1885
Noel, Roden Berkeley Wriothesleu	1834-1894
Nordau, Max Simon	1848-1923
Normanby, Constantine Henry Phipps	1797-1863
Norris, Frank	1870-1902
Norris, William Edward	1847-1925
Norton, Caroline Elizabeth Sarah	1808-1877
Norton, Charles Eliot	1827-1908
Nunez De Arce, Gaspar	1834-1903
O'Grady, Standish James	1846-1928
Ohnet, Georges	1848-1918
Oliphant, Laurence	1829-1888
Oliphant, Margaret Oliphant	1828-1897
Oliveira, Martins Joaquim Pedro De	1845-1894
Oman, Sir Charles William Chadwick	1860-1946
Opie, Amelia	1769-1853
Oppenheim, Edward Phillips	1866-1946
Opzoomer, Cornelius William	1821-1892
Orczy, Baroness Emmuska	1865-1947
Orzeszkowa, Eliza	1842-1910
Osbourne, Lloyd	1868-1947
O'Shaughnessy, Arthur William Edgar	1844-1880
Ostrovsky, Alexander Nikolaevich	1823-1886
Ouida	1839-1908
Ozanam, Antoine Frederic	1813-1853
Page, Thomas Nelson	1853-1922
Page, Walter Hines	1855-1918
Pain, Barry Eric Odell	1865-1928
Palacio Valdes, Armando	1853-1938
Palacky, Frantisek	1798-1876
Palamas, Kostes	1859-1943
Paleologue, Maurice Georges	1859-1944
Palfrey, John Gorham	1796-1881
Palgrave, Francis Turner	1824-1897
Paludan-Muller, Frederik	1809-1876
Panzini, Alfredo	1863-1939
Paoli, Cesare	1840-1902
Pardo Bazan, Emilia	1851-1921
Pares, Sir Bernard	1867-1949
Paris, Gaston	1839-1903
Parker, Sir Gilbert	1862-1932
Parker, Theodore	1810-1860
Parkman, Francis	1823-1893
Parton, James	1822-1891
Pascoli, Giovanni	1855-1912
Pater, Walter Horatio	1839-1894
Paterson, Andrew Barton ("Banjo")	1864-1941

Patmore, Coventry Kersey Dighton	1823-1896
Pattison, Mark	1813-1884
Paul, Charles Kiegan	1828-1902
Paulding, James Kirke	1778-1860
Pauli, Reinhold	1823-1882
Paulsen, Friedrich	1846-1908
Payn, James	1830-1898
Payne, John Howard	1791-1852
Paz Soldan, Mariano Felipe	1821-1886
Peabody, Andrew Preston	1811-1893
Peabody, Josephine Preston	1874-1922
Peacock, Thomas Love	1785-1866
Peesemsky, Alexey Feofilictovich	1820-1881
Peguy, Charles	1873-1914
Peirce, Charles Sanders	1839-1914
Pelham, Henry Francis	1846-1907
Pellico, Silvio	1788-1854
Pemberton, Sir Max	1863-1950
Percival, James Gates	1795-1856
Pereda, Jose Maria De	1833-1906
Perez Galdos, Benito	1845-1920
Perry, Bliss	1860-1945
Pertz, Georg Heinrich	1795-1876
Pfleiderer, Edmund	1842-1902
Phillips, Stephen	1868-1915
Phillpotts, Eden	1862-1960
Pinero, Sir Arthur Wing	1855-1934
Pirandello, Luigi	1867-1936
Pirenne, Henry	1862-1935
Planche, James Robinson	1796-1880
Plekhanov, Georgy Valentinovitch	1857-1918
Plieksans, Jan	1865-1929
Pollard, Alfred Frederick	1869-1948
Ponsard, Francois	1814-1867
Pontoppidan, Henrik	1857-1943
Poole, William Frederick	1821-1894
Porter, Eleanor Hodgman	1868-1920
Porter, Gene Stratton	1868-1924
Porter, Noah	1811-1892
Porto-Riche, Georges De	1849-1930
Post, Melville Davisson	1871-1930
Potgieter, Everhades Johannes	1808-1875
Potter, Beatrix	1866-1943
Potthast, August	1824-1898
Powell, Frederick York	1850-1904
Powyss, John Cowper	1872-1963
Powyss, Theodore Francis	1875-1953
Prantl, Karl Von	1820-1888
Prati, Giovanni	1815-1884
Prel, Karl	1839-1899
Prescott, Harriet Elizabeth	1835-1921
Prescott, William Hickling	1796-1859

Prevost, Eugene Marcel	1862-1941	Richardson, Henry	
Pribram, Alfred Francis	1859-1942	Handel	1870-1946
Procter, Adelaide Anne	1825-1864	Richepin, Jean	1849-1926
Procter, Bryan Waller	1787-1874	Ridge, William Pett	1857-1930
Proudhon, Pierre Joseph	1809-1865	Ridgway, Robert	1850-1929
Proust, Marcel	1871-1922	Riley, James Whitcomb	1849-1916
Prus, Boleslaw	1847-1912	Rilke, Rainer Maria	1875-1926
Prutz, Hans	1843-1929	Rimbaud Jean Arthur	1854-1891
Przybyszewski, Stanislaw	1868-1927	Ritchie, Anne Isabella	
Psichari, Ernest	1883-1914	Lady	1837-1919
Purnell, Thomas	1834-1889	Ritter, Heinrich	1791-1869
Pusey, Edward Bouverie	1800-1882	Rivas, Angel De	
Quental, Anthero De	1842-1891	Saavedra	1791-1865
Quicherat, Jules Etienne		Roberts, Sir Charles	
Joseph	1814-1882	George Douglas	1860-1943
Quiller-Couch, Sir Arthur		Roberts, Morley	1857-1942
Thomas	1863-1944	Robertson, Thomas	
Quincy, Josiah	1772-1864	William	1829-1871
Quinet, Edgar	1803-1875	Robinson, Edwin	
Quintana, Manuel José	1772-1857	Arlington	1869-1935
Quintero, Joaquin Alvarez	1873-1944	Robinson, Lennox	1886-1958
Quintero, Serafin Alvarez	1871-1938	Rod, Edouard	1857-1910
Ragabe, Alexandros Rizos	1810-1892	Rodo, Jose Enrique	1872-1917
Raleigh, Sir Walter		Roe, Edward Payson	1838-1888
Alexander	1861-1922	Rogers, Randolph	1825-1892
Rambaud, Alfred Nicolas	1842-1905	Rogers, Samuel	1763-1855
Ranc, Arthur	1831-1908	Rolland, Romain	1866-1944
Randall, James Ryder	1839-1908	Rolleston, Thomas	
Rands, William Brighty	1823-1882	William Hazen	1857-1920
Ranke, Leopold Von	1795-1886	Roosevelt, Theodore	1858-1919
Rashdall, Hastings	1858-1924	Rose, John Holland	1855-1942
Raumer, Fredrich Ludwig		Rosegger, Peter	1843-1918
George Von	1781-1873	Rosenkranz, Karl	1805-1879
Ravaisson-Mollien, Jean		Rosmini-Serbati, Antonio	1797-1855
Gaspard Felix	1813-1900	Rosny, Joseph Henri	1856-1940
Rawlinson, George	1812-1902	Rosny, Seraphin Justin	
Reade, Charles	1814-1884	Francois	1859-1948
Realf, Richard	1834-1878	Ross, Janet Anne	1842-1927
Reclus, Jean Jacques		Rossetti, Dante, Gabriel	1828-1882
Elisée	1830-1905	Rossetti, Christina	
Redgrave, Richard	1804-1888	Georgina	1830-1894
Regnier, Henri Francois		Rossetti, Gabriele	1783-1854
Joseph De	1864-1936	Rossetti, William Michael	1829-1919
Reid, Thomas Mayne	1818-1883	Rostand, Edmond	1869-1918
Reinach, Joseph	1856-1921	Roumanille, Joseph	1818-1891
Remusat, Charles Francois		Royce, Josiah	1855-1916
Marie	1797-1875	Rozanov, Vasili	
Renan, Ernest	1823-1892	Vasilievich	1856-1919
Rennell, James Rennell		Rückert, Friedrich	1788-1866
Rodd 1st Baron	1858-1941	Ruffini, Giovanni	
Renouvier, Charles		Domenico	1807-1881
Bernard	1815-1903	Ruge, Arnold	1802-1880
Reuter, Fritz	1810-1874	Runeberg, Johan Ludvig	1804-1877
Reuter, Gabriel	1859-1941	Ruskin, John	1819-1900
Reymont, Wladyslaw		Russell, Bertrand Arthur	
Stanislaw	1868-1925	William	1872-
Rhys, Ernest Percival	1859-1946	Russell, George William	1867-1935
Rice, James	1843-1882	Rutherford, Mark	1831-1913
Richards, Frank	1875-	Rydberg, Abraham Viktor	1828-1895
Richardson, Dorothy Miller	1873-1957	Sabatier, Paul	1858-1928

Sabatini, Rafael	1875-1950
Safarik, Pavel Josef	1795-1861
Sainte-Beuve, Charles	
Augustin	1804-1869
Saint-Marc, Girardin	1801-1873
Saintsbury, George	
Edward Bateman	1845-1933
Sala, George Augustin	
Henry	1828-1895
Salten, Felix	1869-1945
Saltykov, Michael	
Evgrafovich	1826-1889
Salvemini, Gaetano	1873-
Samain, Albert Victor	1858-1900
Sand, George	
(Dudevant)	1804-1876
Sanday, William	1843-1920
Sandeau, Leonard	
Sylvain Julien	1811-1883
Sant, James	1820-1916
Santayana, George	1863-1952
Santine, Joseph Xavier	1798-1865
Sardou, Victorien	1831-1908
Sarmiento, Domingo	
Faustino	1811-1888
Saxe, John Godfrey	1816-1887
Schaffner, Jakob	1875-1944
Scheffel, Joseph Viktor	
Von	1826-1886
Schelling, Friedrich	
Wilhelm Joseph Von	1775-1854
Scherer, Wilhelm	1841-1886
Schimmelpenninck, Mary	
Ann	1778-1856
Schlaf, Johannes	1862-1941
Schnitzler, Arthur	1862-1931
Schonner, Karl	1869-1942
Schopenhauer, Arthur	1788-1860
Shreiner, Olive	1855-1920
Schweitzer, Albert	1875-1965
Schweitzer, Jean Baptista	1833-1875
Scott, Duncan Campbell	1862-1947
Scott-Moncrieff, Charles	
Kenneth Michael	1889-1930
Scribe, Eugene	1791-1861
Seaman, Sir Owen	1861-1936
Sedgwick, Anne Douglas	1873-1935
Seebohm, Frederick	1833-1912
Seeley, Sir John Robert	1834-1895
Segur, Philippe Paul	
Comte De	1780-1873
Seignobos Charles	1854-1942
Sellar, William Young	1825-1890
Serao, Matilde	1856-1927
Sergeyev-Tsensky, Sergey	1875-1958
Service, Robert William	1874-1958
Seth, Andrew	1850-1931
Settembrini, Luigi	1813-1877
Sewell, Anna	1820-1878
Sharp, John Campbell	1819-1885

Sharp, William	1856-1905
Shaw, George Bernard	1856-1950
Shaw, Henry Wheeler	1818-1885
Sheil, Richard Lalor	1791-1851
Shelley, Mary	
Wollenstonecraft	1797-1851
Sherwood, Mary Martha	1775-1851
Shevchenko, Taras	1814-1861
Shorter, Clement King	1857-1926
Shorthouse, Joseph Henry	1834-1903
Sidgwick, Henry	1838-1900
Sienkiewicz, Henryk	1846-1916
Sigourney, Lydia Huntley	1791-1865
Sill, Edward Rowland	1841-1887
Simmel, Georg	1858-1918
Simms, William Gilmore	1806-1870
Simon, Jules Francois	1814-1896
Simrock, Karl Joseph	1802-1876
Sims, George Robert	1847-1922
Sinclair, May	1864-1946
Skeat, Walter William	1835-1912
Skene, William Forbes	1809-1892
Smiles, Samuel	1812-1904
Smith, Alexander	1830-1867
Smith, Francis	
Hopkinson	1838-1915
Smith, Goldwin	1823-1910
Smith, Logan Pearsall	1865-1946
Smith, Norman Kemp	1872-1958
Smith, Walter Chalmers	1824-1908
Smith, Sir William	1813-1893
Snoilsky, Carl Johan	
Gustaf	1841-1903
Sokolov, Nahum	1859-1936
Sologub, Fedor	1863-1927
Soloviev, Sergei	
Mikhailovich	1820-1879
Soloviev, Vladimer	
Sergeivich	1853-1900
Sorabji, Cornelia	1866-1954
Sorel, Albert	1842-1906
Sorel, Georges	1847-1922
Sparks, Jared	1789-1866
Spence, Lewis	1874-1955
Spencer, Herbert	1820-1903
Spender, Edward Harold	1864-1926
Spielhagen, Friedrich Von	1829-1911
Spitteler, Carl	1845-1924
Stacpoole, Henry de Vere	1863-1951
Stahl, Frederich Julius	1802-1861
Stanley, Arthur Penrhyn	1815-1881
Stanley, Sir Henry Morton	1841-1904
Stedman, Edmund	
Clarence	1833-1908
Steed, Henry Wickham	1871-1956
Stein, Gertrude	1874-1946
Steiner, Rudolf	1861-1925
Stephen, Sir Leslie	1832-1904
Stepnyak	1852-1895
Stern, Daniel (Agoult)	1805-1876

Stevenson, Robert Louis	
Balfour	1850-1894
Stifter, Adalbert	1805-1868
Stirling, James	
Hutchinson	1820-1909
Stirling-Maxwell, Sir	
William Bart	1818-1878
Stirner, Max	1806-1856
Stocker, Helene	1869-
Stockton, Francis Richard	1834-1902
Stoddard, John Lawson	1850-1931
Stoddard, Richard Henry	1825-1903
Stoddard, William Osborn	1835-1925
Storm, Theodor Wolsden	1817-1888
Stout, George Frederick	1860-1944
Stowe, Harriet Elizabeth	
Beecher	1811-1896
Strauss, David Friedrich	1808-1874
Street, Alfred William	1811-1881
Streuvels, Styn	1871-
Strickland Agnes	1806-1874
Strindberg, Johan August	1849-1912
Stubbs, William	1825-1901
Stuckenberg, Viggo	1863-1905
Sudermann, Hermann	1857-1928
Sue, Eugene	1804-1857
Sully-Prudhomme, Rene	
Francois Armand	1839-1907
Surtees, Robert Smith	1803-1864
Sutro, Alfred	1863-1933
Suttner, Bertha	1843-1914
Svevo, Italio	1861-1928
Swan, Annie	1860-1943
Swanwick, Anna	1813-1899
Swetchine, Madame	1782-1857
Swinburne, Algernon	
Charles	1837-1909
Sybel, Heinrich Von	1817-1895
Symonds, John Addington	1840-1893
Symons, Arthur	1865-1945
Synge, John Millington	1871-1909
Tabley, John Byrne	
Leicester Warren	1835-1895
Tagore, Sir Rabindranath	1861-1941
Taine, Hippolyte, Adolphe	1828-1893
Talfourd, Sir Thomas	
Noon	1795-1854
Tamayo, Baus Manuel	1829-1898
Tarkington, Newton Booth	1869-1946
Taylor, Alfred Edward	1869-1945
Taylor, Ann	1782-1866
Taylor, Bayard	1825-1878
Taylor, Sir Henry	1800-1886
Taylor, Isaak	1787-1865
Taylor, Isaak	1829-1901
Taylor, Tom	1817-1880
Tedder, Henry Richard	1850-1924
Tennyson, Alfred Lord	1809-1892
Thackeray, William	
Makepeace	1811-1863

Tharaud, Jerome	1874-1953
Thaxter, Celia Laighton	1835-1894
Thayer, William Roscoe	1859-1923
Theuriet, Claude Adhemar	
Andre	1833-1907
Thierry, Jacques Nicolas	
Augustin	1795-1856
Thiers, Louis Adolph	1797-1877
Thirlwall, Connop	1797-1875
Thomas, Augustus	1857-1934
Thomas, Brandon	1849-1914
Thompson, Francis	1859-1907
Thomson, James	1834-1882
Thoreau, Henry David	1817-1862
Thurston, Katherine Cecil	1875-1911
Ticknor, George	1791-1871
Tiek, Johann Ludwig	1773-1853
Tischendorf, Lobegott	1815-1874
Tocqueville, Alexis	
Charles Henri Clarel	1805-1859
Tolstoy, Alexei,	
Konstantinovich	1817-1875
Tolstoy, Leo Nokolayevich	1828-1910
Tomlinson, Henry Major	1873-1958
Tommaseo, Niccolo	1802-1874
Tompa, Mihaly	1817-1868
Topelius, Zachris	1818-1898
Toru, Dutt	1856-1877
Tout, Thomas Frederick	1855-1929
Toynbee, Arnold	1852-1883
Traill, Henry Duff	1842-1900
Treitschke, Heinrich Von	1834-1896
Trelawny, Edward John	1792-1881
Trench, Frederick Herbert	1865-1923
Trench, Richard Chevenix	1807-1886
Trendelenburg, Friedrich	
Adolf	1802-1872
Trevelyan, Sir George	
Otto	1838-1928
Trevelyan, Robert	
Calverley	1872-1951
Trollope, Anthony	1815-1882
Trollope, Frances	1780-1863
Trollope, Thomas	
Adolphus	1810-1892
Tucker, Charlotte Marie	1821-1893
Tupper, Martin Farquhar	1810-1889
Turgenev, Ivan	
Sergeyevich	1818-1883
Turner, Charles Tennyson	1808-1879
Turner, Frederick Jackson	1861-1932
Twain, Mark	1835-1910
Tyler, Moses Coit	1835-1900
Tynan, Katherine	1863-1931
Tyndall, John	1820-1893
Tyuchev, Fydor Ivanovich	1803-1873
Uberweg, Friedrich	1826-1871
Uhland, Johann Ludwig	1787-1862
Unamuno, Miguel De	1864-1936
Underhill, Evelyn	1875-1941

Uspenski, Gleb Ivanovich	1840-1902	Wasserman, Jakob	1873-1933
Vachell, Horace Annesley	1861-1955	Watson, Sir William	1858-1935
Vacherot, Etienne	1809-1897	Watts-Dunton, Walter	
Vaihinger, Hans	1852-1933	Theodore	1832-1914
Valera Y Alcala,		Waugh, Edwin	1817-1890
Galiano Juan	1824-1905	Webb, Beatrice	1858-1943
Valery, Paul	1871-1945	Webb, Sidney James	1859-1947
Valle-Inclan, Ramon Del	1869-1936	Wedekind, Frank	1864-1918
Valles, Jules	1832-1885	Welhaven, Johann	
Van, Beers Jan	1821-1888	Sebastian Cammermeyer	1807-1873
Van Dyke, Henry	1852-1933	Wells, Charles Jeremiah	1798-1879
Vaperau, Louis Gustave	1819-1906	Wells, Herbert George	1866-1946
Varnhagen, Francesco		Wennerberg, Gunnar	1817-1901
Adolpho De	1816-1878	Weyman, Stanley John	1855-1928
Varnhagen, Von Ense		Wharton, Newbold Edith	1862-1937
Karl August	1785-1858	White, Richard Grant	1821-1885
Vazoff, Ivan	1850-1921	White, William Hale	1831-1913
Veblen, Thornstein B.	1857-1929	Whitehead, Charles	1804-1862
Veitch, John	1829-1894	Whitlock, Brand	1869-1934
Verdaguer, Mosen Jacinto	1845-1902	Whitman, Walt	1819-1892
Verga, Giovanni	1840-1922	Whittier, John Greenleaf	1807-1892
Verhaeren, Emile	1855-1916	Widmann, Joseph Victor	1842-1911
Verlaine, Paul	1844-1896	Wieniawski, Henri	1835-1880
Verne, Jules	1828-1905	Wiggin, Kate Douglas	1856-1923
Verplanck, Gulian		Wilcox, Ella	1850-1919
Crommelin	1786-1870	Wilde, Oscar Fingall	
Verwey, Albert	1865-1937	O'Flahertie Wills	1854-1900
Viaud, Louis Marie Julien	1850-1923	Wilde, Speranza Lady	1826-1896
Vidyasagar, Iswar,		Wildenbruch, Ernst Van	1845-1909
Chandra	1820-1891	Willis, Nathaniel Parker	1806-1867
Viebig, Clara	1860-1952	Wills, William Gorman	1828-1891
Viele-Griffen, Francis	1864-1937	Wilson, John	1785-1854
Vigfusson, Gudbrandir	1828-1889	Winsor, Justin	1831-1897
Vigny, Alfred De	1797-1863	Winther, Christian	1796-1876
Villari, Pasquale	1827-1917	Wister, Owen	1860-1938
Villemain, Abel Francois	1790-1870	Wodsworth, Dorothy	1771-1855
Villiers de L'Isle, Auguste		Wolff, Pierre	1865-1944
Compte De	1838-1889	Wood, Mrs. Henry	1814-1887
Vinje, Aasmunde Olavson	1816-1870	Woods, Margaret Louisa	1856-1945
Vinogradoff, Sir Paul	1854-1925	Woolf, Virginia	1882-1941
Vischer, Friedrich		Wright, Thomas	1810-1887
Theodor	1807-1887	Wright, William Aldis	1836-1914
Vogue, Eugene Melchior	1848-1910	Wundt, Wilhelm Max	1832-1920
Voss, Richard	1851-1918	Wyatt, Sir Matthew	
Vrchlicky, Jasoslav	1853-1912	Digby	1820-1877
Vuillard, Jean Edouard	1868-1940	Wyndham, George	1863-1913
Waagen, Gustav Friedrich	1794-1868	Yates, Edmund	1831-1894
Wallace, Alfred Russel	1823-1913	Yeats, William Butler	1865-1939
Wallace, Edgar	1875-1932	Yonge, Charlotte Mary	1823-1901
Wallace, Lewis	1827-1905	Yriarte, Charles	1832-1898
Wallace, William	1844-1897	Zahn, Ernst	1867-1952
Wallon, Henri Alexandre	1812-1904	Zangwill, Israel	1864-1926
Warburton, Eliot	1810-1852	Zeller, Eduard	1814-1908
Ward, Artemus	1834-1867	Zeromski, Stephen	1864-1925
Ward, Mary Augusta		Zhukovsky, Vasili	
(Mrs. Humphrey)	1851-1920	Andreyevich	1783-1852
Warner, Charles Dudley	1829-1900	Zola, Emile Edouard	
Warner, Susan Bogert	1819-1895	Charles Antoine	1840-1902
Warren, Samuel	1807-1877	Zorrilla, Jose	1817-1893

Abbey, Edwin Austin	1852-1911	Boelkin, Arnold	1827-1901
Achenbach, Andreas	1815-1910	Bonheur, Rosa	1822-1899
Adams, Herbert	1858-1945	Bonnard, Pierre	1867-1947
Adamsen, Amandus		Bonnat, Leon Joseph	
Heinrich	1855-1929	Florentin	1833-1922
Ainmuller, Maximilian		Borglum, Gutzon	1871-1941
Emmanuel	1807-1870	Borglum, Solon Hannibal	1868-1922
Alexander, John White	1856-1915	Boudin, Louis Eugene	1824-1898
Anderson, Sir Robert		Bough, Samuel	1822-1878
Rowand	1834-1921	Boughton, George Henry	1833-1905
Ansdell, Richard	1815-1885	Bouguereau, Adolphe	
Armitage, Edward	1817-1896	William	1825-1905
Armstead, Henry Hugh	1828-1905	Bourdelle, Emile Antoine	1861-1929
Auberjonois, Rene	1872-	Boutet de Monvel,	
Audubon, John James	1785-1851	Maurice	1851-1913
Bacon, Henry	1866-1924	Boyle, John	1851-1917
Baer, William Jacob	1860-1941	Bracquemond, Felix	1833-1914
Baily, Edward Hodges	1788-1867	Bradford, William	1827-1892
Bakst, Leon	1866-1924	Braekeleer, Henri Jean	
Ball, Thomas	1819-1911	Augustin De	1840-1888
Balla, Giacomo	1871-1958	Brangwyn, Sir Frank	1867-1956
Bandel, Ernst Von	1800-1876	Brascassat, Jacques	
Barker, Thomas	1815-1882	Raymond	1804-1867
Barnard, George Grey	1863-1938	Breitner, George Hendrik	1857-1923
Bartels, Hans Von	1856-1913	Breton, Jules Adolphe	
Barry, Sir Charles	1795-1860	Aime Louis	1827-1906
Bartholdi, August	1834-1904	Bridgman, Frederic	
Bartholomé, Paul Albert	1848-1928	Arthur	1847-1928
Barye, Antoine Louis	1796-1875	Brierly, Sir Oswald	
Bastien-Lepage, Jules	1848-1884	Walters	1817-1894
Bates, Harry	1850-1899	Bright, Henry	1814-1873
Baudry, Paul Jacques		Brock, Sir Thomas	1847-1922
Aime	1828-1886	Brodie, William	1815-1881
Beardsley, Aubrey Vincent	1872-1898	Brough, Robert	1872-1905
Beaux, Cecilia	1863-1942	Brown, Ford Madox	1821-1893
Beckwith, James Carroll	1852-1917	Brown, George Loring	1814-1889
Begas, Karl	1794-1854	Brown, Henry Kirke	1814-1886
Begas, Reinhold	1831-1911	Brown, John George	1831-1913
Behrens, Peter	1868-1938	Browne, Hablot Knight	1815-1882
Bell, John	1811-1895	Bruce-Joy, Albert	1842-1924
Bellows, Albert F.	1829-1883	Brunner, Arnold William	1857-1925
Benlliure, Y Gil Jose	1855-1937	Brush, George de Forest	1855-1941
Benson, Frank Weston	1862-1951	Brymner, William	1855-1925
Bentley, John Francis	1839-1902	Burgess, John Bagnold	1830-1897
Berlage, Hendrik Petrus	1856-1934	Burn, William	1789-1870
Besnard, Paul Albert	1849-1934	Burne-Jones, Sir Edward	
Beverley, William Roxby	1814-1889	Burne	1833-1898
Bierstadt, Albert	1830-1902	Burne-Jones, Sir Philip	1861-1926
Birch, Samuel	1813-1885	Burnham, Daniel Hudson	1846-1912
Bissen, Herman Vilhelm	1798-1868	Burton, Decimus	1800-1881
Blakelock, Ralph Albert	1847-1919	Butler, Lady Elizabeth	1851-1933
Blanche, Jacques Emile	1862-1942	Butterfield, William	1814-1900
Blashfield, Edwin		Cabanel, Alexandre	1823-1889
Howland	1848-1936	Calame, Alexandre	1810-1864
Blomfield, Sir Arthur		Caldecott, Randolph	1846-1886
William	1829-1899	Calderon, Philip	
Blomfield, Sir Reginald	1856-1942	Hermogenes	1833-1898
Blore, Edward	1787-1879	Calvert, Charles	1785-1852
Blum, Robert Frederick	1857-1903	Calvert, Edward	1799-1883
Boehm, Sir Joseph Edgar	1834-1890	Cameron, Sir David Young	1865-1945

Camphausen, Wilhelm	1818-1885	Dantan, Antoine Laurent	1798-1878
Capronnier, Jean-Baptiste	1814-1891	Dantan, Edward Joseph	1848-1897
Caran D'ache	1858-1909	Dantan, Jean-Pierre	1800-1869
Carolus-Duran	1837-1917	Darley, Felix Octavius	
Carpeaux, Jean Baptiste	1827-1875	Carr	1822-1888
Carrier, Eugene	1849-1906	Daubigny, Charles	
Cassatt, Mary	1845-1926	Francois	1817-1878
Catlin, George	1796-1872	Daumet, Pierre Jerome	
Cattermole, George	1800-1868	Honore	1826-1911
Cazin, Jean Charles	1841-1901	Daumier, Honore	1808-1879
Cezanne, Paul	1839-1906	David, Pierre Jean	1789-1856
Chalmers, George Paul	1836-1878	Davies, Arthur B.	1862-1928
Chapu, Henri	1833-1891	Davis, Charles Harold	1857-1933
Chase, William Merrit	1849-1916	Dawson, Henry	1811-1878
Chasseriau, Theodore	1819-1856	Dawson-Watson, Dawson	1864-1939
Church, Frederick Edwin	1826-1900	Decamps, Alexandre	
Clarke, Thomas Shields	1860-1920	Gabriel	1803-1860
Claus, Emile	1849-1924	Defregger, Franz Von	1835-1921
Clausen, Sir George	1852-1944	Degas, Hilaire Germain	
Clays, Paul Jean	1819-1900	Edgar	1834-1917
Cockerell, Charles Robert	1758-1863	Delacroix, Ferdinand	
Cole, Vicat	1833-1893	Victor Eugene	1798-1863
Collier, Hon Jon	1850-1934	Delaroche, Hippolyte	1797-1856
Colman, Samuel	1832-1920	Delaunay, Elie	1828-1891
Conder, Charles	1868-1909	Denis, Maurice	1870-1943
Constant, Benjamin Jean		Despiau, Charles	1874-1946
Joseph	1845-1902	Detaille, Edouard	1848-1912
Cooper, Abraham	1787-1868	Diaz, Narcisse Virgile	1809-1876
Cooper, Thomas Sidney	1803-1902	Dicksee, Sir Francis	
Cope, Charles West	1811-1890	Bernard	1853-1928
Corbett, Harvey Wiley	1873-1954	Dielman, Frederick	1847-1935
Corbould, Edward Henry	1815-1905	Dillens, Julien	1849-1904
Corinth, Louis	1858-1925	Dobson, William Charles	
Cormon, Fernand	1845-1924	Thomas	1817-1898
Cornelius, Peter Von	1783-1867	Dodge, William de	
Corot, Jean-Baptiste		Leftwich	1867-1935
Camille	1796-1875	Dore, Paul Gustave	1832-1883
Costa, Giovanni	1826-1903	Doyle, Richard	1824-1883
Cottet, Charles	1863-1925	Drake, Friedrich	1805-1882
Courbet, Gustav	1819-1877	Drury, Alfred	1857-1944
Couture. Thomas	1815-1879	Dubois, Paul	1829-1905
Cox, David	1783-1859	Dumont, Augustin	
Cox, David the younger	1809-1885	Alexandre	1801-1884
Cram, Ralph Adams	1863-1942	Dupre, Giovanni	1817-1882
Crane, Thomas	1808-1859	Dupre, Jules	1811-1889
Crane, Walter	1845-1915	Durand, Asher Brown	1796-1886
Crauck, Gustav	1827-1905	Duveneck, Frank	1848-1919
Crawford, Thomas	1814-1857	Dyce, William	1806-1864
Creswick, Thomas	1811-1869	Eakins, Thomas	1844-1916
Cruikshank, George	1792-1878	East, Alfred	1849-1913
Dagnan-Bouveret, Pascal		Eastlake, Sir Charles	
Adolphe Jean	1852-1929	Lock	1793-1865
Daguerre, Louis Jacques		Eaton, Wyatt	1849-1896
Mande	1789-1851	Eberlein, Gustav	1847-1926
Dahl, Johann Kristen	1788-1857	Eberz, Josef	1801-1882
Daingerfield, Elliott	1859-1932	Eckersberg, Kristoffer	1783-1853
Dallin, Cyrus Edwin	1861-1944	Edelfelt, Albert Gunter	1854-1905
Dalou, Jules	1838-1902	Egg, Augustus Leopold	1816-1863
Danby, Francis	1793-1861	Elliott, Charles Loring	1812-1868
Dannat, William T.	1853-1929	Ensor, James	1860-1942

Etex, Antoine	1808-1888	Goldschmidt, Hermann	1802-1866
Faed, Thomas	1826-1900	Goodall, Frederick	1822-1904
Falguiere, Jean Alexandre		Goodhue, Bertram	
Joseph	1831-1900	Grosvenor	1869-1924
Fantin-Latour, Ignace Henri		Gordon, Sir John	
Jean Theodore	1836-1904	Watson	1788-1864
Farquharson, David	1840-1907	Grafly, Charles	1862-1929
Farquharson, Joseph	1846-1935	Grant, Sir Francis	1803-1878
Feininger, Lyonel	1871-1956	Greenough, Horatio	1805-1852
Feuerbach, Anselm	1829-1880	Greenaway, Kate	1846-1901
Fielding, Copley	1787-1855	Gregory, Edward John	1850-1909
Fildes, Sir Luke	1844-1927	Grossmith, Weedon	1853-1919
Finch, Alfred William	1854-1930	Gudin, Theodore	1802-1880
Flagg, Ernest	1857-1947	Guillamin, Armand	1841-1927
Flandrin, Jean Hyppolyte	1809-1864	Guillaume, Jean Baptiste	
Fogelberg, Benedict		Claude Eugene	1822-1905
Erland	1786-1854	Guthrie, Sir James	1859-1930
Foley, John Henry	1818-1874	Guys, Constantin	1805-1892
Fontaine, Pierre Francois		Gwilt, Joseph	1784-1863
Leonard	1762-1853	Haag, Carl	1820-1915
Forain, Jean Louis	1852-1931	Haas, Johannes Hubertus	
Ford, Edward Onslow	1852-1901	Leonhardus De	1832-1908
Forster, Ernst	1800-1885	Habermann, Hugo Freiherr	
Fortuny, Mariano Jose		Von	1849-1929
Maria Bernardo	1838-1874	Hacker, Arthur	1858-1919
Foster, Myles Birket	1825-1899	Haider, Karl	1846-1912
Fowler, Charles	1792-1867	Hamon, Jean Louis	1821-1874
Frampton, Sir George	1860-1928	Hansom, Joseph Aloysius	1803-1882
Francais, Francois Louis	1814-1897	Harding, Chester	1792-1866
Fremiet, Emmanuel	1824-1910	Harpignies, Henri	1819-1916
French, Daniel Chester	1850-1931	Harrison, Thomas	
Fripp, Alfred Downing	1822-1895	Alexander	1853-1930
Fripp, George Anthony	1814-1896	Hartley, Jonathan Scott	1845-1912
Frith, William Powell	1819-1909	Harvey, Sir George	1806-1876
Fromentin, Eugene	1820-1876	Hassall, John	1868-1948
Frost, William Edward	1810-1877	Hayter, Sir George	1792-1871
Fry, Roger Elliot	1866-1934	Henner, Jean Jacques	1829-1905
Fuertes, Louis Agassiz	1874-1927	Henri, Robert	1865-1929
Fuhrich, Joseph Von	1800-1876	Herbert, John Rogers	1810-1900
Fuller, George	1822-1884	Hildebrand, Adolf	1847-1921
Furse, Charles Wellington	1868-1904	Hilderbrandt, Eduard	1818-1869
Gallait, Louis	1810-1887	Hiroshege	1797-1858
Gallen-Kallela, Akseli		Hittorff, Jacques Ignace	1792-1867
Valdemar	1865-1931	Hockert, Johan Frederick	1826-1866
Garnier, Jean Louis		Hodgkins, Francis Mary	1869-1947
Charles	1825-1898	Hodler, Ferdinand	1853-1918
Gauguin, Paul	1848-1903	Hoffman, Josef	1870-
Gaul, Gilbert William	1855-1919	Holiday, Henry	1839-1927
Gavarni, Paul	1801-1866	Holl, Frank	1845-1888
Gay, Walter	1856-1937	Holmes, Sir Charles John	1868-1936
Gebhardt, Eduard Von	1830-1925	Holroyd, Sir Charles	1861-1917
Gerome, Jean Leon	1824-1904	Homer, Winslow	1836-1910
Gervex, Henri	1852-1929	Hook, James Clarke	1819-1907
Gibson, Charles Dana	1867-1944	Horsley, John Callcott	1817-1903
Gibson, John	1790-1866	Hosmer, Harriet	
Gifford, Robert Swain	1840-1905	Goodhue	1830-1908
Gilbert, Sir Alfred	1854-1934	Hovenden, Thomas	1840-1895
Gilbert, Cass	1859-1934	Hubner, Julius	1806-1882
Gilbert, Sir John	1817-1897	Hughes, Arthur	1832-1915
Gleyre, Charles	1806-1874	Hunt, Alfred William	1830-1896

Hunt, Richard Morris	1828-1895	Lemaire, Philip Honore	1798-1880
Hunt, William Henry	1790-1864	Lenbach, Franz Von	1836-1904
Hunt, William Holman	1827-1910	Leslie, Charles Robert	1794-1859
Hunt, William Morris	1824-1879	Lethaby, William Richard	1857-1931
Huntingdon, Daniel	1816-1906	Leutze, Emanuel	1816-1868
Hurlstone, Frederick		Leys, Hendrik	1815-1869
Yeates	1800-1869	Liebermann, Max	1847-1935
Hut, Paul	1804-1869	Lindsay, Sir Coutts	1824-1913
Ingres, Jean Auguste		Linnell, John	1792-1882
Dominique	1780-1867	Linton, Sir James Dromgole	1840-1916
Inness, George	1825-1894	Llewellyn, Sir William	1863-1941
Isabey, Jean Baptiste	1767-1855	Lockhart, William Ewart	1846-1900
Israels, Josef	1824-1911	Lockwood, Wilton	1861-1914
Jackson, Sir Thomas		Lucas, John Seymour	1849-1923
Graham	1835-1924	Lukeman, Henry Augustus	1871-1935
Jacque, Charles	1813-1894	Lutyens, Sir Edwin	
Jalabert, Charles Francois	1819-1901	Landseer	1869-1944
Jawlesky, Alexei Van	1864-1941	Macbeth, Robert Walker	1848-1910
John, Sir William		MacColl, Dugald	
Goscombe	1860-1952	Sutherland	1859-1948
Johnson, Eastman	1824-1906	Macculoch, Horatio	1805-1867
Jonkind, Johann Barthold	1819-1891	McEntee, Jervis	1828-1891
Jonsson Einar	1874-1954	McKim, Charles Follen	1847-1909
Jordan, Rudolf	1810-1887	Mackintosh, Charles	
Kandinsky, Vasily	1866-1944	Rennie	1868-1928
Keene, Charles Samuel	1823-1891	Maclise, Daniel	1806-1870
Keller, Albert Von	1844-1920	MacMannies, Frederick	
Kemp-Welch, Lucy		William	1863-1937
Elizabeth	1869-	MacNee, Sir Daniel	1806-1882
Khnopff, Fernand	1858-1921	MacNeil, Hermon Atkins	1866-1947
Kirkup, Seymore Stocker	1788-1880	MacTaggart, William	1835-1910
Klinger, Max	1857-1920	Macwhirter, John	1839-1911
Knaus, Ludwig	1829-1910	Madrazo Y Kunt, Don	
Knight, Daniel Ridgway	1845-1924	Frederico De	1815-1894
Knight, Harold	1874-1961	Magonigle, Harold Van	
Knowles, Sir James	1831-1908	Buren	1867-1935
Kupka, Frank	1871-1957	Maillol, Aristide Joseph	
Kyosai, Sho-Fu	1831-1889	Bonaventure	1861-1944
La Farge, John	1835-1910	Makart, Hans	1840-1884
Lalique, René	1860-1945	Manes, Josef	1820-1871
Lambeaux, Jef	1852-1908	Manet, Edouard	1832-1883
Lanchester, Henry		Manson, George	1850-1876
Vaughan	1863-1953	Marees, Hans Von	1837-1887
Landseer, Sir Edwin Henry	1802-1873	Marin, John	1870-
Laszlo, Sir Philip	1869-1937	Maris, Jacob	1837-1899
Lathrop, Francis	1849-1909	Maris, Matthiss	1839-1917
La Touche, Gaston	1854-1913	Maris, Willem	1843-1910
Lauder, Robert Scott	1803-1869	Marochetti, Carlo	1805-1867
Laurens, Jean Paul	1838-1921	Marquet, Albert	1875-1947
Lavery, Sir John	1856-1941	Marr, Carl	1859-1936
Lawson, Cecil Gordon	1851-1882	Marshall, William Calder	1813-1894
Lazlo De Lombos, Philip		Martin, Homer Dodge	1836-1897
Alexius	1869-1937	Martin, John	1789-1854
Lear, Edward	1812-1888	Matejko, Jan Alois	1838-1893
Leech, John	1817-1864	Matisse, Henri	1869-1954
Legros, Alphonse	1837-1911	Mauve, Anton	1838-1888
Lehmann, Rudolf	1819-1905	Mead, Larkin Goldsmith	1835-1910
Leibl, Wilhelm	1844-1900	Mead, William Rutherford	1846-1928
Leighton, Frederick		Meissonier, Jean Louis	
Leighton	1830-1896	Ernest	1815-1891

Melchers, Gari	1860-1932	Peale, Rembrandt	1778-1860
Menzel, Adolph Friedrich		Pearce, Charles Sprague	1851-1914
Erdmann-Von	1815-1905	Pearson, John	
Mercie, Marius Jean		Loughborough	1817-1897
Antonin	1845-1916	Pennell, Joseph	1860-1926
Mesdag, Hendrik Willem	1831-1915	Peploe, Samuel John	1871-1935
Meunier, Constantin	1831-1905	Perrett, Auguste	1874-1955
Millais, Sir John Everett	1829-1896	Pettie, John	1839-1893
Millet, Francis Davis	1846-1912	Piloty, Karl Von	1826-1886
Millet, Jean Francois	1814-1875	Pinwell, George John	1842-1875
Mondrian, Pieter Cornelis	1872-1944	Pissaro, Camille	1830-1903
Monet, Claude	1840-1926	Platt, Charles Adams	1861-1933
Monticelli, Adolphe Joseph		Playfair, William Henry	1789-1857
Thomas	1824-1856	Poelzig, Hans	1869-1936
Moore, Albert Joseph	1841-1893	Poole, Paul Falconer	1807-1879
Moore, Henry	1831-1895	Pope, John Russell	1874-1937
Moore, William	1790-1851	Portaels, Jean Francois	1818-1895
Moran, Edward	1829-1901	Post, George Browne	1837-1913
Moreau, Gustave	1826-1898	Powers, Hiram	1805-1873
Morel-Ladeuil, Leonard	1820-1888	Poynter, Sir Edward John	1836-1919
Morisot, Berthe Marie		Pradilla, Francisco	1848-1921
Pauline	1841-1895	Prinsep, Valentine	
Morris, William	1834-1896	Cameron	1838-1904
Morse, Samuel Finley		Proctor, Alexander	
Breese	1791-1872	Phimister	1862-1950
Moses, Anna Mary		Prout, Samuel	1783-1852
(Grandma)	1860-1961	Pugin, Augustus Welby	
Mosler, Henry	1841-1920	Nortmore	1812-1852
Motte, William De La	1775-1863	Purvitis, Vilhelms Karlis	1872-1945
Mount, William Sidney	1807-1868	Puvis De Chavannes	
Mowbray, Harry Siddons	1858-1928	Pierre Cecile	1824-1898
Muenier, Jules A.	1863-1934	Pyle, Howard	1853-1911
Mulready, William	1786-1863	Rackham, Arthur	1867-1939
Munch, Edvard	1863-1944	Raemaekers, Louis	1869-1956
Munkacsy, Michael	1846-1900	Rauch, Christien Daniel	1777-1857
Murphy, John Francis	1853-1921	Raven Hill, Leonard	1867-1942
Murray, Sir David	1849-1933	Redon, Odilon	1840-1916
Nesfield, William Eden	1835-1888	Regnault, Henri	1843-1871
Neuville, Alphonse		Reid, Sir George	1841-1913
Marie De	1836-1885	Reid, Robert	1862-1929
Nicholson, Sir William	1872-1949	Remington, Frederic	1861-1909
Nicol, Erskine	1825-1904	Renoir, Pierre Auguste	1841-1919
Niehaus, Charles Henry	1855-1935	Renwick, James	1818-1895
Nolde, Emil	1867-1956	Repin, Ilya Yefimovich	1844-1930
Ochtmann, Leonard	1854-1934	Rethel, Alfred	1816-1859
Orchardson, Sir William		Retzsch, Friedrich August	
Quiller	1832-1910	Moritz	1779-1857
Oudine, Eugene Andre	1810-1887	Richardson, Henry	
Overbeck, Johann		Hobson	1838-1886
Frederick	1789-1869	Richmond, George	1809-1896
Page, William	1811-1885	Richmond, Sir William	
Palmer, Samuel	1805-1881	Blake	1842-1921
Parsons, Alfred	1847-1920	Ricketts, Charles	1866-1931
Parsons, William Edward	1872-1939	Rietschel, Ernst	1804-1861
Partridge, Sir Bernard	1861-1945	Riviere, Briton	1840-1920
Partridge, William		Roberts, David	1796-1864
Ordway	1861-1930	Robinson, William Heath	1872-1944
Paton, Sir Joseph Noel	1821-1901	Rodin, Auguste	1840-1917
Paul, Bruno	1874-	Roerich, Nikolai	
Paxton, Sir Joseph	1801-1865	Constantinovich	1874-1947

Rogers, John	1829-1904	Strachan, Douglas	1875-1950
Rops, Felicien	1833-1898	Strang, William	1859-1921
Rossetti, Dante Gabriel	1828-1882	Street, George Edmund	1824-1881
Rothenstein, Sir William	1872-1945	Sturgis, Russell	1836-1909
Rouault, Georges	1871-1958	Sullivan, Louis Henri	1856-1924
Rousseau, Henri	1844-1910	Sully, Thomas	1783-1872
Rousseau, Pierre Etienne		Svabinsky, Max	1873-
Theodore	1812-1867	Szinye-Merse, Paul De	1845-1920
Rude, Francois	1784-1855	Taft, Lorado	1860-1936
Ryder, Albert Pinkham	1847-1917	Tanner, Henry Assawa	1859-1937
Sargent, John Singer	1856-1925	Tarbell, Edmond C.	1862-1938
Salisbury, Frank Owen	1874-1957	Tenniel, Sir John	1820-1914
Schadow, Friedrich		Thayer, Abbott Handerson	1849-1921
Wilhelm	1789-1862	Thoma, Hans	1839-1924
Scheffer, Ary	1795-1858	Thompson, Launt	1833-1934
Schilling, Johannes	1828-1910	Thornycroft, Sir William	
Schnorr Von Karolsfeld,		Hamo	1850-1925
Julius	1794-1872	Tiffany, Louis Comfort	1848-1933
Schreyer, Adolf	1828-1899	Tissot, James Joseph	
Schwartze, Teresz	1852-1918	Jacques	1836-1902
Schwind, Moritz Von	1804-1871	Tite, Sir William	1798-1873
Scott, Sir George Gilbert	1811-1878	Tonks, Henry	1862-1937
Seganti, Giovanni	1858-1899	Toulouse-Lautrec,	
Semper, Gottfried	1803-1873	Henri De	1864-1901
Serusier, Paul	1863-1927	Travies De Villers,	
Seurat, Georges	1859-1891	Charles Joseph	1804-1859
Severn, Joseph	1793-1879	Troubetzkoy, Amelie	
Shannon, Charles		Rives	1863-1945
Hazelwood	1863-1937	Troubetzkoy, Pierre	1864-1936
Shannon, Sir James		Troyon, Constant	1810-1865
Jebusa	1862-1923	Trubner, Wilhelm	1851-1917
Shaw, Richard Norman	1831-1912	Tryon, Dwight William	1849-1925
Shields, Frederick James	1833-1911	Tuke, Henry Scott	1858-1929
Short, Sir Frank Job	1857-1945	Turner, Joseph Mallord	
Sickert, Walter Richard	1860-1942	William	1775-1851
Signac, Paul	1863-1935	Tweed, John	1869-1933
Simmons, Edward		Valadon, Suzanne	1869-1938
Emerson	1852-1931	Vallotton, Felix	1865-1929
Simpson, Sir John	1858-1933	Vanderlyn, John	1776-1852
Sisley, Alfred	1840-1899	Van Der Stappen, Charles	1843-1910
Slevogt, Max	1868-1932	Van De Velde, Henri	1863-1957
Smillie, James David	1833-1909	Van Gogh, Vincent	1853-1890
Smirke, Sir Robert	1781-1867	Vedder, Elihu	1836-1923
Somerscales, Thomas		Veit, Philipp	1793-1877
Jacques	1842-1928	Verboeckhoven, Eugene	
Somov, Konstantin		Joseph	1798-1881
Andreevich	1869-	Vereshchagin, Vassili	
Sorolla Y Bastida, Joaquin	1863-1923	Vassilievich	1842-1904
Stanfield, William		Vernet, Emile Jean	
Clarkson	1794-1867	Horace	1789-1863
Stark, James	1794-1859	Vierge, Daniel	1851-1904
Steell, Sir John	1804-1891	Vigeland, Adolf Gustav	1869-1943
Steer, Philip Wilson	1860-1942	Vigne, Paul De	1843-1901
Steinle, Eduard	1810-1886	Villon, Jacques	1875-
Steinlen, Theophile		Vinton, Frederic Porter	1846-1911
Alexandre	1859-1923	Viollet Le Duc, Eugene	
Stevens, Alfred	1818-1875	Emmanuel	1814-1879
Stevens, Alfred	1828-1906	Vivin, Louis	1861-1936
Stillman, William James	1828-1901	Volk, Leonard Wells	1828-1895
Story, William Wetmore	1819-1895	Vonnoh, Robert William	1858-1933

Vorosmarty, Mihaly	1800-1855
Vuillard, Edward	1868-1940
Wainewright, Thomas Griffiths	1794-1852
Waldo, Samuel Lovett	1783-1861
Walker, Frederick	1840-1875
Walker, Henry Oliver	1843-1929
Walker, Horatio	1858-1938
Ward, Edward Matthew	1816-1879
Ward, John Quincy Adams	1830-1910
Warren, Whitney	1864-1943
Waterhouse, Alfred	1830-1905
Waterhouse, John William	1847-1917
Waterlow, Sir Ernst Albert	1850-1919
Watts, George Frederic	1817-1904
Wauters, Emile	1846-1933
Webb, Sir Aston	1849-1930
Webb, Philip Speakman	1831-1915
Weir, Robert Walter	1803-1889
Westmacott, Sir Richard	1775-1856
Weyr, Rudolf Von	1847-1914
Whistler, James Abbott McNeill	1834-1903
White, Stanford	1853-1906
Whymper, Edward	1840-1911
Wiertz, Anton Joseph	1806-1865
Willems, Florent Joseph Marie	1823-1905
Willette, Leon Adolphe	1857-1926
Willumsen, Jens Ferdinand	1863-1958
Winterhalter, Franz Xavier	1806-1873
Woolner, Thomas	1826-1892
Wright, Frank Lloyd	1869-1959
Wyant, Alexander	1836-1892
Wyspienski, Stanislaw	1869-1907
Yeames, William Frederick	1835-1918
Yeats, Jack Butler	1871-1957
Ziem, Felix Francois George	1821-1911
Zorn, Anders	1860-1920
Zuluago, Ignacio	1870-1945

COMPOSERS

Abt, Franz	1819-1885
Adam, Adolphe Charles	1803-1856
Albeniz, Isaac	1860-1909
Albert, Eugen Francis Charles D'	1864-1932
Arditi, Luigi	1822-1903
Arensky, Anton Stephanovich	1861-1906
Auber, Daniel Francois Eprit	1782-1871
Audran, Edmond	1842-1901
Bache, Francis Edward	1833-1858
Balakirev, Milly Aleivich	1836-1910
Balfe, Michael William	1808-1870
Bantock, Sir Granville	1868-1946
Bargiel, Woldemar	1828-1897
Barnby, Sir Joseph	1838-1896
Barnett, John	1802-1890
Barnett, John Francis	1837-1916
Bemberg, Herman	1861-
Bendl, Karel	1838-1897
Benedict, Sir Julius	1804-1885
Bennett, Sir William Sterndale	1816-1875
Benoit, Pierre Leonard Leopold	1834-1901
Beriot, Charles Auguste De	1802-1870
Berlioz, Hector	1803-1869
Bishop, Sir Henry Rowley	1786-1855
Bizet, Georges	1838-1875
Blumenthal, Jacob	1829-1908
Boelmann, Leon	1862-1897
Boito, Arriego	1842-1918
Borodin, Alexander Porfyrievich	1834-1887
Bottesini, Giovanni	1822-1889
Brahms, Johannes	1833-1897
Bruch, Max	1838-1920
Bruckner, Anton	1824-1896
Bruneau, Alfred	1857-1934
Buck, Dudley	1839-1909
Burleigh, Henry Thaker	1866-1949
Busoni, Ferruccio	1866-1924
Chabrier, Alexis Emmanuel	1841-1894
Chaminade, Cecile	1861-1944
Charpentier, Gustave	1860-1956
Chvala, Emanuel	1851-1924
Clay, Frederick	1838-1889
Coleridge-Taylor, Samuel	1875-1912
Cowen, Sir Frederick Hynam	1852-1935
Cornelius, Carl August Peter	1824-1874
Costa, Sir Michael	1810-1884
Cui, Cesar Antonovitch	1835-1918
Czerny, Karl	1791-1857
D'Albert, Eugen Francis Charles	1864-1932
Damrosch, Leopold	1832-1885
Dargomijsky, Alexander Sergeivich	1813-1869
David, Felicien	1810-1876
Davies, Sir Henry Walford	1869-1941

Debussy, Claude Achille	1862-1918	Herbert, Victor	1859-1924
De Koven, Reginald	1861-1920	Herve, Florimond Rounger	1825-1892
Delibes, Clement Philbert		Herz, Henri	1806-1888
Leo	1836-1891	Hiller, Ferdinand	1811-1885
Delius, Frederick	1863-1934	Holst, Gustave	1874-1934
Diabelli, Anton Antonio	1781-1858	Hubay, Geno De	1858-1937
D'Indy, Paul Marie		Hullah, John Pyke	1812-1884
Theodore	1851-1931	Humperdinck, Engelbert	1854-1921
Dopper, Cornelis	1870-1939	Jacques-Dalcroze, Emile	1865-1950
Doppler, Albert Franz	1821-1883	Janacek, Leos	1854-1928
Dreyschock, Alexander	1818-1869	Jarnefelt, Edvard Armas	1869-1958
Dubois, Francois Clement	1837-1924	Jensen, Adolf	1837-1897
Dukas, Paul	1865-1935	Joachim, Joseph	1831-1907
Dupark, Henri	1848-1933	Joncieres, Victorin	1839-1903
Dvorak, Antonin	1841-1904	Jongen, Joseph	1873-1953
Dykes, John Bacchus	1823-1876	Kajanus, Robert	1856-1933
Eitner, Robert	1832-1905	Kienzl, Wilhelm	1857-1941
Elgar, Sir Edward	1857-1934	Kjerulf, Holfdan	1815-1868
Elvey, Sir George Job	1816-1893	Kovarovic, Karel	1862-1920
Engel, Karl	1818-1882	Lacomb, Louis Trouvillon	1818-1884
Erlanger, Camille	1863-1919	Lalo, Edouard	1823-1892
Ernst, Heinrich Wilhelm	1814-1865	Lamond, Frederick	1868-1948
Faure, Gabriel	1845-1924	Lassen, Eduard	1830-1904
Fetis, Francois Joseph	1784-1871	Lecocq, Alexandre Charles	1832-1918
Fibich, Zdenko	1850-1900	Lehar, Franz	1870-1948
Finck, Heinrich		Lekeu, Guillaume	1870-1894
Theophilus	1854-1926	Lemmens, Nicolas Jacques	1823-1881
Flotow, Friedrich		Leoncavallo, Ruggiero	1858-1919
Freiherr Von	1812-1883	Liadov, Anatol	1855-1914
Foerster, Josef Bohuslav	1859-	Liszt, Franz	1811-1886
Foote, Arthur William	1853-1937	Loeffler, Charles Martin	1861-1935
Foster, Stephen Collins	1826-1864	Loewe, Johann Karl	
Franck, Cesar	1822-1890	Gottfried	1796-1869
Franz, Robert	1815-1892	Lortzing, Albert	1801-1851
Gade, Niels Vilhelm	1817-1890	Maccun, Hamish	1868-1916
Gatty, Nicholas Comyn	1874-1946	Macdowell, Edward	
German, Sir Edward	1862-1936	Alexander	1861-1908
Glazunov, Alexander		Macfarren, Sir George	
Constantinovich	1865-1936	Alexander	1813-1887
Glinka, Michael Ivanovich	1803-1857	Mackenzie, Sir Alexander	
Godard, Benjamin	1849-1895	Campbell	1847-1935
Godowsky, Leopold	1870-1938	Mahler, Gustav	1860-1911
Goldmark, Karl	1832-1915	Marschner, Heinrich	
Goss, Sir John	1800-1880	August	1795-1861
Gounod, Charles Francois	1818-1893	Mascagni, Pietro	1863-1945
Granados Y Campina,		Mason, Daniel Gregory	1873-1953
Enrique	1867-1916	Massenet, Jules Emile	
Gretchaninov, Alexander		Frederic	1842-1912
Tikhonovich	1864-1956	Mengelberg, Willem	1871-1951
Grieg, Edvard Hagerup	1843-1907	Merikanto, Oskar	1868-1924
Gung'l, Josef	1810-1889	Messager, Andre Charles	
Hadley, Henry Kimball	1871-1937	Prosper	1853-1929
Halevy, Jacques Francois		Meyebeer, Gialomo	1791-1864
Fromental	1799-1862	Monckton, Lionel	1861-1924
Handy, William		Monk, William Henry	1823-1889
Christopher	1873-1958	Moszkowski, Moritz	1854-1925
Hatton, John Liptrot	1809-1886	Mottl, Felix	1856-1911
Hauptmann, Moritz	1792-1868	Moussorgsky, Modest	
Heller, Stephen	1815-1888	Petrovich	1835-1881
Henselt, Adolf Von	1814-1889	Napravnik, Edward	1839-1915

Nathan, Isaac	1791-1864	Scriabin, Alexander	
Nevin, Ethelbert	1862-1901	Nicholaevich	1872-1915
Nielsen, Carl August	1865-1931	Sgambati, Giovanni	1843-1914
Novak, Viteslav	1870-1949	Sibelius, Johan Julius	1865-1958
Offenbach, Jacques	1819-1880	Sinding, Christian	1856-1941
Ouseley, Sir Frederick		Smetana, Bedrich	1824-1884
Arthur	1825-1889	Smyth, Dame Ethel Mary	1858-1944
Paderewski, Ignace Jan	1860-1941	Soderman, August Johan	1832-1876
Parker, Horatio William	1863-1919	Somervell, Sir Arthur	1863-1937
Parry, Sir Charles		Sousa, John Philip	1854-1932
Hubert Hastings	1848-1918	Spohr, Ludwig	1784-1859
Pearsall, Robert Lucas De	1795-1856	Spontini, Gasparo	
Pedrell, Felipe	1841-1922	Luigi Pacifico	1774-1851
Perosi, Lorenzo	1872-1956	Spottiswoode, Alicia Ann	
Pierson, Henry Hugo	1815-1873	Lady John	1811-1900
Planquette, Robert	1850-1903	Stanford, Sir Charles	
Ponchielli, Amilcare	1834-1886	Villiers	1852-1924
Puccini, Giacomo	1858-1924	Straus, Oscar	1870-1954
Rachmaninoff, Sergei		Strauss, Johann the	
Vassilievitch	1873-1943	Younger	1825-1899
Raff, Joseph Joachim	1822-1882	Strauss, Richard	1864-1949
Randegger, Alberto	1832-1911	Suk, Joseph	1875-1935
Ravel, Maurice	1875-1937	Sullivan, Sir Arthur	
Rebikov, Vladimir	1866-1920	Seymour	1842-1900
Reger, Max	1873-1916	Suppe, Franz Von	1820-1895
Reinecke, Carl Heinrich	1824-1910	Svendsen, Johan Severin	1840-1911
Rheinberger, Joseph		Taneiev, Sergius	1856-1915
Gabriel	1839-1901	Tcherepnin, Nicolai	1873-1945
Rimsky-Korsakov,		Thomas, Ambroise	1811-1896
Nikolai Andreivich	1844-1908	Thomas, Arthur Goring	1850-1892
Rockstro, William Smith	1823-1895	Thuille, Ludig	1861-1907
Roger-Ducasse, Jean		Tosti, Sir Francesco	
Jules Aimable	1873-1954	Paolo	1846-1916
Ronald, Sir Landon	1873-1938	Tovey, Sir Donald	
Rossini, Gioachino		Francis	1873-1940
Antonio	1792-1868	Tschaikovsky, Peter Ilyich	1840-1893
Roussel, Albert	1869-1937	Vaughan Williams, Ralph	1872-1958
Rubinstein, Anton	1829-1894	Verdi, Guiseppe Fortunino	
Saint-Saens, Charles		Francesco	1813-1901
Camille	1835-1921	Wagner, Wilhelm	
Satie, Erik Leslie	1866-1925	Richard	1813-1883
Scharwenka, Xavier	1850-1924	Waldteufel, Emil	1837-1915
Schonberg, Arnold	1874-1951	Wallace, William	1860-1940
Schubert, Franz	1808-1878	Wallace, William Vincent	1812-1865
Schumann, Clara		Weingartner, Felix	1863-1942
Josephine	1819-1896	Wesley, Samuel Sebastian	1810-1876
Schumann, Robert		Widor, Charles Marie	1845-1937
Alexander	1810-1856	Wolf, Hugo	1860-1903

S

1876 Bulgarian massacres.
1877 Russia declares war on Turkey.
     Roumania declared independent.
1878 Microphone invented.
1879 Tay Bridge destroyed.
     War in Zululand.
1880 Transvaal declared a republic.
1881 Battle of Majuba Hill.
     Peace arranged with Boers.
1882 Servia declared a kingdom.
1883 Royal College of Music opened.
     Phoenix Park murderers convicted.
1884 Fabian Society founded.
1885 Battle of Abu Klea
     Khartoum captured.
1891 Free education act passed in England.
1894 Japan declares war on China.
     Drevfus convicted of treason.
1896 Discovery of X-Rays.
1897 Turkey declares war on Greece.
1898 Peace between U.S. and Spain.
     Battle of Omdurman.
1899 Battle of Modder River
     Marconi experiments in wireless telegraphy.
1900 Boers attack Ladysmith.
     Relief of Mafeking.

PROMINENT PEOPLE

Baird, John Logie	1888-1946	Hitler, Adolf	1889-1945
Beaverbrook, Lord	1879-1964	Kitchener of Khartoum	1850-1916
Bevin, Ernest	1881-1951	Lessepes, Vicomte	
Bismarck, Leopold Von	1815-1898	Ferdinand de	1805-1894
Booth, General William	1829-1912	Lister, Lord	1827-1912
Caruso, Enrico	1873-1921	Lloyd George, David	1863-1945
Chaliapin, Fedor		Manning, Henry Edward,	
Ivanovich	1873-1938	Cardinal	1808-1892
Curie, Pierre	1859-1906	Marconi, Marchese	
Curie, Marie	1867-1934	Gulielmo	1874-1937
De Gaulle, Charles	1890-	Mussolini, Benito	1883-1945
Diaghilev, Sergei		Nobel, Alfred	1833-1896
Pavlovich	1872-1929	Pankhurst, Emmeline	1858-1928
Edison, Thomas, Alva	1847-1931	Pasteur, Louis	1822-1895
Einstein, Albert	1879-1955	Rasputin, Grigri	
Gandhi, Mahandas		Yefimovich	1871-1916
Karamchand	1869-1948	Rhodes, Cecil	1853-1902
Garibaldi, Giuseppe	1807-1882	Rontgen, Prof. Wilhelm	
		Konrad	1845-1923

EMPERORS OF CHINA (MANCHU (Ch'ing) DYNASTY)

Teh Tsung   1875-1908

POPES

Pius IX   1846-1878   Leo XIII   1878-1903

Macmahon, President, Marshal	1873-1879	Casimir-Perier, President Faure, President,	1894-1895
Grevy, President, Jules	1879-1887	Francois Felix	1895-1899
Carnot, President, Sadi	1887-1894	Loubet, President, Emile	1899-1906

ENGLAND, SOVEREIGNS

Victoria	1837-1901

SWEDEN, KINGS

Oscar II	1872-1907

RUSSIA, TSARS

Alexander II	1855-1881	Nicholas II	1894-1917
Alexander III	1881-1894		

SPAIN, SOVEREIGNS

Alfonso XII	1874-1885	Alfonso XIII	1886-1931

PORTUGAL, KINGS

Luiz I	1861-1889	Carlos I	1889-1908

U.S.A. PRESIDENTS

Grant, Ulysses	1869-1877	Cleveland, Grover	1885-1889
Hayes, Rutherford	1877-1881	Harrison, Benjamin	1889-1893
Garfield, James	1881-	Cleveland, Grover	
Arthur, Chester		(again)	1893-1897
(Vice P)	1881-1885	McKinley, William	1897-1901

PRUSSIA, KINGS

William I (Became Emperor of Germany 1871)	1861-1888

AUSTRIA, EMPERORS

Josef, Franz	1848-1916

NETHERLANDS, SOVEREIGNS

William III	1849-1890	Wilhelmina	1890-1948

BELGIUM KINGS

Leopold II	1865-1909

ITALY, KINGS

Emmanuel, Victor	1861-1878	Umberto I	1878-1900

GERMANY, EMPERORS

William I	1871-1888	William II	1888-1918

Aakjaer, Jeppe	1866-1930	Alcott, Louisa May	1832-1888
Aanrud, Hans	1863-1953	Alcover, Joan	1854-1926
Aansen, Ivar	1813-1896	Aldanova, Mark	
Abbott, Edwin Abbott	1838-1926	Alexandrovitch	1889-
Abbott, Evelyn	1843-1901	Alden, Isabella	1841-1930
Abbott, George	1899-	Alden, Joseph	1807-1885
Abbott, Jacob	1803-1879	Aldington, Richard	1892-1962
Abbott, Lyman	1835-1922	Aldrich, Thomas Bailey	1836-1907
Abbott, Wilbur Cortez	1869-1947	Aleardi, Aleardo	1812-1878
Abercrombie, Lascelles	1881-1938	Alecsandri, Vasile	1821-1890
Aberigh-Mackay, George		Alexander, Cecil Francis	1818-1895
Robert	1848-1881	Alexander, Samuel	1859-1938
About, Edmond Francois		Alexander, William	1826-1894
Valentin	1828-1885	Alger, Horatio	1834-1899
Ackerman, Louis		Alin, Oscar Josef	1846-1900
Victorine Choquet	1813-1890	Alington, Cyril Argentine	1872-
Acton, John Emerich		Allen, Charles Grant	
Edward Dolbey	1834-1902	Blairfindie	1848-1899
Adam, Juliette	1836-1936	Allen, James Lane	1849-1925
Adam, Paul	1862-1920	Allen, William Hervey	1889-1949
Adamic, Louis	1899-1951	Allibone, Samuel Austin	1816-1889
Adams, Andy	1859-1935	Allingham, William	1824-1889
Adams, Charles Follen	1842-1918	Allmers, Hermann	1821-1902
Adams, Henry Brooks	1838-1918	Alma Tadema, Sir	
Adams, James Truslow	1879-1949	Laurence	1836-1912
Adams, Oscar Fay	1855-1919	Alonso, Dameso	1898-
Adams, Samuel Hopkins	1871-1958	Alvaro, Corrado	1895-1956
Adams, William Taylor	1822-1897	Alvarez Quintero,	
Adamson, Robert	1852-1902	Joaquin	1873-1944
Addams, Jane	1860-1935	Alvarez Quintero,	
Ade, George	1866-1944	Serafin	1871-1938
Adickes, Erich	1866-1928	Amicis, Edmondo de	1846-1908
Adler, Alfred	1870-1937	Amiel, Henri Frederic	1821-1881
Ady, Endre	1877-1919	Ancona, Alessandro	1835-1914
Agate, James Evershed	1877-1947	Anderson, Maxwell	1888-1959
Agoult, Marie Catherine		Anderson, Sherwood	1876-1941
Sophie de Flavigny	1805-1876	Andrews, Charles	
Aguilo I Fuster, Marian	1825-1897	McLean	1863-1943
Aho Juhani	1861-1921	Andreyev, Leonid	
Aicard, Jean Francois		Nicolaevich	1871-1919
Victor	1848-1921	Andric, Ivo	1892-
Aide, Hamilton	1830-1906	Angell, Sir Norman	1874-
Aiken, Conrad Potter	1889-	Angellier, Auguste Jean	1848-1911
Aimard, Gustave	1818-1883	Angus, Marion	1866-1946
Ainger, Alfred	1837-1904	Anker-Larsen, Johannes	1874-1957
Ainsworth, William		Annunzio, Gabrielle D'	1863-1938
Harrison	1805-1882	Anstey, Francis	1856-1934
Aird, Thomas	1802-1876	Antokolski, Mark	
Aitken, Robert Ingersoll	1878-1949	Matveevich	1843-1902
Akhmatova, Arna		Anzengruber, Ludwig	1839-1889
(Gorenko)	1888-	Apollinnaire, Guillaume	1880-1918
Akins, Zoe	1886-1958	Arany, Janos	1817-1882
Aksakov, Ivan Sergelvich	1823-1886	Arbois De Juainville,	
Alain-Fournier, Henry	1886-1914	Marie Henri d'	1827-1910
Alarcon, Pedro Antonio	1833-1891	Archer, William	1856-1924
Alas, Leopoldo	1852-1901	Arcos, Rene	1881-
Albert, Eugen Francis		Arlen, Michael	1895-1956
Charles d'	1864-1932	Arnason, Jon	1819-1888
Albiker, Karl	1878-	Arneth, Alfred	1819-1897
Alcott, Amos Bronson	1799-1888	Arnold, Sir Edwin	1832-1904

Arnold, Matthew	1822-1888	Barbellion, W.N.P.	1889-1919
Arthur, Timothy Shay	1809-1885	Barbey D'Aurevilly, Jules	
Artzybashev, Mikhail		Amedee	1808-1889
Petrovich	1878-1927	Barbier, Henri Auguste	1805-1882
Asbjornsen, Peter		Barbier, Paul Jules	1825-1901
Christian	1812-1885	Barbusse, Henri	1873-1935
Asch, Sholem	1880-1957	Baring, Maurice	1874-1946
Ashbee, Charles Robert	1863-1942	Baring-Gould, Sabine	1834-1924
Ashe, Thomas	1836-1889	Barlow, Jane	1860-1917
Asnyk, Adam	1838-1897	Barnes, Harry Elmer	1889-
Atherton, Gertrude		Barnes, Margaret Ayer	1886-
Franklin	1857-1948	Barnes, William	1800-1886
Attlee, Clement Richard	1883-	Baroja, Pio	1872-1956
Aubanel, Theodore	1829-1886	Barr, Amelia Edith	1831-1919
Audoux, Marguerite	1880-1937	Barres, Maurice	1862-1923
Auerbach, Berthold	1812-1882	Barrie, Sir James	
Auersperg, Anton		Matthew	1860-1937
Alexander	1806-1876	Barriere, Theodore	1823-1877
Augier, Guillaume		Barrili, Antonio Giulio	1836-1908
Victor Emile	1820-1889	Barry, Philip	1896-1949
Aukrust, Olav Lom	1883-1929	Barthelemy, Saint-Hilaire	
Aulard, Francois Victor		Jules	1805-1895
Alphonse	1849-1928	Bascom, John	1827-1911
Austin, Alfred	1835-1913	Bashkirtsev, Maine	1860-1884
Austin, Mary Hunter	1869-1934	Bataille, Felix Henri	1872-1922
Autran, Joseph	1813-1877	Bates, Arlo	1850-1918
Avenarius, Richare		Bates, Katherine Lee	1859-1929
Heinrich Ludwig	1843-1896	Bateson, Mary	1865-1906
Axelrod, Pavel		Baudissin, Wolf Heinrich	1789-1878
Borriasovich	1850-1928	Bauer, Bruno	1809-1882
Ayala Y Herrera, Adelardo		Bauernfeld, Eduard Von	1802-1890
Lopez d'	1828-1879	Baumbach, Rudolf	1840-1905
Azorin, Jose Martinez		Bax, Ernest Belfort	1854-1926
Ruis	1874-	Bazin, Rene	1853-1932
Babbitt, Irving	1865-1933	Beard, Charles Austin	1874-1948
Babits, Mihaly	1883-1941	Beaverbrook, William	
Bacheller, Irving Addison	1859-1950	Maxwell Aitken	1879-1964
Bachelli, Riccardo	1891-	Becker, Carl L.	1873-1945
Bacon, Leonard	1802-1881	Becque, Henry Francois	1837-1899
Bagehot, Walter	1826-1877	Bede, Cuthbert	1827-1889
Bahr, Hermann	1863-1934	Bédier, Joseph	1864-1938
Bailey, Philip James	1816-1902	Beecher, Henry Ward	1813-1887
Bain, Alexander	1818-1903	Beerbohm, Sir Max	1872-1956
Baird, Henry Martin	1832-1906	Beets, Nikolaas	1814-1903
Baker, Sir Herbert	1862-1946	Behaine, Rene	1889-
Baker, Ray Stannard	1870-1946	Belasco, David	1854-1931
Balaguer, Victor	1824-1901	Beljame, Alexandre	1842-1906
Baldensperger, Fernand	1871-1958	Bell, John Jay	1871-1934
Baldini, Antonio	1889-	Bellamy, Edward	1850-1898
Ballantine, James	1808-1877	Belloc, Joseph Hilaire	
Ballantyne, Robert		Pierre	1870-1953
Michael	1825-1894	Belloc, Lowndes Marie	
Balmont, Constantine	1867-1943	Adelaide	1868-1947
Bancroft, George	1800-1891	Bemis, Samuel Flogg	1891-
Bancroft, Hubert Hoew	1832-1918	Benavente Y Martinez,	
Banerjee, Satyendranath	1897-	Jacinto	1866-1954
Bang, Herman Joachim	1858-1912	Benchley, Robert	1889-1954
Banning, Margaret Culkin	1891-	Benelli, Sem	1877-1949
Banville, Theodore		Benet, Stephen Vincent	1898-1943
Faullain De	1823-1891	Benjamin, Rene	1885-1948

Bennet, Enoch Arnold	1867-1931	Boisgobey, Fortune	
Benoa, Julien	1867-	Abraham, Du	1824-1891
Benson, Arthur		Bojer, Johan	1872-1959
Christopher	1862-1925	Boker, George Henry	1823-1890
Benson, Edward Frederic	1867-1940	Boldrewood, Rolf	1826-1915
Benson, Robert Hugh	1871-1914	Bonghi, Ruggero	1828-1895
Bentley, Edmund		Bonnard, Abel	1883-
Clerihew	1875-1956	Boothby, Guy Newell	1867-1905
Bercovici, Konrad	1881-	Bordeaux, Henri	1870-
Beresford, John Davys	1873-1947	Borrow, George Henry	1803-1881
Bergman, Bo Hjalmar	1869-	Bosanquet, Bernard	1848-1923
Bergman, Hjalmar		Bosboom, Toussaint, Anna	
Frederick Elgerus	1883-1931	Louisa Geertruida	1812-1886
Bergson, Henri	1859-1941	Bottomley, Gordon	1874-1948
Bernanos, Georges	1888-1948	Bouchor, Maurice	1855-1929
Bernard, Jean Jacques	1888-	Boucicault, Dion	1822-1890
Bernard, Tristan	1866-1947	Bourget, Paul Charles	
Barnhardi, Friedrich Von	1849-1930	Joseph	1852-1935
Bernstein, Henry	1876-1953	Bowen, Elizabeth	1889-
Bertrand, Louis	1866-1941	Bowen, Francis	1811-1890
Besant, Annie	1847-1933	Bowers, Claude G.	1878-
Besant, Sir Walter	1836-1901	Boyd, Andrew Kennedy	
Betti, Ugo	1892-1954	Hutchinson	1825-1899
Bialik, Hayim Nachman	1873-1934	Boyd, Ernest	1887-1946
Biedermann, Friedrich		Boyesen, Hjalmar	1848-1895
Karl	1812-1901	Boylesve, Rene	1867-1926
Bierce, Ambrose	1842-1916	Braddon, Mary Elizabeth	1837-1915
Biggers, Earl Derr	1884-1933	Bradford, Gameliel	1863-1932
Billinger, Richard	1893-	Bradley, Andrew Cecil	1851-1935
Binding, Rudolf George	1867-1938	Bradley, Edward	1827-1889
Binyon, Laurence	1869-1943	Bradley, Francis Herbert	1846-1924
Birrell, Augustine	1850-1933	Braithwaite, William	
Bishop, Isabella	1831-1904	Stanley Beaumont	1878-
Bjornson, Bjornstjerne	1832-1910	Brailsford, Henry Noel	1873-1958
Black, William	1841-1898	Braga, Theophilo	1843-1924
Blackie, John Stuart	1809-1895	Bramah, Ernest	1867-1942
Blackmore, Richard		Brandes, Gorge Maurice	
Doddridge	1825-1900	Cohen	1842-1927
Blackwood, Algernon		Braun, Lily	1865-1916
Henry	1869-1951	Brazil, Angela	1868-1947
Blanc, Jean Joseph		Breasted, James Henry	1865-1935
Charles Louis	1811-1882	Brecht, Berthold Eugen	
Blavatsky, Helena Petrova	1831-1891	Friedrich	1898-1956
Blind, Mathilde	1847-1896	Bremond, Henri	1865-1933
Blixen, Karen, Baroness	1885-1962	Brentano, Franz	1838-1917
Bloch, Jean Richard	1884-1947	Breton, Andre	1896-
Blok, Alexander	1880-1921	Bridie, James	1888-1951
Blok, Petrus Johannes	1855-1932	Bridges, Robert Seymour	1844-1930
Blondel, Maurice	1861-1939	Brierly, Benjamin	1825-1896
Blood, Benjamin Paul	1832-1919	Brieux, Eugene	1858-1832
Blouet, Paul	1848-1903	Brittain, Vera	1893-
Bloy, Leon	1846-1917	Broad, Charles Dunbar	1887-
Blunck, Hans Friedrich	1888-	Brod, Max	1884-
Blunden, Edmund Charles	1896-	Brokmeyer, Henry	
Blunt, Wilfrid Scawen	1840-1922	Conrad	1828-1906
Boas, Franz	1858-1942	Bromfield, Louis	1896-1956
Bodenheim, Maxwell	1892-1959	Brooke, Rupert Chawner	1887-1915
Bodenstedt, Friedrich		Brooke, Stopford	
Martin, Von	1819-1892	Augustus	1832-1916
		Brooks, Phillips	1835-1894

Brooks, Van Wyek	1886-1963	Calvet, Jean	1874-
Broughton, Rhoda	1840-1920	Calvo, Carlos	1824-1906
Broun, Heywood	1888-1939	Cammaerts, Emile	1878-1953
Brown, Alice	1857-1948	Campoamor Y Campoosorio,	
Brown, George Douglas	1869-1902	Raymon De	1819-1901
Brown, Peter Hume	1850-1918	Canth, Minna	1844-1897
Brown, Thomas Edward	1830-1897	Cantu, Cesare	1804-1895
Browning, Oscar	1837-1923	Capek, Karel	1890-1938
Browning, Robert	1812-1889	Capern, Edward	1819-1894
Brownson, Orestes		Capuana, Luigi	1839-1915
Augustus	1803-1876	Capus, Alfred	1858-1922
Brugsch, Heinrich Karl	1827-1894	Caraglia, Joan	1852-1912
Brunner, Henry	1840-1915	Carco, Francis	1886-1958
Bryant, William Cullen	1794-1878	Carducci, Giosue	1835-1907
Bryce, Lloyd Stephens	1851-1917	Carleton, Will	1845-1912
Bryussov, Valery		Carlen, Emilia Smith	
Yakovlevitch	1873-1924	Flygare	1807-1892
Buber, Martin	1878-	Carman, Bliss	1861-1929
Buchan, John	1875-1940	Carlyle, Thomas	1795-1881
Buchanan, Robert		Carmen, Sylva	1843-1916
Williams	1841-1901	Carnap, Rudolf	1891-
Buchner, Ludwig	1824-1899	Carnegie, Andrew	1835-1918
Bucholtz, Johannes	1882-1940	Caro, Emile Marie	1826-1887
Buck, Pearl Sydenstricker	1892-	Carossa, Hans	1878-1956
Buckle, George Earle	1854-1935	Carpenter, Edward	1844-1929
Buckstone, John Baldwin	1802-1879	Carr, Edward Hallett	1892-
Bull, Olav Jacob Martin		Carr, Joseph William	
Luther	1883-1933	Comyns	1849-1916
Bullett, Gerald	1893-1958	Carriere, Moritz	1817-1895
Bunin, Ivan Alexeyevich	1870-1953	Carton, R. C.	1853-1928
Burckhardt, Jakob	1818-1897	Cary, Joyce	1888-1957
Burgess, John Bagnold	1830-1897	Cassirer, Ernst	1874-1945
Burke, Kenneth	1897-	Castello, Branco Camillo	1825-1890
Burke, Thomas	1886-1945	Castro, Eugenio De	1869-1944
Burnand, Frederick		Cather, Willa Sibert	1876-1947
Gustavus	1842-1885	Cavalcaselle, Giovanni	
Burnett, William Riley	1899-	Battista	1820-1897
Burnett, Frances Eliza		Cazalis, Henri	1840-1909
Hodgson	1849-1924	Cecchi, Emilio	1884-
Burroughs, Edgar Rice	1875-1950	Champfleury	1821-1889
Burroughs, John	1837-1921	Chantavoine, Henri	1850-1918
Burrows, Montague	1819-1905	Chapman, John Jay	1862-1933
Burton, John Hill	1809-1881	Chardonne, Jacques	1884-
Burton, Sir Richard		Charles, Elizabeth	1828-1896
Francis	1821-1890	Chase, Mary Ellen	1887-
Bury, John Bagnell	1861-1927	Chase, Stuart	1888-
Butler, Nicholas Murray	1862-1947	Chatrian, Alexandre	
Butler, Samuel	1835-1902	(Erkman, Chatrian)	1826-1890
Buysse, Cyriez	1859-1932	Chatterji Bankim, Chandra	1838-1894
Byron, Henry James	1834-1884	Chausson, Ernest	1855-1899
Caballero, Fernan	1796-1877	Chekhov, Anton Pavlovich	1860-1904
Cabell, James Branch	1879-1958	Cherbuliez, Charles	
Cable, George Washington	1844-1925	Victor	1829-1899
Caine, Sir Thomas Henry		Chernyshevsky, Nikolay	
Hall	1853-1931	Gavrilovich	1828-1889
Caird, Edward	1835-1908	Cheruel, Pierre Adolphe	1809-1891
Caird, John	1820-1898	Chesney, Charles	
Calderon, George	1868-1915	Cornwallis	1826-1876
Calderwood, Henry	1830-1897	Chesterton, Gilbert Keith	1874-1936
Calvert, George Henry	1803-1889	Chevalier, Gabriel	1895-

Chiarelli, Luigi	1894-1947	Couperus, Louis	1863-1923
Chiesa, Francesco	1871-	Courteline, Georges	1860-1929
Child, Francis James	1825-1896	Courthope, William John	1842-1917
Chopin, Kate	1851-1904	Coward, Noel	1899-
Christie, Agatha Mary		Cox, Sir George William	1827-1902
Clarissa	1891-	Craddock, Charles Egbert	1850-1922
Church, Richard	1893-	Craig, Edward Gordon	1872-
Churchill, Winston	1871-1947	Craigie, Pearl Mary	
Churchill, Sir Winston		Teresa	1867-1906
Spencer	1874-1965	Craik, Dinah Maria	1826-1887
Cibrario, Luigi Count	1802-1870	Crane, Harold Hart	1899-1932
Cladel, Leon	1835-1892	Crane, Stephen	1871-1900
Claretie, Jules Arsene		Craven, Pauline	1808-1891
Arnaud	1840-1913	Crawford, Francis Marion	1854-1909
Clark, William George	1821-1878	Creasy, Sir Edward	
Clarke, Charles Cowden	1787-1877	Shepherd	1812-1878
Clarke, Marcus Andrew		Creighton, Mandell	1843-1901
Hislop	1846-1881	Cremazie, Octave	1822-1879
Claudel, Paul	1868-1955	Cremer, Jakobus Jan	1827-1880
Claussen, Sophus Niels		Cremieux, Benjamin	1888-1944
Christen	1865-1931	Croce, Benedetto	1866-1952
Clemencau, George	1841-1929	Crockett, Samuel	
Clifford, William Kingdon	1845-1879	Rutherford	1860-1914
Clowes, Sir William Laird	1856-1905	Cronin, Archibald Joseph	1896-
Cobb, Irwin Shrewsbury	1876-1944	Crothers, Rachel	1878-
Cobbe, Frances Power	1822-1904	Crozier, John Beattie	1849-1921
Cocteau, Jean	1891-1964	Csengery, Antal	1822-1880
Cohan, George Michael	1878-1942	Csiky, Gregor	1842-1891
Cole, Sir Henry	1808-1882	Cullum, George	
Colet, Louise	1810-1876	Washington	1809-1892
Colette, Sidonie Gabrielle	1873-1954	Cummings, Edward Estlin	1894-
Collett, Jacobine Camilla	1813-1895	Cumont, Franz Valery	
Collier, John Payne	1789-1883	Marie	1868-1947
Collingwood, Robin		Cunninghame, Graham	
George	1899-1943	Robert Bontine	1852-1936
Collins, William Wilkie	1824-1889	Curel, Francois	
Colomb, Philip Howard	1831-1899	Vicomte De	1854-1928
Colum, Padraic	1881-	Curtis, George William	1824-1892
Connelly, Marcus (Marc)		Curtius, Ernst	1814-1896
Cook	1890-	Curtius, Georg	1820-1885
Conscience, Hendrik	1812-1883	Curwood, James Oliver	1878-1927
Conrad, Joseph	1857-1924	Cust, Sir Lionel Henry	1859-1929
Conrad, Noel	1899-	Dahn, Julius Sophus Felix	1834-1912
Conway, Hugh	1847-1885	Dalov, Jules	1838-1902
Conway, Moncure Daniel	1832-1907	D'Alviella, Count Goblet	1846-1925
Cook, Sir Edward Dutton	1829-1883	Daly, Augustin	1838-1899
Cook, Sir Edward Tyas	1857-1919	Dana, Richard Henry	1815-1882
Cooke, John Esten	1830-1886	D'Annunzio, Gabriele	1863-1938
Cooke, Rose Terry	1837-1892	Dantas, Julio	1876-
Coolidge, Susan	1835-1905	Dareste De La Chavanne,	
Coolus, Romaine	1868-1952	Cleophas	1820-1882
Coppee, Francois	1842-1908	Darmesteter, James	1849-1894
Coppee, Henry	1821-1895	Darwin, Charles Robert	1809-1882
Cooper, Alfred Duff		Daubler, Theodore	1876-1934
(1st Viscount Norwich)	1890-1954	Daudet, Alphonse	1840-1897
Corelli, Marie	1855-1924	Daudet, Ernest	1837-1921
Cossa, Pietro	1830-1881	Daudet, Leon	1867-1942
Costa, Joaquim	1846-1911	Davidson, John	1857-1909
Coster, Charles Theodore		Davidson, Thomas	1840-1900
Henri De	1827-1879	Davies, Hubert Henry	1869-1917

Davies, William Henry	1871-1940	**Dodgson,** Charles Lutwidge	
Davis, Henry William		(Lewis Carrol)	1832-1898
Carless	1874-1928	**Dollinger,** Johann Joseph	
Davis, Richard Harding	1864-1916	Ignaz Von	1799-1890
Debosis, Adolfo	1863-1924	**Domett,** Alfred	1811-1887
Decelles, Alfred Duclos	1843-1925	**Donnay,** Charles Maurice	1859-1945
De Court, Frans	1834-1878	**Doolittle,** Hilda	1886-1961
Deeping, George Warwick	1877-1950	**Doran,** John	1807-1878
De Gaulle, Charles André		**Dos Passos,** John Roderigo	1896-
Joseph Maurice	1890-	**Dostoievsky,** Fyodor	
De Geer, Louis Gerhard		Mikhaylovich	1821-1881
Baron	1818-1896	**Doughty,** Sir Arthur	
Dehmel, Richard	1863-1920	George	1860-1936
Dekker, Edward Douwes	1820-1887	**Doughty,** Charles	
Delafield, E. M.	1890-1943	Montegu	1843-1926
De La Mare, Walter John	1873-1956	**Douglas,** Lord Alfred	1870-1945
Deland, Margaretta Wade	1857-1945	**Douglas,** Norman	1868-1952
De La Roche, Mazo	1885-1961	**Douglas,** Sir William	
Delbruck, Hans	1848-1929	Fettes	1822-1891
Deledda, Grazia	1875-1936	**Dove,** Alfred	1844-1916
Delisle, Leopold Victor	1826-1910	**Dowden,** Edward	1843-1913
Dell, Ethel Mary	1881-1939	**Dowson,** Ernest	1867-1900
Demongeot, Jacques		**Doyle,** Sir Arthur Conan	1859-1930
Claude	1808-1894	**Dolye,** Sir Francis	
De Morgan, William		Hastings Charles	1810-1888
Frend	1839-1917	**Drachmann,** Holger Henrik	
Denifle, Heinrich Seuse	1844-1905	Herboldt	1846-1908
Dennery, Adolphe		**Drake,** Friedrich	1805-1882
Philippe	1811-1899	**Dragomirov,** Michael	
Dent, John Charles	1841-1887	Ivanovich	1830-1905
De Quincey, Thomas	1785-1859	**Draper,** William	1811-1882
Dereme, Tristan	1889-1941	**Dreiser,** Theodore	1871-1945
Deroulede, Paul	1846-1914	**Drews,** Arthur	1865-1935
De Tabley, John Byrne		**Driesch,** Hans Adolf	
Leicester Warren	1835-1895	Eduard	1867-1943
Deussen, Paul	1845-1919	**Drinkwater,** John	1882-1937
Devere, Aubrey Thomas	1814-1902	**Drobisch,** Moritz Wilhelm	1802-1896
Dewey, John	1859-1952	**Droysen,** Johann Gustav	1808-1884
Dexter, Henry Martyn	1821-1890	**Drummond,** Henry	1851-1897
Diaz, Daniel Vazquez	1882-	**Duboc,** Julius	1829-1903
Dicey, Edward	1832-1911	**Dubois,** William Edward	
Dickinson, Emily	1830-1886	Burghardt	1868-
Dickinson, Goldsworthy		**Du Bos,** Charles	1882-1939
Lowes	1862-1932	**Du Camp,** Maxine	1822-1894
Dieren, Bernard Van	1884-1936	**Ducasse,** Pierre Emmanuel	
Dierx, Leon	1838-1912	Albert	1813-1893
Digby, Kenelm Henry	1800-1880	**Duclauz,** Agnes Mary	
Dilthey, Wilhelm	1833-1911	Frances	1857-1944
Dimitrov-Maistora,		**Duff,** Sir Mountstuart	
Vladimar	1882-	Elphinstone Grant	1829-1906
Dingelstedt, Franz Von	1814-1881	**Duhamel,** George	1884-1966
Dionne, Narcisse Eutrope	1848-1917	**Duhring,** Eugen Karl	1833-1921
Disreali, Benjamin	1804-1881	**Dumas,** Alexandre (fils)	1824-1895
Dixon, Richard Watson	1833-1900	**Du Maurier,** George Louis	
Dixon, William Hepworth	1821-1879	Palmella Busson	1834-1896
Dobree, Bonamy	1891-	**Dummler,** Ernst Ludwig	1830-1902
Dobson, Henry Austin	1840-1921	**Dunbar,** Paul Laurence	1872-1906
Dodge, Mary	1838-1905	**Duncker,** Maximilian	
Dodge, Theodore Aynault	1842-1909	Wolfgang	1811-1886
		Dunne, John William	1875-1949

Dunsany, Edward John	1878-1957
Durkheim, Emile	1858-1917
Duruy, Jean Victor	1811-1894
Duun, Olav	1876-1939
Ebers, George Moritz	1837-1898
Ebert, Karl Egon	1801-1882
Ebner-Eschenbach, Marie	1830-1916
Eca De Queiroz, Jose Maria	1843-1900
Echegaram Y Ezaguire, José	1833-1916
Eddy, Mary Baker Glover	1821-1910
Edgren-Lffeler, Anne Charlotte	1849-1892
Edschmid, Kasimir	1890-
Edwards, Amelia	1831-1892
Eeden, Frederick Willem Van	1860-1932
Egan, Maurice Francois	1852-1924
Egge, Peter Andreas	1869-
Eggleston, Edward	1837-1902
Ehrenburg, Ilya	1891-
Ehrenfels, Christian Frieherr, Von	1859-1932
Einstein, Albert	1879-1955
Eisler, Rudolf	1873-1926
Eisner, Kurt	1867-1919
Eliot, Sir Charles Norton Edgcumbe	1864-1931
Eliot George (Marian Evans)	1819-1880
Eliot, Thomas Stearns (T.S.)	1888-1965
Ellis, Alexander John	1814-1890
Ellis, Henry Havelock	1859-1939
Elton, Godfrey 1st Baron	1892-
Elton, Oliver	1861-1945
Eluard, Paul	1895-1952
Emerson, Ralph Waldo	1803-1882
Eminescu, Mihail	1849-1889
Engels, Friedrich	1820-1895
English, Thomas Dunn	1819-1902
Erckmann, Emile (Erckman-Chatrian)	1822-1899
Erdmann, Benno	1851-1921
Erdmann, Johann Eduard	1805-1892
Ernle, Rowland Edmond Prothero	1851-1937
Ernst, Paul	1866-1933
Ertz, Susan	1894-
Ervine, St. John Greer	1883-
Esenin, Sergius	1895-1925
Esher, Reginald Baliol Brett	1852-1930
Esquiros, Henri Francois Alphonse	1812-1876
Estaunie, Edouard	1862-1942
Eucken, Rudolf Christoph	1846-1926
Evans, George Essex	1863-1909
Ewing, Juliana Horatia Orr	1841-1885
Fabre, Ferdinand	1830-1898
Faesi, Robert	1883-
Fagan, James Bernard	1873-1933
Fagniez, Gustav Charles	1842-1927
Faguet, Emile	1847-1916
Falkberget, Johan Petter	1879-
Falke, Gustave	1853-1916
Falke, Johann Friedrich Gottlieb	1823-1876
Fallada, Hans	1893-1947
Falloux, Frederic Alfred Pierre	1811-1886
Falls, Cyril Bentham	1888-
Farina, Salvatore	1846-1918
Farjeon, Benjamin Leopold	1838-1903
Farjeon, Eleanor	1881-1965
Farjeon, John Jefferson	1883-1958
Farnol, John Jeffrey	1877-1952
Farrar, Frederick William	1831-1903
Farrere, Claude	1876-1957
Farson, James Negley	1890-1960
Faulkner, William	1897-1962
Fazy, Henri	1842-1920
Fechner, Gustav Theodore	1801-1887
Federer, Heinrich	1866-1928
Fenn, George Maniville	1831-1909
Ferber, Edna	1887-
Ferguson, Sir Samuel	1810-1886
Fergusson, James	1808-1886
Ferrari, Giuseppe	1812-1876
Ferrari, Paolo	1822-1889
Ferrero, Guglielmo	1871-1942
Ferri, Luigi	1826-1895
Ferrier, Paul	1843-1920
Feuchtwanger, Lion	1889-1958
Feuillet, Octave	1821-1890
Feval, Paul Henri Corentin	1817-1887
Fichte, Immanuel Hermann Von	1796-1879
Field, Eugene	1850-1895
Fields, James Thomas	1817-1881
Figuier, Louis	1819-1894
Filon, Augustin	1841-1916
Firbank, Ronald	1886-1926
Firth, Sir Charles Harding	1857-1936
Fisher, Ernst Kuno Berthold	1824-1907
Fisher, Herbert Albert Laurens	1865-1940
Fisher, Vardis	1895-
Fiske, John	1842-1901
Fitch, William Clyde	1865-1909
Fitzgerald, Edward	1809-1883

Fitzgerald, Percy			**Fullerton**, Lady Georgiana	
Hetherington	1834-1925		Charlotte	1812-1885
Fitzgerald, Francis Scott	1896-1940		**Fustel De Coulanges**,	
Flach, Geoffroi Jacques	1846-1919		Numa Denis	1830-1889
Flammarion, Nicolas			**Fyffe**, Charles Alan	1845-1892
Camille	1842-1925		**Gachard**, Louis Prosper	1800-1885
Flaubert, Gustave	1821-1880		**Gairdner**, James	1828-1912
Flecker, James Elroy	1884-1915		**Gale**, Zona	1874-1938
Flers, Robert De La Motte			**Galsworthy**, John	1867-1933
Ango	1872-1927		**Ganesh Datta Shastri**,	
Fletcher, John Gould	1886-1950		Shri Jagadguru	1861-1940
Flint, Frank Stewart	1885-		**Ganivet**, Angel	1865-1898
Fogazzaro, Antonio	1842-1911		**Garborg**, Arne Evensen	1851-1924
Fontaine, Theodor	1819-1898		**Gardiner**, Samuel Rawson	1829-1902
Forbes, Rosita	1893-		**Garland**, Hamlin	1860-1940
Ford, Paul Leicester	1865-1902		**Garnett**, David	1892-
Forester, Cecil Scott	1899-		**Garnett**, Edward	1868-1937
Forsell, Hans Ludvig	1843-1901		**Garnett**, Richard	1835-1906
Forster, E. M.			**Garshin**, Vsevolod	
(Edward Morgan)	1879-		Mikhailovich	1855-1888
Forster, John	1812-1876		**Gautier**, Leon	1832-1897
Fort, Paul	1872-1960		**Geddes**, Patrick	1854-1932
Fortescue, Sir John			**Geibel**, Emanuel	1815-1884
William	1859-1933		**Geijer**, Eric Gustav	1783-1877
Fortlage, Karl	1806-1881		**Gentile**, Giovanni	1875-1944
Fouillee, Alfred Jules			**George**, Henry	1839-1897
Emile	1838-1912		**George** Stefan	1868-1933
Fowler, Frank George	1871-1918		**Gerstacker**, Friedrich	1816-1877
Fowler, Henry Watson	1858-1933		**Gervinus**, George	
France, Anatole	1844-1924		Gottfried	1805-1871
Frank, Leonhard	1882-		**Gezelle**, Guido	1830-1899
Frank, Waldo David	1889-		**Ghika**, Helena	1829-1888
Frankau, Gilbert	1884-1953		**Giacometti**, Paolo	1816-1882
Frankl, Ludwig August	1810-1894		**Giacosa**, Guiseppe	1847-1906
Franzos, Karl Emil	1848-1904		**Gibbings**, Robert John	1889-1958
Fraser, Alexander			**Gibbs**, Sir Philip	1877-
Campbell	1819-1914		**Gibson**, Wilfred Wilson	1878-
Frazer, Sir James George	1854-1941		**Gibson**, William Hamilton	1850-1896
Frechette, Louis Honore	1839-1908		**Gide**, Andre Paul	
Frederic, Harold	1856-1896		Guillaume	1869-1951
Freeman, Edward			**Giesebrecht**, Wilhelm Von	1814-1889
Augustus	1823-1892		**Gilbert**, Sir John Thomas	1829-1898
Freeman, John	1880-1929		**Gilbert**, William	1804-1889
Freeman, Mary Eleanor			**Gilbert**, Sir William	
Wilkins	1852-1930		Schwenk	1836-1911
Freiligrath, Ferdinand	1810-1876		**Gilder**, Richard Watson	1844-1909
Frenssen, Gustav	1863-1945		**Gilgik**, Iwan	1858-1924
Freud, Sigmund	1856-1939		**Gill**, Erik	1882-1940
Frey, Adolf	1855-1920		**Gillette**, William Hooker	1853-1937
Freytag, Gustav	1816-1895		**Gillies**, William George	1898-
Fried, Alfred Hermann	1864-1921		**Gilman**, Harold	1878-1919
Friedjung, Heinrich	1851-1920		**Gilson**, Etienne	1884-
Froding, Gustav	1860-1911		**Gindely**, Anton	1829-1892
Frohschammer, Jakob	1821-1893		**Giner De Los Rios**,	
Frost, Robert	1875-1963		Francisco	1840-1915
Frothingham, Octavius			**Giraudoux**, Hippolyte	
Brooks	1822-1895		Jean	1882-1944
Froude, James Anthony	1818-1894		**Gissing**, George Robert	1857-1903
Fryxell, Anders	1795-1881		**Gjellerup**, Karl	1857-1919
Fucini, Renato	1843-1921		**Glasgow**, Ellen	1874-1945

Glaspell, Susan	1882-1948	Gumilev, Nikolai	
Glassbrenner, Adolf	1810-1876	Stepanovich	1886-1921
Gleig, George Robert	1796-1888	Gunn, Neil Miller	1891-
Glinka, Fedor		Gurdjieff, George	
Nikolayevich	1788-1880	Ivanovitch	1868-1949
Glyn, Elinor	1864-1943	Guthrie, Thomas Anstey	1856-1934
Golding, Louis	1895-1958	Gutschmid, Alfred	1835-1887
Goldschmidt, Aaron Meier	1819-1887	Gutzkow, Karl Ferdinand	1811-1878
Gollancz, Victor	1893-	Guyau, Jean Marie	1854-1888
Gomperez, Theodor	1832-1912	Gyp	1849-1932
Goncharov, Ivan		Habberton, John	1842-1921
Alexandrovich	1812-1891	Hacklander, Friedrich	
Goncourt De, Edmond	1822-1896	Wilhelm Von	1816-1877
Gooch, George Peabody	1873-	Haggard, Sir Henry Rider	1856-1925
Gordon, Leon	1831-1892	Hahn-Hahn, Ida	1805-1880
Gorky, Maxim	1868-1936	Hake, Thomas Gordon	1809-1895
Gorst, Harold	1868-1950	Haldane, Elizabeth	
Gorter, Herman	1864-1933	Sanderson	1862-1937
Gosse, Sir Edmund	1849-1928	Haldane, Richard Burdon	
Gottschall, Rudolf Von	1823-1908	Haldane	1856-1928
Gould, John	1804-1881	Hale, Edward Everett	1822-1909
Gould, Nathaniel	1857-1919	Hale, Sarah Josepha	1788-1879
Gourmont, Remy De	1858-1915	Halevy, Daniel	1872-1962
Grahame, Kenneth	1859-1922	Halevy, Elie	1870-1937
Grand, Sarah	1862-1943	Halevy, Leon	1802-1883
Grant, James	1822-1887	Halevy, Ludovic	1834-1908
Granville-Barker,		Hall, Anna Maria	1800-1881
Harley Granville	1877-1946	Hall, Marguerite	
Gratz, Heinrich	1817-1891	Radclyffe	1886-1943
Graves, Alfred Percival	1846-1931	Hall, Samuel Carter	1800-1889
Graves, Robert Ranke	1895-	Hall, William Edward	1835-1894
Green, John Richard	1837-1883	Halliday, Andrew	1830-1877
Green, Julian	1900-	Hamerton, Philip Gilbert	1834-1894
Green, Mary Ann		Hamley, Sir Edward	
Everett	1818-1895	Bruce	1824-1893
Green, Thomas Hill	1836-1882	Hammerstein, Oscar	1895-1960
Greene, George		Hammond, John	
Washington	1811-1883	Lawrence Lebreton	1872-1949
Greg, William Rathbone	1809-1881	Hamp, Pierre	1876-
Gregorovius, Ferdinand	1821-1891	Hamsun, Knut	1859-1952
Gregory, Isabella Augusta	1852-1832	Handel-Mazzetti, Enrica	1871-1962
Grenfell, Julian	1888-1915	Hannay, James Owen	1865-1950
Greville, Henry	1842-1902	Hanotaux, Albert Auguste	
Grey, Zane	1872-1939	Gabriel	1853-1944
Grigorovich, Dmitri		Hansson, Ola	1860-1925
Vaslievich	1822-1900	Hardy, Thomas	1840-1928
Groome, Francis Hindes	1851-1902	Hare, Augustus John	
Grossmith, George	1847-1912	Cuthbert	1834-1903
Grub, George	1812-1892	Harland, Henry	1861-1905
Grundy, Sydney	1848-1914	Harraden, Beatrice	1864-1936
Grunewald, Isaak	1889-1946	Harris, Frank	1856-1931
Gubernatis, Angelo De	1840-1913	Harris, Joel Chandler	1848-1908
Guedalla, Phillip	1889-1944	Harrison, Frederic	1831-1923
Guerin, Charles	1873-1907	Hart, Albert Bushnell	1854-1942
Guerrini, Olinda	1845-1916	Harte, Francis Bret	1836-1902
Guest, Edgar Albert	1881-1959	Hartley, Leslie Poles	1895-
Guest, Edwin	1800-1880	Hartmann, Karl Robert	
Guimera, Angel	1849-1924	Eduard Von	1842-1906
Guitry, Sacha	1885-1957	Hartmann, Nicolai	1882-1950

Hartzenbusch, Juan Eugenio	1806-1880
Harvey, Frederick William	1888-
Hasenclever, Walker	1890-1940
Hauptmann, Gerhart	1862-1946
Haureau, Barthelemy	1812-1896
Haverfield, Francis John	1860-1919
Havet, Julien	1853-1893
Hay, Ian	1876-1952
Hay, John	1838-1905
Haym, Rudolf	1821-1901
Hayward, Abraham	1801-1884
Hazard, Rowland Gibson	1801-1888
Hecht, Ben	1894-
Heckel, Erich	1883-
Heer, Jakob Christoph	1859-1925
Heiberg, Gunnar Edward Rode	1857-1929
Heidegger, Martin	1889-
Heidenstam, Verner Von	1859-1940
Heijermans, Hermann	1864-1924
Helmholtz, Hermann Ludwig Ferdinand Von	1821-1894
Hemingway, Ernest	1898-1961
Henderson, William James	1855-1937
Henley, William Ernest	1849-1903
Henry, O.	1862-1910
Henty, George Alfred	1832-1902
Herbert, Allan Patrick	1890-
Herculano De Carvalho, E Araujo Alexandre	1810-1877
Herczeg, Ferenc	1863-
Heredia, Jose Maria De	1842-1905
Hergesheimer, Joseph	1880-1954
Hermant, Abel	1862-1950
Hernandez, Jose	1854-1886
Herne, Jame A.	1840-1901
Herrick, Robert	1868-1938
Hervieu, Paul	1857-1915
Hesse, Herman	1877-1962
Hewlett, Maurice Henry	1861-1923
Heyse, Paul Johann Ludwig Von	1830-1914
Hichens, Robert Smythe	1864-1950
Higginson, Thomas Wentworth	1823-1911
Hill, George Birbeck Norman	1835-1903
Hillebrand, Karl	1829-1884
Hilton, James	1900-1954
Himly, Louis-Auguste	1823-1906
Hippius, Zinaida	1869-1945
Hitler, Adolf	1889-1945
Hobhouse, Leonard Trelawney	1864-1929
Hocking, Silas Kitto	1850-1935
Hodgkin, Thomas	1831-1913
Hodgson, John Evan	1831-1895
Hodgson, Ralph	1871-1962
Hodgson, Shadworth Holloway	1832-1912
Hoetzsh, Otto	1876-1946
Hofer, Karl	1878-1955
Hoffding, Harald	1843-1931
Hoffmann, Heinrich	1809-1894
Hofmannsthal, Hugo Von	1874-1929
Hogben, Lancelot	1895-
Holl, Karl	1866-1926
Holland, Josiah Gilbert	1819-1881
Holmes, Oliver Wendell	1809-1894
Holst, Hermann Eduard Von	1841-1904
Holtby, Winifred	1898-1935
Holtei, Karl Eduard Von	1798-1880
Holz, Arno	1863-1929
Hope, Anthony	1863-1933
Hopfen, Hans Von	1835-1904
Hopkins, Gerard Manley	1844-1889
Horne, Richard Henry	1803-1884
Hornung, Ernest William	1866-1921
Hosmer, James Kendall	1834-1927
Hostrup, Jews Christian	1818-1892
Houghton, Richard Monckton Milnes	1809-1885
Houghton, William Stanley	1881-1913
Housman, Alfred Edward	1859-1936
Housman, Laurence	1865-1959
Houssaye, Arsene	1815-1896
Houssaye, Henry	1848-1911
Howard, Sidney Coe	1891-1939
Howe, Julia Ward	1819-1910
Howells, Herbert	1892-
Howells, William Dean	1837-1920
Howitt, Mary	1799-1888
Howitt, William	1792-1879
Hubbard, Elbert	1856-1915
Huch, Ricarda	1864-1947
Hudson, William Henry	1841-1922
Huggenberger, Alfred	1867-
Hughes, Clovis	1851-1907
Hughes, Thomas	1822-1896
Hugo, Victor Marie	1802-1885
Hulme, Thomas Ernest	1883-1917
Hume, Fergus	1859-1932
Hutton, Arthur Wollaston	1848-1912
Hutton, Richard Holt	1826-1897
Huxley, Aldous Leonard	1894-1963
Huxley, Sir Julien Sorell	1887-
Huxley, Thomas Henry	1825-1895
Huysmans, Joris Karl	1848-1907
Hyde, Douglas	1860-1949
Hyne, Charles John Cutliffe Wright	1865-1944
Ibanez, Vincent Blasco	1867-1928
Ibsen, Henrick Johan	1828-1906
Ihne, Wilhelm	1821-1902
Ilg, Paul	1876-
Inge, William Ralph	1860-1954

Ingelow, Jean	1820-1897	Kahn, Gustave	1859-1936
Ingleby, Clement		Kaiser, Georg	1878-1945
Manfried	1823-1886	Karr, Alphonse	1808-1890
Ingraham, Prentice	1843-1904	Kate, Jaeds Lodewykten	1819-1884
Innes, Arthur Donald	1863-1938	Kastner, Erich	1899-
Iqbal, Sir Mohammed	1875-1938	Kaufman, George Simon	1889-1961
Isaacs, Jorge	1837-1895	Kaye-Smith, Sheila	1887-1956
Ivanov, Vyacheslav		Keightley, Thomas	1789-1872
Ivanovich	1866-1949	Kellermann, Bernhard	1879-1951
Jacks, Laurence Pearsall	1860-1955	Keller, Gottfried	1819-1890
Jackson, Frederick John		Kendall, Henry Clarence	1841-1882
Foakes	1855-1941	Kenealy, Edward Vaughan	
Jackson, Helen Maria	1831-1885	Hyde	1819-1880
Jacob, Naomi Ellington	1889-1964	Kennedy, Margaret	1896-
Jacob, Violet	1863-1946	Kervyn De Lettenhove,	
Jacobs, William Wymark	1863-1943	Joseph	1817-1891
Jacobsen, Jens Peter	1847-1885	Key, Ellen	1849-1926
James, Henry	1843-1916	Keyserling, Hermann	1880-1946
James, Montague Rhodes	1862-1936	Kielland, Alexander	1849-1906
James, William	1842-1910	Kilmer, Joyce	1886-1918
Jameson, Storm	1897-	Kinck, Hans Ernst	1865-1926
Jammes, Francis	1868-1938	Kinglake, Alexander	
Jane, Frederick Thomas	1870-1916	William	1809-1891
Janssen, Johannes	1829-1891	Kingsley, Henry	1830-1876
Jaspers, Karl	1883-	Kingston, William Henry	
Jebavy, Vaclav	1868-1929	Giles	1814-1880
Jebb, Sir Richard		Kinkel, Johann Gottfried	1815-1882
Claverhouse	1841-1905	Kipling, Rudyard	1865-1936
Jefferies, Richard	1848-1887	Klabund	1891-1928
Jeffers, John Robinson	1887-1962	Klaczko, Julian	1825-1906
Jensen, Johannes Vilhelm	1873-1950	Knox, Edmund George	
Jensen, Wilhelm	1837-1911	Valpy	1881-
Jerome, Jerome Klapka	1859-1927	Koch, Ludwig	1881-
Jesse, Fryn Tennyson	1889-1958	Kolcsey, Ferencz	1790-1888
Jewett, Sarah Orne	1849-1909	Korolenko, Vladimir	
Jewsbury, Geraldine		Galaktionovich	1853-1921
Endsor	1812-1880	Korzybski, Alfred Habdank	
Jimenez, Juan Ramon	1881-1958	Skarbek	1879-1950
Joad, Cyril Edwin		Kraszewski, Joseph	
Mitchinson	1891-1953	Ignatius	1812-1887
Johnson, James Weldon	1871-1938	Kraus, Karl	1874-1936
Johnson, Lionel Pigot	1867-1902	Krehbiel, Henry Edward	1854-1923
Joinville, Francois		Kretzer, Marx	1854-1941
Fernand D'Orleans	1818-1900	Kropotkin, Peter	
Jokai, Maurus	1825-1904	Alexeivich	1842-1921
Jones, Henry	1831-1899	Ku, Hung-Ming	1856-1928
Jones, Henry Arthur	1851-1929	Kulpe, Oswald	1868-1915
Jordan, Wilhelm	1819-1904	Kuprin, Alexander	
Jorga, Nicholas	1871-1940	Ivanovich	1870-1938
Jorgensen, Johannes	1866-1951	Labiche, Euegene Marin	1815-1888
Joyce, James	1882-1941	Lacaita, Sir James	1813-1895
Judson, Edward Zane		Ladd, George Trumbull	1842-1921
Carroll	1823-1886	Laforgue, Jules	1860-1887
Jung, Carl Gustav	1875-1964	Lagerlof, Selma	1858-1940
Junqueiro, Abilio Guena	1850-1923	Lagerkvist, Par	1891-
Jusserand, Jean Adrien		Laing, Samuel	1810-1897
Antoine Jules	1855-1932	Laird, John	1887-1946
Kafka, Franz	1883-1924	Lane, Edward William	1801-1876
Kagawa, Toyohiko	1888-1960	Lane-Poole, Reginald	1857-1939
		Lane-Poole, Stanley	1854-1931

Lanfrey, Pierre	1828-1877	Liebrecht, Felix	1812-1890
Lang, Andrew	1844-1912	Liliencron, Detlev Von	1844-1909
Lanier, Sidney	1842-1881	Lind-Af-Hageby, Emelie	
Lapidoth-Swarth, Helene	1859-1941	Augusta Louisa	1878-
Laprade, Pierre Marin		Lindau, Paul	1839-1919
Victor Richard De	1812-1883	Lindau, Rudolf	1829-1910
Larbaud, Valery	1881-1957	Lindo, Mark Prager	1819-1879
Lardner, Ring W.	1885-1933	Lindsay, Nicholas Vachel	1879-1931
Laski, Harold Joseph	1893-1950	Linklater, Eric	1899-
Laube, Heinrich	1806-1884	Lin, Yutang	1895-
Lauff, Joseph	1855-1933	Lippincott, Sara Jane	
Laurent, Francios	1810-1887	Clarke	1823-1904
Lavedan, Henri Leon		Lissauer, Ernst	1882-1937
Emile	1859-1940	Littlefiel, Walter	1867-1948
Laver, James	1899-	Littre, Maximilien Paul	
Lavissee, Ernest	1842-1922	Emile	1801-1881
Lawless, Emily	1845-1913	Ljunggren, Gustaf Haken	
Lawrence David Herbert	1885-1930	Jordan	1823-1905
Lawrence, George Alfred	1827-1876	Locke, William John	1863-1930
Lawrence, Thomas		Locker-Lampson, Frederick	1821-1895
Edward	1888-1935	Lodge, Henry Cabot	1850-1924
Layard, Sir Austen		London, John Griffith	
Henry	1817-1894	(Jack)	1876-1916
Lazarus, Emma	1849-1887	Longfellow, Henry	
Lazarus, Moritz	1824-1903	Wadsworth	1807-1882
Lea, Henry Charles	1825-1909	Lönnrot, Elias	1802-1884
Leacock, Stephen Butler	1869-1944	Lonsdale, Frederick	1881-1954
Lecky, William Edward		Lorca, Federige, Garcia	1899-1936
Hartpole	1838-1903	Lossing, Benson John	1813-1891
Leconte De Lisle, Charles		Losski, Nikolai	
Marie Rene	1818-1894	Onufreivich	1870-
Lee, Sir Sidney	1859-1926	Loti, Pierre	1850-1923
Le Gallienne, Richard	1866-1947	Lotze, Rudolf Hermann	1817-1881
Legouve, Gabriel Jean		Louys, Pierre	1870-1925
Baptist Ernest Wilfred	1807-1903	Lowell, Amy	1874-1925
Leland, Charles Godfrey	1824-1903	Lowell, James Russell	1819-1891
Lemaitre, Jules	1853-1914	Lubbock, Percy	1879-
Le Moine, James		Lubke, Wilhelm	1826-1893
MacPherson	1825-1912	Lucas, Edward Verrall	1868-1938
Lemonnier, Antoine		Lucas, Frank Lawrence	1894-
Louis Camile	1844-1913	Luchaire, Achille	1846-1908
Lenin, Vladimir Iliych		Lucka, Emil	1877-1941
Ulyanov	1870-1924	Ludwig, Emil	1861-1948
Lenormand, Henri-Rene	1882-1951	Lu Hsun	1881-1936
Leo, Heinrich	1799-1878	Lummis, Charles Fletcher	1859-1928
Le Queux, William		Lunacharsky, Anatoly	
Tufnell	1864-1927	Vasilievich	1875-1933
Leskov, Nikolai		Lund, Troels Frederick	1840-1921
Semenovich	1831-1895	Lyall, Edna	1857-1903
Levertin, Oscar Ivan	1862-1906	Lynd, Robert	1879-1949
Levy-Bruhl, Lucien	1857-1939	Lytton, Edward Robert	
Lewald, Fanny	1811-1889	Bulwer-Lytton	1831-1891
Lewes, George Henry	1817-1878	Maartens, Maarten	1858-1915
Lewis, Clive Staples	1898-1963	Macaulay, Rose	1889-1958
Lewis, Sinclair	1885-1951	MacCarthy, Denis	
Lewis, Wyndham	1884-1957	Florence	1817-1882
Lhote, Andre	1885-	MacCarthy, Sir Desmond	1878-1952
Lie, Jonas Lauritz		M'Carthy, Justin	1830-1912
Edemil	1833-1908	McCord, Louise Susanna	
		Cheves	1810-1879

McDiarmid, Hugh	1892-	Martineau, James	1805-1900
MacDonald, George	1824-1905	Martinez, Gregorio	1881-1947
MacGowan, Kenneth	1888-	Martini, Ferdinando	1841-1928
MacGregor, John	1825-1892	Marx, Karl Heinrich	1818-1883
Mach, Ernst	1838-1916	Masefield, John	1878-
Machado, Antonio	1875-1939	Mason, Alfred Edward	
Machar, Jan Svatopluk	1864-1942	Woodley	1865-1948
Mackay, Charles	1814-1889	Mason, Walt	1862-1939
Mackaye, Percy	1875-	Massey, Gerald	1828-1907
Mackaye, Steele	1842-1894	Masson, David	1822-1907
Mackenzie, Edward		Masson, Frederic	1847-1923
Montague Compton	1883-	Masters, Edgar Lee	1869-1950
MacLeish, Archibald	1892-	Matthews, Brander	1852-1929
M'cMaster, John Bach	1852-1932	Maugham, William	
MacNeill, John Gordon		Somerset	1874-1965
Swift	1849-1926	Maupassant, Henri Rene	
M'Cosh, James	1811-1894	Albert Guy de	1850-1893
M'cTaggart, John		Mauriac, Francois	1885-
M'cTaggart Ellis	1866-1925	Maurois, Andre	1885-
Madariaga, Salvador De	1866-	Maurras, Charles	1868-1952
Maeterlinck, Maurice	1862-1949	Mayakovsky, Vladimir	1894-1930
Magny, Claude Drigon	1797-1897	Mayhew, Henry	1812-1887
Mahan, Alfred Thayer	1840-1914	Medina, Jose Toribio	1852-1930
Maine, Sir Henry James		Mee, Arthur	1875-1943
Sumner	1822-1888	Mehring, Franz	1846-1919
Maironis	1862-1932	Meilhac, Henri	1831-1897
Maitland, Edward	1824-1897	Melville, Herman	1819-1891
Maitland, Frederic		Menard, Louis Nicholas	1822-1901
William	1850-1906	Mendes, Catulle	1841-1909
Major, Richard Henry	1818-1891	Menendez y Pelayo,	
Malet, Lucas	1852-1931	Marcelino	1856-1912
Mallarme, Stephane	1842-1898	Merezhkovsky, Dmitri	
Malleson, George Bruce	1825-1898	Sergeievich	1865-1941
Mallock, William Hurrell	1849-1923	Meredith, George	1828-1909
Maning, Frederick		Merivale, Charles	1808-1893
Edward	1812-1883	Merrick, Leonard	1864-1939
Mann, Heinrich	1871-1950	Mesonero Romanos,	
Mann, Thomas	1875-1955	Ramon De	1803-1882
Mansfield, Katharine	1888-1923	Meurice, Paul	1818-1905
Mao-Tun	1896-	Mew, Charlotte	1870-1928
Marcel, Gabriel	1889-	Meyer, Conrad Ferdinand	1825-1898
Marguerite, Paul	1860-1918	Meyer, Eduard	1855-1930
Marguerite, Victor	1866-1942	Meynell, Alice	1849-1922
Marinetti, Filippo		Mignet, Francois Auguste	
Tommaso	1876-1944	Marie	1796-1884
Maritain, Jacques	1882-	Millay, Edna St. Vincent	1892-1950
Markham, Edwin	1852-1940	Miller, Henry	1891-
Marquand, John Phillip	1893-1960	Miller, Joaquin	1841-1913
Marquardt, Joachim	1812-1882	Milne, Alan Alexander	1882-1956
Marquis, Donald Robert		Milyukov, Paul	
Perry	1878-1937	Nikolayevich	1859-1942
Marradi, Giovanni	1852-1922	Mirbeau, Octave Henri	
Marryat, Florence	1838-1899	Marie	1850-1917
Marston, John Westland	1819-1890	Mistral, Frederic	1830-1914
Marston, Philip Bourke	1850-1887	Mitchell, Donald Grant	1822-1908
Martin Du Gard, Roger	1881-	Mitchell, Margaret	1900-1949
Martin, Henri	1810-1883	Mitchison, Naomi	
Martin, Sir Theodore	1816-1909	Margaret	1897-
Martin, Violet Florence	1862-1915	Moeran, Edward James	1895-1950
Martineau, Harriet	1802-1876	Molesworth, Mary Louisa	1839-1921

Molesworth, William
Nassau — 1816-1890
Molnar, Ferenc — 1878-1952
Mommsen, Theodor — 1817-1903
Monkhouse, William
Cosmo — 1840-1901
Monnier, Marc — 1829-1885
Monod, Gabriel — 1844-1912
Monroe, Harriet — 1860-1936
Montague, Charles Edward — 1867-1928
Montherlant, Henri
Millon de — 1896-
Montufar, Lorenzo — 1823-1898
Moody, William Vaughan — 1869-1910
Moore, George — 1852-1933
Moore, Marianne Craig — 1887-
Morand, Paul — 1889-
More, Paul Elmer — 1864-1937
Moreas, Jean — 1856-1910
Morgan, Charles — 1894-1958
Morley, Christopher
Darlington — 1890-1957
Morley, Henry — 1822-1894
Morley, John Morley — 1838-1923
Morris, Sir Lewis — 1833-1907
Morris, William — 1834-1896
Morrison, Arthur — 1863-1945
Morton, Henry Vollam — 1892-
Morton, John Maddison — 1811-1891
Motley, John Lothrop — 1814-1877
Mottram, Ralph Hale — 1883-
Moulton, Louise Chandler — 1835-1908
Muir, Edwin — 1887-1959
Muir, John — 1838-1914
Muirhead, John Henry — 1855-1940
Munro, Hector Hugh
(Saki) — 1870-1916
Munsterberg, Hugo — 1863-1916
Munthe, Axel — 1857-1949
Murray, Gilbert — 1866-1957
Murry, John Middleton — 1889-1957
Myers, Frederick William
Henry — 1843-1901
Nabokov, Vladimir — 1899-
Naden, Constance
Caroline Woodhill — 1858-1889
Naidu, Sarojini — 1879-1949
Namier, Sir Lewis
Bernstein — 1888-1960
Nazor, Vladimir — 1876-1949
Neal, John — 1793-1876
Nehru, Jawaharlal — 1889-1964
Nekrasov, Nikolai
Alexeyevich — 1821-1877
Neruda, Jan — 1834-1891
Nettleship, Richard Lewis — 1846-1892
Newbolt, Sir Henry John — 1862-1938
Newman, Francis William — 1805-1897
Newman, John Henry
(Cardinal) — 1801-1890

T

Newton, Eric — 1893-
Nexo, Martin Anderson — 1869-1954
Nichol, John — 1833-1894
Nichols, Robert Malise
Bowyer — 1893-1944
Nicholson, Meredith — 1866-1947
Nicoll, Maurice — 1884-1953
Nicolson, Sir Harold
George — 1886-
Nietzshe, Friedrich
Wilhelm — 1844-1900
Nitzsch, Karl Wilhelm — 1818-1880
Noailles, Anna Elizabeth
Comptesse De — 1876-1933
Noailles, Paul Duke of — 1802-1885
Noel, Roden Berkeley
Wriothesleu — 1834-1894
Nordau, Max Simon — 1848-1923
Norris, Frank — 1870-1902
Norris, Kathleen — 1880-
Norris, William Edward — 1847-1925
Norton, Caroline Elizabeth
Sarah — 1808-1877
Norton, Charles Eliot — 1827-1908
Nouy, Pierre Lecompte du — 1883-1947
Noyes, Alfred — 1880-1958
Nunez De Arce, Gaspar — 1834-1903
O'Casey, Sean — 1884-1964
O'Faolain, Sean — 1900-
O'Flaherty, Liam — 1897-
O'Grady Standish James — 1846-1928
Ohnet, Georges — 1848-1918
Oliphant, Laurence — 1829-1888
Oliphant, Margaret
Oliphant — 1828-1897
Oliveira, Martins Joaquim
Pedro De — 1845-1894
Oman, Sir Charles
William Chadwick — 1860-1946
O'Neill, Eugene Gladstone — 1888-1953
Oppenheim, Edward
Phillips — 1866-1946
Opzoomer, Cornelius
William — 1821-1892
Orczy, Baroness Emmuska — 1865-1947
Orzeszkowa, Eliza — 1842-1910
Osbourne, Lloyd — 1868-1947
O'Shaughnessy, Arthur
William Edgar — 1844-1880
Ostrovsky, Alexander
Nikolaevich — 1823-1886
Ouida — 1839-1908
Ouspensky, P. D. — -1947
Owen, Wilfred — 1893-1918
Page, Thomas Nelson — 1853-1922
Page, Walter Hines — 1855-1918
Pain, Barry Eric Odell — 1865-1928
Palacio, Valdes Armando — 1853-1938
Palacky, Frantisek — 1798-1876
Palamas, Kostes — 1859-1943

Paleologue, Maurice	
Georges	1859-1944
Palfrey, John Gorham	1796-1881
Palgrave, Sir Francis	1788-1861
Palgrave, Francis Turner	1824-1897
Paludan-Muller, Frederik	1809-1876
Panzini, Alfredo	1863-1939
Paoli, Cesare	1840-1902
Papini, Giovanni	1881-1956
Pardo Bazan, Emilia	1851-1921
Pares, Sir Bernard	1867-1949
Paris, Gaston	1839-1903
Parker, Dorothy	1893-
Parker, Sir Gilbert	1862-1932
Parkman, Francis	1823-1893
Parton, James	1822-1891
Partridge, Eric	
Honeywood	1894-
Pascoli, Giovanni	1855-1912
Pasternak, Boris	
Leonidovich	1890-1960
Pater, Walter Horatio	1839-1894
Paterson, Andrew Barton	
("Banjo")	1864-1941
Patmore, Coventry Kersey	
Bighton	1823-1896
Pattison, Mark	1813-1884
Paul, Charles Kiegan	1828-1902
Pauli, Reinhold	1823-1882
Paulsen, Friedrich	1846-1908
Payn, James	1830-1898
Paz Soldan, Mariano	
Felipe	1821-1886
Peabody, Andrew Preston	1811-1893
Peabody, Josephine	
Preston	1874-1922
Peacock, Thomas Love	1785-1866
Pearse, Patrick Henry	1879-1916
Pearson, Hesketh	1887-1964
Peesemsky, Alexey	
Feofilactovich	1820-1881
Peguy, Charles	1873-1914
Peirce, Charles Sanders	1839-1914
Pelham, Henry Francis	1846-1907
Pellico, Silvo	1788-1854
Pereda, Jose Maria De	1833-1906
Perez De Ayala, Ramon	1881-1962
Perez Galdos, Benito	1845-1920
Perry, Bliss	1860-1945
Pertz, Georg Heinrich	1795-1876
Petersen, Nis	1897-1943
Pfleiderer, Edmund	1842-1902
Phillips, Stephen	1868-1915
Phillpotts, Eden	1862-1960
Pinero, Sir Arthur Wing	1855-1934
Pilnyak, Boris	1894-1938
Pirandello, Luigi	1867-1936
Pirenne, Henry	1862-1935
Pitter, Ruth	1897-
Planche, James Robinson	1796-1880

Plekhanov, Georgy	
Valentinovich	1857-1918
Plieksans, Jan	1865-1929
Pollard, Alfred Frederick	1869-1948
Pontoppidan, Henrik	1857-1943
Poole, William Frederick	1821-1894
Porter, Gene Stratton	1868-1924
Porter, Katherine Anne	1894-
Porter, Noah	1811-1892
Porto-Riche, Georges De	1849-1930
Post, Melville Davisson	1871-1930
Potter, Beatrix	1866-1943
Potter, Stephen	1900-
Potthast, August	1824-1898
Pound, Ezra	1885-
Powell, Frederick York	1850-1904
Powys, John Cowper	1872-1963
Powys, Llewelyn	1884-1939
Prantl, Karl Von	1820-1888
Prati, Giovanni	1815-1884
Prel, Karl	1839-1899
Prescott, Harriet	
Elizabeth	1835-1921
Prevost, Eugene Marcel	1862-1941
Pribram, Alfred Francis	1859-1942
Priestly, John Boynton	1894-
Proust, Marcel	1871-1922
Prus, Boleslaw	1847-1912
Prutz, Hans	1843-1929
Przybyszewski, Stanislaw	1868-1927
Psichari, Ernest	1883-1914
Purnell, Thomas	1834-1889
Pusey, Edward Bouverie	1800-1882
Quental, Anthero De	1842-1891
Quicherat, Jules Etienne	
Joseph	1814-1882
Quiller-Couch, Sir Arthur	
Thomas	1863-1944
Quintero, Joaquin Alvarez	1873-1944
Quintero, Serafin Alvarez	1871-1938
Radhakrishnan,	
Sir Sarvepalli	1888-
Ragabe, Alexandros Rizos	1810-1892
Raleigh, Sir Walter	1861-1922
Rambaud, Alfred Nicolas	1842-1905
Ramuz, Charles Ferdinand	1878-1947
Ranc, Arthur	1831-1908
Randall, James Ryder	1839-1908
Rands, William Brighty	1823-1882
Ranke, Leopold Von	1795-1886
Ransome, Arthur Mitchell	1884-
Rashdall, Hastings	1858-1924
Rasmussen, Knud Johan	
Victor	1879-1933
Ravaisson-Mollien, Jean	
Gaspard Felix	1813-1900
Rawlinson, George	1812-1902
Read, Sir Herbert	1893-
Reade, Charles	1814-1884
Realf, Richard	1834-1878

Reboux, Paul	1877-1963
Reclus, Jean Jacques Elisée	1830-1905
Regnier, Henri Francois Joseph De	1864-1936
Reichenbach, Hans	1891-1953
Reid, Thomas Mayne	1818-1883
Reinach, Joseph	1856-1921
Remarque, Erich Maria	1898-
Remizov, Alexei	1877-1957
Renan, Ernest	1823-1892
Rennell, James Rennell Rodd, 1st Baron	1858-1941
Renouvier, Charles Bernard	1815-1903
Reuter, Gabriele	1859-1941
Reymont, Wladyslaw Stanislaw	1868-1925
Reynolds, Stephen	1881-1919
Rice, Elmer	1892-
Rice, James	1843-1882
Richards, Frank	1875-1961
Richardson, Dorothy Miller	1873-1957
Richardson, Henry Handel	1870-1946
Richepin, Jean	1849-1926
Ridge, William Pett	1857-1930
Ridgway, Robert	1850-1929
Riisager, Knudage	1897-
Riley, James Whitcomb	1849-1916
Rilke, Rainer Maria	1875-1926
Rimbaud, Jean Arthur	1854-1891
Ritchie, Anne Isabella Lady	1837-1919
Rivière, Jacques	1886-1925
Roberts, Sir Charles George Douglas	1860-1943
Roberts, Morley	1857-1942
Robinson, Edwin Arlington	1869-1935
Robinson, Lennox	1886-1958
Rod, Edouard	1857-1910
Rodo, Jose Enrique	1872-1917
Roe, Edward Payson	1838-1888
Rogers, Randolph	1825-1892
Rohmer, Sax	1886-1959
Rolland, Romain	1866-1944
Rolleston, Thomas William Hazen	1857-1920
Rolvaag, Ole Edvart	1876-1931
Romains, Jules	1885-
Roosevelt, Anna Eleanor	1884-1962
Roosevelt, Theodore	1858-1919
Rose, John Holland	1855-1942
Rosegger, Peter	1843-1918
Rosenkranz, Karl	1805-1879
Rosmini-Serbati, Antonio	1797-1855
Rosny, Joseph Henri	1856-1940
Rosny, Séraphin Justin François	1859-1948

Ross, Janet Anne	1842-1927
Rossetti, Dante Gabriel	1828-1882
Rossetti, Christina Georgina	1830-1894
Rossetti, William Michael	1829-1919
Rostand, Edmond	1869-1918
Roumanille, Joseph	1818-1891
Royce, Josiah	1855-1916
Rozanov, Vasili Vasilievich	1856-1919
Ruffini, Giovanni Domenico	1807-1881
Ruge, Arnold	1802-1880
Runeberg, Johan Ludvig	1804-1877
Runyon, Damon	1884-1946
Ruskin, John	1819-1900
Russell, Bertrand Arthur William	1872-
Russell, George William	1867-1935
Rutherford, Mark	1831-1913
Rydberg, Abraham Viktor	1828-1895
Ryle, Gilbert	1900-
Sabatier, Paul	1858-1928
Sabatini, Rafael	1875-1950
Sackville-West, Victoria Mary	1892-1962
Sadleir, Michael	1888-1957
Saint-Exupery, Antoine De	1900-1944
Saintsbury, George Edward Bateman	1845-1933
Saint-John, Perse	1887-
Sala, George Augustin Henry	1828-1895
Salten, Felix	1869-1945
Saltykov, Michael Evgrafovich	1826-1889
Salvemini, Gaetano	1873-
Samain, Albert Victor	1858-1900
Sand, George (Dudevant)	1804-1876
Sanday, William	1843-1920
Sandburg, Carl	1878-
Sandeau, Leonard Sylvain Julien	1811-1883
Sant, James	1820-1916
Santayana, George	1863-1952
Sardou, Victorien	1831-1908
Sarmiento, Domingo Faustino	1811-1888
Sassoon, Siegfried Lorraine	1886-
Saxe, John Godfrey	1816-1887
Sayers, Dorothy L.	1893-1957
Schaffner, Jakob	1875-1944
Scheffel, Joseph Viktor Von	1826-1886
Scherer, Wilhelm	1841-1886
Schickele, Rene	1883-1940
Schlick, Moritz	1882-1936
Schlaf, Johannes	1862-1941

Schnitzler, Arthur	1862-1931	Soloviev, Vladimir	
Scholes, Percy Alfred	1877-1958	Sergeivich	1853-1900
Schonner, Karl	1869-1942	Sorabji, Cornelia	1866-
Schreiner, Olive	1862-1920	Sorel, Albert	1842-1906
Schweitzer, Albert	1875-1965	Sorel, Georges	1847-1922
Scott, Duncan, Campbell	1862-1947	Sorge, Reinhard Johannes	1892-1916
Scwob, Marcel	1876-1905	Soutar, William	1898-1943
Seaman, Sir Owen	1861-1936	Spence, Lewis	1874-1955
Sedgwick, Anne Douglas	1873-1935	Spencer, Herbert	1820-1903
Seebohm, Frederick	1833-1912	Spender, Edward Harold	1864-1926
Seeley, Sir John Robert	1834-1895	Spengler, Oswald	1880-1936
Seignobos, Charles	1854-1942	Spielhagen, Friedrich Von	1829-1911
Sellar, William Young	1825-1890	Spitteler, Carl	1845-1924
Serao, Matilde	1856-1927	Spring, Howard	1889-1965
Sergeyev-Tsensky,		Squire, Sir John Collings	1884-1958
Sergey	1875-1958	Stacpoole, Hendy de Vere	1863-1951
Service, Robert William	1874-1958	Stanley, Arthur Penrhyn	1815-1881
Seth, Andrew	1850-1931	Stanley, Sir Henry	
Seton-Watson, Robert		Morton	1841-1904
William	1879-	Stedman, Edmund	
Settembrini, Luigi	1813-1877	Clarence	1833-1908
Sewell, Anna	1820-1878	Steed, Henry Wickham	1871-1956
Sharp, John Campbell	1819-1885	Stein, Gertrude	1874-1946
Sharp, William	1856-1905	Steiner, Rudolf	1861-1925
Shaw, George, Bernard	1856-1950	Stephen, Sir Leslie	1832-1904
Shaw, Henry Wheeler	1818-1885	Stephens, James	1882-1950
Sherriff, Robert Cedric	1896-	Stepnyak	1852-1895
Sherwood, Robert Emmet	1896-1955	Stern, Daniel (Agoult)	1805-1876
Shorter, Clement King	1857-1926	Stevens, Wallace	1879-1955
Shorthouse, Joseph Henry	1834-1903	Stevenson, Robert Louis	
Shute, Nevil	1899-1960	Balfour	1850-1894
Sidgwick, Henry	1838-1900	Stirling, James	
Sienkiewicz, Henryk	1846-1916	Hutchinson	1820-1909
Sill, Edward Rowland	1841-1887	Stirling-Maxwell,	
Sillani, Tomaso	1888-	Sir William Bart	1818-1878
Sillanpaa, Frans Eemil	1888-	Stocker, Helene	1869-
Simmel, George	1858-1918	Stockton, Francis Howard	
Simon, Jules Francois	1814-1896	Richard	1834-1902
Simonds, Frank Herbert	1878-1936	Stoddard, John Lawson	1850-1931
Simrock, Karl Joseph	1802-1876	Stoddard, Richard Henry	1825-1903
Sims, George Robert	1847-1922	Stoddard, William Osborn	1835-1925
Sinclair, May	1864-1946	Stopes, Marie Carmichael	1880-1958
Sinclair, Upton	1878-	Storm, Theodor Wolsden	1817-1888
Sitwell, Edith	1887-1964	Stout, George Frederick	1860-1944
Sitwell, Sir Osbert	1892-	Stowe, Harriet Elizabeth	
Sitwell, Sacheverell	1897-	Beecher	1811-1896
Skeat, Walter William	1835-1912	Strachey, Lytton	1880-1932
Skene, William Forbes	1809-1892	Street, Alfred William	1811-1881
Smiles, Samuel	1812-1904	Streuvels, Styn	1871-
Smith, Francis Hopkinson	1838-1915	Strindberg, Johan August	1849-1912
Smith, Goldwin	1823-1910	Strobl, Karl Hans	1877-1946
Smith, Norman Kemp	1872-1958	Strong, Leonard Alfred	
Smith, Walter Chalmers	1824-1908	George	1896-1958
Smith, Sir William	1813-1893	Stubbs, William	1825-1901
Snoilsky, Carl Johan		Stuckenberg, Viggo	1863-1905
Gustaf	1841-1903	Sudermann, Hermann	1857-1928
Sokolov, Nahum	1859-1936	Sully-Prudhomme, Rene	
Sologub, Fedor	1863-1927	Francois Armand	1839-1907
Soloviev, Sergei		Supervielle, Jules	1884-1960
Mikhailovich	1820-1879	Sutro, Alfred	1863-1933

Suttner, Bertha	1843-1914
Svevo, Italio	1861-1928
Swan, Annie	1860-1943
Swanwick, Anna	1813-1899
Swinburne, Algernon	
Charles	1837-1909
Sybel, Heinrich Von	1817-1895
Symonds, John Addington	1840-1893
Symons, Arthur	1865-1945
Synge, John Millington	1871-1909
Tabley, John Byrne	
Leicester Warren	1835-1895
Tagore, Sir Rabindranath	1861-1941
Taine, Hippolyte Adolphe	1828-1893
Tamayo, Baus Manuel	1829-1898
Tardieu, Andre Pierre	
Gabriel Amedee	1876-1945
Tarkington, Newton	
Booth	1869-1946
Tawney, Richard Henry	1880-1962
Taylor, Alfred Edward	1869-1945
Taylor, Bayard	1825-1878
Taylor, Sir Henry	1800-1886
Taylor, Isaak	1829-1901
Taylor, Tom	1817-1880
Tedder, Henry Richard	1850-1924
Teilhard De Jardin,	
Pierre	1881-1955
Tennyson, Alfred Lord	1809-1892
Tharaud, Jerome	1874-1953
Thaxter, Celia Laighton	1835-1894
Thayer, William Roscoe	1859-1923
Theuriet, Claude Adhemar	
Andre	1833-1907
Thiers, Louis Adolph	1797-1877
Thomas, Augustus	1857-1934
Thomas, Brandon	1849-1914
Thompson, Francis	1859-1907
Thomson, James	1834-1882
Thurber, James	1894-1961
Thurston, Ernest Charles	
Temple	1879-1933
Thurston, Katherine Cecil	1875-1911
Tillich, Paul Johannes	1886-
Toland, Hideki	1885-1948
Toller, Ernst	1893-1939
Tolstoy, Count Alexey	
Nikolayevich	1882-1945
Tolstoy, Leo Nokolayevich	1828-1910
Tomlinson, Henry Major	1873-1958
Tonks, Henry	1862-1937
Topelius, Zachris	1818-1898
Toru, Dutt	1856-1877
Tout, Thomas Frederick	1855-1929
Toynbee, Arnold	1852-1883
Toynbee, Arnold Joseph	1889-
Tozzi, Federigo	1883-1920
Traill, Henry Duff	1842-1900
Travers, Ben	1886-
Traz, Robert De	1884-

Treitschke, Heinrich Von	1834-1896
Trelawny, Edward John	1792-1881
Trench, Frederick Herbert	1865-1923
Trench, Richard Chevenix	1807-1886
Trevelyan, George	
Macaulay	1876-1962
Trevelyan, Robert	
Calverley	1872-1951
Trevelyan, Sir George	
Otto	1838-1928
Trollope, Anthony	1815-1882
Trollope, Thomas	
Adolphus	1810-1892
Trotsky, Lev Davidovich	1879-1940
Tupper, Martin Farquhar	1810-1889
Turgenev, Ivan	
Sergeyevich	1818-1883
Turner, Charles Tennyson	1808-1879
Turner, Frederick Jackson	1861-1932
Turner, Walter James	
Redfern	1889-1946
Twain, Mark	1835-1910
Tyler, Moses Coit	1835-1900
Tynan, Katherine	1863-1931
Tyndall, John	1820-1893
Unamuno, Miguel de	1864-1936
Underhill, Evelyn	1875-1941
Undset, Sigrid	1882-1949
Ungaretti, Guiseppe	1888-
Unger, Rudolf	1876-
Unruh, Fritz, Von	1885-
Uspenski, Gleb Ivanovich	1840-1902
Vachell, Horace	
Annesley	1861-1955
Vacherot, Etienne	1809-1897
Vaihinger, Hans	1852-1933
Valera Y Alcala, Galiano	
Juan	1824-1905
Valery, Paul	1871-1945
Valle-Inclan, Ramon Del	1869-1936
Valles, Jules	1832-1885
Van Beers, Jan	1821-1888
Van Doren, Carl Clinton	1885-1950
Van Doren, Mark Albert	1894-
Van Dyke, Henry	1852-1933
Van Loon, Hendrick	
Willem	1882-1944
Vaperau, Louis Gustave	1819-1906
Varnhagen, Francisco	
Adolpho de	1816-1878
Vazoff, Ivan	1850-1921
Veblen, Thornstein B.	1857-1929
Veitch, John	1829-1894
Verdaguer, Mosen	
Jacinto	1845-1902
Verga, Giovanni	1840-1922
Verhaeren, Emile	1855-1916
Verlain, Paul	1844-1896
Verne, Jules	1828-1905
Verwey, Albert	1865-1937

Viaud, Louis Marie Julien	1850-1923	Whitman, Walt	1819-1892
Vidyasagar, Iswar		Whittier, John Greenleaf	1807-1892
Chandra	1820-1891	Widmann, Joseph Victor	1842-1911
Viebig, Clara	1860-1952	Wiechert, Ernst	1887-1950
Viele-Griffin, Francis	1864-1937	Wiggin, Kate Douglas	1856-1923
Vigfusson, Gudbrandir	1828-1889	Wilcox, Ella	1850-1919
Villari, Pasquale	1827-1917	Wilde, Oscar Fingall	
Villiers, De L'isle		O'Flahertie Wills	1854-1900
August Compt de	1838-1889	Wilde, Speranza Lady	1826-1896
Vinogradoff, Sir Paul	1854-1925	Wildenbruch, Ernst Van	1845-1909
Vischer, Friedrich		Wilder, Thorton	1897-
Theodor	1807-1887	Wildgans, Anton	1881-1932
Vogue, Eugene Melchior	1848-1910	Williamson, Henry	1895-
Voss, Richard	1851-1918	Wills, William Gorman	1828-1891
Vrchlicky, Jaroslav	1853-1912	Wilson, Edmund	1895-
Vuillard, Jean Edouard	1868-1940	Wilson, John Dover	1881-
Waddell, Helen	1889-	Winsor, Justin	1831-1897
Wallace, Alfred Russel	1823-1913	Winther, Christian	1796-1876
Wallace, Edgar	1875-1932	Wister, Owen	1860-1938
Wallace, Lewis	1827-1905	Wittgenstein, Ludwig	
Wallace, William	1844-1897	Josef Johannes	1889-1951
Wallon, Henri Alexandre	1812-1904	Wodehouse, Pelham	
Walpole, Sir Hugh		Grenville	1881-
Seymour	1884-1941	Wolfe, Humbert	1885-1940
Ward, Mary Augusta		Wolfe, Thomas Clayton	1900-1938
(Mrs. Humphry)	1851-1920	Wolff, Pierre	1865-1944
Warner, Charles Dudley	1829-1900	Wood, Mrs. Henry	1814-1887
Warner (Susan Bogert)	1819-1895	Woods, Margaret Louisa	1856-1945
Warren, Samuel	1807-1877	Woolf, Virginia	1882-1941
Wasserman, Jakob	1873-1933	Wright, Thomas	1810-1887
Watson, Sir William	1858-1935	Wright, William Aldis	1836-1914
Watts-Dunton, Walter		Wundt, Wilhelm Max	1832-1920
Theodore	1832-1914	Wyatt, Sir Matthew Digby	1820-1877
Waugh, Alec	1898-	Wylie, Elinor Hoyte	1885-1928
Waugh, Edwin	1817-1890	Wyndham, George	1863-1913
Webb, Beatrice	1858-1943	Yates, Dornford	1885-1960
Webb, Mary Gladys	1881-1927	Yates, Edmund	1831-1894
Webb, Sidney James	1859-1947	Yeats, William Butler	1865-1939
Wedekind, Frank	1864-1918	Yonge, Charlotte Mary	1823-1901
Wellesz, Egon Joseph	1885-	Young, Andrew John	1885-
Wells, Charles Jeremiah	1798-1879	Young, Francis Brett	1884-1954
Wells, Herbert George	1866-1946	Yriarte, Charles	1832-1898
Wennerberg, Gunnar	1817-1901	Zahn, Ernst	1867-1952
Werfel, Franz	1890-1945	Zangwill, Israel	1864-1926
West, Rebecca	1892-	Zeller, Eduard	1814-1908
Weyman, Stanley, John	1855-1928	Zeromski, Stephen	1864-1925
Wharton, Newbold Edith	1862-1937	Zola, Emile Edouard	
Wheeler, Sir Robert		Charles Antoine	1840-1902
Mortimer	1890-	Zorrilla, Jose	1817-1893
White, Richard Grant	1821-1885	Zuckmayer, Carl	1896-
White, William Hale	1831-1913	Zweig, Arnold	1887-
Whitlock, Brand	1869-1934	Zweig, Stefan	1881-1942

ARTISTS

Aalto, Alvar	1899-	Abbey, Edwin Austin	1852-1911
Aaltonen, Waino	1894-	Abercrombie, Sir Patrick	1879-1957
Aba-Novak, Vilmos	1894-1941	Achenbach, Andreas	1815-1910

Adams, Herbert	1858-1945
Adamsen, Amandus Heinrich	1855-1929
Alexander, John White	1856-1915
Alonso, Mateo Silva Leitao	1878-
Anderson, Sir Robert Rowand	1834-1921
Ansdell, Richard	1815-1885
Archipenko, Alexander	1880-
Armitage, Edward	1817-1896
Armstead, Henry Hugh	1828-1905
Armstrong, John	1893-
Artzybashev, Boris	1899-
Asplund, Erik Gunnar	1885-1940
Attwell, Mabel Lucie	1879-
Bacon, Henry	1866-1924
Baer, William Jacob	1860-1941
Baker, Bryant	1881-
Bakst, Leon	1866-1924
Ball, Thomas	1819-1911
Balla, Gyacomo	1871-1958
Bandel, Ernst Von	1800-1876
Barker, Thomas	1815-1882
Barlach, Ernst	1870-1938
Barnard, Georges Grey	1863-1938
Bartels, Hans Von	1856-1913
Bartholdi, Auguste	1834-1904
Bartholome, Paul Albert	1848-1884
Bastien-Lepage, Jules	1848-1884
Bates, Harry	1850-1899
Baudry, Paul Jacques Aime	1828-1886
Baumeister, Willi	1889-1955
Beach, Chester	1881-
Beardsley, Aubrey Vincent	1872-1898
Beaudin, André	1895-
Beaux, Cecilia	1863-1942
Beckmann, Max	1884-1950
Beckwith, James Carrol	1852-1917
Begas, Reinhold	1831-1911
Behrens, Peter	1868-1938
Bell, John	1811-1895
Bellows, Albert F.	1829-1883
Bellows, George Wesley	1882-1925
Benlliure Y Gil, Jose	1855-1937
Benson, Frank Weston	1862-1951
Bentley, John Francis	1839-1902
Berlage, Hendrik Petrus	1856-1934
Besnard, Paul Albert	1849-1934
Beverley, William Roxby	1814-1889
Bierstadt, Albert	1830-1902
Bigge, John	1892-
Birch, Samuel	1813-1885
Blakelock, Ralph Albert	1847-1919
Blampied, Edmund	1886-
Blanche, Jacques Emile	1862-1942
Blashfield, Edin Howland	1848-1936
Bloch, Martin	1883-1954

Blomfield, Sir Arthur William	1829-1899
Blomfield, Sir Reginald	1856-1942
Blore, Edward	1787-1879
Blum, Robert Frederick	1857-1903
Boccioni, Umberto	1882-1916
Boehm, Sir Joseph Edgar	1834-1890
Boelkin, Arnold	1827-1901
Bombois, Camille	1883-
Bone, Sir Muirhead	1876-1953
Bonheur, Rosa	1822-1899
Bonnard, Pierre	1867-1947
Bonnat, Leon Joseph Florentin	1833-1922
Borglum, Gutzon	1871-1941
Borglum, Solon Hannibal	1868-1922
Borie, Adolphe	1877-1934
Boudin, Louis Eugene	1824-1898
Bough, Samuel	1822-1878
Boughton, George Henry	1833-1905
Bouguereau, Adolphe William	1825-1905
Bourdelle, Emile Antoine	1861-1929
Boutet De Monvel, Maurice	1851-1913
Boyle, John J.	1851-1917
Bracquemond, Felix	1833-1914
Bradford, William	1827-1892
Braekeleer, Henri Jean Augustin De	1840-1888
Brancusi, Constantin	1876-1957
Brangwyn, Sir Frank	1867-1956
Braque, Georges	1882-1963
Breitner, George Hendrik	1857-1923
Breton, Jules Adolphe Aime Louis	1827-1906
Bridgman, Frederic Arthur	1847-1928
Brierly, Sir Oswald Walter	1817-1894
Brock, Sir Thomas	1847-1922
Brodie, William	1815-1881
Brough, Robert	1872-1905
Brown, Ford Madox	1821-1893
Brown, George Loring	1814-1889
Brown, Henry Kirke	1814-1886
Brown, John George	1831-1913
Brown, Hablot Knight	1815-1882
Bruce-Joy, Albert	1842-1924
Brunner, Arnold William	1857-1925
Brush, George de Forest	1855-1941
Brymner, William	1855-1925
Burgess, John Bagnold	1830-1897
Burne-Jones, Sir Edward Burne	1833-1898
Burne-Jones, Sir Philip	1861-1926
Burnham, Daniel Hudson	1846-1912
Burton, Decimus	1800-1881
Butler, Lady Elizabeth	1857-1933
Butterfield, William	1814-1900

Cabanel, Alexandre	1823-1889	Daumet, Pierre Jerome	
Caldecott, Randolph	1846-1886	Honore	1826-1911
Calderon, Philip		Daumier, Honore	1808-1879
Hermongenes	1833-1898	Davies, Arthur B.	1862-1928
Calvert, Edward	1799-1883	Davis, Charles Harold	1857-1933
Cameron, Sir David		Dawson, Henri	1811-1878
Young	1865-1945	Dawson-Watson, Dawson	1864-1939
Camphausen, Wilhelm	1818-1885	Defregger, Franz Von	1835-1921
Capronnier, Jean Baptiste	1814-1891	Degas, Hilaire Germain	
Carand'Ache	1858-1909	Edgar	1834-1917
Carolus-Duran	1837-1917	Delaunay, Elie	1828-1891
Carra, Carlo	1881-	Delaunay, Robert	1885-1941
Carriere, Eugene	1849-1906	Delvaux, Paul	1897-
Casorati, Felice	1886-	Demuth, Charles	1883-1935
Cassatt, Mary	1845-1926	Denis, Maurice	1870-1943
Cazin, Jean Charles	1841-1901	Derain, Andre	1880-
Cezanne, Paul	1839-1906	Despiau, Charles	1874-1946
Chagall, Marc	1887-	Detaille, Edouard	1848-1912
Chalmers, George Paul	1836-1878	Diaz, Narcisse Virgile	1809-1876
Chapu, Henri	1833-1891	Dicksee, Sir Francis	
Chase, William Merrit	1849-1916	Bernard	1853-1928
Chirico, Giorgio De	1888-	Dielman, Frederick	1847-1935
Church, Frederick Edwin	1826-1900	Dillens, Julien	1849-1904
Clarke, Thomas Shields	1860-1920	Dix, Otto	1891-
Claus, Emile	1849-1924	Dobson, Frank	1887-1963
Clausen, Sir George	1852-1944	Dobson, William Charles	
Clays, Paul Jean	1819-1900	Thomas	1817-1898
Coates, Wells Wintemute	1895-1958	Dodge, William de	
Cole, Vicat	1833-1893	Leftwich	1867-1935
Collier, Hon John	1850-1934	Dore, Paul Gustave	1832-1883
Colman, Samuel	1832-1920	Dougherty, Paul	1877-1947
Conder, Charles	1868-1909	Doyle, Richard	1824-1883
Constant, Benjamin Jean		Drake, Friedrich	1805-1882
Joseph	1845-1902	Drury, Alfred	1857-1944
Cooper, Thomas Sidney	1803-1902	Dubois, Paul	1829-1905
Cope, Charles West	1811-1890	Duchamp, Marcel	1887-
Corbett, Harvey Willey	1873-1954	Dufy, Raoul	1877-1953
Corbould, Edward Henry	1815-1905	Dumont, Augustin	
Corbusier Le, Charles		Alexandre	1801-1884
Edouard	1887-1965	Dupre, Giovanni	1817-1882
Corinth, Louis	1858-1925	Dupre, Jules	1811-1889
Cormon, Fernand	1845-1924	Durand, Asher Brown	1796-1886
Costa, Giovanni	1826-1903	Duveneck, Frank	1848-1919
Cottet, Charles	1863-1925	Eakins, Thomas	1844-1916
Courbet, Gustav	1819-1877	East, Alfred	1849-1913
Couture, Thomas	1815-1879	Eaton, Wyatt	1849-1896
Cram, Ralph Adams	1863-1942	Eberlein, Gustav	1847-1926
Crauck, Gustav	1827-1905	Eberz, Josef	1801-1882
Cruikshank, George	1792-1878	Edelfelt, Albert Gunter	1854-1905
Daingerfield, Elliott	1859-1932	Ensor, James	1860-1942
Dallin, Cyrus Edwin	1861-1944	Epstein, Jacob	1880-1959
Dalou, Jules	1838-1902	Ernst, Max	1891-
Dannat, William T.	1853-1929	Etex, Antoine	1808-1888
Dantan, Antoine Laurent	1798-1878	Faed, Thomas	1826-1900
Dantan, Edward Joseph	1848-1897	Faistauer, Anton	1887-1930
Darley, Felix Octavius		Falguiere, Jean Alexandre	
Carr	1822-1888	Joseph	1831-1900
Daubigny, Charles		Fantin-Latour, Ignace	
Francois	1817-1878	Henri Jean Theodore	1836-1904
		Farquharson, David	1840-1907

Farquharson, Joseph	1846-1935
Feininger, Lyonel	1871-1956
Feuerbach, Anselm	1829-1880
Fildes, Sir Luke	1844-1927
Finch, Alfred William	1854-1930
Flagg, Ernest	1857-1947
Flint, Sir William Russell	1880-
Forain, Jean Louis	1852-1931
Ford, Edward Onslow	1852-1901
Forster, Ernst	1800-1885
Foster, Myles Birket	1825-1899
Frampton, Sir George	1860-1928
Francais, Francois Louis	1814-1897
Fraser, Claud Lovat	1890-1921
Fraser, James Earle	1876-1953
Fremiet, Emmanuel	1824-1910
French, Daniel Chester	1850-1931
Fresnaye, Roger De La	1885-1925
Friesz, Emile Othon	1879-1949
Fripp, Alfred Downing	1822-1895
Fripp, George Arthur	1814-1896
Frith, William Powell	1819-1909
Fromentin, Eugene	1820-1876
Frost, William Edward	1810-1877
Fry, Roger Elliot	1866-1934
Fuertes, Louis Agassiz	1874-1927
Fuhrich, Joseph Von	1800-1876
Fuller, George	1822-1884
Furse, Charles Wellington	1868-1904
Gabo, Naum	1890-
Gallait, Louis	1810-1887
Gallen-Kallela, Akseli Valdemar	1865-1931
Garnier, Jean Louis Charles	1825-1898
Gaudier-Brzeska, Henry	1891-1915
Gauguin, Paul	1848-1903
Gaul, Gilbert William	1855-1919
Gay, Walter	1856-1937
Gebhardt, Eduard Von	1830-1925
Geddes, Norman Bel	1893-1958
Gerome, Jean Leon	1824-1904
Gervex, Henri	1852-1929
Gibson, Charles Dana	1867-1944
Gifford, Robert Swain	1840-1905
Gilbert, Sir Alfred	1854-1934
Gilbert, Cass	1859-1939
Gilbert, Sir John	1817-1897
Gleizes, Albert	1881-1953
Gogh, Vincent Van	1853-1890
Goodall, Frederick	1822-1904
Goodhue, Bertram Grosvenor	1869-1924
Grafly, Charles	1862-1929
Grant, Duncan	1885-
Grant, Sir Francis	1803-1878
Greenway, Kate	1846-1901
Gregory, Edward John	1850-1909
Gris, Juan	1887-1927
Gromaire, Marcel	1892-

Gropius, Walter	1883-
Grossmith, Weedon	1853-1919
Grosz, George	1893-1959
Gudin, Theodore	1802-1880
Guillamin, Armand	1841-1927
Guillaume, Jean Baptiste Claude Euegene	1822-1905
Gunn, James	1893-
Guthrie, Sir James	1859-1930
Guys, Constantin	1805-1892
Haag, Carl	1820-1915
Haas, Johannes Hubertus Leonhardus De	1832-1908
Habermann, Hugo Freiherr Von	1849-1929
Hacker, Arthur	1858-1919
Haider, Karl	1846-1912
Hansom, Joseph Aloysius	1803-1882
Harpignies, Henri	1819-1916
Harrison, Thomas Alexander	1853-1930
Hartley, Jonathan Scott	1845-1912
Harvey, Sir George	1806-1876
Hassall, John	1868-1948
Henner, Jean Jacques	1829-1905
Henri, Robert	1865-1929
Herbert, John Rogers	1810-1900
Hilberseimer, Ludwig	1885-
Hildebrand, Adolf	1847-1921
Hodgkins, Frances Mary	1869-1947
Hodler, Ferdinand	1853-1918
Hoffman, Josef	1870-
Hoffman, Malvina	1887-
Holiday, Henry	1839-1927
Holl, Frank	1845-1888
Holmes, Sir Charles John	1868-1936
Holroyd, Sir Charles	1861-1917
Homer, Winslow	1836-1910
Hook, James Clarke	1819-1907
Horsley, John Callcott	1817-1903
Hosmer, Harriet Goodhue	1830-1908
Hovenden, Thomas	1840-1895
Hubner, Julius	1806-1882
Hughes, Arthur	1832-1915
Hunt, Alfred William	1830-1896
Hunt, Richard Morris	1828-1895
Hunt, William Holman	1827-1910
Hunt, William Morris	1824-1879
Huntingdon, Daniel	1816-1906
Hutchison, Sir William Oliphant	1889-
Innes, James Dickson	1887-1914
Inness, George	1825-1894
Israels, Josef	1824-1911
Jackson, Sir Thomas Graham	1835-1924
Jacque, Charles	1813-1894
Jagger, Charles Sargeant	1885-1934
Jalabert, Charles Francois	1819-1901
Jawlesky, Alexei Van	1864-1941

John, Augustus Edwin	1878-1961
John, Sir William	
Goscombe	1860-1952
Johnson, Eastman	1824-1906
Jonkind, Johann Barthold	1819-1891
Jonsson, Einar	1874-1954
Jordan, Rudolf	1810-1887
Kandinsky, Vasily	1866-1944
Kauffer, Edward	
McKnight	1890-
Keene, Charles Samuel	1823-1891
Keller, Albert Von	1844-1920
Kelly, Sir Gerald Festus	1879-
Kemp-Welch, Lucy	
Elizabeth	1869-
Kennington, Eric Henry	1888-1960
Kent, Rockwell	1882-
Kirchner, Ernst Ludwig	1880-1938
Khnopff, Fernand	1858-1921
Kirkup, Seymore Stocker	1788-1880
Klee, Paul	1879-1940
Klerk, Michel De	1884-1923
Klinger, Max	1857-1920
Klint, Kaare	1888-
Knaus, Ludwig	1829-1910
Knight, Dame Laura	1877-
Knight, Daniel Ridgway	1845-1924
Knight, Harold	1874-1961
Knowles, Sir James	1831-1908
Kokoshka, Oskar	1886-
Koort, Jaan	1883-1935
Kramer, Pieter Lodewijk	1881-
Kubin, Alfred	1877-1959
Kupka, Frank	1871-1957
Kuznetson, Pavel	1878-
Kyosai, Sho-Fu	1831-1889
La Farge, John	1835-1910
Lafresnaye, De Roger	1885-1925
Lalique, René	1860-1945
Lambeaux, Jef	1852-1908
Lanchester, Henry	
Vaughan	1863-1953
Laszlo, Sir Philip	1869-1937
Lathrop, Francis	1849-1909
La Touche, Gaston	1854-1913
Laurencin, Marie	1885-1957
Laurens, Henri	1885-1954
Laurens, Jean Paul	1838-1921
Lavery, Sir John	1856-1941
Lawson, Cecil Gordon	1851-1882
Lazlo De Lombos, Philip	
Alexius	1869-1937
Lear, Edward	1812-1888
Leger, Fernand	1881-1955
Legros, Alphonse	1837-1911
Lehmann, Rudolf	1819-1905
Lehmbruck, Wilhelm	1881-1919
Leibl, Wilhelm	1844-1900
Leighton, Frederick	
Leighton	1830-1896

Lemaire, Philipp Honoré	1798-1880
Lenbach, Franz Von	1836-1904
Lethaby, William	
Richard	1857-1931
Liebermann, Max	1847-1935
Lindsay, Sir Coutts	1824-1913
Lindsay, Norman	1879-
Linnell, John	1792-1882
Linton, Sir James	
Dromgole	1840-1916
Lipchitz, Jacques	1891-
Llewellyn, Sir William	1863-1941
Lockhart, William Ewart	1846-1900
Lockwood, Wilton	1861-1914
Lowry, Stephen	1887-
Lucas, John Seymour	1849-1923
Lukeman, Henry	
Augustus	1871-1935
Lutyens, Sir Edwin	
Landseer	1869-1944
Macbeth, Robert Walker	1848-1910
MacColl, Dugald	
Sutherland	1859-1948
McEntee, Jervis	1828-1891
McEvoy, Ambrose	1878-1927
Macke, August	1887-1914
McKim, Charles Follen	1847-1909
Mackintosh, Charles Rennie	1868-1928
MacMannies, Frederick	
William	1863-1937
MacNee, Sir Daniel	1806-1882
MacNeil, Hermon Atkins	1866-1947
MacTaggart, William	1835-1910
Macwhirter, John	1839-1911
Madrazo Y Kunt,	
Don Federico De	1815-1894
Magonigle, Harold Van	
Buren	1867-1935
Magritte, Réne	1898-
Maillol, Aristide	
Joseph Bonaventure	1861-1944
Makart, Hans	1840-1884
Manet, Edouard	1832-1883
Manship, Paul	1885-
Marc, Franz	1880-1916
Marchand, Jean	1883-1941
Marees, Hans Von	1837-1887
Marin, John	1870-
Maris, Jacob	1837-1899
Maris, Matthiss	1839-1917
Maris, Willem	1843-1910
Marquet, Albert	1875-1947
Marr, Carl	1859-1936
Marshall, Willam Calder	1813-1894
Martin, Frank	1890-
Martin, Homer Dodge	1836-1897
Matejko, Jan Alois	1838-1893
Matisse, Henri	1869-1954
Mauve, Anton	1838-1888
Mead, Larkin Goldsmith	1835-1910

Mead, William Rutherford	1846-1928
Meissonier, Jean Louis Ernest	1815-1891
Melchers, Gari	1860-1932
Mendelsohn	1887-1953
Meninsky, Bernard	1891-1950
Menzel, Adolph Friedrich Erdmann Von	1815-1905
Mercie, Marius Jean Antonin	1845-1916
Mesdag, Hendrik Willem	1831-1915
Mestrovic, Ivan	1883-1962
Meunier, Constantin	1831-1905
Mies Van Der Rohe	1886-
Millais, Sir John Everett	1829-1896
Miro, Joan	1893-
Millet, Francis Davis	1846-1912
Modigliani, Amadeo	1884-1920
Mondrian, Pieter Cornelis	1872-1944
Monet, Claude	1840-1936
Moore, Albert Joseph	1841-1893
Moore, Henry	1831-1895
Moore, Henry Spencer	1893-
Moran, Edward	1829-1901
Morandi, Giorgio	1898-
Moreau, Gustave	1826-1898
Morel-Ladeuil, Leonard	1820-1888
Morisot, Berthe Marie Pauline	1841-1895
Morris, William	1834-1896
Moses, Anna Mary (Grandma)	1860-1961
Mosler, Henry	1841-1920
Mowbray, Harry Siddons	1858-1928
Muenier, Jules, A.	1863-1934
Munch, Edvard	1863-1944
Munk, Kaj	1898-1944
Munkacsy, Michael	1846-1900
Munnings, Alfred	1878-1959
Murphy, John Francis	1853-1921
Murray, Sir David	1849-1933
Nash, Paul	1889-1946
Nervi, Pier Luigi	1891-
Nesfield, William Eden	1835-1888
Neuville, Alphonse Marie De	1836-1885
Nevinson, Christophe Richard Wynne	1889-1946
Nicholson, Ben	1894-
Nicholson, Sir William	1872-1949
Nicol, Erskine	1825-1904
Niehaus, Charles Henry	1855-1935
Nolde, Emil	1867-1956
Ochtmann, Leonard	1854-1934
Orchardson, Sir William Quiller	1832-1910
Orpen, Sir William Newenham Montague	1878-1931

Oud, Jacobus Johann Pieter	1890-
Oudine, Eugene Andre	1810-1887
Ozefant	1886-
Page, William	1811-1885
Palmer, Samuel	1805-1881
Parsons, Alfred	1847-1920
Parsons, William Edward	1872-1939
Partridge, Sir Bernard	1861-1945
Partridge, William Ordway	1861-1930
Paton, Sir Joseph Noel	1821-1901
Paul, Bruno	1874-
Pearce, Charles Sprague	1851-1914
Pearson, John Loughborough	1817-1897
Pennell, Joseph	1860-1926
Peploe, Samuel John	1871-1935
Permeke, Constant	1886-1952
Perrett, Auguste	1874-1955
Pettie, John	1839-1893
Picabia, Francis	1878-1953
Picasso, Pablo	1881-
Piloty, Karl Von	1826-1886
Pissarro, Camille	1830-1903
Platt, Charles Adams	1861-1933
Poelzig, Hans	1869-1936
Poole, Paul Falconer	1807-1879
Pope, John Russell	1874-1937
Portaels, Jean Francois	1818-1895
Post, George Browne	1837-1913
Poynter, Sir Edward John	1836-1919
Pradilla, Francisco	1848-1921
Prinsep, Valentine Cameron	1838-1904
Proctor, Alexander Phimister	1862-1950
Purvitis, Vilhelms Karlis	1872-1945
Puvis De Chavannes, Pierre Cecile	1824-1898
Pyle, Howard	1853-1911
Rackham, Arthur	1867-1939
Raemaekers, Louis	1869-1956
Raven-Hill, Leonard	1867-1942
Redon, Odilon	1840-1916
Redpath, Anne	1895-
Reid, Sir George	1841-1913
Reid, Robert	1862-1929
Remington, Frederic	1861-1909
Renoir, Pierre Auguste	1841-1919
Renwick, James	1818-1895
Repin, Ilya Yefimovich	1844-1930
Richardson, Sir Albert Edward	1880-1963
Richardson, Henry Hobson	1838-1886
Richmond, Sir George	1809-1896
Richmond, Sir William Blake	1842-1921
Ricketts, Charles	1866-1931

Rietschel, Ernst	1804-1861
Rivera, Diego	1886-1957
Riviere, Briton	1840-1920
Roberts, William	1895-
Robinson, William Heath	1872-1944
Rodin, Auguste	1840-1917
Roerich, Nikolai Constantinovich	1874-1947
Rogers, John	1829-1904
Rops, Felicien	1833-1898
Rossetti, Dante Gabriel	1828-1882
Rothenstein, Sir William	1872-1945
Rouault, Georges	1871-1958
Rousseau, Henri	1844-1910
Ryder, Albert Pinkham	1847-1917
Salisbury, Frank Owen	1874-1957
Sargent, John Singer	1856-1925
Schilling, Johannes	1828-1910
Schmidt-Rottluff, Karl	1884-
Schreyer, Adolf	1828-1899
Schwartze, Teresa	1852-1918
Scott, Sir George Gilbert	1811-1878
Scott, Sir Giles Gilbert	1880-
Seganti, Giovanni	1858-1899
Segonzac, André Dunoyer de	1884
Serusier, Paul	1863-1927
Seurat, Georges	1859-1891
Severini, Gino	1883-
Severn, Joseph	1793-1879
Shahn, Ben	1898-
Shannon, Charles Hazelwood	1863-1937
Shannon, Sir James Jebusa	1862-1923
Shaw, Richard Norman	1831-1912
Shields, Frederick James	1833-1911
Short, Sir Frank Job	1857-1945
Sickert, Walter Richard	1860-1942
Signac, Paul	1863-1935
Simmons, Edward Emerson	1852-1931
Simpson, Sir John	1858-1933
Sisley, Alfred	1840-1899
Slevogt, Max	1868-1932
Smillie, James David	1833-1909
Smith, Sir Matthew Arnold	1879-1959
Soffici, Ardengo	1879-
Somerscales, Thomas Jacques	1842-1928
Somov, Konstantin Andreevich	1869-
Sorolla Y Bastida, Joaquin	1863-1923
Spadini, Armando	1883-1925
Spencer, Gilbert	1892-
Spencer, Sir Stanley	1891-1959
Steell, Sir John	1804-1891
Steer, Philip Philip Wilson	1860-1942
Steinle, Eduard	1810-1886

Steinlen, Theophile Alexandre	1859-1923
Stevens, Alfred	1828-1906
Stillman, William James	1828-1901
Story, William Wetmore	1819-1895
Strachan, Douglas	1875-1950
Strang, William	1859-1921
Street, George Edmund	1824-1881
Strobl De Kisfalud, Sigismund	1884-
Sturgis, Russell	1836-1909
Sullivan, Louis Henri	1856-1924
Svabinsky, Max	1873-
Szinye-Merse, Paul De	1845-1920
Szonyi, Stephen	1894-
Taft, Lorado	1860-1936
Tamayo, Rufino	1899-
Tanner, Henry Assawa	1859-1937
Tarbell, Edmund C.	1862-1938
Taut, Bruno	1880-
Tenniel, Sir John	1820-1914
Thayer, Abbott Handerson	1849-1921
Thoma, Hans	1839-1924
Thompson, Launt	1833-1934
Thornycroft, Sir William Hamo	1850-1925
Tiffany, Louis Comfort	1848-1933
Tissot, James Joseph Jacques	1836-1902
Tonks, Henry	1862-1937
Toulouse-Lautrec, Henri De	1864-1901
Troubetzkoy, Amelie Rives	1863-1945
Troubetzkoy, Pierre	1864-1936
Troyon, Constant	1810-1865
Trubner, Wilhelm	1851-1917
Tryon, Dwight William	1849-1925
Tuke, Henry Scott	1858-1929
Tweed, John	1869-1933
Utrillo, Maurice	1883-1955
Valadon, Suzanne	1869-1938
Valloton, Felix	1865-1929
Van Der Stappen, Charles	1843-1910
Van De Velde, Henri	1863-1957
Van Doesburg, Theo	1883-1931
Van Gough, Vincent	1853-1890
Van Meegeren, Han	1889-1947
Vedder, Elihu	1836-1923
Veit, Philipp	1793-1877
Verboeckhoven, Eugene Joseph	1798-1881
Vereschagin, Vassili Vassilievich	1842-1904
Vierge, Daniel	1851-1904
Vigeland, Adolf Gustav	1869-1943
Vigne, Paul De	1843-1901
Villon, Jacques	1875-1963
Vinton, Frederic Porter	1846-1911

Viollet Le Duc, Eugene Emmanuel	1814-1879
Vivin, Louis	1861-1936
Volk, Leonard Wells	1828-1895
Vonnoh, Robert William	1858-1933
Vuillard, Edward	1868-1940
Wadsworth, Edward	1889-1949
Walker, Henry Oliver	1843-1929
Walker, Horatio	1858-1938
Ward, Edward Matthew	1816-1879
Ward, John Quincy Adams	1830-1910
Warren, Whitney	1864-1943
Waterhouse, Alfred	1830-1905
Waterhouse, John William	1847-1917
Waterlow, Sir Ernst Albert	1850-1919
Watts, George Frederic	1817-1904
Wauters, Emile	1846-1933
Webb, Sir Aston	1849-1930
Webb, Philip Speakman	1831-1915
Weber, Max	1881-1961
Weir, Robert Walter	1803-1889
Weyr, Rudolf Von	1847-1914

Wheeler, Sir Charles	1892-
Whistler, James Abbott McNeill	1834-1903
White, Ethelbert	1891-
White, Stanford	1853-1906
Whymper, Edward	1840-1911
Willems, Florent Joseph Marie	1823-1905
Willette, Leon Adolphe	1857-1926
Willumsen, Jen Ferdinand	1863-1958
Woolner, Thomas	1826-1892
Wright, Frank Lloyd	1869-1959
Wyant, Alexander H.	1836-1892
Wyspianski, Stanislaw	1869-1907
Yeames, William Frederick	1835-1918
Yeats, Jack Butler	1871-1957
Young, Mahonri Mackintosh	1877-
Zadkine, Ossip	1890-
Ziem, Felix Francois George Philibert	1821-1911
Zorn, Anders	1860-1920
Zuloago, Ignacio	1870-1945

COMPOSERS

Abt, Franz	1819-1886
Albeniz, Isaac	1860-1909
Albert, Eugen Francis Charles d'	1864-1932
Alfano, Franco	1876-1954
Antheil, George	1900-1959
Arditi, Luigi	1822-1903
Arensky, Anton Stephanovich	1861-1906
Auber, Daniel Francois Esprit	1782-1871
Audran, Edmond	1842-1901
Auric, Georges	1899-
Balakirev, Milly Alexeivich	1836-1910
Bantock, Sir Granville	1868-1946
Bargiel, Woldemar	1828-1897
Barnby, Sir Joseph	1838-1896
Barnett, John	1802-1890
Barnett, John Francis	1837-1916
Bartok, Bela	1881-1945
Bax, Sir Arnold Edward Trevor	1883-1953
Beecham, Sir Thomas	1879-1964
Bendl, Karel	1838-1897
Benedict, Sir Julius	1804-1885
Benjamin, Arthur	1893-1960
Benoit, Pierre Leonard Leopold	1834-1901
Berg, Alban	1885-1935
Berlin, Irving	1888-

Berners, Gerald Hugh Tyrwhitt-Wilson	1883-1950
Bliss, Sir Arthur	1891-
Bloch, Ernest	1880-
Blom, Eric	1888-1959
Blumenthal, Jacob	1829-1908
Boelmann, Leon	1862-1897
Boito, Arriego	1842-1918
Borodin, Alexander Porfyrievich	1834-1887
Bottesini, Giovanni	1822-1889
Brahms, Johannes	1833-1897
Bridge, Frank	1879-1941
Bruch, Max	1838-1920
Bruckner, Anton	1824-1896
Bruneau, Alfred	1857-1934
Buck, Dudley	1839-1909
Burleigh, Henry Thaker	1866-1949
Busoni, Ferruccio	1866-1924
Cadman, Charles Wakefield	1881-1946
Carpenter, John Alden	1876-1951
Casals, Pablo	1876-
Casella, Alfred	1883-1947
Castelnuovo-Tedesco, Mario	1895-
Chabrier, Alexis Emmanuel	1841-1894
Chaminade, Cecile	1861-1944
Charpentier, Gustave	1860-1956
Chvala, Emmanuel	1851-1924
Chavez, Carlos	1899-

Clay, Frederic	1838-1889
Coates, Albert	1882-1953
Coates, Eric	1886-1958
Coleridge-Taylor, Samuel	1875-1912
Costa, Sir Michael	1810-1884
Cowell, Henry Dixon	1897-
Cowen, Sir Frederick Hymen	1852-1935
Cui, Cesar Antonovich	1835-1918
D'Albert, Eugen Francis Charles	1864-1932
Damrosch, Leopold	1832-1885
Davies, Sir Henry Walford	1869-1941
Debussy, Claude Achille	1862-1918
De Koven, Reginald	1861-1920
Delibes, Clement Philibert Leo	1836-1891
Delius, Frederick	1863-1934
D'Indy, Paul Marie Theodore Vincent	1851-1931
Dohnanyi, Ernst Von	1877-1960
Dopper, Cornelis	1870-1939
Doppler, Albert Franz	1821-1883
Dubois, Francois Clement Theodore	1837-1924
Dukas, Paul	1865-1935
Dunhill, Thomas Frederick	1877-1946
Duparc, Henri	1848-1933
Durey, Louis	1888-
Dvorak, Antonin	1841-1904
Eitner, Robert	1832-1905
Elgar, Sir Edward	1857-1934
Elvey, Sir George Job	1816-1893
Enesco, George	1881-1955
Engel, Carl	1883-1934
Engel, Karl	1818-1882
Erlanger, Camille	1863-1919
Falla, Manuel de	1876-1946
Faure, Gabriel	1845-1924
Fibich, Zdenko	1850-1900
Finck, Heinrich Theophilus	1854-1926
Flotow, Friedrich Frieherr Von	1812-1883
Foerster, Josef Bohuslav	1859-
Foote, Arthur William	1853-1937
Franck, Cesar	1822-1890
Franz, Robert	1815-1892
Gade, Niels Vilhelm	1817-1890
Gatty, Nicholas Comyn	1874-1946
German, Sir Edward	1862-1936
Gershwin, George	1898-1937
Glazunov, Alexander Constantinovich	1865-1936
Godard, Benjamin	1849-1895
Godowsky, Leopold	1870-1938
Goldmark, Karl	1832-1915
Goosens, Eugene	1893-1962
Goss, Sir John	1800-1880

Gounod, Charles Francois	1818-1893
Grainger, Percy Aldridge	1882-
Granados Y Campina, Enrique	1867-1916
Gretchaninov, Alexander Tikhonovich	1864-1956
Grieg, Edvard Hagerup	1843-1907
Grofé, Ferde	1892-
Gung'l, Josef	1810-1889
Haba, Alois	1893-
Hadley, Henry Kimball	1871-1937
Handy, William Christopher	1873-1958
Hanson, Howard	1896-
Harris, Roy	1898-
Harty, Sir Herbert Hamilton	1880-1941
Hatton, John Liptrot	1809-1886
Heller, Stephen	1815-1888
Henschel, Sir George	1850-1934
Henselt, Adolf Von	1814-1889
Herbert, Victor	1859-1924
Herve, Florimond Rounger	1825-1892
Herz, Henri	1806-1888
Hiller, Ferdinand	1811-1885
Hindemith, Paul	1895-1963
Hofmann, Josef Casimir	1876-1957
Holbrooke, Josef Charles	1878-1958
Holst, Gustave	1874-1934
Honegger, Arthur	1892-1956
Hubay, Geno De	1858-1937
Hullah, John Pyke	1812-1884
Humperdinck, Engelbert	1854-1921
Ibert, Jacques	1890-
Ireland, John	1879-1962
Jacques-Dalcroze, Emile	1865-1950
Janacek, Leos	1854-1928
Jarnefelt, Edvard Armas	1869-1958
Jensen, Adolf	1837-1897
Joachim, Joseph	1831-1907
Joncières, Victoria	1839-1903
Jongen, Joseph	1873-1953
Kajanus, Robert	1856-1933
Karel, Rudolf	1880-
Kern, Jerome	1885-1945
Kienzl, Wilhelm	1857-1941
Kodaly, Zoltan	1882-
Korngold, Erich Wolfgang	1897-1957
Kovarovic, Karel	1862-1920
Krenek, Ernst	1900-
Kubelik, Jan	1880-1940
Lacomb, Louis Trouvillon	1818-1884
Lalo, Edouard	1823-1892
Lassen, Eduard	1830-1904
Lecocq, Alexandre Charles	1832-1918
Lehar, Franz	1870-1948
Lekeu, Guillaume	1870-1894
Lemmens, Nicolas Jacques	1823-1881

Leoncavallo, Ruggiero	1858-1919	Quilter, Roger	1877-1953
Liadov, Anatol	1855-1914	Rachmaninoff, Sergei	
Liszt, Franz	1811-1886	Vassilievitch	1873-1943
Loeffler, Charles Martin		Raff, Joseph Joachim	1822-1882
Tornov	1861-1935	Randegger, Alberto	1832-1911
Loucheur, Raymond	1899-	Rathaus, Kard	1895-1954
Maccun, Hamish	1868-1916	Ravel, Maurice	1875-1937
MacDowell, Edward		Reger, Max	1873-1916
Alexander	1861-1908	Reinecke, Carl Heinrich	
MacFarren, Sir George		Carsten	1824-1910
Alexander	1813-1887	Respighi, Ottorino	1879-1936
Mackenzie, Sir Alexander		Riegger, Wallingford	1885-
Campbell	1847-1935	Rimsky-Korsakov, Nicolai	
Mahler, Gustav	1860-1911	Andreievich	1844-1908
Malipiero G. Francesco	1882-	Rockstro, William Smith	1823-1895
Martinu, Bohuslar	1890-1959	Roger-Ducasse, Jean Jules	
Mascagni, Pietro	1863-1945	Aimable	1873-1954
Mason, Daniel Gregory	1873-1953	Rogers, Bernard	1893-
Massenet, Jules Emile		Ronald, Sir Landon	1873-1938
Frederic	1842-1912	Roussel, Albert	1869-1937
Medtner, Nikolai	1879-1951	Rubinstein, Anton	1829-1894
Mengelberg, Willem	1871-1951	Saint-Saens, Charles	
Merikanto, Oskar	1868-1924	Camille	1835-1921
Messager, Andre Charles		Satie, Erik Leslie	1866-1925
Prosper	1853-1929	Scharwenka, Xavier	1850-1924
Milhaud, Darius	1892-	Schnabel, Arthur	1882-1951
Monckton, Lionel	1861-1924	Schonberg, Arnold	1873-1951
Monk, William Henry	1823-1889	Schubert, Franz	1808-1878
Morris, Reginald Owen	1886-1948	Schumann, Clara	
Moszkowski, Moritz	1854-1925	Josephine	1819-1896
Mottl, Felix	1856-1911	Schumann, Robert	
Moussorgsky, Modest		Alexander	1810-1856
Petrovich	1835-1881	Scott, Cyril Meir	1879-
Napravnik, Edward	1839-1915	Scott, Francis George	1880-1958
Nevin, Ethelbert	1862-1901	Scriabin, Alexander	
Nielsen, Carl August	1865-1931	Nicholaevich	1872-1915
Novak, Viteslar	1870-1949	Sessions, Roger	1896-
Novello, Ivor	1893-1951	Sgambati, Giovanni	1843-1914
Nystrom, Gosta	1890-	Sibelius, Johan Julius	1865-1958
Offenbach, Jacques	1819-1880	Sinding, Christian	1856-1941
Orff, Carl	1895-	Smetana, Bedrich	1824-1884
Ornstein, Leo	1895-	Smyth, Dame Ethel Mary	1858-1944
Ouseley, Sir Frederick		Soderman, August Johan	1832-1876
Arthur	1825-1889	Somervell, Sir Arthur	1863-1937
Paderewski, Ignace Jan	1860-1941	Sousa, John Philip	1854-1932
Palmgren, Selim	1878-	Souza, Leo	1895-
Parker, Horatio William	1863-1919	Sowerby, Leo	1895-
Parry, Sir Charles Hubert		Spottiswoode, Alicia Ann	
Hastings	1848-1918	Lady John	1811-1900
Pedrell, Felipe	1841-1922	Stanford, Sir Charles	
Perosi, Lorenzo	1872-1956	Villiers	1852-1924
Pijper, Willem	1894-1947	Still, William Grant	1893-
Piston, Walter	1894-	Straus, Oscar	1870-1954
Pizzetti, Ildebrando	1880-	Strauss, Johann	
Planquette, Robert	1850-1903	the younger	1825-1899
Ponchielli, Amilcare	1834-1886	Strauss, Richard	1864-1949
Porter, Cole	1892-1963	Stravinsky, Igor	
Poulenc, Francis	1899-1963	Fedorovich	1882-
Prokofiev, Sergei	1891-1953	Suk, Joseph	1875-1935
Puccini, Giacomo	1858-1924	Sullivan, Sir Arthur	1842-1900

Suppé, Franz Von	1820-1895	Villa-Lobos, Heitor	1887-1959
Svendsen, Johan Severin	1840-1911	Vogel, Vladimir	1896-
Szymanowski, Karol	1883-1937	Vycpalek, Ladislav	1882-
Taneiev, Sergius	1856-1915	Wagner, Wilhelm Richard	1813-1883
Tcherepnin, Nicolai	1873-1945	Waldteufel, Emil	1837-1915
Thomas, Ambroise	1811-1896	Wallace, William	1860-1940
Thomas, Arthur Goring	1850-1892	Warlock, Peter	1894-1930
Thompson, Randall	1899-	Webern, Anton Von	1883-1945
Thomson, Virgil	1896-	Weill, Kurt	1900-1950
Thuille, Ludwig	1861-1907	Weinberger, Jaremir	1896-
Tommasini, Viscenzo	1880-	Weiner, Leo	1885-
Tosti, Sir Francesco Paolo	1846-1916	Weingartner, Felix	1863-1942
Tovey, Sir Donald Francis	1873-1940	Wesley, Samuel Sebastian	1810-1876
Tschaikovsky, Peter Ilyich	1840-1893	Widor, Charles Marie	1845-1937
Turina, Joaquin	1882-1949	Wolf, Hugo	1860-1903
Varese, Edgar	1885-	Wolf-Ferrari, Ermanno	1876-1948
Vaughan Williams, Ralph	1872-1958	Wood, Haydn	1882-1959
Verdi, Giuseppe		Zimbalist, Efrem	1889-
Fortunino Francesco	1813-1901		

INDEX

v

Masters, Edgar Lee	1869-1950	Menendez Y Pelayo,	
Matejko, Jan Alois	1838-1893	Marcelino	1856-1912
Mather, Cotton	1663-1728	Mengelberg, Wilem	1871-1951
Mather, Increase	1639-1723	Mengs, Anton Raphael	1728-1779
Matisse, Henri	1869-1954	Meninsky, Bernard	1891-1950
Matos Fragoso, Juan de	1608-1689	Menzel, Adolf Friedrich	
Matsys, Quentin	1466-1530	Erdmann von	1815-1905
Matthews, Brander	1852-1929	Menzel, Wolfgang	1798-1873
Mattheson, Johann	1681-1764	Mercie, Marius Jean	
Matthisson, Friedrich von	1762-1831	Antonin	1845-1916
Maturin, Charles Robert	1782-1824	Mercier, Sebastien	1740-1814
Maugham, William		Merck, Johann Heinrich	1741-1791
Somerset	1874-1965	Meredith, George	1828-1909
Maupassant, Guy de	1850-1893	Meres, Francis	1565-1647
Maurer, Georg		Merezhkovsky, Dmitri	
Ludwig von	1790-1872	Sergeievich	1865-1941
Mauriac, François	1885-	Merikanto, Oskar	1868-1924
Maurois, André	1885-	Mérimée, Prosper	1803-1870
Maurras, Charles	1868-1952	Merivale, Charles	1808-1893
Mauve, Anton	1838-1888	Merrick, Leonard	1864-1939
May, Thomas	1595-1650	Merrill, Stuart	1863-1915
Mayakovsky, Vladimir	1894-1930	Merriman, Henry Seton	1862-1903
Mayhew, Henry	1812-1887	Mesdag, Hendrik Willem	1831-1915
Mazzoni, Giacomo	1548-1598	Mesonero Romanos	
Mead, Larkin Goldsmist	1835-1910	Ramon de	1803-1882
Mead, William		Messager, Andre Charles	
Rutherford	1846-1928	Prosper	1853-1929
Medina, Jose Toribio	1852-1930	Messalla, Corvinus	
Medtner, Nikolai	1879-1951	Marcus Valerius	B.C. 64-8 A.D.
Medwall, Henry	1462-1505	Mestrovic, Ivan	1883-1962
Mee, Arthur	1875-1943	Metastasio	1698-1782
Mehring, Franz	1846-1919	Metsu, Gabriel	1630-1667
Mehul, Etienne Nicolas	1763-1817	Meulen, Adam	
Meilhac, Henri	1831-1897	Frans van der	1632-1690
Meinong, Alexius von	1853-1930	Meung, Jean de	1250-1305
Meissonier, Jean Louis		Meunier, Constantin	1831-1905
Ernest	1815-1891	Meurice, Paul	1818-1905
Meissonier, Juste Aurele	1693-1750	Mew, Charlotte	1870-1928
Mela, Pomponius	fl. 40	Meyer, Conrad Ferdinand	1825-1898
Melanchthon, Philip	1497-1560	Meyer, Edouard	1855-1930
Melchers, Gari	1860-1932	Meyebeer, Giacomo	1791-1864
Melendez Valdes, Juan	1754-1817	Meynell, Alice	1849-1922
Melo, Francisco		Meyrink, Gustav	1868-1932
Manuel de	1608-1666	Mezieres, Phillipe De	1327-1405
Melozzo Da Forli	1438-1494	Michaud, Joseph Francois	1767-1839
Melville, Hermann	1819-1891	Michel, Claude	1738-1814
Memlinc, Hans	1430-1494	Michel of Northgate, Dan	c. 1340
Mena, Juan de	1411-1456	Michelangelo	1475-1564
Mena, Pedro de	1693-	Michelet, Jules	1798-1874
Menander	B.C. 349-291	Michell, John	1724-1793
Menard, Louis Nicolas	1822-1901	Michelozzi, Michelozzo	
Mencius	fl. B.C. 300	di Bartolommeo	1396-1472
Mendelsohn, Erich	1887-1953	Mickiewicz, Adam	1798-1855
Mendelssohn, Moses	1729-1786	Mickle, William Julius	1735-1788
Mendelssohn, Bartholdi		Middleton, Thomas	1570-1627
Jakob Ludwig Felix	1809-1847	Mierevelt, Michiel	
Mendes, Catulle	1841-1909	Jansz van	1567-1641
Mendoza, Diego		Mieris, Freins Van	1635-1681
Hurtado de	1503-1575	Mies Van Der Rohe,	
		Ludwig	1886-

x